PSALMS IN COMMUNITY

Society of Biblical Literature

Symposium Series

Christopher R. Matthews,
Editor

Number 25

PSALMS IN COMMUNITY
Jewish and Christian Textual, Liturgical, and Artistic Traditions

PSALMS IN COMMUNITY

Jewish and Christian Textual, Liturgical, and Artistic Traditions

Edited by
Harold W. Attridge and Margot E. Fassler

Society of Biblical Literature
Atlanta

PSALMS IN COMMUNITY

Jewish and Christian Textual, Liturgical, and Artistic Traditions

Joyful Noise, written and produced by Margot Fassler with support from the Yale Institute of Sacred Music and the Lilly Endowment, Inc., is a DVD companion piece to this volume and may be ordered online from the SBL at http://www.sbl-site.org (ISBN: 9780974945736).

Cover photo of Pesher Habakkuk, Qumran, courtesy of the D. Samuel and Jeane H. Gottesman Center for Biblical Manuscripts, The Israel Museum, Jerusalem.

Library of Congress Cataloging-in-Publication Data

Psalms in community : Jewish and Christian textual, liturgical, and artistic traditions / edited by Harold W. Attridge and Margot E. Fassler.

p. cm. — (Society of Biblical Literature symposium series ; no. 25)

Papers from the conference "Up with a Shout" held at Yale University in January, 2002.

Includes bibliographical references and indexes.

ISBN 1-58983-078-4 (pbk. : alk. paper)

1. Bible. O.T. Psalms—Liturgical use—History—Congresses. 2. Bible. O.T. Psalms—Criticism, interpretation, etc.—History—Congresses. 3. Bible. O.T. Psalms—Devotional use—History—Congresses. 4. Judaism—Liturgy—History—Congresses. I. Attridge, Harold W. II. Fassler, Margot Elsbeth. III. Series: Symposium series (Society of Biblical Literature) ; no. 25.

BS1435 .P74 2003b

223'.206'09—dc22 2003020845

11 10 09 08 07 5 4 3 2

Printed in the United States of America on acid-free, recycled paper conforming to ANSI/NISO Z39.48-1992 (R1997) and ISO 9706:1994 standards for paper permanence.

Contents

ACKNOWLEDGMENTS

A work of this size and complexity has required the efforts of many people and institutions. We are especially grateful to John Leinenweber, who was the research assistant on the project, did the copy editing for the volume, prepared the index, and worked with us to design the bibliography. His extraordinary skills, patience, and unfailing kindness have made this volume a joy to produce. The following people, some of them ISM staff members, provided invaluable clerical support: Jenna-Claire Kemper, Sarah Hare, Louise Johnson, Gale Pollen, and Trisha Radil. The bibliography was put in final form and typed by Nick D'Alessio, a student at the Yale Institute of Sacred Music and at Yale Divinity School. Technical expertise was necessary too, for which we are indebted to Robert Honstein, Robert Piscatelli, and Sachin Ramabhandran. Robert Honstein prepared the musical examples for this volume. We are thankful for the resources of Yale University Libraries, most especially for those of Yale Divinity Library and for the help of reference librarian Martha Smalley, and head of circulation Susan Burdick; numerous other librarians made our work easier and offered advice and expertise, and we must mention here Robert Babcock, curator of medieval manuscripts at the Beinecke Rare Book and Manuscript Library, and Richard Boursey, the archivist of the Herrick Music Library. Several libraries granted permission for the publication of plates. The book has been supported by a grant from the Lilly Endowment, Inc., and certain other costs were underwritten by the Yale Institute of Sacred Music. We are thankful to Melissa Maier for her work on the conference "Up with a Shout!" that inspired this volume and to Terese Cain, who supervised the camera crew and conducted many interviews with participants. Much of this material will soon be available in the form of a three-volume series of videos on the Psalms. Last of all, and most importantly, we thank the many colleagues and associates who wrote for the volume and who prepared their work in a timely fashion, and thank the several churches and synagogues who have welcomed us and our colleagues into their communities to learn and to be inspired by their knowledge and by their various proclamations of the psalms.

Harold W. Attridge and Margot E. Fassler

Abbreviations

Primary Sources

Ambrose	
Expl. Ps.	*Explanatio super psalmos xii / Explanations on Twelve Psalms*
Hex.	*Hexaemeron libri sex / Six Days of Creation*
Athanasius	
Ep. Marcell.	*Epistula ad Marcellinum de interpretatione Psalmorum / Letter to Marcellinus on the Interpretation of the Psalms*
Athenaeus	
Deipn.	*Deipnosophistae*
Augustine	
Conf.	*Confessionum libri XIII / Confessions*
Enarrat. Ps.	*Enarrationes in Psalmos / Enarrations on the Psalms*
Ep.	*Epistulae / Letters*
Retract.	*Retractationum libri II / Retractations*
b.	Babylonian Talmud
Basil of Caesarea	
Ep.	*Epistulae / Letters*
Ber.	*Berakot*
Cassiodorus	
Exp. Ps.	*Expositio Psalmorum / Exposition on the Psalms*
Cicero	
De or.	*De oratore / On the Orator*
Clement of Alexandria	
Paed.	*Paedagogus / Christ the Educator*
Strom.	*Stromateis Miscellanies*
Diodore	
Comm. Ps.	*Commentarii in Psalmos / Commentaries on the Psalms*
Dionysius of Halicarnassus	
Rhet.	*Ars rhetorica / The Art of Rhetoric*

Eusebius	
Hist. eccl.	*Historia ecclesiastica / Ecclesiastical History*
Gregory of Nyssa	
Inscr. Ps.	*In inscriptiones Psalmorum / On the Inscriptions of the Psalms*
Hilary of Poitiers	
Instr. Ps.	*Instructio Psalmorum / Commentary on the Psalms*
Horace	
Ars	*Ars poetica / The Art of Poetry*
Irenaeus	
Haer.	*Adversus haereses / Against Heresies*
Jerome	
Comm. Ps.	*Commentarioli in Psalmos / Notes on the Psalms*
Tract. Ps.	*Tractatus in Psalmos / Tractates on the Psalms*
Josephus	
Ag. Ap.	*Contra Apionem / Against Apion*
Ant.	*Antiquitates judaicae / Jewish Antiquties*
J.W.	*Bellum judaicum / Jewish War*
Let. Aris.	*Letter of Aristeas*
Longinus	
[*Subl.*]	*De sublimitate / On the Sublime*
LXX	Septuagint
m.	Mishnah
OG	Old Greek
Origen	
Comm. Jo.	*Commentarii in evangelium Joannis / Commentary on the Gospel of John*
Or.	*De oratione (Peri proseuchēs) / Prayer*
Philoc.	*Philocalia / Love of the Beautiful*
Princ.	*De principiis (Peri archōn) / First Principles*
Pesaḥ.	*Pesaḥim*
Philo	
Aet.	*De aeternitate mundi / On the Eternity of the World*
Agr.	*De agricultura / On Agriculture*
Cher.	*De cherubim / On the Cherubim*
Congr.	*De congressu eruditionis gratia / On the Preliminary Studies*
Contempl.	*De vita contemplativa / On the Contemplative Life*
Ebr.	*De ebrietate / On Drunkenness*
Flacc.	*In Flaccum / Against Flaccus*
Leg.	*Legum allegoriae / Allegorical Interpretation*
Mos.	*De vita Mosis / On the Life of Moses*
Plant.	*De plantatione / On Planting*

Prob.	*Quod omnis probus liber sit / That Every Good Person Is Free*
Sobr.	*De sobrietate / On Sobriety*
Somn.	*De somniis / On Dreams*
Spec.	*De specialibus legibus / On the Special Laws*
Plato	
Resp.	*Respublica / Republic*
Quintilian	
Inst.	*Institutio oratoria / The Orator's Education*
SRA	*Seder Rav Amram*
Sextus Empiricus	
Math.	*Adversus mathematicos / Against the Mathematicians*
Sop.	*Sopherim*
t.	Tosefta
Taʿan.	*Taʿanit*
Tertullian	
Apol.	*Apologeticus / Apology*
Marc.	*Adversus Marcionem / Against Marcion*
Or.	*De oratione / Prayer*

SECONDARY SOURCES

AB	Anchor Bible
ABRL	Anchor Bible Reference Library
ACW	Ancient Christian Writers
AGJU	Arbeiten zur Geschichte des antiken Judentums und des Urchristentums
AHR	*American Historical Review*
ASOR	American Schools of Oriental Research
BBR	*Bulletin of Biblical Research*
BEL.S	Bibliotheca "Ephemerides liturgicae," Subsidia
BETL	Bibliotheca ephemeridum theologicarum lovaniensium
BHG	*Bibliotheca hagiographica graeca*. Edited by François Halkin. Brussels: Société des ballandistes, 1969.
Bib	*Biblica*
BJS	Brown Judaic Studies
BZ	*Biblische Zeitschrift*
BZNW	Beihefte zur neutestamentliche Wissenschaft
CBQ	*Catholic Biblical Quarterly*
CCSG	Corpus Christianorum: Series graeca. Turnhout, 1977–
CCSL	Corpus Christianorum: Series latina. Turnhout, 1953–.
CQ	*Classical Quarterly*
CRINT	Compendia rerum iudaicarum ad Novum Testamentum

CSCO	Corpus scriptorum christianorum orientalium. Edited by I. B. Chabot et al. Paris, 1903–.
CSEL	Corpus scriptorum ecclesiastorum latinorum
DACL	*Dictionnaire d'archéologie chrétienne et liturgie*. Edited by F. Cabrol. 15 vols. Paris: Letouzey et Ané, 1907–1953.
DOP	*Dumbarton Oaks Papers*
DSD	*Dead Sea Discoveries*
EncJud	*Enyclopedia Judaica*. 13 vols. Jerusalem: Keter, 1971.
FC	Fathers of the Church
FOTL	Forms of the Old Testament Literature
FRLANT	Forschungen zur Religion und Literatur des Alten und Neuen Testaments
GCS	Die griechische christlilche Schriftseller der ersten [drei] Jahrhunderte
Hen	*Henoch*
HSS	Harvard Semitic Studies
HTR	*Harvard Theological Review*
HUCA	*Hebrew Union College Annual*
Int	*Interpretation*
JE	*The Jewish Encyclopedia*. Edited by I. Singer. 12 vols. New York: Funk & Wagnalls, 1901–6.
JECS	*Journal of Early Christian Studies*
JJS	*Journal of Jewish Studies*
JQR	*Jewish Quarterly Review*
JR	*Journal of Religion*
JSNT	*Journal for the Study of the New Testament*
JSOT	*Journal for the Study of the Old Testament*
JSOTSup	Journal for the Study of the Old Testament Supplement Series
JSJ	*Journal for the Study of Judaism*
JSS	*Journal of Semitic Studies*
JSSSup	Journal of Semitic Studies Supplement
LCC	Library of Christian Classics
LQ	*Lutheran Quarterly*
LQF	Liturgiewissenchaftliche Quellen und Forschungen
MECL	*Music in Early Christian Literature*. Edited by J. McKinnon. Cambridge Readings in the Literature of Music. New York: Cambridge University Press, 1987.
MGWJ	*Monatschrift für Geschichte und Wissenschaft des Judentums*
MMB	Monumenta Musicae Byzantinae
Mus	*Muséon: Revue d'études orientales*
Neot	*Neotestamentica*
NRSV	New Revised Standard Version

NTS	*New Testament Studies*
OCA	Orientalia Christiana Analecta
OCD	*Oxford Classical Dictionary*. 2d ed. Oxford: Clarendon, 1970.
OCP	*Orientalia christiana periodica*
OPA	*Les oeuvres de Philon d'Alexandrine*. Edited by R. Arnaldez, J. Pouilloux, and C. Montdésert. 36 vols. in 35. Paris: Cerf, 1961–92.
OrChr	*Oriens Christianus*
OTP	*The Old Testament Pseudepigrapha*. Edited by J. H. Charlesworth. 2 vols.; Garden City, N.Y.: Doubleday, 1983–85.
OTS	Old Testament Studies
PG	Patrologia graeca [= Patrologiae cursus completus: Series graeca]. Edited by J.-P. Migne. 162 vols. Paris: Migne, 1857–86.
PL	Patrologia latina [= Patrologiae cursus completus: Series latina]. Edited by J.-P. Migne. 217 vols. Paris: Migne, 1844–64.
PO	Patrologiae orientalis
RBén	*Revue bénédictine*
REAug	*Revue des études augustiniennes*
Res	*Res: Anthropology and Aesthetics*
RevExp	*Review and Expositor*
RTAM	*Recherches de théologie ancienne et médiévale*
SBLDS	Society of Biblical Literature Dissertation Series
SBLMS	Society of Biblical Literature Monograph Series
SBLTT	Society of Biblical Literature Texts and Translations
SC	Sources chrétiennes. Paris: Cerf. 1943–.
SJ	Studia Judaica
Spec	*Speculum*
TDNT	*Theological Dictionary of the New Testament*. Edited by G. Kittle and G. Friedrich. Translated by G. W. Bromiley. 10 vols. Grand Rapids: Eerdmans, 1964-1976.
TQ	*Theologische Quartalschrift*
TRE	*Theologische Realenzyklopädie*. Edited by G. Krause and G. Müller. Berlin: de Gruyter, 1977–.
TU	Texte und Untersuchungen
VT	*Vetus Testamentum*
VTSup	Supplements to Vetus Testamentum
WUNT	Wissenschaftliche Untersuchungen zum Neuen Testament
ZNW	*Zeitschrift für die neutestamentliche Wissenschaft und die Kunde der älteren Kirche*
ZTK	*Zeitschrift für Theologie und Kirche*

PREFACE

Harold Attridge and Margot Fassler

> To me, one of the truly striking elements in the Psalms, in addition to their great poetic beauty and moral depth, is the all-encompassing diversity of attitudes, sentiments and affects with which the Divine is approached. Indeed, as has often been commented upon, it is one of the extraordinary things about the Jewish religion that confronting God, even to the point of challenging God's actions and judgment, is acceptable.
>
> —Shulamit Ran, composer, from the notes to a performance of her "Supplications (for Chorus and Orchestra)" (3 November 2002)

> At the practical level the parish musician bears the fundamental responsibility for psalmody. Psalmody is the parish musician's stream of consciousness. The parish musician controls the song of the people of God, is controlled by it, and becomes the real corporate voice and representative of the people.... The parish musician is first of all responsible to what the people sing, and the matrix of that song is Psalmody.
>
> —Professor Paul Westermeyer, writing in *The Hymn* 33, 1980

"Up with a Shout," a major conference on the Psalms in Jewish and Christian textual, liturgical, and artistic traditions, took place at Yale University in January 2002. It was sponsored by numerous Yale entities and planned and designed by a team of scholars and leaders of local faith communities. From the beginning the plan was to study the Psalms from different perspectives, but always with attention to what happens when texts are formed in community and continue to live in community. Because the Psalms form the only canonical collection of song texts in two faith traditions (albeit in very different linguistic and liturgical guises), we needed an interfaith exploration, one that involved both the theoretical and the practical, the scholarly and the performative. Thus, as the concept broadened and developed, the work came to involve scholars, religious leaders, performers, composers, compilers of texts for worship, and healers expert in the use of the Psalms for pastoral care.

We intended not only to talk, listen, and learn over a three-day period; we wished to write a guidebook to accompany the apparent explosion of psalmody taking place in American religious life today, as we sought to answer some of the most basic questions regularly encountered in the classroom, the concert hall, and in the lives of congregations:

- What roles did the Psalms play in the worship life of the people of Israel and for early Christian and Jewish liturgical traditions?
- How and why did the Psalms evolve as major song texts in both traditions?
- What theologies of the Psalms are distinctive in Jewish and Christian traditions?
- How have the Psalms inspired music and art in the histories of our traditions?
- How do contemporary Jewish and Christian communities make use of the Psalms, not only for collective, but also for individual modes of prayer?
- What are the major issues facing translators and liturgical performers of these texts in several traditions?

This book treats these and other questions according to various disciplines, beginning with two liturgical scholars whose different perspectives constituted plenary talks for "Up with a Shout": Robert Taft, of the Pontifical Oriental Institute in Rome and the University of Notre Dame, on the historical formation of Christian psalmody in the Eastern church, especially as related to what we understand of early liturgical practices; and Rabbi Lawrence Hoffman, of Hebrew Union College, on the ways in which the language of the Psalms permeates the fabric of Jewish prayer life in Reformed Judaism. From this historical and practical framework, our study moves to biblical texts and textual communities, seeking to show how the Psalms slowly cohered as a body of poetry, a process still going on at the time of the copying of the Dead Sea Scrolls, and the ways in which this collection came to offer believers a theologically grounded model for praise and for understanding the nature of the relationship between the divine and the human. Building upon this emphasis on community, a small group of New Testament scholars probes the ways in which the various lives of early Christians depended upon the Psalms for creating community, for worship, and for song. Religious historians then offer three studies of the Psalms and early commentaries upon them: the words of a Jew in the first century, the writings of Christian exegetes in the fourth and fifth centuries, and in exploration of the nature and use of the Psalter in the East Syrian tradition.

The textual and exegetical traditions adduced by biblical scholars and historians are encountered in Christian practices in the medieval and early modern period, but in new and sometime strange manifestions. The Rule of Saint Benedict, the most basic document for the study of Western liturgical prayer, inspired the lofty songs of Hildegard of Bingen; commentaries upon the Psalms originating in early centuries were explored through illuminated manuscripts produced in the monastic and cathedral scriptoria of medieval Europe. Of all the cities attempting to "live out" the Psalms, none was quite as intense as Calvin's Geneva. At the same time that Geneva was being ruled through the sounds of its psalmody, the Psalms were also moving from Spain to the New World, to be dressed in a panoply of fabulous feathers and a new understanding of their original liturgical context.

After this historical background, we chose three studies from the astounding array of contemporary practices now coexisting in the United States: one of the life of an African American church in Atlanta, another of the Psalms as sung by the Syrian Orthodox Jews of New York City, and a third of the changes now taking place in Greek Orthodox liturgies. At the end our book returns to the place it began, with the texts themselves, as interpreted by modern poets, as translated for congregational prayer, and as preached and explained in the Jewish and the Christian traditions.

As we began to plan the conference "Up with a Shout" we sought a book about the Psalms from several perspectives, a book to teach from and to serve as an inspiration for theological education in several venues. When we could not find a single volume we decided to write one. In the near future, our work will be supplemented by a series of videos studying the Psalms in a variety of Jewish and Christian liturgical settings. Our purpose is simple: to help worshiping congregations restore their psalmody where it is lost and to understand it more fully where it is not. At a time when the worshiping world is in a state of upheaval, the Psalms, blessedly, have come roaring back. Our book offers a guide to what they have meant throughout the centuries and suggests ways in which contemporary worshipers can sing and know them better.

INTRODUCTION
THE PSALMS IN TWO RELIGIOUS TRADITIONS

Christian Liturgical Psalmody: Origins, Development, Decomposition, Collapse

Robert F. Taft, S.J.
Pontifical Oriental Institute

The title of this paper is deliberately ominous, for Christian liturgical psalmody has come upon bad times, where it has not disappeared entirely. Nor has liturgical scholarship shown itself any less neglectful of psalmody than has liturgical practice. Despite the overwhelming importance of psalms and psalmody in Christian liturgy from the start, there is not a single major, overarching work in any language dealing adequately with Christian liturgical psalmody as a whole, disconcerting as that must seem.[1] One might well ask professionals in the field of Christian liturgy just what they have been doing with their time!

Though I cannot justify this lacuna—nor do I make any pretense of being able to fill it in the space allotted here—I think it only fair to note

---

[1] One overview, John A. Lamb's *The Psalms in Christian Worship* (London: Faith Press, 1962), contains much good material but is outdated and far too general and summary in its treatment of the early and Eastern material. As for Eric Werner's *The Sacred Bridge: The Interdependence of Liturgy and Music in Synagogue and Church during the First Millennium*, vol. 1 (New York: Columbia University Press, 1959, 1984), partially reprinted, though omitting much of the musical material, as *The Sacred Bridge: Liturgical Parallels in Synagogue and Early Church* (New York: Columbia University Press, 1970), see Peter Jeffery, "Werner's *The Sacred Bridge* Volume 2: A Review Essay," *JQR* 77 (1987): 283–98, and the relevant references he cites. There are, however, several fine—some of them superb—studies on particular aspects of psalmody. Even a partial list would have to include the works (listed in the bibliography) by Froyshov, Leeb, McKinnon, Mateos (especially Juan Mateos, ed., *Le Typicon de la Grande Église. Ms. Sainte-Croix no. 40, Xe siècle: Introduction, texte critique, traduction et notes* [2 vols.; OCA 165–166; Rome: Pontificium Institutum Orientalium Studiorum, 1962–63], 1:54; 2:280–81, 283–85, 289, 300–306, 308–17, 319, 321–29; and idem, *Lelya-Sapra: Les offices chaldéens de la nuit et du matin* [2d ed.; OCA 156; Rome: Pontificium Institutum Orientalium Studiorum, 1972], 28–31), Strunk, and Quasten.

that the study of liturgy has been a university discipline only since the middle of the twentieth century.[2] Add to that the number of languages ancient and modern a scholar would need to know to accomplish such a study, and one can begin to grasp the magnitude of the enterprise.

My focus here will be on when, how, and why Christians used biblical psalmody—and why things eventually fell apart, which, as we shall see, they most certainly did. I shall start with the first clear historical evidence for Christian liturgical psalmody, then watch it grow to full development until it begins to decompose in the Middle Ages. As far as the musical execution of the psalmody is concerned, I leave that to the musicologists.[3]

Origins

Psalmody of some sort was a factor in Christian worship from the start, as is clear from several New Testament texts.[4] Just what these texts mean by "psalms, psalmody, psalming" remains moot, however, despite the exegesis to which they are traditionally subjected.[5] Are they referring to the biblical psalms? Possibly, but not certainly. The Greek term ψαλμός was not the only one Christians used for the Psalms of David,[6] nor was this term per se restricted to the biblical psalms. Moreover, although early Christian usage would seem to favor interpreting the term as referring to the biblical psalms where there is no reason to suspect another meaning,[7] as late as the third and fourth centuries we see Greek and Latin writers still using ψαλμός/*psalmus* for what are clearly nonbiblical

---

[2] On the whole question, see my "Über die Liturgiewissenschaft heute," *TQ* 177 (1997): 243–55 and the literature cited there.

[3] I limit myself to a single remark on the issue: when liturgical or other texts in Greek (λέγειν), Latin (*dicere*), Syriac (*ʿemar*) refer to the psalms being "said," this simply means they are executed aloud orally; it in no way implies that they are "spoken" as opposed to "chanted" or "sung": see Mateos, *Le Typicon,* 2:302; Taft, *The Great Entrance: A History of the Transfer of Gifts and Other Preanaphoral Rites of the Liturgy of St. John Chrysostom.* (OCA 200; Rome: Pontificium Institutum Orientalium Studiorum, 1978), 418.

[4] 1 Cor 14:26; Eph 5:18–20; Col 3:16–17; Jas 5:13; and Rev 5:8–9, all cited in James W. McKinnon, *Music in Early Christian Literature* (Cambridge Readings in the Literature of Music; Cambridge: Cambridge University Press, 1987) = *MECL*.

[5] For instance, Lamb, *Psalms in Christian Worship,* 19.

[6] See Marcel Metzger, "Expressions hymniques dans les *Constitutions apostoliques,*" in *L'hymnographie: Conférences Saint-Serge* (ed. A. M. Triacca and A. Pistoia; BEL.S 105; Rome: CLV-Edizioni Liturgiche, 2000), 60.

[7] Geoffrey Lampe, ed., *A Patristic Greek Lexicon* (Oxford: Clarendon Press, 1961), 1539–40; cf. Taft, *Great Entrance,* 85–86.

compositions.[8] However, since numerous New Testament texts refer to singing of one sort or another, and since by this time ψαλμοί had become for hellenophone Jews the Greek proper name for what we know as the Psalms of David (though not exclusively), I shall neither challenge nor attempt to prove the conventional wisdom that the earliest Christians probably used biblical psalms in their gatherings. It is perfectly clear that Christians eventually came to do so, and it is equally obvious that they got these psalms from Judaism. Whether or not they got their liturgical psalmody from Judaism is another matter entirely, and I note with satisfaction a certain skepticism in the more recent good literature on the topic.[9]

Liturgy and Psalmody, Monastic and Cathedral[10]

Essential to any understanding of Christian liturgical psalmody is the by now classic distinction of Christian liturgy and its attendant psalmody into monastic and cathedral.[11] This distinction has, in my view, withstood

---

[8] E.g., Tertullian (d. after 220), *Marc.* 5.8.12 (CCSL 1:688 = *MECL* §81); Eusebius of Caesarea (ca. 260–ca. 340), *Hist. eccl.* 5.38.5, 7.30.10 (SC 41:75, 217 = PG 20:512–13, 713 = *MECL* §§210–11).

[9] James W. McKinnon, "Desert Monasticism and the Later Fourth-Century Psalmodic Movement," *Music and Letters* 75 (1994): 505–19; repr. as ch. 11 in McKinnon, *The Temple, the Church Fathers and Early Western Chant* (Brookfield, Vt.: Ashgate, 1998); idem, *MECL,* introduction, 8; Edward Foley, *Foundations of Christian Music: The Music of Pre-Constantinian Christianity* (Collegeville, Minn.: Liturgical Press, 1996), 96–97.

[10] On all this, full details and sources in Juan Mateos, *La célébration de la parole dans la liturgie byzantine: Étude historique* (OCA 191; Rome: Pontificium Institutum Orientalium Studiorum, 1971), 8–26; Robert Taft, *The Liturgy of the Hours in East and West: The Origins of the Divine Office and Its Meaning for Today* (2d ed.; Collegeville, Minn.: Liturgical Press, 1993), 10–11, 33–35, 39–56, 141–90, 211–13, and see "psalmody" in the index; idem, *The Precommunion Rites* (vol. 5 of *A History of the Liturgy of St. John Chrysostom;* OCA 261; Rome: Pontificium Institutum Orientalium Studiorum, 2000), 270–88; McKinnon, "Desert Monasticism."

[11] The distinction goes back to Anton Baumstark's lectures at Amay-sur-Meuse in 1932, first published as *Liturgie comparée* (Chevetogne: Éditions de Chevetogne, 1939). I cite the English translation, *Comparative Liturgy* (Westminster, Md.: Newman, 1958), 111–18. On Baumstark's original lectures, see Emmanuel Lanne, "Les dix leçons de Liturgie Comparée d'Anton Baumstark au Monastère d'Amay-sur-Meuse en 1932: leur contexte et leur publication," in *Acts of the International Congress Comparative Liturgy Fifty Years after Anton Baumstark (1872–1948)* (ed. R. F. Taft and G. Winkler; OCA 265; Rome: Pontificium Institutum Orientalium Studiorum, 2001), 145–61. On Baumstark and his work, the basic study is Frederick S.

recent challenges,[12] and I will continue to employ it here. "Monastic liturgy" is the common prayer of monastic communities; "cathedral liturgy" is the liturgy of the churches where the laity worship. We call it "cathedral" rather than "parish" liturgy because throughout most of the first Christian millennium, long before the conversion of the *pagani* in the *pagus* or countryside stimulated the growth of the parochial system,[13] the bishop's cathedral church was the center of nonmonastic liturgical life.[14]

West, *Anton Baumstark's Comparative Liturgy in Its Intellectual Context* (Ann Arbor, Mich.: University Microfilms International Dissertation Services, 1988).

[12] On this, see my riposte in "Comparative Liturgy Fifty Years after Anton Baumstark (d. 1948): A Reply to Recent Critics," *Worship* 73 (1999): 532–34. For Byzantium, at least, we see the distinction unambiguously expressed in the liturgical and musical manuscripts and liturgical psalter manuscripts. For example, manuscripts refer to the Rite of the Great Church—i.e., the cathedral rite of Hagia Sophia in Constantinople—as "the ecclesiastical rite" or "ordo," to distinguish it from the Palestinian "hagiopolite monastic office"; see Elena Velkovska, *Il Praxapolstolos A.b.V (XI sec.) della Biblioteca di Grottaferrata* (Rome: Pontificio Istituto Orientale, 1994), 84, citing that eleventh-century manuscript as well as the eleventh/twelfth-centuy *Grottaferrata Db XVII;* also the tenth/eleventh-century Psalter manuscript *Barberini Gr. 285* (f. 152v); see also the tenth/eleventh-century *Grottaferrata Gb 10* (f. 34r) cited in Stefano Parenti, "La celebrazione delle Ore del Venerdì Santo nell'eucologio G.b.X. di Grottaferrata (X–XI sec.)," *Bolletino della Badia Greca di Grottaferrata* 44 (1990): 86.

Musical manuscripts, such as *Vienna Theol. Gr. 185* (c. 1385–91), f. 105v, distinguish monastic usage from that of the "katholikon"—i.e., cathedral church; Kenneth Levy, "A Hymn for Thursday in Holy Week," *Journal of the American Musicological Society* 16 (1963): 157 and n. 50. In addition, sources such as the famous seventh/eighth-century *Narration of the Abbots John and Sophronius* (ed. A. Longo, "Il testo della «Narrazione degli abati Giovanni e Sofronio» attraverso le «Ἑρμηνεῖαι» di Nicone," *Revista di studi bizantini e neoellenici* NS 2–3 = 12–13 [1965–66]: 223–67, here 251–67 *passim*) and Symeon of Thessalonika (d. 1429), *De sacra precatione,* 347, 349 (PG 155:624–29, 636–42; cf. Oliver Strunk, *Essays on Music in the Byzantine World* [New York: Norton, 1977], 113–15, 118, 125), give unambiguous testimony to the validity of this distinction.

[13] See Taft, *Liturgy of the Hours,* 297–99.

[14] Juan Mateos identifies three basic types of the later-developed cathedral/monastic offices: (1) cathedral; (2) Egyptian-monastic or "pure" monastic; and (3) urban-monastic or "hybrid" monastic. The hybrid type of office resulted from the attempt of monks in monasteries not isolated in the wilderness or desert, like those of Egypt, but located in or near urban centers, to take account of the cathedral traditions with which they were in contact; see idem, "The Origins of the Divine Office," *Worship* 41 (1967): 477–85. I later nuanced this distinction further, showing that this synthesis resulted, in different areas, in offices some of which can be considered monastic offices "cathedralized," whereas others are more cathedral offices

MONASTIC LITURGY AND ITS PSALMODY

Early monastic prayer was more a meditation in common on sacred Scripture than a "liturgical ceremony." The monastics paid no attention whatever to symbol or ceremonial, hymns or chant, or to ritualizing the hour or season or feast.[15] Their interest was not in conforming their prayer to the time or season but in conforming their hearts to the word of God. This is quite different from cathedral offices, in which the psalmody is our praise of God rather than his saving word to us. With regard to psalmody, this meant that the monastics usually had a reader recite the psalms aloud slowly, one by one, in the order in which they occur in the Bible, while the listeners meditated in their hearts on the sacred words, making them their own in interior prayer.[16] There is also evidence for the whole monastic brotherhood reciting the psalm together or alternating the verses divided into two choirs.[17]

John Cassian, in the monastic "desert" of Scetis, Egypt, from around 380 to 399, describes the psalmody there. After each psalm the monks rose and prayed in silence with arms extended in the orans position. They followed this with a prostration, praying all the while, then another period of prayer standing with arms outstretched. The presider concluded the prayer with a collect. This was repeated through the course of twelve psalms, the twelfth being always an alleluia psalm. The "Glory be to the Father. . . " concluded the psalmody, followed by two readings from the Bible to complete the synaxis.[18]

The penitential earnestness of these endlessly repeated prostrations has recently been demonstrated by paleopathological research on fifth- to

---

"monasticized," depending on which characteristics, cathedral or monastic, predominate (*Liturgy of the Hours,* 202–4).

[15] Details and sources in Taft, *Liturgy of the Hours,* 66–73.

[16] On this kind of meditative psalmody, see Mateos, *La célébration de la parole,* 26; McKinnon, "Desert Monasticism," 506–9. For the most complete description of the early monastic system, see Taft, *Liturgy of the Hours,* chs. 4, 6, 7, esp. pp. 57–73. Monastic services were not really what we call "liturgy," surprising as that may seem to us today, when monasticism is considered the locus of liturgy par excellence: "In the beginning the liturgy was not a part of monastic life. Even the celebration of the Eucharist did not occupy a special place in it. All this was the affair of the clergy, not the monk. The monk's part was to pray in his heart without ceasing. That was his *Opus Dei,* his *Officium,* that is, fasting, watching, work, contrition of heart and silence" (Friedrich Wulf, "Priestertum und Rätestand," *Geist und Leben* 33 [1960]: 250, English translation from André Louf et al., *The Message of Monastic Spirituality* [New York: Desclée, 1964], 32).

[17] Mateos, *La célébration de la parole,* 26; Taft, *Liturgy of the Hours,* 39–40; *MECL* §139.

[18] Texts and details in Taft, *Liturgy of the Hours,* 58–61.

seventh-century monastic skeletal remains in Palestine, which has uncovered pathologies of the lower limb indicative of sustained, repetitive kneeling.[19] There was a time when we had only to fear the Last Judgment. Now if we do not say our prayers we must worry that the archeologists will not find the right bumps on our shin bones!

Although most ancient church fathers were favorable to melodiously chanted psalmody, what Froyshov calls the "mouvement psalmodique" beginning in the fifth century, when hymns of eccesiastical (i.e., nonbiblical) compositions began to multiply, provoked a reaction from the anchorites of Egypt and Sinai. They vehemently opposed the new music and chant[20] and refused to farce their psalmody with the new-fangled responds or refrains. These monks came to accept such "cathedral psalmody" only later,[21] a remarkable turnabout that began during the flowering of liturgical

---

[19] Susan Guise Sheridan, "Biocultural Reconstruction of Kneeling Pathology in a Byzantine Judean Monastery," *American Journal of Physical Anthropology* Supplement 24 (1996): 209; idem, "'New Life the Dead Receive': The Relationship between Human Remains and the Cultural Record for Byzantine St. Stephen's," *RB* 106 (1999): 1–34; Susan Guise Sheridan and Sarah E. Niebuhr, "Vertebral Pathology from a Byzantine Judean Monastery," Abstract, *American Journal of Physical Anthropology,* Supplement 26 (1996): 170; Susan Guise Sheridan and Michael S. Driscoll, "Every Knee Shall Bend: A Biocultural Reconstruction of Liturgical and Ascetical Prayer in V–VII Century Palestine," *Worship* 74 (2000): 453–68.

[20] Johannes Quasten, *Music and Worship in Pagan and Christian Antiquity* (trans. B. Ramsey; Washington, D.C.: National Association of Pastoral Musicians, 1983), 94–99; Stig S. Froyshov, "La réticence à l'hymnographie chez les anchorètes de l'Égypte et du Sinaï du 6ᵉ au 8ᵉ siècles," in *L'hymnographie: Conférences Saint-Serge* (ed. A. M. Triacca and A. Pistoia; BEL.S 105; Rome: CLV-Edizioni Liturgiche, 2000), 229–30, 245. Indeed, some early anchorites opposed not only cathedral psalmody; they also refused to participate in the liturgical and sacramental life of the church. Though there is considerable variety in the evidence for eremitical usage, it is clear that there was a certain tension between the demands of solitude and participation in the public, ecclesial action of the eucharistic liturgy, and the extant evidence reveals widely varying solutions to this problem. Some Syriac texts attributed to Saint Ephrem (ca. 306–373) seem to imply that monastic asceticism even replaces the eucharistic liturgy; see A. Vööbus, *A History of Asceticism in the Syrian Orient* (CSCO 197, Subsidia 17; Louvain: Secrétariat du CSCO, 1960), 2:311. The same approach is expressed even more trenchantly by Anastasius of Sinai (fl. 640–700), *Quaestio* 2, PG 89:344–52. Some solitaries not only avoid the church's public synaxes but even seem to disdain them; see Palladius (ca. 363–ca. 431), *Historia lausiaca* (ca. 419), 25.2–5, 26.2, 27.2 (Palladio, *La Storia lausiaca* [ed. G. J. M. Bartelink, trans. M. Barchiesi; Vite dei santi 2; Milan: Modadori, 1990], 134–42).

[21] Alexander Lingas, "Hesychasm and Psalmody," in *Mount Athos and Byzantine Monasticism* (ed. A. Bryer and M. Cunningham; Brookfield, Vt.: Variorum, 1996), 156ff.; Robert Taft, *The Byzantine Rite: A Short History* (Collegeville, Minn.:

poetry from the fifth century on and gained momentum during the restoration of monastic and church life in the Holy Land following the Persian depredations in 614.[22]

Egeria's *Diary* describes monastics participating in the liturgical life of the cathedral churches of Palestine during her pilgrimage there in 381–384.[23] By the fifth century, Palestinian monks were even assisting in the performance of the cathedral offices, according to Cyril of Scythopolis (ca. 525–ca. 558), *The Lives of the Monks of Palestine*.[24] So it is not difficult to see how the "cathedralization" of the monastic offices eventually came about.

It did not happen without a struggle, however, for the early monks were less than enthusiastic about such things as liturgical chant, which they considered highly unsuitable for the sober prayer of ascetics. This is clearly reflected in such early texts as a fragment perserved in codex *Vatican Gr. 1579* reporting the teaching of the hermit Saint Antony the Great of Egypt (ca. 251–356) as recorded by his immediate disciples.[25] A similar resistance to the introduction of cathedral psalmody into the monastic usage can be seen in another largely ignored but important text, Dadisho' bar Qatraya's late-seventh-century complaint that the proliferation of new *'onyatha* (antiphons) and other "useless chants," as he brands them, were destroying the pristine purity of the East-Syrian monastic offices.[26]

Liturgical Press, 1992), 58–60, 79–81; and, most recently, Thomas Pott, *La réforme liturgique byzantine* (BEL.S 104; Rome: CLV-Edizioni liturgiche, 2000), 99–124. McKinnon, "Desert Monasticism," 514–21, outlines the first signs of this shift.

22 Taft, *Byzantine Rite,* 58; Froyshov, "La réticence," esp. 243–45; Rainer Stichel, "Homiletik, Hymnographie und Hagiographie im frübyzantinischen Palästina," in *Andrias: Herbert Hunger zum 80. Geburtstag = Jahrbuch der Österreichischen Byzantinistik* 44 (ed. W. Hörander et al.; Vienna: Verlag der Österreichischen Akademie der Wissenschaften, 1994), 404–6.

23 *Diary* 24.1, 12; 25.2, 6–7, 12: Egeria, *Journal de voyage: Itinéraire* (ed. P. Maraval; SC 296; Paris: Cerf, 1982), 234–37, 244–47, 250–51, 254–55.

24 *Life of St. Sabas* (439–532), 6, 31; *Life of St. Theodosius* (ca. 430–529), 1, in *Kyrillos von Skythopolis* (ed. E. Schwartz; TU 49.2; Leipzig: Hinrichs, 1939), 90, 116, 236; English translation in Cyril of Scythopolis, *The Lives of the Monks of Palestine* (trans. R. M. Price; Cistercian Studies 114; Kalamazoo, Mich.: Cistercian Publications, 1991), 90 (cf. 210 n. 8), 125, 262–63; further secondary sources cited in Stichel, "Homiletik, Hymnographie und Hagiographie," 389–406. On the whole question, see Jean-Miguel Garrigues and Jean Legrez, *Moines dans l'assemblée des fidèles à l'époque des pères: IVᵉ–VIIIᵉ siècle* (Théologie historique 87; Paris: Beauchesne, 1990).

25 Gérard Garitte, "Un fragment grec attribué à S. Antoine l'Ermite," *Bulletin de l'Institute historique belge de Rome* 20 (1939): 165–70.

26 Unedited Syriac text from codex *Vatican Syriac 496* (ff. 154v–157v) translated into French in appendix 8 of Mateos, *Lelya-Sapra,* 472–74.

In Palestine the same sentiments are clearly reflected in the famous seventh- or eighth-century *Narration of the Abbots John and Sophronius* recounting the visit those two Palestinian monks made to the anchorite Abbot Nilus of Sinai.[27] Their conversation, preserved in the *Hermeneiai* of Nikon, concerns mostly the Divine Office, the differences between cathedral and monastic services, and cathedral chanting, in particular, the monastic rejection of it. When his visitors express their astonishment at the absence in Nilus's offices of the ecclesiastical poetry they were accustomed to in their own Sabaitic offices,[28] Nilus replies that such refrains are proper to the offices of the ordained clergy (i.e., the cathedral office) but not suitable for monks bewailing their sins:[29] "As for the psalmody executed with singing and tone, and with the people responding the *akrosticha* with melody and chant—these things we [monks] leave to readers, psalmists, subdeacons, and deacons."[30]

However, the adoption of the ecclesiastical system of offices eventually won out, if not without a struggle, as we see in later miracle stories concerning the monks in Sardinia, disciples of Gregory Asbestas, mid-ninth century archbishop of Syracuse in Sicily, who ridiculed Saint Theodore of Studios's (d. 826) Triodion canons for Orthros (Matins) in Lent. In such outlying areas the new poetry had probably not yet been accepted by the monks. Since this important text is rarely cited, I give it in full:

> But it is time for us to describe a miracle which took place for a man living on the island of Sardinia and thereby please the ears of the pious, for it is a remarkable story, combining the amazing with the miraculous. There was a man on the island who loved and honored the writings of the great man [Saint Theodore of Studios] above all else, and especially the poems for Pentecost, which are usually called the Triodia. Once some monks who were travelling happened to visit him during Lent. They were disciples of Gregory of Syracuse, quite unintelligent with hearts full of arrogance, and they attempted to mock the Saint's poems, saying they were not composed according to the rules of poetry and were full of solecisms. So their host, convinced I know not how, quickly changed his mind and stopped chanting them in the morning office [ἐν ὀρθριναῖς ταῦτα

---

[27] Longo edition (see n. 12); see also Taft, *Liturgy of the Hours,* 198–200, 224, 274–75; Juan Mateos, "La psalmodie variable dans l'office byzantin," *Societas Academica Dacoromana Acta philosophica et theologica* 2 (1964): 337. On the date, see Froyshov, "La réticence," 235.

[28] See Taft, *Byzantine Rite,* chs. 5–7 *passim.*

[29] Longo edition, lines 49–55, 61–64.

[30] Ibid., lines 238–41. Earlier (lines 191–95) Nilus uses the exact same expression with reference to the *prokeimena, propsalmata,* and *bematikia* chants but does not mention the *koinonikon.*

ὑποψάλλων δοχολογίας] as he used to do. The Father appeared to him one night, looking very old (as he in fact was at the time), with a pale face and the top of his head bald. With him were other people holding clubs; it was a vision which was horrible enough just to see, and quite unendurable. He ordered the others to obey his orders immediately and to beat with the clubs the man who was so easily led and so unsteady in his opinions. While he was being beaten, the Father stood nearby and said: "You faithless fellow, why do you reject my poems and consider them worthless, though only a short time ago you loved and honored them? You should be able to see for yourself that God's church would not have accepted them and passed them on unless there were some benefit in them. For grandiloquence and rhetorical art do not know how to affect the heart, but rather humble words which are composed for spiritual benefit and which are totally sound. For me, one who honors education above all else is worthy of everything, and he seems far more honorable than one who pays attention only to sounds." When he had been sufficiently beaten and paid the penalty for his turn to the worse, day arrived. Still aching, he jumped out of bed, his heart quivering with fear and his body swollen from the blows. He straightaway showed the marks to everyone and pathetically recounted what had happened to him. After violently insulting those corrupters who had caused his suffering, he drove them from his house. Wishing to placate the Father, he showed greater faith in him than before and loved and honored the great man's poetry. Since he did this with greater veneration than I can describe, he received true healing of the soul.[31]

No wonder the Benedictine monk Eligius Dekkers's ironically entitled article, "Were the Early Monks Liturgical?"[32] poured cold water on the romanticism of the nineteenth-century Benedictine revival à la Guéranger and its resumption of the Cluniac *monachus propter chorum* ideology, which considered the monk a *homo liturgicus* par excellence.

---

31 *Life of St. Theodore Studites* (= *Vita* 2), 113, attributed to Theodore Daphnopates (= *BHG* 1755), PG 99:216B–17A, translated by Mark Herlong, to whom I am indebted for furnishing me a copy of his unpublished version; Vasilij Latyshev, "Zhitie prep. Feodora Studita v mjunxenskoj rukopisi No. 467," *Vizantijskij Vremennik* 21 (1914): 222–54; cf. also Michael the Studite, *Vita* 1, 56 (= *BHG* 1754), PG 99:312C–313B; and *Vita* 3 (= *BHG* 1755d), Vasilij Latyshev, "Vita S. Theodori Studitae in codice Mosquensi musei Rumianzoviani No. 520," *Vizantijskij Vremennik* 21 (1914): 255–304, here 296.33–297.32.

32 Eligius Dekkers, "Were the Early Monks Liturgical?" *Collectanea Cisterciensia* 22 (1960): 120–37. See also Wulf, "Priestertum und Rätestand," 109–18, 246–61; Ghislain Lafont, "The Eucharist in Monastic Life," *Cistercian Studies* 19 (1984): 296–318; and the discussion in Taft, *Liturgy of the Hours*, 362–63.

CATHEDRAL LITURGY AND ITS PSALMODY

So the offices of the secular (i.e., nonmonastic) or "cathedral" churches were totally different in spirit, structure, and content from the purely monastic offices. Focused on the Paschal Mystery, the cathedral offices were services of *latreia* or worship, designed to praise and adore God in thanksgiving for his salvation in Christ Jesus and to implore his aid and favor. As offices of praise and intercession, the cathedral services were not a Liturgy of the Word, designed to edify or instruct.[33] These popular services were characterized by symbol and ceremonial (light, incense, processions, etc.), by congregational chanting (responsorial and antiphonal psalmody, popular refrains and hymns), celebrated under the leadership of ordained presiders (bishops or presbyters), and with the participation of the fully articulated gamut of lesser ordained ministers (deacons, readers, psalmists, etc.).[34]

Furthermore, cathedral offices were popular services for nonprofessionals. Their structure was simple and almost invariable. Petitionary prayer for the needs of the common people occupied a large part of the services, and—most important for our purposes—the psalmody was limited and select rather than current and complete. That is, the psalms were not read continuously according to their numerical order in the Bible, but certain psalms only, or even sections of psalms, were chosen for their suitability to the hour or service according to the text of the liturgical psalter.[35] In the Septuagint, for example, Ps 140 was read at Vespers because verse 2 refers to "the lifting up of my hands like an evening sacrifice"; Ps 62 was read at Matins because verse 2a says, "O God my God, I keep watch before you, my soul thirsts for you," and verse 7, "On my bed I remember you, and meditate on you in the morning watches."

---

[33] There were no scriptural lessons whatever in the daily ferial cathedral offices, contrary to the sixteenth-century "Reformation fallacy" that conceived Christian liturgy as centered essentially on the proclamation of God's Word. One is free to think that is what the cathedral Divine Office ought to be; one is dead wrong to think anyone before Luther conceived of it in that way. Though there were usually no Scripture readings on ordinary days, such lessons were added later to provide feast days with festive coloration. On the whole question, see Taft, *Liturgy of the Hours,* 32–33, 319–20.

[34] Taft, *Liturgy of the Hours,* 32–33; William F. Storey, "The Liturgy of the Hours: Cathedral versus Monastic," *Worship* 50 (1976): 56–58.

[35] That is, the psalms in the Latin Vulgate, Greek LXX, or Syriac Peshitta, which are of course not the same as in the Hebrew Psalter. For the different numbering of the psalms in these liturgical psalters, see Taft, *Liturgy of the Hours,* x.

Christian Cathedral Psalmody, Responsorial and Antiphonal[36]

The psalmody of these cathedral services was designed for popular participation by the ordinary laity, many of whom were illiterate. In any case, before the advent of printing they would not have owned psalters, nor, unlike the monks[37] and professional psalmists, did they know the psalter by heart.[38] Thus their active participation in the psalmody was assured by providing them with short, easily remembered responses or refrains that they could repeat after the psalm verses chanted aloud by a professional soloist. This psalmody took two forms: responsorial psalmody and its later elaboration, antiphonal psalmody.

Responsorial Psalmody[39]

When clear evidence for Christian cathedral psalmody first emerges in the second and third centuries in East and West, it has already assumed the responsorial form still in use today. Responsorial psalmody consists in the congregation repeating a "respond"—a psalm verse or short exclamation such as Alleluia—after each segment[40] or verse of the psalm intoned by the soloist or psalmist (ψάλτης).[41] This respond, if a psalm verse, is almost always from the psalm of the responsory itself. The psalmody opened with the soloist proclaiming the respond, thus instructing the people, who of course did not have books, what they were to sing. The people repeated the respond after the soloist, who then proceeded to proclaim the psalm verses

---

[36] See Mateos, *La célébration de la parole,* 7–26; idem, *Le Typicon,* 2:313–14, 316–17, 323–29; Taft, *Great Entrance,* 83–108, 112–18.

[37] See, e.g., Pachomius (ca. 290–346), *Precepts* 140–142, *MECL* §112; Gregory of Nyssa (ca. 330–ca. 395), *Life of St. Macrina* 3, SC 178:150 = *MECL* §151.

[38] Chrysostom, *In ps 117,* 1, PG 55:328 = *MECL* §170, says so explicitly.

[39] See Taft, *Liturgy of the Hours,* 39–41, 55–56, 59–61, 80, 90, 94–96, 103, 108, 116–20, 123–30, 133, 135, 137–40, 150, 167, 169, 175–77, 180, 187–89, 212.

[40] I say "segment" to avoid the mistaken impression that the verse divisions of the psalter were necessarily as they are today. For this one must consult the liturgical psalters in the respective traditions. See Robert Taft, "Mount Athos: A Late Chapter in the History of the 'Byzantine Rite,'" *DOP* 42 (1988): 181–82; idem, *Liturgy of the Hours,* 227, 230–31, 275, 280; Mateos, "La psalmodie variable"; idem, *Le Typicon,* 1:54; 2:327–28; and, for the Syriac psalters, Juan Mateos, "Une collection syrienne de «prières entre les marmyata»," *OCP* 31 (1965): esp. 56–61, 333–35; Mateos, *Lelya-Sapra,* esp. 28–31.

[41] Mateos, *La célébration de la parole,* 7–13; idem, *Le Typicon,* 2:316–17; McKinnon, introduction to *MECL,* 10. On the ψάλτης, see Mateos, *Le Typicon,* 2:328–29; Neil K. Moran, *Singers in Late Byzantine and Slavonic Painting* (Byzantina Neerlandica, fasc. 9; Leiden: Brill, 1986), ch. 2.

one by one, with the people repeating the respond after each. The soloist signaled the people that the responsory was concluding by intoning the incipit of the respond, as in the Byzantine *prokeimenon* or responsory of Easter Vespers:

Psalmist: Great responsory in the seventh tone! Who is a great god like our God? You are the God who does wonders! (Ps 76:13b–14a).

People: Who is a great god like our God? You are the God who does wonders!

Psalmist: You have made known your power among the nations (Ps 76:14b).

People: Who is a great god like our God? You are the God who does wonders!

Psalmist: And I said: Now have I begun! This is the change of the right hand of the Most High! (Ps 76:10).

People: Who is a great god like our God? You are the God who does wonders!

Psalmist: I remembered the works of the Lord, for I will remember your wonders from the beginning (Ps 76:11).

People: Who is a great god like our God? You are the God who does wonders!

Psalmist: Who is a great god like our God?

People: You are the God who does wonders!

This type of psalmody, still preserved between the Scripture lessons of the Liturgy of the Word in East and West, goes back to the biblical text itself, as for example in the "Alleluia psalms" (LXX Pss 104–106; 110–118; 134–135; 145–150), or Ps 135 in the Septuagint, with its respond "for his mercy is forever" after each verse.

Already by the end of the second century we see responsories employed in Christian worship. Tertullian's treatise *On Prayer* 27, written between 198 and 204 C.E., says: "The more diligent in praying are accustomed to add in prayers the Alleluia *and psalms of this type,* to the conclusions of which those who are together may respond."[42] Moreover, the *agape* chapter (25)[43] of the so-called *Apostolic Tradition,* a third- or

42 CCSL 1:273 = PL 1:1194 = *MECL* §78.

43 On this chapter, not found in the earliest source of the document, see Taft, *Liturgy of the Hours,* 26–27.

fourth-century source,[44] refers thus to the Christian liturgical use of the biblical psalms with built-in responds:

> They shall rise, then, after supper and pray; and the boys and the virgins shall say psalms.
>
> And then the deacon, when he receives the mixed cup of the offering, shall say a psalm from those in which "Alleluia" is written, and then, if the priest so directs, again from the same psalms. And after the bishop has offered the cup, he shall say the whole of a psalm which applies to the cup,[45] with "Alleluia," all joining in. When they recite psalms, all shall say, "Alleluia," which means "We praise him who is God; glory and praise to him who created every age through his word alone." And when the psalm is finished, he shall give thanks over the cup and distribute the fragments to all the faithful.[46]

Somewhat later, Saint Athanasius of Alexandria's (295–373) *Defense of His Flight* 24, shows the exact same tradition in Egypt: "I urged the deacon to read a psalm and the people to respond: *For his mercy endures forever*" (LXX Ps 134).[47]

ANTIPHONAL PSALMODY

With Athanasius we are well into the fourth century, when abundant evidence from everywhere shows that Christians also used another genre of psalmody, called antiphonal. To the student of Western psalmody, the word *antiphonal* automatically conjures up visions of a monastic community divided into two choirs, chanting the verses of a psalm in alternation. If you learn nothing else from what I write here, take away at least this one idea: that is *not* what antiphonal psalmody means. I would like, once and for all, to bury that notion and to impose a new terminology, "alternate psalmody," for that usage.[48]

---

44 Present discussion on the nature, provenance, authorship, etc. of this document, and hence its dating, are in a state of considerable agitation. See Paul F. Bradshaw, Maxwell E. Johnson, and L. Edward Phillips, *The Apostolic Tradition: A Commentary* (ed. Harold W. Attridge; Minneapolis: Fortress, 2002).

45 E.g., Ps 115:4: "I shall take the chalice of salvation, and call upon the name of the Lord."

46 Bernard Botte, *La Tradition apostolique de Saint Hippolyte: essai de reconstitution* (LQF 39; Münster Westfalen: Aschendorff, 1963), 66–67; G. J. Cuming, *Hippolytus: A Text for Students* (Grove Liturgical Studies 8; Bramcote, Notts.: Grove Books, 1976), 24.

47 SC 56:162 = PG 35:676 = *MECL* §102.

48 It is true that medieval Latin writers use the term *antiphonal* for alternate psalmody, but I believe this nomenclature is better avoided, to obviate what

Antiphonal psalmody, from the Greek verb ἀντιφωνεῖν, to respond alternately, is an elaboration of the responsorial method. Tradition assigns its origins to Antioch in the fourth century.[49] In Byzantine usage antiphonal psalmody is distinguished by the following characteristics.

1. Although the entire liturgical unit of psalm verses plus refrain is called "antiphon" by synecdoche, strictly speaking the "antiphon" is the "troparion" (literally "ritornello"). It is usually (but not always) a nonbiblical composition or (especially in earlier sources) Alleluia, used as the refrain to be repeated after the psalm verses.

2. The people, divided into two choirs, *respond alternately*—hence the name "antiphonal"—to the verses of the psalm chanted by a soloist (ψάλτης[50]) or alternately by two soloists, one at the head of each choir.

3. Sometimes each choir has not only its own soloist to whom it responds but even its own proper refrain.

4. Sometimes, as in the antiphons of the "Choral Office" (ἀκολουθία ἀσματική) of Hagia Sophia described by Symeon of Thessalonika (d. 1429),[51] the refrain was Alleluia or a very short phrase,[52] usually an ecclesiastical composition, only rarely a verse from Scripture.

5. At other times, the troparion was a longer composition, of which only the finale (ἀκροτελεύτιον), a self-standing grammatical unit such as "save us," would be repeated after each verse. In this case the whole refrain would be chanted only at the beginning (thrice), then twice again after the doxology at the end of the antiphon.[53]

6. The antiphonal psalmody, unlike the responsorial, always concludes with the "Glory be to the Father. . . ."

7. Sometimes this doxology is split, and one choir repeats the refrain after "Glory be to the Father and to the Son and to the Holy Spirit," the

---

McKinnon (introduction to *MECL,* 10) means when he calls "antiphonal psalmody in the early Christian period . . . one of the perplexities" in the history of psalmody. "In the early medieval sources this type appears in its commonly understood meaning of two choirs singing psalm verses in alternation. . . . There is, however, just one example of dual choir psalmody given in this volume [*MECL*], from Basil's Epistle 207, and it fails to use the term antiphonal."

49 Socrates (ca. 380–450), *Church History* 6.8, GCS neue Folge 1:325–26 = *MECL* §218; Theodoret of Cyrrhus (ca. 393–ca. 466), *Church History* 2.24.8–9, GCS 44:154 = *MECL* §224; Augustine, *Conf.* 9.6.14–7.15, CCSL 27:141–42 = *MECL* §351, calls it "after the manner of the eastern regions."

50 See note 41 above.

51 *De sacra precatione* 347, 349, PG 155:624–29, 636–42; cf. Strunk, *Essays in Music* 113–18, 125.

52 Symeon of Thessalonika, *De sacra precatione* 347, 349, PG 155:624–29, 636–42; Strunk, *Essays on Music,* 122–25; on 140–42, Strunk lists the refrains.

53 Illustrated from the sources in Mateos, *La célébration,* 16–20.

other after the concluding "both now and ever, and unto the ages of ages. Amen!"

8. For this final double-repetition, called περισσή or "appendix," sometimes a variant refrain would be substituted.[54]

In its most developed form, the antiphon opened with the repetition of the refrain(s) by the two choirs.[55] If there was only one refrain, it was sometimes repeated six times, thrice by the soloists, then thrice by the people. The verses of the accompanying psalm were then chanted by a soloist or by two alternating soloists, one at the head of each choir. To these the people, divided into two choirs, responded alternately with the refrain(s). Sometimes each choir in turn responded with the same troparion or refrain; sometimes each choir was assigned a different refrain. If the troparion was rather long, it was sung in its entirety only at the beginning and end of the psalmody. After each psalm verse the respective choir would respond with only the ἀκροτελεύτιον or final phrase of the refrain.[56] This explains why many Byzantine troparia conclude in a final, grammatically independent phrase, intelligible by itself, and hence easily detachable from the rest of the composition. The final psalm verse was always followed by the Gloria Patri. We have a clear example of this type of psalmody in the antiphons that interrupt the readings on the vigils of Christmas and Theophany. The first of these, according to the Typikon and Prophetologion, was executed in the following manner:

> The psalmists together: You were born in the secrecy of a grotto, but heaven, putting up a star to proclaim it, announced You to all, O Savior, and it led the Magi to You, who adored You with Faith: with them have mercy on us! (repeated three times).
>
> Readers and people together: the same troparion, three times.
>
> Psalmist: His foundation upon the holy mountains, the Lord loves. He prefers the gates of Sion more than any dwelling of Jacob. Glorious things are said of you, O city of God: "I reckon Rahab and Babylon among those who know me" (Ps 86:1–4a).
>
> People: With them, have mercy on us!
>
> Psalmist: Tyre, Philistia, or Ethiopia, one such was born there; but Sion, everyone says to her: "Mother," for in her everyone was born. And he who has established her is the Most High. (Ps 86:4b–5).

---

[54] Ibid., 17–20; Mateos, *Le Typicon,* 2:313–14.

[55] On the two choirs, see Mateos, *Le Typicon,* 2:315.

[56] Mateos, *La célébration,* 13–23; idem, *Le Typicon,* 2:88 (apparatus 3), 310, 325; further references to the ἀκροτελεύτιον in Taft, *Great Entrance,* 87 n. 142.

People: With them, have mercy on us!

Psalmist: The Lord inscribes in the book of the nations... (Ps. 86:6–7).

People: With them, have mercy on us!

Psalmist: Glory to the Father ... both now and ever, and unto the ages of ages. Amen!

People: With them, have mercy on us!

The psalmists together: You were born in the secrecy of a grotto, but heaven, putting up a star to proclaim it, announced You to all, O Savior, and it led the Magi to You, who adored You with Faith: with them have mercy on us!

Readers and people together: You were born in the secrecy of a grotto, but heaven, putting up a star to proclaim it, announced You to all, O Savior, and it led the Magi to You, who adored You with Faith: with them have mercy on us! [57]

The ancient manner of beginning an antiphonal psalm with the triple repetition of the whole refrain, first by all the psalmists, then by the people, is preserved in Slavic usage at the beginning of the services of Easter week, although now the priest takes the place of the psalmists, and the troparion is so short it is repeated in its entirety after each verse of the psalm.

Note also the ancient method of concluding the psalmody.[58] After the "Glory be to the Father," the ἀκροτελεύτιον is repeated a final time. Then the psalmists repeat the whole troparion, and, finally, the readers and the people do the same. This double final repetition of the entire troparion was, as I already noted, called περισσή or "appendix." More often, however, the name περισσή was given to a second refrain, which, for variety, was substituted at the end of the antiphon for the final repetition of the troparion. In contemporary Byzantine practice, the "O only-begotten Son" troparion (*Monogenes*) is a περισσή of the second antiphon of the Divine Liturgy. So also is the κοντάκιον of the third antiphon on great feast days in the Slavonic books, which have preserved, on these days at least, the ancient manner of psalmody intact.

Of course, in the later intermingling—and, in some traditions, even fusion—of cathedral and monastic offices, both styles of psalmody came to be used in the Liturgy of the Hours of the various Eastern and Western

---

[57] C. Høeg and G. Zuntz, *Prophetologium* (Monumenta musicae byzantinae, Lectionaria 1, fasc. 1–5; Copenhagen: Munksgaard, 1939–62), 1:39–41, and the respective rubrics. Cf. Mateos, *La célébration,* 17; Taft, *Great Entrance,* 86–89.

[58] Mateos, *La célébration,* 17–19; idem, *Le Typicon,* 2:313–14.

rites, in almost all of which the Divine Office is a hybrid of both types, synthesized in the context of urban monasticism of late antiquity.[59]

In Praise of Psalmody

By all accounts, Christian liturgical psalmody was a huge success, if we can believe the patristic witnesses of late antiquity.[60] The reliability of this positive testimony is reinforced by the fact that psalmody was about the only thing for which the fathers of the church praise rather than berate their congregations with regard to their behavior in church.[61] In Asia Minor Saint Gregory Nazianzen (d. ca. 390), *Oratio 43 in Praise of St. Basil the Great* 52, recounts that when the Arian emperor Valens visited Saint Basil's church at Epiphany, "the thundering psalmody struck his ear."[62] In addition, *Miracle* 33 in the fifth-century Greek *Life and Miracles of Saint Thecla* from Seleucia in Isauria (Silifke in Turkey)[63] recounts how the pilgrims to Hagia-Thekla (Ayatekla), the sanctuary of the saint just south of Seleucia, giving their impression of the feast and its liturgy (synaxis), mention, *inter alia,* "the harmony of the chanting of the psalms."[64] For Ambrose (d. 397), in Milan, too, the psalmody was glorious,[65] and the prayers and responsories of the people resounding with the soft harmony of the waves at sea gave him inexpressible joy.[66] Augustine (d. 430) also took delight in the people's psalmody, though he admitted that his North African Catholics were rather sluggish and that the Donatists sang better, taunting their Catholic rivals with the boredom of their chanting.[67] In Southern Gaul, Caesarius of Arles (d. 542) also praised the way his people chanted the psalms.[68]

---

59 On all this, see Taft, *Liturgy of the Hours.*

60 E.g., Egeria, *Journal* 24.5, 8, SC 296:240–43; Basil, *MECL* §§130, 131, 136, 139; Augustine, *MECL* §§351, 352, 365, 372; other witnesses cited below in notes 62–68.

61 I cite numerous examples in "Women at Church in Byzantium: Where, When—and Why," *DOP* 52 (1998): 82–86; idem, "'Eastern Presuppositions' and Western Liturgical Renewal," *Antiphon* 5 (2000): 13–14.

62 PG 36:561CD = *MECL* §148.

63 Isauria is the southern coast of Turkey directly north of Cyprus.

64 Gilbert Dagron, ed., *Vie et miracles de Sainte Thècle: texte grec, traduction et commentaire* (Subsidia hagiographica 62; Brussels: Société des Bollandistes, 1978), 376–77; on the sanctuary and its location, ibid., 55–79. I am indebted to Alice-Mary Talbot, Director of Byzantine Studies at Dumbarton Oaks, for drawing my attention to this citation.

65 *Expl. Ps.* 1, 9, CSEL 64:7–8 = *MECL* §276.

66 *Hex.* 3.5.23, CSEL 32.1:74–75 = *MECL* §289.

67 *Ep. 55,* 34–35, CSEL 35:208–9 = *MECL* §377.

68 *Sermo 75,* CCSL 103:313–15.

THE BENEFITS OF PSALMODY

The reasons for this praise of psalmody were both spiritual and pastoral. First of all, biblical psalmody was seen as the antidote to "private psalms" (ψαλμοὶ ἰδιοτικοί)—that is, nonbiblical refrains and hymns—often used by heretics to propagate their doctrine.[69] "If you yearn for songs, you have the psalms," the third-century *Didaskalia* 6.3.5 curtly instructed Christians,[70] and nonbiblical songs were expressly prohibited in canon 59 of the Council of Laodicea in Phrygia (ca. 360–390).[71]

The fathers subjected psalmody to a long litany of praise from the spiritual point of view, as well. Psalmody recommended itself first of all because of its scriptural warrant: the Psalms are divinely revealed; they were used by Christ and the apostles;[72] the Psalter contains everything found in all the other books of the Bible: history, law, prophecy, admonition, morality;[73] the Psalms stir piety and the love of God; psalmody calms the passions, teaches love of wisdom, cleanses the soul, stimulates tears of repentence, puts the devil to flight, fosters the ascent to God, and so on.[74]

PSALMODY IN PRACTICE

How the liturgical psalmody "worked," punctuating a cathedral service with frequent elements of active popular participation, can be easily discerned in codex *Rahmani Syr. 33*. This copy of an eighth- or ninth-century Syriac manuscript preserving a still earlier liturgical ordo of the late sixth century details the ritual for the solemn entry of a bishop into town for the liturgy.[75] The ordo describes the Liturgy of the Word and preanaphora as follows:

---

[69] See, e.g., the numerous texts in *MECL* §§71, 165, 211, 218, 226, 232, 377, 385; Taft, *Liturgy of the Hours,* 149, 159, 172.

[70] Franz X. Funk, ed., *Didascalia et Constitutiones apostolorum* (2 vols.; Paderborn: Schoeningh, 1905; repr., Turin: n.p., 1964), 1:15 = *MECL* §71.

[71] Laodicea (Laodikeia) was near modern Denizili on the southern coast of Turkish Asia Minor. The Greek text of the canon is edited in P.-P. Joannou, *Discipline générale antique* (Fonti codificazione canonica orientale 9; Grottaferrata [Rome]: Tipografia Italo-Orientale "S. Nilo," 1962–64), 1.2:154. In the West, canon 12 of the Council of Braga (563 C.E.) legislates the same prohibition; see Taft, *Liturgy of the Hours,* 158–59.

[72] Augustine, *Ep. 55,* 34, CSEL 34:208–9 = *MECL* §377.

[73] *MECL* §§129, 131–33, 138, 276.

[74] *MECL* §§115, 129–32, 164–66, 188, 198–99, 275–76, 305–6, 352.

[75] Ignatius Ephrem II Rahmani, ed., "Ritus receptionis episcopi et celebrationis liturgiae catechumenorum," in *Vetusta documenta liturgica* (fasc. 3 of his Studia Syriaca; Monte Libano: Typis Patriarchalibus in Seminario Scharfensi, 1908), 1–22, and Syriac numerals 1–4, here text 1–5 (Syriac numerals); Latin version 16–22. For

1. At the time of the service, the clergy arrive and he [the bishop] descends with them to the diakonikon, and immediately sits down there until the clergy have put on their vestments.
2. And when the archdeacon, carrying the gospel book, has gone out ahead of the bishop, the vigilers begin the service.
3. And as soon as the bishop enters the church, the archpriest recites the prayer.
4. Afterwards the psalmists chant the Trisagion.
5. And straightaway the bishop says the prayer before the lessons, and sits in his place, and the presbyters sit according to their rank.
6. And straightaway the archdeacon cries: "Be quiet!"
7. And straightaway the reader ascends and announces the name of his book.
8. Then the archdeacon cries: "Let us be attentive!"
9. And as soon as the reader has finished the lesson, the archdeacon makes a sign to one of the priests, who, remaining seated, cries: "Peace to you!" And he does the same until two books, Greek and Syriac, [have been read].
10. And straightaway a psalmist, going up, says: "A psalm of David!"
11. And the archdeacon says: "Intone [the responsory]!"
12. And the psalmist says the respond.
13. And the archdeacon cries: "Sing the respond!"
14. And without delay the vigilers sing.
15. And straightaway [the readers of] two other lections ascend, while the bishop stays at his place on his throne, and those who are seated remain in their places.
16. And the vigilers say six verses of the psalm "Have mercy on me, O God, according to your mercy" [Ps 50:1/51:1], with suitable strophes.
17. And straightaway one of the presbyters [says] "Peace to you!" and they remain seated.
18. Whereupon straightaway the apostle is read.
19. Then straightaway the Alleluia.
20. The archdeacon says: "Intone [the responsory]!"

---

a liturgical analysis of this text, with its Greek and Syriac terms in the original, see Taft, "The βηματίκιον in the 6/7th c. Narration of the Abbots John and Sophronius (BHGNA 1438w): An Exercise in Comparative Liturgy," in *Crossroad of Cultures: Studies in Liturgy and Patristics in Honor of Gabriele Winkler* (ed. H.-J. Feulner et al.; OCA 260; Rome: Pontificium Institutum Orientalium Studiorum, 2000), 685–91.

21. And right after the Alleluia the archdeacon says: "All chant the respond in symphony!"
22. And straightaway the Gospel is read.
23. And the litanies.
24. And the bishop prays.
25. Then the archdeacon carries the gospel book, which had been put on the altar.
26. And the Greek deacon cries: "Catechumens depart!"
27. And after him the Syrian [deacon]: "Whoever has not received the seal, depart!"
28. And all [the deacons] cry out in this way until they enter to the altar.
29. And the archdeacon, bearing the gospel book, cries: "Catechumens depart! The doors!"
30. And the veils and doors are closed.
31. And immediately the vigilers chant the *ma'nyoto* [i.e., antiphon].
32. And water for the ablution is brought to the bishop and all the priests.
33. And the bishop enters and stands before the altar, and straightaway the psalmists begin to sing the Alleluia before the Mysteries [i.e., the chant at the entrance into the sanctuary for the preanaphora].
34. And when they have arrived at the door of the altar, the veils are opened.
35. And as soon as the mysteries [i.e., the gifts of bread and wine for the Eucharist] have been arranged on the altar, the bishop incenses, and they say the creed... [MS *explicit*].

What a striking contrast to the bare-bones early eucharistic service as described around 150 C.E. by Justin Martyr, *Apol.* 1.67![76] From the fourth century on in East and West, the witnesses to this cathedral psalmody are legion, and the testimony of the anchorite Nilus in the seventh- or eighth-century *Narration of the Abbots John and Sophronius* shows that the cathedral chants were still executed with the active participation of the people, who repeated the respond after the verses chanted by the soloists. Leeb draws the same conclusion from the hagiopolite Georgian sources.[77]

---

[76] *MECL* §25.

[77] Helmut Leeb, *Die Gesänge im Gemeindegottesdienst von Jerusalem (von 5. bis 8. Jahrhundert)* (Wiener Beiträge zur Theologie 28; Vienna: Herder, 1970), 128–32.

Overdevelopment and Collapse

Despite the paeans of praise, witnesses to the excessive overgrowth of cathedral psalmody and its consequent collapse were not long in coming.[78] The communion psalmody provides a convenient paradigm. The custom of chanting psalmody during the communion rite emerges in the East in the second half of the fourth century,[79] where we see it for the first time almost simultaneously in Palestine[80] and the environs of Antioch.[81] In its earliest form this communion chant comprised simple responsorial psalmody,[82] initially, it seems, LXX Ps 33, with verse 9, "Taste and see that the Lord is good!" as respond. However, communion antiphons develop by the end of late antiquity, with the first appearance of liturgical books in the proper sense of that term, beginning with the so-called *Hymns of Severus of Antioch,* a sixth- or seventh-century anthology of Greek refrains now extant only in Syriac, one of the earliest collections of nonbiblical Christian liturgical chant texts.[83] This songbook, originally a collection of refrains

---

[78] One of the first to signal this collapse was Frank E. Brightman, *Liturgies Eastern and Western* (Oxford: Clarendon Press, 1896), 570.

[79] See Joseph A. Jungmann, *The Mass of the Roman Rite: Missarum sollemnia* (2 vols.; New York: Benziger, 1951–55), 1:391–94; Henri Leclercq, "Communion (Rite et antienne de)," *DACL* 3/2:2427–33.

[80] Cyril/John II of Jerusalem (after 380), *Myst. Cat.* 5, 20, in *Catéchèses mystagogiques* (ed. A. Piédagnel; SC 126bis; Paris: Cerf, 1966), 168–71. This is confirmed by Jerome, *Commentarius in Esaiam* 2.5:20, written in Bethlehem between 407 and 410; CCSL 73:77 = PL 24:86D = *MECL* §331.

[81] John Chrysostom, still a presbyter in Antioch before being summoned to Constantinople in October 397 to become bishop of that see at the beginning of 398, *Expositio in ps. 144,* 1, PG 55:464 = *MECL* §172; *Const. ap.* (ca. 380 C.E.) 8.13.11–14.2, in *Les Constitutions apostoliques* (ed. Marcel Metzger; SC 336; Paris: Cerf, 1987), 208–10.

[82] Detailed with full documentation in Taft, *Precommunion Rites*, 261–318.

[83] Ernest W. Brooks, ed., *The Hymns of Severus and Others in the Syriac Version of Paul of Edessa as Revised by James of Edessa* (PO 6.1 and 7.5; Paris: Firmin-Didot, 1911). On this source, see Aelred Cody, "The Early History of the Octoechos in Syria," in *East of Byzantium: Syria and Armenia in the Formative Period* (ed. N. G. Garsoïan et al.; Washington, D.C.: Dumbarton Oaks Center for Byzantine Studies, 1982), 90–94; Heinrich Husmann, "Hymnus und Troparion," in *Jahrbuch des Staatlichen Instituts für Musikforschung Preussischer Kulturbesitz 1971* (Berlin: de Gruyter, 1972), 7–86 passim; Peter Jeffery, "The Sunday Office of Seventh-Century Jerusalem in the Georgian Chantbooks (Iadgari): A Preliminary Report," *Studia liturgica* 21 (1991): 60 n. 28; and the still-valuable older studies: Anton Baumstark, *Festbrevier und Kirchenjahr der syrischen Jakobiten* (Studien zur Geschichte und Kultur des Altertums 3.3–5; Paderborn: Schönigh, 1910), "ὀκτώηχος des Severus

in Greek, mostly attributed to Severus (ca. 465–538), patriarch of Antioch 512–518, was translated into Syriac by Paul of Edessa in 619–629 and revised by James of Edessa in 675.[84] It contains for the eucharistic liturgy three categories of *ma'nyata,*[85] the Syriac equivalent of "antiphons,"[86] including twenty-two communion *ma'nyata.* This shows that early on the communion psalmody, originally responsorial, had been "antiphonalized" via the addition of an entire repertory of nonbiblical refrains, a process clearly observable in the sources of Antioch, Jerusalem, and, somewhat later, Constantinople.[87]

The liturgical chants in the so-called Georgian Lectionary of Jerusalem,[88] extant in a series of manuscripts from the fifth to the eighth centuries and thoroughly analyzed by Helmut Leeb,[89] betray the same overgrowth. The very name in Georgian for the communion psalmody, *ganic'adï,* the imperative aorist second-person singular for "taste," betrays the origins of the hagiopolite kononikon. The term comes from the incipit of Ps 33:9, "*Taste* and see how good is the Lord." Eventually the hagiopolite koinonikon repertory will expand beyond Ps 33:9, but the Georgian verb-incipit remains the technical term even for koinonika that have nothing to do with Ps 33.[90]

---

von Antioch" in the index; Jules Jeannin and Julien Puyade, "L'Octoëchos syrien," *Oriens christianus* NS 3 (1913): 82–104, 277–98; Jules Jeannin, "Octoëchos syrien," *DACL* 12/2:1888–90.

84 See Taft, *Great Entrance,* 93.

85 PO 6.1:28–32; PO 7.5:670–92.

86 PO 7.5:674, 681. On the identification of these chants as roughly the equivalent of the Byzantine antiphon, see Husmann, "Hymnus und Troparion," 65–6.

87 For a detailed analysis of the entire evolution, see Taft, *Precommunion Rites,* 278–300, 307–18.

88 Strictly speaking, a lectionary is the liturgical book containing the full text of the lections to be read during the services. The so-called Armenian and Georgian lectionaries are really kanonaria-synaxaria, i.e., a sort of liturgical calendar listing the movable and fixed commemorations of the liturgical cycles of the year and indicating the lections for each day/feast via incipit and explicit, but without providing the actual text of the lessons. The Georgian Lectionary is the earliest hagiopolite document to provide detailed information on the liturgical chants of the Eucharist. The earlier Armenian Lectionary of Jerusalem has no chants: Athanase Charles Renoux, ed., *Le codex arménien Jérusalem 121* (PO 36.1; Turnhout: Brepols, 1971).

89 Leeb, *Gesänge im Gemeindegottesdienst;* on the communion chant, see 124–33. Jeffery, "Sunday Office," 55 n. 12, says he disagrees with some of Leeb's interpretations, but since he does not tell us which or why, his critique is not helpful.

90 Michel Tarchnishvili, ed., *Liturgiae Ibericae antiquiores* (CSCO 122–123 = Scriptores Iberici 1–2, ser. 1, vol. 1; Louvain: Durbecq, 1950), §29 pp. 19, 26; §24 pp. 69, 91; André Jacob, "Une version géorgienne inédite de la Liturgie de S. Jean Chrysostome," *Le Muséon* 77 (1964): 115.

In the process, the Georgian term acquires substantive value by the addition of the nominative suffix *y—ganic'adey.* As Jeffery remarks, this name doubtless indicates that Ps 33:9 was the common hagiopolite communion respond before the expansion of the repertory pari-passu with the development of the festive calendar.[91]

Leeb concludes "that in the ancient church and especially in Jerusalem, Psalm 33:9 was the communion chant pure and simple [*schlechthin*]"[92] and that it was originally responsorial psalmody comprising Ps 33, with verse 9 as respond.[93] Other responds, and eventually even nonbiblical refrains, were added later, such as two (*Agnus Dei;* Ps 148) in the early Georgian recension of the Liturgy of Saint John Chrysostom in the eleventh-century Palestinian manuscript *Sinai Georg 89;*[94] and, in the Georgian Lectionary, eleven of them for the Holy Week services: five for Holy Thursday, three for the Easter Vigil, three for Easter Sunday.[95]

Leeb believes this multiplication of communion chants could have been provoked by the great number of communions on those days.[96] That is not an unreasonable surmise, if one considers that on occasions such as the liturgy fêting Patriarch Eutychius's return to Constantinople from exile on 2 October 577 the distribution of holy communion at the liturgy he celebrated in Hagia Sophia is said to have taken three hours because everyone wanted to receive from the hand of Eutychius himself.[97] Even allowing for the inevitable hagiographical exaggeration, it is obvious that the distribution of communion at such solemnities could take quite some time. It is equally possible that by that time the psalmody had already decomposed and that the number of communions demanded a multiplication of refrains to cover the distribution of the sacrament. At any rate, the hagiopolite communion chant repertory continued to grow, as I have already detailed elsewhere and do not need to repeat here.[98]

---

[91] Jeffery, "Sunday Office," 62 n. 33.

[92] Leeb, *Gesänge im Gemeindegottesdienst,* 125.

[93] Ibid., 128.

[94] Jacob, "Une version géorgienne," 115.

[95] Michel Tarchnishvili, ed., *Le Grande lectionnaire de l'Église de Jérusalem* (CSCO 188–189, 204–205 = Scriptores Iberici 9–10, 13–14; Louvain: Secrétariat du CSCO, 1959–60), §§639, 739, 751 in the apparatus; commentary, precisions, and corrections in Leeb, *Gesänge im Gemeindegottesdienst,* 129, 134–36.

[96] Leeb, *Gesänge im Gemeindegottesdienst,* 129–30.

[97] Eustratius, *Vita et conversatio S. Eutychii* 78 (= *BHG* 657), PG 86.2:2364B. The same *Vita,* 94, has Eutychius celebrating the whole Divine Liturgy on the Easter before he died and giving communion in the Body of Christ to all the faithful (PG 86.2:2380B).

[98] Taft, *Precommunion Rites,* 284–88.

In the hagiopolite sources, then, we see the following step-by-step evolution of the communion chant:

1. The pristine chant is responsorial psalmody comprising Ps 33 with Ps 33:9 as respond.
2. To this, Ps 70:8 (*Plerotheto*[99]), perhaps expanded beyond the biblical text, is later appended as περισσή.
3. Still later, nonbiblical refrains or other psalms enter the repertory, in some instances replacing the original psalmic respond.
4. Eventually the doxology and the full *Plerotheto* refrain are added to conclude the psalmody—exactly as in Byzantium.[100]
5. This overgrowth of the entire system ultimately induces collapse.[101]

The reasons for this collapse of the hagiopolite communion psalmody can only be guessed, but I have traced the same evolution in the Byzantine communion responsory,[102] and in other instances the responsorial psalmody in the Eucharist and other offices has suffered at least a reduction to only one psalm verse, with the respond intoned before and after it.

A similar collapse is observable in the history of antiphonal psalmody, which fell apart in a variety of ways once its clearly defined scope was no longer evident. In the Eucharist, for example, as I have shown elsewhere,[103] the three principal "soft points" of the ancient structure of the Eucharist as it emerges already around 150 C.E. in Justin, *Apol.* 1.65, 67,[104] the opening of the liturgy, the transfer of gifts and preparation for the anaphora, and the communion[105]—originally three points of "action without words"—

[99] On the *Plerotheto* refrain, so-called because its incipit is from LXX Ps 70:8, "May my mouth be filled with your praise" (Πληρωθήτο τὸ στόμα μου αἰνέσεως), see Taft, *Precommunion Rites,* 268–69, 286, 288–300.

[100] Jacob, "Une version géorgienne," 115–16.

[101] Leeb, *Gesänge im Gemeindegottesdienst,* 127–32.

[102] Taft, *Precommunion Rites,* 269–70, 288–318.

[103] Robert F. Taft, *Beyond East and West: Problems in Liturgical Understanding* (2d ed.; Rome: Edizioni Orientalia Christiana, Pontifical Oriental Institute, 1997), 204 and ch. 11 *passim.*

[104] Anton Hänggi and Irmgard Pahl, eds., *Prex eucharistica* (3d ed.; Spicilegium Friburgense 12; Fribourg: Universitätsverlag, 1998), 68–71.

[105] For the Roman Mass this material is detailed in the yet to be superseded history by Jungmann, *Mass of the Roman Rite*. For the Byzantine rite, the history of the introit antiphon is studied in Mateos, *La célébration,* 46–57, 106–26; of the preanaphoral antiphon in Taft, *Great Entrance,* 53–118; of the communion psalmody in Taft, *Precommunion Rites,* 261–318.

eventually came to be filled in everywhere with prayer and chant formulas to form a threefold structure comprising (1) an action, (2) covered by a chant, (3) concluded by a prayer. Saint Augustine (d. 430) is an early witness to this when he refers in *Retract.* 2.37 to a certain "Tribune [*vir tribunitius*] Hilarius" who opposed the liturgical custom, recently introduced in Carthage, of chanting psalmody at the people's communion: "singing at the altar hymns from the book of psalms, either before the anaphora or when what had been offered [in the anaphora] was distributed to the people [in communion]."[106]

This pristine system, too, would ultimately degenerate in various ways. For instance, in the Byzantine Trisagion, originally the fixed and invariable introit antiphon of the eucharistic liturgy, the psalm verses were simply suppressed, leaving the opening triple repetition of the refrain and the concluding doxology, ἀκροτελεύτιον, and περισσή.[107] This strangling, in favor of the ecclesiastical refrain, of what was the most important element of the whole liturgical unit, the scriptural text, is a common phenomenon throughout the history of liturgical hymnody.[108] Why such changes occur the sources almost never say, but the reasons can be legion: (1) fluctuations in the amount of time needed for the ritual action the antiphon was destined to "cover": in the case of the communion

---

[106] CSEL 36:144 = *MECL* §385.

[107] Taft, *Beyond East and West,* 198–99, 215–16.

[108] See Mateos, *La célébration,* 22. A classic instance is the nine-ode canon of Byzantine Orthros (Matins), where the riotous development of liturgical poetry has completely suffocated the text at the original basis of the Odes, the nine biblical canticles; see John Ė. Klentos, *Byzantine Liturgy in Twelfth-Century Constantinople: An Analysis of the Synaxarion of the Monastery of the Theotokos Evergetis* (Ann Arbor: University Microfilms International Dissertation Service, 1997), 152–57. On the complexities of these Odes in the history of the Byzantine office, see most recently Gregor Hanke, "Der Odenkanon des Tagzeitenritus Konstantinopels im Licht der Beiträge H. Schneiders und O. Strunks—eine *Relectur,*" in Feulner et al., *Crossroad of Cultures,* 345–67. Certain "temps forts" of the liturgical year preserve remnants of the original system of biblical canticles, following the law of Anton Baumstark concerning the conservative nature of such times: Anton Baumstark, "Das Gesetz der Erhaltung des Alten in liturgisch hochwertiger Zeit," *Jahrbuch für Liturgiewissenschaft* 7 (1927): 1–23; in *Comparative Liturgy* he formulates it thus: "primitive conditions are maintained with greater tenacity in the more sacred seasons of the Liturgical Year" (27). On the whole question, see Taft, "Comparative Liturgy," esp. 527, 536–40; idem, "Anton Baumstark's Comparative Liturgy Revisited," in Taft and Winkler, *Acts of the International Congress,* 191–232; Enrica Follieri, "L'innografia bizantina dal contacio al canone," in *Da bizanzio a San Marco: Musica e liturgia* (ed. G. Cattin; Quaderni di "Musica e storia" 2; Venice: Societá editrice "Il mulino," 1997), 1–32.

psalmody, for instance, the precipitous decline in the frequency of communion from the fourth century on; (2) the multiplication of the poetic refrains at the expense of the scriptural text; (3) the elaboration and complication of the music of these refrains to the detriment of the clear declamation of the scriptural text; and (4) the problem of adapting to small village churches and monasteries a system designed for huge urban basilicas such as Justinian's Hagia Sophia.

In the case of the Trisagion antiphon, one can presume that the later addition of variable antiphons to the Byzantine introit forced the reduction of the original fixed Trisagion antiphon to its present skeletal remains. Why it was kept in reduced form instead of being simply suppressed, or made one among the several new variable antiphons, is probably because of its antiquity and popularity. However, those are the sort of rational questions that only moderns, ever in quest of the logic of things, would dream of asking—except for the historian, long inured to the arbitrariness of reality.

Later, the new variable introit antiphons will also collapse in various ways according to the circumstances. The alternation between soloists and choir(s) disappears as the choirs take over the roles of both soloists and people, a state of evolution we see reflected in the thirteenth-century Otrantan codex *Karlsruhe Ettenheimmünster 6*.[109] Then the alternation between the choirs is suppressed as the two choirs are collapsed into one, the psalm verses are reduced to a few and ultimately, in some present-day usages, disappear entirely.

These degenerations result in the total destruction of the pastoral purpose of the antiphonal psalmody. The execution of the psalm verses by choir instead of soloist results in the usual choral muffling we all know from the opera: the music may be beautiful, but no one—not even fluent Italian speakers—understands the words. The whole point of having the soloist declaim the scriptural verse was so that the sacred words of Scripture would be understood, as fathers of East and West such as Athanasius (d. 373)[110] and Augustine (d. 430)[111] make crystal clear. Finally, the people's participation via the refrain, which was the point of it all, dies out. This, by and large, is the impasse in which we still find ourselves today.

---

[109] Richard Engdahl, *Beiträge zur Kenntnis der byzantinischen Liturgie* (Neue Studien zur Geschichte der Theologie und der Kirche 5; Berlin: Trowitzsch, 1908), 8–9; cf. Mateos, *La Célébration,* 14–15.

[110] *MECL* §§98–101

[111] *Conf.* 10.33.49–50, CCSL, 27:181–82 = *MECL* §352; *Ep.* 211, 7, CSEL 67:361 = *MECL* §379.

Hallels, Midrash, Canon, and Loss: Psalms in Jewish Liturgy

Lawrence A. Hoffman
Hebrew Union College

Rolling around in the deep recesses of memory is a scene from my childhood, with someone saying in Yiddish, *m^e^ darf zog^e^n tehillim:* "You should say psalms." In all probability, the occasion prompting the advice was some family illness, against which reciting psalms was considered a reasonable remedy. The speaker may even have been a member of a *hevra tehillim,* a "society for reciting psalms," a voluntary organization devoted to the special piety of psalm recitation: according to one custom, the psalter would be divided into seven sections, one for each day of the week; another practice associated psalms with weekly Torah portions and the holiday cycle, so that not a Sabbath or a holiday passed without some psalm being added because it was indicative of the day in question. Similarly, Ps 19 was read for weddings, Ps 12 for a circumcision, other psalms still to bring rain in times of drought or healing for those in pain.[1]

This privatized recitation of psalms emerged from sixteenth- and seventeenth-century kabbalistic lore and was outfitted with an introductory and a concluding prayer requesting every known and even unknown benefit. "Let my recitation be as if King David himself were saying it," said the worshiper. Not just the sentences, but the words, the letters, the vocalization scheme, the cantillation marks, and the names of God formed by combining the letters of the beginning and ends of sentences would atone for sin, provide long life, placate divine wrath, and bring about the *yichudim* (as they were called), the unification of the male and the female sides of God that represented the uniquely kabbalistic metaphor for redemption.[2] The kabbalist Isaiah Horowitz (1565?–1630) reports what he

---

[1] Judah David Eisenstein, *Otsar Dinim Uminhagim* (New York: Aizenshtain, 1917), 433–34.

[2] Seligmann Baer, *Seder Avodat Yisrael* (Rödelheim: Lehrberger, 1868), "Introduction to Psalms," 5.

thinks is an old custom of staying up all Yom Kippur eve to read through the psalter in its entirety! "Nothing is greater than Psalms," he adjured his reader, "for it contains everything: much praise for the Holy One, Blessed be He, as well as many psalms that evoke penitence and seek divine pardon."[3]

Typically, as each of the five books of psalms was concluded, worshipers prayed especially that on account of the merit of the words, letters, mystical names, and the like sin would be forgiven, sick friends and family healed, captives redeemed, travelers protected, stillbirths avoided, pregnancies brought to fruition with scholarly children, and even croup or whooping cough eliminated. Unfriendly governments would look kindly on their Jewish populations, evil decrees would be eliminated, business would prosper, and redemption would arrive. *m^e^ darf zog^e^n tehillim,* indeed. Powerful things, these psalms.

If the listener from my childhood was also a synagogue-goer, he or she would have recognized the regular use of psalm collections in the statutory liturgy as well. The regular morning service begins with an entire section largely given over to psalms, its centerpiece being Pss 145–150. The Sabbath is ushered in by Pss 92/93; 95–99; and 29. Other psalms appear here and there with regularity, either whole or in snippets, sometimes readily recognizable, sometimes not.

In addition, the listener from my childhood, if a scholar, would have known that psalms were an integral part of the cult that ceased functioning with the razing of the temple by the Romans in 70 C.E. The best-known instances were known as Hallels, including, first and foremost, the Egyptian Hallel, nowadays (and perhaps in temple times already) Pss 113–118, which was recited for the three pilgrim festivals.[4] In addition, the Levites were said to have sung a different psalm every day of the week.[5] Talmudic tradition further assigns a different psalm for the offering of each intermediate day of Sukkoth.[6] Other traditions assign

---

[3] *Shnei Luchot Habrit, amud hat'shuvah*.

[4] See *m. Pesaḥ.* 5:7; *b. Taʿan.* 28b; *b. ʿArak.* 10a. *Pesaḥ.* 5:7 cites Ps 116:1 as part of it, and independently, but connected to the Seder meal, not the temple sacrifice. Pss 113 and 114 are associated with the first-century C.E. Hillelite/Shammaite debate (*m. Pesaḥ.* 10:6; *t. Pesaḥ.* 10:9).

[5] Ps 24 on Sunday, Ps 48 on Monday, Ps 82 on Tuesday, Ps 94 on Wednesday, Ps 81 on Thursday, Ps 93 on Friday, and Ps 92 on the Sabbath day itself (*m. Tamid* 7:4).

[6] See *b. Sukkah* 55a. The identification of the psalms is somewhat difficult, as only one verse is cited in each case. Traditional interpretation gives them as Pss 29 (day one), 50 (day 2), 94:16 to end of psalm (day three), 94:8–15 (day four), 81 (day five), and 82 (day six). A Sabbath falling within the days called for Ps 92, in which case the psalm for day six was dropped.

Ps 105:1–15 and Ps 96 to the temple rite every morning and every evening, respectively.[7]

I can hardly trace here the history of every single psalm in Jewish liturgy, but I can conveniently cluster the most important insights into three sections: (1) collections of "Praise psalms" known as Hallels; (2) individual psalms for holidays, especially as we know of the custom from medieval Palestinian usage; and (3) psalms as proof texts in what I will call liturgical midrash.

The Hallels

From the earliest of times, groups of psalms that praise God were allotted calendrically. The best-known instance is the festival liturgy's Hallel, known more precisely as "The Egyptian Hallel," after Ps 114:1, which begins, "When Israel left Egypt." At the Passover Seder this Egyptian Hallel was accompanied by another, called (for reasons unclear) "The Great Hallel" and variously identified in the Talmud as Ps 136 or Ps 23—an anomaly, if true, since only a single psalm is mentioned, whereas a Hallel usually refers to more than one.[8] A third Hallel was an optional recitation of psalms prior to the statutory morning service. Rabbi Yose ben Halafta, a second-century sage, is cited as saying, "May my lot be among those who complete a Hallel every day."[9] Nowadays, that Hallel, differentiated as "The Daily Hallel" (*Hallel sheb'khol yom*), is invariably associated with Pss 145–150, but that was purely a Babylonian preference, attested to in the ninth-century *Seder Rav Amram,* our first extant comprehensive prayer book, which hails from Babylonia. Amram explains the custom by noting that Pss 146–150 all begin and end with "halleluyah." His reasoning is circular, however, since he himself admits, "After Psalm 145:21 [its final verse], we add [Ps 115:81] 'We will bless the Lord now and forever: *Halleluyah,*' in order to create a chain of *Halleluyahs,* one after the other."[10]

Amram's reasoning cannot be historically accurate, then. He added a halleluyah verse to the end of Ps 145 because he had inherited the custom of saying that psalm along with the rest, but did not know why. Since Pss 146–150 all began and ended with halleluyah, he assumed that the common halleluyah was the rationale for their selection; and, since Ps 145

[7] *Seder Olam* 14: a midrashic pseudo-history of Israel, variously dated, but possibly referred to by Rabbi Yochanan (third century), who attributed it to Yose bar Halafta (see *b. Nid.* 46b; *b. Yebam.* 82b).

[8] *b. Pesaḥ.* 118a, cited in the name of Rabbi Tarfon (second century). Ps 23 may be a later gloss.

[9] *b. Šabb.* 118b.

[10] *Seder Rav Amram,* 1:10/11.

began but did not end that way, he added a final halleluyah line to harmonize it with the others and thereby justify its inclusion.

There is some logic behind the selection of Pss 145–150, but the common halleluyah has nothing to do with it. All that needs explaining is why the Babylonian selection ended with Ps 150 and began with Ps 145.

The ending is derived from a literal reading of Rabbi Yose's dictum, "May my lot be among those who complete a Hallel every day." The verb "complete" was taken to imply that people should complete the Psalter daily, and Rabbi Yose may have meant just that—saying all 150 psalms every day. But did he? The context of his remark suggests otherwise. His teaching is included in a lengthy talmudic list of overly pious wishes attributed to him: eating an extra meal in honor of the Sabbath, for instance, and keeping the Sabbath an extra-long time. The latter is particularly instructive, as he wishes he could begin Shabbat in Tiberias and end it in Sepphoris. Now, Tiberias is east of Sepphoris, in a valley, while Sepphoris is west of Tiberias, in the mountains. By beginning the Sabbath in the east, he would see the sun rise sooner. By crossing the mountain and moving west, he would enjoy an extra hour or so of the Sabbath day. Such a practice was patently impossible, so Yose's statements should be taken as metaphorical exaggerations of idealized piety, not as practical things that anyone would necessarily do.

What we have is a collection of statements by Rabbi Yose, all in rhetorical form: "May my lot be among those who. . . . " His wish that he might "complete a Hallel daily" is not necessarily related to an actual communal liturgy. To say psalms at all, publicly or privately, was to "say a Hallel." To say the entire Psalter was to "complete a Hallel," something Rabbi Yose held out as a specially pious ideal, even though he probably did not do it.

Other people did, however, as we learn from an anonymous sage who bans the custom as being overly pietistic.[11] Since the literary form of Rabbi Yose's sayings is, technically speaking, a *memra* list—that is, a list of various things that a rabbi once said, which was later memorized and reproduced without the context in which the individual items had been spoken—it is impossible now to reconstruct the circumstances in which the sayings arose. Yose may, for instance, have been thinking about the pietists who said 150 psalms daily, offering approbation for the custom in the face of those who banned it. Whatever the case, he was either talking about a personal pietistic gesture that some people actually followed, or he was speaking in exaggerated terms so as to emphasize the marvelous rhetoric of psalmody. He was not yet talking about psalms in the daily statutory liturgy.

---

[11] *b. Šabb.* 118b.

That is not how his words were taken by the Talmud, however. The Talmud distinguishes Yose's Hallel from the Egyptian Hallel for festivals by identifying it as something called the "Daily Hallel." It is hard to know if the Talmud coins that phrase anew or if a liturgical practice of saying a daily Hallel already existed. If the latter, we can date the daily use of synagogal psalmody as a standard (but optional) liturgical rubric to the late Tannaitic or Amoraic era (that is, prior to the seventh century). Alternatively, it may be that only after the Talmud's compilation, as late as the seventh century or so, did readers of the Talmud read into the words "Daily Hallel" the desirability of having such a rubric, although that is less likely, since the rubric was the norm in both Palestine and Babylon, not just in Babylon, where the Babylonian Talmud was taken as normative. In either case, this use of such psalms is standard today as a lengthy morning introduction to the statutory public liturgy.

Somewhere in the first several centuries C.E., then, it became customary to recite psalms prior to the morning call to prayer. However, the psalms to be said differed widely. The Palestinian Genizah fragments, for instance, vary considerably, frequently having no complete psalms at all, but only collections of psalm verses from here and there, strung together with no obvious rationale for their having been selected.[12] Others, however, who read Rabbi Yose's dictum literally, sought to "complete a Hallel" every morning. Thus one Genizah fragment calls for Pss 120–150 then, a somewhat Herculean task.[13] Like our inherited Babylonian custom of saying Pss 145–150, it too ends with the very last psalm, thus "completing the Psalter" in the sense of reading its last several psalms.

So we know why Ps 150 ends the morning psalmody, but why does Ps 145 (or Ps 120, in Palestine) begin it? We can only speculate, but Ps 120 may have been chosen because it begins the fourteen psalms that are outfitted with the superscription, "A song of ascent." It was an appropriate place to start. The Babylonian case for Ps 145 is easier to explain. The Babylonian Talmud rules that saying Ps 145 daily assures a share in the world to come.[14] Here too its recitation may have been, at first, a matter of private spirituality, but the need to identify a beginning point for public morning psalmody made Ps 145 an obvious choice. Morning psalmody in Babylon thus completed the psalter with Ps 150 (as in Palestine) but began

---

[12] Jacob Mann, "Genizah Fragments of the Palestinian Order of Service," in *Contributions to the Scientific Study of Jewish Liturgy* (ed. J. J. Petuchowski; New York: Ktav, 1970), 386.

[13] Ibid.

[14] *b. Ber.* 4b. Later, in the Middle Ages, after the custom of saying it three times daily developed, the words "three times [daily]" were inserted.

that act of completion with Ps 145, the psalm that Babylonians took as guaranteeing a share in the world to come (not, as in Palestine, Ps 120). Amram inherited that custom; then, noting the use of "halleluyah" in Pss 146–150, he added a halleluyah verse to Ps 145 so as to explain the choice.

Psalms 145-150 are attested elsewhere as well. The eighth-century *Massekhet Sofrim* has the same selection, even though, generally speaking, its liturgical customs are Palestinian.[15] The tenth-century gaon, Saadiah, calls for them too, although our manuscripts of his Siddur inexplicably omit Ps 146, probably in error. Practice remained fluid, however, as we see from the Genizah in general, and as late as the thirteenth century Jacob ben Asher (in Spain) reports that even though Pss 145–150 have become universally the norm, at least in Europe, "In some places, people say *mizmor l'todah* ['A psalm of grateful acknowledgment,' Ps 100]"; his words imply that others did not. "In some places," he continues, "people add other verses, every place according to its own custom."[16] Even in the sixteenth century, Joseph Caro in Palestine felt free to dispense with the halleluyah verse that Amram had added to Ps 145.[17]

Individual Psalms for Holidays

So by the gaonic era (ca. 750–1034), in addition to the Egyptian and the Great Hallels, both Babylonian and Palestinian Jewry "completed" a Daily Hallel, though not necessarily with the same psalms. In addition, specific psalms were assigned to other occasions still.

One such assignment was the daily Levitical psalms, recited "in memory of the temple cult." In varying forms, the practice is known to Amram (ninth century), *Sofrim* (eighth century), and Maimonides (1135–1204), but only as a custom and by no means a universal one.[18] Amram, however, does not actually say the psalms. He merely appends the Mishnah's description of the psalms as those said while the temple stood. Commonly, liturgical descriptions of cultic activity from the Bible or rabbinic literature entered the service in lieu of performing the actual sacrifices, an impossibility after 70. These recitations were actually called *korbanot,* "sacrifices,"

---

[15] Debra Reed Blank, "It's Time to Take Another Look at 'Our Little Sister' Soferim: A Bibliographic Essay," *JQR* 90 (1999): 1–26. Some of *Massekhet Sofrim* was redacted in Babylonia.

[16] *Tur* Orah Ḥayyim 51.

[17] *Bet Yosef* to *Tur* 51, s.v. *v acharav.*

[18] *Sofrim* 18:1; *Seder Rav Amram,* no. 60; *Seder Hat fillah shel Harambam* (ed. E. D. Goldschmidt; Jerusalem: Magnes, 1979), 205. See the discussion on these and other psalms in Ezra Fleischer, *T'fillah Uminhagei T'fillah Erets Yisra'eliyim Bit'kufat Hagenizah* (Jerusalem: Magnes, 1988), 162.

in line with the general rabbinic theory that prayer is "the [sacrificial] offering of our lips." Amram gives us another example of *korbanot,* then—not actual psalmody, just the reading of the passage that describes the Levites' saying of them.

Sofrim, however, does call for the daily psalm being recited, since "reciting a verse in its proper time is like building a new altar and offering a sacrifice on it." Maimonides concurs, but says only, "*Some* of the people are accustomed to reciting" them. We should like to conclude, therefore, that the recitation of these daily Levitical psalms is Palestinian, since *Sofrim* is generally said to be a Palestinian document, and Maimonides lived in Egypt, where the Genizah evidence (also Palestinian) was later found. However, curiously, not a single Genizah fragment contains this custom. Ezra Fleischer therefore assumes that it was the Babylonians who practiced it, even though Amram is content with merely mentioning it, not actually doing it.[19]

Whether that be so or not (and it is hard to conclude with certainty either way), it is indubitably correct that Palestinian Jewry led the way in a second custom: if not reciting the daily Levitical psalm, then at least adopting special psalms for other calendrical events. *Sofrim,* for instance, includes psalms for Hanukkah, Purim, festivals, and Tisha B'av; and the Genizah fragments agree. The holiday and Sabbath psalms offered praise in honor of the occasion that evoked them, and the custom is early. Though we have no Genizah fragments prior to the eighth century, and even though most of them cannot be dated even that early, we can deduce the use of psalms from the synagogue poetry of Eliezer Kalir, who already in the fifth century embeds holiday psalms as proof texts in his festival poetry.[20] Eventually these liturgical psalms were copied into separate scrolls that could be rolled to the right selection as the yearly holiday cycle progressed.

As we would expect, given such early liturgical fluidity—especially in Palestine, where canonization of the service never occurred—practice varied. Only *Sofrim* knows of psalms for the Ninth of Av, for instance (Pss 99; 137). Genizah fragments assign psalms not just to holidays but to Sabbaths that feature specific lections, such as V'zot Habrakhah and Hahodesh. (The former is the final scripture reading of the year; the latter announces the Passover season so is a "first" reading in that it heralds the first biblical month of Nisan, a day that enjoyed special status in medieval Palestine.[21]) All variations aside, however, Palestinian synagogues universally

---

[19] Fleischer, *T'fillah,* 163.

[20] Fleischer, "Chekrei Fiyut V'shirah," *Tarbiz* 39 (1970): 19–38, 248–67.

[21] See Fleischer, "Chekrei Fiyut V'shirah"; idem, "Chadashot L'inyan 'Rosh Roshei Chodashim,'" in *Mechkarim B'aggadah, Targumim, Ut'fillot Yisrael L'zekher Yosef*

said psalms in the evening service of major holidays and with remarkable agreement as to which psalm should be said and when: Pss 135 for the first day of Passover, 136 for the last day, 47 for Rosh Hashanah, 103 for Yom Kippur, 29 for Shavuot, 98 for Rosh Hodesh, 30 for Hanukah, 7 or 22 for Purim, and so on.[22]

As time went on, holiday psalms were further outfitted with other psalms to introduce them. Psalm 93 was usually used for that purpose, and when holidays fell on the Sabbath, Ps 92 ("A psalm for the Sabbath day") preceded it. However, then it was felt that the Sabbath psalm (92) deserved its own preliminary psalm, so Ps 121 was appended as an apt introduction, giving us four psalms in a row: 121 (to introduce Ps 92), 92 (the psalm for the Sabbath), 93 (to introduce the holiday psalm), and the psalm for whatever holiday it was.[23] Soon the practice was generalized to Sabbaths even when no holiday fell on them. At such times, congregations read Ps 121 and then 92. But Ps 92 was by now associated with Ps 93, the psalm that followed it on festivals, so the average Sabbath now featured three psalms: 121 (to introduce the Sabbath psalm); 92 (the Sabbath psalm); and 93 (to introduce the festival psalm, even though there was none to introduce). This, at least, is Fleischer's reconstruction; if he is correct, the process by which Pss 92 and 93 were closely associated had been completed by the fifth century, since poetry written for the Sabbath by then, and based on Ps 92, already included citations from Ps 93 as well.[24]

Liturgically, this practice of "hard wiring" together two originally disparate units so that the recitation of one inevitably brings with it the second, can be called "modularization." Such ritual modularization is well attested liturgically, possibly as part of ritual's inherent tendency toward invariance of wording and its penchant for binding together linguistic fragments rather than, as in normal cognitive discourse, the very reverse: separating linguistic units and recombining them for the sake of

---

Heinemann (ed. E. Fleischer and J. Petuchowski; Jerusalem: Magnes, 1981), esp. 117, where Ps 19:8–15 occurs at the end of Rosh Chodesh Nisan, if it coincided with Saturday night.

22 Fleischer, *T'fillah,* 163–75. Psalms for Sukkoth seem to have varied more than those of other holidays. Ps 122 was most frequently recited, but *Sofrim* knows Ps 76 for the occasion, and the sole extant psalm scroll in our possession carries Ps 113. Shemini Atseret featured Pss 12; 9; 111; or 6. Early *piyyutim* for the occasion assume Pss 6; 148; or 122.

23 The list might even be longer. The Romaniot liturgy, probably of Palestinian provenance, provides Pss 93; 98; 136; and 121 for Rosh Hodesh (the new moon) alone. See E. D. Goldschmidt, *Mechkarei Tefillah Ufiyut* (Jerusalem, Magnes, 1979).

24 Fleischer, *T'fillah,* 176–78.

information-bearing specificity.[25] A good example in Jewish liturgy is the set of blessings that conclude the Sabbath reading of the *Haftarah* (the prophetic lection). The first blessing is apt: it thanks God for sending prophets and assuring the fulfillment of their messages. However, the blessings that follow are irrelevant to the occasion and even redundant to blessings said earlier in the rubric known as the Amidah. Apparently, the entire set of blessings had been fused together ritually into a single module, so that when the first blessing was moved to the *Haftarah* position, the others came along with it.[26] Here too, then, Ps 92, the "psalm for a Sabbath day," was early on fused with Ps 93, an introduction to festival psalmody. In our current rite, we say them both on Friday nights, even though only the first is topically relevant.

Curiously, however, we now say Pss 92 and 93 on Friday nights without an introductory blessing. I say "curiously" because the rabbis of antiquity usually adopted such an introductory blessing (and sometimes a concluding one as well) when Scripture was cited liturgically. The festival use of Pss 113–118 and the daily inclusion of Pss 145–150, for example, begin with blessings that identify them as cases of liturgical Hallel and acknowledge the obligation to recite them as such. Similarly, the daily Shema (Deut 6:4–9; 11:13–21; Num 15:37–41) is prefaced with a Birkat Hatorah ("blessing over Torah") affirming God's supreme act of grace in giving the Torah at Sinai; and the weekly lections also (as we saw above, in part, regarding the *Haftarah*) call for bracketing blessings as part of their proclamation. Here too, then, we would have expected a blessing at least before, if not after, these evening psalms; in fact, in the Genizah we find one. Preceding the entire string of psalms is the following:

> Blessed are You, Adonai our God, ruler of the universe, who chose David your servant, and took pleasure in his praise and sacred songs, to extol, praise and glorify Him for his many acts of greatness throughout all time. Blessed are You, Adonai, who cause full and imminent deliverance to spring up for his people, and who build up Jerusalem.[27]

In some cases, only the first part was said: "Blessed are You, Adonai our God, ruler of the universe, who chose David your servant." The tenth-

---

[25] Roy Rappaport, *Ecology, Meaning and Religion* (Berkeley: North Atlantic Books, 1979), esp. 206.

[26] Joseph Heinemann, *Prayer in the Talmud: Forms and Patterns* (trans. R. S. Sarason; SJ 9; Berlin: de Gruyter, 1977), 227–29.

[27] See Simchah Assaf, "Miseder Hatefillah Me'erets Yisra'el," in *Sefer Dinaburg* (ed. Y. Baer et al.; Jerusalem: Kiryat Sefer, 1949), 124; A. Scheiber, *Geniza Studies* (Hildesheim: Olms, 1981), 10; Fleischer, *T'fillah,* 181.

century Palestinian Karaite, Jacob Al Kirkisani, railed against the blessing as an instance in which the rabbinites transgressed the Bible's own command to praise God "as King David of Israel had ordained" (Ezra 3:10), which is to say (in Kirkisani's view) by psalms alone.[28]

What about a concluding blessing? As we saw regarding the *Haftarah* reading, the rabbis often framed discrete units of biblical citation with concluding blessings, and that is indeed the case with our extant Hallels. Both the Daily and the Egyptian Hallel are followed by a liturgical staple called the Birkat Hashir, literally, "Blessing of Song." The blessing's exact wording varies with the rites and harks back to a talmudic debate in which different versions are known. The Palestinian preference begins with "All that you have made will praise You" (*y'hallelukha kol ma'asekha*). Significantly enough, a version of that blessing also appears, in some cases, for the Palestinian evening psalm collections. In other words, Sabbath and festival eve psalmody were originally structured with opening and closing benedictions, the latter being a version of the standard closing blessing for Hallels generally.

A single conclusion follows: calendrically driven psalmody should properly be seen as just another example of a Hallel, that is, a set of psalms offering God praise but tied, as is the Egyptian Hallel, to the calendar.[29]

However, as we saw with regard to Amram's added "halleluyah" ending to Ps 145 in the daily Hallel, the rabbis were equally likely to frame whole psalms with single verses from elsewhere in the Psalter. Psalm 145 is also introduced with Pss 84:5 and 144:15 because the two verses combined mention the word "happy" three times. This refers to the fact that certain recensions of the Talmud promise eternal reward to anyone who says Ps 145 "three times" daily. Some Genizah manuscripts, therefore, omit the introductory blessing and have, instead, Ps 106:48, "Blessed is Adonai, God of Israel, from eternity to eternity. Let all the people say 'Amen, Halleluyah.'" This is one of the five verses (known as doxologies) that close the five books of Psalms. Typically, a doxology asserts, without any substantiating reason, praise of God or of God's name, forever.[30] Its opening use of "Blessed is" makes it stylistically akin to a blessing. It represents the use of one psalm to contextualize another.

---

[28] From Leon Nemoy's study of Kirkisani (5 vols.; New York: Alexander Kohut Memorial Foundation, 1939-43), cited by Fleischer, *T'fillah,* 181.

[29] Fleischer (*T'fillah,* 185) thinks the absence of the final blessing in so many fragments betrays the fact that the rabbinites took the critique of Al Kirkisani to heart and removed it. Alternatively, it seems to me, customs varied.

[30] For discussion of liturgical usage, see Eric Werner, *The Sacred Bridge: Liturgical Parallels in Synagogue and Early Church* (New York: Columbia University Press, 1970; orig. 1959), ch. 9.

This properly introduces my final topic: psalmody that is used exegetically like midrash, not just, as here, to set the context for other psalms that follow, but to provide proof texts for the rabbinic writings that constitute the bulk of the Jewish prayer service.

Psalms as Midrash

My analysis so far has been diachronic, thoroughly historical: an analysis of when and how Hallel psalms came into being, a replication of what we know about Palestinian practice before it ended with the coming of the Crusaders, and an identification of Palestinian psalmody as just another case of Hallel. My historicist teachers would be proud of me. I, like them, have charted the historical use of liturgical psalmody in this era and in that.

However, liturgy is not a document like the Talmud, or even the Bible. The prayerbook is less a book than it is a script for a sacred drama performed regularly by a changing cast of worshipers across the generations, who care little when the lines they say were drafted. The playwright here is the sacred community through time, which periodically alters the script and hands the newest version down to the next generation. Our English "tradition" and the parallel "*masorah*" in Hebrew both mean "that which is handed down, as property."[31] We should be as interested in how the final script is played out, and thereby handed down to each new generation of worshipers, as we are in when the individual lines of the script were drafted and by whom.

Having done my duty historically, I turn to what is to me a more interesting question: the use of psalms as worship, regardless of when each particular psalm was first said. Beginning with the rabbis of antiquity, but continuing through the ages, we find psalms being used not just as Hallels to offer God praise but also as a means of midrashic intertextuality. They are woven throughout the liturgy, providing context for other material and proof texts for later rabbinic assertions.

The specific rhetorical devices of Jewish liturgy are many, of course, but a particularly overwhelming one stands out: the selective citation of psalm verses. Yes, individual psalms are recited whole, as we have seen, but by and large the psalms are stitched into the liturgical narrative, sentence by sentence, one verse here and another there, so skillfully that unless one knows the Psalter by heart the snippets are easy to miss. In addition to citing verses out of context, the liturgy sometimes deliberately alters the biblical text for its own ends. Alterations may be merely stylistic

---

[31] See Lawrence A. Hoffman, *Beyond the Text: A Holistic Approach to Liturgy* (Bloomington: Indiana University Press, 1991), 9–13.

(e.g., a change in person) or a matter of content, an alteration that amends biblical theology so that the liturgy reports the Bible differently from the way that the Bible itself does.[32]

Selective citation wrenches sentences away from their biblical context to make them do duty as units in the liturgical narrative, completely independently of how they fit in the Bible. However, the opposite could theoretically occur as well. Psalm fragments might be cited metonymically, cited, that is, precisely because the worshiper is expected to recognize the biblical context in which the snippet occurs. I began my study expecting to find this happening and thereby to reveal covert layers of intended meaning in the citations. I was disappointed to find that happening rarely, if at all. At least with the psalms, looking at their original context seems hardly to increase understanding of a prayer in which a psalm is cited. The rabbis cite psalms with abandon but usually because of what the cited excerpt says expressly, not because of its original context.

This literal (and limited) usage suggests that the rabbis composed at least some prayers for the masses, not for themselves alone. They assumed that worshipers had enough familiarity with the biblical text to recognize a biblical citation when they saw it, but not to know its context.

This use of selective citation is familiar to us as a common rabbinic genre. It is called midrash. I want, then, to characterize rabbinic liturgy as a branch of midrash, a sacred drama in which the midrashic meaning of the Bible is enacted. Psalms are used with many of the midrashic tropes in mind: wordplays, for example, and even the express use of formal midrashic style—a verse preceded by *shene'emar,* for instance, or *ka'amur* ("as it is said," in English)—a certain indication that a proof text is at hand. Rabbinic liturgy, then, does what midrash does. It represents a sacred universe beyond the world of the senses and beyond even the literal world of Scripture. It shanghais scripture selectively to demonstrate the truth of rabbinic cosmology, theology, and anthropology, the ultimate truths of the universe, of God, and of human nature, for which the rabbis stood.

Biblical citations and rabbinic writing thus intersect in a mutually interpretive fashion. As we saw, psalms are rarely said without a rabbinic blessing to tell the worshiper what they are to mean; similarly, however, even blessings are apt to include a verse or more from psalms to anchor the rabbis' worldview in biblical reality and to contextualize the way rabbinic prayers are to be heard by those who say them.

A few examples will suffice, but let me first indicate the extent to which, of all the Bible, the psalms are overwhelmingly favored for this

---

32 See below (p. 50) on the use of Ps 92.

midrashic work. Using the standard Birnbaum *siddur* as my text,[33] I computed the percentage of lines from the morning liturgy that come from the psalms and the percentage of biblical quotations in the liturgy that are psalmic rather than from other biblical books. In both cases, as the following chart reveals, the results are nothing short of astounding.

	Psalms as Percent of Liturgy	Psalms as Percent of All Biblical Citations
Weekday		
P'sukei D'zimrah	54.0	74.0
Shema and its blessings	0.9	12.5
Amidah	4.5	31.0
Torah liturgy	76.0	52.0
Shabbat		
P'sukei D'zimrah	68.0	88.0
Shema and its blessings	0.7	12.5
Amidah	4.7	40.0
Torah liturgy	25.0	50.0
Musaf	7.5	53.0

To be sure, the count is open to some haggling. Different rites, for instance, contain different prayers, and Birnbaum's choice of what to include was, to some extent, subjective. Nonetheless, the overall impression of these figures cannot be denied. We would expect the high psalm count in the P'sukei D'zimrah—the introductory morning rubric that contains the Daily Hallel. What is striking, however, is the high percentage of psalms in the Torah liturgy and the relatively low percentage in the two main rubrics, the Shema and the Amidah.

The Torah liturgy is a relatively late compilation, containing material that ranges from late antiquity to the medieval period and even beyond. Apparently, the Jewish fascination with psalms is not just early rabbinic. It seems to have manifested itself especially in the post-talmudic era, when the Torah liturgy came into being. However, the low percentage of psalm content in the two early rabbinic rubrics (Shema and Amidah) by no means indicates a rabbinic dismissal of them, since the right-hand column demonstrates the high percentage, even there, of psalmic to other biblical citations. The 12.5 percent for the Shema is to be expected, since most of the Shema is, after all, the Shema (Deut 6:4–9; 11:13–21; Num 15:37–41), which is toraitic. However, look at the Amidah, a wholly rabbinic

33 Philip Birnbaum, ed., *Daily Prayer Book: Ha-Siddur Ha-Shalem* (New York: Hebrew Publishing Company, 1949, 1993).

invention. There all the biblical citations are individual verses, so no lengthy citations skew the whole. There, where the rabbis could have cited anything at all in their prayers, 31 percent of the daily and 40 percent of the Shabbat liturgy is from the single book of Psalms. Was this a deliberate attempt to include psalms in rabbinic prayer material? We can only speculate, but I think it was, and the question then arises: Why? One possible explanation has to do with the nature of rabbinic prayer, and the other deals with the nature of the rabbis.

The first is simply that Jewish prayer is overwhelmingly praise-oriented, and the psalms are ideal citations for giving praise. The very nature of rabbinic liturgy, then, preselected the psalms for emphasis. However, the rabbis themselves cannot be overlooked. If we conceptualize rabbinic liturgy as a ritual typical of an oral culture, we recognize that our written prayers today are merely the chance remnants of a much larger prayer repertoire of antiquity. Without written documents, rabbinic prayer leaders made it up as they went along, much like a master African American preacher who laces sermons with biblical snippets committed to memory and drawn upon at will. The large psalm percentage indicates the rabbis' extensive familiarity with the psalms. They simply knew them well.

Let me turn next to some illustrations of how psalms are used in the liturgy. Although I can hardly cite every instance, I can provide enough examples to demonstrate the midrashic role that I am claiming.

PROOF TEXTS

The most common midrashic use of Scripture is simple proof-texting, which is exactly what we get in the prayers.

1. An evening extension of the prayer that requests safekeeping while we sleep acknowledges, "In your hand are the souls of the living and the dead," then offers proof by citing Job 12:10 and Ps 31:6: "In his hand is the soul of every living thing, the soul of every human being; I entrust my soul into your hand. You save me, O Lord, faithful God."

2. The first morning blessing preceding the Shema pictures angels praising God, "who renews daily the work of creation, as it is said (Ps 136:7), 'The One who makes the great lights, for his mercy endures forever.'"[34]

SECONDARY MIDRASHIC EXPLANATION

I said above that psalms are rarely cited with the prior understanding that the worshiper is expected to associate the citation with the original biblical context. However, ex post facto, psalms that occur liturgically

---

[34] Ibid., 73.

sometimes attract a secondary layer of midrashic exegesis that "justifies" their use in prayer.[35]

1. Psalm 24, for instance, is the Levitical psalm for Sunday, day one of the week—we might guess because it begins, "The earth is the Lord's and all it holds. . . . For He founded it upon the ocean and set it on the nether streams." That does seem fitting for the day when "God began to create the heaven and the earth," but this psalm is also cited to accompany the liturgical act of replacing the Torah scroll in the ark.[36] Why so? The *Midrash to Psalms* explains that when Solomon was bringing the ark of the testimony into the temple, the gates were too small for the ark to fit through, at which time he shouted Ps 24:7, "O gates, lift up your heads, up high, you everlasting doors."[37]

2. Similarly, we find Ps 27 associated with the High Holy Days and recited each day of the preceding preparatory month of Elul.[38] Any number of verses stand out as appropriate for the Days of Awe: "God is my light and my help; whom should I fear?" (27:1), perhaps; or "One thing I ask of Adonai, only that do I seek: to live in the house of Adonai all the days of my life" (27:4). However, the midrash tells us:

> The Rabbis interpreted the whole psalm as referring to Rosh Hashanah and Yom Kippur. "Adonai is my light" (v. 1) on Rosh Hashanah. "Adonai is my help" (v.1) on Yom Kippur. . . . The numerical value of the letters in the word *hasatan* [Satan] is 364, one short of the number of days in the year. He [Satan] thus has authority to accuse Israel of sin every day in the year except Yom Kippur, when God says to him, "You have no authority to touch them, but you may go out and see how they keep busy." He goes out and sees them all fasting and praying, dressed in white and cloaked like ministering angels, at which time he returns ashamed and confused. God asks, "What did you learn about my children?" And Satan replies, "In truth, they are like ministering angels so I cannot touch them." Thereupon, God chains up Satan and declares to Israel, "I have forgiven

---

35 My examples are from *Midrash to Psalms,* a compilation variously dated to somewhere between the fifth and the eighth century, so probably after Kalir. See William G. Braude, trans., *The Midrash on Psalms* (Yale Judaica Series 13; New Haven: Yale University Press, 1959), 27–31. Since psalmody for special days seems to have been common as early as Kalir, it would follow that the midrashic connections postdate the use of psalms and explain their selection, rather than predating their selection and constituting the actual reason for their inclusion liturgically.

36 Birnbaum, *Daily Prayer Book,* 140, 128.

37 *Midr. Ps.* 24:10.

38 Birnbaum, *Daily Prayer Book,* 148.

you." [Israel thus says Ps 27:3:] "Though an army besiege me, my heart would have no fear. . . ."[39]

PSALM STRUCTURE

Though I cannot say for sure, it would seem that sometimes a psalm is chosen not for its content but for its structure, which facilitates a liturgical act: the use of a psalm to count a *minyan.* Certain Jewish prayers—those expressly assumed to deal with the theme of sanctity—require a quorum of ten worshipers if they are to be said. However, counting those present by pointing to them was (and in some quarters still is) considered a source of bad luck, since it drew the evil eye, so to speak, toward the worshipers. All sorts of subterfuges have arisen over time to prevent such bad fortune from falling on those engaged in prayer. Even today, on occasion, one hears people numbering off as "Not 1," "Not 2," for instance.

In the Middle Ages, prayers were used to count. Medieval France, for instance, featured the introduction of Balaam's description of Israel: "How goodly are your tents, O Jacob, your habitations O Israel" (Num 24:5). Manuscripts of *Machzor Vitry,* an eleventh-century French work, leave no doubt, however, that what mattered was the following line: "By your abundant grace I enter your house. I worship before your holy shrine with reverence." As much as the content of this line may seem appropriate, its cognitive content is largely beside the point. The significant thing is that, in Hebrew, the line has ten words. People could count off by reciting the words, one after another. When the last word was spoken, ten worshipers were present.

So too, we find Ps 20 recited before a prayer known as the K'dushah d'sidra. Prior to that prayer, on days when the Torah is read, the Torah scrolls have been replaced in the ark and Ps 145 has been said. On days without Torah readings, the prior prayers would be Tachanun, a lengthy silent confessional liturgy, followed by Ps 145. On a weekday the major rubrics of prayer would have ended well before that. Can we imagine that some worshipers might have left by the time the K'dushah d'sidra was said? Congregations were apt to be tiny in the Middle Ages, hardly more than a quorum at best. Psalm 20 has nothing in terms of content to suggest that it should be said here, but it does have ten verses for recounting the house before launching a prayer that requires the presence of ten.

INTERNAL MIDRASHIC ELABORATION

Lastly, I want to look at prayers that use psalms internally for the midrashic elaboration they provide. In such cases psalms may be juxtaposed

---

[39] *Midr. Ps.* 27:4.

to other rabbinic lore or even taken out of context—deliberately misread, that is—so as to render the prayer in question rhetorically interesting. I begin with the service for putting on *tallit* and *tefillin.*

1. Each weekday morning the liturgy calls for blessings to accompany the acts of donning these two sacred garments, the first being a prayer shawl, the second two small boxes with leather straps attached; the boxes hold sections of Torah. The boxes are attached with straps to the forehead and arm. The arm strap is then tied to the hand in such a way as to spell out by its shape the name of God.

As the liturgy now stands, the blessings are expanded by sixteenth- or seventeenth-century Lurianic *kavvanot,* that is, by mystical meditations that link the act of donning these prayer accouterments to esoteric ultimates. Wearing a *tallit,* for instance, reflects the robing of the soul in the world to come.[40] In addition, however, we find psalm verses that gratuitously introduce or follow the *kavvanot.* Before putting on the *tefillin* that go on the hand and arm, one says Ps 145:16: "You open your hand and satisfy every living thing with favor." Similarly, before donning the *tallit,* one says Ps 104:1–2, "Bless Adonai, O my soul; Adonai, my God, You are very great. You are robed in glory and majesty. You wrap yourself in light as a garment. You spread the heavens like a curtain."[41]

Here is a fine example of using psalms as exegetical contextualization. They make the act of putting on prayer garments more than what they appear to be on the surface. The worshiper is implicitly portrayed as imitating God. God too opens his hand and wraps himself up. The *tefillin* are no longer just ritual wrappings but a reminder of the need to "satisfy every living thing with favor," and the *tallit* is the equivalent of "glory and majesty." The worshiper, is, as it were, enwrapped alongside God in the very heavens themselves.

However, beyond the obvious metaphoric parallels that the psalm verses present, contrary to the general rule (pp. 43–44 above) we find here allusions to talmudic haggadah. This is a case where worshipers are really expected to know deeper rabbinic lore. Psalm 145, as we saw, is especially well known liturgically since it is said three times daily under the belief that "saying it daily guarantees a share in the world to come."[42] Moreover, of the entire psalm, it is verse 16 ("You open your hand and satisfy every living thing with favor") that the rabbis identify

---

[40] Our standard *kavvanot* are generally attributed to Isaiah Horowitz (ca. 1565–1630), the kabbalist we encountered above, p. 33.

[41] Birnbaum, *Daily Prayer Book,* 8, 4.

[42] *b. Ber.* 4b; later manuscripts (and thus our current version) add "three times daily."

as central.[43] Even more striking is the tradition that when Moses asked God how Israel would be saved from sin, God himself donned a *tallit* and promised to pardon Jews who recited the divine attributes of Exod 34:8–9.[44] The author of the liturgy has thus employed psalms to portray the worshiper as imitating God, by alluding to a well-known talmudic tale that provides the paradigmatic instance of so doing. An ordinary act of worship becomes a transcendent instance of *imitatio Dei.*

2. A second example is the use of Ps 92. We saw above that its biblical superscription identifies it as "A psalm for the Sabbath day." Its opening verse continues, "It is good to give thanks to God." However, the liturgy recasts that meaning midrashically in this prayer from the Sabbath morning service:

> To God who rested from all the work of creation on the seventh day and ascended to sit upon his throne of glory. He wrapped the day of rest with beauty and called the Sabbath day a "delight." This is the praise of the seventh day, for on it God rested from all his work. The seventh day offered praise, saying, "This is the psalm of the seventh day: It is good to give thanks to God. . . . "[45]

The author has deliberately mistranslated the superscription to read not "A psalm *for* the Sabbath day" but "*of* the Sabbath day," that is, a psalm "*belonging to* the Sabbath day." He then personifies the Sabbath day, imagining it to be, like God, wrapped in a virtual *tallit* of beauty and moved to utter its own psalm of praise in gratitude for being so endowed.

Conclusion: Prayer and Study; the Liturgical Canon

The recognition that psalms (and other biblical snippets too) recur liturgically as proof texts for rabbinic propositions provides insight into the connection of rabbinic liturgy to rabbinic texts in general, as well as the relative position of prayer and study within the evolving rabbinic religious system.

As to the first, one cannot help but be struck by the fact that Christian church fathers wrote regularly about their liturgies while rabbis from the same era did not. To be sure, we have mishnaic and talmudic commentary on what prayers to say and how to say them, but the amount of material is exceptionally sparse relative to the entire corpus of rabbinic literature—a condition that, I think, is not the case in early Christian writing. Of the

---

[43] Ibid.

[44] *b. Roš. Haš.* 17b.

[45] For Hebrew prayer, see Birnbaum, *Daily Prayer Book,* 339–41.

Mishnah's sixty-three tractates, only one (*Berakhot*) deals, as its main topic, with the daily and Shabbat statutory public service, and over half of that is related to mealtime prayer and occasional blessings, such as seeing a rainbow or hearing bad news. The Passover Seder gets only one chapter out of ten in the tractate on Passover. High-holiday liturgy cannot even be reconstructed from the Mishnah, so tiny is its coverage in either tractate *Roš Haššanah* or tractate *Yoma* (i.e., Yom Kippur). Moreover, we almost never get full texts of prayers, nothing at all akin, say, to the *Didache*'s celebrated table prayers or the Eucharist of Hippolytus, both of which hail from the period that parallels the Mishnah. The only exceptions in tannaitic literature (and they are several) are cultic events long gone: for example, the Sukkot water celebration, the Second Tithe confession, the Firstfruit affirmation, or the Ma'amad fast-day liturgy in the town square.[46] Jews have nothing like the Christian pilgrim Egeria's fourth-century diary, which is less a travelogue of the Holy Land than a guide to the holy worship she encountered there.[47] Partly, we assume, this is a matter of chance, and partly not. There are talmudic traditions, after all, of travelers from Palestine observing diverse liturgical customs in Babylonia,[48] and small studies of liturgical diversity between the two great centers in the early post-talmudic or gaonic era are to some extent available.[49] So it is not as if Jews paid no attention to what the liturgy was. However, the topic is rarely the evolving set of prayer texts; rather, it is the halakic issues of when a prayer gets said, who says it, and so forth.

An easy and obvious conclusion is that whatever the act of prayer meant to the rabbis, their discussion of praying was simply one more facet of their discussion of everything else: an investigation into its halakah—the playing out of the rabbinic paradigm of investigation, roughly equivalent to asking, "What does God want and how do we know it?" So far so good. We now know how rabbinic literature relates to liturgy. It discusses liturgy

---

[46] For Christian examples, see Joseph A. Jungmann, *The Mass of the Roman Rite: Missarum sollemnia* (2 vols.; New York: Benziger, 1951–55; repr., Westminster, Md.: Christian Classics, 1986), 12, 22–23; and Theodor Klauser, *A Short History of the Western Liturgy* (Oxford: Oxford University Press, 1979), 16–17. For the Sukkot Water Ceremony, see *m. Sukkah* 5:2–4. For Second Tithe Confession, see *m. Maʿaś. Š.* 5:10–13. For the Firstfruits Ceremonial, see *m. Bik.* 3:1–6. For the fast-day ritual, see *m. Taʿan.* 2:1–4.

[47] *Egeria's Travels to the Holy Land* (trans. J. Wilkinson; rev. ed.; Jerusalem: Ariel, 1981).

[48] The most noted, perhaps, being Rav's observation of the use of the half Hallel there on Rosh Hodesh; see *b. Taʿan.* 28b.

[49] Most notably, Joel Müller, ed., *Chiluf Minhagim Bein Bavel V'erets Yisra'el* (Jerusalem: Makor, 1970; orig. 1870).

as part of the undifferentiated whole of human experience, the way it discusses anything else.

However, what of the reverse? What is the relationship of the evolving liturgical text to rabbinic literature? Traditionally, the study of liturgy has been subsumed under the category of rabbinics. I, for example, teach liturgy as part of a rabbinics department and was appointed as a professor of "Liturgy and Rabbinic Literature," with the subtle assumption that some relationship must exist even if no one was quite sure what it was. By contrast, my Christian counterparts generally teach in departments of theology. The difference is that classical Christian discussion is patently theological. That is why Christians worry more about the words of prayer. Christians organize knowledge, liturgical and otherwise, around theology, a content, while Jews organize their knowledge around halakah, a method.

To be sure, method and content overlap. Theology is method too, just as halakah is also content. However, talmudic texts are strikingly method-centered, their discussions often ending with no decision at all, simply a black hole of unresolved debate. Early rabbinic prayer obeyed this tendency toward method, in that as long as basic halakic instructions were obeyed, the specific content of prayers was changeable. Prayers were not cited in detail because there was nothing permanent to cite. Eventually, more or less canonized versions of what had been a massive set of evolving options became the norm, and that is what we have by the ninth century or so, in the first comprehensive prayer book, which was promulgated by Rav Amram. Analyzing the use of psalms in the Birnbaum Siddur, a prayer version typical of the most common Western rite—but that is overall descended from Amram's paradigm—provides insight into how that original liturgy related to the larger rabbinic enterprise. The answer, I suggest, is that liturgy was a form of exegetical midrash.

I have labeled the original rabbinic project as "method" rather than "content" and identified the method as mostly halakic (legal). It is now time to consider the relationship of midrash to halakah. Again, the way we organize our knowledge matters. Because of the privileged status accorded to legal discussion over the years, midrash as a genre has been split off from halakah. However, clearly they were not originally separate. The earliest midrashim, prior to 200, are halakic through and through, the explication of law via midrashic method. Talmud too is filled with midrashic proof for halakic propositions. Even the Mishnah and Tosefta, which are more code-like in their form, sometimes cite proof texts midrashically to buttress legal claims. Eventually, to be sure, other rhetorical conceits came to constitute part of the halakic method, but the midrashic citing of sources is never lost sight of; this, in fact, is preferred by the Babylonian Talmud, which seems intent on restoring it to primacy.[50] In general, then, one can say that the halakic method contains within it an extension of a midrashic method, whereby citation of scriptural proof texts, often with creative and deliberate misreadings, remains central.

That is exactly what the liturgy is: another example of the midrashic method, but without the halakic end in view. Instead, the end is theological. Just as halakah needs scriptural underpinnings, so too does liturgy. We can now array liturgy alongside other rabbinic works as another instance of the general rabbinic method, the utilization of Scripture (in this case, largely psalms) to defend rabbinic propositions (in this case, theological ones).

The issues vary, depending on the rabbinic work in question, but the method does not.

1. Mishnah: How do we know that a boat is insusceptible to ritual impurity? Because it says (Prov 30:19), "It is the way of a ship to ply the sea."[51]

2. Mekhilta: How do we know that a perpetrator is guilty of theft as long as the stolen property is within the suspect's possession, though not necessarily "in his hand"? Because even though (referring to theft) the Torah says the stolen property must be discovered "in his hand," Gen 24:10 also says, "having all the bounty of his master in his hand." In Genesis, "in his hand" refers to all Abraham's "bounty," which is loaded on camels, so it cannot mean, literally, "*in his hand.*" So too, everywhere else "in his hand" must mean only "in his possession."[52]

3. Passover Haggadah: We eat bitter herbs on Passover "because the Egyptians embittered the lives of our ancestors in Egypt, as it is written (Exod 1:13–14), 'They embittered their lives with hard work. . . .' "[53]

4. Morning Liturgy: How do we know that "at the end of time every mouth, every tongue, every knee and every heart shall praise God? Because it says (Psalm 35:10) 'All my being shall say, O Lord, who is like

---

[50] For the claim that the Babli, though connected to other rabbinic works, has its own systemic agenda, see Jacob Neusner, "System or Tradition? The Babli and Its Sources," in *Judaic and Christian Interpretation of Texts* (ed. J. Neusner and E. S. Frerichs; New Perspectives on Ancient Judaism 3; Lanham, Md.: University Press of America, 1987), 127–83; for the Babli's specific interest in scriptural proof texts, see Jacob Neusner, *The Formation of the Jewish Intellect* (BJS 151; Atlanta: Scholars Press, 1988), esp. 158–59.

[51] *m. Šabb.* 9:2.

[52] *Mek. Nez.* in *Mekilta d'Rabbi Ishmael* (ed. J. Z. Lauterbach; 3 vols.; Philadelphia: Jewish Publication Society of America, 1949 [5709]), 3:104.

53. Philip Birnbaum, ed., *Birnbaum Haggadah* (New York: Hebrew Publishing Company, 1953), 94.

You ?' . . . Therefore, we will praise, laud and glorify You and bless your holy name, as it is said by David (Psalm 103:1) 'Bless the Lord, O my soul, and let my whole being bless his holy name.'"

The first example is Mishnah, a halakic code, where midrashic proof-texting is relatively rare but is found occasionally—as here. The second is a pre-200 halakic midrash, where the midrashic rhetoric is ubiquitous and central. The third and fourth are liturgical but nuanced differently. The example from the Passover Haggadah justifies a specific eating practice, while the fourth justifies the entire act of prayer as praise and thus occurs in that section of the morning liturgy given over to praising God.

We can now move on to a related point: the putative distinction between prayer and study as alternative, even dichotomous, rabbinic roads to deliverance. It is clear that before 70 C.E. the temple cult atoned for sin and brought salvation. After 70, study seems to have taken its place. Following E. E. Urbach, Stefan Reif posits another candidate for a post-temple nexus with the divine—*ma'asim tovim,* "good deeds"—but believes that Rabbi Akiba anticipated the ultimate victory of study in holding that "study leads to deeds."[54] On this view, even though prayer arose within the rabbinic study circles, it was always seen as tertiary at best, a Johnny-come-lately to the rabbinic regimen, entirely separate from Torah study and demanding ideological justification as a continuation of the defunct temple cult in order for it to take hold.

We can now see, however, that the presumed dichotomy between prayer and study exists more in the minds of twentieth- and twenty-first-century critics than it did in rabbinic imagination. Midrash was the common form that united the two enterprises. Though their contents and organization differ, the liturgy is no less midrashic than the Talmud. Talmudic writing determines and justifies halakah; liturgical writing defines and justifies theology. Prayer is a form of study. Now, I recall some teachers of mine justifying prayer that way because it followed that prayer was not really prayer—precisely what these wholly ethnic and secular mentors of mine despised. They could justify prayer by referring to the obvious study components of the prayer book: the Shema, for example, or even the psalms that compose the various Hallels. When I say that prayer is study, however, I do not mean to demote it in order to save it. On the contrary. We now know that rabbinic study itself was a far cry from the secular sense of study that permeates, say, public school systems or even the furthest reaches of academia. True to the gnostic environment in which rabbinic notions of study arose, "study,"

[54] Stefan C. Reif, *Judaism and Hebrew Prayer* (Cambridge: Cambridge University Press, 1993), 96.

for the rabbis, was a means to salvation. To describe prayer in that way is hardly to denigrate it.

This is, however, to define prayer rabbinically as something different from the current popular notion of prayer as personal conversation with God. The rabbis would not have objected to such a conversational agenda, but they would, apparently, have expanded it to include the midrashic linking of biblical text to the expression of theological realia. That is the role of biblical proof-texting in the rabbinic liturgy, the role especially of the psalms, which appear so much more frequently than the rest of the Hebrew Scripture.

We should see my claim as a further insight into what has been called canonical biblical criticism. For my purposes, the work of James Sanders in response to Brevard Childs is critical here. Childs had offered an alternative to the atomizing sort of biblical scholarship that dissected redacted biblical books into their various documentary parts and then privileged the early parts as being more authentic than the ultimate canonical whole. By contrast, Childs drew our attention to the creative work entailed in redacting the books as they ultimately appear to us; he asked why the raw material used by the redactors should be any more "authentic" or "real" than the final version.

Sanders carried Childs's thinking further. For the believing community, which accepts the canon as theologically necessary, the entirety of any given canonical book is less important than the way that book is presented to and perceived by the believing community.

> Canon *and* community go together. Neither truly exists without the other. ... [The canon's] life setting is the believing communities ... which find their identities in it and try to live their lives in the light of it. Its proper life setting is not the scholar's but the liturgical and instructional programs of the believing communities.[55]

Constantly stressing the adaptability, not the stability, of canon, Sanders defines canon as a people's story; canon is canon not only because it survives but "because it can give its survival power to the community that recites it."[56]

Sanders's evolving and working canon, then, is a far cry even from Childs's literary canon, in that the *real* canon turns out to be the literary canon as it is "liturgically and instructionally recited by believing

---

[55] James A. Sanders, *Canon and Community* (Philadelphia: Fortress, 1983), xv.

[56] James A. Sanders, *From Sacred Story to Sacred Text* (Philadelphia: Fortress, 1987), 19.

communities," that is to say, for our purposes, the canon as proclaimed liturgically, whether as worship or as lectionary.

The same atomistic tendency that Brevard Childs condemned when he considered the breaking down of biblical books into their constitutive parts, rather than seeing those parts too as living canonical Scripture, led students of the liturgy to take apart a worship service, reducing it to its own constitutive elements and dealing with them as if they were not part of a living liturgical whole. In Jewish circles, for instance, the lectionary was treated academically under the rubric of "homiletics" or "midrash," while the rest of the service was entitled "liturgy." Our study of psalms has shown us just how far off the mark that dichotomy is. The real canon is not even just the particular Torah and *Haftarah* readings of the week but the midrashic underpinning that roots the liturgy's claims in biblical proof texts, of which the psalms are paramount. Scholars may emphasize the disjunction between biblical and postbiblical Judaism, but believing Jews are given a liturgy with selective citations that establish hermeneutic claim to continuity between Torah and the rabbis. That is the whole point of midrash and, to some extent, it now turns out, of the liturgy too, which approaches God in the present but from the vantage point of a sure and certain biblical past.

What is at stake is the effective canon, by which I mean the canon *de facto,* not *de jure.* In theory, the canon is the sum total of biblical books held to be sacred. In practice, it is just those books (or selections from books) that are regularly read or proclaimed and therefore known. My overall claim is that *as midrash, liturgy is the presentation of an alternative world of reality supported by the selective perception of Scripture, largely psalms. Regular worshipers encounter this* de facto *canon, on which they stake their lives.*

Jews today no longer approach their liturgy with this fine appreciation of its intertextuality, and a final word is in order to conceptualize this loss of textual richness. Brian Stock traces the idea of a textual community beyond the old and established anthropological dichotomy that had juxtaposed orality and literacy.[57] Since even illiterate medieval cultures depended on texts, the proper issue is whether or not a society uses texts and, if it does, how it does so. Jews, for instance, were not always a thoroughly literate community, but they were a "textual" one. The question here is the role of the text.

Literate communities always have an oral cultural lag, so Jews who had discovered literacy were, at some point, still oral. They knew that literacy

---

57 Brian Stock, *Listening for the Text* (Baltimore: Johns Hopkins University Press, 1990).

mattered, but they themselves did not regularly or necessarily read and write. That is to say, they had a text, but the text was not one the average person poured over. Rather, the text was the validating part of their orality. To quote the text was to justify oral tradition. That is why *kakatuv* ("as it is written") or *shene'emar* ("as it is said [in the text]") mattered. It justified oral proclamations by quoting written text. When prayer leaders cited Scripture, their hearers *knew* it. They *heard* the connection between the oral claims of the liturgy and the canonical demonstration of their veracity.

Eventually, however, the prayer corpus became a book, and *all* the liturgy began looking and sounding the same: just a single surface set of words with no canonical depth. Today, to the extent that people pay heed at all to what it says, they judge it like a magazine on the newsstand. Fiction or nonfiction? If nonfiction, as it claims to be, it must be open to ordinary scientific demonstration, depending on empirical evidence of whether or not the world accords with what the liturgy says. However, that was never the way prayer was supposed to work. The liturgy's claims were rooted in textual, not sensory, evidence. It described an alternative world that was believable despite our senses; this was accomplished by the artistry with which a rabbinic universe was substantiated by sacred texts. Will the righteous be justified in a world to come? Certainly; not because of what our senses tell us, but because sacred Scripture does. Prayer was a textual, not an empirical, pastime.

By using psalms to establish its claims about the universe, classic Jewish liturgy provided not just a dialogue with God but a set of theological verities to explain, and sometimes to oppose, our everyday perception of a frightening and uncertain world. With ears now deadened to textual intricacies, we moderns no longer hear the psalms as our ancestors did. They are still there, echoing through the liturgical text with their claims on reality, but we rarely notice them, and even when we do they speak without authority—while the world remains as frightening and uncertain as ever.

PART 1
PSALMS IN THE LIFE OF ANCIENT ISRAEL

Sweet Singer of Israel: David and the Psalms in Early Judaism

Esther M. Menn
Lutheran School of Theology

The biblically inspired imagination most intimately associates the figure of David—the "sweet singer of Israel"—with the psalms. This perfect match between traditional author and treasured verse seems to have been made in heaven, whatever the actual connection between Israel's greatest king and its classic corpus of religious poetry in more mundane, historical terms.[1] Only a legendary figure as psychologically complex and biographically multidimensional as David could ever embrace so completely the diverse contents of the Psalter and encompass so many of its aspects and usages within Judaism and Christianity. Already nascent in different parts of the Hebrew Bible itself are at least three not entirely reconcilable depictions of David's relation to the psalms: as royal sponsor of corporate liturgy, as private man of prayer and praise, and as inspired author of revelatory literature.[2] These distinct portraits of David vis-à-vis the psalms not only endure in early Judaism but appear magnified in the creative biblical interpretation of the rabbis known as midrash. Exploring the development of David's roles as patron, supplicant, and prophet from their origins in the Bible to their later expression in the classic rabbinic commentary on the psalms entitled *Midrash Tehillim*[3] promises to deepen our delight in the

[1] Allen Cooper discusses the literary significance of the traditional attribution of the Psalms to David, despite its dubious historical basis; see "The Life and Times of King David according to the Book of Psalms," in *The Poet and the Historian: Essays in Literary and Historical Biblical Criticism* (ed. R. E. Friedman; Chico, Calif.: Scholars Press, 1983), 117–31.

[2] James L. Mays explores the beginnings of these three portraits of David's relation to the Psalms in the Bible itself in "The David of the Psalms," *Int* 40 (1986): 143–55.

[3] Much of the material in the first and earliest part of *Midrash Tehillim* (commenting on Pss 1–119) stems from the Amoraic period (third to fifth centuries C.E.), although the final form of the commentary emerged from a gradual process of

psalms and our appreciation of their broad range of application. The persistent diversity of David's roles highlights the equally persistent diversity of the psalms' resonance in public worship, in personal communion with God, and in contemplation of the theological significance of human history, even until the present day.

Royal Sponsor of Corporate Liturgy

Most consonant with the traditional use of the psalms in communal worship settings is the figure of David as royal sponsor of liturgical music. The biblical book of 1 Chronicles, a postexilic work from the fifth or fourth century B.C.E. (fully half a millennium after David's reign), portrays the king as a patron of compositions for the temple destined to be built by his son Solomon. Not yet an author himself even at this late date, David instead charges musical guilds, under the leadership of professionals, including Asaph, Heman, and Jeduthun, with providing inspired performances of thanksgiving and praise.[4] The Chronicler's innovative portrait of Israel's archetypal king as promoter of temple music, entirely absent in the earlier account in 2 Samuel, provides a prestige of origins and a legitimacy through association for the liturgical performances at the newly rebuilt sanctuary of the restoration period.

Midrash Tehillim builds upon this portrayal of David's interest in worship music, although it uniformly overlays the biblical role of sponsor with the later consensus that the king himself personally composed psalms, including those introduced by the superscription "of David."[5] This conflation of perspectives concerning David's relation to the psalms is of course not exclusive to *Midrash Tehillim*. Its beginnings are evident already in the apocryphal book of Ben Sira, from the second century B.C.E., which sequentially calls attention first to David's own exuberant praise of his Maker through his songs of thanksgiving (Sir 47:8) and next to his provision for singers before the altar to exalt God's holy name through sweet

---

compilation continuing until the thirteenth century. For the Hebrew text, see Solomon Buber, ed., *Midrasch Tehillim* (Vilna: Wittwe & Gebrüder Romm, 1891); for an English translation, see William G. Braude, *The Midrash on Psalms* (Yale Judaica Series 13; New Haven: Yale University Press, 1959).

[4] 1 Chr 15:16; 16:4; 23:6; 25:1; and 2 Chr 7:6.

[5] The phrase "of David" (*ldwd*) that introduces 73 of the 150 psalms in the Hebrew Psalter does not itself indicate whether the king should be considered patron, subject, or author. The maximal position that David composed the entire Psalter (*Midr. Teh.* 72.6; 104.2) extends his authorship not only to the "orphan psalms" that bear no superscription but even to those psalms introduced by superscriptions that include the names of other biblical figures.

melody (Sir 47:9–10). The description of "David's Compositions" in the Qumran *Psalms Scroll,* perhaps from the early part of the first century C.E., draws the further conclusion that the 4,050 works attributed to the prolific king include songs to be sung before the altar over sacrifices and to be performed at various festivals.[6] *Midrash Tehillim* stresses this theme of David's personal contribution to the temple liturgy when it portrays God's promise that the "Psalms of David" would continue to be sung in their author's honor at every sacrifice offered in Jerusalem.[7] Another tradition in this commentary asserts that the psalms served as accompaniment not only for temple sacrifices but also for the very construction and later destruction of the sanctuary where they were offered.[8]

In response to the destruction of the Second Temple in 70 C.E. and the emergence of the rabbinic institutions of synagogue and school, David takes on different responsibilities in his role as sponsor of corporate worship in *Midrash Tehillim.* Within this transformed religious context, the David of this commentary seeks new venues for his literary immortality when he implores God to promise that his psalms will be recited forever in houses of prayer and houses of study.[9] While rabbinic prayers eventually come to replace the biblical psalms as the liturgy of the synagogue, *Midrash Tehillim* nevertheless presents David's compositions as a template for elements of contemporary worship. For example, David's first eighteen psalms establish a pattern for the eighteen benedictions at the heart of the rabbinic prayer service.[10] In addition, the great king's preparation of his heart for prayer by reciting psalms provides a model for what becomes standard practice before the corporate prayers of the synagogue.[11] *Midrash Tehillim* even portrays David praying three times a day, like the patriarchs before him and like participants in synagogue liturgy long after him.[12]

From his beginning as royal patron of temple music in Chronicles, David becomes even more personally invested as author of liturgical compositions and spiritual ancestor of the rabbinic synagogue in *Midrash Tehillim.* Although this public persona is not emphasized in *Midrash Tehillim* to the

---

[6] 11QPs^a xxvii 5–10. James Sanders, ed., *The Psalms Scroll of Qumran Cave 11 (11QPs^a)* (Oxford: Clarendon Press, 1965), 48, 91–93.

[7] *Midr. Teh.* 30.3.

[8] *Midr. Teh.* 92.9; cf. 79.3; 94.6. *Midr. Teh.* 147.3 further maintains that the restoration of the temple will be accompanied by psalms.

[9] *Midr. Teh.* 30.3; 61.3.

[10] *Midr. Teh.* 6.1; 20.2; cf. 29.2.

[11] *Midr. Teh.* 1.2; 10.7; 108.1–2. This practice eventually came to be known as P'sukei D'zimrah ("Verses of Song"), although this term does not appear in *Midrash Tehillim.*

[12] *Midr. Teh.* 55.2; cf. 17.6; 72.4; 96.1.

same extent as the other two roles still to be explored, David as royal sponsor of corporate liturgy nevertheless continues to embody the practice of community worship, whether based on the psalms or of later provenance, that has been characteristic of both Judaism and Christianity throughout the centuries.

Private Man of Prayer and Praise

Contrasting with this public role is the depiction of David's deeply personal connection with the psalms, understood as his own addresses to the divinity. This understanding of the psalms as David's prayers and praises is already implied by the historicizing headings that introduce some thirteen psalms.[13] These secondary prefaces attest to the emergence of a practice of canonical relecture, a type of interpretation that correlates the originally anonymous compositions collected in the Psalter with specific events in David's life recounted elsewhere in scripture (specifically, in 2 Samuel, which portrays a fully human David). Through the addition of superscriptions, the moving penitential prayer found in Ps 51 becomes "a psalm of David, when Nathan the prophet came to him, after he had gone into Bathsheba" (cf. 2 Sam 11–12); the lament of an individual surrounded by threatening enemies found in Ps 3 becomes "a psalm of David, when he fled from Absalom his son" (cf. 2 Sam 15–18); and the expression of thanksgiving for victory in battle in Ps 18 becomes "a psalm of David the servant of the Lord, who addressed the words of this song to the Lord on the day when the Lord delivered him from the hand of all his enemies, and from the hand of Saul" (2 Sam 22).[14] This understanding of the psalms as David's personal supplications and spontaneous expressions of gratitude is supported by the brief colophon at the end of Ps 72, apparently marking the conclusion of an earlier and shorter version of the book: "The prayers of David, son of Jesse, are ended." A rabbinic tradition preserved in *Midrash Tehillim* interprets this statement expansively to mean, "All of these [namely, all the psalms in the Psalter] are the prayers of David."[15]

In *Midrash Tehillim,* the occasions for David's personal prayers are multiplied to include biblical situations not mentioned in any of the historical superscriptions to the psalms. For example, the commentary associates

---

[13] Pss 3; 7; 18; 34; 51; 52; 54; 56; 57; 59; 60; 63; and 142.

[14] Brevard Childs discusses the historical superscriptions as instances of early Jewish biblical interpretation; see "Psalm Titles and Midrashic Exegesis," *JSS* 16 (1971): 137–50.

[15] *Midr. Teh.* 1.6; cf. *b. Pesaḥ.* 117a.

Ps 53 with David's encounter with Nabal and Abigail in 1 Sam 25. It does so in part through the application of the opening line of the psalm ("A fool [in Hebrew, *nābāl*] says in his heart, 'There is no God'") to the character of Nabal.[16] In addition, postbiblical embellishments of the king's legendary career become associated with particular psalms. For example, the petition found in Ps 22:22 ("Save me from the lion's mouth, for you have answered me from the horns of the reem [wild ox]") becomes David's desperate prayer as a shepherd boy when threatened by this dangerous beast.[17] This plethora of contexts for David's prayer in *Midrash Tehillim* suggests that he constantly called on God during the many moments of danger and distress in his life and that he experienced deliverance and comfort.

David does not only pray for himself in *Midrash Tehillim.* According to this commentary, the psalms also contain David's intercessions with God on behalf of all Israel[18] as well as his requests that the people's own prayers be received favorably.[19] In anticipation of future crises in Israel's history, David composes prayers with particular biblical characters in mind, including Solomon,[20] Daniel,[21] and Esther.[22] He also prays more generally for vulnerable classes of people, including Israel's school children,[23] the sick,[24] the oppressed righteous of the community,[25] and sinners in need of divine mercy.[26] According to *Midrash Tehillim,* a number of psalms present David's supplications for those who will live under foreign subjugation and in exile.[27] The king also prays for the people's welfare in the yet more distant future, during the final, eschatological battle with Gog and Magog[28]

---

16 *Midr. Teh.* 53.1. For additional examples, see *Midr. Teh.* 36.1, 2, which associates Ps 36 with David's combat with Goliath (1 Sam 17), and *Midr. Teh.* 55.1, 5, which associates Ps 55 with the treason of his counselor Ahithophel during Absalom's rebellion (2 Sam 15–17).

17 *Midr. Teh.* 22.28. For an additional example, see *Midr. Tehillim* 24.10, which identifies the concluding petition in Ps 86:17 as David's plea that the people assembled at the dedication of Solomon's temple receive a sign that God had indeed forgiven his sin with Bathsheba.

18 *Midr. Teh.* 25.5, 14; 31.2, 3, 6; 36.7; 90.7.

19 *Midr. Teh.* 20.4; cf. 116.1.

20 *Midr. Teh.* 72.2, 6.

21 *Midr. Teh.* 55.4; 64.1.

22 *Midr. Teh.* 22.7.

23 *Midr. Teh.* 7.7.

24 *Midr. Teh.* 41.8.

25 *Midr. Teh.* 9.7–14; 17.9; 68.1.

26 *Midr. Teh.* 38.1.

27 *Midr. Teh.* 6.5; 9.7; 17.9; 31.2; 68.1.

28 *Midr. Teh.* 17.9.

and even in the world to come.[29] This dual function of the praying David as extemporaneous petitioner on his own and Israel's behalf is apparent even in a cursory perusal of the commentary preserved in *Midrash Tehillim,* and it is summarized elegantly in the statement, "All that David says in the book of Psalms is said of himself, or of the congregation of Israel."[30]

In keeping with this emphasis on the psalms as an expression of David's personal piety, one tradition in *Midrash Tehillim* explicitly acknowledges the king's special skill in prayer. All of the members of David's ancestral tribe of Judah were effective in offering petitions, since Moses blessed Judah with the words, "Lord, hear the voice of Judah!" (Deut 33:7). Within that tribe, however, David and his house are singled out as especially gifted in intercession.[31] According to *Midrash Tehillim,* the psalms amply illustrate David's masterful crafting of his prayers and his strategic offering of multiple petitions in order to elicit a positive divine response.[32] As private man of prayer and praise, David's model of personal piety continues to be worthy of emulation by his spiritual heirs, whether through the recitation of the ancient king's own words to the divinity or through the offering of original addresses in the tradition of petition and exaltation that David represents.[33]

Inspired Author of Revelatory Literature

The most surprising portrayal of David's association with the Psalter involves a decisive shift in the genre of the psalms, as David becomes not merely a dedicated sponsor of liturgy or a pious author of prayers and praises but also a prophet who composed revelatory poetry under divine inspiration.[34] This transformation—that numbers David, too, among the

---

[29] *Midr. Teh.* 31.2–3, 6; 71.1.

[30] *Midr. Teh.* 4.1; cf. 18.1; 24.3; 35.1.

[31] *Midr. Teh.* 4.1; 102.2; cf. 5.6; 27.5; 84.4; 86.1.

[32] *Midr. Teh.* 27.5; cf. 25.14. Even the alternate tradition in *Midr. Teh.* 1.6 that credits a group of ten notable biblical figures with the composition of the psalms identifies David as the most preeminent of them all, known as the "sweet singer of Israel."

[33] For a fuller discussion of David as an exemplar of prayer in rabbinic psalms commentary, see Esther Menn, "Praying King and Sanctuary of Prayer, Part I: David and Temple Origins in Rabbinic Psalms Commentary (*Midrash Tehillim*)," *JJS* 52 (2001): 1–26, and "Part II: David's Deferment and the Temple's Dedication in Rabbinic Psalms Commentary (*Midrash Tehillim*)," *JJS* 53 (2002): 298–323.

[34] James L. Kugel reconstructs the emergence of the motif of David as prophet from clues in the Bible, Second Temple literature, and rabbinic midrash; see "David the Prophet," in *Poetry and Prophecy: The Beginning of a Literary Tradition* (ed.

prophets—is so remarkable that its development and consequences deserve extended treatment.

Clearly, in 1 and 2 Samuel and in 1 Kings David is a royal figure who relies on others—including Samuel, Nathan, and Gad—to serve the mediating role of the prophet. In this connection one immediately thinks of the prophet Nathan's conveyance of the oracle in 2 Sam 7, to the effect that David is not to build a house for the Lord, or of the same prophet's more confrontational message to the king in 2 Sam 12, following his adultery with Bathsheba and his arrangement of Uriah the Hittite's death in battle. Although king and prophet are originally two distinct offices, there are a number of suggestive details in the Hebrew Bible that contribute to the eventual vesting of King David himself in the prophet's mantle.

One of these prophetic details involves the descent of the spirit of the Lord on David from the moment that Samuel anoints him (1 Sam 16:13). This incident recalls Saul's similar experience, when, after his anointing, God's spirit possesses Saul and he begins prophesying, so that people ask in amazement, "Is Saul, too, among the prophets?" (1 Sam 10:9–13). It also recalls the effect of the spirit in the lives of other Israelite prophets, including Ezekiel, whose visions are often accompanied by dramatic interventions of the spirit. It is perhaps no wonder, then, that the Jewish historian Josephus understands the significance of David's anointment as the beginning of his prophetic career. Writing in the first century C.E., Josephus explains, "The spirit abandoned Saul and passed to David, who when the divine spirit had moved over to him began to prophesy."[35] The epithet, "the anointed of the God of Jacob," applied to David in the preface to his last words in 2 Sam 23:1, may itself have facilitated the identification of David as a prophet, since in the Hebrew Bible not only kings and priests are anointed, but also prophets, including Elisha (1 Kgs 19:16) and the figures alluded to in the parallel lines of Ps 105:16: "Do not touch my anointed ones, nor harm my prophets."

The story of David's introduction into Saul's court, later in 1 Sam 16, similarly suggests that from his youth David possessed a supernatural power, for "whenever the evil spirit from God was upon Saul, David took his lyre and played it with his hand, so Saul was refreshed, and was well, and the evil spirit departed from him" (1 Sam 16:23). David's uncanny employment of the lyre to control the spirit world recalls the prophet

J. L. Kugel; Ithaca, N.Y.: Cornell University Press, 1990). For a discussion of the genres associated with King David's authorship, see Harry Nasuti, *Defining the Sacred Songs: Genre, Tradition, and the Post-Critical Interpretation of the Psalms* (Sheffield: Sheffield Academic Press, 1999).

[35] *Ant.* 6.8.2 §166.

Elisha's use of stringed accompaniment to stimulate his prophetic capacity in 2 Kgs 3:14–16. Although 1 Sam 16 implies that it was David's instrumental music alone that caused the evil spirit to depart from Saul,[36] the later version of the same story in the *Biblical Antiquities* of Pseudo-Philo introduces the actual words that David recited through the guidance of the spirit. Similarly, the four apocryphal "Songs of David" preserved in a manuscript from the Cairo Genizah present incantations for the exorcism of spirits. These four compositions, dating perhaps from the first century C.E., correspond in number to the four "songs for the possessed" listed among David's compositions in the Qumran *Psalms Scroll* (11QPs[a]). This interpretive trajectory claims for David's lyre-accompanied speech an extraordinary efficacy, akin to the prophetic word. Rabbinic tradition makes this claim explicit when it portrays David's invocation of the holy spirit by playing his lyre until he is able to compose an inspired psalm.[37]

Prophetic status for David's speech is more directly claimed in 2 Sam 23:1, the introduction to David's last words.[38] In full, the heading reads, "Now these are the last words of David, the oracle of David son of Jesse, the oracle of the man whom God exalted, the anointed of the God of Jacob, the sweet singer of Israel." Two aspects of this introduction deserve further comment. The first is that the opening phrase, "The *oracle* of David, son of Jesse, the *oracle* of the man whom God exalted," strikingly resembles the phrase that introduces the utterance of the foreign prophet Balaam in Num 23:3: "The *oracle* of Balaam, son of Beor, the *oracle* of the man whose eye is clear." The second point of interest is that the last phrase, which has traditionally been translated as "the sweet singer of Israel," is cryptic and may be translated in a variety of ways. Most suggestive for our present purposes is the translation, "the one granted an affirmative omen by the Strong One of Israel." The composition extolling God's eternal covenant with David that follows also begins with an apparent allusion to David's prophecy: "The spirit of the Lord speaks through me; his word is upon my tongue" (2 Sam 23:2). Whereas the scenes introducing David's career in 1 Sam 16, including the gift of the spirit at his anointing and the success of his career as a musical exorcist in Saul's court, anticipate the future king's prophetic potential, the culminating speech in 2 Sam 23 openly describes the inspired nature of the mature king's speech.

---

36 For David's enduring reputation as an instrumentalist, see Amos 6:5.

37 *Midr. Teh.* 24.3; 57.4. According to this tradition, psalms composed through David's intentional invocation of the holy spirit are labeled by the title "a psalm, to David," whereas psalms composed after a spontaneous visitation of the holy spirit are labeled by the title, "to David, a psalm."

38 Mentioned in passing above, p. 67.

Significantly, the preceding chapter (2 Sam 22) implies that David is the author of at least one psalm when it presents a version of Ps 18 as his song of victory. The historical superscription identifying the context of this composition is essentially the same in Ps 18:1 and in 2 Sam 22:1, both of which indicate that David addressed the words of this song to the Lord "on the day when the Lord delivered him from the hand of all his enemies and from the hand of Saul." The juxtaposition of psalmic material and prophetic claims in 2 Sam 22 and 23 no doubt facilitated the inference that the psalms themselves are the inspired speech of the great king himself.

Additional material contributing to the construction of a prophetic David may be found in 1 Chronicles and the historical superscriptions on a number of the psalms, even though (as noted previously) these sources forward very different understandings of David's relation to the psalms. For example, the Chronicler's description of David as "the man of God" (2 Chr 8:14) helps assimilate the great king to a prophetic model, since elsewhere in the Bible this title is given to prophetic figures, including Moses, Samuel, Elijah, Elisha, and others. In addition, the assertion that David directly received plans for the temple from the Lord (1 Chr 28:11–19), much as the great prophet Moses originally received plans for the tabernacle, bolsters his prophetic credentials. Similarly, the appearance of a Davidic superscription (*ldwd,* which may be translated "to David," "for David," or "of David") in headings of psalms referring to events occurring long after the king's death suggests that he must have employed prophetic foresight in composing them, since this superscription eventually came to be understood as an indication of authorship. For example, Ps 137, a Davidic psalm (at least in the Masoretic Text), refers to the Babylonians' destruction of the Jerusalem temple in the sixth century B.C.E., even though this structure was not even completed in David's lifetime! This historical anachronism was negotiated by attributing special powers of insight into the future to David.

Apparently it was sometime between the second century B.C.E. and the first century C.E. when David came to be commonly perceived as the prophetic author of the psalms. This development can be dated to this period through a comparison of the treatments of David's relation to the psalms in the apocryphal book of Ben Sira and in the Qumran *Psalms Scroll* (11QPs[a]). Ben Sira, writing in the second century B.C.E., never suggests that David composed the psalms through *prophecy*. As noted previously, he places his emphasis instead on David's exuberance in thanking and praising God and on his patronage of liturgical music growing out of his own enthusiasm for exalting the divinity. In fact, Ben Sira credits Nathan as the preeminent prophet active in David's time (Sir 47:1). A century or so later, the Qumran *Psalms Scroll* (11QPs[a]) similarly conflates the traditions of David as sponsor of liturgical music and of David as author of the psalms when it presents a literary inventory of

"David's Compositions" for various festivals and worship contexts. The Qumran *Psalms Scroll* goes far beyond Ben Sira, however, when it clarifies that David uttered all 4,050 of these compositions "through *prophecy* given to him by the most high God." Similarly, the pesher-type interpretation of certain psalms (including 37, 47, 60, and, possibly, 108) in terms of contemporary events in the Qumran community, such as the unjust persecution and anticipated vindication of their leader, the Teacher of Righteousness, exactly parallels the pesher-type interpretation of the prophetic books, including Habakkuk and Nahum. This common exegetical treatment of the psalms and the prophets implies that at Qumran David's compositions were considered revelatory literature, even if extremely cryptic and therefore demanding a similarly inspired interpreter.

Since the idea that David was the prophetic author of the psalms had become an established interpretive tradition by the first century C.E., it comes as no surprise that the followers of Jesus considered David a prophet. The authors of the New Testament literature employed the psalms along with the other prophetic books, including Isaiah, Jeremiah, and even Daniel (who himself received a belated induction into the prophetic guild), to stress the working out of God's ancient, providential plans for humanity through the coming of the expected Messiah and Savior of the world. Acts 2:29–30, for example, explicitly calls David a "prophet" ("David, therefore, being a prophet"), who disclosed in Ps 132:11 God's oath to put one of his descendants on the throne and who predicted in Ps 16:10 that God would resurrect the Messiah, whom he would not abandon to Hades nor allow his flesh to experience corruption. Similarly, according to Acts 1:16, the Holy Spirit "spoke beforehand by the mouth of David" concerning Judas's betrayal of Jesus, and "what is written in the book of Psalms" is quoted in Acts 1:20 as David's prophecy concerning the grim fate of this disciple who guided the soldiers when they arrested Jesus.

The list of explicit citations of the psalms, and of more covert allusions to them in the New Testament, as David's predictive discourse concerning the details and significance of Jesus' life, death, and resurrection is too long to rehearse here. It must suffice to note that the book of Psalms is the most often quoted book of the Jewish scriptures within the New Testament corpus and that both Greek and Latin patristic authors continued and further developed the interpretation of the psalms as David's christological prophecy, nascent in the New Testament. To give just one example, Augustine in his *Sermons on the Psalms* interprets the entirety of Ps 22 (to him, Ps 21) in terms of Jesus' death on the cross and his resurrection. In his systematic exegesis, he goes far beyond the isolated references to particular verses of Ps 22 in the Gospels, including the quotation of the opening line, "My God, my God, why have you forsaken me?" as Jesus' last words in Mark and Matthew and the note in John 19:24 that the soldiers divided Jesus' clothing and cast lots for his tunic, "in order to fulfill what scripture says" in Ps 22:18.[39]

Within rabbinic Judaism, however, the motif of David's prophecy addressed very different issues, including the status of the psalms within the scriptural canon and the intentional nature of Israel's providential history as viewed through the single, panoramic perspective of the inspired king. With respect to the first issue of the canon, no doubt the original impetus for the development of David as a prophetic figure emerged at least in part from reflection concerning how the apparently human prayers and praises of the Psalter might be considered part of a corpus of sacred scripture. The elevation of David as a prophet at least partially assimilates the psalms to the genre of prophecy that becomes the dominant model for understanding the canonical writings as authoritative and revelatory. Comparisons between David and the greatest prophet of all, Moses, precisely on the topic of their respective compositions, confirms that the issue of the canonical status of the psalms underlies the portrayal of David as a prophet. A tradition in *Midrash Tehillim* asserts, "As Moses gave five books of law to Israel, so David gave five books of psalms to Israel." Following this assertion, *Midrash Tehillim* continues with a review of the seams of the fivefold division of the book of Psalms that mark it as a parallel work to Moses' Pentateuch.[40]

Despite this comparison and the inspired status that it claims for the Psalter, the psalms nevertheless retain a secondary status vis-à-vis the Torah. An especially poignant indication of this subordinate ranking in *Midrash Tehillim* is the expression of David's insecurity when he prays that his compositions not be mistakenly read as Homer (in other words, as human poetry inspired only by the poet's muse) but rather understood as Torah (or revelatory instruction from God himself).[41] This petition from the traditional author, although answered favorably in *Midrash Tehillim,* gives voice to persistent reservations about the standing of the psalms within the Jewish biblical canon.

---

39 Esther M. Menn, "No Ordinary Lament: Relecture and the Identity of the Distressed in Psalm 22," *HTR* 93 (2000): 327–35, highlights some of the applications of Ps 22 to the passion of Christ in the early Christian tradition.

40 *Midr. Teh.* 1.2; cf. *Midr. Teh.* 24.5. Uriel Simon articulates the medieval commentator Saadya Gaon's extreme position that David's Psalter was for all intents and purposes a second Torah; see *Four Approaches to the Book of Psalms: From Saadiah Gaon to Araham Ibn Ezra* (Albany: State University of New York Press, 1991).

41 *Midr. Teh.* 1.8.

While the initial issue in the development of David as a prophetic figure may have been the status of the psalms within the canon of the Hebrew Bible, a remarkable outcome of this development in rabbinic Judaism is the emergence of David as a unifying voice, commenting on the whole of Israel's providential history. In *Midrash Tehillim,* David's prophecy does include an element of inspired foresight into the future. Unlike the interpretations of the psalms at Qumran or in the New Testament in terms of contemporary characters and events, however, in this commentary application of the psalms seldom extends beyond the confines of the biblical narrative into the world of the rabbis and their contemporaries.

Instead of rabbinic events, the prophetic David in *Midrash Tehillim* more typically envisions future biblical events, including how his own son Solomon will receive wisdom enabling him to judge righteously,[42] how Daniel and his three companions will resist the pressures of Nebuchadnezzar to compromise their faith,[43] how Esther will risk her life to save her people,[44] and how the temple will be rebuilt in the time of Ezra.[45] David's inspired vision of the biblical future is difficult to summarize further, for it appears over the course of commentary on many psalms. Two short passages defining Ps 22 (a "psalm of David" according to the superscription) as David's composition concerning Queen Esther's prayer before approaching the Persian king Ahashuerus will serve as illustrations:

> My God, my God, why have you forsaken me? (Ps 22:1). On the first day of a fast, one says: "My God." On the second, one says, "my God." Only on the third may one say "why have you forsaken me?" So it was only after Esther cried in a loud voice, "why have you forsaken me?" that her cry was heard.[46]

In this commentary, the three parts of the first line of Ps 22, "My God, my God, why have you forsaken me," become addresses to God over the course of a three day fast. David apparently discerns through prophetic clairvoyance Esther's utterance of these words and God's response. *Midrash Tehillim* is even more explicit in its assertion that David composed Ps 22 concerning Esther's prayer in another passage:

---

[42] *Midr. Teh.* 72.2.
[43] *Midr. Teh.* 9.17; 64.1.
[44] *Midr. Teh.* 22.7.
[45] *Midr. Teh.* 22.9.
[46] *Midr. Teh.* 22.6.

> When David foresaw by the help of the holy spirit that Esther would call on the Holy One, blessed be he, using the title, "my Strength" (Ps 22:20), he, thinking of Esther, composed [Ps 22], "For the leader, concerning the Strength of the Dawn" (Ps 1:1).[47]

As a prophet, David also sees the distant eschatological restoration of Israel's fortunes and writes about them in the psalms. For example, the repetition of the verb "to awake" in Ps 57:9 ("Awake, my glory; awake, psaltery and harp; I will awaken the dawn!") refers sequentially to the fate of the Jerusalem temple, not yet built in David's own life, and to its destiny at the end of days. Specifically, the first "Awake, my glory" alludes to the First Temple, which was destroyed by the Babylonians and rebuilt by the hands of Ezra, whereas the second, "awake, psaltery and harp; I will awaken the dawn," alludes to the Second Temple, which was destroyed by the Romans and will be rebuilt ultimately by God's own hand.[48]

Perhaps surprising in light of our common understanding of prophetic clairvoyance as clear vision concerning the future is the additional information that David's inspired poetry supplies about the formative past in *Midrash Tehillim,* including the period of the patriarchs, the exodus, and the receiving of the law at Sinai (all events recounted in the five books of the Torah). We may have to adjust our idea about the direction of clairvoyance to understand how in *Midrash Tehillim* David's prophetic gift allows him to see the past clearly. Josephus's understanding of prophetic accuracy in ancient matters may help us make this adjustment. He writes about scripture's presentation of history:

> So it naturally, or rather necessarily follows, seeing the accounts, that there is no discrepancy in what is written, seeing that, on the contrary, the prophets alone had this privilege, obtaining their knowledge of the most distant and ancient history through inspiration which they owed to God.[49]

David as a prophet in *Midrash Tehillim* thus clarifies such things as how Abraham and his small band of men were able to withstand the combined forces of all the indigenous kings in Gen 14: "It was not Abraham himself who fought the battle, but rather God himself." As *Midrash Tehillim* explains: "Who fought all the battles? It was the Holy One, blessed be he. He said to Abraham, 'Sit at my right hand' (Psalms 110:1), and I will fight

---

47 *Midr. Teh*. 22.7. The superscription to the psalm contains a word that is generally translated as "hind" but would, if pointed with different vowels, be the same word for "strength" used in Ps 22:20.

48 *Midr. Teh*. 22.9.

49 *Ag. Ap*. 1.7 §37.

the battles for you. That God did so is not made plain in the narrative. Who made it plain? David, who said, "The Lord said to my Lord, 'Sit at my right hand.'"[50]

David's prophetic involvement with Israel's biblical past and future is not limited to objectively dispensing additional information, however. Instead, his emotional involvement is clearly evident in his engagement in intercession, dialogue, and praise. For example, David blesses Israel for their many merits leading to the exodus from Egypt,[51] and he chides God for holding his peace when the temple is destroyed.[52]

The tradition of David as prophetic author of the psalms therefore bequeaths an inspired and panoramic vision of biblical history, surveying the magnificent scope of divine providence both before and after him. The unfolding of the biblical story through the psalms in so passionate a consciousness as the prophet David is no mean accomplishment, and *Midrash Tehillim's* commentary offers its ancient and modern readers a new and compelling vantage point from which to consider God's history with Israel.

Conclusion

The "sweet singer of Israel" in *Midrash Tehillim* thus remains the public sponsor of liturgical music, the personal exemplar of recourse and devotion to the divinity, and the prophetic lens through which to view divine providence at work in human history. Because of the multiplicity of his own roles, David is uniquely suited to represent the multiplicity of the psalms, in all of their senses and in all of their employments within religious communities. As multifaceted traditional author, the complex figure of David ensures that the rich treasury of the Psalter remains open for every generation.

---

[50] *Midr. Teh.* 110.4. Similarly, according to *Midr. Teh.* 23.4, Ps 23 provides additional details about God's providential care for Moses and his generation as they wandered in the wilderness following the exodus from Egypt.

[51] *Midr. Teh.* 1.1; cf. 114.5.

[52] *Midr. Teh.* 109.1.

Amazing Grace: The Transformation of the Thanksgiving Hymn at Qumran

John J. Collins
Yale University Divinity School

The Dead Sea Scrolls, discovered in caves near the site of Qumran approximately fifty years ago, have provided a rich trove of primary resources for a period of Jewish history that had previously been poorly documented. The topics on which new light has been cast include the formation of the Psalter,[1] the transmission of traditional hymns and prayers,[2] and the early history of Jewish liturgy.[3] The finds also include a corpus of religious poems that were not traditional but were evidently composed in and for the sectarian community that preserved the Scrolls. The original find of seven carefully preserved scrolls in the cave that became known as Cave 1 included one that was taken up with a collection of more than thirty poems, each of which opens with a distinctive formula, "I thank you, Lord" (אודכה אדוני) or "Blessed are you, O Lord" (ברוך אתה אדוני). Consequently, these poems were dubbed *Thanksgiving Psalms* or *Hodayot*.[4] Six other manuscripts containing copies of these

---

[1] Peter W. Flint, *The Dead Sea Psalms Scrolls and the Book of Psalms* (STDJ 17; Leiden: Brill, 1997).

[2] Eileen M. Schuller, *Non-canonical Psalms from Qumran: A Pseudepigraphic Collection* (HSS 28; Atlanta: Scholars Press, 1986); idem, "Prayer, Hymnic and Liturgical Texts from Qumran," in *The Community of the Renewed Covenant* (ed. E. Ulrich and J. VanderKam; Notre Dame, Ind.: University of Notre Dame Press, 1994), 135–72; Esther G. Chazon, "Hymns and Prayers in the Dead Sea Scrolls," in *The Dead Sea Scrolls after Fifty Years* (ed. P. W. Flint and J. C. VanderKam; Leiden: Brill, 1998), 1:244–70.

[3] Lawrence H. Schiffman, "The Dead Sea Scrolls and the Early History of Jewish Liturgy," in *The Synagogue in Late Antiquity* (ed. L. I. Levine; Philadelphia: ASOR, 1987), 33–48; Daniel F. Falk, *Daily, Festival, and Sabbath Prayers from Qumran* (STDJ 27; Leiden: Brill, 1997).

[4] E. L. Sukenik, *The Dead Sea Scrolls of the Hebrew University* (Jerusalem: Magnes, 1955). They are often called Thanksgiving Hymns. The term *hymn* in

psalms were later discovered in Qumran Cave 4.[5] The number of manuscripts would seem to indicate that these psalms were of some importance to the community that preserved them. They provide evidence of an ongoing tradition of composing religious poetry in Hebrew in the period between the Bible and the Mishnah.

The initial editor of the *Hodayot,* E. L. Sukenik, was impressed that "most of these hymns strike a distinctive personal note."[6] He suggested that they were written by none other than the Teacher of Righteousness, the founding father of the Dead Sea sect. This suggestion was generally accepted at first but was later challenged, especially by the Danish scholar Svend Holm-Nielsen, who denied that the *Hodayot* were a literary unity and concluded that "it is barely possible to say anything at all decisive about the actual authorship."[7] Of course, any identification of an anonymous collection of writings is hypothetical, and an attribution to a figure about whom we know very little is all the more hazardous. Nonetheless, the question of the authorship of these hymns launched a fruitful discussion, which even yielded one of the few points of consensus in the study of the Dead Sea Scrolls. Holm-Nielsen was right that the *Hodayot* are not a literary unity. We can distinguish two quite distinct collections, conventionally known as Teacher Hymns and Hymns of the Community, which are distinguished both by their choice of vocabulary and by the kinds of claims they make.[8] In the original *Hodayot* scroll from Cave 1, the so-called Teacher Hymns are found in a block in columns 10–17 (columns 3–9 in Sukenik's enumeration) surrounded by Hymns of the Community. The manuscripts from Cave 4 include some smaller collections, one of which appears to have only Teacher Hymns.[9] Whether the Teacher Hymns were actually written by the founding Teacher or not, the distinction raises the question of the relationship between psalms that bear the strong imprint

---

biblical scholarship is usually reserved for a song of praise, but there is obvious overlap between hymns and psalms of thanksgiving.

5 Eileen M. Schuller, "Hodayot," in *Qumran Cave 4.XX: Poetical and Liturgical Texts, Part 2* (ed. E. Chazon; DJD 29; Oxford: Clarendon Press, 1999), 69–254.

6 Sukenik, *Dead Sea Scrolls,* 39.

7 Svend Holm-Nielsen, *Hodayot: Psalms from Qumran* (Acta theologica Danica 2; Aarhus: Universitetsforlaget, 1960), 316.

8 Gert Jeremias, *Der Lehrer der Gerechtigkeit* (SUNT 2; Göttingen: Vandenhoeck & Ruprecht, 1963); Jürgen Becker, *Das Heil Gottes* (SUNT 3; Göttingen: Vandenhoeck & Ruprecht, 1964); Heinz-Wolfgang Kuhn, *Enderwartung und Gegenwärtiges Heil* (SUNT 4; Göttingen: Vandenhoeck & Ruprecht, 1966); Michael C. Douglas, "The Teacher Hymn Hypothesis Revisited: New Data for an Old Crux," *DSD* 6 (1999): 239–66.

9 4QH[c], Schuller, "Hodayot," 187–94.

of an individual and communal liturgical usage. Related to this is the question whether the *Hodayot* were in fact used in community worship. Some scholars have assumed that they were,[10] while others have argued that they were used primarily in an instructional or didactic context or for private meditation.[11]

The Biblical Thanksgiving Psalm

It will be useful to begin by considering the genre of thanksgiving psalms as it is found in the biblical Psalter. In accordance with the classic analysis of Hermann Gunkel,[12] these psalms typically begin with a more or less expanded introduction that communicates the intention and content: "I will thank you," "I will praise you," or "Give thanks," "Praise." They invariably mention the name of the Lord as the one who is to be thanked or praised. An essential element is "the narrative of the fate of the one offering thanks." It is usually directed to a human audience and refers to the Lord in the third person, but it can also be addressed to the Lord directly. According to Gunkel, the most important thing the psalmist has to say is how he has passed from death to life, by the grace of God. The account typically has three parts: the reports of distress, the call to the Lord, and the deliverance. The distress is often described in hyperbolic terms: the psalmist has gone down to the grave, or to Sheol. In contrast, realistic details of the psalmist's experience are in short supply. (This may be due to the fact that the psalms were meant to be broad enough to fit a range of experiences. Gunkel suggests that these psalms were originally composed by officials at the temple for use by worshipers.) The distress of the psalmist is often attributed to the opposition of enemies.

Another essential element is the confession to the Lord as the one who delivered from distress. The verb *hôdâ,* to give thanks, also means to confess. The point of a thanksgiving psalm is to give public acknowledgement to the salvation wrought by the Lord. By its very nature, this acknowledgement is directed toward others and speaks of the Lord in the third person. Sometimes the psalm mentions a thanksgiving sacrifice or the fulfillment of a vow. Sometimes, too, there is a communal thanksgiving at the end, presumably spoken by bystanders or festival guests. Most of the thanksgiving psalms of the Psalter are cast as the confession of individuals.

---

[10] E.g., Holm-Nielsen, *Hodayot,* 348.

[11] Schiffman, "Dead Sea Scrolls," 36; see the summary of the discussion by Schuller, "Prayer, Hymnic and Liturgical Texts," 166–67.

[12] Hermann Gunkel, *An Introduction to the Psalms* (completed by J. Begrich; trans. J. D. Nogalski; Macon, Ga.: Mercer University Press, 1998), 199–221.

Examples include Pss 18; 30; 32; 41; 66B; 118; and 138.[13] Communal thanksgivings are less common and less clearly defined, but are attested. Psalms 124 and 129 are sometimes cited as examples. Communal thanksgiving psalms, however, are difficult to distinguish from hymns of praise. There are several examples in the Chronicler's history where priests and Levites give thanks and praise to the Lord in ceremonial contexts.[14]

The classical psalm of thanksgiving may be illustrated by Ps 118. There we find, first, a call to give thanks, then an affirmation that the Lord answered the psalmist's prayer "and set me in a broad place," followed by several affirmations of the value of trust in the Lord. The description of the distress is quite vague ("all nations surrounded me"). The fact that the enemies are nations suggests that the speaker is the king. The psalmist confesses that the Lord has punished him but gives thanks that he was not given over to death. There are indications of a procession to the temple (118:19: "Open to me the gates of righteousness"; cf. 118:27: "bind the festal procession with branches"), and in 118:22–27 the speaker is in the plural. The psalm concludes with another call to give thanks. We are given the impression that the psalmist goes to the temple in procession with friends and that they participate in the thanks and praise.

Another example is found in Ps 30, where the psalmist says that God has rescued him from the netherworld (Sheol). There are no statements with plural subjects, but there is a call to "his faithful ones" to give thanks and praise. In Ps 30, the psalmist admits to a false sense of security before he was humbled, but a confession of fault is not a necessary part of the genre. In Ps 18, for example, the speaker claims that God has "rewarded me according to my righteousness" (18:20).

Gunkel inferred that these thanksgiving psalms had their *Sitz im Leben* in a ritual of thanksgiving in the temple.[15] The thanksgiving may accompany a sacrifice or may itself be the offering. The individual does not approach the altar alone, but surrounded by a community of friends or perhaps by other people giving thanks for their own deliverance. It is of the essence of this thanksgiving that it is a public act. Hence, there is a necessary interplay between the individual and the community. The deliverance is experienced by an individual, but the assembled congregation joins in the thanks and praise.

---

[13] Erhard S. Gerstenberger, *Psalms: Part 1, with an Introduction to Cultic Poetry* (FOTL 14; Grand Rapids: Eerdmans, 1988), 15–16.

[14] E.g., Ezra 3:11; 2 Chr 20:21; see Patrick D. Miller, *They Cried to the Lord: The Form and Theology of Israelite Prayer* (Minneapolis: Fortress, 1994), 205.

[15] Gunkel, *Introduction to the Psalms,* 199–200.

The Teacher Psalms

Against this background, we turn now to consider the Teacher Hymns from Qumran. For an illustration, let us turn to the hymn that begins in 1QH[a] 12:5.[16] There is no opening call to praise here and nothing to suggest a ceremonial setting. Neither is there any praise spoken with a plural subject at the end of the psalm. In short, the psalm has much more the character of a private prayer than was the case with its biblical counterparts. The psalmist gives thanks here for illumination: "you have lightened my face for your covenant.... Like perfect dawn you have revealed yourself to me with perfect light." Some other *Hodayot* are closer to the biblical prototype at this point. For example, the psalm that begins in 1QH[a] 11:19 (a Community Psalm) declares: "I thank you, Lord, because you saved my life from the pit, and from the Sheol of Abaddon have lifted me up to an everlasting height, so that I can walk on a boundless plain." In column 12, too, the psalmist reports adversity, specifically, opposition by enemies: "For I have been rejected by them, and they do not esteem me when you made yourself great through me." The psalm goes on to describe conflict with "mediators of fraud and seers of deceit" who are evidently rival teachers. These people have "driven me from my land like a bird from its nest."

All of this has a specific, personal ring to it that is unusual in the canonical psalms. Moreover, it is apparent that these opponents have not yet been vanquished. Rather, the psalmist expresses his conviction that God will act "to annihilate all men of deception." For now, the psalmist is giving thanks for the illumination and revelation that enables him to remain resolute and rise above those who scorn him. The psalm gives praise to God, but it serves simultaneously to assert the legitimacy of the psalmist as the person who articulates God's way. The thanksgiving is not only for deliverance from death or the netherworld but also for giving the speaker a certain status. There are some analogies for this in the canonical Psalter, primarily in the case of the king. (Consider, for example, Ps 18:43–44: "you have made me head of the nations; people whom I had not known served me. As soon as they heard of me they obeyed me.")

This thanksgiving psalm does not call on bystanders to join in the praise, but it has a communal dimension nonetheless. The speaker gives thanks that through him God has enlightened the face of the many. This is a reflex of the exaltation of the speaker, since it strengthens his position and supports his claims. However, it is important to note that the speaker does not stand before God in isolation. His role is that of a mediator of

---

[16] See Florentino García Martínez and Eibert J. C. Tigchelaar, *The Dead Sea Scrolls Study Edition* (Leiden: Brill, 1997), 1:166–67.

revelation, and his validity depends on his acceptance by a community. Those who accept him share in his illumination and in his security over against enemies. There is an analogy here between the role of the king in the canonical Psalter and that of the psalmist (teacher?) here. The community (the many) attain their deliverance by sharing in the experience of the psalmist.

One other aspect of this psalm requires comment. Toward the end of the poem the author reflects on his own unworthiness. In part this is ontological; he is a creature of clay. The same point is made more extensively in the Community Psalm in 1QH^a 11:19–24: "But I, a creature of clay, what am I? Mixed with water, as whom shall I be considered? What is my strength? For I find myself at the boundary of wickedness." In column 12, the author also "remembered my guilty deeds, together with the unfaithfulness of my ancestors," but he is quickly rescued from these thoughts by remembering the mercy of God. The author has a strong sense of human unworthiness, but his own guilt is acknowledged only as an occasion for praising God that he has been purified and exalted.

Psalms of the Community

The Psalms of the Community differ from the so-called Teacher Psalms primarily insofar as they lack the concern for the authority of the speaker and also the apparent allusions to personal experience (such as being driven from his land). The opening verses of the hymn in 1QH^a 11:19–36 may be taken as representative: "I thank you, Lord, because you saved my life from the pit, and from the Sheol of Abaddon have lifted me up to an everlasting height, so that I can walk on a boundless plain." Presumably the author was not actually in the netherworld, but there is no indication of a more realistic cause of distress. The description of salvation seems equally hyperbolic: "the depraved spirit you have purified from great offense so that he can take a place with the host of the holy ones and can enter into communion with the congregation of the sons of heaven." Fellowship with the angels was the destiny of the righteous after death in the early apocalypses of Daniel and Enoch (Dan 12; *1 En.* 104). Human beings were also thought to mingle with angels in the cult and in warfare. There are several passages in the Dead Sea Scrolls that indicate that the sectarian community aspired to live permanently with and like the angels "in the council of the holy ones" (see, e.g., 1QSa 2:8–9). Again in 1QH^a 19:10–14 God is praised because "for the sake of your glory you have purified man from offense, so that he can make himself holy for you from every impure abomination and guilt of unfaithfulness, to become united with the sons of your truth and in the lot with your holy ones, to raise the worms of the dead from the dust, to an everlasting community." The language here is of death and resurrection, as is also often the case in the biblical psalms when they speak of rescue from Sheol. Some scholars have read this passage as evidence for a belief in physical resurrection at Qumran,[17] but this is not necessarily so. The passage may mean that life outside the community is tantamount to living in the netherworld, while life within the community is tantamount to living with the angels.[18] Here again we find a strong sense of human unworthiness, but only as a foil to the certainty of the salvation that has been experienced. One might compare the modern hymn "Amazing Grace": "I was blind, but now I see." The blindness here is not so much a matter of personal sin as of the impurity of the unsanctified human condition.

The Psalms of the Community are written in the first person, just like the Teacher Psalms, and they include no calls to bystanders to join in praise nor speech in plural form. However, the designation "Psalms of the Community" is not unreasonable, since there is little indication here of distinctive personal experience. The transformation reported in these hymns is similar to that claimed in the Teacher Psalms, but it lacks the specificity of those compositions. They are not psalms for specific occasions, like those in the Psalter, to be recited upon recovery from sickness or danger. Rather, they give thanks for a state of being: the sanctified, quasi-angelic life of members of the sectarian community. We can only guess at the use to which these psalms were put, although it is clear from the number of copies preserved at Qumran that they were used in some way. They could have been recited in unison in a synagogal service, or they could have been used for personal meditation. Of course, the Teacher Hymns could also have been recited in common or appropriated by other members of the community, insofar as they identified with the sentiments expressed in those hymns.

A Clearly Liturgical Psalm among the *Hodayot*

A new complication is introduced into the discussion of the *Hodayot* by the publication of the fragments from Cave 4. These fragments include some that have no parallel in 1QH[a], including a remarkable hymn found in 4Q427 fragment 7. We do, however, have other copies of this hymn in 4Q491c and 4Q471b, both of which were originally regarded as copies of the *War Scroll*. More precisely, we have

---

[17] E.g., Emile Puech, *La croyance des Esséniens en la vie future* (EBib NS 21–22; Paris: Gabalda, 1993), 2:375–81.

[18] John J. Collins, *Apocalypticism in the Dead Sea Scrolls* (London: Routledge, 1997), 110–29.

two recensions of this hymn, the shorter form in 4Q491c and the longer in 4Q427 7 and 4Q471b. Further fragments of the longer recension are found in 4Q431, which is part of the same manuscript as 4Q471b, and in 1QH^{a} 25:35–26:10.[19]

This composition is remarkable in two respects. It contains a claim of self-exaltation that is without parallel in the Dead Sea Scrolls, and this first-person hymn is followed by an imperatival call to the righteous to join in the praise of God.

Unfortunately, all copies of this hymn are very fragmentary, and the opening formula is not preserved in the longer copies. There is, however, a tiny fragment of 1QH^{a} (25:35–26:10) that appears to be a copy of the same work. (The text is too fragmentary to permit certainty, but it includes some distinctive phrases. Wise offers an extensive reconstruction.[20]) This fragment has the title "for the maskil, a psalm," which is at once an indication of liturgical use and a distinctive marker that sets it apart from other hymns in the *Hodayot.* The short recension of the self-glorification hymn in 4Q491 evidently began with praise of God for his marvelous deeds and went on to speak of "a mighty throne in the congregation of the gods," on which none of the kings of the East shall sit. (The Hebrew term for "gods," **אלים**, can refer to heavenly beings other than the Most High, so, in effect, to angels.) The speaker boasts "I am reckoned with the gods, and my dwelling is in the holy congregation," and "there is no teaching comparable [to my teaching]." He also asks "who suffers evil like me" and boasts that his glory is with the sons of the king (i.e., God).

Some other striking phrases are found in the other fragments. The speaker is "beloved of the king, companion of the holy ones" and even asks, "Who is like me among the gods?" (4Q471b). In 4Q491, this "self-exaltation hymn" is marked off from the following "canticle of the righteous" by a large *lāmed,* which has been taken to indicate that it was regarded as a separate composition.[21] This marker is not found in the other copies of the text. The canticle is most fully preserved in 4Q427: "Sing a hymn, beloved ones, to the king.... Exalt together with the eternal host, ascribe greatness to our God and glory to our King." This is clearly a liturgical composition that provides precisely the kind of call to praise that is conspicuously lacking in the *Hodayot.*

---

[19] For a comprehensive discussion, see Esther Eshel, "The Identification of the 'Speaker' of the Self-Glorification Hymn," in *The Provo International Conference on the Dead Sea Scrolls* (ed. D. W. Parry and E. Ulrich; STDJ 30; Leiden: Brill, 1999), 619–35; Michael O. Wise, "**מי כמוני באלים**: A Study of 4Q491c, 4Q471b, 4Q427 7 and 1QH^{a} 25:35–26:10," *DSD* 7 (2000): 173–219.

[20] Wise, "**מי כמוני באלים**," 204.

[21] So ibid., 193.

Most of the discussion of this hymn has focused on the identity of the speaker in the "self-glorification" part. There is no parallel for such self-glorification on the part of a human being in ancient Judaism; the closest parallel is perhaps the self-praise of wisdom in Sir 24. Accordingly, the first editor, Baillet, felt that the speaker must be an angel and dubbed the piece "the canticle of Michael."[22] As the late Morton Smith rather caustically observed, however, an archangel would not need to boast about being reckoned with the "gods" or heavenly beings. The speaker must be a human.[23] Those who have sought a human author have usually suggested the Teacher of Righteousness, who is the only personality about whom we know anything in the Dead Sea sect.[24] In this case, the suggestion is supported by the fact that the hymn boasts about the author's teaching. However, the tone of this hymn is very different from that of the so-called Teacher Hymns. There is no reflection here on being a creature of clay; on the contrary, the author boasts that his desire is not like that of flesh. Consequently, two other suggestions have been made. The author might not be the Teacher but a later teacher in the history of the sect; one scholar has even offered a specific identification with Menahem the Essene, who is mentioned by Josephus, but this is not compelling.[25] Alternatively, the speaker may not be a historical person at all but an ideal, imaginary one, such as the eschatological high priest who would also hold a teaching office.[26] None of these suggestions, however, has commanded a consensus. The identity of the speaker is likely to remain controversial.

The most recent study of this text, by Michael Wise, has the merit of proposing yet another solution: that "each member of the user group spoke of himself or herself. At least by the stage of the Hodayot redaction, they declaimed in unison and chanted, singing of their singular significance at the behest of a worship leader, the Maskil."[27] Wise admits that the

---

[22] Maurice Baillet, *Qumrân Grotte 4.III (4Q482–4Q520)* (DJD 7; Oxford: Clarendon Press, 1982), 26–29.

[23] Morton Smith, "Ascent to the Heavens and Deification in 4QMa," in *Archaeology and History in the Dead Sea Scrolls: The New York University Conference in Memory of Yigael Yadin* (ed. L. H. Schiffman; JSPSup 8; JSOT/ASOR Monographs Series 2; Sheffield: JSOT Press, 1990), 181–88.

[24] Martin G. Abegg, "Who Ascended to Heaven? 4Q491, 4Q427 and the Teacher of Righteousness," in *Eschatology, Messianism, and the Dead Sea Scrolls* (ed. C. A. Evans and P. W. Flint; Grand Rapids: Eerdmans, 1997); cf. Wise, "מי כמוני באלים," 218.

[25] Israel Knohl, *The Messiah before Jesus: The Suffering Servant of the Dead Sea Scrolls* (Berkeley and Los Angeles: University of California Press, 2000), 52–55.

[26] John J. Collins, *The Scepter and the Star* (New York: Doubleday, 1995), 148; Eshel, "Identification of the 'Speaker.'"

[27] Wise, "מי כמוני באלים," 216.

claims made in the self-glorification part of the hymn "are too specific to one person's situation, too individualistic to have been a group's self-description *ab origine*. What group, for example, each and every one, could stake a literal claim to teaching beyond compare?"[28] However, the problem is not only with the original composition. Does it make sense to suggest that each member of the group recited the hymn, thinking of his or her own singular significance? How could every member of the community apply such unique claims to himself or herself?

Some light may be thrown on this question by going back to consider the biblical thanksgiving psalms, with which we started. These psalms typically recount the experience of an individual, however stylized, and then conclude by calling on the assembled congregation to join in praising and thanking God. It is not necessarily implied that each member of the congregation applies the narrative of deliverance to himself or herself. They are to praise God for the deliverance of the person making the thanksgiving offering. So it is also in the case of the self-glorification hymn. The "righteous" are called on to praise God for the wonderful exaltation of the speaker, who has been reckoned with the gods. The biblical precedent for concluding a psalm with a call to praise must cast some doubt on the view that the two poems were regarded as separate compositions in 4Q491. In any case, the recension of this psalm in the *Hodayot* regards both canticles as integrally related, and in this it corresponds to the biblical genre.

There is, to be sure, an affinity between the congregation and the individual speaker. Both are called "beloved" (Hebrew ידיד), and both are given a place in "the council of the gods" (עדת אלים). The claim made in the communal canticle is typical of what we find in the Hymns of the Community: God "raises the poor from the dust ... and up to the clouds he extols him in stature, and together with the gods in the congregation of the community" (4Q427 frag. 7, col. 2, 8–9). Despite the reference to raising from the dust, this is not exaltation after death.[29] For the congregation, the fellowship with the gods or angels takes place in the congregation of the community on earth. The individual in the self-glorification hymn, however, claims more than this: he is not only reckoned with the אלים but even asks who among the "gods" can be compared with him. The analogy that springs to mind here is Christ in Heb 1, who is also affirmed as superior to the angels. The relationship between the congregation of righteous ones and the exceptional individual is not unlike that between Christ and those who are "in Christ" in Christian texts.

---

28 Ibid., 281.

29 Contra Wise, "מי כמוני באלים," 217–8.

The self-glorification hymn, however, cannot be taken as a key to the *Hodayot* without reservation. The claims it makes go far beyond anything we find in the Teacher Hymns and lack the acknowledgement of human unworthiness that is typical of the *Hodayot.* It seems unlikely, then, that the original speaker was the same in both cases. Moreover, the genre is different. Even though one copy of the self-glorification hymn is found in a manuscript of *Hodayot,* it is not strictly a thanksgiving psalm. It lacks the narrative of trials and tribulations that is typical both of the biblical thanksgiving psalms and of the Teacher Psalms. The fragment in 1QH^{a} 25–26 labels it a *mizmôr,* a generic psalm, so to speak. The call to the congregation to join in praise, while typical of biblical thanksgiving psalms, is exceptional in the *Hodayot.* Rather than conclude that such a call was implied in other cases in the *Hodayot,* I am inclined to think that it shows the exceptional nature of this hymn. We cannot infer that the *Hodayot* as a whole was a liturgical collection.

Rather, it seems to me that the *Hodayot* are more easily read as texts for personal devotion. The Teacher Hymns recorded the experience of an individual, but they were surely read and pondered by members of the community for several generations. The Hymns of the Community make more general claims on behalf of the typical members of the community. Typically they give thanks not for deliverance from a specific crisis but for their membership in an elect community, in fellowship with the angels. The members who read and prayed these hymns could also praise God for the deliverance of their Teacher and for the exceptional exaltation of the figure in the "self-glorification hymn." It does not follow that they applied everything they found in those psalms to themselves. They could also praise God for the wonders he had wrought in one whose destiny was greater than their own.

The Psalter as a Book of Theology

Patrick D. Miller
Princeton Theological Seminary

In various ways the assumptions in the title above may seem to be immediately in question, both the claim to think of the Psalter as a book and, secondly, to think of it as a work of theology. The first claim comes into question in light of the character of the Psalter as a collection of many different and separate pieces that do not seem to reflect any particular order, much less continuity of subject matter. One may call a hymnbook a "book," but one does not approach it with the customary expectations one brings to a work of fiction or nonfiction that deals with a particular subject matter or develops an account or tells a story. Inasmuch as the Psalter has as its Hebrew title "Tehillim," that is, "hymns," its book character may be debatable. Is it simply a collection of individual psalms, each standing alone with its own integrity, unrelated to other psalms except by various similarities owing to genre?[1] Or can it be read in any sense as a continuous text whose message is more than the sum of its parts?

That last question raises the issue of reading Psalms not simply as a book but as a theological book, a systematic-theological work in the sense of a comprehensive presentation of divine revelation, of theology proper, that is, words about God. Inasmuch as the psalms are notable for their character as human words to God rather than the word of God to human beings, as a collection of prayers and hymns rather than comprehensive theological argument, the characterization of this collection as a book of theology seems problematic. When that is accentuated by the collective character of the Psalter, by the spasmodic movement from one complete psalm to another—and to a psalm that may have nothing to do with the one that precedes it—then the case for reading the Psalter as a book of theology appears thin.

[1] See Norbert Lohfink, "Psalmen in Neuen Testament: Die Lieder in der Kindheitsgeschichte bei Lukas," in *Neue Wege der Psalmenforschung* (ed. K. Seybold and E. Zenger; Herder's Biblical Studies 1; Freiburg: Herder, 1994), 105–25.

Despite those formidable problems for reading the psalms as an intelligible and coherent book that is in fact more than a collection, and for reading it as a comprehensive theological work, a number of interpreters are arguing just that claim about the Psalter. That some coherence has been brought to the book at the editing or redactional level is evident in a number of ways:

1. The presence of an introduction (Pss 1–2) and a conclusion (Ps 150 and, in more elaborated form, Pss 145–150). These psalms function so as to introduce the Psalter and what it is about and to bring it to an end in a conclusive way that leads the reader to say, "It is ended," "Enough said," "Amen"—or as the Psalter itself puts it, "Hallelujah." Furthermore, the introductory psalm—with its exaltation of a continuous meditation on the instruction of the Lord—suggests that what is before us in the psalms that follow is instruction about the Lord and the Lord's way.

2. The sense of movement that is discernible at the simplest level as one moves through the book and experiences the gradual lessening or muting of the loud and constant voices of lament in favor of the increasing, equally loud voices of praise and thanksgiving.[2]

3. The division of the whole into five separate collections, or books, as they are called (Pss 3–41; 42–72; 73–89; 90–106; 107–145 [or 107–150]), identified as such by doxological conclusions (Pss 41:13; 72:18–20; 89:40; 106:48).[3] The purpose of this division is not altogether clear, but many have noted its parallel with the five books of the Torah, itself a collection that is to be read as in some sense a coherent whole. As *Midrash Tehillim* says: "As Moses gave five books of laws to Israel, so David gave five books of Psalms to Israel.... as Moses blessed Israel with the words 'Blessed art thou, O Israel' (Deut 33:29), so David blessed Israel with the words 'Blessed is the man.'"[4] The Psalter thus presents the reader with a "Torah of David" alongside the "Torah of Moses."[5] Furthermore, the books and their doxologies have been seen to represent theologically prominent stages in the history of Israel: the first two doxologies at the end of Pss 41

---

[2] Claus Westermann, "The Formation of the Psalter," in *Praise and Lament in the Psalms* (trans. K. R. Crim and R. N. Soulen; Atlanta: John Knox, 1981), 250–58.

[3] Erich Zenger has suggested that the doxologies, even though they go back to different hands, provide a complete Psalter hermeneutic. See "Der Psalter als Buch: Beobachtungen zu seiner Enstehung, Komposition und Funktion," in *Der Psalter in Judentum und Christentum* (ed. E. Zenger; Herder's Biblical Studies 18; Freiburg: Herder, 1998), 1–57.

[4] William G. Braude, *The Midrash on Psalms* (Yale Judaica Series 13; New Haven: Yale University Press, 1959), 5.

[5] Bernd Janowski, "Die 'Kleine Biblia': Zur Bedeutung der Psalmen für eine Theologie des Alten Testaments," in Zenger, *Psalter in Judentum und Christentum,* 403.

and 72 have to do with and reflect on the monarchical time under David and Solomon; the third book brings the downfall of the monarchy into view, as indicated by the conclusion of the final Ps 89; the fourth book, with its echoes of the prayer of repentance of the people at the end of Ps 106, and the concluding verses describing the scattering of the peoples among the nations has in mind the exile of Israel among the nations. A final transition in Ps 107 leads, with the final book of the Psalter, into the period of restoration.[6]

4. The many subcollections within the whole and within the individual books. In the past these have usually been identified by their superscriptions ("David psalms" or "Korah psalms" or "Asaph psalms") or by the way the divine name is used (thus reference is made to the "Elohistic Psalter" for those psalms in the middle of the Psalter that have a preference for the use of the divine name *Elohim* in the A or first colon of the poetic line). Contemporary investigation of the Psalter, however, has recognized that the coherence of many groups of psalms has to do with their present placing. This is reflected in concatenation of words across two or more psalms, in beginnings and endings that link psalms, in thematic resonances, and in even larger groupings under very general but intelligible notions.[7] Once the reader begins to think about the possibility of a more continuous thematic reading of psalms, it is difficult, for example, to read Ps 22—the paradigmatic lament of the Psalter and the chief New Testament hermeneutical key to the passion of Jesus—without being aware of its adjacency to a series of royal psalms (Pss 18; 20; 21). This brings the possibility of reading Ps 22 as the voice of the royal Messiah as

---

[6] Ibid., 403–4. See Reinhard Gregor Kratz, "Die Tora Davids: Psalm 1 und die doxologische Fünfteilung des Psalters," *ZTK* 93 (1996): 1–34, esp. 21–24; Rolf Rendtorff, *Kanonishe Grundlegung* (vol. 1 of *Theologie des Alten Testaments;* Neukirchen-Vluyn: Neukichener, 1999), 99.

[7] See, e.g., Frank-Lothar Hossfeld and Erich Zenger, "Die Psalmen 1–50" in *Die Neue Echter Bibel: Commentar zum Alten Testament mit der Einheits Übersetzung* (Würzburg: Echter, 1993), 11–14. They suggest that Book 1 of the Psalter (Pss 3–41) is comprised of the following groups: Pss 3–14 (the suffering existence of the poor and the righteous); 15–24 (the Lord delivers the righteous); 25–34 (the Lord delivers the poor); 35–41 (the suffering existence of the poor and the righteous). To characterize these psalms or even group them in another way may be possible, and it cannot be proven that the editing or redacting had the thematic order above clearly in mind; however, the proposal is a sensible one when the psalms are read together and with these rubrics in mind. For an independent identification of the literary and theological coherence of Pss 15–24, see Patrick D. Miller, "Kingship, Torah Obedience, and Prayer: The Theology of Psalms 15–24," in Seybold and Zenger, *Neue Wege der Psalmenforschung,* 127–42.

well as a consciousness of the way it moves from lament into thanksgiving for divine deliverance and onward by means of Ps 23 to a powerful expression of trust in the Lord on the part of one who has been through the valley of the shadow of death but who has received the divine word of deliverance: "Fear not, I am with you; I will comfort you with my rod and staff," and who now professes an enduring confidence in the Lord.

Theological Message of the Psalter

I want to suggest, then, that the Psalter can be seen as a theological work, in the full sense of that term, in two ways. One manifestation of its character as a work of theology is the theological presentation of the Psalter as a whole. That is, a reading of the book from beginning to end confronts the reader with a point of view about God and humankind and God's purpose and work in and through Israel as well as in relation to the larger community of humankind. It is at one and the same time historical and theological. One might naturally expect that for a book as disparate in its contents, and as evidently a collection of individual pieces, as the Psalter, this would be a difficult case to make. As a matter of fact, a good bit of consensus about the theological presentation of the book does exist in the current discussion. I would articulate it this way, drawing upon the work of a number of other scholars, especially the Yale dissertation of Gerald Wilson.[8] Primary ingredients or vehicles of the theological message of the book are the introduction in Pss 1–2 and the conclusion in Pss 145–150, the division into five books, and the royal psalms scattered throughout the book. These are often in strategic places, specifically at the seams of the first three books, but also at one of the climactic points of the Psalter in Ps 101.

The introduction to the Psalter in Pss 1 and 2 first of all identifies two ways that lie before each person: the way of righteousness and the way of wickedness. The determining factor is the degree to which individuals ally themselves and devote themselves to God's instruction, God's law. The text is not more explicit about what comprises that instruction, but one's wholehearted appropriation of it is what defines a way of life that is rich, productive, durable, and watched over by the Lord. The second part of the introduction, Ps 2, sets before the reader a quite different agenda, the rule of God over the nations as mediated through the anointed one, the chosen Messiah of the Lord. The conclusion to the whole of the introduction—"Blessed are all who take refuge in him"—alerts the reader

[8] Gerald Wilson, *The Editing of the Hebrew Psalter* (SBLDS 76; Chico, Calif: Scholars Press, 1985).

both to the dangers that lie along the way of the righteous and to the positive possibilities for those who walk that way in confident trust in the Lord.[9]

In this double introduction, therefore, both an individual's walk and its outcome—a way that often involves a conflict between righteousness and wickedness, between the good and the bad—and the larger realm of politics, the affairs of rulers and nations, are seen to be the concern of God's rule and the focus of God's attention. The psalms that follow spell out the way of the righteous, often in the face of terrible deeds done by the wicked, as testified to again and again in the lament psalms, and lift up the representation of God's rule through the human ruler. The subject of these psalms is at one and the same time the ruler anointed by God, and the individual man or woman whose royal status is well indicated in the words of Ps 8, "You have crowned him with glory and honor.... you have put all things under his feet."[10] The attribution of the psalms that follow to David makes us think of the king as the one who cries out for help and gives praise and thanksgiving. However, as the representative Israelite, David also evokes the experience of every human being. Thus the subject matter of the book is simultaneously the devotion to God's instruction of the individual who is also ruler and the rule of God through the human ruler, whose responsibility is to be a model Israelite, fully attentive to and obedient to the instruction or law of God.[11]

Midway in book 1 this combination of devotion to God's instruction as the way of life and the establishment of the rule of God through the human ruler is lifted up in the chiastically arranged sequence of Pss 15–24. These begin and end with the so-called torah liturgies that identify the way of righteousness expected of any who would stand in the presence of the

[9] For a reading of the Psalter as a whole, and of the editing process, that sees it as setting forth thematically the virtue of seeking refuge in the Lord, see Jerome F. D. Creach, *Yahweh as Refuge and the Editing of the Hebrew Psalter* (JSOTSup 217; Sheffield: Sheffield Academic Press, 1996).

[10] See Patrick D. Miller, "The Beginning of the Psalter," in *The Shape and Shaping of the Psalter* (ed. J. C. McCann; JSOTSup 159; Sheffield: Sheffield Academic Press, 1993), 83–92.

[11] See the summary comment of James L. Mays (*The Lord Reigns: A Theological Handbook to the Psalms* [Louisville: Westminster John Knox, 1994], 132–33): "This intricate pairing as introduction says that all the psalms dealing with the living of life under the Lord must be understood and recited in the light of the reign of the Lord, and all psalms concerned with the kingship of the Lord are to be understood and recited with the torah in mind." Cf. the summary comment of Jerome Creach (*Yahweh as Refuge,* 16): "Within this matrix of meditation on *tôrâ* and submission to Yahweh's rule the whole Psalter is to be read and understood."

Lord and then place at their center two things: the victories of the king and his righteous conduct (reflected in the royal Pss 18; 20; and 21), and the great value and reward of the law (Ps 19). The anointed person as one who lives by the law and the community as those whose presence before God is a testimony to their devotion to God's way in the law lead climactically to the declaration of God's kingship at the end of Ps 24: "Who is this king of glory? The Lord of hosts, he is the king of glory." In various ways these notes are sounded in the rest of book 1, and in book 2, until, as the ending of book 2 says, "The prayers of David are ended."[12]

With book 3 there is a change, reflected in several ways. The opening of the third book raises in the starkest terms the experience of wicked persons at ease and the righteous constantly afflicted (Ps 73). The claim of Ps 1 would seem to be undone by experience, as attested now by the Psalter. However, the psalm goes on to say that all this is incomprehensible until the psalmist comes into the sanctuary and there sees "their end," their fate—that is, the ultimate doing-in of the wicked, a reality only clarified in the presence of the one whose rule is over all and will not be undone. The rest of the third book bears significant witness to the doing-in of the people and ultimately of their human ruler. The largest number of communal laments are laid out here, and the conclusion of the book, Ps 89, acknowledges the downfall of the human ruler. Having articulated the Lord's promise not to take away "my steadfast love" from the anointed one or to "violate my covenant," the psalmist now declares, in light of the defeat and overthrow of God's anointed ruler, "you have renounced the covenant with your servant," and asks at the end: "Lord, where is your steadfast love of old, which by your faithfulness you swore to David?" (Ps 89:49 [MT 50]).[13]

In book 4 the climax of the Psalter's theology is reached. In this book the voices of both Moses (Ps 90) and David (Pss 101; 103) are heard. The anointed of the Lord is still in view, but the larger picture of God's rule and of God's work in creation and history is to the fore. That is indicated in several ways. These include the placing of the other great leader of the people, Moses, as the opening voice;[14] the presence of two extended

[12] Ps 72:20. Technically, of course, that is not the case because, as the Psalter grew, other Davidic psalms were added, particularly near the end, to keep the Davidic model before the reader.

[13] For suggestions about how books 1–3 begin to address the problem of defeat and exile, as well as identifying it, see J. Clinton McCann, "Books I–III and the Editorial Purpose of the Psalter," in McCann, *Shape and Shaping of the Psalter*, 93–107.

[14] For further indications of allusions to Mosaic speeches, see Erich Zenger, "The God of Israel's Reign over the World (Psalms 90–106)," in *The God of Israel and the Nations: Studies in Isaiah and the Psalms* (ed. N. Lohfink and E. Zenger; Collegeville, Minn.: Liturgical Press, 2000), 161–90.

recapitulations of Israel's history at the end of the book, one recounting the Lord's acts of deliverance (Ps 105) and one recounting the many deeds of rebellion that brought the people of Israel under judgment but not to full abandonment (Ps 106); and especially the sustained and repeated exaltation of the rule of Yahweh over the whole world. Yahweh's rule over Israel and all the nations is declared again and again in the enthronement psalms at the center of book 4, Pss 93–99, with their ringing cry: "The Lord is king!"; "The Lord rules!"[15] The book concludes with a response to the claims and queries at the end of book 3, declaring that "for their sake he *remembered his covenant* and showed compassion according to the abundance of his *steadfast love*" (Ps 106:45), notes that have been sounded again and again in different ways in book 4 (e.g., 92:2; 94:18; 98:3; 100:5; 103:4, 8, 11, 17; 105:8–10, 42; 106:2, 7).

In this declaration of the universal rule of the Lord of Israel the king does not disappear. On the contrary, Ps 101 follows immediately with a pledge on the part of the king to study and walk in the blameless way. The failure of the human king does not mean that this way has been abandoned by the Lord who is king over all. As the beginning of the Psalter (Pss 1–2) and Pss 15–24 bring together the centrality of the torah and the rule of the Lord through the Lord's anointed, so at its end this shared way of the Lord is evident again. At the center of book 5, standing massively over the whole, is Ps 119, the full-hearted expression of commitment to and delight in the Lord's instruction. However, the king's voice is there also, as the book includes three royal psalms. The first, Ps 110, declares (echoing Ps 2) that the Lord will indeed establish his rule through the Messiah, the anointed king; the second, Ps 132, confirms the oath sworn to David but, in the light of all that has gone before, makes that covenant dependent upon the obedience to the Lord's covenant of the kings who follow; the last, Ps 144, is set in the final collection of David prayers, joining with them in reminding the community that this representative of the Lord's rule will yet be beset by others and in need of the Lord's deliverance.[16]

The way of torah is the way to go. It is the way that the Lord's anointed one will walk, and as such, in good Deuteronomic style, that ruler will

---

[15] The climactic character of the enthronement psalms, and of book 4 in relation to the whole Psalter, has been observed by a number of scholars, e.g., Wilson, *Editing of the Psalter,* 214–15; and James L. Mays "The Center of the Psalms: 'The Lord Reigns' as Root Metaphor," in idem, *Lord Reigns,* 12–22.

[16] That the reading proposed here, while not specifically christological, is capable of being interpreted eschatologically, or in relation to Christian convictions about the Messiah whom Christians see in Jesus Christ, is surely evident and not to be denied, even if it is not intended or a necessary interpretive outcome of the reading.

model the way that every individual should go. There is finally only one way, and its outcome is clear and predictable. The joy of the torah, the declarations of God's universal rule, and the experience of God's response to all the outcries and laments of the king and others end up in full and extravagant praise. As it comes to an end, the Psalter becomes a theological ground for what one of the Reformed confessions of faith has called the chief end of human existence: to glorify God and enjoy him forever. The Psalter does that in all its words, and it evokes that glorification and joy as the last word of all: the sound of all the voices in the cosmos and all the instruments in the universe join together in incessant praise of God, one never-ending hallelujah, the true music of the spheres.

A Doctrine of God

One way, therefore, of perceiving the Psalter as a book of theology is in the exploration of its comprehensive and coherent testimony to the Lord's way, as a theological interpreter of what is going on and what it means for those who live in trust of this God. However, that is not the only way that the Psalter is a book of theology. As I have indicated earlier, there are smaller segments, psalms that resonate with one another or are joined together in specific ways that become in some fashion authentic theological voices bearing witness to the God of Israel. As one example of many, I would cite the pairing of Pss 103 and 104 in book 4, a significant elaboration of the doctrine of God that underlies the praises of the enthronement psalms.

The two psalms are inescapably linked by their shared inclusions. Each begins and ends with an expression that appears only here in the Psalter: "Bless the Lord, O my soul." In the first of these two psalms, the Lord's rule (103:19)—the thematic claim of book 4 and ultimately the center of the Psalter as a whole—is elaborated in terms of the character of God in relation to human life.[17] In traditional theological categories, the psalm speaks of the attributes of God. However, it speaks of what are commonly called the relative attributes, those that have to do with God's relation to the world and humanity—mercy, love, holiness, and the like—rather than the absolute attributes that have to do with God *a se*—eternity, omnipotence, immutability, and the like.[18]

---

[17] See Mays, "Center of the Psalms."

[18] The latter attributes are hardly dealt with in the psalms in quite the absolute way that they are often and popularly conceived. In Ps 139, for example, God's omniscience is not an abstract attribute of deity. It is an experienced reality: the psalmist realizes, "God knows all about me!" Psalm 139 attests to the omnipresence

In Ps 103 the focus is upon the character of God as demonstrated in interaction with individuals and communities. It is, in effect, a psalmic elaboration upon the ancient confessional formula: The Lord is compassionate and gracious, slow to anger and abounding in steadfast love (see Exod 34:6–7). God's fundamental attributes are *ḥesed* ("steadfast love, lovingkindness") and *raḥămîm* ("compassion"). This is manifest in the particular experiences of individuals ("my soul" is addressed in the first part of the psalm) through forgiveness, healing, deliverance from death, and the provision of good in life. However, the character of God as compassionate and faithful to the relationship is also an experience of a community, revealed through justice for the oppressed and forgiveness for the sins of a community that often turns from the ways of the Lord. God's compassion is comparable only to that of a parent for a child, but its breadth is wider than the widest breadth imaginable, its duration longer than any experience of duration human life can know.

Psalm 104, now inextricably linked to Ps 103 by its beginning and end and in many concatenations, says that more can be said about this God. It speaks in an equally poetic voice about this same God in relation to the world as its Creator and provider.[19] The most repeated words in the psalm are "works/made" and "satisfy/fill." The God who is experienced in compassion and love is the one who made the universe and sustains it—particularly its inhabitants, both human and animal. Creation and providence can be talked about separately in Hebrew as well as in theological discourse, but in the poetry of creation they are a continuous reality. Creation does not simply occur but is a process of past and present. It is as much the providing of food and places for refuge as it is the creation of the heavens, of light and darkness. Indeed, even light and darkness are provided by God as the context in which human beings and animals go forth for their labor and their food (104:20–23). If Gen 1 puts the stamp of goodness on creation, Ps 104 does so equally with God's provision and sustenance: "These all look to you. . . . When you open your hand, they are filled with good things" (104:27–28).

---

of God not as an inherent divine attribute but as the psalmist's often-troubling experience of God's being behind and before, everywhere he is, whether he wants that or not. This way of thinking about an absolute attribute belongs to the Psalter's way of resisting abstract theology on behalf of a realistic theology that is directly related to human experience of the divine.

[19] On this psalm and for elaboration of some of the points made here, see now Patrick D. Miller, "The Poetry of Creation: Psalm 104," in *God Who Creates: Essays in Honor of W. Sibley Towner* (ed. W. P. Brown and S. D. McBride Jr.; Grand Rapids: Eerdmans, 2000), 87–103.

The psalm artfully depicts a highly interdependent creature and a Creator who interacts in various ways with the creation. For example, light is both the clothing of God and the first creation, and so it is at one and the same time the creation of God and the revealing and mysterious nature of God. So also heaven is the abode of God, but it is also created. In the creation of light and the creation of heaven we encounter a view of Creator and creation that understands that an intimate tie exists between the two, while the Creator is neither identical with nor contained in the created realities. The two images of the garment of light that clothes the deity and the heaven that houses the deity serve to create a strong bond between the divine and the created orders even as they are distinct and separate.

The work of divine creation and providence is marked by order and purpose; it harnesses the forces of chaotic nature, sending the waters "to the place that you appointed for them" (104:8) and providing a proper place for the different creatures to live. The world God made is a complex but coherent whole, its intelligibility evident to all and sung out in this psalm. The varied purposes of God's creative activity are especially lifted up in this theological poem of praise, as exemplified by the provision of water—for the animals, but also to make the trees grow, so that the birds will have a place to nest and can sing among their branches. "A whole sequence of creative acts has bird songs as its goals."[20]

God's creative work is also a source of beauty and pleasure. The beauty is in the order of a carefully and intricately crafted universe. Its capacity to evoke pleasure is an even more marked outcome of the Creator's work. That is revealed in several ways: in the songs of birds, in the sea as a place for Leviathan to play, and through wine to gladden the heart. The word for "joy" and "take pleasure in" (*śāmaḥ*) occurs frequently in the psalm. One of the goals of creation, in its details and as a whole, is to provide pleasure and delight. So the psalmist asks: "May the Lord rejoice in his works" (104:31). In other words, this psalm develops with specificity and concreteness the meaning of the divine evaluation in Genesis: "And God saw everything that he had made, and indeed, it was very good" (Gen 1:31).

A feature of Ps 104's presentation of God's creative work is that no hint of human domination, of hierarchy in the creation, occurs. The world is a place for humans and animals, and the vegetation sustains and shelters them. The whole is an intricate and complex creation, one of shared habitation and participation, of appropriate places and times for the well-being of each part of the creation. God is the source of life for all creatures, the breath of life breathed into everyone, animal and human alike. The psalm

---

[20] Ibid., 97.

is an elaboration of the definition of creation suggested by the theologian Michael Welker in his reflection on Gen 1 and 2:

> creation is the construction and maintenance of associations of different, interdependent creaturely realms. God creates by bringing different creaturely realms into fruitful associations of interdependent relations that promote life. The creature is drawn into and bound up into the process of creation by developing and relativizing itself ... into these associations of relations of interdependence, without which the creature would not exist.[21]

One comes to see in all of this something of the character of God, and not only God's creative and sustaining activity. For the psalmist, creation is particularly a testimony to the wisdom of God. That wisdom is often associated theologically with creation is not surprising. Psalm 104 offers grounds for this view. The whole creation is a testimony to the wisdom of God, to the sensibility and order, to the skill and intelligence and practicality of the Lord.

Much more could be said about the way in which this psalm works to spell out the substance of a doctrine of God the Creator, that is, to elaborate the first article of the Apostles' Creed. I will mention, however, only two other matters. One is what the text identifies as elements of human life: "wine to gladden the human heart" and "bread to strengthen the human heart" (104:15). The terms are parallel and so are clearly brought into conjunction with each other. This evokes two observations. One is that these elements are presented as basic elements of life so that God's provision for human existence can be seen to incorporate both the daily sustenance of our lives and a more festive libation for our enjoyment and relaxation. When the Christian community later incorporated these elements into its central ritual, it was not only because of their symbolic potential to represent body and blood but because they were what God had provided for human life. The elements of life become the elements of the church in its sacramental life.

A second observation about the Creator's provision of bread and wine is that these are products of both nature and culture, products of divine origin and of human productivity. The text does not specify seed and fruit, but wine and bread. Human activity—cultivating, harvesting, preparing, cooking, or aging the stuff of God's creation—is a part of God's creative work. This is a clear example of the interdependency of associated creaturely

---

[21] Michael Welker, *Creation and Reality* (trans. J. F. Hoffmeyer; Minneapolis: Fortress, 1999), 13.

realms, as Welker puts it, as well as an indication that the creaturely realms are both natural and cultural, that God's creation cannot be understood as nature on its own apart from cultural involvement with nature.

Finally, one hears at the end a somewhat abrasive note: "Let sinners be consumed from the earth, and let the wicked be no more." The realism of the psalmist's praise of the Creator alerts him to the reality of evil and wickedness in this beautiful and orderly world. Psalm 104 thus echoes Gen 3 as well as Gen 2 and, like Ps 103, knows that iniquity is present and capable of shattering the beauty and order and good of the world God made.

The book of theology that is the Psalter thus gives us a chapter on the character and work of the Lord, whose rule is celebrated in the preceding psalms. The two psalms that make up this chapter go a long way to form the community in its own praise of the nature and character of the divine rule. The works of the Lord are manifold and complex: creating, sustaining, providing, redeeming, forgiving; they are righteous and just, loving and compassionate. One may not flee the hard realities of human life, with its injustice and oppression, its evil and wickedness, its sickness and death, for a cosmic praise unrelated to the way individual and communal life is actually lived. However, the one who redeems and heals the sufferer, who forgives the gravest of sins, is the very one who stretched out the heavens and built up the mountains and who provides for the continuities and processes of nature and culture. And all of that theological understanding of who God is and what God does is worked out in the context of praise. Theology as doxology is what the Psalter as a book is all about. Poetry and music are its medium. That is what we are here in these days to discern and declare, to hear and to feel, to sing and to say.

PART 2
PSALMS IN CHRISTIAN ORIGINS

Giving Voice to Jesus: Use of the Psalms in the New Testament

Harold W. Attridge
Yale Divinity School

As Professor Menn reminds us in her contribution to this volume, the Psalms are the most cited portion of the Old Testament in the New. Of the 150 canonical psalms, 129 make at least a cameo appearance in the pages of the New Testament.[1] Of many psalms there appear only the briefest of glimpses. For example, Ps 26:6, "I wash my hands in innocence," may lurk behind the report in Matt 27:24 that Pilate ostentatiously washed his hands of the blood of Jesus. Or Ps 134:1, "Come bless the Lord all you servants of the Lord," may echo in Rev 19:5, "Praise our God, all you his servants," unless, of course, that verse is a more generic echo of common psalmodic terminology, as in Pss 22:24 and 135:1, 20.

Some psalms have a special prominence. Psalm 22 finds numerous echoes in the passion narratives of Matthew, Mark, and Luke as well as in a few other crucial passages, as we shall see. Psalm 110:1, "The Lord says to my Lord, 'Sit at my right hand until I make your enemies your footstool,'" found wide use as a description of the ultimate fate of Jesus. It expressed the conviction of Jesus' followers that God vindicated him and exalted him to heavenly glory as Messiah and eschatological judge.[2] Such psalms were often construed as prophetic texts, fulfilled in Jesus or his early followers, all of which might exemplify Professor Menn's third category, David as prophet.

---

[1] To judge from Nestle-Aland's index (*Novum Testamentum Graece* [27th ed.; Stuttgart: Deutsche Bibelgesellschaft, 1993]), all but the following are attested in some fashion: 3; 12; 13; 30; 52; 56; 57; 58; 59; 60; 64; 81; 83; 120; 121; 124; 127; 129; 131; 133; 142.

[2] See Matt 22:44; Mark 12:36; Luke 20:42–43; Acts 2:34–35; 1 Cor 15:25; Eph 1:20; Col 3:3; Heb 1:3, 13; 8:1. In general, see David M. Hay, *Glory at the Right Hand: Psalm 110 in Early Christianity* (SBLMS 18; Nashville: Abingdon, 1973).

A full account of the Christian appropriation of the psalms would have to explore all types of data, ranging from explicit citations to vague allusions. This essay will focus on a class of explicit citations of the psalms, citations in which the voice of the psalmist becomes the voice of Jesus, where the eschatological Son of David (Rom 1:3), that is, adopts or is given the persona of his purported ancestor. The phenomenon does not appear throughout the New Testament but only in texts that focus on the passion of Jesus, namely, the Gospels, Acts, the Epistle to the Hebrews, and, ever so briefly, in Paul. The phenomenon has usually been treated as a bit of literary apologetics. Without denying the obvious, I want to suggest that the practice probably has experiential roots in the liturgical life of early Christian communities.

First, a brief review of the major texts is in order. The best known case is, of course, Jesus' cry on the cross, as reported by Mark and Matthew, "My God, my God, why have you forsaken me?" (Mark 15:34; Matt 27:46), from Ps 22:2.[3] As commentators have long noted,[4] the citation is deliberately ambiguous. It sounds a note of agony and despair, but it also evokes the whole prayerful lament that is Ps 22, the prayer of one who suffers yet expresses hope in God who delivers.

Luke resembles Matthew and Mark but finds another verse from the Psalms to express his understanding Christ's death. In Luke's account, Jesus' dying words are: "Father, into your hands I commend my spirit" (Luke 23:46). This citation of Ps 31:5 (LXX 30:6) avoids the anguished cry of the lament used by Matthew and Mark. For Luke, Jesus' death is a more serene and noble affair, in tune with the ideals of his largely Gentile audience.[5]

Matthew and Mark both portray Jesus praying a psalm of lament on the cross. Both put verses from the Psalms on Jesus' lips in other passages. Both do so at the agony in the garden, where Jesus says to Peter, James, and John, "I am deeply grieved," words derived from Pss 42:6, 11; 43:5 (LXX 41:6, 12; 42:5). Luke's garden scene differs, and although the account has textual problems, no manuscript witness to his Gospel has a citation of a verse from the Psalms.

Outside of the passion narratives the phenomenon appears once more in both Matthew and Luke. Both cite Ps 6:9, although in different contexts

---

[3] Biblical quotations are from the NRSV except where indicated. Numeration and versification of the psalms also follows the convention of the NRSV, although the enumeration of the Septuagint is also listed.

[4] See, e.g., Raymond E. Brown, *The Death of the Messiah* (ABRL; New York: Doubleday, 1994), 2:1043–58, 1085–88.

[5] On Luke's passion narrative, see Robert J. Karris, *Luke: Artist and Theologian: Luke's Passion Account as Literature* (New York: Paulist, 1985).

and according to slightly different versions. In Matthew's version (Matt 7:21–23), the citation appears at the end of a saying in which Jesus castigates those who say "Lord, Lord" but do not do the will of God. He issues a warning, saying that "on that day," presumably the day of judgment, many will say that they have prophesied in his name, but he will declare to them, "I never knew you; go away from me you who work lawlessness" (NRSV modified). Luke's application of the saying makes a similar point, although the specific context differs. In response to the claim of familiarity, "We ate and drank with you and you taught in our streets," Luke's Jesus says at 13:27: "I do not know where you come from; go away from me, all you evildoers!"

Of the two versions of the verse, Matthew's more closely corresponds to the reading of the Septuagint text of Ps 6:9. Luke has probably changed "who work lawlessness" to the more generally applicable "evildoers" in line with his general understanding of the relevance of the law.

Although the immediate context of the saying in both Matthew and Luke lacks any reference to the passion, the psalm itself, a classic lament, would be at home in that environment. It deserves citation because that relevance will become apparent in due course:

> 1 O LORD, do not rebuke me in your anger,
> or discipline me in your wrath.
> 2 Be gracious to me, O LORD, for I am languishing;
> O LORD, heal me, for my bones are shaking with terror.
> 3 My soul also is struck with terror,
> while you O LORD—how long?
> 4 Turn, O LORD, save my life;
> deliver me for the sake of your steadfast love.
> 5 For in death there is no remembrance of you;
> in Sheol who can give you praise?
> 6 I am weary with my moaning;
> every night I flood my bed with tears;
> I drench my couch with my weeping.
> 7 My eyes waste away because of grief;
> they grow weak because of all my foes.
> 8 Depart from me, all you workers of evil,
> For the LORD has heard the sound of my weeping.
> 9 The LORD has heard my supplication;
> The LORD accepts my prayer.
> 10 All my enemies shall be shamed and struck with terror;
> they shall turn back, and in a moment be put to shame.

The Gospels offer one last example in Matt 13:34, in a citation introduced with a common Matthean formula. After recounting many of Jesus' parables the narrator adds Ps 78:2: "This is to fulfill what had been spoken by the prophet, 'I will open my mouth to speak in parables, I will proclaim what has been hidden from the foundation of the world.'" This citation, unlike other psalms cited in the Synoptics, has no connection with the passion, either direct or indirect. It is, therefore, interesting that it is not attributed to Jesus but is construed as a prophecy fulfilled in Jesus. Hence the voice of the psalm is that of Jesus only by inference, not by dramatic presentation.

The book of Acts, the second volume of Luke's tale of Christian origins, supplies one further instance rather like the last case from Matthew. Peter's sermon at Pentecost cites several scriptural texts as prophecies of what has been fulfilled in the experience of Jesus and his followers. One of these is Ps 16 (LXX 15):8–11, cited at Acts 2:25–28:

> 8 I saw the Lord always before me,
> for he is at my right hand so that I will not be shaken;
> 9 therefore my heart was glad, and my tongue rejoiced;
> moreover my flesh will live in hope.
> 10 For you will not abandon my soul to Hades,
> or let your Holy One experience corruption.
> 11 You have made known to me the ways of life;
> you will make me full of gladness with your presence."

Peter's introductory comment, "For David says concerning him," indicates Luke's hermeneutical stance. The "I" of the psalm remains David, who reports a vision of God that presages what God will do to his "Holy One." In the hands of other early Christians the psalm could have been construed differently. Without Luke's contextualizing remarks the phrases "you will not abandon my soul to Hades, or let your holy one experience corruption" could well have been construed not as disjunctive but as synonymous, with Jesus expressing the conviction that he would not see corruption. Luke does not follow that path, and both in Peter's speech and again in 13:34, in a speech of Paul, he cites the psalm in the same way, as Davidic prophecy.

The dossier of psalm verses set on the lips of Jesus grows considerably when we turn to the Fourth Gospel, which has no fewer than seven, only one of which substantially coincides with the passages in the Synoptic Gospels.[6]

The collection begins in John 2:17 with a citation of Ps 69:9 (LXX 68:10). The narrator cites the verse at the end of John's version of the cleansing of the temple, and his introductory comment is suggestive: "His disciples

---

[6] See Margaret Daly-Denton, *David in the Fourth Gospel: The Johannine Reception of the Psalms* (AGJU 47; Leiden: Brill: 2000).

remembered that it was written, 'Zeal for your house will consume me.'" Psalm 69 was one of the major contributors to the intertextual fabric of the passion narratives, most obviously in the reference in 69:21, "They gave me poison for food, and for my thirst they gave me vinegar to drink." John's Jesus does not recite a psalm on the cross, although he may allude to the verse in his terse "I thirst" (John 19:28). Nonetheless, the citation in John 2 obviously retains a reference to the passion.

Two things about the explicit citation are worthy of note. The introduction offers a frank admission of the environment in which the practice of attributing such verses arose, the post-Easter "memory" of the disciples, a memory that may have been less about what Jesus himself said and more about the fact that the significance of his mission could be expressed through the words of David.

This psalm citation also says something significant about that mission, the "zeal for God's house." As with so much else in the Fourth Gospel, the phrase could have a variety of senses. Whatever the attitude of the historical Jesus to the temple,[7] John's Jesus claims to become the temple, the place where God is present to his people.[8] To realize that mission consumes his life. Ironically, as "bread of life," the vehicle of the continuing presence of God with his people, he in turn is "consumed" by his followers (John 6:51–58).

The next instance is also complex. In John 10:34 Jesus cites a scriptural text as part of an argument in defense of the Gospel's claims about Jesus' status as Son of God. The text, oddly cited as part of the "law," is from Ps 82 (LXX 81):6: "I said, 'You are gods.'" The psalm describes God taking his place in the heavenly council and castigating the heavenly counselors, who are threatened with "death like any mortals." The Johannine interpretation argues that the addressees are "those to whom the word of God came." However, the precise identity of the addressees is not important, as long as they are not God. If, argues Jesus, the divine "I" could address those nondivine figures as "gods," can he, God's authentic messenger, be blamed for being called God's Son? As often in John, the argument begs a central

---

[7] For reconstructions of Jesus' mission that focus on the temple event as an indication of Jesus' critical stance, see E. P. Sanders, *Jesus and Judaism* (Philadelphia: Fortress, 1985); and Richard A. Horsley, *Jesus and the Spiral of Violence* (San Francisco: Harper & Row, 1987).

[8] The importance of the symbolism of the temple in the Fourth Gospel is widely recognized. See, e.g., Craig R. Koester, *Symbolism in the Fourth* Gospel (2d ed.; Minneapolis: Fortress, 2003); Gale Yee, *Jewish Feasts in the Gospel of John* (Wilmington, Del.: Glazier, 1989); and Norman Petersen, *The Gospel of John and the Sociology of Light: Language and Characterization in the Fourth Gospel* (Valley Forge, Pa.: Trinity Press International, 1993).

question, but more important for our purposes is the identity of the voice that speaks through the psalm. John does not explicitly identify that "I," and the next verse (10:35, "he said") puts some distance between Jesus and the voice of the psalmist. Nonetheless, the reader who has heard Jesus declare his solemn "I am" (8:58) might be forgiven for suspecting that the Evangelist issues an invitation to hear Jesus himself speaking on behalf of the Father through David's words. The claim would be audacious and unparalleled in other attributions of psalmodic verses to Jesus but not beyond the bounds of what is possible in the Fourth Gospel.[9]

John 12:27 returns to more familiar territory. The setting is the end of Jesus' public ministry. Greeks have come seeking him, and he realizes that his "hour," the time of simultaneous suffering and glorification, has arrived.[10] His response, citing two successive verses of Ps 6 (6:3, 4 [LXX 6:4, 5]), expresses his terror at what lies ahead: "'Now my soul is troubled.' And what should I say—'Father save me from this hour'? No, it is for this reason that I have come to this hour."

The brief passage functions as the Johannine equivalent of the Synoptics' Gethsemane scene. Interestingly, it utilizes a verse not from Ps 42 or 43,[11] which had appeared in Mark 14:34 and parallels, but from Ps 6, cited, as already noted, in Matt 7:23 and Luke 13:37. Even more significant is the way in which the Evangelist handles the citation. Jesus asks whether he should pray the psalm's petition to be delivered from death and answers in the negative. To utter such a prayer would be contrary to John's understanding of Jesus as the one who does perfectly the Father's will. The fact that he has Jesus pose the question, and thus hints at a Gethsemane scene, suggests that the Evangelist was struggling with an unwelcome bit of tradition.

The next "I" psalm appears as prophecy fulfilled at the Last Supper when Judas dips his bread with Jesus before departing to betray him. As the narrator tells us at 13:18, "It is to fulfill the scripture, 'The one who ate my bread has lifted his heel against me,'" a citation of Ps 41:9 (LXX 40:10).[12] The formula recalls the introduction to the Matthean citation of Ps 78 and the citation of Ps 16 in Acts. A fulfillment formula also prefaces the next

---

[9] If there is an intertextual allusion to the whole psalm, then its claim that its addressees "judge unjustly" (82:2) may also resonate with the dramatic confrontation between Jesus and his opponents in the Gospel.

[10] For the significance of the passage, see Johannes Beutler, "Greeks Come to See Jesus (John 12:20f)," *Bib* 71 (1990): 333–47.

[11] For these psalms in John, see Johannes Beutler, "Psalm 42/43 im Johannesevangelium," *NTS* 23 (1978–79): 33–57.

[12] On the text of the citation, see Maarten J. J. Menken, "The Translation of Psalm 41:10 in John 13:18," *JSNT* 40 (1990): 61–79.

citation from the Psalms at John 15:25: "They have hated me without cause," which appropriates Ps 35:19 (LXX 34:19) or Ps 69:5 (LXX 68:5).

The final "I" psalm in John also exemplifies the fulfillment of prophecy. This is a familiar psalm, the text, in fact, with which we began this survey, Ps 22:19 (LXX 21:19). It appears, in fact, in all accounts of the passion (Mark 15:24; Matt 27:35; Luke 23:34), although only in John 19:24 does a first-person pronoun appear: "They divided my clothing among themselves and for my clothing they cast lots."[13]

The Gospels thus offer a rich literary tapestry that connects Jesus and the psalms in two interrelated ways. Some psalmodic verses appear as formal scriptural prophecies fulfilled in the life and death of Jesus. David is understood, in these cases, as a seer who foretells what Jesus will say or do. In other cases, the relationship lacks the mediating element of a prophetic text. The words of the psalms are the words of Jesus; Jesus becomes David and David Jesus.

What justifies the equation? Matthew and Luke, with their use of formulaic introductions, make David into a prophet whose poems anticipate situations in the life of Jesus. The Fourth Gospel knows this convention but also seems to have a larger framework for explaining the practice. Jesus, as God's self-expression from all eternity, may be understood to speak in the words of Scripture and may even speak in the person of God both in Scripture and in the flesh. This understanding of Jesus as the Divine Word will come to fuller expression in the apologetic program of Justin Martyr in the second century. However, does the framework of a Logos theology generate the practice or simply rationalize it?

The phenomena explored thus far seem to be interesting literary devices scoring predictable apologetic and didactic points. There are, however, several other examples of psalms giving voice to Jesus that are not found in a narrative context. These instances reveal another context for the development of the practice of giving voice to Jesus through the psalms. Four passages, two from the Epistle to the Hebrews and two from Paul's Epistle to the Romans, offer a window into early Christian practices of giving voice of Jesus.

The Epistle to the Hebrews, which is neither an epistle nor by Paul nor to Hebrews,[14] uses the device extensively. The text is an elaborate early

---

[13] For the text, see Maarten J. J. Menken, "The Use of the Septuagint in Three Quotations in John: Jn 10:34; 12:38; 19:24," in *The Scriptures in the Gospels* (ed. C. Tuckett; BETL 131; Louvain: Leuven University Press, 1997), 367–93.

[14] For review of the introductory issues, see Harold W. Attridge, *The Epistle to the Hebrews* (Hermeneia; Philadelphia: Fortress, 1989), 1–13; or Craig R. Koester, *Hebrews: A New Translation with Introduction and Commentary* (AB 36; New York: Doubleday, 2001), 41–53,

Christian homily, probably composed sometime in the last third of the first century, to encourage a community to remain faithful to its commitments.[15] To fulfill this rhetorical program, Hebrews paints an elaborate portrait of Christ as the true high priest, whose death on the cross had two significant consequences. As the antitype of the Yom Kippur ritual, that death effected expiation of sins. It also fulfilled ancient prophecy, particularly Jeremiah's prediction (Jer 31) of a new covenant, the same prediction that caught the attention of the community of the Dead Sea Scrolls.[16] Despite the elaborate imagery that draws on Jewish apocalyptic traditions and conventional Platonism, the fundamental thrust of Hebrews is to sketch a Christian virtue ethic by focusing on the ultimate paradigm of commitment to God. Christ's willing acceptance of God's will earned him his seat at God's right hand and showed his followers what they must do to accompany him.

In developing this elaborate literary portrait, the homilist cites two clusters of sayings of Jesus. The first appears in Heb 2, after the homilist had, in good encomiastic fashion, celebrated the Son's incarnation and exaltation with a catena of scriptural citations, most from the Psalms.[17] That catena prominently highlights the voice of God speaking to his Son, as in Ps 2:7, the first royal psalm. Such an address deserve a response, and the Son finally gives one in Heb 2.[18]

The response consists of three brief statements. The first (Heb 2:12), derives from Ps 21:23, a key text in the passion narratives (Mark 15:24, 34 and par.). The second and third citations both come from contiguous verses in Isaiah (Isa 8:17–18), but the formula introducing the third indicates that the two verses are to be construed as independent utterances.

The resulting chiastic pattern frames a simple statement, "I will put my trust in him," with two characterizations of the "many children" for whom the Son serves as "pioneer" or "forerunner" (*archēgos* [2:10]). The first utterance, "I will proclaim your name to my brothers and sisters; in the midst of the congregation I will praise you," establishes the solidarity between the Son and other children, which is the surface argument of the text at this point. It also efficiently scores three points significant for the text's theology. It first defines an important element of the Son's work, to

---

[15] See also David deSilva, *Perseverance in Gratitude: A Socio-rhetorical Commentary on the Epistle "to the Hebrews"* (Grand Rapids: Eerdmans, 2000).

[16] E.g., 1QS 1:8; 5:8; CD 3:12–14.

[17] For the Psalms in Hebrews in general, see Simon J. Kistemaker, *The Psalm Citations in the Epistle to the Hebrews* (Amsterdam: van Soest, 1961).

[18] Pamela Michelle Eisenbaum calls attention to the use of the Psalms as direct divine speech in Hebrews but does not note the dialogical element involved. See *The Jewish Heroes of Christian History: Hebrews 11 in Literary Context* (SBLDS 156; Atlanta: Scholars Press, 1997), 90–133.

proclaim the name of God, emphasizing the text's ultimate focus on God. It also defines the sphere where the response to the proclamation of God's name takes place, the congregation or *ekklēsia,* a pregnant term in Hebrews that will appear again at 12:23 referring to the community of "firstborn ones" enrolled in heaven. Hebrews 2:12 finally describes how the Son responds to God's call: by singing God's praise. The final verse of the triptych, 2:13b (from Isa 8:18: "Here I am and the children whom God has given me"), also scores two points. The actions that Jesus claims for himself in the previous verses are not his alone but are to be shared with his "brothers and sisters," who also must trust in God and sing God's praise. Furthermore, those siblings are, like all else in the salvific process, also a gift of God.

The dialogue and response established in the first two chapters forms a pattern at work throughout the text. The next instance of such dialogue reveals a passionate God who appeals to all who hear scripture "today" not to harden their hearts (Heb 3:8). God, speaking in the psalm, reports his own reaction to the rebellious members of the exodus generation: "In my anger I swore, 'they will not enter my rest'" (Heb 3:11, citing Ps 95:11). There follows considerable exegetical play with the psalm (3:12–4:10), all of which emphasizes the immediacy of God's call to the addressees of the homily. Finally, the homilist himself articulates the desired response in his exhortation to his addressees to hold fast, to stay the course, and to enter God's "rest" (4:11).

Chapters 8 through 10 develop the image of the heavenly high priest, effecting final and permanent atonement for sins by his unique sacrifice, consummated by his entry to heaven, the "true tent" (8:2). This exposition culminates in a quotation of the Son's words, which ultimately constitute the response to his appointment by God as high priest. These words also show how God fulfills the promise recorded in the citation of Jeremiah at 8:8–12, how, that is, God makes a new covenant by inscribing laws onto human hearts. The Son's words in Heb 10:5–6, like his comments in Heb 2, come from Scripture, Ps 40:7–9 (LXX 39:7–9). They contrast the "burnt offerings and sin offerings" in which God does not take delight with willing obedience, expressed in the words of the psalmist, now Jesus, "See, God, I have come to do your will, O God."

The homilist's exegetical comment (Heb 10:8–10) underlines the importance of this dialogue, which operates at several levels. The traditional contrast between external sacrifices and a faithful, obedient heart distinguishes the key feature of the promised new covenant. Of equal importance is the exemplary function of the Son's response to the divine initiative. Just as the Son's earlier words in Heb 2 modeled the kind of behavior expected of all God's sons and daughters, this final comment of the dutiful priestly Son models the fidelity that his siblings should exhibit. It is precisely as an example of virtue that Christ establishes the new-covenant community.[19]

Hebrews presents Christ as a model of faith and, of equal importance, as a model of one who prays. One instance is particularly germane to our theme. Hebrews 5:7 makes what some have taken to be an allusion to the Gethsemane story: "In the days of his flesh, Jesus offered up prayers and supplications with loud cries and tears to the one who was able to save him from death, and he was heard because of his reverent submission." Although an appeal to the Gethsemane stories known from the Synoptic Gospels is unlikely, the passage does evoke in a dramatic way the language of Ps 6, another part of which was cited as a word of Jesus in Matthew and Luke and also in a prepassion context in John 12.

The crucial point, however, is the inference that Hebrews makes from this allusion to Ps 6: that because of his faithful obedience Jesus became "the source of eternal salvation for all who heed him." One way in which he so functioned is as a model of faithful prayer.

Two later passages underscore the point. Hebrews 13:15 indicates the bottom line of its homiletic advice: "Through him, then, let us continually offer a sacrifice of praise to God, that is, the fruit of lips that confess his name." Just before that comment the homilist had given an example of what he meant. Imitating the example of the author and perfecter of faithful service to God, he had prayed a psalm, a quotation from Ps 117:6: "The Lord is my helper; I will not be afraid. What can anyone do to me?" For Hebrews, the followers of Jesus assume the role in his dialogue with God. Their prayer of the psalm is a response to the divine promise quoted in Heb 12:5 "I shall not leave you nor abandon you" (Deut 31:6 and Gen 28:15). Their prayer affirms their faith in God's fidelity.

Hebrews, then, displays a dialogical use of psalmody that, by giving a dramatic voice to Jesus, also offers a model for Christian liturgical life, a model that says, in effect, that in the psalms his followers will find their relationship to God.

The final way station on our journey through early Christian psalmody is Paul. While Paul uses Scripture in many fascinating ways,[20] the concern of this essay is only with a subset of his citations. There are three explicit citations of the Psalms featuring a first-person voice in the Pauline corpus.

---

[19] Margaret Daly-Denton sees echoes of this psalm in the Johannine motif of Jesus as the one sent to do the Father's will; see *David in the Fourth Gospel,* 252–53. For a similar analysis, see Günter Reim, "Vom Hebräerbrief zum Johannesevangelium, an hand der Psalmzitate," *BZ* NS 44 (2000): 92–99.

[20] On Paul's use of scripture in general, see Richard B. Hays, *Echoes of Scripture in the Letters of Paul* (New Haven: Yale University Press, 1989).

In 2 Cor 4:13 Paul comments on his own apostolic activity, citing Ps 116 (LXX 115): "Just as we have the same spirit of faith that is in accordance with scripture—'I believed, and so I spoke'—we also believe and so we speak." This passage shows Paul finding an analogy between the psalmist and himself. The analogy suggests a scriptural grace note to accompany his autobiographical reflection. It illustrates an appropriation of the persona of the psalmist, but without the mediating figure of Jesus as a model.

Romans offers examples closer to what was seen in Hebrews. In Rom 15 Paul is engaged in a hortatory finale to his great epistle. Romans 15:3 cites Ps 69:10 (LXX 68:10): "For Christ did not please himself; but, as it is written, 'The insults of those who insult you have fallen on me.'" This citation supports the admonition to "please our neighbor for the good purpose of building up the neighbor. For Christ did not please himself." Again Rom 15:9 cites Ps 18:50 (LXX 17:50). Drawing a homiletic conclusion from his conviction that the gospel is for Gentiles as well as Jews, Paul argues:

> Welcome one another, therefore, just as Christ has welcomed you, for the glory of God. For I tell you that Christ has become a servant of the circumcised on behalf of the truth of God in order that he might confirm the promises given to the patriarchs, and in order that the Gentiles might glorify God for his mercy. As it is written, "Therefore I will confess you among the Gentiles, and sing praises to your name."

Paul goes on to quote other passages on the Gentiles, but it is that first-person citation that is relevant to our concern.

Although both verses lack the dramatic immediacy of the passion narratives or the subtlety of Hebrews, they confirm our analysis of the social setting and literary dynamics encountered in Hebrews. The first citation, transparently presenting the psalmist's voice as that of Jesus, depicts Christ modeling an attitude of forbearance that the Roman audience is to imitate. The latter case is less transparent, and some have taken the "I" to be Paul.[21] Although the parallel is not decisive, it is remarkable how closely this citation parallels the citation of Ps 22:23 in Heb 2:12. Both portray the psalmist standing in solidarity, either with God's children who share flesh and blood (Hebrews) or with the Gentiles (Paul). In both, the psalmist promises to sing God's praises. Paul's first citation of Ps 69, one of the most common passion psalms, may indicate a familiarity with the dramatic portrayal of Jesus as the suffering psalmist. His liturgical tradition probably included the other great passion psalm, Ps 22, and in the form cited in Hebrews. However, for Paul, general solidarity with humankind was

---

[21] See ibid., 72, with references to alternative positions.

not enough to affirm. His specific argument, emphasizing the inclusion of both Jew and Gentile in God's salvific plan, required another emphasis, for which Ps 18 served nicely.

However Paul came to use these particular texts, his citations of Pss 69 and 18 as texts appropriately expressing what Jesus was all about also serve as examples that Jesus' followers are supposed to use in prayer. If the first is particularly apt for disciples who need to be told to bear one another's burdens, the latter is particularly appropriate for Paul himself. He seldom tired of setting himself up as an example to follow but did so as one who followed the example of Christ. Here in Romans, in adopting the "I" of a David become Christ, he was giving voice to the One for whom and in whom he now lived. His claim in Gal 2:20, "It is no longer I who live, but it is Christ who lives in me," had its correlation, and perhaps its roots, in the liturgical practice of giving a voice to Christ that his followers too could share.

The Psalms and the Origins of Christology

Adela Yarbro Collins
Yale University Divinity School

Paul admonished the Corinthians, "When you gather, each one has a psalm, a teaching, a revelation, a tongue, or an interpretation. Let them all take place for edification."[1] The context makes it clear that by "psalm" here Paul did not mean one of the canonical psalms.[2] This admonition gives us a valuable glimpse of the creative liturgical activity of some of the earliest Christians. Paul clearly alludes to the practice of composing religious songs and presenting them in communal worship. About ten years later, a close associate of Paul wrote in his name to the Colossians, urging them to "let the word of Christ dwell among you abundantly, as you teach and admonish one another with all wisdom and gratefully sing with your hearts to God in psalms, hymns, and spiritual songs."[3] It is unlikely that the text refers to three sharply differentiated kinds of liturgical expression here. Rather, taken together, the three terms stand for the full range of liturgical singing.[4] The use of a variety of terms, however, may be an indication of the pluralistic social situation of these early Christians and how they interacted with it. In this presentation, I would like to explore how Phil 2:6–11 fits into the liturgical life of early Christians in their multicultural social settings.

First of all, it should be noted that the early Christians did not have a monopoly of creativity and cultural diversity with regard to liturgy. The Dead Sea Scrolls attest to the fact that the canonical book of Psalms had not attained a fixed form by the first century of the Common Era and that members of the community at Qumran continued to write psalms and other songs.[5] The Hebrew Bible uses a variety of terms for the songs of

---

[1] 1 Cor 14:26.

[2] Gerhard Delling, "ὕμνος, κ.τ.λ.," *TDNT* 8:499.

[3] Col 3:16.

[4] Eduard Lohse, *Colossians and Philemon* (Hermeneia; Philadelphia: Fortress, 1971), 151.

[5] Delling, "ὕμνος," 497.

the Psalter, and the Greek translators used a corresponding variety of Greek terms. Some of them, such as מזמור and ψαλμός, emphasize the fact that the songs are sung to the accompaniment of stringed instruments. Others, such as תהלה and ὕμνος, emphasize the content of the most typical songs: praise of God. The choice of the Greek word ὕμνος ("hymn") had the effect of associating the canonical psalms and other Jewish songs with the long tradition of Greek hymns to the gods.

In his work *On the Contemplative Life,* written in the early first century of the Common Éra, the Jewish exegete and philosopher Philo describes a community of ascetics, the Therapeutae, who had withdrawn from the life of the city in order to pursue a contemplative life centered on the philosophical study of Scripture and gatherings for liturgy on Sabbaths and festivals. It is debated whether such a Jewish community actually existed or whether it is a fiction expressing Philo's ideals.[6] In either case, this work indicates how at least one Jew at the turn of the era related Jewish liturgy to Hellenistic culture. It is striking that Philo conceptualizes the Psalter in terms of the various types of Greek cultic songs:

> Then the President rises and sings a hymn composed as an address to God, either a new one of his own composition or an old one by poets of an earlier day who have left behind them hymns in many measures and melodies, hexameters and iambics, lyrics suitable for processions or in libations and at the altars, or for the chorus whilst standing or dancing, with careful metrical arrangements to fit the various evolutions. After him all the others take their turn as they are arranged and in the proper order while all the rest listen in complete silence except when they have to chant the closing lines or refrains, for then they all lift up their voices, men and women alike.[7]

Here and elsewhere Philo refers to the canonical psalms as "hymns."[8] It is striking that, just like Paul, he assumes that the members of the community may perform new psalms or hymns of their own composition. In his *Apology,* written about two hundred years later, Tertullian states, in a way similar to Philo's description of the Therapeutae, that in the Christian feast

---

[6] Troels Engberg-Petersen, "Philo's *De vita contemplativa* as a Philosopher's Dream," *JSJ* 30 (1999): 40–64.

[7] Philo *Contempl. Life* 80 (trans. LCL). Delling ("ὕμνος," 491–92) cites this passage as evidence that Philo was aware of the various types of Greek cultic songs but does not comment on his assertion that the Jewish Psalter contained all these types.

[8] Delling, "ὕμνος," 496.

called Agape, each person present is asked to stand and sing to God, either a song from the Scriptures or one of his own composing.[9]

Josephus, the Jewish historian who was a younger contemporary of Philo, also uses terminology that stresses the similarity between Jewish songs and Greek hymns. He calls the psalms of the Hebrew Bible "hymns to God" (ὕμνοι εἰς τὸν θεόν)[10] and refers to the Song of the Sea in Exod 15 as "a song to God in hexameter verse" (ᾠδὴ εἰς τὸν θεόν ... ἐν ἑξαμέτρῳ τόνῳ). He describes this song as ἐγκώμιος, that is, "belonging to the praise of a conqueror," a term that assimilates it to processions escorting home a victor in the games. The same term, used as a noun, means a song or speech in praise of someone.[11] Josephus also calls the Levites of the Hebrew Bible "choral singers" (ὑμνῳδοί).[12] This was a technical term in the first century of the Common Era for cultic officials in the cities of Asia Minor.[13] Finally, Josephus says that David composed "songs to God and hymns" (ᾠδᾶς εἰς τὸν θεὸν καὶ ὕμνους) in various meters.[14]

It is clear from their works that Philo and Josephus, as Greek-speaking and writing Jews, appropriated their Jewish heritage in a way shaped by Hellenistic culture. It is equally clear that Paul, as a Hellenistic Jew engaged in a mission to the nations, expressed the significance of Jesus as the Jewish Messiah in cultural forms that were intelligible and accessible to his audiences. After the discussion of some preliminary matters, I will investigate how Paul did so in the case of Phil 2:6–11.

At least since Ernst Lohmeyer's study published in 1928, Phil 2:6–11 has been defined as a hymn by New Testament scholars.[15] Lohmeyer referred to the passage as "ein carmen Christi in strengem Sinne," alluding to a letter of Pliny to Trajan stating that Christians of Asia Minor were in the habit of singing antiphonally a hymn to Christ as to a god.[16] Lohmeyer argued that the vocabulary and style of the psalm or hymn indicated that it had been composed in Greek by a poet whose mother tongue was a Semitic language. He concluded, therefore, that it was

---

9 Tertullian, *Apol.* 39.

10 Josephus *Ag. Ap.* 1.40.

11 Josephus *Ant.* 2.346.

12 Josephus *Ant.* 7.364. See Delling, "ὕμνος," 496.

13 H. W. Pleket, "An Aspect of the Emperor Cult: Imperial Mysteries," *HTR* 58 (1965): 343.

14 Josephus *Ant.* 7.305.

15 Ernst Lohmeyer, *Kyrios Jesus: Eine Untersuchung zu Phil. 2, 5–11* (Heidelberg: Winter, 1928; repr., Darmstadt: Wissenschaftliche Buchgesellschaft, 1961).

16 Citation of Lohmeyer by Ralph P. Martin, *A Hymn of Christ: Philippians 2:5–11 in Recent Interpretation and in the Setting of Early Christian Worship* (Downers Grove, Ill.: InterVarsity Press, 1997), 25; translation of Pliny's letter, ibid., 1.

pre-Pauline and that it belonged to the eucharistic liturgy of the Christian community in Jerusalem. A few scholars have concluded that the passage was originally composed in Aramaic.[17] Most notably, Joseph A. Fitzmyer has shown that the passage can be retroverted "into a tolerable form of contemporary Aramaic." Certain words, however, have no equivalent in Middle Aramaic, and Fitzmyer was forced to use Late Aramaic equivalents for these.[18]

Since Lohmeyer, scholars have generally agreed that the passage is a liturgical composition, usually described as a hymn, and that it belongs to the subtype "christological hymn" or "hymn to Christ."[19] Lohmeyer's argument that the hymn is pre-Pauline effected a near consensus, but it has eroded considerably lately.[20] With regard to content, most studies have focused on the contribution of the passage to the emergence of christological doctrine. A debate has raged over the relative weight and importance of the theological focus of the passage itself and the ethical and pastoral application of it in the context of Philippians as a whole.[21]

The definition of the passage in Phil 2 as a "hymn" implies that it is a poetical composition. If it was composed in Aramaic, it can be understood as a "hymn" in the same way that modern critics define certain canonical psalms as hymns.[22] Like the psalms of the Hebrew Bible, it would not have a particular meter, as Greek and Latin poetry would.[23] Rather, its poetic character would lie to some degree in its distinctive phonology, vocabulary, grammar, and syntax, but especially in its use of metaphors, symbolic

---

17 Martin, *Hymn of Christ,* 27, 30 n. 1, 39–41.

18 Namely, ἁρπαγμός, ὑπήκοος, and κάμπτω; Joseph A. Fitzmyer, "The Aramaic Background of Philippians 2:6–11," *CBQ* 50 (1988): 470–83, esp. 481–82.

19 Martin, *Hymn of Christ,* xliii–xlv.

20 Martin, ibid., xxxiv, 55–61, 315; Gordon D. Fee, "Philippians 2:5–11: Hymn or exalted Pauline Prose?" *BBR* 2 (1992): 29–46; Ralph Brucker, *"Christushymnen" oder "epideiktische Passagen"? Studien zum Stilwechsel im Neuen Testament und seiner Umwelt* (Göttingen: Vandenhoeck & Ruprecht, 1997), 17, 21–22, 349–50; Samuel Vollenweider, "Der 'Raub' der Gottgleichheit: Ein religionsgeschichtlicher Vorschlag zu Phil 2.6(–11)," *NTS* 45 (1999): 413 and n. 2. Martin and Vollenweider continue to argue that the passage is pre-Pauline; Fee and Brucker argue for Pauline composition.

21 Martin, *Hymn of Christ,* vii–viii, xii–xix, xxxiii–xxxv, xli, xliii.

22 Erhard S. Gerstenberger, *Psalms: Part 1, with an Introduction to Cultic Poetry* (FOTL 14; Grand Rapids: Eerdmans, 1988), 16–19.

23 A number of scholars, however, have argued that Phil 2:6–11 has a stress-accentual meter, on the assumption that accentual meter was typical of Hebrew and Aramaic poetry; Fitzmyer, "Aramaic Background," 471–74; Barbara Eckman, "A Quantitative Metrical Analysis of the Philippians Hymn," *NTS* 26 (1980): 258–66, esp. 258.

expressions, and characteristic themes.[24] The postcanonical psalms and thanksgiving hymns from Qumran are poetic in the same ways.

Lohmeyer argued that the Greek hymn consisted of eighteen lines that were structured into two strophes of three verses each. Each line has three accents or stresses. The first retroversion of the passage into Aramaic had the same structure advocated by Lohmeyer, but the second did not.[25] Fitzmyer's retroversion has the same structure as Lohmeyer's analysis of the Greek text, but Fitzmyer does not think that it is possible to arrive at a perfect pattern of three beats to a line.[26] Advocates of a Semitic original of Phil 2:6–11 have also generally agreed with Lohmeyer's conclusion that Paul made at least one addition to the hymn.[27] The most important literary similarity that Phil 2:6–11 has with the psalms of the Hebrew Bible and Second Temple Judaism is the synonymous, antithetical, and climactic relationships among some of its phrases and clauses.[28]

Several recent studies of Phil 2:6–11 have challenged the current consensus. Gordon D. Fee published an article in 1992 in which he argued that the passage is not a hymn; rather, it is exalted prose written by Paul himself.[29] In his view, "it contains nothing at all of the nature of Greek

---

24 Gerstenberger, *Psalms,* 34.

25 Fitzmyer, "Aramaic Background," 473–74, 475 n. 20.

26 Ibid., 483.

27 Martin, *Hymn of Christ,* 26, 33, 36–37; Fee, "Philippians 2:5–11," 32–33; Fitzmyer, "Aramaic Background," 476.

28 Verse 6, ὃς ἐν μορφῇ θεοῦ ὑπάρχων οὐχ ἁρπαγμὸν ἡγήσατο τὸ εἶναι ἴσα θεῷ is antithetically parallel to the first part of verse 7, ἀλλὰ ἑαυτὸν ἐκένωσεν μορφὴν δούλου λαβών. The last two phrases of verse 7 are synonymously parallel to one another: ἐν ὁμοιώματι ἀνθρώπων γενόμενος and καὶ σχήματι εὑρεθεὶς ὡς ἄνθρωπος. The main clause of verse 8, ἐταπείνωσεν ἑαυτόν is synonymously parallel to the following participial phrase, γενόμενος ὑπήκοος μέχρι θανάτου. The last phrase of verse 8, θανάτου δὲ σταυροῦ is climactically parallel to the preceding participial phrase, γενόμενος ὑπήκοος μέχρι θανάτου. In verse 9, the two coordinated main clauses, ὁ θεὸς αὐτὸν ὑπερύψωσεν and ἐχαρίσατο αὐτῷ τὸ ὄνομα τὸ ὑπὲρ πᾶν ὄνομα are synonymously parallel. In verse 10, the clause πᾶν γόνυ κάμψῃ ἐπουρανίων καὶ ἐπιγείων καὶ καταχθονίων is synonymously parallel to a clause in verse 11, πᾶσα γλῶσσα ἐξομολογήσηται ὅτι κύριος Ἰησοῦς Χριστός. See Martin, *Hymn of Christ,* xxxiv.

29 Brucker argues that Paul himself composed Phil 2:6–11 and that its differences from the surrounding context can be explained by the ancient practice of deliberately shifting from one style to another. The letter as a whole belongs to the category of deliberative rhetoric, but it contains a number of epideictic passages, including 2:6–11 (see Brucker, *"Christushymnen" oder "epideiktische Passagen,"* 349–50). See also Ewen L. Bowie's discussion of prose writers who imitate standard poetic forms and insert the poems into their larger prose works in "Greek Sophists

hymnody or poetry. Therefore, it must be Semitic in origin." However, he argues, the type of parallelism found in this passage is "quite unlike any known example of Hebrew psalmody."[30] The Philippians passage actually contains three types of parallelism: synonymous, antithetical, and climactic. These general types are also found in the Hebrew Psalter, but the Philippians passage does not have the structure typical of canonical psalms, namely, a line made up of two cola that often relate to each other in synonymous, antithetical, or synthetic ways.[31]

Fee agreed with a long line of commentators going back to the Greek exegetes and theologians of the early church that the word ἁρπαγμός in verse 6 should be understood as *res rapta.* In other words, Christ was equal to God from the beginning; he did not consider this equality as a "prize" or a "gain" to be held tightly but rather chose to let it go. The other main view has been that the Greek word should be understood as *res rapienda.* According to this view, the word expresses something to be attained, not something already possessed. This interpretation makes far better sense of the climactic statement in 2:9–11 that God highly exalted Jesus. The plot of the passage requires that the final state of Jesus be higher than the initial state.

In another important study, Samuel Vollenweider argued that ἁρπαγμός in 2:6 should be understood as *res rapienda.* He concluded that 2:6 means that Christ did not consider being equal to God as booty, as something to be seized by force. Although the exact Greek word ἁρπαγμός does not occur in the Jewish Scriptures written in or translated into Greek, its word family occurs frequently in these works, always with the negative connotation of robbery or taking plunder. Except for the usage of being snatched up to heaven, the word group usually has a negative connotation in the Greek Pseudepigrapha, Philo, Josephus, and the New Testament.[32] Furthermore, the notion of equality with God on the part of entities that are not aspects of God has a strongly negative connotation in biblical, Jewish, and early Christian literature.[33] Finally, he makes a case for its primary context

---

and Greek Poetry in the Second Sophistic," *ANRW* 33.1:221–29, 253. In light of Bowie's discussion, it is plausible that Paul imitated the form of a prose hymn in writing to the Philippians about the example of Christ. This hypothesis is further supported by the ancient convention that the style employed should be appropriate to the subject matter.

30 Fee, "Philippians 2:5–11," 30–31, 42–43.

31 Gerstenberger, *Psalms,* 35. Grelot seems to have attempted to structure his retroversion in lines made up of two cola, but Fitzmyer does not follow him in this; cited by Fitzmyer, "Aramaic Background," 475, 482–83.

32 Vollenweider, "Der 'Raub' der Gottgleichheit," 417–18.

33 Ibid., 418; see, e.g., John 5:18.

in the history of religions as traditions about the typical ruler who is violent and who presumes to take a divine role.[34] Verse 6, in his view, means that, although Christ had a divine form, unlike the typical arrogant ruler he did not attempt to make himself equal to God.[35] Vollenweider argued that Phil 2:6–11 is a pre-Pauline Jewish Christian composition, but his arguments would apply equally well if Paul himself were the author.[36]

Next I would like to offer a hypothesis about the literary nature of Phil 2:6–11 and some reflections on its social setting and purpose. Fee described the passage as "exalted prose." It would be more precise to define it as "rhythmic prose," a "prose hymn," or a brief encomium.[37] Prose-rhythm, as a branch of ancient rhetoric, concerned the quantitative or accentual arrangement of syllables of a sentence, especially its opening and ending. Only the quantitative type of arrangement is relevant to the first century of the Common Era. According to the ancient authorities, rhythmic prose should be distinct from poetic meter and not too obvious.[38] Fee argued that the Philippians passage consists of three sentences, but it seems more appropriate to conclude that it consists of two sentences, each containing two main verbs. The first sentence is found in 2:6–8; the second in 2:9–11.[39] The first sentence begins with the rhythm: one short element followed by three long;[40] the second begins with the pattern: two short elements, a long and then a short.[41] The first sentence ends with four long elements;[42] the second ends with a short, two long, and a short element.[43]

---

[34] Ibid., section 2, beginning on p. 419. With this argument, Vollenweider revives and updates an older interpretation that has had few recent advocates.

[35] Ibid., 429.

[36] Ibid., 428.

[37] Klaus Berger has argued that the passage is an encomium ("Hellenistische Gattungen im Neuen Testament," *ANRW* 25.2:1173–91). Brucker has argued that it is a rhetorical epainos (*"Christushymnen" oder "epideiktische Passagen,"* 350). He criticizes Berger's proposal as imprecise (ibid., 11).

[38] W. H. Shewring and K. J. Dover, "Prose-Rhythm," *OCD*², 888. For ancient criticism of the use of rhythmic prose, see Bowie, "Greek Sophists," 212.

[39] The two main verbs of the first sentence are ἡγήσατο in 2:6 and ἐκένωσεν in 2:7. Those of the second sentence are ὑπερύψωσεν and ἐχαρίσατο, both in 2:9.

[40] Ὃς ἐν μορφῇ. The *epsilon* and *omicron* are long by position; see Herbert Weir Smyth, *Greek Grammar* (Cambridge: Harvard University Press, 1966), §144.

[41] Διὸ καὶ ὁ.

[42] -τοῦ δὲ σταυροῦ. The *epsilon* is long by position; see Smyth, *Greek Grammar,* §144. This rhythmic pattern is avoided as a sentence-ending by prose writers in the Hellenistic period, but it is little avoided by classical writers; Shewring and Dover, "Prose-Rhythm," 889.

[43] Assuming that the α of πατρός is long by position; if not, the pattern is short, long, short, short. See Smyth, *Greek Grammar,* §145.

A characteristic of exalted prose that Fee does not mention is that the ends of clauses often rhyme. There may also be a parallelism of sound between two clauses, either at the beginning, middle, or end.[44] Taking the arrangement of clauses in the Nestle-Aland text of the Greek New Testament as a starting point, one finds end-rhyme in two places in the first sentence (γενόμενος and ἄνθρωπος in 2:7 and θανάτου and σταυροῦ in 2:8) and in one place in the second (Χριστός and πατρός in 2:11).[45]

The character of the passage as exalted or rhythmic prose is compatible with the hypothesis that it is a prose hymn.[46] The most famous author of prose hymns is Aelius Aristides, who lived in the second century of the Common Era. I give here two selections from his prose hymn to Dionysos as an example:

> Zeus lies with Semele;
> and when Semele was with child,
> Zeus, wishing to be both to Dionysus—
> both father and mother—
> sent Semele from earth to Olympus in fire
> and himself taking up his child
> stitched him into his thigh
> and carried him ten months
> dwelling at first in Nysa beyond Ethiopia;
> and, when the time came,
> he summoned the Nymphs and undid the stitching;
> and so Dionysus was born,
> his father's child on both sides.
>
> And so Zeus honored him especially above all gods and men;
> for neither he nor any other
> stood in both these relationships to any being.
> The God, therefore, so they say, is both male and female,
> because his father partook of both natures to bring him to birth.
>
> I have heard some tell another tale about this,
> that Dionysus is Zeus himself.

---

[44] The technical terms are *homoioteleuton* (end-rhyme) and *paromoiosis* (parallelism of sound between two clauses); see Smyth, *Greek Grammar,* §§3026, 3039. See also the discussion by Quintilian, *Inst.* 9.3.75–79. I am grateful to my former colleague at the University of Chicago, Elizabeth Asmis, for calling the end-rhyming of exalted prose to my attention.

[45] If the repetition of ὄνομα may count as rhyme, then there is a second case of end-rhyme in the second sentence in 2:9.

[46] On prose hymns, see Brucker, *"Christushymnen" oder "epideiktische Passagen,"* 6 and n. 35.

What greater thing could be said?
. . .
He oversees the limits of night and day,
the one by being torchbearer and guide of sight himself,
the other by entrusting it to others;
Yet even then he is not idle,
but passes his time always in movement and activity.
He is both the oldest of gods and the youngest
and a lover of every passing hour and happening.

Hail to Iacchus, under all his many names,
the cup of friendship is for the moment full.[47]

Aristides' hymn is longer than Phil 2:6–11. Literary hymns, like those of Aristides, tended to be longer than liturgical hymns, and the passage in Philippians may be modeled on the liturgical ones.

Aristides claimed to be an innovator in writing prose hymns, but this claim is exaggerated. An inscription from the first century before the Common Era records the victory of a writer of a prose encomium to a deity in a public competition.[48] Prose encomia also had a place in worship of the deities. Officials called θεολόγοι had the task of delivering such encomia in cultic settings.[49] The author of a rhetorical handbook in Latin in the first century, Quintilian, gives comprehensive rules for composing prose hymns to the gods. This fact is an indication that such hymns were already commonplace in the first century of the Common Era.[50] Quintilian states that some gods may be praised because they were born immortal, whereas others may be praised because they attained immortality by means of their excellence. The context makes clear that the latter group included the Roman emperors Vespasian and Titus.[51]

Typically, Greek hymns included an invocation of the god, praise of his birth and of his acts, and a prayer for his coming.[52] The fact that the Philippians passage lacks the invocation of the deity at the beginning and the prayer at the end may be explained in either of two ways. One is that it was originally a cultic hymn that included these elements but Paul

---

[47] Translation from Donald A. Russell, "Aristides and the Prose Hymn," in *Antonine Literature* (ed. D. A. Russell; Oxford: Clarendon Press, 1990), 211, 215.

[48] Bowie, "Greek Sophists," 213 and n. 9.

[49] Ibid.

[50] Quintilian *Inst.* 3.7.7–8; for discussion, see Russell, "Aristides and the Prose Hymn," 207–8.

[51] Quintilian *Inst.* 3.7.9.

[52] Delling, "ὕμνος," 492. See the similar list of typical elements of the hymns of the Psalter given by Gerstenberger, *Psalms,* 17.

omitted them in order to fit the hymn better into its context in the letter. The other possibility is that the passage was composed for the context. As a literary hymn it could omit the opening and closing elements, as many of the Homeric hymns do.[53] Aristides' hymn to Dionysos begins with a prologue rather than with a typical invocation of the god.

An alternative to the hypothesis that Phil 2:6–11 is a prose hymn is that it is a prose encomium. There is a close relationship between the two, since sophists and others studied classical hymns as models for their prose encomia.[54] The implicit contrast created in Phil 2 between Jesus and arrogant rulers is similar to a contrast made in Philo's encomiastic *Life of Moses.* Philo states that Moses was appointed leader of the multitude departing from Egypt and held this office and kingship, not like those "who thrust themselves into positions of power by means of arms ... but on account of his goodness and his nobility of conduct and the universal benevolence which he never failed to shew."[55] Philo goes on to say that God bestowed kingship upon Moses as a gift of honor that he deserved. Although as the son of the daughter of the reigning king he was a ruler of Egypt, he renounced his expected inheritance. God therefore thought fit to requite him with the kingship of a nation destined to be consecrated above all others.[56] Since he rejected material wealth and power, God granted him the greatest and most perfect wealth by making him a partner in the divine rule of the universe. This partnership was magnified by the honor of being accounted worthy to bear the same name as the deity, for Moses was called god and king of the whole nation.[57]

The hypothesis that Phil 2:6–11 is a prose hymn or a brief encomium in rhythmic prose and that it compares Jesus favorably with typical rulers raises intriguing possibilities about its social setting and purpose. In the Hellenistic and Roman periods, prose hymns to deities became more and more important, and the responsibility for composing them was assigned to those possessing the office or honorary position of θεολόγος. Before long, this or a similar office was established in the imperial cult. A decade or two before Paul wrote to the Philippians, the imperial cult in a city of Asia Minor included the services of a σεβαστολόγος, one who composed

---

[53] According to William Keith Chambers Guthrie, the Homeric hymns were literary, not devotional, and in them the myth is the chief feature ("Hymns," *OCD*², 534). One could say the same for Phil 2:6–11.

[54] Bowie, "Greek Sophists," 221.

[55] Philo, *Moses* 1.27 (§148).

[56] Ibid., §§148–149.

[57] Ibid., 1.28 (§§155–158). See Shewring and Dover for a discussion of Philo's use of prose-rhythm ("Prose-Rhythm," 889).

prose hymns in honor of the emperor.[58] Later on, the term θεολόγος was used for such officials in the imperial cults in Pergamon, Ephesus, and Smyrna.[59] Since Paul spent an extended period of time in Ephesus, it is likely that he was familiar with the writing of prose hymns or encomia in honor of the emperor. The Philippians were probably familiar with the practice as well. Philippi was a Roman colony and thus, at first and officially, was governed by the laws of Rome. Following Roman practice, the imperial cult in Philippi included *flamines,* that is, priests of Augustus, and *augustales,* that is, associations of ex-slaves devoted to the imperial cult.[60] However, Roman colonies in the Greek East soon came under the influence of the dominant Greek culture,[61] so it is likely that the worship of the emperor included composers of prose hymns to the emperor, whatever they were called.

One of the duties of the composer of such hymns or encomia was to make widely known the powers, achievements, and benefactions of the deity or emperor.[62] Paul once declared, "I have become all things to all people, in order that I might by all means save some."[63] For the sake of the gospel, he adapted the form of the Greek prose hymn in order to instruct the Philippians in cultural terms familiar to them. Before turning to Christ, they had their θεολόγοι and their σεβαστολόγοι. These venerable traditions may have inspired Paul to become a Χριστολόγος.

---

58 In Didyma in the cult of Gaius Caligula; see Martin P. Nilsson, *Geschichte der griechischen Religion* (3d ed.; Munich: Beck, 1974), 2:380–81.

59 Ibid.; Allen Brent, "John as Theologos: The Imperial Mysteries and the Apocalypse," *JSNT* 75 (1999): 90, 95.

60 Michel Sève and Patrick Weber, "Un monument honorifique au forum de Philippes," *Bulletin de correspondence hellénique* 112 (1988): 470 n. 6; on the *flamines* and *augustales,* see S. R. F. Price, *Rituals and Power: The Roman Imperial Cult in Asia Minor* (Cambridge: Cambridge University Press, 1984), 88.

61 Price, *Rituals and Power,* 88–89.

62 Nilsson, *Geschichte der griechischen Religion,* 2:381, citing Lucian, *Alexander the False Prophet* 19.

63 1 Cor 9:22.

Christian "Rock" Music at Corinth?

Diana M. Swancutt
Yale University Divinity School

> The LORD is my stronghold, my fortress, and my champion,
> my God, my rock where I find safety....
> Therefore, LORD, I will praise you among the nations
> and sing psalms to your name,
> to the one who gives his king great victories
> and in all his acts keeps faith with his anointed king,
> with David and his descendants forever. (2 Sam 22:2–3, 50–51)

Bedecked in stunning yellow and black nylon-lycra, the hard-rock band Stryper stormed the American Christian music scene in 1984. Wedding the generically Protestant message of contemporary Christian music with the screaming riffs of their electric guitars, the group gained popularity among evangelicals and eventually popularized the hard-rock musical style among Christian bands of the late 1980s.[1] In 1984, however, Stryper had to labor long to sanction their song-making. They did so in part by evoking a long-standing scriptural and musical commonplace: according to the lyrics of their signature song, "The Rock That Makes Us Roll," Stryper claimed the supreme endorsement of God their Rock.

Stryper's self-authorization through the praise of God as Rock was hardly a novel way to identify or empower their group. Generations of Christians have sung Augustus Toplady's "Rock of Ages" and Martin Luther's "A Mighty Fortress Is Our God" both to praise their God and to declare his incomparability.[2] Similarly, many American Jews still sing the traditional

---

[1] On the lively role of Christian rock music in evangelical Christian worship and politics, see Michael R. Smith, "In the 'Christian Rock' Sound You Can Hear God Whisper," *Fundamentalist Journal* 5/2 (1986): 22–23; Barbara Claire Freeman, "Practicing Christian Rock," in *One Nation under God? Religion and American Culture* (ed. M. Garber and R. L. Walkowitzt; New York: Routledge, 1999), 221–31.

[2] Note verse two of "A Mighty Fortress Is Our God": "Did we in our own strength confide, our striving would be losing / were not the right man on our side, the man

hymns "Our Rock" and "Rock of Ages" and in their Sabbath and festival liturgies affirm that God is "our Rock ... our Shield that saves through every generation."[3] Indeed, Jews from Philo of Alexandria and Maimonides to the authors of the *Mekhilta of Rabbi Ishmael* and the qabbalistic *Sha'arei Orah* have claimed that the epithet expresses the matchless singularity of the God of Israel.[4] As Michael Knowles said, "with a remarkable uniformity of interpretation" generations of Jews have sung psalms to the Rock because the title expressed the unique power of the deity as Creator, sovereign, and savior of his people.[5]

This essay argues that Paul knew the social power of these Rock psalms and that he and his associates "handed on" a collection of them to Christ-confessing Gentiles at Corinth and Rome for their οἰκοδομή, their edification or instruction in their new identity in Christ (1 Cor 11:2). Making this case is by no means easy. Our knowledge of early Christian worship practices is limited.[6] In the first century C.E., literacy was low, books were rare among common people, the Scriptures did not exist as a canonical collection, and individual texts such as Isaiah and the psalms were expensive and time-

---

of God's own choosing/dost ask who that may be? Christ Jesus it is he/Lord Sabaoth his name, from age to age the same."

[3] See Rabbinical Assembly of America and the United Synagogue of America, *Sabbath and Festival Prayer Book* (New York: Rabbinic Assembly of America, 1988), 361, 363, 365, 375, and, e.g., 23, 32, 41, 66, 88, 90, 94, 99, 106, 108, 118, 131, 143, 145, 154, 162, 165. Verse one of "Rock of Ages": "Rock of Ages, let our song praise Thy saving power; / Thou amidst the raging foes wast our shelt'ring tower. / Furious they assailed us, but Thine arm availed us, / and Thy word broke their sword, When our own strength failed us." Cf. "Our Rock": "Rock from whose store we have eaten— / Bless him, my faithful companions. / ... Holy is none like the Lord."

[4] For a discussion of these examples, see Ithamar Gruenwald, "God the 'Stone/Rock': Myth, Idolatry, and Cultic Fetishism in Ancient Israel," *JR* 76 (1996): 428–49; J. T. A. G. M. van Ruiten, "The Use of Deuteronomy 32:39 in Monotheistic Controversies in Rabbinic Literature," in *Studies in Deuteronomy* (ed. F. García-Martínez; VTSup 53; Leiden: Brill, 1994), 223–41.

[5] Michael P. Knowles, "'The Rock, His Work is Perfect': Unusual Imagery for God in Deuteronomy 32," *VT* 39 (1989): 321.

[6] James T. Burtchaell, *From Synagogue to Church: Public Services and Offices in the Earliest Christian Communities* (Cambridge: Cambridge University Press, 1992), 52–272. For the origin of Christian hymnody, see Philip Sigal, "Early Christian and Rabbinic Liturgical Affinities: Exploring Liturgical Acculturation," *NTS* 30 (1984): 63–90; Henry Chadwick, *The Early Church* (Harmondsworth: Penguin, 1967) 258–77; Paul F. Bradshaw, *Daily Prayer in the Early Church: A Study of the Origin and Early Development of the Divine Office* (London: SPCK, 1981).

consuming to copy.[7] There are also no extant psalms collections earlier than that preserved in the fifth-century Codex Alexandrinus. In other words, we cannot be sure how mid-first-century believers would have accessed a collection of Rock psalms. This essay is therefore an act of historical imagination: it aims not to assert "the truth" in a strict, philological sense but to sketch a probable Pauline usage of Israel's Scriptures that cogently explains odd citational patterns in Paul's letters, while also illuminating early socialization practices of Christ-confessing communities composed predominantly of Gentiles being introduced to the narrative and ethos of messianic Judaism. In other words, this essay invites us to imagine both that, and how, Paul may have used the psalms to teach Gentile believers about the character and high status of the Jewish God and to give them a shared history and identity as Israel.[8]

The "Rock" in Israelite Psalmic Traditions

Evidence for this argument derives, first, from the origin of the divine title in psalmic texts depicting the God of Israel as a צור or "Rock." Surprisingly, the epithet only occurs in a slim selection of poetic texts: thirteen of the 150 canonical psalms (18; 19; 28; 31; 62; 71; 73; 78; 89; 92; 94; 95; 144; cf. 49:15), the prophecies of Isaiah (Isa 8:14; 17:10; 26:4; 44:8), and four songs inset within narratives (Deut 32; 1 Sam 2; 2 Sam 22; 23).[9] (Occurring even less frequently as names for God, the Hebrew terms for "stone," אבן and סלע, function similarly in such texts as Gen 49:24; Isa 8:14; Ps 118:22; and in the Rock Pss 18:3; 31:4; 71:3; and 2 Sam 22:2, where סלע is paired with צור.) The social power of the divine name belies the infrequency of its appearance in the Scriptures, however. Statistically speaking, צור in the Hebrew canon functions most frequently as

[7] Harry Y. Gamble, *Books and Readers in the Early Church : A History of Early Christian Texts* (New Haven: Yale University Press, 1995).

[8] Sigal, "Early Christian and Rabbinic Liturgical Affinities," 63. This essay takes seriously both the lack of a developed Christianity distinct from Judaism in Paul's day and Paul's expressed efforts to write the Gentiles *into* rather than *out of* the ethnic history of Israel (e.g., 1 Cor 10; Rom 4; 9–11). For this position, especially as it is expressed in Paul's letter to the Romans, see Diana M. Swancutt, "*Pax Christi:* Romans as Protrepsis to Live as Kings" (Ph.D. diss., Duke University, 2001).

[9] References include Deut 32:4, 15, 18, 30, 31; 1 Sam 2:2; 2 Sam 22:3, 32, 47 (twice); 2 Sam 23:3; Pss 18:3, 32, 47; 19:15; 28:1; 31:3; 62:3, 7, 8; 71:3; 73:26; 78:35; 89:27; 92:16; 94:22; 95:1; 144:1 (cf. 49:15); Isa 8:14; 17:10; 26:4; 44:8. צור was also used metaphorically to refer to other gods (Deut 32:31, 37; Isa 44:8; Hab 1:12), to Abraham (Isa 51:1), and to Jerusalem (Isa 30:29).

a divine title.[10] The number of metaphorical allusions to God as Rock (thirty-four, if we include Ps 61:3) equals in number the instances when צור is a literal reference.[11] In fact, a full 70 percent of the occurrences of צור in the psalms are allusions to God.

These statistics, in turn, reflect both the great age of the title and its importance to early Israelite identity and worship practices.[12] A well-known feature of Yahwistic poetry, the epithet occurs in four of the earliest, independent biblical songs (Deut 32; 1 Sam 2; 2 Sam 22; 23).[13]

---

[10] The same cannot be said for אבן and סלע, which are usually literal references to stones and rocks.

[11] Knowles, "The Rock," 307: "The metaphoric uses of the term outnumber the literal forty-four to thirty-four. Of the former, at least thirty-three refer directly to God."

[12] For full discussions of cult practices associated with rocks, see Gruenwald, "God the 'Stone/Rock'"; Knowles, "The Rock"; and Herbert Schade, "Zur 'beseelten Säule' (= lithos empsychos) als Ursprung des Gottesbildes: Ein Beitrag zur kosmologisch-psychologischen Hermentituk der älteren Kunstgeschichte," in *Aufsätze zur Kunstgeschichte: Festschrift für Hermann Bauer zum 60. Geburtstag* (ed. K. Möseneder and A. Prater; Hildesheim; Olms, 1991), 1–32.

[13] The approximate dates of composition for Deut 32 and other independent hymns inset within Hebrew biblical narrative (e.g., Exod 15; 1 Sam 2; 2 Sam 22) range from the eleventh to ninth centuries B.C.E. Based on textual and poetic archaisms, William Foxwell Albright argues that Deut 32 and 1 Sam 2 date to the eleventh century; see *Yahweh and the Gods of Canaan* (Garden City, N.Y.: Doubleday, 1968). J. T. Willis places 1 Sam 2, together with Exod 15; Judg 5; Hab 3; and Ps 68, in the same period; see "The Song of Hannah and Psalm 113," *CBQ* 35 (1973): 139–54. Based on his typology of divine names within Yahwistic poetry, however, D. N. Freedman dates 1 Sam 2 to ca. 1000 B.C.E. but puts Deut 32 later; see "Divine Names and Titles in Early Hebrew Poetry," in *Magnalia Dei, the Mighty Acts of God: Essays on the Bible and Archaeology in Memory of G. Ernest Wright* (ed. F. M. Cross et al.; Garden City, N.Y.: Doubleday, 1976), 55–107. Similarly, G. E. Wright argues that themes shared by 1 Sam 2 and Deut 32 are better viewed as ninth-century Israelite emphases; see "The Lawsuit of God: A Form-Critical Study of Deuteronomy 32," in *Israel's Prophetic Heritage: Essays in Honor of James Muilenberg* (ed. B. W. Anderson and W. Harrelson; New York: Harper, 1962), 26–67. P. Kyle McCarter concurs, dating both psalms to the period of the monarchy; see *1 Samuel: A New Translation with Introduction and Commentary* (AB 8; Garden City, N.Y.: Doubleday, 1980). Cf. Paul Sanders, *The Provenance of Deuteronomy 32* (OTS 37; Leiden: Brill, 1996); and Andreas Reichert, "The Song of Moses (Deut 3) and the Quest for Early Deuteronomic Psalmody," in *August 1985 Proceedings: Ninth World Congress of Jewish Studies, Jerusalem* (Jerusalem: World Union of Jewish Studies, 1986), 53–60. On the subject of psalms inset within biblical narratives, see now the excellent treatments of James W. Watts, *Psalm and Story: Inset Hymns in Hebrew Narrative* (JSOTSup 139; Sheffield: JSOT Press,

The Genesis narrative also portrays the patriarch Jacob as blessing stones as places of worship and associating them with the divine presence. According to Gen 28:18, 22, "Jacob rose early in the morning, took the stone on which he had laid his head, set it up as a sacred pillar, and poured oil on the top of it. He named that place Beth-El [... and said] 'and this stone that I have set up as a sacred pillar shall be a house of God'" (cf. 31:45; 35:13–15). Memorialized in Gen 49:24 ("The sinews of the arms [of Joseph's enemies] were torn apart by the power of the Strong One of Jacob, the Shepherd, the Stone (**אבן**) of Israel"), the patriarchal practice of stone veneration continued through the period of the judges and early kings, when great rocks dedicated to Yahweh served as places of ritual sacrifice, worship, and atonement (e.g., 1 Sam 6:14–15; 7:12; 14:34; cf. 1 Kgs 8:9).

Significantly, over time this practice of stone veneration functioned ideologically to elevate the status of the Israelites over the other peoples of Canaan, from whom they had assimilated the custom. As is well known, Canaanites and other inhabitants of Syro-Palestine associated divine spirits with the surrounding mountains and sacred stones, some of which even became the foundations for local temples.[14] Texts such as Deut 29:16 record the Israelites' condemnation of their worship of "gods of wood and stone" (cf. Isa 37:19; 2 Kgs 19:18). Nevertheless, the Rock psalms testify that Israelites also assimilated the practice (Ps 118:22; Isa 8:14; cf. "Jacob's iniquity," Isa 27:9).[15] Listen to the psalmist in Deut 32:3–4, 31: "I will proclaim the name of the LORD / praise the greatness of our God. He is the Rock/his works are perfect, and all his ways, just ... for the enemy have no rock like our Rock." A didactic ode appended to help conclude the book, Deut 32 invokes the epithet seven times to teach Israel the signal lesson of the wilderness wandering, that Yahweh was faithful despite their

---

1992); and S. Weitzman, *Song and Story in Biblical Narrative: The History of Literary Convention in Ancient Israel* (Bloomington: Indiana University Press, 1997); for these references I wish to thank Robert Wilson. On Hebrew poetry and poems in general, see Frank Moore Cross Jr. and David Noel Freedman, *Studies in Ancient Yahwistic Poetry* (Grand Rapids: Eerdmans, 1997); Robert Alter, *The Art of Biblical Poetry* (New York: Basic Books, 1985); Elaine R. Follis, ed., *Directions in Biblical Hebrew Poetry* (JSOTSup 40; Sheffield: JSOT Press, 1987); and Susan E. Gillingham, *The Poems and Psalms of the Hebrew Bible* (Oxford: Oxford University Press, 1994).

[14] Knowles, "The Rock," 321.

[15] Frank Moore Cross Jr. is perhaps the most famous scholar to point out the connection between Canaanite mythology and Israelite titles for God such as El-Shaddai ("mountain-god"); see *Canaanite Myth and Hebrew Epic* (Cambridge: Harvard University Press, 1973).

periodic idolatry.[16] Likewise, the prayer of Hannah claims that "there is no Rock like our God/Cease your proud boasting" (1 Sam 2:2–3). Formerly a sovereign's victory song, in its current narrative context the song's praise of the Rock and call to humble worship together presage the divine reversal of political fortunes that Hannah's son Samuel would bring Israel by anointing David as its king. In fact, divine rock imagery was so valuable politically that Rock psalms frame the Davidic history of the books of Samuel: 1 Sam 2 stands at its inception, 2 Sam 22 and 23 at its end. As 2 Sam 23:1–3 reflects, the Israelites bolstered the power of the monarchy by embracing the practice of stone veneration, transforming the Canaanite cultic "rocks" into a title for "the God of Jacob," aligning it with the Davidic kingship of Israel, and sacralizing that relationship in psalms.[17] As they would millennia later for modern Jews, Christians, and even the hard-rock band Stryper, God-as-Rock psalms had a striking currency in Israel as communal instructions about the preeminence of their God and their worth as his people.[18]

The Psalms in the Pauline Churches

Like other first-century Christian Jews, Paul was heir to this tradition, and his letters offer an oddly suggestive array of evidence that he used such psalms to fix Gentile believers' identification with the God of Israel. To begin, letters in the Pauline tradition describe psalm-singing as a major part of early Christian worship and link it explicitly with group instruction. In 1 Cor 14:15, 19, 26, Paul exhorted the Corinthians, "when you congregate, each person has a psalm [ψαλμὸν ἔχει], a teaching, a revelation, a tongue, or an interpretation. Let everything be done for upbuilding [οἰκοδομή of the church]."[19] Letters from Paul's followers to

---

[16] The theme of avoiding idolatry has traditionally been associated with the Josianic reform (621 B.C.E.), and, thus, Deuteronomy has often been dated to the eighth to seventh centuries B.C.E.

[17] On the political function of Hebrew prophecy and poetry, see David Aberbach, *Imperialism and Biblical Prophecy, 750–500 BCE* (New York: Routledge, 1993).

[18] For more on this subject, see Robert L. Platzner, "In the Cleft of a Rock: Metaphors of Divine Concealment and Disclosure in the Hebrew Bible," in *Metaphor, Canon, and Community: Jewish, Christian, and Islamic Approaches* (ed. R. Bisschops and J. Francis; New York: Lang, 1999), 29–37; and Samuel Terrien, "The Metaphor of the Rock in Biblical Theology," in *God in the Fray: A Tribute to Walter Brueggemann* (ed. T. Linafelt and T. K. Beal; Minneapolis: Fortress, 1998), 157–71.

[19] The psalms are linked to instruction not only through the connection to upbuilding but also through the proximity between psalm-singing and instruction

churches at Colossae and Ephesus likewise commanded believers that "the word of Christ [should] dwell in you richly; teach and admonish one another in all wisdom, and sing psalms [ψαλμοῖς] and hymns and spiritual songs with thankfulness in your hearts to God" (Col 3:16; cf. Eph 5:19–20).[20] The testimony of the Roman official Pliny the Younger provides outside confirmation of this worship practice. In 111 C.E. he wrote to the emperor Trajan that Christians in Asia Minor "met regularly before dawn on a fixed day to chant verses alternately among themselves in honor to Christ as a god."[21] Pauline believers in Asia Minor sang psalms together and used them to confirm their common identity in Christ.

Further, Pauline communities could have used and collected Rock psalms; non- and post-Pauline believers certainly recited, cited, reconfigured, and collected specific psalms—including Rock psalms—that they deemed relevant to their developing identity as Christians. The Gospels themselves testify to the importance of select psalms to the activities and Christology of the Jesus movement.[22] Matthew 26:30 and Mark 14:26 portray Jesus and the disciples as having followed Passover custom at the Lord's Supper by "singing a hymn" (ὑμνήσαντες)—probably the last Hallel psalm (Ps 118; see again 118:22)—before they departed for the Mount of Olives. The Gospel of John also repeatedly cites psalms to prove that the passion of Christ fulfilled the Scriptures (e.g., 13:18; 19:24, 28, 36). In fact,

---

in the list. I argue below that the instructions actually derived from the psalms. See 1QS 6:6–7, which suggests that the Qumran community followed a similar practice; assemblies there were required to include "a man to interpret the law" so that "a third of each night ... [the Many shall] read the book, explain the regulation, and bless together." I am grateful to Yonder Gillihan, a graduate student at the University of Chicago and teaching fellow at Yale, for this reference.

[20] Contra Gerhard Delling, "ὕμνος, κ.τ.λ.," *TDNT* 8:499; Eduard Lohse, *Colossians and Philemon: A Commentary on the Epistles to the Colossians and to Philemon* (Hermeneia; Philadelphia: Fortress, 1971), 151, cited by Professor Adela Yarbro Collins in her essay in this volume, "The Psalms and the Origins of Christology." The psalms (ψαλμοί) mentioned in 1 Cor 14:26 and Col 3:16 do not necessarily refer to poetic compositions of believers *rather than* the scriptural psalms. As Collins recognizes, Philo of Alexandria (*Contempl.* 80) and Josephus (*Ant.* 2.346; 7.305) both characterized the scriptural psalms, on a Hellenistic model, as "hymns" or "odes" to God, and Tertullian (*Apol.* 39) said that at agape meals Christians sang either scriptural songs or those of their own composition. In other words, there is definitional overlap between the terms ψαλμός and ὕμνος. Hence, references to "hymns" in the Pauline corpus could denote either scriptural psalms or newly composed hymns, and Paul's allusion to psalms in 1 Cor 14:26 may well refer to the scriptural psalms.

[21] *Ep.* 10.96; cf. Eusebius, *Hist. eccl.* 5.28.5.

[22] See especially the contribution to this volume by Professor Harold Attridge.

the well-known, consistent use of Pss 22; 69; 110; and 118 in first-century Christian writings reflects an early consensus that the psalms were particularly apt witnesses to the messianic identity of Jesus.[23]

Importantly, both New Testament and patristic authors treated the Rock songs Deut 32 and 1 Sam 2 as two such independent, christological hymns. For example, 1 Sam 2 forms the foundation of the Magnificat of Mary (Luke 1:46–55) and Zechariah's prophecy (Luke 1:68–79), christological songs composed of excerpts from 1 Sam 2 interlaced with fragments of canonical psalms (such as Pss 34; 41; 98; 107; the Rock Pss 71; 89; and 2 Sam 22/Ps 18).[24] Similarly, Deut 32 is the scriptural basis of the "Songs of Moses and the Lamb" in Rev 15:3–4.[25] Called "the second Song of Moses" in the Greek Odes of the Codex Alexandrinus (see below), it is dubbed the "great hymn" by Origen, Eusebius, and Hippolytus of Rome and quoted as an independent song by Justin Martyr.[26] Indeed, Justin's *Dialogue with Trypho,* which is riddled with quotations from Isaiah and the Psalms (thirty-six citations), cites Deut 32 (five times) as often as any canonical psalm (Ps 110, five times). The *First Apology* repeats this trend. Of eleven quoted psalms only the two Rock psalms, Deut 32 and Ps 19, are cited twice. In other words, the emerging church treated 1 Sam 2 and Deut 32 as they did other select psalms, as independent scriptural witnesses to the legitimacy of the movement. This fact increases the likelihood that Paul used Rock psalms similarly.

---

[23] E.g., C. H. Dodd, *According to the Scriptures: The Sub-structure of New Testament Theology* (London: Nisbet, 1952); E. Earle Ellis, *Paul's Use of the Old Testament* (Edinburgh: Oliver & Boyd, 1957).

[24] See H. Ringgren, "Luke's Use of the Old Testament," in *Conflict and Context: Hermeneutics in the Americas* (ed. M. L. Branson and C. R. Padilla; Grand Rapids: Eerdmans, 1986).

[25] W. Fenske, "'Das Lied des Mose, des Knechtes Gottes, und das Lied de Lammes' (Apokalypse de Johannes 15,3 f): Der Text und seine Bedeutung für die Johannes-Apokalypse," *ZNW* 90 (1999): 250–64.

[26] For the patristic characterization of Deut 32, see C. E. Hill, "Chrysostom's Commentary on the Psalms: Homilies or Tracts?" in *Prayer and Spirituality in the Early Church* (ed. P. Allen et al.; Queensland: Australian Catholic University, 1998), 301–17; Paul F. Bradshaw, "From Word to Action: The Changing Role of Psalmody in Early Christianity," in *Like a Two-Edged Sword: The Word of God in Liturgy and History: Essays in Honour of Canon Donald Gray* (ed. M. R. Dudley; Norwich: Canterbury, 1995), 21–37; A. Bastiaensen, "Psalmi, Hymni and Cantica in Early Jewish-Christian Tradition," in *Second Century: Tertullian to Nicaea in the West, Clement of Alexandria and Origen, Athanasius* (vol. 3 of *Papers Presented to the Tenth International Conference on Patristic Studies Held in Oxford, 1987;* ed. E. A. Livingstone; StPatr 21; Leuven: Peeters, 1989), 15–26.

Finally, the possibility that Rock psalms were gathered for this purpose is supported by a Christian collection of odes preserved within the Old Greek Scriptures of the fifth-century Codex Alexandrinus. Concluded by a matitudinal hymn composed of psalm fragments,[27] twelve of the collection's fourteen songs are excerpts from poetic Scriptures, and the second and third of these are the Rock psalms, Deut 32 and 1 Sam 2.[28] The presence of Deut 32 and 1 Sam 2 among ten other carefully selected scriptural odes underscores the longevity of the Christian treatment of these texts as independent songs. As important, because this collection arose after Origen reacted to gnostic and Greek song-making by compiling biblical songs for liturgical use,[29] the collection testifies to the Christian impulse to define its group identity by collecting specific psalmic texts and singing them liturgically.[30] Since the Christian *Odes of Solomon* were composed around 100 C.E.,[31] and since Jews actively wrote and collected psalms-based poetry and

---

[27] The matitudinal hymn is similar to *Const. ap* 7.47 and is composed of excerpts from Pss 145:2; 90:1; 6:2; 36:10.

[28] The Odes include the first Song of Moses (Exod 15:1–9), the second Song of Moses (Deut 32:1–43), the Prayer of Hannah (1 Sam 2:1–10), the Prayer of Habakkuk (3:2–19), the Prayer of Isaiah (26:9–20), the Prayer of Jonah (2:3–10), the Prayer of Azariah (Dan 3:26–45 OG), the Hymn of the Three Youths (Dan 3:52–88 OG), the Prayer of Mary (Luke 1:46–55, 68–79), the Ode of Isaiah (5:1–9), the Prayer of Hezekiah (Isa 38:10–20), the *Prayer of Manasseh* (second century B.C.E.–first century C.E.), the Prayer of Simeon (Luke 2:29–32), and a matitudinal hymn.

[29] H. Schneider, "Die biblischen Oden im christlichen Altertum," *Bib* 30 (1949): 28–65. Cf. Everett Ferguson, "Psalm-Singing at the Eucharist: Liturgical Controversy in the Fourth Century," *Austin Seminary Bulletin: Faculty Edition* 98 (1983): 52–77. The early "canon" included Judg 5:1–31; 1 Sam 2:1–10; Hab 3:1–19; Jonah 2:3–10; and Isa 5:1–2.

[30] For a discussion of the liturgical setting of the odes, see Eric Werner, "Hebrew and Oriental Christian Metrical Hymns: A Comparison," *HUCA* 23 (1950–51): 414–15.

[31] The *Odes* were based in part on the psalms. See Lonappan Arangassery, "The Odes of Solomon and the Psalms of David [Thematic Comparison]," *Christian Orient* 19 (1998): 63–72; Brian McNeil, "The Odes of Solomon and the Scriptures," *OrChr* 67 (1983): 104–22; cf. Jack T. Sanders, "Nag Hammadi, the Odes of Solomon and NT Christological Hymns," in *Gnosticism and the Early Christian World: In Honor of James M. Robinson* (ed. J. E. Goehring et al.; Sonoma, Calif.: Polebridge, 1990), 51–66. On dating, see James H. Charlesworth, "The Odes of Solomon," *OTP* 2:725–27; William Horbury, "Old Testament Interpretation in the Writings of the Church Fathers," in *Mikra: Text, Translation, Reading, and Interpretation of the Hebrew Bible in Ancient Judaism and Early Christianity* (ed. M. J. Mulder; CRINT 2/1; Assen: Van Gorcum; Minneapolis: Fortress, 1990), 752. On hymn writing, see ibid., 751–55; cf. David Flusser, "Psalms, Hymns, and Prayers," in *Jewish Writings of the Second Temple Period: Apocrypha, Pseudepigrapha, Qumran, Sectarian*

hymns well before the beginning of the Jesus movement,[32] we cannot preclude the existence of a psalms collection in first-century Pauline churches. Given that Pauline churches sang psalms in worship and for edification and that the earliest believers employed selected psalms, including Deut 32 and 1 Sam 2, for group definition, Pauline churches could have employed a collection of selected Rock psalms likewise.

That Pauline churches did so best explains odd citational patterns and recurring thematic emphases in Paul's letters to Corinth; his letter to Rome, which was written from Corinth; and *1 Clement,* a first-century letter sent from the church in Rome to that in Corinth. These letters prominently quote eleven of the seventeen psalms and odes that refer to God as Rock, including Pss 18 (2 Sam 22); 19; 28; 31; 62; 71; 73; 89; and 94; 1 Sam 2; and Deut 32.[33] Within these letters, citations from Rock psalms occur both individually and in clusters, and on important occasions they even structure whole rhetorical movements. Moreover, the psalms have the same functions in the letters of Paul and Clement, to describe the character of the God of Israel and to call believers to humility and community harmony. In order to teach strong Corinthians to accommodate their table fellowship to the needs of weaker believers, lest it become a "stumbling stone" to them (πρόσκομμα, 1 Cor 8:9; 10:32; cf. Rom 9:33 below), Paul even calls Christ the "spiritual Rock" from which Israel drank in the wilderness (1 Cor 10). Taken together, the evidence of Romans, *1 Clement,* and the Corinthian correspondence suggests that Pauline communities used a Rock psalms collection for group instruction and identity formation in at least Corinth and Rome.

Writings, Philo, Josephus (ed. M. E. Stone; CRINT 2/2; Assen: Van Gorcum; Minneapolis: Fortress, 1984), 551–77; Jacques Fontaine, *Naissance de la poésie dans l'Occident chrétien: Esquisse d'une historie de la poésie latine chrétienne du IIIe au VIe siécle* (Paris: Etudes augustiniennes, 1981); Markus Jenny, "Cantica," *TRE* 7:624–28. The practice of hymn writing and collection only expanded after the end of the first century, as Christian hymns and metrical faith statements in a variety of sources indicate (see Eph 5; Col 1; 1 Tim 3; Phil 2; Clement of Alexandria, *Paed.* 3.12; *Acts of Thomas;* Melito of Sardis's *Concerning the Pasch;* Methodius, *Symp.* 11).

[32] See, e.g., the Qumran *Hodayot,* the *Psalms of Solomon,* and the *Sibylline Oracles.* See also Horbury, "Old Testament Interpretation," 751–52.

[33] Rock psalms not cited by Paul or Clement are 2 Sam 23 and Pss 92; 95; and 144. Paul's citations from Deut 32 make up 22 percent of his citations of Deuteronomy; Paul's treatment of Deut 32 as an independent song cannot therefore be proven. However, Paul clearly treated 1 Sam 2 as an independent song. His two citations from 1 Samuel are both from 1 Sam 2:10 (1 Cor 1:31; 2 Cor 10:17; Nestle-Aland suggests 1 Sam 12:22 as the source of Rom 11:2, but the quotation probably came from Rock Ps 94:14). One of two of Paul's citations of 2 Samuel derives from Rock psalm 2 Sam 22 (see 2 Sam 22:50 in Rom 15:9; cf. 2 Sam 7 in 2 Cor 6:18).

"ROCK" PSALMS IN ROMANS

While Paul's letters repeatedly cite Rock psalms, Romans is the best starting point for an examination of the evidence for a collection because it exhibits the clearest case of citational clustering. Not only does it contain three of the New Testament's five quotations of Deut 32 (e.g., Deut 32:35 in Rom 12:20), an allusion to 1 Sam 2:10 OG, and a christological reference to the Isaian "stone of stumbling" (Isa 8:14), each of these allusions is linked to one of two catenae of Rock psalms citations positioned at critical junctures in Paul's argument. The first such catenae, Rom 10:18–11:2, is the rhetorical culmination of the central argument (9:30–11:11) of Rom 9–11, a demonstration of God's justice in welcoming the Gentiles into Israel (9:6–29) that is aimed ultimately to call them to humility toward the Jews (11:13–36). Romans 9:30–10:17 builds toward this end by asserting that Gentiles apprehended by faith what Israel failed to see, that God alone produced the righteousness of the law (10:1–3) and, thus, that Christ was the law's true goal (10:4, 5–17). As Paul put it in Rom 9:30–33, conflating Isa 28:16 and 8:14, Israel had stumbled over the "stone of stumbling and the rock of falling" (λίθος προσκόμματος καὶ πέτραν σκανδάλου, 9:33).[34] Although the "rock" in Isa 8:14 originally referred to God, the repetition of Isa 28:16 in Rom 10:11 indicates that Paul identified Christ as the promised "rock" to whom the law pointed and over whom, in the "proclamation of Christ" (10:17), Israel had stumbled.

Given Paul's allusive play with Isaian rock imagery at the beginning of this argument (9:30–33), it should hardly surprise us that Paul seals his point in Rom 10:18–11:2 with a cluster of citations from Rock psalms Deut 32:21 and Pss 18:5 and 94:14. Asking rhetorically whether Jews had heard God's scriptural proclamation about Christ (10:18), Paul answers yes by citing Rock Ps 18:5. The psalm had taught them so. To his next rhetorical

---

[34] Note as well the possible echo of Isa 8:14 in Rom 11:9–11. Paul cites Ps 68:23 (OG) to prove that table fellowship has become a "snare [τράπεζα] and a trap [παγίδα], a pitfall [σκάνδαλον] and a retribution" for some Jews. However, σκάνδαλον in Ps 68:23 (OG) links, *gezara shewa,* to Isa 8:14. Isaiah 8:14–15—the MT of which is closer to Rom 11:10–11 than the Old Greek—also treats themes found in Rom 11:11 but that are missing in Ps 68 (OG). Isaiah 8:15 says, "many shall fall and be broken, snared and caught"; Rom 11:11 counters that "they have not stumbled so as to fall" (μὴ ἔπταισαν ἵνα πέσωσιν). In other words, Rom 11:11 reverses the Isaian judgment of Israel for stumbling over the "rock," a stumbling whose eschatological function in Romans was to welcome the Gentiles into the covenant (9:30–32; 11:11–16). In terms of Paul's use of the Scriptures, the implication is that while the christological conjunction of Isa 28:16 and 8:14 may have been traditional (cf. 1 Pet 2:8), Paul knew and could use, for his own ends, the larger Isaian prophecies in which such texts were embedded.

question, Did Israel not understand God's scriptural good news? (10:19), Paul again assents, simultaneously detailing in Moses' voice the consequence of idolatry described in Deut 32: "I will make you jealous of those who are not a nation; with a foolish nation I will make you angry."[35] According to Paul's Deuteronomic logic, God embraced the Gentiles because Israel "stumbled over the stumbling stone" (9:30–33), a point Paul then elaborates through a citation of Isa 65 (10:20–21). Significantly, however, Paul's most important diatribal question then follows in 11:1. Has God therefore rejected his people Israel? Psalm 94 delivers a resounding no: "'God has not rejected his people' whom he foreknew." In other words, a catenae of Rock psalm citations structures the rhetorical conclusion of 9:30–10:21 and acts as the *inclusio* of a rhetorical movement inaugurated by christological rock imagery (9:33). It also forecasts the main point of Rom 9–11. Gentiles newly embraced by the God of Israel must not lord their position over unbelieving Jews (11:11–32) because their prophesied stubbornness was the means by which God opened the covenant to include Gentiles in his salvation (11:11–16, 26). In short, the heaping of God-as-Rock psalms in Rom 9–11 teaches Gentiles to honor the supreme judgment of the God of Israel, as it is recorded in the Scriptures, and to act with humility toward Jews.

Romans 15:9–21 repeats these sentiments in another catenae of Rock psalm citations that comprise the rhetorical summation of the letter. Preceding it are three chapters of paraenetic instruction that end with the call for the Gentile "strong" to act like Christ, thinking first of the needs of their neighbors, of οἰκοδομή (15:2), rather than setting a "stumbling block" in the path of "weaker" believers (πρόσκομμα, 14:13, 20). Evoking Ps 69 as proof, Paul declares that Scriptures like it "were written for our instruction, that by the steadfastness and encouragement of the Scriptures we might have hope" and "live in harmony with one another," with one voice glorifying God (15:4–5). This psalmic exhortation forms the bridge to Paul's summing call, largely constituted by Rock psalms, for Gentiles to worship God together with their Jewish brothers (15:7–13). Paul declares that Christ became and remains God's servant to the circumcised in order to prove God's truthfulness to his scriptural promises (15:8). The Rock Pss 89 (88:3 OG); 18:50; Deut 32:43; and Hallel Ps 117 then form the proof for Paul's main point: Gentiles should glorify God for his mercy by praising him in song (ψαλῶ) together with the circumcised of Israel (15:9–12). In an Isaian inclusio on Rom 15:7–9, Paul concludes that the Gentiles' hope lies in their

[35] On the importance of Deuteronomy to the motif of jealousy in Rom 9–11, see Richard H. Bell, *Provoked to Jealousy: The Origin and Purpose of the Jealousy Motif in Romans 9–11* (Tübingen: Mohr Siebeck, 1994).

oneness with Israel, for they are ruled by the messianic "root of Jesse" (Isa 11:1). How could it be otherwise? It is the Jewish Messiah, Paul claims, who taught the Gentiles to pray the psalms he has just invoked (15:9).[36] In other words, Paul implies that the Rock psalms they now sing were written as Christ's instructions in community harmony.

If we recognize Paul's "boast" of 15:16–17 as a final allusion to 1 Sam 2:10 OG, "He who boasts should boast in ... the Lord" (an attribution made more likely by Paul's citation of it in 1 Cor 1:31 and especially 2 Cor 10:17),[37] then we can draw an important conclusion about Paul's citation of Rock psalms in Romans. He cites different Rock psalms and different verses of those psalms in independent clusters that include Deut 32 and 1 Sam 2. This finding suggests, in turn, that Paul, like other early Christians, treats Deut 32 and 1 Sam 2 as independent, scriptural songs; that Paul is not proof-texting verses but rather groups the psalms (Pss 18; 19; 89; 94; Deut 32; 1 Sam 2) based on their common emphasis on God as Rock; and that Paul's audience is expected to recognize the thematic connection among them. Finally, the Rock psalms are invoked as both scripture and liturgical poetry to deal with two of the letter's key themes, the messianic identity of the "stone of stumbling" (πρόσκομμα) and the need for harmony between Gentile and Jewish believers in Rome. Hence, the social functions of the Rock psalms in Romans are compatible with their functions among ancient Israelites. They educate the faithful about the incomparability of the God of Israel, correct their arrogance, and call them to worship God unreservedly.

---

36 For this argument and the identification of Christ as the speaker of Ps 18 in Rom 15:9, see the essay in this volume by Professor Attridge.

37 See below for the discussion of the text in 1 Cor 1:31. In a context similar to Rom 15:17, that of a self-recommendation, 2 Cor 10:17 cites 1 Sam 2:10 OG. The OG of 1 Sam 2:10 reads: "The knowledgeable should not boast in their knowledge, nor the powerful in their might, nor the wealthy in their wealth, but *the one who boasts should boast in* this, understanding and knowing *the Lord* and doing justice upon the earth." Paul claims that "in Christ Jesus [he has] reason to boast" that his preaching to the Gentiles is a priestly service and that the Gentiles are his offering to the Lord. The ground for his boast is that his actions bring glory to God rather than to himself. As an allusion to 1 Sam 2, the text has a threefold impact here. The arrogant boastfulness of the Roman Gentiles toward Jews is contrasted with his own humble boastfulness in acting for God on behalf of the Gentiles. Paul casts himself as an example of humility that they should imitate. Finally, 1 Sam 2 provides the scriptural foundation for Paul's ministry to Gentiles and for his command that they live and worship in unity with Jewish believers.

"ROCK" PSALMS IN *1 CLEMENT*

The *First Letter of Clement* supports these findings. Written at the end of the first century, *1 Clement* was sent by the Roman church to the Corinthians to correct them for arrogance and disunity. In the process of calling them to humility, the author of *1 Clement* quotes twenty-nine psalm texts, ten of which are Rock psalms. Given how few of the canonical psalms call God Rock, this proportion of Rock psalm citations is remarkable. *First Clement*'s citational practice is also intriguing since the letter cites different verses of the Rock psalms than Paul uses (89:21 in *1 Clem.* 18; cf. 89:3 in Rom 15:8, 89:12 in 1 Cor 10:26) and cites a psalm Paul does not use (Ps 28:6 in *1 Clem.* 26). On one occasion (*1 Clem.* 15), three Rock psalms Paul never used together (Pss 62; 78; and 31) even form a single scriptural proof against the Corinthians' boasting. On another (*1 Clem.* 18), Ps 89 is cited to highlight David as an example of humility. Finally, Deut 32 is cited twice (32:15 in *1 Clem.* 3; 32:8–9 in *1 Clem.* 29), and 1 Sam 2:10 is used against arrogance once (*1 Clem.* 13), but the larger books of Deuteronomy and 1 Samuel are not quoted at all—again underscoring the treatment of these texts as independent psalms. In short, *1 Clement* provides strong non-Pauline evidence for the use and possible collection of these Rock psalms. The fact that the letter originated at Rome at the end of the first century indicates that the Roman church, to whom Paul cited them some forty years earlier, knew these psalms well, that their authority had lasted beyond Paul's lifetime, and that the Roman church could use the Rock psalms independently of him, but for a similar purpose—to humble and unite the Corinthians.

"ROCK" PSALMS IN 1 CORINTHIANS

Given the endurance of the social functions of the Rock psalms, as witnessed in Romans and *1 Clement,* the question is whether coincidence is the best explanation for Paul's use of them for the same end in his earlier letters, 1 and 2 Corinthians. A careful reading of 1 Corinthians suggests that it is not. Rather, Paul, seeking to unify a church divided along status lines between "strong" and "weak" believers, introduces a "reversal of fortunes" motif found in 1 Sam 2 and, after a four-chapter exegesis of the text meant to call them to humility, declares, in a passage riddled with allusions to Rock Ps 78 and Deut 32, that Christ is their Rock.

Paul begins in 1 Cor 1:17 by asserting that the gospel of the crucified Messiah is folly to sages and scribes but the power of God for believers (1:19–25). As is well known, the rhetorical effect of this claim is to shame the few powerful Corinthians into ceasing to lord their status over the majority of believers, who are neither sages (σοφοί) nor powerful (δυνατοί) nor wellborn (εὐγενεῖς; 1:26–27). Paul clinches this result, as Dietrich-Alex Koch and Ross Wagner have shown, by citing 1 Sam 2:10

OG ("the one who boasts should boast in the Lord," Rom 1:31),[38] an ideal proof text for this purpose not only because it explicitly exhorts the wise (φρόνιμος, σοφός), the powerful (δυνατός, ἰσχυρός), and the wealthy (πλούσιος) to boast in God alone[39] but also because the Song of Hannah (1 Sam 2) is itself a "reversal of fortunes" story. It praises God the Rock for delivering the weak from the clutches of the strong and empowering them to sit with the mighty; it demands that people stop boasting in the face of God's superior knowledge and judgment making (2:3); it chronicles the enfeebling of the powerful (2:4, 6–9); and it ends by exalting God's anointed or "christ." As Ross Wagner has shown, Paul employs the themes found in 1 Sam 2 through the next three chapters of 1 Corinthians to exalt his "lowliness" as an apostle while humbling high-status Corinthians. The culmination of this argument, which Paul delivers with a scathing rhetorical flourish, comes in 4:8–13: "already you are filled ... rich ... kings, and I wish you would reign, so that we might share the rule with you! [But God has shown us apostles to be] ... a spectacle to the world .... we are fools for Christ's sake, but you are wise [φρόνιμοι]. We are weak, but you are strong [ἰσχυροί]." Paul finishes with something less than his usual modest candor ("I do not write this to make you ashamed," 4:8–13): his goal is precisely to shame them for their arrogance by teaching them "to not go beyond what is written."

The critical question here is, What is "what is written" (4:6)? The rest of the letter indicates that Paul gave the Corinthians traditions about the

---

[38] With the exception of Dietrich-Alex Koch (*Die Schrift als Zeuge des Evangeliums: Untersuchungen zur Verwendung und zum Verstandnis der Schrift bei Paulus* [Tübingen: Mohr Siebeck, 1985]) and, more recently, J. Ross Wagner ("'Not beyond the Things Which Are Written': A Call to Boast Only in the Lord [1 Cor 4.6]," *NTS* 44 [1998]: 179–87), most scholars attribute the quotation to Jer 9:23. However, as Koch has recognized, Jer 9:23 and 1 Sam 2:10 are practically identical linguistically. Indeed, a careful comparison of *Ode* 3, 1 Sam 2, and Jer 9:23 suggests that the differences between the three versions probably result from independent translations and/or oral Greek transmission of an original Hebrew hymn. As it stands, Jer 9:23 is a free-floating verse thematically and structurally dissimilar from the surrounding context. Jeremiah 9 also lacks contextual features (except the reference to the wise, strong, and rich) that might commend it here. On the other hand, the text of 1 Sam 2:10 OG, which occurs only in *Ode* 3 and in the OG of the Song of Hannah, is imbedded in a larger song that, as I show, contains motifs clearly analogous to 1 Corinthians.

[39] All three versions of the verse (1 Sam 2:10 OG; Jer 9:23–23 OG; *Ode* 3.10 OG) censure the wise (φρόνιμος [1 Sam 2:10 OG]; σοφός [Jer 9:23–23 OG; *Ode* 3.10 OG]), the mighty (δυνατός [1 Sam 2:10 OG]; ἰσχυρός [Jer 9:23–23 OG; *Ode* 3.10 OG]), and the wealthy (πλούσιος). No individual version agrees with 1 Cor 1:26–27 exactly.

resurrection and the Lord's Supper. However, the presence of the same phrase in Rom 15:4 as an explicit reference to the Scriptures indicates that in 1 Cor 4:6 "what is written" probably referred to scriptural traditions that were used in worship and for instruction. Given that Paul calls Christ the "foundation stone" (θεμέλιον) and the Corinthians his sanctuary (οἰκοδομή, νάος) in 1 Cor 3:10–17 and that he quotes Rock Ps 94 in 1 Cor 3:19, the repeated allusions to 1 Sam 2 through the epistle's first four chapters may indicate that "what is written" refers to Rock psalms. In other words, it may well be that Rock psalms were among the traditions Paul passed on to the Corinthians to be sung and used as teaching tools, to "remind them [of Paul's] ways in Christ" (4:17).

Toward Unity in Corinth: Invoking the "Rock"

This likelihood is increased by the fact that 1 Cor 10 deploys the image of Christ as Rock and allusions to Ps 78 and Deut 32 to call believers to community harmony. There Paul discusses the social disunity that results when believers eat meat sacrificed in local pagan temples and then share the Lord's Supper (1 Cor 8–10): the consciences of weak believers can be harmed by the practice (10:30–33). To address this social dilemma, Paul evokes the story of the Israelites' wilderness wandering, as told in Exod 15 and retold in Rock Ps 78 (see 78:24, 15 in 10:3–4; 78:31 in 10:6; and 78:18 in 10:9). Placing the Corinthians squarely in that history by describing the Israelites as their ancestors (10:1), Paul claims that Christ was the spiritual Rock that fed and watered Israel (10:4–5). Paul then argues that not even Christ's presence as their spiritual Rock prevented some of the Corinthians' forefathers from straying to idolatry (10:5). The rhetorical point is that even though the same nourishing "Rock" feeds the Corinthians at the Lord's Supper, they, like some of their forebears, can be led astray to idolatry through the eating of idol meat (10:19). Paul then cites Deut 32 twice (Deut 32:17 in 10:20; Deut 32:21 in 10:22) to show that eating idol meat can lead weak believers astray since to them it represents participation (κοινωνία) in a realm of spirits diametrically opposed to that of the body of Christ (10:15–22). In short, Paul uses the Exodus account, allusions to two Rock psalms, and a reference to Christ as the "spiritual Rock" to instruct the Corinthians about their identity in Christ and to prevent the Corinthians from provoking the Lord to jealousy (Deut 32:21) by participating in the cult practices of those who were not Israel.

One question still remains, however. How does Christ-as-Rock imagery support Paul's case against the consumption of idol meat? The answer may be found in ancient assumptions about stone veneration, which illuminate the phrase "sharers in the altar" (10:18; cf. 10:20). As Ithamar Gruenwald details, the practice of stone veneration across several Near

Eastern cultures included the belief that the spirit of the deity resided in sacred stones and altars. This was true even for the Israelites. As Gruenwald says, commenting on the *Mekhilta* on Exod 17:6:

> "Behold, I will stand before you there on *the rock* at Horeb; and you shall strike *the rock* and water shall come out of it." The midrashic comment of the *Mekhilta de Rabbi Ishmael* suggests this: "God said to him [Moses]: In every place in which you find the imprint of a man's legs, there I am before you." What the *Mekhilta* appears to imply is that God's image can take a physical shape, and even leave a physical—humanlike—imprint in or on a rock. Although *strictu sensu,* what the *Mekhilta* says is that Moses could see vestiges of the divine presence in that particular rock . . . we can safely say that, since the scripture verse reads "there I am before you," the Midrash actually implies that God's imprints in the rock indicate his presence there.[40]

The assumption that the divine presence dwelt *in* the rock explains why Philo (*Leg.* 2.86) claimed that the rock at Horeb *was* the divine Wisdom of God. It also explains why, several centuries earlier, the poet of Deut 32 anthropomorphized God as Rock and contrasted his power to feed, shelter, and punish Israel (32:31, 37–38) with the relative impotence of flinty, foreign spirits whom some Israelites had idolatrously worshiped (32:17). For the Deuteronomist, there was *literally* no Rock like their Rock (32:31). Natives of the Roman Near East may have responded similarly to Greek worship of sacred stones and altars, assimilating the cultic practice in order to usurp its political power.[41] According to Fergus Millar, temples dedicated in Greek to Zeus Bomos (Zeus the Altar) and Zeus Betylos (Zeus the Betyl/Stone) were built during the imperial period in Damascus, Antioch, the Orontes, and Dura Europas, and ancient sources such as Philo of Byblos portray the altars or stones as housing divine spirits.[42] As the historian Herodian (5.3.5) says, "There was no actual man-made statue of the god, the sort Greeks and Romans put up. But there was an enormous black stone, rounded at the base and coming to a point at the top. . . . This stone is worshipped as though it were sent from heaven."[43] Millar speculates that the cults of Zeus Bomos and Zeus Betylos may have offered non-Greeks and non-Romans, "as a contrast to the multiplicity of gods portrayed in the

---

[40] Gruenwald, "God the 'Stone/Rock,'" 439, see also 435–36.

[41] Greeks similarly worshiped sacred stones. See Pausanius 4.154; 5.314, 354; Arnobius, *Adv. Nationes* 1.39; Clement of Alexandria, *Strom.* 7.4.26.

[42] Fergus Millar, *The Roman Near East, 31 B.C.–A.D. 337* (Cambridge: Harvard University Press, 1993), 12–15, 250–56.

[43] Cited by ibid., 15.

cult-status of Graeco-Roman paganism, a fundamental preference for monotheism and the conception of a single deity who could not be represented in human form."[44]

However speculative this final point, Millar's insights explain how Roman-era Greeks could appreciate the claims that Christ was a Rock (or an Altar, 1 Cor 10:18; cf. ἱλαστήριον, Rom 3:25) and Israelite idolaters "sharers in a [different] Altar" (10:18): they were aware of the idea that spirits dwelt in sacred rocks or altars. More important, it explains why Paul uses Rock psalms and the image of Christ as Rock to contrast Christian cultic practices with those of Greeks, who sacrificed meat to idols. In a typically Deuteronomic move, Paul claims that the spiritual Rock of Israel is distinctly superior to, and will not abide interaction with, the altars or spirits of Corinth (10:21). That is why Paul argues that Israelites who ate the food of foreign daimons died even though their Rock fed them with his spirit in the wilderness. They were sharers in different altars or spirits (10:7–8, 18). The implication of Paul's psalmic exegesis is, thus, that the spirit of Christ and daimonic spirits cannot inhabit the same body. One cannot both share in the life of daimons (10:20) and also become "partners in the (true) Altar" (κοινωνοὶ τοῦ θυσιαστηρίου, 10:18) by consuming the body of Christ (10:16, 21). Such a partnership is antithetical to life in the spiritual Body/Rock of Christ (3:10–16; 10:1–4). In short, it is the assumption that Christ was the Corinthians' Rock or Spirit that explains Paul's call for strong believers to stop eating food sacrificed to idols: because "weak" believers thought that daimonic spirits lived on in idol meat and thus that their consumption made them partners with different altars or spirits, the actions of the strong could actually make weak believers who ate the Lord's Supper vulnerable to death-by-daimon (11:29–30; cf. Rom 14:13–23). Hence, Paul adjures the strong, "Let no one seek his own good but the good of the other" (10:24).

One of the most consistent Pauline teachings is that all Christian practices, from the eating of meals to liturgical uses of "psalms, instruction, revelation, glossolalia, and interpretation," should lead to unity and community upbuilding (1 Cor 14:26). This essay has demonstrated that Paul pursued those goals by encouraging psalm-singing in his churches, emphasizing psalmic Scriptures as a basis for community instruction, and using Rock psalms for christological instruction and moral formation. These practices were repeated fifty years later in *1 Clement*. If this evidence coheres, then Paul sought to knit together his newly forming churches in part by giving them a group of psalms that extolled God as their Rock.[45] Further,

---

[44] Ibid., 20–21.

[45] The explicit equation of Christ as Rock is particularly interesting, since the Greek psalms whose Hebrew originals honor God as Rock rarely render צור with

the communal singing of those psalms taught Gentile believers to embrace Israel's history and God's promises as their own, to form identities as his children in Christ, and to live in unity with those who were unlike themselves in matters of status, opinion, or ethnic heritage. As Paul said in Rom 15:5–13, they, together with their Jewish siblings, were to sing psalms to God and to glorify him with one harmonious voice.

πέτρα (2 Sam 22:1 being a notable exception). The reason is that in classical Greek, πέτρα, πετρός, and λίθος (the normal Greek equivalents for צור) almost always represented a stone or pebble. When used symbolically in classical Greek, the terms usually described hard-hearted or block-headed people. Calling the God of Israel a Rock would therefore be akin to describing him as stubborn or foolish. Unsurprisingly, Old Greek translators of the Rock psalms either omitted an equivalent for צור or changed it to θέος, κύριος, δίκαιος, ἰσχυρός, φύλαξ, or βοήθη. This shift in translation raises questions that will have to be more fully explored elsewhere. (For explanations of this shift, see Staffan Olofsson, *God Is My Rock: A Study of Translation Technique and Theological Exegesis in the Septuagint* [Stockholm: Almqvist & Wiksell, 1990], C. T. Fritsch, "Studies in the Theology of the Greek Psalter," in *Zer li-qevurot* [ed. B.-Z. Luria; Jerusalem: World Union of Jewish Studies, 1973], 729–41, and H. M. Erwin, "Theological Aspects of the Septuagint of the Book of Psalms," Ph.D. diss., Princeton University, 1962.) First, who might have gathered the Hebrew Rock psalms and translated them into Greek? I have found no evidence for a Rock psalms collection in pre-Christian Jewish sources, so the collection may have originated among Christ-confessors. Further, that person or persons would have had to know Hebrew. Could Paul have been the collector? He usually cited OG versions of the Scriptures. However, my examination of his *gezara shewa* linkages between Greek and Hebrew texts indicates that he knew Hebrew. Can this be demonstrated? Finally, was the name of God as צור preserved in the Greek "Rock" psalms used by Paul and his churches (even if there were no collection)? The evidence of the letters (1 Cor 10:1; Rom 9:33) indicates that the title held currency among Gentile believers and thus that a literal equivalent for צור, such as πέτρα, could have been used. More study of these questions is needed.

PART 3
PSALMS IN FORMATIVE JUDAISM AND CHRISTIANITY

Philo's Impact on Christian Psalmody

Peter Jeffery
Princeton University

A Sacred Bridge?

Of all the treasures that the church has inherited from Israel, none is more beloved than the book of Psalms. The Psalter is quoted a good eighty times in the New Testament, more than any other book. The few Hebrew words that are still used in Christian worship—amen, hallelujah, hosanna—come mostly from the psalms.[1] The psalms have been recited, sung, and meditated upon throughout history, providing models for innumerable prayers and hymns composed in most of the world's five thousand languages. Even Christians who do not know the Hebrew scriptures very well often know that the Lord is my shepherd, that my soul thirsts for God as the hart pants for flowing streams, that his steadfast love endures forever, that everything that has breath praises the Lord (Pss 23:1; 42:1; 136:1; 150:6). Though many Christians may value the Sermon on the Mount more than the law given from Sinai or identify more with the sufferings of Jesus than the sufferings of Job, the hymns and prayers of the New Testament have never supplanted the psalms—only supplemented them. Both Christians and Jews, therefore, may look on the Psalter as the most eagerly shared portion of our common ground, from which leaders of worship, preachers, and spiritual authors of both religions have endlessly drawn on the wide range of human feeling and experience that the psalms reveal: joy, anger, remorse or contrition, sadness and longing, acceptance and peace.

[1] "Amen" may have had its main liturgical context in covenant ceremonies such as Deut 27:14–26 and Neh 8:6, but the word is also used to close four of the five sections of the book of Psalms (41:13; 72:19; 89:52; 106:48; cf. 1 Chr 16:36); see Bruce Chilton, "Amen," *ABD* 1:184–86. "Hosanna" comes from Ps 118:25, filtered through the New Testament (Matt 21:9, 15; Mark 11:9–10; John 12:13; cf. Luke 19:38; see Marvin H. Pope, "Hosanna," *ABD* 3:290–91). "Hallelujah," of course, is a refrain found with Pss 104–106; 111–118; 120–136; 146–50; as well as 1 Chr 16:36; Neh 5:13.

Where Jews and Christians find common spiritual ground, it is easy to assume that they also have common historical ground: that Christianity received from Israel not only the bare texts of the psalms but also traditional Jewish ways of singing them. To put it another way, what the church received was not only the Psalter but also psalmody. In that case, at least some of the many Christian methods of psalm-singing that developed over the centuries would owe their origin to Jewish practices that the church preserved and continued. The most extended expression of this supposal is Eric Werner's classic pair of volumes entitled *The Sacred Bridge.*[2] Werner deserves credit for the important issues he raised and the interesting phenomena he called attention to; his provocative work fascinated and challenged scholars in many disciplines for much of the twentieth century. However, while no one could ever be fully competent in all the languages and periods that Werner sifted for evidence (he himself certainly was not), it can nonetheless be shown that virtually all of Werner's parallels are illusory, resting ultimately upon mere coincidence, unjustified interpretations, forced distortions, or outright errors.[3]

In fact, Judaism as it has existed in all its varied forms for most of the last two millennia is not the ancestor of Christianity. The two are siblings or perhaps cousins, each descended from the ancient Israelite religion by a unique route that the other has historically regarded as illegitimate. To find the origin of a Christian practice, therefore, we cannot merely discover a similar Jewish practice and identify it without further ado as the likely ancestor of the Christian one. Instead, one would have to trace back two different paths of historical descent over many centuries, one in each religion, to find the original "missing link" or common ancestor—if indeed there was one.

For example, it is popularly believed that at least some of the psalms may originally have been sung in the temple in Jerusalem; thus the Psalter has been called "a manual for the Temple service"[4] and the "Hymn Book of the Second Temple."[5] However, the historical sources

---

[2] *The Sacred Bridge: The Interdependence of Liturgy and Music in Synagogue and Church during the First Millennium,* vol. 1 (New York: Columbia University Press, 1959; partially reprinted [omitting much of the musical material] as *The Sacred Bridge: Liturgical Parallels in Synagogue and Early Church* [New York: Schocken, 1970]), and vol. 2 (New York: Ktav, 1984).

[3] Peter Jeffery, "Werner's *The Sacred Bridge,* Volume 2: A Review Essay," *JQR* 77 (1986–87): 283–98.

[4] Marie Pierik, *The Psalter in the Temple and the Church* (Washington, D.C.: Catholic University of America Press, 1957), 2.

[5] H. H. Rowley, *Worship in Ancient Israel: Its Forms and Meaning* (London: SPCK, 1967, 1981), 176.

that report on psalmody in the temple—the books of Chronicles,[6] the Mishnah and Talmuds,[7] the titles in the Psalter itself[8]—present many problems of interpretation and verification. In any case, there is unlikely to have been a direct historical connection between the priestly sacrificial cult of the temple and the worship of early Christians: no New Testament writer gives the impression of having actually attended services in the temple, for example. Paul, the earliest of them, wrote while the temple was still standing and was later said to have visited it (Acts 21:26–29; 22:17), yet in his writings the temple is mentioned rarely, and then as the basis of an analogy (1 Cor 3:16–17; 6:19; 9:13; 2 Cor 6:16; 2 Thess 2:4). Some New Testament

---

[6] 2 Chr 3:1–7:22 (paralleling 1 Kgs 6:1–9:9); 2 Chr 6:41–42 (paralleling Ps 132:8–10, 1); and 2 Chr 7:3 (paralleling Ps 136:1). At a minimum, the Chronicler is imaginatively reading the temple practices of his own time back to the period of David and Solomon—but these may not be the practices of the Chronicler's time, either. According to Joachim Braun ("Some Remarks on the Music History of Ancient Israel/Palestine: Written or Archaeological Evidence?" in *Musikarchäologie früher Metallzeiten* [vol. 2 of *Studien zur Musikarchäolgie;* ed. E. Hickmann et al.; Orient-Archäologie 7; Rahden: Leidorf, 2000], 138), there is "a total lack of archaeological evidence" to support the Chronicles description of the temple cult: "we have here a case of mythologisation, heroisation and beautification of the past, ... the invention of a fictitious, subordinated musical culture."

[7] Mishnah tractates describing the special occasions of the year sometimes indicate the psalms that were sung: *Bik.* 3:4; *Pesaḥ.* 5:7; 9:3; 10:7; *Sukkah* 4:1, 8; 5:4; *Mid.* 2:5; and *Taʿan.* 2:3; 3:9; 4:4–5. As Richard S. Sarason pointed out, however, the rabbis who compiled the Mishnah and Talmuds did not have firsthand experience of the temple cult, which ceased a century or more before they were born. They reported traditions that may ultimately have originated in the temple but have since been filtered through the rabbis' own very different perspective; see "Religion and Worship: The Case of Judaism," in *Take Judaism, For Example* (ed. J. Neusner; Chicago: University of Chicago Press, 1983), 59–65.

[8] The titles of certain psalms appear to indicate their usage in the temple cult, but the interpretation of some of them is debatable (see the convenient listing in Nahum M. Sarna et al., "Psalms, Book of," *EncJud* 13:1318–19). Moreover, the Hebrew and Greek texts of the Psalter contain some divergences. The most interesting case is to be made for the so-called Daily Psalms (24; 48; 82; 94; 81; 93; 92), which according to the Mishnah were recited on the seven days of the week after the daily sacrifice (*Tamid* 7:4, cf. *Sop.* 18:4). In the Hebrew Psalter, only Ps 92 has a title mentioning its weekly assignment: "A psalm, a song for the sabbath day." Some manuscripts of the Greek Psalter, however, also indicate weekday assignments for Pss 24; 48; 94; and 93; see J. A. Smith, "The Ancient Synagogue, The Early Church and Singing," *Music and Letters* 65 (1984): 6. For an English translation of the Greek text, see Albert Pietersma, trans., *The Psalms: A New English Translation of the Septuagint and Other Greek Translations Traditionally Included under That Title* (Oxford: Oxford University Press, 2000).

authors exhibit a hostile attitude toward the temple[9]—but even those with a relatively positive view seem to lack a firsthand knowledge of the actual building and what went on inside it. Instead, they describe a spiritual, symbolic temple, based on information obtained from the Jewish scriptures and at times even conflating the temples of Solomon, Zerubbabel, and Herod with their predecessor, the tabernacle in the wilderness.[10] Later generations of Christians made no effort to rebuild the temple after its destruction in 70 C.E.,[11] and it may not have been until the sixth century

---

9 Thus the Stephen tradition in Acts 6:8–8:1 seems to identify the temple with a Jewish failure to recognize that "the Most High does not dwell in houses made with hands" (7:44–50), a viewpoint possibly influenced by Samaritanism (cf. John 4:20–24). The Gospel of John sees the temple as a place where Jesus regularly encountered opposition, and the destruction of which he foretold (2:13–22; 4:20–24; 7:14–30; 8:20, 59; 10:22–39; 11:55–57; 18:20). See Raymond E. Brown, *The Community of the Beloved Disciple: The Life, Loves, and Hates of an Individual Church in New Testament Times* (New York: Paulist, 1979), 38–39, 49, 118; Stephen Motyer, "The Fourth Gospel and the Salvation of Israel: An Appeal for a New Start," in *Anti-Judaism and the Fourth Gospel: Papers of the Leuven Colloquium, 2000* (ed. R. Bieringer et al.; Jewish and Christian Heritage Series 1; Assen: Van Gorcum, 2001), 97–103.

10 Thus Luke's temple scenes (1:8–23; 2:41–51; and perhaps Acts 2:46–3:11; 21:26–29; 22:17) are clearly composed out of Old Testament elements, particularly the story of Samuel (1 Sam 1:1–2:26); they include a historically implausible synthesis (2:22–39) of the redemption of the firstborn (Exod 13:11–16) with the purification of the mother (Lev 12); see Raymond E. Brown, *The Birth of the Messiah: A Commentary on the Infancy Narratives in Matthew and Luke* (Garden City, N.Y.: Doubleday, 1977), 265–71, 280–81, 447–51, 485–86. In 1 Pet 2:4–10 the temple is a metaphor for the Christian community. Hebrews 4:14–5:10; 7:1–10:22 describe the temple ritual and its paraphernalia and priesthood as mere earthly copies of the heavenly reality, but the temple this author imagines is the desert tent of Moses' time rather than the building of Solomon or its successors (9:1–14). Revelation reinterprets the temple menorahs (1:12–20; cf. Exod 27:20–21; Lev 24:2–4; 2 Chr 4:7), the incense (5:8 and 8:3–5; cf. Exod 30:1–10), and possibly the great bronze basin or "molten sea" (4:6; 15:2; cf. 1 Kgs 7:23–26). The seer is told to measure the earthly temple (11:1–2; cf. Ezek 40:3–42:20; Zech 2:1–5), sees the ark of the covenant in the heavenly temple (11:19), and ultimately envisions a heavenly Jerusalem with no temple at all (21:22). For symbolic temples in Jewish writings of roughly the same period, see Neil S. Fujita, *A Crack in the Jar: What Ancient Jewish Documents Tell Us about the New Testament* (Mahwah, N.J.: Paulist, 1986), 140–50. Passages in Jewish literature referring to the messianic rebuilding of Jerusalem and the temple are conveniently collected in English in Raphael Patai, *The Messiah Texts: Jewish Legends of Three Thousand Years* (Detroit: Wayne State University Press, 1979), 220–28.

11 An anonymous Christian pilgrim of the year 333 took note of a pierced rock on the site, presumably the one now covered by the Dome of the Rock. Once a

that temple symbolism began to be incorporated into Christian architecture or worship.[12]

If not the temple, what of the synagogue? Here too there is little to support the idea of a direct relationship to the worship of the early church. The New Testament picture of the synagogue is consistently more negative than that of the temple, for the synagogue was the place where Christians, beginning with Jesus himself, were misunderstood, rejected, punished, and expelled.[13] Affirmations that, in spite of this, early Christians somehow

---

year, he reported, Jews came and anointed the rock, tore their garments in mourning, and left (see John Wilkinson, ed., *Egeria's Travels* [3d ed.; Warminster: Aris & Phillips, 1999], 30, 199–200). On the authorship of this work, see Laurie Douglass, "A New Look at the *Itinerarium Burdigalense,*" *JECS* 4 (1996): 313–33; Skusan Weingarten, "Was the Pilgrim from Bordeaux a Woman? A Reply to Laurie Douglass," *JECS* 7 (1999): 291–97. Most Christian accounts of the holy places fail to mention even this much.

[12] Martin Harrison, *A Temple for Byzantium: The Discovery and Excavation of Anicia Juliana's Palace Church in Istanbul* (Austin: University of Texas Press, 1989).

[13] Wayne Meeks ("Breaking Away: Three New Testament Pictures of Christianity's Separation from the Jewish Communities," in *Essential Papers on Judaism and Christianity in Conflict: From Late Antiquity to the Reformation* [ed. J. Cohen; Essential Papers on Jewish Studies; New York: New York University Press, 1991], 89–113) sees "three New Testament pictures of Christianity's separation from the Jewish communities": the Johannine documents preserve a particularly bitter memory of a conflict that resulted in their exclusion from the local synagogues (see also Brown, *Community of the Beloved Disciple,* 22–23, 41–43, 66–69, 71–73, 172–73; Reimund Bieringer, Didier Pollefeyt, and Frederique Vandecasteele-Vanneuville, "Wrestling with Johannine Anti-Judaism: A Hermeneutical Framework for the Analysis of the Current Debate," in Bieringer et al., *Anti-Judaism and the Fourth Gospel,* 23–30); the Pauline communities were organized in urban households that were organizationally unconnected with neighboring synagogues, but in which there were internal debates about the relevance of preserving Jewish customs; though the Synoptic Gospels also preserve traditions about Christian expulsion from synagogues, Matthew in particular seems to have been shaped by leadership struggles within Jewish communities, between followers of Jesus and "the scribes and the Pharisees"—representatives of an emerging Judaism that was close to the rabbinic type that eventually predominated (compare Krister Stendahl, *The School of St. Matthew and Its Use of the Old Testament* [2d ed.; Philadelphia: Fortress, 1968; repr., Ramsey, N.J.: Sigler, 1991). In none of these scenarios is it easy to imagine much continuity with synagogue worship as it is known from the Mishnah and later Jewish sources. A fourth and even more complicated picture may be seen in the Acts of the Apostles, which gives an important role to Gentile "God-fearers" who attended synagogues without full conversion to Judaism (John G. Gager, "Jews, Gentiles, and Synagogues in the Book of Acts," in *Christians among Jews and*

continued to follow practices they had learned in the synagogue are extremely difficult to confirm. First, there is much uncertainty about what was actually done in synagogues at the time of Jesus and his disciples.[14] Most of our early textual evidence relates to the rabbinic stabilization of the synagogue services that took place after the destruction of 70 C.E., when the synagogue was in some respects being made to substitute for the lost temple[15]—but these developments are already part of the history of formative Judaism, not of pre-Christianity. Archaeological evidence takes us back somewhat earlier than 70,[16] but though we can say that synagogue worship probably included at least the public reading of the Scriptures and the recital of certain prayers, it is not at all clear that it regularly or usually included any psalms or whether these psalms were performed as readings, prayers, or songs.[17] It is even possible to argue that the synagogue services originally had no singing of any kind.[18] Moreover, the Christian liturgy is structured very differently from that of the synagogue, and the

---

Gentiles: Essays in Honor of Krister Stendahl on His Sixty-Fifth Birthday [ed. G. W. E. Nickelsburg and G. W. MacRae; Philadelphia: Fortress, 1986], 91–99).

[14] Paul F. Bradshaw, *The Search for the Origins of Christian Worship: Sources and Methods for the Study of Early Liturgy* (2d ed.; New York: Oxford University Press, 2002), 36–46.

[15] Joseph Heinemann, *Prayer in the Talmud: Forms and Patterns* (Studia Judaica; Forschungen zur Wissenschaft des Judentums 9; Berlin: de Gruyter, 1977), which I reviewed in *Worship* 51 (1977): 558–60; Richard S. Sarason, "On the Use of Method in the Modern Study of Jewish Liturgy," in *Theory and Practice* (vol. 1 of *Approaches to Ancient Judaism;* ed. W. S. Green; BJS 1; Missoula, Mont.: Scholars Press, 1978), 97–172; Lawrence A. Hoffman, *The Canonization of the Synagogue Service* (University of Notre Dame Center for the Study of Judaism and Christianity in Antiquity 4; Notre Dame, Ind.: University of Notre Dame Press, 1979); Jacob J. Petuchowski, "The Liturgy of the Synagogue: History, Structure, and Contents," in *Studies in Liturgy, Exegesis, and Talmudic Narrative* (vol. 4 of *Approaches to Ancient Judaism;* ed. W. S. Green; BJS 27; Chico, Calif.: Scholars Press, 1983), 1–64.

[16] Joseph Gutmann, ed., *The Synagogue: Studies In Origins, Archaeology and Architecture* (New York: Ktav, 1975); Paul Virgil McCracken Flesher, "Palestinian Synagogues before 70 C.E.: A Review of the Evidence," in *Studies in the Ethnography and Literature of Judaism* (vol. 6 of *Approaches to Ancient Judaism* ed. J. Neusner and E. S. Frerichs; BJS 192; Atlanta: Scholars Press, 1989); Lee I. Levine, *The Ancient Synagogue: The First Thousand Years* (New Haven: Yale University Press, 2000), 42–159.

[17] Bradshaw, *Search for the Origins,* 38–39. The evidence for psalm-singing in the ancient synagogue is so meager that there is not even a section on it in the liturgy chapter of Levine, *Ancient Synagogue,* 501–60.

[18] Smith, "Ancient Synagogue,"

two traditions have very few texts in common apart from the Bible itself.[19] Finally, the sad history of rivalry and bad feeling between the two religions has only obscured any common features their worship may once have had. There is reason to believe that both Christians and Jews, as their communities were separating, sought to discourage Christians from taking part in Jewish ceremonies, that each group even made a point of formulating its rites to ensure such exclusion.[20]

---

[19] For a rare exception, see David A. Fiensy, *Prayers Alleged to be Jewish: An Examination of the Constitutiones Apostolorum* (BJS 65; Chico, Calif.: Scholars Press, 1985); Pieter W. van der Horst, "The Greek Synagogue Prayers in the Apostolic Constitutions," in *From Qumran to Cairo: Studies in the History of Prayer: Proceedings of the Research Group Convened under the Auspices of the Institute for Advanced Studies of the Hebrew University of Jerusalem, 1997* (ed. J. Tabory; Jerusalem: Orhot Press, 1999), 19–46. On the complicated problem of the Sanctus/Qeduššah, derived from Isa 6:3, see Petuchowski, "Liturgy of the Synagogue," 37–40, 51–53; Bryan D. Spinks, *The Sanctus in the Eucharistic Prayer* (Cambridge: Cambridge University Press, 1991), 46–54, 104–21; Levine, *Ancient Synagogue,* 540–45.

[20] According to talmudic tradition, for example, the Ten Commandments were originally recited in the daily service, but this practice was suspended because it seemed to support a Christian interpretation that these had special status above the other commandments of the Torah; see Ismar Elbogen, *Jewish Liturgy: A Comprehensive History* (ed. J. Heinemann et al; trans. R. P. Scheindlin; Philadelphia: Jewish Publication Society, 1993), 193. Early phylactery scrolls support the hypothesis that the Decalogue was once recited with the Shema but later omitted; see Ruth Satinover Fagen, "Phylacteries," *ABD* 5:368–70. For a possible historical context, see Charlotte Elisheva Fonrobert, "The *Didascalia Apostolorum:* A Mishnah for the Disciples of Jesus," *JECS* 9 (2001): 503–4. On Birkat Haminim ("the blessing of the sectarians") and similar texts, see also Samuel E. Karff, "The Perception of Christians in Jewish Liturgy: Then and Now," in *The Changing Face of Jewish and Christian Worship in North America* (ed. P. F. Bradshaw and L. A. Hoffman; Two Liturgical Traditions 2; Notre Dame, Ind.: University of Notre Dame Press, 1991), 34; Elbogen, *Jewish Liturgy;* S. J. Joubert, "A Bone of Contention in Recent Scholarship: The 'Birkat ha-Minim' and the Separation of Church and Synagogue in the First Century AD," *Neot* 27 (1993): 351–63; John Gurrieri, "The Perception of Jews in Christian Liturgy: Then and Now," in Bradshaw and Hoffman, *Changing Face of Jewish and Christian Worship,* 46–65; Motyer, "Fourth Gospel," 94–95, 133–35. On the Christian side, much effort was expended on revising the calendar so that Easter could not possibly coincide with Passover (see, e.g., David Brakke, "Jewish Flesh and Christian Spirit in Athanasius of Alexandria," *JECS* 9 [2001]: 453–81) and on slandering Jewish practices (Robert Wilken, *John Chrysostom and the Jews: Rhetoric and Reality in the Late Fourth Century* [Berkeley and Los Angeles: University of California Press, 1983]), even to the point of characterizing heterodox and nonstandard Christian practices as "Jewish" (Brakke as above).

If indeed there was a "sacred bridge," if Christians ever performed psalms in a way that had been learned from Jews, it should be sought in a less formalized type of worship that both religions shared even in their earliest stages of development: the group banquet. According to the earliest history of the church, it was the banquets that provided the characteristic environment for the emergence of a distinctively Christian identity: "they regularly went to the temple but met in their houses for the breaking of bread" (Acts 2:46–47). It has been proposed that the significance of the shared meal and of the many rituals connected with eating were two of the central issues that distinguished the early Christian movement from the contemporary Pharisees.[21] However, behind such disputes was an extensive common cultural background, for social meals were universal in the ancient world, among Jews and Greeks, Christians and pagans. Many of them included practices that are still familiar to us today: speeches and discussion on philosophical and ethical topics, the reading and exposition of holy books, the lighting of lamps, the recital of prayers, the offering and distribution of bread and wine and other foods that had become charged with special religious meanings. All of these have parallels or counterparts in services as diverse as the Passover Seder, the Friday night supper and Qiddush blessing that opens the Jewish Sabbath, the Christian Eucharist, and the Agape or love feast, from which survived such practices of Christian Vespers as the *lucernarium,* the *artoklasia*[22] and the loving cup.[23] In particular, ancient Greek banquets often concluded with a *symposium* ("drinking together") that, depending on the interests of the participants, could include games, various kinds of entertainment, and/or philosophical conversation, preceded by libations of wine with the singing of special hymns to pagan deities and ending with other sacred and secular songs.[24] Because these occasions began with idolatry and often ended in drunken carousing, ancient Jewish and Christian writers firmly disapproved, both echoing the New Testament admonition, "Do not get drunk

---

[21] Jacob Neusner, "Cultic Piety and Pharisaism before 70," in *The Glory of God Is Intelligence: Four Lectures on the Role of Intellect in Judaism* (Salt Lake City, Utah: Religious Studies Center, Brigham Young University, 1978), 20–28.

[22] George Galavaris, *Bread and the Liturgy: The Symbolism of Early Christian and Byzantine Bread Stamps* (Madison: University of Wisconsin Press, 1970), 132–33.

[23] Peter Jeffery, *A New Commandment: Toward a Renewed Rite for the Washing of Feet* (Collegeville, Minn.: Liturgical Press, 1992), 21, 28.

[24] François Lissarrague, *The Aesthetics of the Greek Banquet: Images of Wine and Ritual* (trans. A. Szegedy-Maszak; Princeton: Princeton University Press, 1990); Oswyn Murray, ed., *Sympotica: A Symposium on the Symposion* (Oxford: Clarendon Press, 1990); William J. Slater, ed., *Dining in a Classical Context* (Ann Arbor: University of Michigan Press, 1991).

with wine, but be filled with the Spirit, addressing one another in psalms and hymns and spiritual songs, singing and making melody to the Lord with all your heart" (Eph 5:18–19).[25] If only we had a detailed description of a first-century Jewish religious banquet, it might offer our best glimpse of the context in which early Christian worship—and particularly psalmody—may have emerged.

An Ideal Banquet

In fact, we do have such a description, and it is of interest not only because of what it can teach us, some twenty centuries later, about Jewish singing at the beginning of the Christian era, but also because, long after Christianity and Judaism had parted ways, it continued to influence Christian perceptions of the history and Jewish origins of psalmody and thus to shape the actual use of the psalms in Christian worship. This is the well-known work *On the Contemplative Life* by the first-century Jewish writer Philo of Alexandria. It portrays the life, ideals, and worship of a (fictional?) Egyptian Jewish monastic sect that Philo called the Therapeutai; by his own account, the name could mean the "Healers" or the "Worshipers" (*Contempl.* 1.2).

The Therapeutai and Their Hymns

As Philo described it, this group lived a rather Carthusian lifestyle. Each member had his or her own dwelling and spent most of the time studying in a private room. One of the names for this room, *monastērion,* is the earliest recorded use of the word "monastery."

> In each is found a sacred room called a "sanctuary [σεμνεῖον]" or "solitary [μοναστήριον = monastery]" where they isolate themselves to accomplish the mysteries of the sanctified life. Nor do they bring anything in: neither drink, nor food, nor any of those things necessary to the wants of the body, but laws and sayings prophesied by the prophets and hymns [ὕμνους] and the other things by which knowledge and piety are increased and fulfilled. (*Contempl.* 3.25)

But what interests us most is what they studied: laws, prophetic sayings, and hymns. Doubtless what was intended was the three-part canon of the Hebrew Bible, which Philo's contemporary Jesus referred to as "the law of Moses, the prophets, and the psalms" (Luke 24:44). Surely the Psalms, which dominate the third section of the Hebrew canon (now usually called

---

[25] See Hans Lewy, *Sobria ebrietas: Untersuchungen zur Geschichte der antiken Mystik* (BZNW 9; Giessen: Töpelmann, 1929).

the Writings or Ketuvim) had an important place among the hymns the Therapeutai studied.

However, the Therapeutai had other writings also, which clearly were not part of the Bible but helped facilitate biblical study.

> Also with them are writings of old men, who became founders of the sect, [and] left behind many memorials of the allegorizing principle. Taking these as archetypes of a sort, they imitate the procedure of this approach. Thus they not only contemplate, but also make songs [ἄσματα] and hymns [ὕμνους] to God in all kinds of meters and melodies which, of course, they inscribe with very solemn rhythms. (*Contempl.* 3.29)

Philo approved the fact that the Therapeutai studied and interpreted the scriptures allegorically. This delving into hidden meanings seems to have inspired them to compose their own songs and hymns as a response to or meditation on the biblical text. We immediately think of the many surviving Jewish and Christian hymns that seem to imitate the psalms: the noncanonical psalms of Qumran, the psalms and odes ascribed to David's son Solomon, the canticles of the New Testament, and the numerous hymns preserved in apocryphal and gnostic writings.[26]

However, this passage also tells us something else: the Therapeutai composed not only the words of songs and hymns but also the music; careful analysis of Philo's musical terminology is therefore essential to understanding what he thought these songs and hymns were like, what he really meant by "all kinds of meters and melodies ... with very solemn rhythms." From his other writings it is evident that Philo, a highly educated man, was well-informed about music theory and that he used its terminology knowledgeably.[27] Since he regarded meter, melody, and rhythm as the

---

[26] See, e.g., Bonnie Kittel, *The Hymns of Qumran* (SBLDS 50; Missoula, Mont.: Scholars Press, 1981); James H. Charlesworth et al., eds., *The Dead Sea Scrolls: Hebrew, Aramaic, and Greek Texts with English Translations.* Vol. 4A: *Pseudepigraphic and Non-Masoretic Psalms and Prayers.* Vol. 4B: *Angelic Liturgy: Songs of the Sabbath Sacrifice* (Tübingen: Mohr Siebeck; Louisville: Westminster John Knox, 1993); Geza Vermes, *The Complete Dead Sea Scrolls in English* (London: Penguin, 1997), 243–383; James H. Charlesworth "A Prolegomenon to a New Study of the Jewish Background of the Hymns and Prayers in the New Testament," *JJS* 33 [*Essays in Honour of Yigael Yadin*] (1982): 265–85.

[27] *Prob.* 49–51 (ed. M. Petit; *OPA* 28:176–79); *Spec.* 2.230 (ed. S. Daniel; *OPA* 24:374–75); Louis H. Feldman, "Philo's Views on Music," in *Studies in Hellenistic Judaism* (AGJU 30; Leiden: Brill, 1996; repr. from *Journal of Jewish Music and Liturgy* 9 [1986–87]: 36–54); Siegmund Levarie, "Philo on Music," *Journal of Musicology* 9 (1991): 124–30; Jutta Leonhardt, *Jewish Worship in Philo of Alexandria* (Texts and Studies in Ancient Judaism 84; Tübingen: Mohr Siebeck, 2001), 159–60, 287–88.

three essential components of music,[28] he was clearly trying to say that the Therapeutai made full use of the resources available to them in the musical learning of the time: melody, meter, and rhythm. However, what did each of these three terms actually describe?

Philo's threefold conception of music was echoed by late antique writers on ancient Greek music theory, such as Aristides Quintilianus (late third or early fourth century C.E.), Alypius (late fourth to early fifth century C.E.?), and the Latin encyclopedist Cassiodorus (died 585 C.E.).[29] However, these authors all lived centuries after Philo; he could not have learned it from them. The preserved writings of Aristoxenos (late fourth century B.C.E.), a disciple of Aristotle and the most important ancient Greek theorist, suggest only two subfields within music theory: harmonics and rhythm.[30] Nor is a ternary structure characteristic of the mathematical tradition of music study attributed to Pythagoras or the ethical approach ascribed to Damon.[31] In fact, Philo's understanding of music appears to be rooted in Plato's theory of poetry, for in the ancient world poems were always songs.[32] Philo's own thinking seems closest, both in

---

[28] Philo, *Cher.* 105 (ed. J. Gorez; *OPA* 3:68–71); *Sobr.* 36 (ed. J. Gorez; *OPA* 11–12:144–45).

[29] Thomas J. Mathiesen, *Apollo's Lyre: Greek Music and Music Theory in Antiquity and the Middle Ages* (Publications of the Center for the History of Music Theory and Literature, Indiana University 2; Lincoln: University of Nebraska Press, 1999), 527, 595, 638.

[30] Mathiesen, *Apollo's Lyre,* 294–344. For the extant fragments on rhythm, see Aristoxenos, *Elementa Rhythmica: The Fragment of Book II and the Additional Evidence for Aristoxenean Rhythmic Theory,* (ed. L. Pearson; Oxford: Clarendon Press, 1990). Thus the treatise ascribed to Plutarch, which is explicitly dependent on Aristoxenus, seems to divide musical learning into harmonics and rhythmics (*Mus.* 33, 36; Andrew Barker, ed., *Greek Musical Writings* [2 vols.; Cambridge Readings in the Literature of Music; Cambridge: Cambridge University Press, 1984, 1989], 1:239–42, 243), even though it also reports information on metrics (12, 28; Barker, *Greek Musical Writings,* 1:218, 233–35) and echoes Plato in saying, "Three minimal items must always fall on the hearing simultaneously, the note, the duration, and the syllable" (35; Barker, *Greek Musical Writings,* 1:243). If this work actually dates from the lifetime of Plutarch (ca. 50–ca. 120 C.E.), it was written within a century of Philo's death (Mathiesen, *Apollo's Lyre,* 355–66).

[31] Neither has left us any extant writings, though a writing of Damon circulated in ancient times. On Pythagoras, see Barker, *Greek Musical Writings,* 2:28–52; Mathiesen, *Apollo's Lyre,* 344–53. On Damon, see Barker, *Greek Musical Writings,* 1:168–69; Eric Csapo and William J. Slater, *The Context of Ancient Drama* (Ann Arbor: University of Michigan Press, 1995), 343–45.

[32] In Plato's *Republic* (398–403) Socrates states that a song or ode has three parts: the words, the melody, and the rhythm (Barker, *Greek Musical Writings,* 1:130;

content and in historical date, to certain minor commentators on Plato, such as Thrasyllus the Astrologer (fl. 5 B.C.E.–36 C.E.), whose writings survive only as lengthy quotations in a fragmentary work entitled "Mathematics Useful for Reading Plato" by Theon of Smyrna (second century C.E.).[33] Philo himself seems to have believed that the music theory he knew was of Egyptian origin rather than Greek, a preposterous idea that nonetheless could have been derived, once again, from Plato.[34] While we still await a comprehensive study of Philo's musical ideas and vocabulary, he should probably be connected to a lesser-known tradition of music theory that was based on the study of the philosopher whom Philo went so far as to call "the most holy Plato."[35]

---

trans. R. W. Sterling and W. C. Scott [New York: Norton, 1985], 95–96). In *Gorgias* (502c; trans. R. E. Allen [New Haven: Yale University Press, 1984], 291) Socrates argues that poetry is a kind of rhetoric, because if it is stripped of melody, rhythm, and meter, the words will remain (Warren D. Anderson, *Music and Musicians in Ancient Greece* [Ithaca, N.Y.: Cornell University Press, 1994], 145–69).

33 Barker, *Greek Musical Writings,* 2:209–29.

34 Following the Hellenistic Jewish belief that Moses "was instructed in all the wisdom of the Egyptians" (Acts 7:22), Philo imagined the following course of study: "The learned ones handed on to him arithmetic and geometry, the rhythmic and harmonic and metric theory, and the whole of music, through both instrumental practice and Egyptian teachings on the arts and other subjects, as well as philosophy through symbols, which are expounded in the so-called sacred writings and through the veneration of animals, which they even worship with honors due to gods. But the other educational curriculum the Greeks taught [him], while people from the neighboring countries [taught him] the Assyrian letters and the Chaldean knowledge of the heavens" (*Mos.* 1.23 [ed. R. Arnaldez et al.; *OPA* 22:36–37]). I am indebted to Brian Noelle for calling my attention to this passage; see also *Prob.* 49–51 (*OPA* 28:176–79). Robert Anderson, "Egypt, Arab Republic of. 1: Ancient Music," in *The New Grove Dictionary of Music and Musicians* (ed. S. Sadie and J. Tyrrell; 2d ed.; London: Macmillan, 2001), 8:1, shows that a number of late antique writers believed Greek music owed something to Egyptian music. Philo could have found such views in Plato, *Laws* 656d; 799a; 819a–c (trans. T. L. Pangle; New York: Basic Books, 1980), 36–37, 187, 210–11. However, the Egyptian culture of Philo's time had already undergone much Hellenization. It is very difficult to see any relationship between classical Greek music and the music of Pharaonic times before Alexander the Great, in so far as the latter can be reimagined from surviving instruments, depictions in visual artworks, and texts. For a general introduction to ancient Egyptian music, see Lise Manniche, *Music and Musicians in Ancient Egypt* (London: British Museum, 1991).

35 *Prob.* 13 (*OPA* 28:144–45). As Petit's footnote points out, in most manuscripts of Philo the word ἱερώτατον ("holiest"), which Philo usually reserved for Moses, has been changed to λιγυρώτατον ("sweetest"). The dependence of Philo's musical thinking on Plato is also emphasized in Feldman, "Philo's Views on Music," 507–17.

From the treatise of Aristides, the most detailed exposition of ancient Greek music theory that follows a tripartite arrangement,[36] it is clear that "rhythmics," or "rhythmic composition," refers to patterns of duration, counted in *chronoi* ("beats") and articulated by the alternation of *theses* (dance steps, hand claps, the sounds of rhythm instruments) and *arses* (the time intervals in between theses). "Metrics" or "poesy" had to do with measuring the lengths of syllables combined into feet, to form Greek quantitative poetry, which was always sung and often danced, never merely spoken as in a modern poetry reading.[37] "Melic composition" or "harmonics" included all uses of musical pitch, beginning with the categories of tuning and including intervals, modes, and what we would call both melody and harmony.[38] In fact most ancient Greek music theorists, following Aristoxenos, called this subject "harmonics" rather than "melody," as Philo did.[39]

The fact that rhythm and meter were so highly developed as to form two distinct branches of music theory may seem strange to us, but it demonstrates "the unity of music, text, and movement that [was] so important to the musical culture of the Greeks."[40] The three elements of poetry, song, and dance combined most fully in the Greek chorus, which played an essential role not only in the classical theater but also in the education of both girls and boys to take their adult places in the *polis*—to be untrained in the choral arts was to be uneducated.[41] Thus it is telling that

---

[36] Thomas J. Mathiesen, "Rhythm and Meter in Ancient Greek Music," *Music Theory Spectrum* 7 (1985): 167; idem, *Apollo's Lyre,* 527, 538–41.

[37] Bruno Gentili and Roberto Pretagostini, eds., *La Musica in Grecia* (Bari: Editori Laterza, 1988), 5–71, 123–218.

[38] Philo, *Somn.* 1.205 (ed. P. Savinel, *OPA* 19:110–11); *Agr.* 137 (ed. J. Pouilloux, *OPA* 9:78–79). A brief outline of the theory of melos or melody, from close to Philo's period, can be found in Vitruvius, *De architectura* 5.4 (trans. Ingrid D. Rowland in *Ten Books on Architecture* [Cambridge: Cambridge University Press, 1999], 66–68, 243–45). This text is the earliest account in Latin of Greek music theory, dating from the first century B.C.E.

[39] Mathiesen, *Apollo's Lyre,* 294–344, 595.

[40] Ibid., 37.

[41] Leo Aylen, *The Greek Theater* (Madison, N.J.: Fairleigh Dickinson University Press, 1985), 114–20; Arthur Pickard-Cambridge, *The Dramatic Festivals of Athens* (2d ed. with supplement; rev. J. Gould and D. M. Lewis; Oxford: Clarendon Press, 1988), 246–62; L. P. E. Parker, *The Songs of Aristophanes* (Oxford: Clarendon Press, 1997); Wayne B. Ingalls, "Ritual Performance as Training for Daughters in Archaic Greece," *Phoenix: Journal of the Classical Association of Canada* 54 (2000): 1–20; Anton Bierl, *Der Chor in der alten Komödie: Ritual und Performativität (unter besonderer Berücksichtigung von Aristophanes' Thesmophoriazusen und der Phallslieder fr. 851 PMG)* (Munich: Saur, 2001); Claude Calame, *Choruses of Young*

the playwright Aristophanes, even before Plato, saw rhythmics and metrics as two discrete subjects.[42]

In the modern West, on the other hand, "music is often informally divided into three domains: melody, harmony, and rhythm."[43] In this scheme meter is a subcategory within rhythm; it is the pitch aspects of music that are so highly developed as to form two distinct categories: melody, dealing with relationships among successive pitches; and harmony, dealing with pitches that are sounded simultaneously. The reason for this is simply that the art of harmony is much more developed among us than it was in ancient Greece, because of our long history of vocal and instrumental polyphony and the central popularity of keyboard and string instruments that can play chords. The Greeks, in contrast, made use of what we would call heterophony: the skilled instrumentalist played an ornamented variation on the singer's melody.[44] One can get a sense of this by contrasting our experience of singing to a chordal guitar accompaniment with Plato's advice on teaching young people to accompany songs on the lyre: he thought they should be taught only the simplest method, in which the lyre-player reproduced the singer's melody note for note, "in unison with the sounds of the song." Plato was opposed to teaching the more complex techniques, "with the strings uttering tunes [μέλη] one way, and the melody [μελῳδίαν] composed by the poet another way," for these involved doing the opposite of what the singer was doing: filling in the melodic skips of the voice with stepwise instrumental passages, playing figurations in short, quick notes while the singer held a longer note, or harmonizing the melody at a higher or lower pitch, by playing "symphonies" (i.e., concordant fourths and fifths) or "antiphons" (i.e., octaves; σύμφωνον καὶ ἀντίφωνον). "No such things should be taught to those who must assimilate quickly.... For the opposites disrupt one another and make learning difficult, whereas the young ought to learn everything as easily as possible, since the subjects that are prescribed for them are neither small nor few."[45]

Women in Ancient Greece: Their Morphology, Religious Role, and Social Functions (rev. ed.; trans. D. Collins and J. Orion; Lanham, Md.: Rowman & Littlefield, 2001).

[42] *Clouds* 635–692, partly translated in Barker, *Greek Musical Writings,* 1:100–101.

[43] Harold S. Powers, "Melody," *The New Harvard Dictionary of Music* (ed. D. M. Randel; Cambridge: Harvard University Press, 1986), 481.

[44] Andrew Barker, "*Heterophonia* and *Poikilia:* Accompaniments to Greek Melody" in *Mousike: Metrica, ritmica e musica greca in memoria di Giovanni Comotti* (ed. B. Gentili and F. Perusino; Pisa: Istituti Editoriali e Poligrafici Internazionali, 1995), 41–60.

[45] Plato, *Laws* 812d–e (trans. Pangle, 203–4); Barker, *Greek Musical Writings,* 1:162–63. See also Mathiesen, *Apollo's Lyre,* 73, 361–62; Barker, "*Heterophonia* and *Poikilia.*"

When interpreting ancient texts, therefore, it is essential to keep in mind these differences between ancient and modern music: in Philo and other ancient writers we encounter a certain ambiguity between melody and harmony that seems confusing to us, for it would be intolerable in descriptions of our own music. However, for them, combining simultaneous pitches (what we call "harmony") was only a way of elaborating a melody, one alternative among a repertoire of techniques a musician could choose from, such as adding melodic ornaments or filling in intervals of pitch or time with accompanying figurations. Thus the same ancient Greek terms can refer indiscriminately to harmonic ("vertical") or melodic ("horizontal") relationships, where we demand greater explicitness.

On the other hand, rhythm and meter were distinguished with a degree of specificity that seems to us too punctilious. Thus, though the Therapeutai composed their songs and hymns "in all kinds of meters and melodies," Philo thought that it was particularly the rhythms that endowed a composition with the requisite solemnity and seriousness, for "of course, they inscribe [them] with very solemn rhythms" (*Contempl.* 3.29). Other Greek writers on both music and literary style make clear that long syllables and long notes were what conveyed a sense of grandeur, seriousness, solemnity, even masculinity, because they called for a dignified, deliberate dance step.[46] Thus Aristides associated "very long durations" with a "calming effect on the mind," a "concern for things sacred" and "sacred hymns." Hence the spondaic meter, in which long durations of equal length were balanced in pairs, recalled "people whose steps are of good length and equal," people who are "stable and manly in character." The slow, even beats suggested a healthy pulse and even a mental state of "good order" that constituted "the health of the soul," in contrast to unequal and faster rhythms that implied more agitated emotional states.[47] This was in fact the meter typically used in the libation hymns that were sung at the beginning

---

46 Thomas J. Mathiesen, "Harmonia and Ethos in Ancient Greek Music," *Journal of Musicology* 3 (1984): 270, 276; M. L. West, *Ancient Greek Music* (Oxford: Clarendon Press, 1992), 157–59, 246–53. Thus the treatise *On Style* (*De elocutione*) by a certain Demetrius, earlier than or contemporary with Philo, states that long syllables naturally convey a sense of grandeur (μεγαλεῖον): Demetrius, *On Style* 39 (trans. D. C. Innes; 2d ed.; LCL 199; Cambridge: Harvard University Press, 1995), 374–75). The much more detailed discussion of the Greek meters by Dionysius of Halicarnassus (first century B.C.E.) makes clear that it is the long durations that imbue a text with worthiness (ἀξιωματική): Dionysius, *On Synthesis* 6.17–18, in *La composition stylistique* (vol. 3 of *Opuscules rhétoriques;* ed. G. Aujac and M. Lebel; Collection des Universités de France; Paris: Les Belles Lettres, 1981), 25–28, 120–36.

47 Barker, *Greek Musical Writings,* 2:485–86.

of the symposium—that is why the spondaic meter is named after the *spondai* or libations.[48]

THERAPEUTAI CELEBRATIONS

The Therapeutai studied and composed hymns for six days, pursuing philosophy—the love of wisdom—without leaving the solitude of their "monasteries." Many of them hardly ate the entire time but were sustained by their songs, like crickets that, so far as Philo knew, subsisted mainly on air, "having strength enough, it would seem, to be nourished by air like the genus of crickets, [their] hunger being alleviated, as I believe, by song [τῆς ᾠδῆς]" (*Contempl.* 4.35).[49] On the Sabbath, however, the Therapeutai assembled in a common sanctuary (also called *semneion*) to hear the teaching of their wisest member. On these occasions they sat in order by age, segregated by gender with a chest-high partition.

However, the most important gatherings for the Therapeutai were their communal banquets, which Philo called *symposia*.[50] Philo emphasized at great length that these symposia were not like those of the Greeks, with their excessive drinking, libations to pagan deities, and ribald entertainment. Just as the New Testament warned against "godless persons..., blemishes on your love feasts as they carouse fearlessly" (Jude 4, 12), Philo

---

48 Aylen, *Greek Theater,* 359; West, *Ancient Greek Music,* 155–56.

49 This idea evidently comes from Plato's *Phaedrus* 259a, which says that crickets were once human beings. When the Muses brought them the gift of song, they were so delighted that they sang incessantly, without thinking to stop for food or drink. As a result they died, so the Muses had them reincarnated as crickets, and they now do nothing but sing (G. R. F. Ferrari, *Listening to the Cicadas: A Study of Plato's Phaedrus* [Cambridge: Cambridge University Press, 1987], 1–2, 28). It would seem that the Therapeutai also were being transformed into a new kind of being that sings (praises) instead of eating.

50 Philo seems to say that the Therapeutai gather every seven weeks, and this has launched all kinds of speculation as to what sort of calendar they may have followed. Some, as early as Jerome (David T. Runia, *Philo in Early Christian Literature: A Survey* [CRINT 3/3; Assen: Van Gorcum; Minneapolis: Fortress, 1993], 315), have thought he really meant the day of Pentecost, which occurs annually as the end, the fiftieth day, of the seven-week period beginning at Passover. Others imagine a calendar divided into periods of seven weeks, which would allow seven such celebrations every 350 days, not quite fitting into the solar year. Parallels with Qumran and Syrian Christian calendars have also been alleged (*The Contemplative Life* [trans. D. Winston; Classics of Western Spirituality; New York: Paulist, 1981], 320 n. 38; Jean LaPorte, *Eucharistia in Philo* [Studies in the Bible and Early Christianity 3; New York: Mellen, 1983], 82–84; Leonhardt, *Jewish Worship in Philo of Alexandria,* 48–50). However, for our purposes what matters is not how often they gathered but what they did there.

wrote that the Gentile Greeks would get drunk and fight all night until someone got hurt. He found even more offensive the luxurious banquets in the so-called "Italian style": lavish with furnishings, bejewelled dishes, and especially comely teenage male waiters, with the guests refraining from pederasty only because, having stuffed themselves to the point of impotence, they could do nothing but drink.[51] Most shameful of all, in his estimation, were the two famous philosophical dialogues involving Socrates, both entitled *Symposion*: the one by Xenophon, which includes the most detailed surviving descriptions of the erotic acrobatics and salacious singing that professional entertainers often provided at these apparently all-male affairs;[52] and the one by Plato, at which the guests held forth in praise of natural and unnatural loves. Both texts were widely read in Philo's time as "models of philosophy," but he lets us know in no uncertain terms that "the disciples of Moses, trained from their earliest years to love the truth, regard them with supreme contempt and continue undeceived."[53]

In spite of all this, the practice of having entertainment during banquets (still familiar to us today) was not inherently objectionable to religious Jews, provided it was entertainment of a morally acceptable kind. For instance, in the *Letter of Aristeas,* a Jewish writing of the second century B.C.E., the seventy wise Israelites who translated the Old Testament into Greek are shown pausing from their work every night of the week for lavish banquets that included profound philosophical discussions with the Gentile king who had commissioned the project. It is the king who asks the questions, and he rewards the men for their sagacious answers with

---

51 The attribution of homosexual behavior to the "Italians," the other great culture of antiquity, parallels the Latin tendency to see it as a Greek vice, see J. N. Adams, *The Latin Sexual Vocabulary* (Baltimore: John Hopkins University Press, 1982), 123, 202, 228; Craig A. Williams, *Roman Homosexuality: Ideologies of Masculinity in Classical Antiquity* (New York: Oxford University Press, 1999), 72. For pictorial evidence of homosexual behavior at *symposia,* see Lissarrague, *Aesthetics,* 33; K. J. Dover, *Greek Homosexuality* (Cambridge: Harvard University Press, 1978), plate R295. On sex and fighting at the *symposia,* see Murray, *Sympotica,* 114, 135–48, 181–82, 190, 201.

52 The passages that are most informative about music are translated and discussed in Barker, *Greek Musical Writings,* 1:117–23. On the participation of women in banquets, see Blake Leyerle, "Meal Customs in the Greco-Roman World," in *Passover and Easter: Origin and History to Modern Times* (ed. P. F. Bradshaw and L. A. Hoffman; Two Liturgical Traditions 5; Notre Dame, Ind.: University of Notre Dame Press, 1999), 43–45.

53 *Contempl.* 63 (trans. F. H. Colson; rev. ed.; LCL 363 [Philo vol. 9]; Cambridge: Harvard University Press, 1954; repr., 1995), 151

drink and "merriment."[54] Indeed for Philo himself the combination of dining and entertainment could support a remarkable allegory: the creation of humankind was like a summons to a cosmic party, with God inviting humans both to participate in a great banquet and to enjoy a wonderful show. The banquet consists of all the good things that the earth brings forth for our use and enjoyment, while the show is the grand spectacle of creation: the mysteries of life and the universe that we explore in the arts and sciences, and particularly the cosmic dance of the stars and planets, which, as Plato learned from the Pythagoreans,[55] were governed by the same numerical proportions as the harmonies of music.[56]

THERAPEUTIC LITERARY AND MUSICAL GENRES

The *symposia* of the Therapeutai began with prayer. Then they were seated in order of admission to the community and segregated by gender, with the young male waiters, who were called "deacons," standing by. Bread and water were prepared, the only items on the menu, for these were people who took moderation to extremes. Everyone became silent and the president spoke, commenting on some point from the Holy Scriptures or solving some problem put to him, talking plainly without resorting to the tricks of rhetoric, masterfully employing the procedures of allegorical interpretation. After general applause he stood up and burst into song, followed in turn by other members of the group. Philo seems to have identified five possible genres for these songs.

---

[54] *Let. Aris.* 182–294 in Moses Hadas, ed. and trans., *Aristeas to Philocrates (Letter of Aristeas)* (Jewish Apocryphal Literature; New York: Harper & Brothers for the Dropsie College for Hebrew and Cognate Learning, 1951), 170–215. Note that at the last meal, on the Sabbath, the king asks, "How ought one to conduct himself in banquets [*symposia*]?" The Jewish sage answers, "One ought to invite lovers of learning and men capable of suggesting what may be useful to the realm and the lives of its subjects—more harmonious and sweeter music you could not find" (286, pp. 212–13).

[55] Plato, *Resp.* 530–531, 600, 616–617 (trans. Sterling and Scott, 224–25, 290, 306–7). A handbook of what we now call "Middle Platonism," dating from shortly after Philo's time, put it this way: "even as the eyes are naturally suited to astronomy, so is the sense of hearing to harmony; and even as in applying our minds to astronomy we are led from visible objects to invisible and intelligible essence, so in listening to harmonious sound we in the same way transfer our attention from things audible to what is contemplated by the mind itself.... For one must pass swiftly from what is visible and audible to those things which may be seen only by the rational activity of the soul" (Alcinous, *The Handbook of Platonism* [trans. J. Dillon; Oxford: Clarendon Press, 1993], 14, 89).

[56] *Opif.* 77–78; 53–54; 69–71 (ed. R. Arnaldez; *OPA* 1:190–93, 174–77, 186–89).

> And finally having risen, he sings a hymn [ὕμνον ᾄδει] made to God, either a new one he made himself, or some old one of the poets of long ago—for they have left behind many meters and melodies:
>
> [1] trimeter verses [ἐπῶν τριμέτρων],
> [2] processional hymns [προσοδίων ὕμνων],
> [3] paraspondees [παρασπονδείων],
> [4] altar songs [παραβωμίων],
> [5] choric set pieces well-measured with strophes and polystrophes [or: with many-twisted turns] [στασίμων χορικῶν στροφαῖς πολυστρόφοις εὐδιαμεμετρημένων].
>
> After him also the others according to rank in proper order, all [the rest] listening in complete silence, except when they have to sing [ᾄδειν] the verse-ends [τὰ ἀκροτελεύτια] and refrains [ἐφύμνια]. For then all, male and female, sing out [ἐχηξοῦσι]. (*Contempl.* 10.80)

Singing by turns was a general practice at Greek *symposia*. After all had sung a paean together, with a libation or wine offering to the gods, each participant was expected to sing or lead a skolion ("crooked") when the myrtle branch was passed to him at random or "crookedly."[57] An oboe-like aulos provided accompaniment, often played by a girl.[58] Finally, a lyre would be brought out, so that those who had learned to play it could provide music of a more accomplished kind.[59] It is important to understand that the hymns and songs of the *symposium* were not necessarily like the beer-hall table-thumpers we (some of us) hear today: they included sophisticated poetry, songs that even in those days were revered for their antiquity, texts that were designed to educate the young male waiters and wine-pourers in the learning of Greek ways. Thus it is possible for a modern scholar to argue that "all Archaic poetry composed for solo delivery ... was in origin intended for the *symposion,*" while ancient authors valued the symposium poetry by cultured,

---

57 Mathiesen, *Apollo's Lyre,* 142; Gentili and Pretagostini, *La Musica,* 238–45

58 Thus a skolion partially preserved in a first-century Egyptian papyrus (*Oxyrhynchus* 1795) included a refrain that began with an address to the piper: "Pipe to me" (Neil Hopkinson, ed., *A Hellenistic Anthology* [Cambridge: Cambridge University Press, 1988, 1999], 80–81, 271–72. For pictures of aulos- and kithara-playing at *symposia,* see Lissarrague, *Aesthetics,* 33, 66, 101, 136; Murray, *Sympotica,* plates 11, 17, 18, 22. On the meanings associated with the aulos, see Peter Wilson, "The *aulos* in Athens," in *Performance Culture and Athenian Democracy* (ed. S. Goldhill and R. Osborne; Cambridge: Cambridge University Press, 1999), 58–95.

59 A. E. Harvey, "The Classification of Greek Lyric Poetry," *CQ* 49 (= NS 5) (1955): 162; Lissarrague, *Aesthetics,* 33, 123–39; Murray, *Sympotica,* plates 2, 11, 19, 20; Parker, *Songs of Aristophanes,* 4

aristocratic amateurs above the technically skilled compositions of professional musicians.[60]

The songs at the Therapeutai banquets had comparable cultic, artistic, and educational associations. Philo says that the president may sing one of his own compositions "or some old one of the poets of long ago," presumably including the biblical psalms. At least some of these hymns were responsorial, with the entire group chiming in at the ends of verses or on the refrains. Let us look at the five genres of "meters and melodies" that the old poets had bequeathed. Three have names that are suggestive of pagan rituals: *prosodia* or processional hymns (item 2) were originally sung while approaching the altar for pagan sacrifices.[61] Upon arriving at the altar one sang a paean: Philo does not mention this genre, but perhaps *parabomion* (item 4), a rare word literally meaning "next to the altar," was a substitute Jewish usage that avoided the paean's association with Apollo.[62] *Paraspondees* (item 3), an even rarer term, may be Philo's way of indicating the dignified, long rhythms of the spondaic meter, while also implying some distinction (*para-*) from the pagan wine libations (*spondai*) at which songs in this meter were sung.

The first and last genres are reminiscent of classical Greek dramas: trimeters (item 1) were iambic lines of three metra, with each metron consisting of two iambic feet.[63] Considered a more elementary kind of poetry closer to speech, it was often used in Greek drama for the dialogue or recitative between the solo and choral songs.[64] Most interesting of all is the *stasimon* (item 5), which I have translated with the modern operatic term "set piece"—it was sung by the chorus in Greek drama.[65] As its name suggests (cf. *stasis*), the chorus would be standing in one place at the time;

---

[60] Murray, *Sympotica,* 177, 294. For more on the poetry of *symposia,* see ibid., 20–22, 135–48, 177–83, 185–95, 221–29, 230–37, 240, 252, 254, 257, 272–76, 289–307.

[61] Mathiesen, *Apollo's Lyre,* 81.

[62] Ian Rutherford, *Pindar's Paeans* (Oxford: Oxford University Press, 2001), 3–136.

[63] D. S. Raven, *Greek Metre* (2d ed.; London: Faber & Faber, 1968; repr., London: Bristol Classical Press, 1998), 27–43.

[64] Aylen, *Greek Theatre,* 357; Csapo and Slater, *Context of Ancient Drama,* 331–32, 334–35; Parker, *Songs of Aristophanes,* 27–35. Cf. the trimeters Philo quoted in *Prob.* 48 and 141 (*OPA* 28:176–77, 236–37). The latter are from a lost work of Euripides.

[65] See Mathiesen, *Apollo's Lyre,* 74, 97, 99, 101–2; Claude Calame, "Performative Aspects of the Choral Voice in Greek Tragedy: Civic Identity in Performance," in *Performance Culture and Athenian Democracy* (ed. S. Goldhill and R. Osborne; Cambridge: Cambridge University Press, 1999), 125–53.

the songs it sang while entering and exiting had other names. However, standing does not mean standing still, for this is a choric set piece, and the root meaning of *choros* is "dance," as in the word "choreography."[66] Thus a certain etymological ambiguity besets the rest of the phrase. If Philo was thinking mainly of the texts that were sung, the strophes and polystrophes would have been well-metered stanzas. However, the word "strophe" originally referred to the chorus's turn in a new direction as it began each new stanza; therefore, the passage could also mean something like "many-twisted turns," if Philo was thinking more of the dance.[67] The Therapeutai actually did dance, as Philo will indicate later on.

Thus Philo's five genres seem to have been listed hierarchically, from the relatively mundane iambic trimeter, through the grand processional prosodion and the even more dignified paraspondeion, finally arriving, as it were, "next to the altar" with a parabomion. The whole then culminated in the stanzas of choric song and dance.[68] If they were actually performed in this sequence, the effect would have been one of growing solemnity, with a graduated increase in complexity. If Philo's use of the rare terms "paraspondee" and "parabomion" were indeed intended to avoid the pagan implications of "spondee" and "paean," it is interesting that he did not object to "prosodion" or "stasimon," even though the ancient Greek

---

[66] Pickard-Cambridge, *Dramatic Festivals of Athens,* 251–52.

[67] On the choral dance in Greek theater, see Aylen, *Greek Theater,* 120–33. For detailed analyses of some stasimon texts, with attempts to imagine aspects of the lost music and dance, see William C. Scott, *Musical Design in Aeschylean Theater* (Hanover, N.H.: University Press of New England for Dartmouth College, 1984), 43–68; idem, *Musical Design in Sophoclean Theater* (Hanover, N.H.: University Press of New England for Dartmouth College, 1996), xiv–xviii, 23, 37–59, 103–14, 127–43, 157–87. Frederick C. Conybeare's translation ("Philo. Concerning the Contemplative Life," *JQR* 7 [1895]: 768) attempts to cover both textual and performance possibilities by rendering "hymns of station or of the dance, deftly proportioned for turning and returning."

[68] Compare the description in the medieval Greek text known as *Etymologicum Magnum: "Prosodia* are songs recited as the offerings are being borne forward to the altar. . . . *Huporchēmata,* in turn, are songs they would recite while dancing and running in a circle around the altar as the offerings were being burnt. *Stasima,* finally are songs they would recite while standing still, resting from their running in a circle around the altar. When they ran around the altar, they would set off first from the left hand to the right, in imitation of the circle of the zodiac since it makes the opposite motion from the sky as it is borne from west to east. They would then go back from right to left in imitation of the sky" (trans. from William Mullen, *Choreia: Pindar and Dance* [Princeton: Princeton University Press, 1982], 226–27).

theater was thoroughly integrated with pagan religious ritual.[69] On the other hand, names of musical genres can be handed down for centuries, long after their original meaning has lost its associations or even been forgotten completely. In our culture words such as "ballad" and "carol" no longer imply dancing, as they did in the Middle Ages. Our "preludes" no longer precede anything, and the symphony has developed well beyond its original function as an opera overture, just as its name has little to do with the ancient notion of "symphony," meaning "consonance." Thus it is possible that the Therapeutai took the pagan origins of their five genres less seriously than we are inclined to do. The metrical and melodic conventions associated with these terms may by that time have become such a pervasive part of the culture that their use by the Therapeutai implied no more religious compromise than the use of Helios, Orpheus, and imperial motives in early Christian art.[70] Nor should we too glibly perceive a precedent for what Catholic liturgists today call "inculturation," worship that deliberately apes popular culture, as in the modern folk mass. We should, rather, keep in mind that Philo, like the church fathers, was extremely critical of the theater of his time as a place that fomented immorality, even though he himself attended plays and knew the works of the great playwrights.[71]

Nor should we forget that the "meters and melodies" left behind by "the poets of long ago" probably included the psalms and other biblical poems. There seems to have been a general belief among Jews who read the Bible

---

[69] Ancient Greek drama grew out of the cult of Dionysos, to which it retained an attachment; see Margarete Bieber, *The History of the Greek and Roman Theater* (Princeton: Princeton University Press, 1961), 51–73; Aylen, *Greek Theater,* 41–87; Pickard-Cambridge, *Dramatic Festivals of Athens;* Jennifer Wise, *Dionysus Writes: The Invention of Theatre in Ancient Greece* (Ithaca, N.Y.: Cornell University Press, 1998), 89–90. The plays included hymns to a wide range of gods (Calame, "Performative Aspects of the Choral Voice"), and the orchestra area, where the choros performed, had an altar located nearby (Clifford Ashby, *Classical Greek Theatre: New Views of an Old Subject* [Studies in Theatre History and Culture; Iowa City: University of Iowa Press, 1999], 42–61).

[70] André Grabar, *Christian Iconography: A Study of Its Origins* (Bollingen Series 35/10; Princeton: Princeton University Press, 1968).

[71] *Agr.* 34–35 (*OPA* 9:34–37); *Congr.* 63–64 (*OPA* 16:148–49). At the same time, Philo admitted that he "often happened to be at the theater" (*Ebr.* 177; *OPA* 11–12:96–97), and he was not above citing the works of Euripides (*Aet.* 5, 30; *OPA* 30:78–79, 94–97) and Sophocles (*Prob.* 19; *OPA* 28:150–51). For much interesting material on this issue in early Christianity, see Christine Catharina Schnusenberg, *The Relationship between the Church and the Theatre, Exemplified by Selected Writings of the Church Fathers and by Liturgical Texts until Amalarius of Metz—775–852 AD* (Lanham, Md.: University Press of America, 1988).

in Greek that the Hebrew originals were equal in artistic quality to the most sophisticated Greek poetry. Philo's near contemporary Josephus tells us that Moses composed his two hymns (Exod 15 and Deut 32) in hexameters, while David wrote the psalms in "varied meters," including trimeters and pentameters.[72] Taken literally, these assertions are false, but the underlying idea seems to have been that the Jewish scriptures lacked nothing, that if Greek poetry could be admired for the artistry of its metrical complexities, ancient Hebrew poetry would somehow prove to be equally "well-metered."[73] Of course, the songs and hymns that the Therapeutai composed in imitation of these ancient models may indeed have followed Greek principles of meter and form, like the Christian hymns of Synesius of Cyrene or Clement of Alexandria.[74] Unfortunately, no extant hymns from this period can be identified as certainly Therapeutic in origin, though some scholars have proposed a Therapeutai background for the *Testament of Job,* a Greek retelling of the biblical story that includes several hymns.[75]

THE HARMONIES OF THE VIGILS

After the supper the Therapeutai kept an all-night vigil, which again is called by the same word used in the Greek Christian liturgy: *pannychis.*[76]

---

[72] Josephus, *Ant.* 2.16.4 §346; 4.8.44 §303; 7.12.3 §305.

[73] On the belief that the psalms were composed in meter, see James L. Kugel, *The Idea of Biblical Poetry: Parallelism and Its History* (New Haven: Yale University Press, 1981), 135–42; Adam Kamesar, "Philo and the Literary Quality of the Bible: A Theoretical Aspect of the Problem," *JJS* 46 (1995): 55–68; Jutta Leonhardt, *Jewish Worship in Philo of Alexandria,* 146. Jean Irigoin ("Le Psaume 26 dans la Septante: Étude de compositions rythmique," in Κατά τούς Ο': *Selon les Septante: Trente études sur la Bible grecque des Septante en hommage à Marguerite Harl* [ed. G. Dorival and O. Munnich; Paris: Cerf., 1995], 287–97, and earlier articles cited therein) has proposed in a series of publications that the Greek translations of the psalms have a kind of accentual rhythm, based on syllable count rather than metrical feet.

[74] Wilhelm Schmid, *Die nachklassische Periode der griechischen Literatur* (vol. 2 of *Wilhelm von Christs Geschichte der griechischen Literatur;* ed. Walter Otto; rev. ed.; Handbuch der Altertumswissenschaft 7; Munich: Beck, 1924), 2:957, 1118, 1311, 1400).

[75] See R. P. Spittler's translation, "Testament of Job," *OTP* 1:829–68. The arguments for a Theraeputai background are given on pages 833–34; they include: prayer facing east (40:3, cf. Philo, *Contempl.* 89), well-developed female characters suggesting an audience that included women, and many hymns (25:1–8; 32:1–12; 33:3–9; 43:4–17; 49–50; 53:2–4). On the other hand, the work also mentions slaves (13:4; 14:4), and angelic languages (48:3; 50:1), which are not mentioned in Philo's account of the Therapeutai.

[76] For another report of Jews holding an all-night vigil until dawn with hymns and odes, see Philo, *Flacc.* 121–124 (*OPA* 31:120–23).

Men and women formed two choirs, each with its own leader. They sang hymns that, like those mentioned earlier, were composed in "many meters and melodies." The description seems to make it explicit that the performance involved dance, gesticulating with the hands but also moving the feet, reaching a heightened emotional level that can be likened to the inspired frenzy of a pagan conjurer or prophet.

> After the supper they do the holy all-night vigil [παννυχίδα]. The all-night vigil is done this way: All stand up together, and in the middle of the symposium they first become two choirs [χοροί], one of men, the other of women. The most honored and also the most musical [ἐμμελέστατος] [individuals are] chosen as guide [ἡγεμών] and leader [ἔξαρχος] for each [choir]. (11.83).
>
> Then they sing hymns [ὕμνους] to God in many meters and melodies, both sounding together [συνηχοῦντες] and also with antiphonal harmonies [ἀντιφώνοις ἁρμονίαις], gesturing with their hands [ἐπιχειρονομοῦντες] and dancing [ἐπορχούμενοι], and performing with inspired frenzy [ἐπιθειάζοντες] now the processionals, now the set pieces, making strophes and antistrophes [or: turns and counterturns] in the choral dance [χορείᾳ]. (*Contempl.* 11.84)

Again we are told that they sang prosodia or processionals and set pieces involving multiple strophes, this time with dancing movements that involved both hands and feet. What is most interesting, however, is the reference to "antiphonal harmonies." A long Christian tradition identifies the word "antiphonal" with singing in alternation, as when one choir sings a psalm verse, the opposite choir sings the second verse, the first choir sings the third verse, and so on. This seems a natural enough interpretation of the verb *antiphōneō,* which can mean "reply," "answer," or even "contradict." However, since Philo used musical terminology knowledgeably, that is certainly not what he had in mind. The word for "sounding together" (*sunēcheō*) or "co-echoing" refers to singing simultaneously: sounding in accord, resonating together, echoing in the sense of "ringing to," not in the sense of alternating back and forth. The expression "antiphonal harmonies" makes this resounding more explicit, for it refers to singing in what we would call "parallel octaves."

The most common word for "octave" in ancient Greek music theory is *diapasōn,* the octave conceived melodically as a succession through all (διὰ πασῶν) eight pitches, plucking the strings of a lyre one at a time in the same way one would now play a scale on the piano.[77] The word *antiphōnon* or "corresponding sound," on the other hand, referred to the

[77] Mathiesen, *Apollo's Lyre,* 245.

octave conceived as a harmony, when two pitches an octave apart sounded simultaneously. Thus when we encounter references to "antiphons" in ancient Greek literature, it is usually in the context of simultaneous singing by men and boys or of instruments with double strings tuned in octaves, as on a modern twelve-string guitar.[78] In short, Philo was describing what naturally happens when men and women attempt to sing in unison: the difference in their natural ranges produces two concurrent renditions an octave apart. With the usual ancient Greek ambiguity between melody and harmony, this kind of singing can be perceived in two different ways: either the men and women were singing the same melody in unison but in different voice ranges, or they were harmonizing at the octave, the pre-eminent consonance in ancient Greek theory, for it had the simplest numerical ratio: 2/1.[79]

The etymology of the word "antiphon" ("corresponding sound") and the very fact that there was a special term for "octave" among the consonances reflect the Greek understanding of what we now call "octave equivalence": the sensation that two pitches an octave apart, though obviously different, sound somehow "the same," so that if one begins at any pitch and then moves up or down an octave, one arrives at "the same" note again. Many world cultures (and reportedly even some animal species) recognize this phenomenon: that is why in modern times we repeat the same seven pitch names, *A* through *G* or *Do* through *Ti,* over and over again as we ascend through every level, so that any two pitches that are an octave apart will have the same name and belong to the same pitch class or chroma.[80]

The acoustical basis of octave equivalence is the simple fact that the higher pitch vibrates exactly twice as fast as the lower one, producing the very Pythagorean 2/1 ratio, closer than any other to perfect 1/1 unity. As Philo's contemporary Thrasyllus put it, "antiphony" was a species of "symphony" (consonance), opposed to "diaphony" (dissonance), because in antiphony the two pitches corresponded across an octave (or a double octave). The fifth and the fourth, on the other hand, were consonant by "paraphony," because the two pitches were similar rather than

---

[78] Ibid., 273–74, 361; Barker, "*Heterophonia* and *Poikilia,*" 44 n. 2. See the theoretical discussion in the *Aristotelian Problemata* 4.17, translated in Barker, *Greek Musical Writings,* 2:92. A modern twelve-string guitar has six courses or pairs of strings: the four lower-pitched pairs are tuned in octaves, while the two higher-pitched pairs are tuned at the unison—that is, to the exact same pitch.

[79] West, *Ancient Greek Music,* 8, 40–41, 224.

[80] Diana Deutsch, ed., *The Psychology of Music* (2d ed.; San Diego: Academic, 1999), 252–57, 350, 398–99, 734–43, 775–76; Bob Snyder, *Music and Memory: An Introduction* (Cambridge, Mass.: MIT Press, 2000), 130–32.

corresponding, their ratios being 3/2 and 4/3 respectively.[81] We know that Philo understood all this, for he made allegorical use of the octave when he wrote that, in the demeanor of the wise person, childlike happiness and joy mix with honorable praiseworthiness, "as if they resonated together [συνηχοῦσαν] in antiphonal notes on a well-tuned lyre, [combining] into a blend of one melody."[82] This passage even uses the same verb (*synēcheō*) that Philo used to describe the Therapeutai singing in accord, co-echoing, or resonating together.

Blending and mixing was, indeed, what the Therapeutai increasingly did as the night wore on. The experience of resonating together produced a profound sense of oneness—not only between the men and the women, but between the Therapeutai and the long-ago Israelites of the exodus, who sang of thanksgiving and victory at the Red Sea, led by Moses and his sister Miriam.[83]

> Then when each of the choirs has feasted individually and by itself, carried away as if in the Bacchic rites by the undiluted wine of the God-beloved [θεοφιλοῦς], they mix and become one choir out of both, a representation of the one set up long ago by the Red Sea on account of the wonders wrought there.... (11.85) Seeing and experiencing this, which was a work greater than word and thought and hope, both men and women together becoming one choir, rapt in ecstasy, were singing [ᾖδον] hymns of thanksgiving [εὐχαριστηρίους ὕμνους] to God the savior, with the men led by Moses the prophet, and the women by Miriam the prophetess. (11.87)
>
> Modeled above all on this, the [choir] of Therapeutai, male and female, with re-echoing and antiphonal melodies [μέλεσιν ἀντήχοις καὶ ἀντιφώνοις], to the low voice of the men mingling [ἀνακιρνάμενος] the high

---

81 Barker, *Greek Musical Writings,* 2:213. The second-century C.E. Alexandrian theorist Ptolemy (*Harmonics* 1.7 [trans. and commentary by J. Solomon; Mnemosyne: Bibliotheca Classica Batava, supplementum 203; Leiden: Brill, 2000], 22–24) has a more technical discussion of the fact that "the octave and the double octave plainly differ from the other concords," though he uses the word "homophone" rather than "antiphon" (Barker, *Greek Musical Writings,* 2:289–90). Porphyry's commentary on Ptolemy 1.6 and 2.3 (Ingemar Düring, ed., *Porphyrios Kommentar zur Harmonielehre des Ptolemaios* [Göteborgs Högskolas Årsskrift 38; Göteborg: Elanders Boktryckeri Aktiebolag, 1932; repr. New York: Garland, 1980], 104, 160) explains that simultaneous octaves "are also called antiphons."

82 *Plant.* 167 (*OPA* 10:100–102); see also *Ebr.* 116–117 (*OPA* 11–12:72–73).

83 On the Song of the Sea as a model for Jewish song and Christian antiphony, see Heidy Zimmermann, *Tora und Shira: Untersuchungen zur Musikauffassung des rabbinischen Judentums* (Publikationen der Schweizerischen Musikforschenden Gesellschaft 2/40; Bern: Lang, 2000), 225–347.

> [voice] of the women, achieves well-tuned concord [ἐναρμόνιον συμφωνίαν] and true music [μουσικήν ὄντως]. All beautiful are the thoughts, all beautiful are the words, holy are the choristers [χορευταί], but the perfection of thoughts and words and choristers is piety. (*Contempl.* 11.88)

The adjectives *antēchois* ("re-echoing" or "countervoiced") and *antiphōnois* ("antiphonal"), constructed with the same prefix (*anti-*) might be seen as more strongly suggestive of answering or alternating verses, especially since they modify the word "melodies" rather than "harmonies." However, this is simply an example of a skilled author striving for variety of expression, for we are told in the very next phrase that the high and low voices mingled, or mixed, with the same word one would use for mixing wine and water in a punch bowl or making an alloy of metals (*kirnaō*). The result is therefore an "enharmonic symphony"or "well-tuned concord," that is, a harmony.[84] After achieving this ideal of "true music," they prayed facing the newly risen sun and went home.

The singing at the Red Sea is mentioned many times in Philo's works, always with a similar vocabulary that describes a harmonic mixture of male and female voices. The most detailed such passage, accurately interpreted, confirms that Philo imagined men and women blending simultaneously, not alternating, as in medieval Christian antiphonal psalmody.

> That is why Moses reasonably honored the [divine] benefactor with hymns of thanksgiving, for he divided the people into two choirs, one of men, the other of women, and himself led the men while he appointed his sister to lead the women, so that they might sing hymns to the Father and Creator, resounding together in antiphthongal harmonies [ἀντιφθόγγοις ἁρμονίαις συνηχοῦντες], through a mixture [κράσεως] of performers [ἠθῶν] eager for the same recompense [ἀμοιβήν], and of melody combined into a consonance [συμφωνίαν] of low and high. For the notes [φθόγγοι] of the men are low, [those] of the women high; from these [notes], when the mixture [κρᾶσις] is made in the right proportion, the most pleasant and perfectly harmonious melody results. All these myriads [Moses] persuaded to be of one mind, and in that [mind] to sing together the same hymn [about] those wondrous mighty works.... Joyous over these things, and seeing the rejoicing of the people, but no longer able to contain his own pleasure, the prophet made the beginning of the song, and those hearing him, assembled in two choirs, sang the aforesaid things with him.[85]

---

[84] On the meaning of *enharmonios* as "attuned" see Theon of Smyrna 47–48 in Barker, *Greek Musical Writings,* 2:212 and n. 4.

[85] *Mos.* 2.256–257 (*OPA* 22:150–1); see also Levarie, "Philo on Music," 128.

Again we are told that the choirs resound together, with the same verb (*synēcheō*), but this time the harmonies are said to be "antiphthongal" rather than antiphonal. The words are nearly synonyms, but *phthongos* ("note") has a more specific meaning than *phōnē* ("sound"). Like the word *antēchois* ("re-echoing") we encountered earlier, either "antiphthongal" or "antiphonal" can mean "answering" or "responding," and this meaning could be supported if the word translated "recompense" (*amoibē*) were rendered "exchange" or "reply." However, *antiphthongos* can also refer to a combination of simultaneous sounds, in which case it could be translated "note against note" or "counterpoint."[86] That this is what Philo meant is clear from his references to "melody combined into a consonance of low and high," from which "when the mixture [*krasis*] is made in the right proportion, the most pleasant and perfectly harmonious melody results." Therefore, one cannot insist that the "performers eager for the same recompense" (they are called *ēthoi,* like the characters of a drama) must have been singing in alternation, as in the later meaning of "antiphonal." They could have been "replying" to Moses' leadership merely by joining in the song or even by singing responsorial refrains. In any case, their participation certainly involved "replying" in the sense of "harmonizing," men and women mixing their respective notes in just the right proportions to produce symphony or consonance.

Philo's most allegorical description of the Song at the Sea does in fact say that the first verse (Exod 15:1) served as "a wondrous refrain beautifully responded," using the classical Greek terms *epode* and *ephymnion*.[87] However, this did not contradict the fact that "two choirs, this of the masculine, that of the feminine household," combined to form one sound, since "standing they will raise the strain [of] a re-echoing and antiphonal harmony" (ἄντηχον καὶ ἀντίφωνον ἀναμέλψουσιν ἁρμονίαν). The leadership of Moses and Miriam, representing the union of Perfect Mind with Purified Sense Perception, was like two instruments struck harmoniously (ἐμμελῶς).[88] Philo

---

[86] Thus, according to Athenaeus, *Deipn.* 14.635b (a literary work that presents itself as an extended *symposium* discussion expanded to encyclopedic dimensions), Aristoxenos interpreted the ψαλμὸν ἀντίφθογγον ("antiphthongal pluck") in one of Pindar's skolia to refer to simultaneous octaves, i.e., "two kinds of instruments together (ἅμα), in octaves (διὰ πασῶν), produce the concerted melody (συνῳδίαν) of men and boys" (Barker, *Greek Musical Writings,* 1:295). Cf. Solon Michaelides, *The Music of Ancient Greece: An Encyclopedia* (London: Faber & Faber, 1978), 21; Mathiesen, *Apollo's Lyre,* 272–75, 361.

[87] The latter word, *ephymnion,* was used earlier (*Contempl.* 10.80) to describe the refrains of the Therapeutai.

[88] *Agr.* 79–82 (*OPA* 9:54–57); Levarie, "Philo on Music," 128. For further allegories related to the singing at the Red Sea, see Dorothy Sly, *Philo's Perception of Women*

may have imagined this against the background of the ancient Greek teacher and leader of the choir, who also handled its expenses and logistics like a modern producer.[89] Elsewhere he likened the role of virtuous people in society to "those leaders [ἔξαρχοι] of force and power, and guides [ἡγεμόνες] of the choir that sings the victory song and thanksgiving hymn."[90] It was no small thing, then, that among the Therapeutai "the most honored and also the most musical [ἐμμελέστατος] [individuals are] chosen as guide [ἡγεμών] and leader [ἔξαρχος] for each [choir]" (*Contempl.* 11.83).

The Therapeutai and the Christians

A common heritage?

As Judaism adjusted to the destruction of the temple, Roman military conquest, and the emergence of an officially Christian empire, the writings of Hellenistic Jewry ceased to circulate among Jews, so that Philo's work was preserved and read only by Christians. His account of the Therapeutai began to attract new attention when it was quoted at length by Eusebius of Caesarea, the early fourth-century "father of church history" who was a friend and admirer of the emperor Constantine. Eusebius was convinced that the Therapeutai must have been a Christian group, because their practices seemed so familiar to him. He therefore enlisted Philo in support of his belief that Saint Mark the Evangelist had preached in Egypt. If Mark had not done so, how could a first-century Egyptian writer such as Philo have described such an obviously Christian organization as the Therapeutai?

> The above mentioned man has given a description of all this in his own writing—which agrees precisely with the manner observed up to now by us alone—of the vigil celebrations on the great feast, the practices associated with them, the hymns [ὕμνους] customarily said [λέγεσθαι] by us skillfully, and how, as one person sings moderately with rhythm [ἑνός μετὰ ῥυθμοῦ κοσμίως ἐπιψάλλοντος], the rest listen in silence and join in singing only the verse-ends [ἀκροτελεύτια] of the hymns.[91]

(BJS 209: Atlanta: Scholars Press, 1990), 105, 111, 112–17, 119–23; LaPorte, *Eucharistia in Philo,* 97, 218; Leonhardt, *Jewish Worship in Philo of Alexandria,* 163–67.

[89] Pickard-Cambridge, *Dramatic Festivals of Athens,* 86–93; Csapo and Slater, *Context of Ancient Drama,* 351–53.

[90] *Ebr.* 121; cf. 115–120 (*OPA* 11–12:72–75).

[91] Eusebius, *Hist. Eccl.* 2.17; PG 20:181–84 = SC 31:77. Translation adapted from *MECL* §208. The proposition that the Therapeutai were Christians was defended by church historians as late as the nineteenth century; see Runia, *Philo in Early Christian Literature,* 227–31. On the possibility that Philo had contact with Christians,

Writers of the century before Eusebius confirm that these practices were indeed widespread among Christians. In Tertullian's account of the Agape or love feast (not the Eucharist), people took turns leading the group, singing either scriptural or newly composed hymns.

> Our meal reveals its meaning in its very name; it is called that which signifies love [*dilectio*] among Greeks [i.e., ἀγάπη]. . . . One does not recline at table without first savoring a prayer to God; and then one eats what the hungry would take and drinks what would serve the needs of the temperate. . . . After the washing of hands and the lighting of lamps [*lumina*], each is urged to come into the middle and sing to God, either from the sacred scriptures or from his own invention [*de proprio ingenio*]. In this way is the manner of his drinking tested. Similarly the banquet [*conuiuium*] is brought to a close with prayer.[92]

Elsewhere Tertullian wrote that the word "alleluia" was sung as a refrain at the verse endings (*clausulis*) of psalms, recalling the responsorial refrains of the Therapeutai. The singing of psalms with an "alleluia" refrain, over a cup of wine at the end of a meal, is also described in Hippolytus, *Apostolic Tradition*.[93] Clement of Alexandria explicitly compared the songs of the Greek *symposium* with the psalmody of Jewish and Christian banquets.

> Just as it is appropriate for us to praise the creator of all before partaking of food, so too is it proper while drinking to sing [ψάλλειν] to him as the beneficiaries of his creation. For a psalm is a harmonious and reasonable blessing, and the Apostle calls a psalm a spiritual song. . . .
>
> And among the ancient Greeks, at their drinking parties [συμποτικάς], a song called the scolion was sung over their brimming cups after the manner of the Hebrew psalms, as all together raised the paean in one voice, and sometimes passed around in order the toasts of song, while the more musical among them sang to the lyre. But let erotic songs be far removed from here; let hymns to God be our songs. "Let them praise his name in dancing [χορῷ]," it is said, "let them play to him on tympanum and psaltery" (Ps 149:3). And who is this singing chorus? The Spirit will explain it to you. "His praise is in the assembly of the faithful; let them rejoice in their king" (Ps 149:1–2).[94]

---

see Birger A. Pearson, "Christians and Jews in First-Century Alexandria," in Nickelsburg and MacRae, *Christians among Jews and Gentiles,* 216.

92 Tertullian, *Apol.* 39.16–18; PL 1:474–77 = CCSL 1:152–53 = *MECL* §74.

93 Gregory Dix, ed., *The Treatise on the Apostolic Tradition of St Hippolytus of Rome, Bishop and Martyr* (rev. H. Chadwick; London: Alban, 1992), 51–52.

94 Clement of Alexandria, *Paed.* 2.4; PG 8:440–45 = GCS 1:181–84 = *MECL* §§51, 55. Eric Werner's attempt (*Sacred Bridge,* 2:122–26) to reconstruct an ancient scale

Thus Eusebius, Clement, Tertullian and Hippolytus, like Philo, attest to the singing of psalms and similar hymns after meals, with individuals taking turns in the leadership roles and with the group sometimes responding by repeating a refrain after the verses. These practices seem to have been a common heritage of Jews and Christians (at least those who spoke Greek); perhaps they were also used by other ancient religious sects, contrary to Eusebius's belief that they were "observed up to now by us alone." However, none of these writers describes alternation between two choirs, and only Philo used any form of the word "antiphon," by which he meant "harmonizing in octaves."

ALTERNATING HALF-CHOIRS

The first Christians to refer to alternating choirs were the Cappadocian fathers, active in the second half of the fourth century. Highly educated, familiar with both Eusebius and Philo, this group was dominated by Saint Basil the Great, his brother Saint Gregory of Nyssa, and their sister Saint Macrina. All were involved in early forms of monasticism, and Macrina was the leader of an ascetic community, including both men and women, that developed in their home. In a well-known letter of the year 375 to the clergy of Neocaesarea, Basil defended the psalmody of such a community against a charge of innovation, describing practices that are not unlike those of the Therapeutai: a vigil service lasting from night to dawn, the singing of psalms in two groups, followed by responsorial psalmody with everyone replying to a leader, after which "all in common" sing a certain "psalm of confession." This may have been Ps 51 (LXX 50), a frequent component of the Christian morning office in contemporary and later sources. It is not clear what, exactly, Basil's opponents found objectionable, but the biggest difference between Basil and Philo is what the two choirs do. Though the Therapeutai men and women sang in octaves, the two choirs in Basil's community sing in alternation, or "counter-psalm to each other."

> Concerning that complaint about psalmody, with which our accusers have intimidated the simpler souls especially, I have this to say: that our customs as now established are in full accord and harmony with all the churches of God. Among us the people [λαός] arise at night and go to the house of prayer; in pain, distress and anguished tears they make confession to God, and finally getting up from prayer they commence the singing of psalms.
>
> [1] At first they divide themselves into two groups (διχῇ διανεμηθέντες) and sing psalms in alternation with each other [ἀντιψάλλουσιν

(the "tropos spondeiakos") on the basis of this passage was completely misguided; see Mathiesen, *Apollo's Lyre,* 357–60.

> ἀλλήλοις], at once intensifying their carefulness over the sacred texts, and focusing their attention and freeing their hearts from distraction.
>
> [2] And then they entrust the lead of the chant [κατάρχειν τοῦ μέλους] to one person, while the rest sing in response.
>
> [3] After thus spending the night in a variety of psalmody with interspersed prayer, now that the light of day has appeared, all in common, as if from one mouth and one heart, offer the psalm of confession to the Lord, while each fashions his personal words of repentance.
>
> Now if you shun us because of these practices, you will shun the Egyptians, you will shun the Libyans as well, and the Thebans, Palestinians, Arabians, Phoenicians, Syrians, and those who live by the Euphrates; and indeed all those among whom vigils, prayers and common psalmody are esteemed.[95]

Gregory of Nyssa's description of Macrina's funeral shows us another vigil, apparently with the male monks and female virgins forming distinct choirs, to which he added the crowds of ordinary men and women who had come to mourn for Macrina. The two choirs seem to have sung simultaneously rather than in alternation, for the result is described as one psalmody out of both sides, well-rhythmed or coordinated, well-tuned or enharmonious, gracefully mixed together through the common song of all, a result that is compared to a professional or institutional chorus. However, Gregory no longer had access to the technical term "antiphon" to describe this phenomenon; the vocabulary of classical Greek music theory was no longer widely understood, even by learned Greeks.[96]

> While we were involved in these activities, and as the psalmody of the virgins, mingled with lamentation, was heard about the place—the rumor of her death, I know not how, having circulated everywhere—all those who lived in the area gathered for the sad event, so that the forecourt was not adequate to house all those assembled. At day-break, when the hymnic vigil [παννυχίδος ... ἐν ὑμνῳδίαις] in her honor was completed after the manner of martyrs' celebrations, the crowd of men and women who

---

[95] Basil the Great, *Ep.* 207 = *MECL* §139 (Saint Basil, *The Letters* [ed. and trans. R. J. Deferrari; 4 vols.; LCL; Cambridge: Harvard University Press, 1926–34], 3:186–91, quote from 186–88). A detailed discussion can be found in Benoît Gain, *L'église de Cappadoce au IVe siècle d'après la correspondance de Basile de Césarée (330–379)* (OCA 225; Rome: Pontificium Institutum Orientale, 1985), 168–79.

[96] On the study of ancient Greek music theory between late antiquity and the eleventh-century revival of Michael Psellus, see Thomas J. Mathiesen, "Hermes or Clio? The Transmission of Ancient Greek Music Theory" in *Musical Humanism and Its Legacy: Essays in Honor of Claude V. Palisca* (ed. B. R. Hanning and N. K. Baker; New York: Pendragon, 1992), 3–35; idem, *Apollo's Lyre,* 641–646.

> had come together for the entire region, broke in on the psalmody with their loud wailing. But I, though my spirit was in so sorry a state because of my misfortune, contrived as much as possible from the circumstances that nothing befitting a funeral of this sort be omitted. So I separated the assembled people according to sex, and mixed the crowd of women with the choir of virgins and the male population with the band of monks, thus bringing about one well-coordinated [εὐρυθμόν] and well-tuned [ἐναρμόνιον] psalmody out of both sides, gracefully mixed together [συγκεκραμένην] through the common song [συνῳδίας] of all, like a professional chorus [χοροστασίᾳ].[97]

The word "antiphon" first reappears in the writing of another Cappadocian, Saint Gregory of Nazianzen (biologically unrelated to the other three). However, he was thinking not of human psalmody but of the heavenly host, classically described in Isaiah's vision according to the Septuagint as singing back and forth in alternation.

> And they cried one to the other [ἐκέκραγον ἕτερος πρὸς τὸν ἕτερον] and said, "Holy, holy, holy..." (Isa 6:3 LXX).

Gregory referenced this familiar scene at least three times in his large corpus of hymnlike poetry. Once he expressed the wish "that the hymn-singing [ὑμνῳδόν] tongue may not be deadened for long, nor your creation silence the antiphon [ἀντίφωνον] of the angels," without specifying what kind of performance "antiphon" implied.[98] Another time he wrote of the "consonant, antiphonal, two-fold company of angels [Σύμφωνον ἀντίφωνον ἀγγέλων στάσιν / Δισσήν] arrayed above and below [ἄνω τε καὶ κάτω]," which company he described in the singular as "hymn-singer [ὑμνῳδόν] of the divine dignity and nature."[99] Here the angels were clearly imagined as one group divided in two, positioned in heaven and on earth, an arrangement inspired by the rephrasing of Isa 6:3 found in the Christian Sanctus: "Heaven and earth are full of his glory."[100] Thus the two half-choirs were evidently crying out "one to the other" across a distance, not singing simultaneously. The word "consonant," therefore, was not used in a technical sense to mean "harmonizing" but with a more casual meaning, such as "sounding good." The words used here for "above and below" are not the

---

97 Gregory of Nyssa, *Vita Sanctae Macrinae* 33, SC 178:246–48 = *MECL* §152. Gregory's *De Virginitate* shows that he knew of Philo's Therapeutai; see Ruina, *Philo in Early Christian Literatuare,* 229, 249–51.

98 From the evening hymn *Carmina Dogmatica* 32, lines 35–38; PG 37:513.

99 *Carmina Moralia* 10, lines 923–24; PG 37: 747.

100 Spinks, *Sanctus in the Eucharistic Prayer,* 19, 54, 60, 117.

terms that Gregory would have had to use if he had meant high and low musical pitches. The word "antiphonal," then, is probably also used in its nontechnical, ordinary Greek meaning of "answering" or "responding," rather than "harmonizing at the octave," as in Philo. This is spelled out more plainly in the third instance, where the angelic choirs sing in opposition, in an "opposed voice," out of which comes the abstract harmony or Pythagorean numerical framework of the cosmos, not the sounding harmony of a musical interval.

> I sing the great God who rules on high, and the splendor of my shining Trinity united into one; the great hymns [ὕμνους] sounding forth from the angelic choirs [ἀγγελικῶν τε χορῶν] who stand close by; from [their] opposed voice [ἐξ ὀπὸς ἀντιθέτου] the harmony [ἁρμονίην] of the world, and a better one to come, for which I hope.[101]

ANTIPHONAL PSALMODY

The application of the word "antiphon" to alternating human choirs is encountered in the early fifth century among writers who sought to continue Eusebius's history. They say that this type of singing emerged in fourth-century Antioch, then spread to Constantinople while Saint John Chrysostom was bishop (398–404), in the context of conflicts between orthodox Christians and followers of the heresy of Arius. Socrates Scholasticus described the two groups competing in the singing of antiphons during the night, though he gave no details about the performance except to say that a eunuch of the empress was hit by a stone while leading the singing of the orthodox.[102]

> The Arians, as I have said, conducted their assemblies outside the city. Each week when the festivals took place—I refer to the Sabbath and the Lord's Day on which the synaxes were accustomed to be held in the churches—they gathered within the gates of the city about the porticoes and sang antiphonal songs [ᾠδας ἀντιφώνους] composed in accordance with Arian doctrine. This they did for the greater part of the night. At dawn, after reciting the same sort of antiphons [ἀντίφωνα], they passed through the middle of the city and went out through the gates and came

---

[101] *Carmina de se ipso* 2.1.34, lines 77–82; PG 37:1313. Translation adapted from Gregory, *Autobiographical Poems* (trans. and ed. C. White; Cambridge: Cambridge University Press, 1996), 170–71. For another translation, see Čelica Milovanović-Barham, "Gregory of Nazianzus: Ars Poetica (In suos versus: Carmen 2.1.39)," *JECS* 5 (1997): 508. Both translate "from opposed voice" as "antiphonal."

[102] Neil Moran, "Byzantine Castrati," in *XXe Congrès international des Études byzantines: Collège de France-Sorbonne, 19–25 août 2001: Pré-Actes 3: Communications libres* (Paris: Diffusion, 2001), 166.

> to the places where they were wont to assemble. Now since they did not cease to speak in provocation of those who held the homoousian position—often they even sang some song such as this: "Where are they who tell of the three as one power?"—John [Chrysostom], concerned lest any of the more simple be drawn away from the church by such songs, set in opposition to them some of his own people, so that they too, by devoting themselves to nocturnal hymnody, would obscure the efforts of others in this regard, and render their own people steadfast in their faith. But while John's purpose appeared to be beneficial, it ended in confusion and peril. Since the homoousian hymns proved to be more splendid in their nightly singing—for John had devised silver crosses, bearing light from wax tapers, provided at the expense of the Empress Eudoxia—the Arians, numerous as they were and seized by jealousy, resolved to avenge themselves and to instigate conflict. Due to their inherent strength, they were anxious to do battle and despised the others. Without hesitation, then, they struck one night and threw a stone at the forehead of Briso, a eunuch of the Empress, who was leading the singers [ὑμνῳδούς] at the time. A number of people from both sides were also killed. The Emperor, moved by these occurrences, forbade the Arians to perform their hymnody in public.

While Socrates attested to the Antiochene origin of antiphonal singing, he evidently had no historical information about it, for he resorted to mythology instead, tracing the custom back to Isaiah's seraphim by way of a vision ascribed to Saint Ignatius, an early bishop of Antioch whose extant writings mention no such thing.

> It must further be told whence the custom of antiphonal hymns [ἀντιφώνους ὕμνους] had its beginning in the Church. Ignatius of Antioch in Syria, the third bishop after the Apostle Peter, and an acquaintance of the Apostles themselves, saw a vision of angels, hymning the Holy Trinity with antiphonal hymns, and passed on to the church of Antioch the manner of singing he saw in the vision. Whence the same tradition was handed down to all the churches.[103]

Socrates could plausibly have linked the spread of antiphonal singing to John Chrysostom, who came to Constantinople from Antioch, but he did not take this opportunity.

Sozomen's account of the same events adds the information that the Arians composed tendentious refrains, for which he uses the same word as Philo and Eusebius: *akroteleutia.*

---

[103] This and the previous quotation from Socrates Scholasticus, *Historia Ecclesiastica* 6.8; PG 67:688–92 = *MECL* §218.

> Since those who follow the Arian heresy had been deprived of their churches in Constantinople during the reign of Theodosius, they held their assemblies outside the city wall. First they gathered at night in the public porticoes, and dividing themselves into groups, they sang [ἔψαλλον] according to the manner of antiphons [τῶν ἀντιφώνων τρόπον], devising refrains [ἀκροτελεύτια] composed in conformity with their doctrine.[104]

Socrates had not used the word *akroteleutia,* though he may have preserved an actual refrain when he quoted the Arians as singing "Where are they who tell of the three as one power?" Quarrels over the theological import of nonscriptural refrains added to the psalms were already occurring in the time of Basil, whose treatise *On the Holy Spirit* was prompted by a dispute over the wording of the doxology we now know as the Gloria Patri, a staple feature of antiphonal psalmody as we know it from later centuries.[105] Sozomen also knew of conflicting doxologies.

> As was their custom, they assembled in choruses when singing hymns to God, and at the end of the songs they declared their individual positions. Some praised the Father and Son as equally worthy of honor, while others praised the Father in the Son, indicating by the insertion of the preposition that the Son played a secondary role.[106]

Theodoret of Cyrrhus, an Antiochene who was more sensitive to music than most church fathers, also wrote that the custom of alternating choirs started in Antioch. However, he was able to name its innovators. There too, the practice was connected with an all-night vigil.

> That remarkable pair, Flavianus and Diodorus, though not yet engaged in their priestly ministry and still numbered among the laity, urged on all, night and day, in the pursuit of piety. They were the first to divide in two [διχῇ διελόντες] the choruses of psalm singers, and to teach them to sing the Davidic song [μελῳδίαν] in alternation [ἐκ διαδοχῆς]. And what was introduced at Antioch spread everywhere, reaching to the ends of the earth. They gathered lovers of holy things into the shrines of the martyrs and spent the entire night with them singing hymns to God.[107]

---

[104] Salaminius Hermias Sozomen, *Historia Ecclesiastica* 6.8; GCS 50:360 = *MECL* §223. Sozomen also saw the Therapeutai as forerunners of Christian monasticism, according to Ruina, *Philo in Early Christian Literature,* 229–30.

[105] Basil, *De Spiritu Sancto* 2.3; Benoît Pruche, ed., *Sur le Saint-Esprit* (2d ed.; SC 17bis; Paris: Cerf, 1968), 256–59.

[106] Sozomen, *Historia Ecclesiastica* 3.20; GCS 50:135 = *MECL* §219.

[107] Theodoret of Cyrrhus, *Historia Ecclesiastica* 2.24.8–9; GCS 44:154 = *MECL* §224.

Until recently, we could not go behind these reports of Antiochene origin. However, Diodore, who died around 390 as bishop of Tarsus, is a figure about whom much is now being learned. As a leading exponent of the Antiochene approach to theology and exegesis, he was the teacher of both John Chrysostom and Theodore of Mopsuestia, but his writings fell into disfavor following the posthumous condemnation of Theodore's works by the fifth ecumenical council (Constantinople II) in 553. Though long out of circulation, Diodore's commentary on the psalms has been recovered, though still only partly published and yet to be translated.[108] The introduction clearly states that Diodore wrote this commentary for the brothers of his monastic community so that they would understand the psalms while they sang them.

> Of this so necessary scripture, then—I speak of the psalms—I thought it right to make a brief exposition of the considerations specifically appropriate to the psalms, and of the literal [κατὰ λέξιν] interpretation as I myself received [it], so that at the time of psalm-singing [ψάλλειν], the brothers would not be able to be led astray by the sounds [ταῖς φωναῖς], nor occupy their thought with other matters from not knowing these things: but having learned to know the order of the words, to "sing wisely" as it is written (Ps 46:8 [47:7])—from the depth of the heart itself, and not superficially from the lips above.[109]

In a later section that has yet to be critically edited and published, Diodore apparently took credit for restoring a "custom of saying antiphons," as if he had revived an ancient practice.[110] His comments on specific psalms sometimes imagined alternating performance: here, for example, is a typically Antiochene exegesis that attempts to place Ps 24 (LXX 23) in a historical context, though it hardly seems "historical" by modern standards. According to Diodore, the psalm depicts the Israelites who, suffering

---

108 Jean Nöel Guinot, "L'*In Psalmos* de Théodoret: une relecture critique du Commentaire de Diodore de Tarse," in *Le Psautier chez les Pères* (Cahiers de Biblia Patristica 4; Strasbourg: Centre d'analyse et de documentation patristiques, 1994), 97–134.

109 Diodore of Tarsus, *Commentarii in Psalmos,* from the prologue; CCSG 6:4. See also p. civ; Louis Mariès (*Études préliminaires à l'édition de Diodore de Tarse sur les Psaumes: La tradition manuscrite, deux manuscrits nouveaux, le caractère diodorien du commentaire* [Collection d'Études anciennes; Paris: Les Belles Lettres, 1933], 152) discusses his own changing views on the translation of this passage.

110 "[A]ccording to the custom of saying antiphons [ἔθος τῶν λεγομένων ἀντιφώνων], now retained [κρατούμενον] by us"; from the introduction to Ps 84 in Diodorus's commentary, quoted in Mariès, *Études préliminaires,* 153. For other Greek and Syriac sources that connect Diodorus to antiphonal psalmody, see ibid., 151–53.

during the Babylonian captivity, greet God their deliverer in alternating antiphonal song.

> RAISE THE GATES, O RULERS OF YOURS! AND BE RAISED UP, O PERPETUAL GATES! AND THE KING OF GLORY SHALL COME IN.
>
> [David speaks] as it were of God their leader, loosing captivity and, having conquered, displaying the captives and entering the bright city for the showing of the trophies, with the people crying, "Raise the gates, O rulers of yours!" He calls them "perpetual gates" [because] they have been closed for a long time. Then, since it was necessary to say such sounds from an antiphon [ἐξ ἀντιφόνου], the other part answers, as it were replying:
>
> WHO IS THIS KING OF GLORY?
>
> Then the other part echoes [ἀντιφθέγγονται]:
>
> THE LORD, STRONG AND POWERFUL, THE LORD, POWERFUL IN BATTLE.
>
> So the others, also, necessarily take up the same sounds [φωνάς] and say:
>
> RAISE THE GATES, O RULERS OF YOURS!
>
> Certainly then, they say, let that be:
>
> AND BE RAISED UP, O PERPETUAL GATES! AND THE KING OF GLORY SHALL COME IN.
>
> The ones who replied before reply back again and say:
>
> WHO IS THIS KING OF GLORY?
>
> So they answer reasonably, having the testimony from the things that were done, and all together cry out:
>
> THE LORD OF HOSTS, HE IS THE KING OF GLORY.[111]

Nor was Diodore the only Antiochene exegete who found the contemporary practice of alternating antiphony attested in the Psalter itself. A long-misdated psalm commentary ascribed to a certain Asterius has recently been shown to have been written in the area of Antioch about 385–410 and to have used the same Antiochene text of the Greek psalms as Diodore.[112] In the comment on Ps 18:3 LXX [RSV 19:2] the words "day to day spews forth utterance" are glossed "as if counter-singing in antiphons [ὡς ἐν ἀντιφώνοις ἀντιψάλλουσαι]."[113]

---

111 Diodore of Tarsus on Ps 23:7–10 LXX [RSV 24:7–10], CCSG 6:141–42. The translation of the psalm is from Pietersma, *Psalms.*

112 Wolfram Kinzig, *In Search of Asterius: Studies on the Authorship of the Homilies on the Psalms* (Forschungen zur Kirchen- und Dogmengeschichte 47; Göttingen: Vandenhoeck & Ruprecht, 1990), 159–68, 223–27.

113 Asterius, *Commentarii in Psalmos, Homily* 29.13 (Marcel Richard, ed., *Asterii Sophistae Commentariorum in Psalmos quae supersunt accedunt aliquot homiliae anonymae* [Symbolae Osloenses fasc. suppl. 16; Oslo: Brøgger, 1956], 234,14–15; Asterius, *Psalmenhomilien* (trans. W. Kinzig; 2 vols.; Bibliothek der griechischen Literatur 56; Stuttgart: Hiersemann, 2002), 2:481. The translation of Ps 18:3 LXX is by Pietersma, *Psalms.* The word ἀντιψάλλω has also been used by Basil's *Ep.* 207 (see above, where it is translated, "sing psalms in alternation").

Conclusion

"The Greeks speak of allegory when something is understood in one way but said in another.... Holy Scripture does not ... repudiate in any way the underlying prior history but 'theorizes,' that is, it develops a higher vision ... without abrogating history."[114] It is not surprising that Antiochenes such as Diodore, so attentive to "history," would have been particularly interested in reviving early Christian practices that they read about in Eusebius and his sources. Ironically, though, the main source of information about early Christian singing would have been the Alexandrian Philo, a major exponent of allegorical exegesis, who was writing about a group that was not even Christian and whose use of technical terms from ancient Greek music theory was no longer understood. As a result, a new practice involving alternation between two choirs was read into Philo's account of men and women singing together, and Philo's term "antiphon," referring to parallel octaves, was understood in its nontechnical meaning as "answer" or "response." Reformers and revivalists throughout history have often made such mistakes. One need think only of the "pastoral musicians" of our own time who seek to depict guitar-accompanied pop songs (mislabeled "folk" songs) as a return to the spirit of early Christian worship. Making this case compels them to discount and ignore the church fathers' relentless polemic against the popular music of ancient times and even more to denigrate Gregorian chant as the degenerate product of a medieval decline and fall, with the stultifying result that the modern program of promoting congregational singing is based on juvenilia most adults are too embarrassed to sing.

On the other hand, thorough study of Philo's terminology makes it possible to trace a remarkable continuity between the music of Hellenistic Jewish worship and medieval chant and to show that the Eusebian rereading of Philo had an important role in shaping Christian musical development. Philo and the church fathers through the third century seem to have shared a Hellenistic musical culture in which much of the singing was connected with group banquets imbued with special religious significance. The bulk of the singing took place after the meal proper and was valued for being in sharp contrast with the idolatrous and lascivious songs that often followed the banquets of polytheists and unbelievers. The repertory included biblical psalms and other traditional texts as well as new compositions, some of which may have imitated the style of the psalms,

---

[114] Diodore of Tarsus, "Preface to the Commentary on Psalm 118," as translated in Karlfried Froehlich, ed., *Biblical Interpretation in the Early Church* (Philadelphia: Fortress, 1984), 87–88.

while others made use of the poetic meters and notions of rhythm and melody that were in use among learned poets and composers of the time. Individuals took turns leading these songs, though a reputation for ethical behavior and musical talent tended to focus attention on certain people as the most suitable leaders. Some songs, but not all, were sung responsorially, with the entire group repeating a refrain at the ends of the verses: the *akroteleutia* or *clausulae*.

In the fourth century another type of singing emerged, in which two choirs sang psalm verses in alternation. This kind of singing often included newly composed, nonscriptural refrains, some of which were challenged as doctrinally questionable or explicitly unorthodox. There may have been more than one reason for the development of alternating choirs: the separation of men and women on different sides of the worship space may have been a factor; imagery of Isaiah's seraphim crying out to one another certainly seems to have played a role. However, fourth-century Antiochene exegetes, reading this type of singing into Eusebius's interpretation of Philo's Therapeutai, began calling it "antiphonal," using Philo's term in its ordinary Greek meaning rather than in the technical sense in which Philo intended it.

Medieval chant, both Latin and Byzantine, preserved all these features, though space does not allow a detailed demonstration here. Leadership of a choir, including the privilege of starting the choral performance by intoning the opening words, continued to be connected with an individual's reputation for virtue and standing within the community. Textual pauses and syntactic breaks—the *akroteleutia* and *clausulae*—were marked by punctuating melismas such as the *differentiae*.[115] Alleluias, scriptural and nonscriptural refrains, and doxologies were interpolated at these points, preserving both the ancient responsorial alternation between soloist and group and the fourth-century innovation of alternation between equal choirs, each with a soloist leader. The meanings of various terms based on the word "antiphon" can be shown to stand in a recoverable historical trajectory from the fourth century: from the full complex of "psalm for two choirs with refrain(s) and doxology,"[116] through "sequence of psalms or verses for alternating performance,"[117] to

[115] Joseph Dyer, "The Singing of Psalms in the Early-Medieval Office," *Speculum* 64 (1989): 535–78.

[116] Adalbert de Vogüé, "Le sens d''antifana' et la longueur de l'office dans la 'Regula Magistri'," *Revue Bénédictine* 71 (1961): 119–24; Robert Taft, *The Liturgy of the Hours in East and West: The Origins of the Divine Office and Its Meaning for Today* (2d ed.; Collegeville, Minn.: Litugical Press, 1993), 94–95, 103, 122–25.

[117] Oliver Strunk, *Essays on Music in the Byzantine World* (New York: Norton, 1977), 112–50, 165–90.

"the refrain itself."[118] After a generation of pretending that what Vatican II called "the treasury of sacred music" stands in diametric opposition to the spirit of early Christian worship, a more exact reading of Philo can demonstrate that the church music tradition conserves significant continuity with the music of the first Christian centuries, while the history of Christian misunderstanding of Philo can remind us of the perennial difficulties and perils involved in interpreting and recovering the past.

---

[118] E.g., Taft, *Liturgy of the Hours,* 118; Strunk, *Essays on Music,* 208–19. There is a large bibliography on the meanings of "antiphon" and related terms, but much of it has become confused due to lack of attention to the musical aspects and performance practice. For example, Juan Mateos, *La célébration de la parole dans la liturgie byzantine: Étude historique* (OCA 191; Rome: Pontificium Institutum Studiorum Orientalium), 7–26, sometimes conflates different categories of psalmody by ignoring their musical characteristics. The example on page 17, for instance, is not called "antiphon" but "stichology" in the sources Mateos cited (the Typikon and Prophetologion of Constantinople). It has long verses performed by soloists; this makes it quite different from the psalms that are associated with the word "antiphon," which have short verses sung by choirs, each choir led by a soloist. One unresolved issue is whether choral psalmody represents a newer practice that widely replaced older solo psalmody, a position argued by Joseph Dyer, "Monastic Psalmody of the Middle Ages," *Revue Bénédictine* 99 (1989): 41–74, who thinks solo psalmody persisted in the West into the eighth century. My position on these issues is still developing but leans toward an earlier emergence of choral antiphonal psalmody in the West; see Peter Jeffery, "Monastic Reading and the Emerging Roman Chant Repertory," in *Western Plainchant in the First Millenium: Studies of the Medieval Liturgy and Its Music in Memory of James W. McKinnon* (Aldershot, U.K.: Ashgate, forthcoming), 45–103.

Finding the Right Key: The Aims and Strategies of Early Christian Interpretation of the Psalms

Brian Daley, S.J.
University of Notre Dame

For the early church, the book of Psalms was "daily bread," clearly one of the most important and familiar books of the Bible. Early Christian commentary on the psalms is more abundant than on any other book of the Hebrew and Christian canon; we still possess partial or complete sets of homilies or scholarly commentaries on the psalms—sometimes more than one set—by at least twenty Latin or Greek patristic authors before 600, and this interest did not abate in the medieval church. The main reason, undoubtedly, was the fact that the psalms were in constant use, both in public worship and in private prayer and meditation.

How the Christian liturgical use of the biblical psalms began remains a matter of scholarly debate. The earliest documentary evidence that Christians regularly sang the psalms at worship comes from the early third century of our era, in the work that is usually called Hippolytus of Rome's *Apostolic Tradition.*[1] Throughout the second century, the psalms were widely used by Christians as a prophetic text from the Hebrew Scripture and seem to have been used also for family and private prayer.[2] Because there is no clear evidence of their liturgical use, however, some scholars have suggested that the earliest Christians may have preferred to sing original compositions in praise of Christ in public worship; in fact, it may only

[1] *Apostolic Tradition* 25 (Ethiopic text with trans. and collation from Ethiopic and Arabic manuscripts: G. Horner, ed., *The Statutes of the Apostles, or, Canones ecclesiastici* [London: Williams & Norgate, 1904]); for singing the psalms at the third, sixth and ninth hours, see ibid., 31–38.

[2] See Clement of Alexandria, *Strom.* 7.7 (psalms as table prayer and prayer before going to bed). See also, from the early third century, Origen, *Or.* 12.2; Tertullian, *Or.* 24–25; Cyprian, *Dom. or.* 34. The best general survey of early Christian practices of prayer is still Adalbert-G. Hamman, *Les trois premiers siècles* (vol. 2 of *La prière;* Paris: Desclée, 1963).

have been the proliferation of such poetry in gnostic circles that led orthodox leaders to decide, around the end of the second century, that biblical psalms be used more regularly as their communities' liturgical song.[3] By the mid-fourth century, at any rate, a synod at Laodicaea in Phrygia could lay down as a canon, "It is not permitted that privately composed psalms or non-canonical books be read out in Church, but only the canonical books of the New and Old Testament."[4]

With the meteoric rise of monasticism and ascetical piety during the fourth century, the recitation and chanting of the psalms grew to be the mainstay of Christian daily prayer, both private and communal;[5] "meditation"—the quiet, ruminative "chewing" on the words of the psalms—was recommended by many spiritual guides as the most effective spiritual weapon against inner demons, a medicine for diseased thoughts.[6] The

---

[3] For a summary of this theory and for further references to the scholarly literature supporting it, see Balthasar Fischer, "Die Psalmenfrömmigkeit der Märtyrerkirche," in *Die Psalmen als Stimme der Kirche* (ed. A. Heinz; Trier: Paulinus Verlag, 1982). See now also James W. McKinnon, *Music in Early Christian Literature* (Cambridge: Cambridge University Press, 1983), 10–11. For a good, brief survey of the development of the liturgical use of the Psalter in the first eight centuries, see Joseph Gélineau, "Les psaumes à l'époque patristique," *La Maison-Dieu* 135 (1978): 99–116.

[4] Canon 59; see E. J. Jonkers, ed., *Acta et Symbola Conciliorum quae saeculo quarto habita sunt* (Brill: Leiden, 1954), 96; Jonkers dates this synod, about which little is known, between 341 and 381. See also Basil of Caesarea, *Ep.* 207.3, for a description of his own congregation's custom of singing the psalms antiphonally during the night vigils; apparently the practice was unusual enough in 375 to elicit sharp criticism from the church of Neocaesaraea in Pontus. Augustine says he wrote a tract against a Carthaginian layman named Hilary, who had criticized the singing of psalms during the eucharistic liturgy "before the oblation" and during the distribution of communion, a custom Augustine says was of recent origin in the Church of Carthage (*Retract.* 2.37, CSEL 36:144). See also Everett Ferguson, "Psalm-Singing at the Eucharist: A Liturgical Controversy in the Fourth Century," *Austin Seminary Bulletin* 98 (1983): 52–77.

[5] The growing monastic use of the psalms seems to have had its effect, in turn, on nonmonastic liturgy; James McKinnon remarks that by the mid-fourth century in the East, "the monastic office virtually inundated the cathedral office with psalmody" (*MECL,* 9).

[6] The fifth-century Latin writer John Cassian insists that the apex of prayer, and indeed of the human spiritual journey, is to be united to God in a total, wordless concentration of mind and heart, free from all material images and concepts (*Conference* 10.5–6). As the first step toward this habitual state, Cassian recommends a version of "meditation" that anticipates later practices of both Eastern and Western Christianity, as well as of some Eastern religions: constantly repeating to oneself the

desert monks seem to have learned large portions of the Psalter, in some cases even the whole of it, by heart and to have chanted the psalms constantly as they worked. Epiphanius of Salamis, the pugnacious defender of orthodoxy of the late fourth century, is said to have chided a Palestinian abbot for allowing his monks to restrict their psalmody to three canonical hours, for "the true monk should have prayer and psalmody continually in his heart."[7] The great sixth-century spiritual guide of the Gaza desert, Barsanuphius, gave familiar, well-tested advice to a young monk who asked how to be freed from the awful slavery of irreligious trains of thought (λογισμοί): resist them forthrightly, throw oneself on God's mercy, confide in one's spiritual director, concentrate on one's manual work. "And as far as the psalms are concerned," he adds, "do not give up studying them, for they are a source of energy; struggle to learn them by heart, for that will be completely beneficial."[8] However, Barsanuphius immediately warns his correspondent against seeking too exalted a knowledge of divine mysteries, presumably through speculation on the meaning of the psalms; he mutters: "As for hearing things that are beyond your powers, don't attempt it; for you have knowledge, for the moment, fitting your own limitations, which will serve you well."[9]

Writers of a more intellectual bent, however, recognized that it was those who used the psalms every day, giving a scriptural voice to their

---

opening words of Ps 70, "O God, come to my assistance; O LORD, make haste to help me!" Since this verse, in Cassian's view, perfectly represents the right attitude of the creature before God, its constant use has a formative effect on the human spirit, as well as practical value for focusing the thoughts. On Cassian's approach to the psalms, see Columba Stewart, *Cassian the Monk* (Oxford: Clarendon Press, 1998), 100–105, 110–13. For general discussion of the use of the psalms in both the common and private prayer of the early monks, see García Colombás, *El monacato primitivo* (Madrid: Biblioteca de autores cristianos, 1975), 2:330–35, 345–46; Lucien Régnault, *La vie quotidienne des Pères du déserte en Égypte au IVe siècle* (Paris: Hachette, 1990), 118–21.

[7] *Apophthegmata Patrum, Alphabetical Collection,* Epiphanius 3 in *The Desert Christian: Sayings of the Desert Fathers: The Alphabetical Collection* (trans. B. Ward; New York: Macmillan, 1980), 57. Theodoret of Cyrus attests to this same practice as his reason for undertaking his own commentary on the Psalter: "For the pupils of piety, both in the cities and in remote places, have all undertaken to focus their minds on the psalms with particular dedication; those who have embraced the ascetic life, for example, recite the Psalter orally by night and by day, as their way of singing the praises of the God of all things and of bringing under control the passions of the body" (PG 80:857D).

[8] Barsanuphius and John of Gaza, *Letter* 215 (Lucien Régnault, trans., *Correspondence* [vol. 1.2; SC 427; Paris: Cerf, 1997], 666–67).

[9] Ibid., 13–15.

prayer and using them as a structuring principle for their daily struggle, who most needed thoughtful and accurate Christian exegesis of the psalms if their *meditatio* was to be different from magical incantation. Diodore of Tarsus, the great Antiochene commentator of the 360s and 370s, gives this as the main reason for his own grammatical labors:

> Since this book of Scripture [he writes in the well-known prologue to his commentary]—I mean the psalms—is so important, I have decided to put together, just as I have myself been taught, a concise explanation of the narrative settings [ὑποθέσεις] specifically corresponding to each of the Psalms, and of their word-for-word meaning, so that in the moment when they are singing them, the brethren may not simply be swept along by the sounds, or find their minds occupied by other things because they do not understand the text; but that, by recognizing the train of thought [τὴν ἀκολουθίαν] in what is said, they may "sing praise with understanding" (Ps. 46:8b LXX), as Scripture puts it—from the depths of each psalm's meaning, and not simply from the top of their heads or the tip of their lips.[10]

The driving concern of early Christian exegesis of the Psalter, in fact, seems to have been somewhat different from that which animated the interpretation of other books of the Bible: except perhaps for the psalm homilies of Ambrose, Augustine, and Chrysostom, its audience seems to have been clergy or monks rather than congregations of "ordinary" believers, and its point was not simply to identify the referent of a particular verse or passage, to find the "prophetic" significance of a text for the Christian reader, but to facilitate the *internalization* of these biblical prayers-in-verse, to enable the reader so to feel and grasp them, as works of divinely inspired poetry, that the reader's own thoughts and emotions, desires and passions, might be purified and transformed. Only if this could be achieved would the psalms really succeed in healing the heart of its ills and driving away its demons.

In its overall aims and methods, of course, ancient Christian exegesis of the psalms rested on the same assumptions and used the same general strategies of interpretation as all Christian biblical exegesis. It assumed, first and foremost, that God is ultimately real—transcending ordinary experience but actively present in all human history and so actively involved in both the composition and the interpretation of the scriptural text. Just as

---

[10] Diodore of Tarsus, *Comm. Ps., Prologue* (CCSG 6:4.33–42). Diodore's more "centrist" heir in the Antiochene tradition of exegesis, Theodoret of Cyrus, expresses a similar concern in the preface to his commentary on the psalms (PG 80:857A–860A); see also Athanasius, *Ep. Marcell.* 1 and 33 (PG 27:12A, 45C).

the divine artistry is constantly involved in the creation and continuance of the world, even down to the tiniest leaf and insect, Origen observes in his preliminary remarks on the first psalm,

> so we must realize, with regard to everything written under the inspiration of the Holy Spirit, that the divine providence which has bestowed superhuman wisdom on the human race through the written word has sown, one might say, saving oracles [λόγια σωτήρια] in every letter—footprints of Wisdom, to the degree that that is possible.[11]

Second, ancient Christian exegesis from Origen on assumed that these inspired Scriptures formed a single book that told, together, a single story of creation, instruction, judgment, and salvation by a single God; thus, if one confessed Jesus to be the Messiah longed for by Israel, the promised Savior who brought to fulfillment God's historical campaign to form for himself a holy people, one was justified in seeing Jesus as the ultimate referent, the "bottom line," in every book and every verse of the whole collection.[12] Third, early Christian interpreters certainly recognized, in varying degrees, that the Scriptures were written in a variety of particular times and places, by particular authors, about particular people and events; far from being unimportant, that particularity provided the "plain sense" on which all interpretation, all discovery of "deeper" or more "spiritual" references, had to be based.[13] Nonetheless, most of them also assumed that the *meaning* of any given passage in the Bible is not simply its reference to the author's own world, its "original" intentionality, but that it also involves *us:* the preacher, the hearer, the community that receives it as part of God's Word. So the task of the interpreter was not simply to reconstruct the *Sitz im Leben* of the "original" version of the text but also to point out its *Sitz in unserem Leben,* the relevance for the community's faith and life that was seen as shaping the text's ultimate meaning within the whole Bible.

Fourth, and most strikingly, early Christian exegetes tended to speak of their task—in language reminiscent of the mystery cults—as that of

---

[11] *Philoc.* frag. 2.4.19–24 (Marguerite Harl, trans., *Sur les Écritures: Philocalie, 1–20* [SC 302; Paris: Cerf, 1983], 246, 11–13).

[12] For a classic statement of this understanding of the Scriptures, see Origen, *Comm. Jo.* 1.6–15; cf. Irenaeus, *Haer.* 4.1–15, 22–26.

[13] See, e.g., Origen, *Princ.* 4.3.4; for a more emphatic insistence on the necessity of searching out the original situation in the narrative (ἱστορία) of Israel to which a given passage in the Bible refers, in order to avoid an arbitrary and "pagan" style of exegesis by ἀλληγορία, see again Diodore's preface to his *Commentarii in Psalmos* (CCSG 6:7.124–132)

penetrating divine secrets: all Scripture, as Origen says in the passage on Ps 1 we have already quoted, is a "locked door" that only "the key of David" can open, a scroll whose seal only the "lamb who was slain" can break.[14] What some may think of as mere literary obscurities, Cassiodorus later insists, often "bear the secret sign of a great mystery."[15] Borrowing Origen's image, Jerome compared the book of Psalms to a house full of locked rooms for which all the keys lie scattered and hopelessly confused; the exegete's task is to enter the house by the "great door" of the Holy Spirit and then to sort through the keys to the "mysteries" of the individual psalms, matching each of them to the right door.[16] The point of such language is not simply to suggest that the central meaning of the psalms, or of any scriptural text, may be difficult to come by but also to describe the quest itself in religious, even mystagogical terms. So Hilary writes, at the beginning of his homily on Ps 13:

> We ought not to treat Scripture with the vulgar familiarity of our ordinary speech; rather, when we speak of what we have learned and read, we should give honor to the author by our care for the way we express ourselves.... Preachers must think that they are not speaking to a human audience, and hearers must know that it is not human words that are being offered to them, but that they are God's words, God's decrees, God's laws. For both roles, the utmost reverence is fitting.[17]

These assumptions lay behind all early Christian biblical interpretation, even though they were applied by different interpreters in very different ways. The Psalter, however, presented distinctive problems for interpretation and called for distinctive strategies: above all, because it is not a book of continuous narrative or instruction but a collection of *poems*. Early Christian commentators on Scripture were virtually all highly trained in the grammatical and rhetorical skills of classical *paideia* and realized that poetry is a distinctive use of language, designed to speak to the feelings as well as to the mind, to "beguile" or "divert" (ψυχαωγεῖν) as well as to

---

[14] *Philoc.* frag. 2.1.1–10 (Harl, *Sur les Écritures*, 240).

[15] *Exp. Ps., praefatio* 9 (CCSG 97:3.9).

[16] Jerome, *Tract. Ps. 1* (CCSL 78:3.1–9), alluding to Origen, *Philoc.* frag. 2.3.1–12 (Harl, *Sur les Écritures*, 244), where the image of the "houseful of locked rooms" is applied to the Bible as a whole; see also Hilary of Poitiers, *Instr. Ps.* 5–6 (CCSL 61:6–8), who takes from the same text of Origen the more general image of the risen Christ as the only "key" who can unlock the meaning of the Bible, "through the mystery of his incarnation and his divinity" (ibid., 8, lines 32–33).

[17] *Tractatus super Psalmos* 13.1 (CCSG 91:76.3–6, 21–24).

inform.[18] A common way of referring to this effect in the ancient world was to speak of the "delight" or "sweetness" that the hearer of poetry was intended to drink in—either as added motivation for taking to heart a poem's intended lesson or simply as a poem's ultimate purpose.[19] The ancient theorist of literary criticism usually known as "Longinus" spoke in somewhat more exalted terms of the "sublimity" or exalted character of the very best classical texts: their ability, recognized only by a person of great experience, to "lift up the soul" and fill it with "joy and exultation," giving it food for lasting thought and making "a strong and ineffaceable impression on the memory."[20]

Patristic commentators, in this same tradition, tended to speak of the Psalter as characterized not primarily by its contents—which often simply mirrored or summarized what is said more at length in the Bible's narrative, prophetic, and wisdom books—but by its "sweetness," its beguiling effect. "Although every part of holy Scripture breathes forth the graciousness [*gratiam*] of God," Ambrose writes (perhaps paraphrasing 2 Tim 3:16), "the book of Psalms is especially sweet."[21] So other biblical figures—Moses, Miriam, Anna—occasionally burst into song, Ambrose observes, but David was chosen by God to do continually, in an entire biblical book, what the others do only rarely[22] and so helps us fulfill our natural desire as creatures to find delight (*delectatio*)

---

[18] For a discussion of the various theories held by ancient theorists on the relative importance of teaching and ψυχαγωγία in poetic diction, see Donald A. Russell, *Criticism in Antiquity* (Berkeley and Los Angeles: University of California Press, 1981), 94–95. For the Epicurean Philodemus's discussion of this issue, see Michael Wigodsky, "The Alleged Impossibility of Philosophical Poetry," in *Philodemus and Poetry* (ed. D. Obbink; New York: Oxford University Press, 1995), 66–69.

[19] See the famous dictum of Horace, *Ars* 343–344: "omne tulit punctum qui miscuit utile dulci, / lectorem delectando pariterque monendo." Horace here reflects more of the Stoic insistence that poetry should also have a moral and didactic purpose than the usual Epicurean view that poetry is simply for amusement. Even Cicero seems to have assumed that poetry, unlike good rhetorical prose, is simply devised to please the ears by its sounds and meter (*De or.* 162). Philodemus, however, the Epicurean thinker who exercised a great deal of influence on the Augustan literary world, seems to have shared Horace's position and may well have inspired much of his *Ars poetica;* see Wigodsky, "Alleged Impossibility of Philosophical Poetry," 67, and the further references there.

[20] Longinus, *[Subl.]* 6 in *Classical Literary Criticism* (ed. D. Russell and M. Winterbottom; World's Classics; Oxford: Oxford University Press, 1989), 148.

[21] *Explanatio Psalmi* 1.4 (Luigi Franco Pizzolato, ed., *Sancti Ambrosii Episcopi Mediolanensis Opera* 7 [Milan: Bibliotheca Ambrosiana; Rome: Città Nuova, 1980], 40).

[22] Ibid., 6 (Pizzolato, *Opera* 7, 42).

in praising God.[23] Basil of Caesarea stresses the paedagogical, medicinal effect of this aesthetic dimension of the psalms:

> When the Holy Spirit saw that the human race was guided only with difficulty toward virtue, and that, because of our inclination toward pleasure, we were neglectful of an upright life, what did he do? The delight of melody he mingled with the doctrines, so that by the pleasantness and softness of the sound heard we might receive without perceiving it the benefit of the words, just as wise physicians who, when giving the fastidious rather bitter drugs to drink, frequently smear the cup with honey.[24]

At the beginning of a homily, no longer completely preserved, on Ps 41 (42), John Chrysostom speaks in a similar vein of the providential work of the Holy Spirit in "mixing melody with prophecy" by causing the psalms to be written and so drawing recalcitrant human minds to the "philosophic life" by the allure of pleasure:

> For nothing so arouses the soul, gives it wing, sets it free from the earth, releases it from the prison of the body, teaches it to love wisdom, and to condemn all the things of this life, as concordant melody and sacred song composed in rhythm.[25]

The task of the early Christian exegete, then, was clearly not only a matter of reading the psalms for their content as moral instructions or prophecies or as witnesses to the long divine narrative that would culminate in the story of Christ and the church but also to read them as poems—and that meant using all the analytical tools and theoretical principles that ancient literary criticism, the art and science of γραμματική, had developed for interpreting and judging secular verse.

The study called "grammar," in the ancient Greek and Roman world, after all, was understood to be principally the art of organized literary exegesis: explaining the meaning of a classic literary work, usually a poetic

---

[23] Ibid., 1–2: "Delight is something natural." On the transforming effect of the psalms' beauty and sweetness on the one who prays, see also Cassiodorus, *Exp. Ps., Prefatio* (CCSL 97:4.39–6.120). On the idea that the pleasure of singing is "natural to the soul," see John Chrysostom, *Homily-Fragment on Psalm 41* 1 (PG 55:157).

[24] Basil, *Homily on Psalm 1* 1 (PG 29:212 B1–9; Agnes Clare Way, trans., *Exegetic Homilies* [FC 46; Washington, D.C.: Catholic University of America Press, 1963], 152). A similar thought appears in the homily "On the Benefit of Singing the Psalms" (*De psalmodiae bono* 5) by Augustine's Dacian contemporary, Niceta of Remesiana (Andrew E. Burn, ed., *Niceta of Remesiana: His Life and Works* [Cambridge: Cambridge University Press, 1905], 73.4–10).

[25] *On Psalm 41* 1 (PG 55:157; *MECL* §80).

text: epic, tragedy, or comedy; analyzing prose classics was considered the parallel work of the rhetorician. Such exegesis moved principally on a linguistic level, beginning often with an explanation of difficult words—proper names, dialect forms, unusual metaphors or allusions—but would also include a wider discussion of the passage's narrative content, its "plot" or ὑπόθεσις. The crowning moment of the grammarian's skill, however—what won his art the name "criticism"—was thought by many to be his "judgment" (κρίσις) of the poem's or the passage's value as a whole.[26] Dionysius of Halicarnassus, the antiquarian and critic active at Rome in the mid-first century B.C.E., wrote a whole essay "On the Examination of Speeches," in which he tried to elaborate criteria for judging the value of prose works by objective standards rather than simply being "led along" (ψυχαγωγοῦμεθα) by the authors' reputations.[27] For philosophically sophisticated critics, this involved commenting not simply on the success of its formal composition—the "arrangement" or σύνθεσις of its images, sounds, and rhythms—but also on its ideas, its moral implications, the example and "teaching" it offered. In fact, it was in such judgment of the philosophic and ethical worth of classical epic poetry that the Stoic art of allegorical interpretation was developed.[28]

---

[26] For references to the use of critical judgment, see, e.g., Sextus Empiricus, *Math.* 1.248; Quintilian, *Inst.* 10.1.40. "Longinus," in the passage referred to above (note 20), remarks that "literary judgment comes only as the final product of long experience" (Russell and Winterbottom, *Classical Literary Criticism,* 148). On the actual practice of some ancient critics in making literary judgments, see J. W. H. Atkins, *Literary Criticism in Antiquity* (2 vols.; Cambridge: Cambridge University Press, 1934), 1:107–16 (Aristotle); 2:39–43 (Cicero), 92–96 (Horace).

[27] Dionysius of Halicarnassus, "On the Examination of Speeches" (περὶ λόγων ἐξετάσεως): *Rhet.* 11 (Hermann Usener and Ludwig Rademacher, eds., *Dionysii Halicarnassi opera* [Leipzig: Teubner, 1904], 2:374–87).

[28] For a description of the intentions and techniques of classical grammarians, see the old but still comprehensive account of Henri-Irénée Marrou, *Histoire de l'éducation dans l'Antiquité* (6th ed.; Paris: Seuil, 1965), 1:250–57 (Greece); 2:81–85 (Rome). On the allegorical interpretation of Homer and other classical texts by philosophically minded grammarians, see Robert Lamberton, *Homer the Theologian* (Berkeley and Los Angeles: University of California Press, 1986), esp. 1–43. On the importance of intellectual as well as aesthetic judgments of poetry, see especially Philodemus, *On Poems* 27 (ed. Richard Janko [Oxford: Oxford University Press, 2000], 215); 151 (ibid., 361); etc. Philodemus constantly argues against the earlier grammarians he calls "the Κριτικοί," whom he accuses of judging poetry solely by its sound; for discussion, see ibid., 120–28; cf. James Porter, "Content and Form in Philodemus: The History of an Evasion," in *Philodemus and Poetry* (ed. D. Obbink; New York: Oxford University Press, 1995), 139–41.

Christian interpreters of the psalms were all influenced, if in varying degrees, by the classroom practice of professional grammarians. Some, like the fourth-century Antiochene exegete Diodore of Tarsus or the sixth-century scholar-bureaucrat Cassiodorus, closely followed the formal procedures of grammatical commentary in their approach to the psalms. Diodore begins his treatment of each psalm with a brief statement of the poem's ὑπόθεσις or theme and makes a conjecture on its probable original setting within the narrative history of Israel; he then moves on to give terse explanatory paraphrases of the "plain sense" of each verse, understood within that historical setting. Cassiodorus, ever the humanist, offers a much more technical, self-consciously academic commentary on each psalm: beginning with a discussion of its number and *titulus* (if there is one); then moving on to a brief analysis of its literary structure and of the presumed speakers to whom various sections can be assigned; then on to a verse-by-verse, often word-by-word explanation of its meaning, frequently identifying the etymologies of significant words and the logical and rhetorical figures he discovers; finishing with his own *conclusio,* in which he offers his judgment of the psalm's importance and summarizes its theological and spiritual "message" for the Christian user. All of this was, in his view, a way of demonstrating the unique *eloquentia,* the heart-transforming beauty, of these biblical poems.[29]

In the introductions—a standard feature of the grammatical genre—to their commentaries or sets of homilies on the psalms, patristic exegetes tended to concern themselves with the sort of general literary questions any grammarian might address in beginning to comment on a body of poems: the unity and arrangement of the collection, its authorship and historical origin, and the peculiar significance of the "titles" or "inscriptions" that are attached to many of them in both the Hebrew and Greek traditions. The answers they gave to these questions varied widely. Diodore, for instance—ever sceptical of attempts to find deeper significance in the apparent incoherences of the Bible—assumed that the psalms had all been written by David and that they referred prophetically to specific events—whether past, present, or future—in Israel's history.[30] However, he argued

[29] See Cassiodorus, *Exp. Ps., Praefatio* 15 (CCSL 97:18–21), on the distinctive "eloquence" of all Scripture; *Exp. Ps., Praefatio* 16 (CCSL 97:21–22), on the particular eloquence of the Psalter.

[30] The Antiochene commentators' attempts to see each psalm as referring to some concrete situation within the history of Israel in some ways resembles the practice of early rabbinic commentators, as represented in the somewhat later (ninth–tenth century) *Midrash Tehillim.* Braude remarks, in the introduction to his translation of this commentary, "For the authors of Midrash Tehillim, historical past, present and future are rolled up into God's single and all embracing vision of

that the present ordering of the psalms was haphazard and that the "titles" represented simply the pious guesswork of later editors.[31] Hilary of Poitiers, on the other hand, as well as Theodoret of Cyrus and later Cassiodorus, were convinced that the present arrangement and numbering of the psalms and the "titles" given to particular psalms, although certainly the work of later editors and of the Greek translators of the Septuagint, also were due to the inspiration of the Spirit and are an essential part of the psalms' full significance.[32] In fact, the numbering and ordering of the psalms were, in Cassiodorus's view, a constitutive element of the "particular eloquence of the Psalter," challenging the reader to divine the meaning of each psalm's number in relation to the text. For these commentators, as for Gregory of Nyssa in his elaborate treatise on the titles of the psalms, the Psalter as a whole was a kind of detailed map for growth in Christian holiness: in Hilary's phrase, an image of the *dispensatio salutis nostrae.*[33] Gregory of Nyssa, as later Jerome, took seriously the traditional Hebrew division of the Psalter into five parts or "books," perhaps in imitation of the Torah, each part ending with a solemn "Amen and Amen."[34] Hilary, on the other hand, followed by Cassiodorus, rejects this view and prefers—on the scriptural authority of Acts 1:20, which refers to "the book of Psalms"—to consider the Psalter a single whole, conceived in three units of fifty poems corresponding to the biblical years of Jubilee and hinting together at three stages of ascent in the spiritual life toward "our blessed hope," the eternal Sabbath.[35]

More important, even, than decoding the structure and order of the Psalter, for early Christian interpreters, was the task of identifying its peculiar effectiveness in guiding its users along this path of spiritual growth, as

---

things, a glimpse of which he occasionally vouchsafes to Patriarchs, kings and prophets who move through the pages of Scripture." (William G. Braude, trans., *The Midrash on Psalms* [2 vols.; Yale Judaica Series 13; New Haven: Yale University Press, 1959], 1:xxiv).

[31] *Comm. Ps., Prologue* 107–108, 120–22 (CCSG 6:6).

[32] So Hilary, *Instr. Ps.* 8 (CCSL 61:9). Theodoret, *Commentary on the Psalms, Prologue* (PG 80:864 A1–B6), does not want to discard the titles, precisely because of their presence in the Septuagint, though he admits his uncertainty about their origin.

[33] See Hilary, *Instr. Ps.* 9, 11 (CCSL 61:9–11); Gregory of Nyssa, *On the Inscriptions of the Psalms* 1.5–8 (37–112); Cassiodorus, *Exp. Ps., Praefatio* 16 (CCSL 97:21–22).

[34] Gregory of Nyssa, *Inscriptions* 1.5 (37); Jerome, *Comm. Ps. 40;* see Cassiodorus, *Exp. Ps., Praefatio* 12 (CCSL 97:15).

[35] Hilary, *Instr. Ps.* 10–11 (CCSL 61:10); Cassiodorus, *Exp. Ps., Praefatio* 12 (CCSL 97:15).

poetry written to be prayed and sung. In this regard, perhaps the fullest and most original treatment of the distinctive working of the psalms was Athanasius's *Letter to Marcellinus on the Interpretation of the Psalms,* a work so highly valued in antiquity that it was included in the early-fifth-century Codex Alexandrinus of the Greek Bible, as an introduction to the book of Psalms. Athanasius presents his essay as embodying the teaching he received from "a scholarly old man"[36]—presumably an *abba* from the Egyptian desert. By this device, he situates his own explanation of the peculiar character and "grace" of the Psalter within the thought world of monastic prayer. Athanasius begins by suggesting, as Basil of Caesarea would also do, that the actual thematic content of the psalms is not really different from that of the other books of the Hebrew Bible but rather "contains in itself what is found in all of them, like a garden, and expresses this in song."[37] What is distinctive about the Psalter in relation to other books is its more personal element, which allows the reader to identify the message with his or her inmost feelings: "It contains within itself the movements of each soul, their changes and adjustments, written out and thoroughly portrayed, so that if someone should wish to grasp himself from it, as from an image, and to understand on that basis how to shape himself, it is written there."[38]

The point of portraying the whole range of human spiritual "movements" or emotions, Athanasius goes on to explain, is not simply poetic imitation—Aristotle's μίμησις—but *therapy.* The person who recognizes his own inner state in the psalms "can possess from this, once again, the image contained in the words, so that he does not simply hear them and move on, but learns what one must say and do to heal one's disordered feelings."[39] The psalms, in other words, do not simply command us to repent of our sins, to bear suffering patiently, or to praise God for his gifts; they actually give us the words by which we can come to say and do these things for ourselves.[40]

> For this, once again, is the curious thing about the psalms: that in reading the other books lectors tend to proclaim the sayings of the holy

---

[36] *Ep. Marcell.* 1 (PG 27:12).

[37] Ibid., 2 (PG 27:12); see Basil of Caesarea, *Homily on Psalm 1* 1 (PG 29:212 A4–9).

[38] Athanasius, *Ep. Marcell.* 10 (PG 27:20), following the suggestion of the eighteenth-century editor, Johann Ernst Grabe, to read ἀπ' εἰκόνος instead of ἄπειρον. Unfortunately, there is not yet a critical edition of this important treatise; Migne's collection reprints Grabe's scholarly but obsolete edition (Venice, 1707), based on the Codex Alexandrinus of the Bible.

[39] Ibid.

[40] Ibid. (PG 27:21).

> authors, whatever subjects they are talking about, as concerning those about whom the books are written, and listeners understand that they themselves are different people from those dealt with in the text.... But while the person who takes up this book will certainly marvel, in the same way as in other books, at the prophecies concerning the Savior, and will make an act of adoration and read on, still he will read out the rest of the psalms as if they are his own words; and the one who hears them will be deeply moved, as if he himself were speaking, and will be affected by the words of these songs as if they were his own.[41]

Athanasius's argument, in this central section of his work, is that in becoming "like a mirror to the one singing them,"[42] the psalms act as a providential corrective to the imbalance of our desires and emotions. In hearing and singing them as our own prayers, in recognizing our present needs and deepest longings in them, we allow them subtly to reshape our inner life to conform with God's own Word, "for what psalm-singers express in words can become forms and models of ourselves."[43] Athanasius also recognizes in this mimetic, modeling role of the psalms an anticipation of the healing effect of the incarnation: just as the Word, in becoming one of us, not only taught us how to live by his words, but "did what he taught," providing us with a living image of "perfect virtue" in his own life,

> for the same reason, even before his life among us, he made this resound from the lips of those who sing the psalms. Just as he revealed the model of the earthly and the heavenly human being in himself, so also anyone who wishes can learn in the psalms about the motions and conditions of souls, and can find in them the remedy and corrective measure for each of these motions.[44]

Toward the end of the treatise, Athanasius draws on Hellenistic music theory to argue that the reason the psalms are sung, and not simply read—besides the fact that this adds "breadth" and solemnity to our praise of God—is to enable them to create a harmony and order in our inner selves that parallels the harmony that the Logos, as Creator and sustainer, perpetually secures in the universe.[45]

---

[41] Ibid., 11 (PG 27:21); Athanasius is thinking of the liturgical chanting of the psalms by a cantor. John Cassian also describes, albeit briefly, the same process of discovering one's own feelings mirrored in the psalms, which enables us to perceive the psalms as expressing our own experience (*Conferences* 10.11.6).

[42] Athanasius, *Ep. Marcell.* 12 (PG 27:24).

[43] Ibid.

[44] Ibid. (PG 27:25).

[45] Ibid., 27 (PG 27:40).

> For just as we recognize the thoughts of the soul, and signify them through the words [of the psalms] we utter, so the Lord wishes that the song that springs forth from the words should be a symbol of spiritual harmony in the soul, and has decreed that the odes be sung to melodies, and the psalms also be chanted musically.[46]

Gregory of Nyssa, in his treatise *On the Titles of the Psalms,* written a few decades after Athanasius's work, elaborates this point at much greater length, comparing the "music" produced by the order of the whole cosmos with the inner harmony of the well-ordered, virtuous human person: "the philosophy that comes through melody."[47] The psalms are given to us precisely as a way of restoring and preserving that "microcosmic" order of mind and body by the "sweetness" of poetry and music.

> Since everything which is in accord with nature is pleasing to nature, and since the music which is in us has been shown to be in accord with nature, for this reason the great David combined singing with philosophical instruction concerning the virtues, thereby pouring the sweetness of honey, as it were, over these sublime teachings. In this singing, nature reflects on itself in a certain manner, and heals itself. For the proper rhythm of life, which singing seems to me to recommend symbolically, is a cure of nature.[48]

What continually amazed early Christian interpreters of the psalms, in fact, was the apparently universal ability of these poems to transform the hearts and minds of the people who regularly prayed them. Like the rest of the Bible, their eloquence and power was not quite the same as that of classical poetry; "it speaks to the heart," Cassiodorus observed (with perhaps a hint of *apologia* toward the secular connoisseurs of his time), "not to the body's ears."[49] The music of the psalms, he suggests, is in fact what "leads the words to God," giving them a "divine eloquence" that even the

---

[46] Ibid., 28 (PG 27:40). Athanasius seems here to be referring to the "odes" or canticles contained in other books of the Bible as a separate, musically more elaborate category of sung liturgical text, alongside the book of Psalms.

[47] Gregory of Nyssa, *Inscr. Ps.* 1.3.18 (James McDonough, ed., *Gregorii Nysseni opera* [Leiden: Brill, 1962], 5:30.23). In the parlance of the fourth-century Greek fathers, "philosophy" meant above all the practice of asceticism, grounded in Christian faith and Scripture.

[48] Gregory of Nyssa, *Inscr. Ps.* 1.3.23 (McDonough, *Gregorii Nysseni opera,* 5:33.7–11; Ronald E. Heine, trans., *Gregory of Nyssa's Treatise on the Inscriptions of the Psalms* [Oxford: Clarendon Press, 1995], 91 [alt.]).

[49] *Exp. Ps., Praefatio* 15 (CCSL 97:18.5–6; Patrick G. Walsh, trans., *Cassiodorus: Explanation of the Psalms* [ACW 51; Mahwah, N.J.: Paulist, 1990], 1:36).

heart of God will presumably find persuasive.[50] The core of the Psalter's power to move and delight was its truth, its "perfect theology,"[51] its richness of moral example.[52] However, as he and other authors insisted, it could do this in the simplest and most direct of terms, so that beginners in the spiritual life could learn from it,[53] people of every rank could sing it and understand it, people of every age could find it engaging, summoning them to silence and uniting them in a single song.[54] For everyone who was prepared to read or chant them in faith, the psalms worked as both a mysterious inner medicine against the passions, and a rigorous workout program, an *askesis,* for the heart. Thus Ambrose describes the paedagogy of the psalms, within the larger context of biblical revelation, in athletic as well as medicinal terms:

> History informs, the law instructs, prophecy announces, correction chastises, moral teaching persuades; but in the book of psalms we find the progress [*profectus*] of each person, a kind of medicine for human healing. Whoever reads it, has the means of curing the wounds of passion by a special remedy. Whoever wants to see, as if in a common training-ground for souls [*in communi animarum gymnasio*] and a stadium of the virtues, can choose for himself various kinds of imaginative situation, all prepared for him, which he knows will suit him well; by using them, he can more easily win the crown of victory.[55]

However, for all their human effectiveness, this therapeutic instrument remained, at a deeper level, God's music rather than our own: a body of songs given to us by God, to enable us to speak to him in the words he is most disposed to hear. As Augustine observes at the beginning of his homily on Ps 99:

---

50 *Exp. Ps., Praefatio* (CCSL 97:4.65–5.68): "Psalmi sunt denique, qui nobis gratas faciunt esse vigilias, quando silenti nocte psallentibus choris humana vox erumpit in musicam, verbisque arte modulatis ad illum redire facit, a quo pro salute humani generis divinum venit eloquium."

51 Basil, *Homily on Psalm 1* (Way, *Exegetic Homilies,* 153); Diodore of Tarsus, *Comm. Ps., Prologue* 45–67.

52 So Cassiodorus, *Exp. Ps., Praefatio* 15; Diodore of Tarsus, *Comm. Ps., Prologue* 1–13.

53 Cassiodorus, *Exp. Ps., Praefatio* 16.

54 Ambrose, *Expl. Ps.* 1.9 (CSEL 64:7); cf. Niceta of Remesiana, *De psalmodiae bono 5* (Burn, *Niceta of Remesiana,* 72).

55 Ambrose, *Expl. Ps.* 1.7 (CSEL 64:6.4–11). For a perceptive study of this same image of the psalms as an athletic training ground for the Christian affections, in patristic literature and in Luther's exegesis, see Günter Bader, *Psalterium affectuum palaestra* (Tübingen: Mohr Siebeck, 1996).

> The voice of God, whatever instrument it sounds through, is still the voice of God, and there is nothing that gives pleasure to his ears except his own voice. For even when we speak, we only give him pleasure when he speaks through us![56]

In the ninth book of his *Confessions,* Augustine describes the peaceful yet excited state of his own heart when he and his companions had made a final decision, after years of searching for truth, to enroll themselves for baptism and to take on the yoke of being a committed disciple of Christ, a *servus Dei.* Most of his intellectual difficulties with mainstream Christian doctrine had been solved, he has told us in book 7, by an immersion into neo-Platonist philosophy at Milan; his old distaste for the apparent harshness of doctrine and literary rusticity of the Bible had also found a cure there, in Ambrose's preaching. His final need was for internal transformation, a healing of the "swelling tumor" of pride that philosophy, even neo-Platonic philosophy, only seemed to aggravate[57] and with that healing a new freedom to move toward the goal he so desired but seemed unable to reach on his own.[58] It was only after that freedom was given him as a gift, in the garden of his house in Milan, that he came to find, in prayer and in the Scriptures, the medicine for his inner ills. He found it above all, he tells us, in the psalms:

> My God, how I cried to you when I read the psalms of David, songs of faith, utterances of devotion which allow no pride of spirit to enter in! I was but a beginner in authentic love of you, a catechumen resting at a country villa.... How I cried out to you in these psalms, and how they kindled my love for you! I was fired by an enthusiasm to recite them, were it possible, to the entire world, in protest against the pride of the human race. Yet they are being sung in all the world, and "there is none who can hide himself from your heat" (Ps 18:7).[59]

For Augustine, as for Ambrose and so many of his contemporaries, it was essential to "sing the psalms with understanding," to seek out their meaning as texts within the context of the whole Christian narrative of salvation. However, it was the emotive and aesthetic power of the psalms—their music, their "sweetness"—that enabled them to touch and transform these readers in a way no other book of Scripture, no preaching or theological

---

[56] *Enarrat. Ps.* 99.1 (CCSL 39:1393.5–8).

[57] So *Conf.* 7.20.26.

[58] Ibid., 7.21.27.

[59] Ibid., 9.4.8 (CCSL 27:137.20–28; Henry Chadwick, trans., *Confessions* [Oxford: Oxford University Press, 1992], 160).

argument, was able to do. Augustine's own later interpretation of the psalms, delivered chiefly in the setting of public worship, would focus more often on their role as the voice of the church as the body of Christ, the *totus Christus* crying out to God in the midst of a hostile society, or as the voice of Christ, the divine Bridegroom, calling to his spouse, the church, to imitate him. However, here at Cassiciacum, in the autumn of 386, Augustine had discovered the power of the psalms in a much more intimate and personal way, as Athanasius and the desert monks had done before him: their power to become part of our inner selves and to form our very thoughts and desires in the image of God.

A Note on the Peshitta Psalms and Their Use at Ramsa (Evening Prayer) in the East Syrian Tradition

Bryan D. Spinks
Yale Divinity School

The Syriac Psalter

The Psalter of the Peshitta, or Syriac Bible, presents scholars with a number of puzzles, three of which are paramount: the origin and nature of the translation, the headings of the psalms, and the five additional non-canonical psalms found in some manuscripts. Each of these requires some discussion before we turn to the use of the psalms in Evening Prayer of the East Syrian Church, or Church of the East.

Our earliest reference to the origin of the Peshitta of the Old Testament comes from Theodore of Mopsuestia, who contrasted what he thought was the poor work of an obscure individual with the masterpiece of Greek translation, the Septuagint, which was accomplished by a task force of seventy scholars.[1] Present-day studies have shown that at least as regards the whole Old Testament Theodore was mistaken, and different hands had been at work throughout the Peshitta translation. Thus it is generally thought that the Pentateuch had a Jewish origin, though whether that origin was Jewish or Christian in faith is unclear. Some have argued that there are traces of dependency on Aramaic Targums, but while that may be true of the Pentateuch, it should not be concluded that the same influences and origins hold good for each Old Testament writing.

The researches of Michael P. Weitzman suggest that such a search in the case of the Psalter is illusory and that the evdience points to the Hebrew as being the base text of the translation.[2] Weitzman pointed out that there are idiosyncrasies, such as the persistent rendering of Hebrew root *ḥwš* by *kattar,* "wait," at Pss 22:20; 38:23; 40:14; 55:9; 70:2, 6; 71:12;

---

1 *Commentarium in Habacucum prophetam,* PG 66:437.

2 "The Origin of the Peshitta Psalter," in *Interpreting the Hebrew Bible* (ed. J. Emerton and S. Reif; Cambridge: Cambridge University Press, 1982), 277–98.

and 141:1 and signs of fatigue in the translation of Ps 119, suggesting "the valiant if erratic efforts of an individual translator."[3] On the other hand, Weitzman noted that there are traits of theological significance. Here he cited the tendency to render the Hebrew *ḥāsîd* as "chosen one" or "elect" and the usage of *paroqa*, "savior." These seem to indicate a Christian theological influence on the translation. The community regarded itself, rather than all Israel, as elect and looked favorably on the Gentiles. In the view of Weitzman, the Peshitta Pentateuch reflects a time when the Syriac community was a Jewish community but the Psalter a time when the community was Christian. However, he might have considered the possibility that it is not the community, but the theological stance of the particular translators, that are reflected in the translation. In a subsequent study he has suggested that the translator of the Psalter at times consulted the Septuagint version.[4]

A second distinct puzzle of the Peshitta psalms is the headings. Both in manuscripts and printed texts the psalms are either without titles, or they have titles that differ completely from those that accompany the Hebrew and Greek texts. They give a longer or shorter interpretation of the psalm. Nowhere in the East or West Syrian traditions do we come across the titles found in the Masoretic text or the Septuagint. This tradition goes back at least to the Psalter *British Library Add 17110,* which is dated around 600 and is East Syrian, and also to Codex Ambrosianus, which is sixth century and West Syrian. It is clear from the study by Willem Bloemendaal that the basis of these titles is the commentaries by Theodore of Mopsuestia.[5] Theodore rejected the Hebrew titles of the psalms and instead categorized them into four groups: historical psalms; prophet psalms; ethical psalms; and four messianic psalms. Theodore was one of the major teachers of the Antiochene school, and his works survive in Syriac. Although he was regarded as a great teacher in his day, the fact that he had been the teacher of Nestorius meant that his Christology came under a cloud—and then in 553, over a hundred years after his death, he was condemned as a heretic. However, his writings were translated into Syriac, and Theodore the Interpreter, as he was called, was the foundational theologian for the Church of the East; his writings maintained their influence in the West Syrian communities as well. The esteem in which he was held is illustrated by the fact that his commentaries provide the basis for the titles of the Syriac Psalms.[6]

---

[3] Ibid., 284.

[4] Michael P. Weitzman, "The Peshitta Psalter and Its Hebrew *Vorlage*," *VT* 35 (1985): 341–54.

[5] Willem Bloemendaal, *The Headings of the Psalms in the East Syrian Church* (Leiden: Brill, 1960).

[6] See Bloemendaal for the discussion of the texts.

A third puzzle of the Syriac psalter is the fact that some manuscripts preserve five additional psalms. As they appear in the *Syriac Manuscript 12t4*,[7] Ps 151 tells of how David was exalted from shepherd to anointed ruler; Ps 152 has six verses and is a plea by David to be delivered from the attack by a lion and bear on his flock; Ps 153 is a thanksgiving for having killed two animals, possibly the lion and bear of the previous psalm; Ps 154 is an exhortation to praise God, supposedly by Hezekiah; and Ps 155 is a plea for deliverance. Some of these extracanonical or apocryphal psalms are known from other sources. Psalm 151 is similar to Ps 151 in the Septuagint, and so a translation from the Greek was at one time a favored theory. However, with the discovery of the Qumran psalms, it is evident that $11QPs^a$ 151 is related to both the Septuagint and Syriac versions, and hence a Hebrew *Vorlage* is possible. However, Pss 154 and 155 also have counterparts in the Qumran *Psalm Scroll*, and thus three of the five extra Syriac psalms have a Hebrew origin. These must date at least to the first century C.E., when the Qumran manuscript was written. Psalms 152 and 153 of *Syriac Manuscript 12t4* have no counterpart in Hebrew, and scholars speculate as to whether or not they had a Hebrew *Vorlage*. Liturgically, however, these psalms do not seem to have been used.

The Psalms in East Syrian Ramsa

The East Syrian, Assyrian, or Church of the East had its original center at Seleucia-Ctesiphon on the Tigris River. Because of its later refusal to condemn Nestorius, it became a persecuted church and found refuge in the Persian Empire where, in some isolation, its Semitic thought forms were conserved. Its liturgical forms, while certainly developed, sometimes exhibit features of a more primitive era. Its Divine Office, as in all churches, represents a combination of "cathedral" and "monastic" usages, though in certain respects the "cathedral" usage alone has been preserved. For the Divine Office, the Syriac Psalter as used in this tradition is divided into twenty *ḥullale*, and each *hullale* is divided into two or three *marmyata*, each of which includes two, three, or four psalms. Ramsa itself has the following structure for festivals:[8]

(opening formulae)
Marmita

---

[7] Harry F. van Rooy, *Studies on the Syriac Apocryphal Psalms* (JSSSup 7; Leiden: Brill, 1999).

[8] See Arthur Maclean, *East Syrian Daily Offices* (London: Rivingtons, 1894); and Sylvester Pudichery, *Ramsa* (Pachalam: Dharmaram College, 1972).

'Onita of incense
Laku Mara Hymn and its collect
Surraya da-qdam (alleluia psalm before the evening psalmody)
Fixed evening psalmody: Pss 140; 141; 118:105–112; 116
Surraya d-batar (alleluia psalm after the evening psalms)
'Onita d-batar (antiphon after the evening psalms)
Intercessions
Trisagion and collect
Prayer of Blessing
Stational procession:
'Onita d-basiliqe (antiphon of the procession)
Surraya
Lord's Prayer
Final prayers

Ferial Ramsa omits the *'onyata de-qdam* and *d-batar* and concludes with:

Trisagion and Collect
'Onita d-ramsa
Surraya
Procession with antiphon of the martyrs
Subba'a (compline)
Final prayers

It is generally agreed among historians of this Office that the original core is the fixed psalmody for the evening, which is shared with the West Syrian and Maronite Ramso. Psalms 140 and 141 are also found in the evening Office of the Byzantine and Armenian rites, and Ps 116 is found in the Coptic and Ethiopic rites. Psalm 140:2 mentions the evening sacrifice; Ps 141 begins in the same fashion as 140:1 and asks for protection and deliverance; and Ps 118:105 is about a lamp and light. Psalm 116 is a short psalm of praise.

However, what of the psalmody of the *Marmita*? It is generally agreed that this is the remains of the service of None, which has become attached to the beginning of Ramsa. For Sundays and feasts the psalms appointed are as follows:

- Annunciation (Advent) to Epiphany: Pss 87 and 88. Psalm 87 is a song about Zion (which inspired the hymn "Glorious Things of Thee Are Spoken"), whereas Ps 88 is penitential in character.
- Other Sundays and feasts: Pss 65; 66; and 67. These are all psalms of praise.

- For memorials on Fridays: Pss 85 and 86. These pray for steadfast love, and for God's help.
- For memorials on other days: Pss 25; 26; and 27. In this selection a whole number of themes are covered—lifting the soul to God, vindication, and patient trust.

Even if the use of these psalms was not original to Ramsa, nevertheless psalm verses are scattered throughout the various components that make up Ramsa. Thus with *'Onita* of Incense (a chant that accompanies the incense) we find psalm verses surrounding the chant: on Sundays Ps 84:1 and 2 ("How lovely are your dwellings") and on feasts also 84:3 and 6. On memorial days, Ps 34:1 and 2 feature ("I will praise the Lord at all times"). Likewise, the hymn *Laku Mara,* a very short hymn repeated several times, is also interspersed with psalmic verses: Ps 121:1, and on feasts, also 121:2.

The *Surraya de-qdam* is the alleluia psalm said or sung before the fixed evening psalms. Provision is made for the seven cycles that divide the liturgical calendar. On the first Sunday of each cycle (*Sawu'a*) Ps 47:1–5 is appointed, and 47:6–9 are added in the period from the Ascension to the season of the Annunciations. The second has Ps 65:1–6 (to the word "earth"); the third, Ps 89:1–5; the fourth, Ps 93:1–3; the fifth, Ps 125:1–5; the sixth, Ps 49:1–5; and the seventh, Ps 136:1–3. Each verse is sung or recited, followed by three alleluias. The *Onita de-qdam* or antiphon before the fixed evening psalms is a poetic strophe that usually begins with a verse of a psalm.

The *Surraya d-batar* has the same format as the *Surraya de-qdam.* In this latter case the sevenfold provision is as follows:

First Sunday: Ps 48:1–3
Second Sunday: Ps 66:1–4
Third Sunday: Ps 89:6–9
Fourth Sunday: Ps 148:1–7
Fifth Sunday: Ps 126:1–3
Sixth Sunday: Ps 129:1–7
Seventh Sunday Ps 137:1–4

The *'Onita d-batar,* which scholars regard as not belonging to the earliest stratum of Ramsa, seems to be a parallel to the *'Onita d-qdam* and to have a similar structure, using, for example, Ps 98:8: "For he comes to judge the earth. The king who raises the dead will shine from above in his glory, and will give life to the dead and will raise those in the grave, and indeed the dead will rise from the graves and praise the one who gives life to the dead."

This short note illustrates not only the distinctive nature of the Peshitta psalms but also demonstrates how the content of the Psalter pervades the whole structure and content of Ramsa, even though the actual formal selection of the Psalter (the fixed evening psalms) are few in number. East Syrian evening prayer is the heart in pilgrimage, drawn and sustained by the spirituality of the psalms.

PART 4

PSALMS IN THE LATIN MIDDLE AGES AND THE EARLY MODERN PERIOD

Hildegard and the Dawn Song of Lauds: An Introduction to Benedictine Psalmody

Margot Fassler

Hildegard of Bingen: Evangelist and Psalmodist

Hildegard of Bingen, a twelfth-century nun from the Rhineland, is unique to medieval theology and music for a number of reasons. She is the only distinguished theologian and exegete who was also a composer of major importance, and this claim holds not only for the centuries of the Middle Ages but also when one considers the entire Western Christian canon.[1] She considered her first theological treatise, *Scivias Domini* (*Know the Ways of the Lord*)—which she wrote after the age of forty—to be another book of the Bible and herself to be a designated transmitter of the Word of God.[2] The famous opening scene from the only illuminated copy of the treatise, a copy whose illuminations may have been directly inspired by the author, suggests the ideals embodied in her writings.[3] She is moved by the power of the fiery Spirit; as she hears God speak, her secretary Volmar writes down what she says of received truth, and—one could argue through iconographical evidence—what she sings of it as well.[4]

---

[1] For an introduction to Hildegard's life and times, see Barbara Newman, ed., *Voice of the Living Light* (Berkeley and Los Angeles: University of California Press, 1998). For the broader context of women and their education in the twelfth-century Rhineland, see Constant J. Mews, ed., *Listen, Daughter: The Speculum Virginum and the Formation of Religious Women in the Middle Ages* (New York: Palgrave, 2001).

[2] See Barbara Newman's introduction to the English translation of the treatise (Columba Hart and Jane Bishop, trans., *Scivias* [Classics of Western Spirituality; New York: Paulist, 1990]) for further discussion.

[3] The miniatures are fully reproduced in color and studied by Lieselotte E. Saurma-Jeltsch in *Die Miniatauren im "Liber Scivias" der Hildegard von Bingen: Die Wucht der Vision und die Ordnung der Bilder* (Wiesbaden: Reichert, 1998).

[4] See ibid., 25–31, for discussion of the opening illumination and its visual sources. The miniature depicting Hildegard receiving the inspired visions underlying her writings is much reproduced.

Through this visual preface, Hildegard is situated in two realms. The first is that of the Evangelists, who are often depicted as receiving the word as they write, within a familiar iconic framework. But other elements of the picture are borrowed from another tradition. This one shows Gregory the Great, who sang psalms to melodies he received from the Holy Spirit, melodies that were recorded by a scribe, much as Volmer transcribed Hildegard's divine messages.[5] The way Hildegard is depicted proclaims that she is both evangelist and composer.

Hildegard accounts for the nature of divine inspiration several times, in her treatises and in her correspondence. Her words reflect the mind of a religious reformer, cast in the mode of prophet. According to the seer, elected officials of the church universal were failing by offering only a lukewarm message, not fit for the salvation of souls. To instruct them God chose the weakest of his vessels to hold the finest wine, a woman, an undereducated nun.[6]

> And I heard the voice saying to me from the aforementioned living fire:
>
> Oh you who are wretched earth and, as a woman, untaught in all learning of earthly teachers and unable to read literature with philosophical understanding, you are nonetheless touched by My light, which kindles in you an inner fire like a burning sun; cry out and relate and write these things My mysteries that you see and hear in mystical visions. So do not be timid, but say those things you understand in the Spirit as I speak them through to you; so that those who should have shown My people righteousness, but who in their perversity refuse to speak openly of the justice they know, unwilling to abstain from the evil desires that cling to them like their masters and make them fly from the face of the Lord and blush to speak the truth, may be ashamed. Therefore, O diffident mind, who are taught inwardly by mystical inspiration, though because of Eve's transgression you are trodden on by the masculine sex, speak of that fiery work this sure vision has shown you. (*Scivias* 2.1)

Hildegard's writings and her music are designed to help restore a failed order of things in the church and to offer a corrective for leaders who could no longer lead—or sing—effectively. She is prophet, evangelist, and psalmodist by divine fiat, and her words and her music come from God. Her works offer a way of reforming the church, both through new

---

[5] Leo Treitler, "Homer and Gregory: The Transmission of Epic Poetry and Plainchant," *MQ* 60 (1974): 333–72.

[6] See Barbara Newman, *Sister of Wisdom: St. Hildegard's Theology of the Feminine* (2d ed.; Berkeley and Los Angeles: University of California Press, 1997), and Constant Mews, "Religious Thinker: 'A Frail Human Being' on Fiery Life," in Newman, *Voice of the Living Light*, 52–69, for discussion of Hildegard's reform theology.

"Scripture" and through a new model of ecclesial song. They also point the way toward an apocalyptic new age in which Hildegard believed all people would sing in modes of praise mystically resembling those described in her writings and mirrored in her compositional art.[7] Hildegard's unique talents allowed her to move freely back and forth from speculative to practical, as she attempted to describe monastic and ecclesial ideals in the actual, sounding exercise of song and drama, as well as in the prose of theological treatises.

Hildegard's compositions included music written for her convent's psalmody: her entire corpus of compositions is conditioned by a lived understanding of the Divine Office and its psalmody.[8] Her reworking of the texts, and her offering of a new book of Scripture, point to some basic facts of Christian psalmody for most of the ages: it is a heavily revised and reworked body of texts, texts recontextualized in a liturgy that transformed their original meaning while preserving many basic elements of the tradition. This essay seeks to indicate several of the ways in which Latin psalmody shaped the Christian imagination in the Middle Ages. The subject is vast, and Hildegard provides a useful point of entry. She works within the frame of an ancient tradition, yet she illustrates various modes of renewal.

The Psalmody of the Benedictine Office

In its larger context, Hildegard's work as a composer can be seen as part of the massive songbook created by monastic and cathedral musicians during the Middle Ages. The psalmody of the Latin church, with its complex layerings of entire psalm texts and of individual verses, set to countless tones and melodies, occupied the creativity of liturgists, melodists, cantors, exegetes, and copyists for centuries. The psalms have always been, as they remain, the basic texts for prayer and praise in Christian monasticism, even as they are texts that have been transformed. The *opus Dei*—the work of God—includes communal singing of the psalms, all 150 of them, according to a regular cursus or plan. One disciplined desert father claimed to sing the entire Psalter every day, but monastic rules, including that ascribed to Saint

---

[7] For discussion of Hildegard's brand of apocalyptic thought, see Kathryn Kerby-Fulton, "Prophet and Reformer: 'Smoke in the Vineyard,'" in Newman, *Voice of the Living Light,* 70–90.

[8] Hildegard's music and its relationship to her monastic ideals are discussed in Margot Fassler, "Composer and Dramatist: 'Melodious Singing and the Freshness of Remorse,'" in Newman, *Voice of the Living Light,* 149–75; and idem, "Music for the Love Feast: Hildegard of Bingen and the Song of Songs," in *Women's Voices across Musical Worlds* (ed. J. Bernstein; Boston: Northeastern University Press, 2003).

Benedict, provide for weekly singing of the book of Psalms.[9] From the time the Rule of Saint Benedict was adapted by Carolingian liturgical reformers in the ninth century, the Rule, with its fairly precise outline of psalmody, has shaped not only the daily offices of Benedictine monasteries but the ordered prayer lives of many other monastic communities and of secular communities as well. For centuries all members of Christian monastic orders in the West had the psalms by heart and knew them within a liturgical, a festive, and, it should be said, a pedagogical context.

Several recent scholarly publications contain outlines of the weekly plan of psalmody Hildegard would have known as a Benedictine nun in the twelfth century and the changes that occurred when major feasts disrupted this ferial cursus.[10] Scholars compare this monastic plan of psalmody with that followed in secular churches and likewise by religious orders whose liturgies were governed by the Rule of Saint Augustine rather than that of Saint Benedict.

Benedictines in Hildegard's era knew the Office psalms in the Latin translation of Jerome. This was a heavily Christianized version of the texts, primarily dependent upon the Septuagint.[11] Although the Vulgate provided the texts for psalms intoned in the Office, psalm verses in the Mass liturgy were frequently taken from even earlier Latin translations. Thus, although the psalms were the primary texts of both the Office and the Mass, they were present in different Latin translations. The commentators and faith communities who prayed the texts had to resolve any difficulties, and as they did so much of the Christian theological understanding of the texts and their meaning evolved.

---

[9] See the essays in *RB 1980: The Rule of St. Benedict in Latin and English with Notes* (ed. T. Fry; Collegeville, Minn.: Liturgical Press, 1981) for an introduction to the psalmody of the Rule of Saint Benedict.

[10] These comparative tables are found in Roger Reynolds, "Divine Office," in *Dictionary of the Middle Ages* (ed. J. Strayer et al.; New York: Scribner, 1982–89), 4:221–31; John Harper, *Forms and Orders of Western Liturgy from the Tenth to the Eighteenth Century: A Historical Introduction and Guide for Students and Musicians* (New York: Oxford University Press, 1991); and Lila Collamore, "Prelude: Charting the Divine Office," in *The Divine Office in the Latin Middle Ages* (ed. M. E. Fassler and R. A. Baltzer; New York: Oxford University Press, 2000), 3–11.

[11] Jerome made three translations of the Psalter, and it is his second translation, the so-called Gallican Psalter, that was used in the Office in the West as well as in the Vulgate Bible. Jerome was heavily influenced by Origen's *Hexapla;* on his texts of Scripture see Gilles Dorival and Alain Le Boulluec, *Origeniana Sexta: Origène et la Bible* (Leuven: Leuven University Press; Peeters, 1995); for an overview of various early Latin translations, see Colette Estin in *Le monde latin antique et la Bible* (ed. J. Fontaine and C. Pietri; Paris: Beauchesne, 1985), 67–88.

Most modern translations of the Bible are of the Hebrew text, little influenced by the Vulgate or by any Latin translation, and thus they may not convey the precise meaning embedded in the Latin or offer the subtle flavor known to the medievals who sang and prayed these texts for so many centuries.[12] Without consultation with the Latin versions we may not understand why certain psalms or psalm verses were chosen for particular liturgical occasions, or the elaborate net of meanings that was woven for the liturgical arts—from poetry and drama to glass, sculpture, mosaics, wall paintings, and manuscript illuminations—by the liturgical psalmody of the Latin Middle Ages.[13]

The first way the psalms of the Latin liturgy were turned into Christian texts was through the translations themselves, but just as important for transforming the texts into Christian poems were their various settings in the liturgy. As a nun, Hildegard would have known each psalm text in several guises: each psalm was sung in its entirety in the Office, framed by interpretive antiphons, and various psalm verses were employed in the Mass and Office liturgies in accord with a feast and its themes. Thus, each psalm was present many times to the mind of a medieval monk or nun, and each singing was surely ripe with multifold references. The modern way of knowing the Psalter, by reading it silently and alone, formed but a small part of the range of ways medievals knew the texts. Also the modern ideal of studying psalms in translations that are as close as possible to the Hebrew original was far removed from the medieval ideal of a deliberately appropriated, transformed, and recontextualized text. It would be false to suppose that the psalms of the Hebrew Bible were the psalms known by medieval Christian nuns and monks. The texts they knew, and their modes of knowing them, mean that these psalms were very different from the parent texts, although still related to them.

One of the best ways to begin to understand the complexities of medieval Christian psalmody is by analyzing the relationships of Office psalms to their antiphons. Antiphons are sung texts of several kinds: they may consist of a particular psalm verse chosen to comment upon the whole psalm; they may be newly written texts created to link a given

---

12 In *The Love of Learning and the Desire for God* (trans. C. Misrahi; 3d ed.; New York: Fordham University Press, 1982) Jean Leclercq discusses the ways in which medieval writers exploited textual resonances in their works, appealing to an audience that had vast quantities of the Bible memorized. It is especially important to remember that the Bible was known primarily through the liturgy throughout the Middle Ages.

13 For an introduction to the monastic liturgy of the Latin Middle Ages, see especially Leclercq, *Love of Learning*.

psalm to a particular hour of the day, to a feast, or to a season; or they may be either a simple or complex Alleluia (these antiphons dominate the liturgy of the Paschal season). Regardless of the style an antiphon might take, each was meant to be sung before and after the intoned text of the entire psalm itself. This way of singing the psalms has long been central to Christian understanding of these poems and is at the heart of many modern practices as well.[14]

In addition to this, the custom in many Christian psalmodic practices—and throughout the Latin Middle Ages—was to seal the text of the psalm with the lesser doxology, "Glory to the Father and to the Son and to the Holy Spirit, as it was in the beginning and will be now and forever. Amen." Thus the texts were sung according to the formula: antiphon, intoned psalm with the doxology as its final verse, and a repeat of the antiphon.[15]

Figures 12.1–3 offer three types of antiphon, all of which were used to frame Ps 62.[16] The first antiphon employs a verse from the psalm itself; the second is a setting of the word *Alleluia;* and the third antiphon was created—both text and melody—by Hildegard. By framing the text of the psalm an antiphon transforms it in several ways.

The antiphon comments upon the psalm text, transforming its meaning in the process. In figure 12.1, the antiphon for Ps 62 is the first half of verse 8, "Thy right hand has received me." That the psalm was rendered with this antiphon in the Office of prayer for the dead explains the reason for its selection: it invokes a sense of God's love and acceptance of human souls in the afterlife.

---

[14] The evolution of this practice in the formative centuries of the late antique period is a difficult subject; two views of it are found in the essays in this collection, by Robert Taft and by Peter Jeffery. By the tenth century the practice had become fairly standardized, although regional differences still existed.

[15] For a general introduction to antiphonal psalmody, see David Hiley, *Western Plainchant: A Handbook* (Oxford: Clarendon, 1993).

[16] The Latin (Greek) number of the psalm as used in Latin liturgical books is given. All translations from the Vulgate Bible are taken from the so-called Douay Rheims Version, the Old Testament first published by the English College at Douay in 1609, and the New Testament by the English College at Rheims in 1582. Although it has been modified several times, most substantially by Challoner in the mid-eighteenth century, its basic character has not been altered. The original translation was made by scholars who knew the Latin liturgy, albeit as reformed by the various church councils held in Trent in the sixteenth century. I have used an edition whose copyright was held by the John Murphy Company (1914), printed by P. J. Kennedy & Son in New York City (n.d.). This particular reprint bore the approbation of James Gibbons, Archbishop of Baltimore; John Farley, Archbishop of New York; and William O'Connell, Archbishop of Boston.

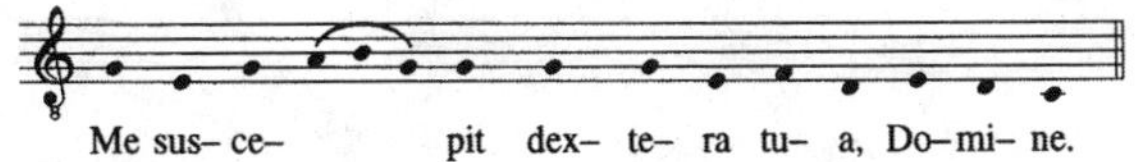

Fig. 12.1. Antiphon, Mode 7. *Antiphonale Monasticum, 1163.* For the full text of the psalm, see the outline of Lauds below.

A different character emerges when the psalm was sung as in the Office of Lauds during Paschal time, with the antiphon a joyful alleluia in mode 8 (fig. 12.2).

Fig. 12.2. Antiphon, Mode 8. *Antiphonale Monasticum, 474.*

Hildegard's third antiphon for Lauds of the Nativity, or a Marian feast, frames the text in yet a third way, by relating it to a complex of ideas connected with a season and with a saint, with reference to her role in the history of human salvation (fig. 12.3).

Hildegard of Bingen's musical compositions contain two sets of psalter antiphons, both apparently composed to be sung with psalms at the Office of Lauds. One of these was specifically for the Feast of the 11,000 Virgins; the other, more general and appropriate either for the Christmas season or for Marian feasts, is the subject of this essay.[17]

Hildegard's writings reveal that she, who sang Lauds every day, had long contemplated its position in the liturgical day. Indeed, her lively imagination seems especially well attuned to the themes of this morning hour of prayer and its incarnational symbolism. Analysis of Lauds as an hour of prayer, and subsequently of Hildegard's Marian antiphons for Lauds, demonstrates a central truth about Christian psalmody in the Middle Ages: the psalms were primarily known as heard rather than as read phenomena.

---

[17] The liturgical poetry of Hildegard of Bingen has been edited, translated, and commented upon by Barbara Newman in *Symphonia* [*Symphony of the Harmony of Celestial Revelations*] (Ithaca, N.Y.: Cornell University Press, 1998); further discussion appears in the second of her essays contained in *Voice of the Living Light,* 176–92: "Poet: 'Where the Living Majesty Utters Mysteries.'"

Fig. 12.3. Wiesbaden, Hessian State Library, 2, f. 467r
(retaining medieval spellings; translated below, p. 227)

Hildegard takes this even further: singing makes an indwelling of the Logos possible, both literally and figuratively. Even medieval authors of written commentaries surely "heard" the familiar musical settings of the words in their minds as they wrote. In the Middle Ages, monastic choirs were usually divided into two parts, singing the psalms in alteration. In monastic and cathedral practice, even at the present time, the halves of the choir are seated so as to watch each other as they sing. This practice offers yet another dimension to the texts and the praise they embody, making antiphonal singing the most profoundly communal of all modes of rendering the psalms. The members of monastic communities were and are bound together on the breath of their antiphonal psalmody.

The composer of antiphon texts and music was a creator of commentary as well, in this case, of exegesis of the texts of the Psalter. Of all commentaries, those sung in community were the most influential, shaping minds, hearts, and human relationships in conjunction with the psalm texts themselves. Hildegard uses a reference to Rev 14:3 to describe the power of monastic song, music that finds a parallel in the court of the Lamb. In her chapter on religious orders in *Scivias,* she offers this description:

> "And they sang, as it were, a new song before the throne, and before the four living creatures and the ancients." What does this mean? In those faithful ones who embrace chastity for a good purpose and preserve their virginity unstained for love of God, good will bursts forth wonderfully in praise of their Creator. How? In the dawn-light of virginity, which always surrounds the Son of God, steadfast praise is hidden; no worldly office and no tie of law can resist it, and it sings in the voice of exultation a celestial song to the glory of God. (*Scivias* 2.5.8)

Psalmody and the Office of Lauds

Lauds is one of the major hours of prayer in the Divine Office.[18] It had a central role to play in monastic rites as the time for the greeting of dawn and the opening of a new day. For Christian monks and nuns, it was a time to contemplate the transition between death and life, between temporal existence and eternity, and for heralding the coming of the Messiah into human flesh. Some monastic rules and customaries from the medieval period have a specific instruction about waiting for the coming of dawn before beginning Lauds—Benedict states that *matutini* (which is usually rendered "Lauds") *incipiente luce agendi sunt,* that is, "is to be performed at daybreak" (Rule 8:4). The influential ninth-century liturgical commentator Amalarius of Metz interprets Lauds in terms of change and the new creation.[19]

The Rule of Saint Benedict includes two chapters concerning Lauds, listing the psalms to be rendered during this, the monastic dawn song.

---

[18] The background of this hour of prayer in the Christian East is found in Robert Taft, *The Liturgy of the Hours in East and West* (2d ed.; Collegeville, Minn.: Liturgical Press, 1993). Taft calls the Office of Lauds "Matins" throughout most of his study—for the problems posed by terminology see the note on p. 77 in Taft. The term "Lauds" came to be used for the morning office because of the importance of the so-called Laudate psalms within it (Pss 148–150). The term was favored only in the West, after the time of the Rule of Saint Benedict, who calls Lauds "Matins" and the Night Office either "Vigils" or "Nocturns." Contemporary scholars who work with the Latin rite of the Middle Ages commonly call the morning office "Lauds" and the office of prayer in the middle of the night "Matins," and this is the practice that will be followed in this essay.

[19] See his *Liber Officialis* 4.10, in *Opera liturgica omnia* (ed. J. M. Hanssens; Studi e Testi 138–40; Vatican City: Biblioteca apostolica vaticana, 1948–50), 2:448–54.

Chapter 12. *How the Morning Office is to Be Said.* The Morning Office on Sunday shall begin with Psalm 66 recited straight through without an antiphon. After that let Psalm 50 be said with Alleluia, the Psalms 117 and 62, the Canticle of Blessing and the Psalms of praise; then a lesson from the Apocalypse to be recited by heart, the responsory, the Ambrosian hymn, the verse, the canticle from the Gospel book, the litany and so the end.

Chapter 13. *How the Morning Office Is to Be Said on Weekdays.* On weekdays the Morning Office shall be celebrated as follows. Let Psalm 66 be said without an antiphon and somewhat slowly, as on Sunday, in order that all may be in time for Psalm 50, which is to be said with an antiphon. After that let two other Psalms be said according to custom, namely: on Monday Psalms 5 and 35, on Tuesday Psalms 42 and 56, on Wednesday Psalms 63 and 64, on Thursday Psalms 87 and 89, on Friday Psalms 75 and 91, and on Saturday Psalm 142 and the canticle from Deuteronomy, which is divided into two sections each terminated by a "Glory be to the Father." But on the other days let there be a canticle from the Prophets, each on its own day as chanted by the Roman church. Next follow the Psalms of praise, then a lesson of the Apostle to be recited from memory, the responsory, the Ambrosian hymn, the verse, the canticle from the Gospel book, the litany, and so the end.

Thus Saint Benedict provided for two variable psalms and a canticle to be sung each morning between the unchanging psalms, that is, Ps 66 and the penitential Ps 50 at the opening, and the joyful "Laudate" psalms, 148–150, sung as a group, to close.[20] The order as set out in table 12.1 created a rhythm of praiseful supplication, slowly turning into ecstatic joy as the skies filled with the light of day, and the prophetic voices of varying canticles reminded the worshipers of God's promises to his people. This weekly plan, in which the changing elements of each day were bracketed by fixed texts, offered the community both consistency and change.

Another set of psalms, as displayed in table 12.2, came to have special prominence. To underscore its festive and joyful character, the Paschal season was marked not only by alleluiatic antiphons but also by a festive set of psalms for Sundays. In time this cursus for the Lauds psalmody of Sundays in Paschal time was adapted for feasts of high rank in many uses, including the Benedictine. Table 12.3 gives the psalms of this festive series in a translation made from the Vulgate Bible and framed by a set of Lauds antiphons written by Hildegard of Bingen. To provide their context, other parts of the

[20] More detailed discussion is found in Nathan Mitchell, appendix 3, "The Liturgical Code in the Rule of Benedict," in Fry, *RB 1980,* 379–414. The translation of chapters 12 and 13 above is by Leonard J. Doyle, St. Benedict's Rule for Monasteries (Collegeville, Minn.: Liturgical Press, 1948).

Table 12.1. Lauds Psalms for the Week, according to the Benedictine Use (Vulgate Psalm numbers)

Sunday	66	50	117	62	Dan 3:57–88 and 56	148–150
Monday	66	50	5	35	Isa 12:1–6	148–150
Tuesday	66	50	42	56	Tob 13:1–10	148–150
Wednesday	66	50	63	64	1 Kgs 2:1–10	148–150
Thursday	66	50	87	89	Exod 15:1–19	148–150
Friday	66	50	75	91	Hab 3:1–19	148–150
Saturday	66	50	142	Deut 32:1–21	Deut 32:22–52	148–150

Table 12.2. Lauds Psalms for Sundays in Paschal Time and for Other Highly Ranked Feasts

66	92	99	62	Dan 3:57–88 and 56	148–150

service are indicated as well. As on all Sundays in the year, the canticle was the Song of the Three Boys in the Fiery Furnace (the so-called *Benedicite,* named from its Latin incipit[21]) as found in the Latin text of the book of Daniel. In this festal cursus the two opening psalms prescribed by the Rule of Benedict for Sundays were replaced with the two opening psalms of the Roman office of Lauds.[22] This set of Sunday psalms, with the *Benedicite* in fourth place, inspired many sets of antiphons for major feasts of the temporal and sanctoral cycles. When one studies groups of antiphons from the Middle Ages, those for Lauds are consistently stable from region to region, the nature of the psalmody apparently promoting fixity in the accompanying antiphon sets as well.[23] These pieces could be adopted for Vespers as

[21] For discussion of the use of this text in the Office, see Mitchell, "Liturgical Code," 403–4; and Ruth Steiner, "Antiphons for the Benedicite at Lauds," *Journal of the Plainsong and Mediaeval Music Society* 7 (1984): 1–17.

[22] For comparison of the reconstructed psalmody of the primitive Roman Office to that of the Rule of Saint Benedict, see Taft, *Liturgy of the Hours,* 130–40.

[23] The classic reference tool for the study of antiphon and responsory texts from the Latin Middle Ages is René-Jean Hesbert's monumental *Corpus antiphonalium officii* (Rerum ecclesiasticarum documenta, Series maior, Fontes 7–12; Rome: Herder, 1963–79), now to be supplemented by the several volumes indexed through the Cantus project, originated by Ruth Steiner at the Catholic University of America, and available online. For discussion of Cantus, see Fassler and Baltzer, *Divine Office in the Latin Middle Ages,* 546–60.

well. Vespers consists of four psalms, with no canticle, and when a set of antiphons was adopted the fourth antiphon (which framed the canticle at Lauds) was the one omitted. It is noteworthy that the Rule requires the recitation by heart of a verse of the book of Revelation for Lauds on Sundays, a practice adopted for major feasts in some uses as well. Through this intoned text the worshiper is reminded that the incarnational powers of transformation point toward the second coming and the apocalytic end of time.

Table 12.3. The psalms of Lauds for Sundays in Paschal Time and for Highly Ranked Feasts. (The antiphons are those composed by Hildegard for a feast of the Virgin Mary. The psalms are divided into lines according to the chanted practice, with a pause at the asterisk. In this practice the lines are sung by alternate choirs.)

Lauds

Psalm 66 [*Deus misereatur,* sung to a tone and without an antiphon]

May God have mercy on us, and bless us: * may he cause the light of his countenance to shine upon us, and may he have mercy on us.
That we may know thy way upon earth: * thy salvation in all nations.
Let people confess to thee, O God: * let all people give praise to thee.
Let the nations be glad and rejoice: * for thou judgest the people with justice, and directest the nations upon earth.
Let the people, O God, confess to thee: let all the people give praise to thee: * the earth hath yielded her fruit.
May God, our God bless us, may God bless us: * and all the ends of the earth fear him.

Antiphon 1: Today a closed gate has opened to us, that which the serpent choked in a woman. So the flower from the Virgin Mary gleams in the dawn.

Psalm 92 [*Dominus regnavit*]

The Lord hath reigned, he is clothed with beauty: * the Lord is clothed with strength and hath girded himself.
For he hath established the world * which shall not be moved.
Thy throne is prepared from of old: * thou art from everlasting.
The floods have lifted up, O Lord, * the floods have lifted up their voice.
The floods have lifted up their waves, * with the noise of many waters.
Wonderful are the surges of the sea: * wonderful is the Lord on high.
Thy testimonies are become exceedingly credible: * holiness becometh thy house, O Lord, unto length of days.
Doxology

Repeat of Antiphon 1

Antiphon 2: Because a woman constructed death, a bright virgin demolished it. Therefore the supreme blessing comes in the form of a woman beyond all creation: for God became man in the Virgin, most sweet and blessed.

Psalm 99 [*Jubilate Deo*]

Sing joyfully to God, all the earth. * Come in before his presence with exceeding great joy.
Know ye that the Lord he is God: * he made us, and not we ourselves.
We are his people and the sheep of his pasture. * Go ye into his gates with praise, into his courts with hymns: and give glory to him.
Praise ye his name: for the Lord is sweet, his mercy endureth forever, * and his truth to generation and generation.
Doxology

Repeat of Antiphon 2

Antiphon 3: While the handiwork of God's finger, formed after the image of God, was born of the mingling of blood though the exile of Adam's fall, the elements received joy in you, O Mary all-praised, as heaven blushed and resounded in praise.

Psalm 62 [*Deus Deus Meus*]

Oh God, my God, * to thee do I watch at break of day.
For thee my soul hath thirsted; * for thee my flesh, O how many ways!
In a desert land, and where there is no way, and no water: * so in the sanctuary have I come before thee, to see thy power and thy glory.
For thy mercy is better than lives: * thee my lips shall praise.
Thus will I bless thee all my life long: * and in thy name I will lift up my hands.
Let my soul be filled as with marrow and fatness: * and my mouth shall praise thee with joyful lips.
If I have remembered thee upon my bed, I will meditate on thee in the morning: * because thou hast been my helper.
And I will rejoice under the covert of thy wings: my soul hath stuck close to thee: * thy right hand hath received me.
But they have sought my soul in vain, they shall go into the lower parts of the earth: * They shall be delivered into the hands of the sword, they shall be the portions of foxes.
But the king shall rejoice in God, all they shall be praised that swear by him: * because the mouth is stopped of them that speak wicked things.
Doxology

Repeat of Antiphon 3

Antiphon 4: While the unhappy parents were blushing at their offspring, walking in the exile of the fall, then you cry out with a clear voice, lifting humankind in this way from that malicious fall.

Song of the Three Boys [*Benedicite:* Dan 3: 57–88 and 56]

All ye works of the Lord, bless the Lord: * praise and exalt him above all for ever.
O ye angels of the Lord, bless the Lord: * praise and exalt him above all for ever.

O ye heavens, bless the Lord: * praise and exalt him above all for ever.
O all ye waters that are above the heavens, bless the Lord: * praise and exalt him above all for ever.
O all ye powers of the Lord, bless the Lord: * praise and exalt him above all for ever.
O ye sun and moon, bless the Lord: * praise and exalt him above all for ever.
O ye stars of heaven, bless the Lord: * praise and exalt him above all for ever.
O every shower and dew, bless ye the Lord: * praise and exalt him above all for ever.
O all ye spirits of God, bless the Lord: * praise and exalt him above all for ever.
O ye fire and heat, bless the Lord: * praise and exalt him above all for ever.
O ye cold and heat, bless the Lord: * praise and exalt him above all for ever.
O ye dews and hoar frosts, bless the Lord: * praise and exalt him above all for ever.
O ye frost and cold, bless the Lord: * praise and exalt him above all for ever.
O ye ice and snow, bless the Lord: * praise and exalt him above all for ever.
O ye nights and days, bless the Lord: * praise and exalt him above all for ever.
O ye light and darkness, bless the Lord: * praise and exalt him above all for ever.
O ye light and darkness, bless the Lord: * praise and exalt him above all for ever.
O ye lightnings and clouds, bless the Lord: *praise and exalt him above all for ever.
O let the earth bless the Lord: * let it praise and exalt him above all for ever.
O ye mountains and hills, bless the Lord: * praise and exalt him above all forever.
O all ye things that spring up in the earth, bless the Lord: * praise and exalt him above all for ever.
O ye fountains, bless the Lord: * praise and exalt him above all for ever.
O ye seas and rivers, bless the Lord: * praise and exalt him above all for ever.
O ye whales, and all that move in the waters, bless the Lord: * praise and exalt him above all for ever.
O all ye fowls of the air, bless the Lord: * praise and exalt him above all for ever.
O all ye beasts and cattle, bless the Lord: * praise and exalt him above all for ever.
O ye sons of men, bless the Lord: * praise and exalt him above all for ever.

O let Israel bless the Lord: * let them praise and exalt him above all for ever.
O ye priests of the Lord, bless the Lord: * praise and exalt him above all for ever.
O ye servants of the Lord, bless the Lord: * praise and exalt him above all for ever.
O ye spirits and souls of the just, bless the Lord: * praise and exalt him above all for ever.
O ye holy and humble of heart, bless the Lord: * praise and exalt him above all for ever.
O Ananias, Azarias, and Misael, bless ye the Lord: * praise and exalt him above all forever.
For he hath delivered us from hell, and saved us out of the hand of death, * and delivered us out of the midst of the burning flame, and saved us out of the midst of the fire.
Blessed art thou in the firmament of heaven: * and worthy of praise and glorious forever.

Repeat of Antiphon 4

Antiphon 5: O leafy branch, standing in your nobility as the dawn breaks: Now rejoice and be glad, and deign to set us frail ones free from our bad habits, and stretch forth your hand to raise us up.

Psalms of Praise [Psalms 148–150]

Praise ye the Lord from the heavens: * praise ye him in the high places.
Praise ye him, all his angels: * praise ye him, all his hosts.
Praise ye him, O sun and moon: * praise him, all ye stars and light.
Praise him, ye heavens of heavens: * and let all the waters that are above the heavens praise the name of the Lord.
For he spoke, and they were made: * he commanded, and they were created.
He hath established them for ever, and for ages of ages: * he hath made a decree, and it shall not pass away.
Praise the Lord from the earth, * ye dragons, and all ye deeps:
Fire, hail, snow, ice, stormy winds, * which fulfil his word:
Mountains and all hills, * fruitful trees and all cedars:
Beasts and all cattle: * serpents and feathered fowls:
Kings of the earth and all people: * princes and all judges of the earth:
Young men and maidens: let the old with the younger, praise the name of the Lord. * For his name alone is exalted.
The praise of him is above heaven and earth: * and he hath exalted the horn of his people.
A hymn to all his saints: * to the children of Israel, a people approaching to him. Alleluia.

[Psalm 149]

Sing ye to the Lord a new canticle: * let his praise be in the church of the saints.
Let Israel rejoice in him that made him: * and let the children of Sion be joyful in their king.

Let them praise his name in choir: * let them sing to him with the timbrel and the psaltery.
For the Lord is well pleased with his people: * and he will exalt the meek unto salvation.
The saints shall rejoice in glory: * they shall be joyful in their beds.
The high praises of God shall be in their mouth: * and two-edged swords in their hands:
To execute vengeance upon the nations, * chastisements among the people:
To bind their kings with fetters, * and their nobles with manacles of iron.
To execute upon them the judgment that is written: * this glory is to all his saints. Alleluia.
[Psalm 150]
Praise ye the Lord in his holy places: * praise ye him in the firmament of his power,
Praise ye him for his mighty acts: * praise ye him according to the multitude of his greatness.
Praise him with sound of trumpets: * praise him with psaltery and harp.
Praise him with timbrel and choir: * praise him with strings and organs.
Praise him on high sounding cymbals: praise him on cymbals of joy: * let every spirit praise the Lord. Alleluia.

Repeat of Antiphon 5

Chapter [Rev 7:12]: Benediction, and glory, and wisdom, and thanksgiving, honour, and power, and strength to our God for ever and ever. Amen.
Response: Thanks be to God.

Short Responsory

Hymn

Antiphon
Canticle of Zachariah (Luke 1:68–79)
Repeat of Antiphon

Kyrie eleison
Pater Noster
Prayer
Litany
Prayer

Marian Psalter Antiphons Composed by Hildegard of Bingen

Coherence of the Group

Besides her sung play *Ordo Virtutum,* Hildegard composed over seventy chants, and the great majority of these are works for the Divine

Office. The Office was doubly important to Hildegard: first, it was less fixed in its elements than was the Mass and allowed more opportunity for expansion, for exerting the individual voice of a given church or community, or even of an individual composer; second, it was managed by the women themselves, without the necessity of male supervision and celebration, as was the case with the Mass liturgy. Hildegard's music for the Office invokes the sounds appropriate for a reformed church at the end of time; it is chant for an apocalyptic new age, one that Hildegard believed was imminent. Her most favored set of themes unfolds within the set of antiphons composed for the psalms of Lauds, and appropriate for this Office when sung during feasts at Christmastide, and for feasts celebrating the Incarnation of Jesus (March 25) and the Nativity of the Virgin Mary (September 8). Through the framing power of the antiphon texts, which have the Virgin Mary and the incarnational act as their centerpiece, the psalms and the canticle for the day become texts about the fall of humankind and the act of redemption made possible through Mary's flesh, the reversal of Eve's carnal disobedience. The discussion that follows refers to the antiphon texts, and the psalms they may have been written for, as translated in table 12.3 above.

We should note that the psalms joined with these antiphons are the most likely ones: as the choice is not specified in the sources of Hildegard's music, the scholar must offer this arrangement only as most plausible. Because Lauds antiphons were also sung with the psalms of Vespers, flexibility was built in. Indeed, another set of psalms with these same antiphons would beget other valid interpretations. The antiphons do stand together as a group, however, and advance a particular set of themes, as is often the case with a newly composed set of antiphons in the medieval practice.

Meanings, then, were made in several ways in monastic psalmody: by the way antiphons interacted with each other; by the way they framed the particular psalm texts with which they were associated (as well as with other psalm and canticle texts sung during the same day or hour); by the way the antiphons and psalm texts were tied to themes found elsewhere in the liturgy, especially as found in the Office readings or in the Mass liturgy; and by the overarching character of particular hours, feast days, and seasons. The complexity of monastic antiphonal psalmody made it a well from which individuals could drink all their lives, always finding new ideas and sources of inspiration no matter how familiar the texts became over the course of time. The psalms were made alive to an ever-changing range of interpretations through their varied modes of liturgical organization.

The first way Hildegard's antiphons make sense is as a group of poetic texts, especially as a group composed specifically for Lauds.

These five antiphons are found as a group only in one of the two major sources of Hildegard's compositions, a manuscript found today in Dendermonde, Belgium (a work that has been published in facsimile).[24] This source was prepared at Hildegard's own monastery, the Rupertsberg, in around 1175. It was most likely compiled under the composer's supervision and sent to the monks of Villers at the back of her *Book of Life's Merits*. Because the music was otherwise unknown to the monks, it had to be written in heightened neumes, and these are placed on lines as well.[25] Chant manuscripts from the region in Hildegard's time were usually provided with unheightened neumes, which required knowing the music by memory. The presence of these melodies as a group in this early source gives them a mark of authenticity. A similar set, that written for the Feast of 11,000 Virgins, is labeled "In Matutinis Laudibus," a common appellation for Lauds in manuscripts from Hildegard's time and region.

As can be seen in the poetic texts (provided in Barbara Newman's translation in table 12.3), the poems abound with dawn imagery and offer two views of the light: the original primordial dawn of Eden, and the new dawn heralded by the coming of the blessed Virgin Mary, the flower who "gleams in the dawn." The fire in between these two dawns is not named in the lyrics, but it is the flaming sword of the angel who guards the gate of Eden, keeping the children of Eve from their original home: "And he cast out Adam; and placed before the paradise of pleasure Cherubims, and a flaming sword, turning every way, to keep the way of the tree of life" (Gen 3:24). The luminous brilliance of the new light is expressed in the second antiphon as well, for Mary is *clara virgo,* "the bright virgin." Singers are advised in this chant to find the highest blessing *in feminea forma,* "in the form of a woman," for God chose her to create a new order of things and restore the first dawn in a new age.

Motives of light and new creation continue in the third antiphon, "Cum processit," as the finger of God's hand is seen making his image; but, after the fall, through a mingling of blood. Mary offers a new creation, she who is the *laudabilis* from whom the sky grows red and sounds *laudibus,* "with praises." The words the poet uses invoke the hour of Lauds and the splendor of the dawn, not only of the day, but of a new age. In the fourth antiphon, as Adam and Eve's offspring rush headlong into hell, Mary's high

---

[24] Peter van Poucke, ed., *Symphonia harmoniae caelestium revelationum* (Peer, Belgium: Alamire, 1991).

[25] For discussion of the notation of the surviving music manuscripts, see Michael Klaper's commentary to his facsimile edition of the Riesencodex in *Lieder* (Wiesbaden: Reichert, 1998).

voice (*clara voce*) calls them back from the malicious fall. Here Hildegard uses the force of music to paint the words in a powerfully dramatic way, capitalizing upon her highly melismatic musical style and her penchant for rapid register change. As can be seen in figure 12.4, the antiphon contains two setting of the word "fall." The first time the word occurs, the music does indeed fall, and rapidly, almost an octave, from C to the D below. In the next phrase, Hildegard paints the high voice of Mary's cry with a glorious melisma that rises to the E above C, the highest point of the entire chant. In the Middle Ages cantors could pitch a particular piece wherever it was most comfortably sung, as long as the whole was kept consistent and the relationships established by the mode were preserved. A particular magnificence was achieved in a series of antiphons or other pieces that worked their way through the entire set of musical modes, a practice Hildegard did not adapt for any of her compositions. Regardless of where this particular antiphon and its psalm were pitched, the extreme highs and lows used in the word painting would have been evident to singers and listeners alike. Hildegard's cadences are often marked by dramatic melismas; here she exploits her own convention.

In the fifth antiphon of the set, "O frondens virga," the image of Christ as a flower from Mary (found in antiphon 1) returns. Here Mary is the verdant branch producing the flower "just as the dawn breaks." The creating finger of the triune God has reached forth again through Mary's own extended hand, transforming humans through a new procreative action. This final antiphon is the most stable musically of the entire set, and indeed it was not included with the other four in the later complete manuscript containing Hildegard's music, Wiesbaden, *Landesbibliothek,* Hs.2, the so-

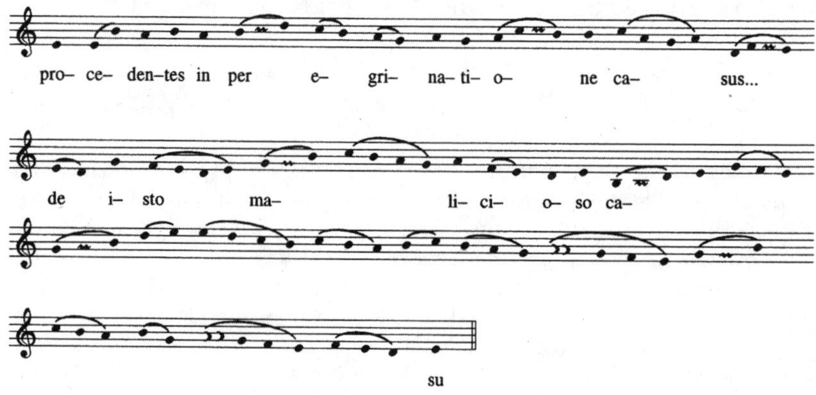

Fig. 12.4. Wiesbaden, Hessian State Library, 2, f. 467r
Two settings of "fall" from "Cum erubuerint"

called Reisencodex.[26] The antiphon is easy to sing, and the command it offers to praise and rejoice is forcefully expressed.[27]

The entire group of poems has moved creation through three states and stockpiled a series of images evoking newness: the finger of God and the hand of the Virgin; the lucent flower of the newborn Messiah; the green branch sustaining it; the blushing, glowing dawn which is first to see him and the miracle of his birth; and the praising voice of the singers who greet a remade universe and embrace the joy of rebirth in a new day. Hildegard, a nun who practiced medicine and wrote medical treatises, had witnessed many births and understood full well the effects birthing has upon the female body.[28] These Marian poems proclaim a body that remains unspoiled and unwounded as it bears a child. It is not difficult to imagine how miraculous and wonderful this idea would have been for women in the medieval period, when death by childbirth was so common. The rigors of monastic life were life-saving for the women who chose them, and Hildegard writes at length about the slavery of marriage in contrast with the freedom of the cloister.[29] Her Mariology must be understood against the backdrop of this social history, as well as, of course, its position within a venerable theological tradition.

THE ANTIPHONS WITH THE PSALMS

Antiphons, Hildegard's or any, were never meant to be read or sung as free-standing poems but were always linked to a series of psalms. When we replace them in the context of the psalms their ability to transform the texts through Christian commentary becomes clear. In the Benedictine use, Lauds for a major feast day such as Christmas, or a Marian feast, began with Ps 66, intoned without an antiphon. As can be seen in the translation from the Vulgate, the Psalm was well chosen to open Lauds, or any Office of morning prayer. With its unadorned plea that God let his light shine upon

---

[26] Now available in facsimile edition with commentary in German and in English.

[27] Hildegard's music has been edited and transcribed by Prudentiana Barth, M. Immaculata Ritscher, and Josef Schmidt-Görg, *Lieder* (Salzburg: Mueller, 1969).

[28] Selections from Hildegard's medical treatises have recently appeared in translation by Margret Berger in *Hildegard of Bingen: On Natural Philosophy and Medicine* (Cambridge; Rochester, N.Y.: Brewer, 1999). For discussion of Hildegard's medical writings, see the introductory article by Berger; and Florence Eliza Glaze, "Medical Writer: 'Behold the Human Creature,'" in Newman, *Voice of the Living Light,* 125–48.

[29] A variety of topics concerning medieval women and social conditions, with updated bibliographies, is covered in Linda E. Mitchell, ed., *Women in Medieval Western European Culture* (New York: Garland, 1999).

the worshipers as they both confess their weaknesses and offer gifts of praise, Ps 66 established the tone of the entire day and set up the series of psalms to follow, as well as their antiphons. Its stark, unadorned state made this psalm a contrast with the others, each of which was sung with an antiphon.

Antiphon 1, when sung with Ps 92, reworks the incarnation, reshaping the verses of the text through allusion to Mary and the virgin birth. In this new guise, the "Lord clothed with beauty" is the flower gleaming in the dawn, the Christ who has come clothed with human flesh.[30] The throne prepared from of old is the Virgin Mary, who becomes here the *sedes sapientiae,* the throne of wisdom.[31] This was an archaic theme, and one that achieved visualization in the late antique period, but was especially popular in the twelfth century. Hildegard used the image of the *sedes sapientiae* in her depiction of the pillar of the humanity of the Savior, a Jesse tree made from Jacob's ladder.[32] In this depiction, several of the virtues are shown in *sedes* position to indicate their power to invoke goodness, to stimulate rebirth through God's grace. The interpretation of the psalm in a Marian context also stimulated the learned imagination with the sounds of sea, for Mary is "the star of the sea" in numerous Christian liturgical and exegetical texts, most famously in the hymn "Ave Maris stella," one of the best known and most beloved of all Christian songs. The final verse of Ps 92 includes the words "holiness becomes thy house," and this too would resonate with a Marian interpretation of the psalm text, Mary being the most common Christian type for the church, the house of the Lord.[33]

Antiphon 2, with its emphasis upon joyful acknowledgement of creative powers, creates a christological context for Ps 99, a powerful text

---

[30] The first verse of Ps 92, *Dominus regnavit,* was also sung as the verse of the Alleluia for the second Mass on Christmas day. Liturgical associations such as this, and others supplied in this essay, would have been present in the minds of all religious people who sang this psalm at Lauds, and especially at Christmastide.

[31] Verse 2 of Ps 92, referring to "sedes tua," was sung in the Mass of the Roman rite as the Offertory for the second Mass of Christmas.

[32] For Hildegard's utilization of the Jesse tree in the *Scivias* and in her liturgical poetry, see Fassler, "Composer and Dramatist."

[33] During the Middle Ages, in the region in which Hildegard lived, this verse was sung as the Invitatory for the Office of the Feast of the Dedication of the Church. For discussion of Hildegard's use of Mary as a type of the church and the importance of light imagery in this exegetic complex, see Margot Schmidt, "Maria: 'materia aurea' in der Kirche nach Hildegard von Bingen," in *Hildegard von Bingen: Prophetin durch die Zeiten* (ed. E. Forster; Freiburg im Breisgau: Herder, 1997), 262–83.

associated with Christ's birth and his healing ministry through its use elsewhere in the medieval liturgy. The first two verses of this psalm were employed at Epiphany, as an Alleluia verse, and as the Offertory on the Sunday within the Octave. The psalm was also sung on Quinquagesima Sunday, the Sunday before the beginning of Lent, just before the reading of the Gospel, Luke 18:31–43, the story of the blind man of Jericho. In this story Jesus restores the beggar's sight and declares that "your faith has made you whole." The allusions point as well to the third antiphon and to association with another scene of restoring sight, that of John 9, when Jesus made mud of dirt and spittle and applied it to the sightless eyes of a beggar. The connection was made powerfully in the liturgy for Ash Wednesday in the week following Quinquagesima Sunday; this included three texts from John 9, two for the Office, and one as the communion text at Mass. Hildegard's antiphon 3 in this set, which was sung with Ps 62, would have worked well with the themes of creation already advanced and complemented the newness of a Christian dawn song. As the antiphon states that the heavens blush and ring in the praise of Mary and the renewal of the elements, the psalm longs for change during a period of waiting "at break of day." Indeed various verses of Ps 62 were themselves used as texts for antiphons at Lauds, both for the daily liturgy and for specific feasts. This psalm, surrounded by Hildegard's dawn-struck Mariological antiphon, brings new water to the thirsty, new hope to the agony of flesh.[34] The mud of the new creation is the body of the Virgin.

Hildegard's fourth antiphon refers to hell and to the fall, as the Virgin's clarion call summons those in the pit to new hope. In the festive plan for Lauds, this antiphon would have framed the Canticle of the Three Boys in the Fiery Furnace, a canticle customarily interpreted by Christians as referring to hell and the Messiah's ability to save, especially as represented by the Harrowing of Hell. In this apocryphal story, which dates back to the late antique period, Christ is said to have drawn Adam, Eve, and many faithful Old Testament figures with him to paradise. Verses of the canticle were used in many other places in the liturgy, often as the fourth antiphon of Lauds. The position of the canticle was well established,

---

[34] The liturgy Hildegard knew was doubtless in the sphere of influence of the Abbey of Hirsau. *Karlsruhe, Badische Landesbibliothek, Aug. LX,* a late twelfth-century antiphoner that originated in Zwiefalten, has been consulted here as a readily available and indexed source whose use was close to that of Hildegard; see *The Zwiefalten Antiphoner: A Cantus Index* (intro. by Hartmut Möller; Musicological Studies 55/5; Ottawa: Institute of Mediaeval Music, 1996). The liturgical use of Hildegard is the subject of a paper now in progress.

and Hildegard wrote an antiphon that complemented the magnificent song by putting Mary's female voice in the pit, calling to the three boys who represent all humankind.

The last antiphon of the set as it appears in the earliest source of Hildegard's compositions was undoubtedly sung with the Laudate Psalms (148–150), the three psalms that always closed the service of Lauds and that were among the most prominent of all psalms in the medieval monastic use. As might be expected with such an important group, several verses were selected for use as the fifth antiphon of Laudes, in a variety of ferial and festive sets of Lauds antiphons. The medieval Latin rite, with some variations, contains verses of these three psalms sung as antiphons at Lauds for the Common of Martyrs, Septuagesima, Sexagesima, and Quinquagesima Sundays, for the feast of Michael the Archangel, and for the Votive Office for Angels. In many regions, verses from these psalms were employed for the first, second, third, and fourth Sundays in Lent and for the Feast of All Saints; selected verses from these psalms commonly formed the texts of the fifth antiphon at Lauds for ferial days as well, for all days of the week, including Saturday. To the medieval mind, the Laudate Psalms were themselves a dawn song, and the opening of Hildegard's antiphon 5 locates Mary, the greening bough, as she stands in the splendor of the dawn, the light of which is refracted through her particular beauty.

In the second half of Hildegard's antiphon 5, the Virgin Mary is asked to join the praising throng, charged to "rejoice and be glad," *gaude et laetare*. The words would have brought to practiced minds an antiphon text that adapted words from the prophet Zacharias (Zechariah). The antiphon text—*Gaude et laetare filia Jerusalem: ecce Rex tuus veniet tibi: Sion, noli timere, quia cito veniet salus tua* ("Rejoice and be glad, daughter of Jerusalem: behold your king will come to you")—was sung as an antiphon at Matins for the Second Sunday of Advent, and in Hildegard's region for the Annunciation as well. It depends upon Zacharias 9:9: *Exsulta satis, filia Sion, iubila, filia Jerusalem: Ecce Rex tuus veniet tibi* ("Rejoice greatly, O daughter of Sion, shout for joy O daugher of Jerusalem: Behold thy King will come to thee. . . ").

Hildegard's liturgical texts commonly trade upon words and phrases found in the texts appropriate to the liturgical occasion she composed for, establishing these new works in the liturgy and yet expanding the imagery in new directions. Antiphon 5 offers a simple example. The phrase *gaude et laetare* allows Mary to offer praise as the daughter of Zion who welcomes her Son, who is also her King. She expects him at Advent; she offers her body for his enfleshment at the Annunciation; she greets him at the dawn, blushing, fresh, and whole.

Conclusion

Hildegard's liturgical texts and music were conceived in the context of the Divine Office and meant to be sung either in close proximity with chanted psalms or, in the case of the pieces studied here, directly with a group of specific texts. When studied with Hildegard's theological writings, the liturgical songs take on new meaning as well. Hildegard ends her treatise *Scivias* with a magnificent commentary upon the third of the Laudate Psalms, Ps 150, the text that closed the psalmody of Lauds every day in the monastic liturgy.

Her final words are a warning to all to praise with the words of the psalms, but as understood in a Christian messianic sense.[35] Hildegard takes us directly to the way Christians have so often understood the Psalms, as Christian texts, translating them into Greek, Latin, and other languages to make them their own, and interpreting them for their own uses. Of course Christians have, in this process, often ignored the meaning of the originals, or worse, even turned them against the faith tradition that owned them first. What are we to do with this? What has Hildegard to do with Jews and Christians in the postmodern world, in the post-Holocaust world? The end of *Scivias* referred to above suggests an answer. In the apocalyptic end of time, Hildegard's hope is that all will join in the virgins' song, all will sing the music that has been the angelic model all along. The virgins whose song Hildegard used as a model are a goad, calling us to the higher life that most mortals simply do not have the power and the grace to achieve in the flesh. Clearly she thought that all would conform at the end of time to a Christian view, but her view nonetheless is of a singing of Ps 150, originally a text from the Hebrew Bible. For all its glories Hildegard's tradition was triumphalist: it was a psalmody that too often makes its meaning by celebrating the triumph of one faith tradition over another, of making Christianity work at Judaism's expense. That is the limit of it.

In order to live with each other better, every tradition needs to acknowledge differences and to understand as fully as possible both the problems and the beauties inherent in the others. The psalms have

---

[35] "Praise, therefore, praise God, ye blessed hearts, for the miracles God has wrought in the frail earthly reflection of the beauty of the Most High; as He Himself foreshadowed when He first made Woman from the rib of the man He had created.

"But let the one who has ears sharp to hear inner meanings ardently love My reflection and pant after My words, and inscribe them in his soul and conscience. Amen."

belonged to both Judaism and Christianity for centuries. The new song of our new millennium will not forget the past that used these texts as swords, but remembering the beauty of the arts that kept the texts alive and part of both traditions for their use and reuse today is equally important. Hildegard provokes us to remember the worst; she calls us as well to something new.[36]

---

[36] In a recent document, published since I wrote this essay, the Roman Catholic Church has endorsed the idea that Christian expectation of the messianic second coming and the Jewish expectation of the Messiah are parallel events that can draw the two faiths together. There is much in the medieval understanding of the psalms and of the liturgy to endorse this position.

Illuminated Psalter Commentaries

Walter Cahn
Yale University

The title of the symposium at which this essay was first presented, "Up with a Shout" (Ps 47:1), in the modern understanding, at least, can fairly be said to lay stress on the lyrical, the performative, and the ecstatic dimensions of the psalms, those qualities that a Donne, a Blake, or a Claudel would have found especially meaningful. If I were to seek among medieval illustrations of the psalms an image that could be said to embody these qualities, I would perhaps choose the painting of King David in the mid-ninth-century Vivian Bible from Tours, who is shown in a state of partial undress, dancing to the accompaniment of his psaltery (fig. 13.1).[1] However, this is mild stuff. The public display of bodily abandon by a personage of royal standing no doubt raised ambivalent feelings, and such images are in fact rather rare.

My concern in the remarks that follow, however, is not with the performative aspects of the psalms, with singing, dancing, let alone shouting, but with a contrasting if not contradictory dimension of their significance for the Middle Ages and later times, the impetus that their interpretation gave to the more reflective discipline of scholarly commentary and theological speculation. As an emblem of this aspect of concern with the psalms, I would offer the historiated initial that introduces the preface sometimes attached to Saint Augustine's vast commentary (a work about which I will have more to say in a moment) in a manuscript of the late twelfth or early thirteenth century that possibly originated in the Bavarian monastery of Oberaltaich (fig. 13.2).[2] Here we see a more reflective portrait of King David, shown in the act of tuning his instrument by tightening or

---

[1] *Paris, Bib. Nat. lat. 1,* fol. 215v. Herbert L. Kessler, *The Illustrated Bibles from Tours* (Princeton: Princeton University Press, 1977).

[2] *Munich, Bayerische Staatsbib. Clm. 9505,* p. 1. Elizabeth Klemm, *Die romanischen Handschriften der Bayerischen Staatsbibliothek,* 1, 3 (Wiesbaden: Reichert, 1980), 87, no. 125. It might be noted that many images conventionally described as "David harping" actually show him tuning his instrument.

Fig. 13.1. Psalms frontispiece with David and his musicians, from the Vivian Bible, Tours, ninth century. Paris, Bib. Nat. lat. 1, fol. 215v (Bibliothèque Nationale de France)

loosening its strings with the help of a key, an act implying greater deliberation than untrammeled, divinely inspired performance and freighted

Fig. 13.2. David and Augustine, from Augustine, *Enarrationes in Psalmos,* Bavaria, twelfth century. Munich, Bayer. Staatsbib. Clm. 9505, fol. 1 (Bayerische Staatsbibliothek).

with a large symbolic resonance of its own. The psalmist is not alone but somewhat awkwardly shares the space defined by the letter O with the attentive bishop of Hippo, the author of the work, whose labor as a scribe is intended to furnish us with a privileged and indispensable access into the meaning of the psalms.

While the biblical word as a whole was deemed in the Middle Ages to be filled with hidden meaning that required decoding, the psalms belonged with the Song of Songs and the Pauline Epistles to a category of sacred writings that posed special difficulties for the reader and thus required arduous efforts of explanation. The major figures in the galaxy of early Christian authors, Jerome, Ambrose, Augustine, Cassiodorus, and Hilary of Poitiers, all wrote commentaries on the psalms, and after them, representative figures of the Carolingian Renaissance and of prescholastic exegesis of the following centuries, who built their works on this patristic foundation.[3] However, this enumeration of famous names should not obscure the fact that explanation of some sort seems to have been the natural accompaniment of the psalms from the beginning. The titles added to the individual psalms by Hebrew editors or by Latin scribes in late antiquity, which purport to identify the authors of these poems and specify the circumstances of their creation, supply them with an abbreviated form of contextualization that our modern printed Bibles have retained. The handsome illuminated Psalter from Canterbury written by the scribe Eadwine liberally sprinkles the sacred text with explanatory glosses and, like other manuscripts of the psalms, presents itself through an exegetical filter, as it were, of multiple prefaces, prologues and *tituli* attached to them (fig. 13.3).[4]

What were some of the questions that the commentators posed and sought to answer? Did the collection of 150 psalms form a single book, or were they an ensemble of originally separate parts later brought together by a redactor? Was David the author of all the psalms, as most commentators maintained, or were some composed by other writers, following various attributions made by the titles, and as might seem to be suggested

---

[3] For medieval exegesis of the psalms, see Beryl Smalley, *The Study of the Bible in the Middle Ages* (Oxford: Blackwell, 1941; 2d rev. ed. 1952); Damien Van den Eynde, "Literary Notes on the Earliest Scholastic Commentarii in Psalmos," *Franciscan Studies* 14 (1954): 121–54; Valerie J. Flint, "Some Notes on the Early Twelfth-Century Commentaries on the Psalms," *RTAM* 38 (1971): 80–88; Nikolaus M. Häring, "Commentary and Hermeneutics," in *Renaissance and Renewal in the Twelfth Century* (ed. R. L. Benson and G. Constable: Cambridge: Harvard University Press, 1982); Marcia Colish, "'Psalterium scholasticorum.' Peter Lombard and the Development of Scholastic Psalms Exegesis," *Speculum* 67 (1992): 531–48; idem, *Peter Lombard* (2 vols.; Leiden: Brill, 1994); Nancy Van Deusen, ed., *The Place of the Psalms in the Intellectual Culture of the Middle Ages* (Albany, N.Y.: State University of New York Press, 1999); and, on a more general plane, Mark Stansbury, "Early Medieval Biblical Commentaries, Their Writers and Readers," *Frühmittelalterliche Studien* 33 (1999): 49–82.

[4] *Cambridge, Trinity College, Ms. 8.17.1.* Margaret Gibson, Timothy A. Heslop, and Richard A. Pfaff, *The Eadwine Psalter: Text, Image and Monastic Culture in Twelfth-Century Canterbury* (University Park: Pennsylvania State University Press, 1992). See especially chs. 4 and 5 for a discussion of these textual components.

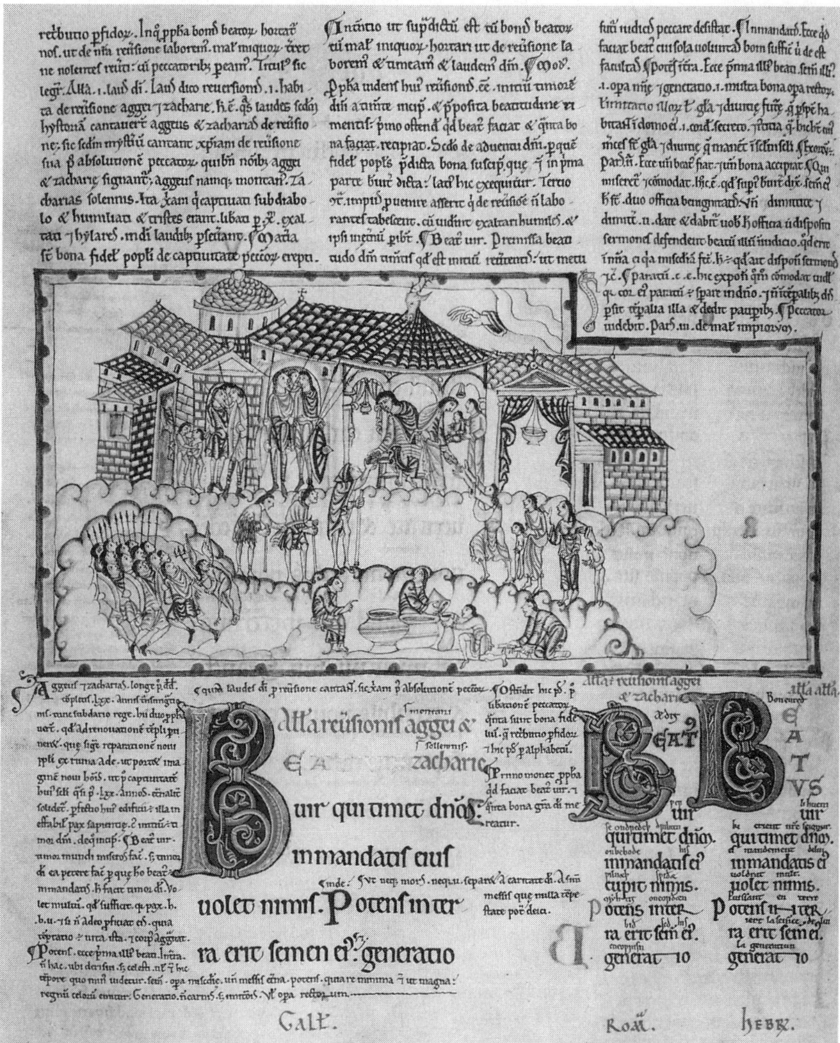

Fig. 13.3. Psalm 111, from the Eadwine Psalter, Canterbury, twelfth century. Cambridge, Trinity College, Manuscript R. 17.1, p. 122 (after Gibson, Heslop, and Pfaff, *Eadwine Psalter*).

by the variety of moods and modes of address that the poems exhibit? Divinely inspired, the psalms (according to a preface found in some manuscripts of Augustine's *Enarrationes*) "truly contain all that is useful. They predict the future, commemorate great deeds of former times, proclaim laws for the living, govern conduct, and, to put it succinctly, constitute a treasury of right doctrine from which everyone may draw, whatever the occasion."[5] It was for the commentators, Augustine among them, to draw out the moral and prophetic implications of this vast treasure house.

Many, perhaps most, manuscripts of commentary on the psalms are sober productions of no particular artistic interest, but some, indeed a remarkable number, received a handsome and sometimes ambitious graphic presentation that lavished upon them the attentions that heretofore had been reserved for liturgical books and copies of the entire Bible. The phenomenon I am describing, which is not yet well explained, reaches back to the earliest phases of medieval book illumination for which we have tangible documentation. A sixth-century copy of Jerome's commentary thought to have been written in Ravenna has typical pen-drawn ornamental initials with fish components,[6] and a Northumbrian manuscript of the commentary of Cassiodorus, preserved at Durham and datable in the second quarter of the eighth century, has full-page framed portraits of David preceding Pss 51 and 101.[7] However, the production of illuminated Psalter commentaries as a more or less habitual practice was a development primarily of the later eleventh and twelfth centuries. Some of the volumes that I will mention were written and illuminated for monastic libraries eager to acquire the classic works of the patristic literature, among which Bible commentaries figure prominently, but also, in due course, newer examples of the genre by contemporaries such as Gilbert de la Porrée and Peter Lombard. Prominent among the instigators of the luxury production of these more recent exegetical writings was a new class of bibliophiles, composed of members of a clerical elite often trained in the invigorating environment of the schools in Paris and who went on to fill administrative and ecclesiastical offices throughout Europe.

I will begin with Augustine's commentary, known by the title *Enarrationes in Psalmos* that Erasmus gave to his edition of it, published in 1529.

---

5 "Psalmorum vero liber quaecumque utilia sunt ex omnibus continent. Futura praedicit, veterum gesta commemorat, legem viventibus tribuit, gerendorum statu it modum: et ut breviter dicam, communis quidam bonae doctrinae thesaurus est, apte singulis necessaria administrans" (PL 36:65).

6 *Paris, Bib. Nat. lat. 2235.* Carl Nordenfalk, Die spätantiken Zierbuchstaben (Stockholm: Egnellska boktr., 1970), 100, 119, 122, 167; François Avril and Yolanta Zaluska, *VIe–XIIe siècles* (vol. 1 of *Manuscrits enluminés d'origine italienne;* Paris: Bibliothèque nationale, Département des manuscrits, 1980), 2, no. 4.

7 *Durham, Cathedral Library, Ms. B.II.30.* Jonathan J. G. Alexander, *Insular Manuscripts, Sixth to the Ninth Century (A Survey of Manuscripts Illuminated in the British Isles)* (London: Miller, 1978), 46, no. 17. The developments of the Carolingian period are traced in detail by Margaret Gibson, "Carolingian Glossed Psalters," in *The Early Medieval Bible: Its Production, Decoration, and Use* (ed. R. Gameson; Cambridge: Cambridge University Press, 1994), 78–100.

It is one of the author's most capacious works, filling nearly nineteen hundred columns in Migne's Patrologia.[8] Written in the early decades of the fifth century, it accomplished the unprecedented feat of interpreting the entire 150 psalms, some of them more than once; Jerome and Ambrose, among Augustine's older colleagues, confined their labors to a selection of the poems. The work enjoyed a wide circulation. André Wilmart's tally, published in 1931, listed a total of no fewer than 368 surviving manuscript copies of it, a number that could no doubt now be increased still further.[9] Wilmart's approximate tabulation also enables us to track the relative distribution of the manuscripts over time. The seventh and the eighth centuries account for twelve copies, most of them fragmentary. There are seventeen for the ninth and twenty for the tenth. Thereafter, the number rises from fifty in the eleventh to 129 for the twelfth, then descends to twenty-six in the thirteenth, and twenty-three in the fourteenth, before registering a modest increase to thirty-two in the fifteenth, when Augustinian spirituality enjoyed a certain rise in esteem in church-reforming and humanistic circles.

In Augustine's *Enarrationes,* the psalm text and commentary are combined to form a continuous sequence, a few words or a phrase of the psalm being followed by its explanation and so forth onward. The words of the psalm are sometimes underlined or written in red in order to give them added salience. The entire text is usually distributed over three stout volumes, each containing fifty psalms, but other kinds of subdivisions can also be found. The tripartite scheme serves a practical or functional purpose, though it may not be without some significance that this subdivision is also encountered in some liturgical psalters, especially in those of Irish or Celtic origin, as reflected in the Northumbrian Cassiodorus already mentioned.

In the absence of authoritative models or an established tradition, the artisans faced with the task of illuminating these manuscripts focused their energies on the opening words of the psalm, to which attention is called (as in luxury psalters) by large drawn and painted initials. However, while the emphases marked by the size and location of these initials may echo customary rhythms of liturgical usage, the pattern is less predictable or systematic. Tuscany and central Italy furnish a substantial number of datable

[8] PL 36:61–1028 and 37:1033–1966. On the work, see most recently the dissertation of Michael Fiedrowicz, *Psalmos vox totius Christi: Studien zu Augustins "Enarrationes in Psalmos"* (Freiburg im Breisgau: Herder, 1997).

[9] André Wilmart, "La tradition des grands ouvrages de Saint Augustin," *Miscellanea augustiniana* 11 (1931): 295–315, and the more recent, ongoing inventory of manuscripts of the works of Augustine published under the auspices of the Österreichische Akademie der Wissenschaften.

manuscripts from the later years of the eleventh century onward.[10] In northern Europe there was a roughly contemporaneous development, exemplified by a copy of the *Enarrationes* in three volumes with partly ornamental, partly historiated initials, given to the abbey of Saint-Amand by a man named Floricus, of whom unfortunately nothing else is known, at some time before 1087.[11] Copies of the work from the Norman houses of Saint-Evroul, Jumièges, and Lyre, executed a decade or two later, exhibit monumental initial letters for the opening psalm, *Beatus vir,* enlivened by a depiction of the combat of David against Goliath, among other subjects, an evident sign of the scribe or illuminator's dependence on habits acquired from the illumination of liturgical psalters.[12] Where three separate volumes were involved, the scribes sometimes tried to devise appropriately imposing frontispieces for each of them. A single folio with a monumental letter D followed by the beginning of Ps 101 (*Domine exaudi orationem meam*), now preserved in the museum of a small town in central France, and all that remains of a manuscript of the *Enarrationes* from the Cistercian abbey of Pontigny, must once have been the opening page of the third volume of such a set (fig. 13.4).[13] It has to be said that the realization of such a large body of writing, with its required complement of embellishment—a total of 150 initials—taxed the capacities of all but the best-staffed scriptoria. Some volumes on Wilmart's list are thus parts of larger wholes left unfinished, or

---

[10] See, for some of these, Edward B. Garrison, *Studies in the History of Medieval Italian Painting* (4 vols.; Florence: L'Imprenta, 1953–63); and Knut Berg, *Studies in Twelfth-Century Tuscan Illumination* (Oslo: Universitetsforlaget, 1968).

[11] *Valenciennes, Bib. Mun. Mss. 39* and *41,* completed by *Paris, Bib. Nat. lat. 1991.* André Boutemy, "Les enlumineurs de l'abbaye de Saint-Amand," *Revue belge d'archéologie et d'histoire de l'art* 12 (1942): 137–38, 141–44. In the middle and third quarter of the twelfth century, several finely illuminated copies of the work were produced in the same area: *Valenciennes, Bib. Mun. Ms. 250,* from Marchiennes (Walter Cahn, *Romanesque Manuscripts: The Twelfth Century* [2 vols.; London: Harvey Miller, 1996], 2:130–32, no. 108); *Ms.* 253, from Anchin (ibid., 132–33, no. 110); and *Florence, Bib. Laurenziana, San Marco 622,* probably from Hasnon (Alexander, *Insular Manuscripts;* François Dolbeau, "La bibliothèque de l'abbaye de Hasnon, O.S.B., d'après un catalogue du XIIe siècle," *REAug* 34 [1988]: 209–29).

[12] *Rouen, Bib. Mun. Mss. 456* (Saint-Evroul) and *458* (Jumièges); Evreux, *Bib. Mun. Ms. 131* (Lyre, described in the exhibition catalogues of Rouen (1975), 54, no. 48, and 69–70, no. 73, and (1979), 1288–89, no. 147, and 132, 135, no. 156. A copy of the *Enarrationes* from Saint-Père, Chartres with related decoration (*Rome, Bibl. Angelica, Mss. 1085–1087*) is published by François Avril, "Notes sur quelques manuscrits bénédictins normands du XIe au XIIe siècle," *Mélanges d'archéologie et d'histoire publiés par l'École Française de Rome* 77 (1965): 237–46, no. 9.

[13] On this fragment preserved in the Musée d'art et d'histoire of Clamecy (Nièvre), see Cahn, *Romanesque Manuscripts,* 1:16 and fig. 6.

Fig. 13.4. Psalm 101 initial page of an Augustine, *Enarrationes in Psalmos,* Pontigny, twelfth century. Clamecy, Musée d'art et d'histoire (Photo Arthaud).

what might be called "mixed sets," with parts begun in Romanesque times but finished decades later with different scribal means.

It is fair to ask whether the substance of the commentary is reflected in the illumination and in what manner. This is a large question, best answered on a case-by-case basis and with a full awareness of the fact that text and interpretation did not ordinarily present themselves as separate (or separable) entities. An instructive instance that may speak to the contrary, however, is supplied by a copy of a work at least partly dependent on Augustine's treatise, the psalm commentary of Odo of Asti, a little-known author who is thought to have been a monk of Monte Cassino active in the first or second decade of the twelfth century. Some twenty-four copies of the work have been identified, a modest though not insignificant number.[14] One of these is a luxury production executed in central Italy, perhaps in the abbey of Farfa in the Sabine Hills north of Rome. This was probably a special commission undertaken on behalf of the kneeling monk proffering an open book with veiled hands at the feet of the enthroned Christ in the elaborate painted frontispiece that graces the volume (fig. 13.5).[15] In the fourteenth century the manuscript belonged to Petrarch, who left some notes in it. The manuscript also features a sequence of marginal drawings enhanced with washes. These track in literal fashion the sometimes arduous constructions of Odo's moral-allegorical readings. As Hélène Toubert has noted, this disposition evokes the appearance of Middle Byzantine "monastic" psalters, the illuminator's likely source of inspiration, where polemical illustrations in the margins similarly extract concrete lessons from the words of the adjoining text.[16] The sketches in the lower margin of Ps 1 in the Odo of Asti manuscript thus draw inspiration from the opening words, with the distinction between the righteous man (*Beatus vir*), who does not dwell in the counsel of the wicked or sit among them in *cathedra pestilentiae,* interpreting these contrasting actions in the sense of a radical opposition between orthodox belief and heresy.[17] The marginal drawings appended to Odo's commentary on Ps 75 are inspired by the image of the Lord with a cup of wine (75:8–9), elaborated by the author in the same terms as an allegorical

---

[14] PL 165:1141–1298. Friedrich Stegmüller, ed., *Repertorium biblicum medii aevi* (11 vols. Madrid: Consejo Superior de Investigationes Cientificos, Institut Francisco Súarez, 1940–80), 3:110–11, no. 6051.

[15] *Paris, Bib. Nat. lat. 2508.* Avril and Zaluska, *VIe–XIIe siècles,* 32–33, no. 57.

[16] Hélène Toubert, "Contribution à l'iconographie des psautiers: Le commentaire des psaumes d'Odon d'Asti, illustré à l'abbaye de Farfa," *MEFR* 88 (1976); 589, for the Byzantine psalters, Kathleen A. Corrigan, *Visual Polemics in the Ninth-Century Byzantine Psalters* (New York: Cambridge University Press, 1992).

[17] Toubert, "Contribution à l'iconographie des psautiers," 593–95; Walter Cahn, "Heresy in the Interpretation of Romanesque Art," in *Romanesque and Gothic: Essays for George Zarnecki* (ed. N. Stratford; Woodbridge, Suffolk: Boydell Press, 1987), 32, repr. in *Studies in Medieval Art and Interpretation* (London: Pindar, 2000), 272–73.

Fig. 13.5. Christ in Majesty with David and his musicians. Odo of Asti, *Commentary on Psalms,* Central Italy, twelfth century. Bib. Nat. lat. 2508, fol. 2v (Bibliothèque Nationale de France).

confrontation of true and false belief. The hot, spiced wine offered to humankind is destined, following the commentary, for the enjoyment of the faithful adherents of true doctrine, while the dregs are reserved for those whom the psalmist calls *omnes peccatores terrae*—for Odo, pagans, heretics and Jews (fig. 13.6).[18]

Around the time when these remarkable designs were executed, biblical commentary was no longer the exclusive province of the monastery and increasingly the concern of schools located in the burgeoning cathedral towns of northwestern Europe. For my topic, a consequence of this new situation is illustrated by the psalm commentary of Gilbert of Poitiers, or, more accurately, *Porretanus,* Gilbert de la Porrée. Born around 1080, Gilbert studied in the influential school of Anselm of Laon, where the continuous commentary on Scripture known as the *Glossa ordinaria* is thought to have been compiled. He later taught at Chartres, in Paris, and he finished his career as bishop of Poitiers, where he died in 1154. He was regarded by contemporaries as an immensely learned and subtle thinker, *incomparabiliter eruditus,* as one of them put it.[19] His commentary on the psalms is thought by some scholars to have been composed as early as 1117, though somewhat later by others, and manuscripts of it that have come down to us do not antedate the 1140s. The latest and most thorough study of the work identifies fifty-one copies of it, nearly all of them dating from the twelfth and thirteenth centuries.[20] Unlike Augustine's *Enarrationes,* which seems to have been diffused in every part of Latinate Europe, the manuscripts of Gilbert's commentary stem in the main from libraries of northeastern France and England, with a good representation from Cistercian houses.

Most, if not all, of them exhibit a characteristic layout that Gilbert himself may have devised, though this is not certain. This layout institutes a clear division between the psalm text and that of the commentary. The

---

[18] Toubert, "Contribution à l'iconographie des psautiers," 601–3. The text printed by Migne (see above, note 14), said to be based on the Venice edition of 1651, has a gap between Pss 45 and 85.

[19] Christopher de Hamel, *Glossed Books of the Bible and the Origins of the Paris Booktrade* (Woodbridge, Suffolk: Brewer, 1984), 5 n. 34, quoting the Auxerre chronicler Robert of Saint-Marien.

[20] Theresa Gross-Diaz, *The Psalms Commentary of Gilbert of Poitiers: From Lectio Divina to the Lecture Room* (Leiden: Brill, 1996), 160–80. On the diffusion of Gilbert's gloss and manuscripts of the *Glossa ordinaria,* see also Patricia Stirnemann, "Où ont été fabriqués les livres de la Glose Ordinaire dans la première moitié du XIIe siècle?" in *Le XIIe siècle: Mutations et renouveau en France dans la première moitié du XIIe siècle* (Cahiers du Léopard d'Or 3. Paris: Le Léopard d'Or, 1994).

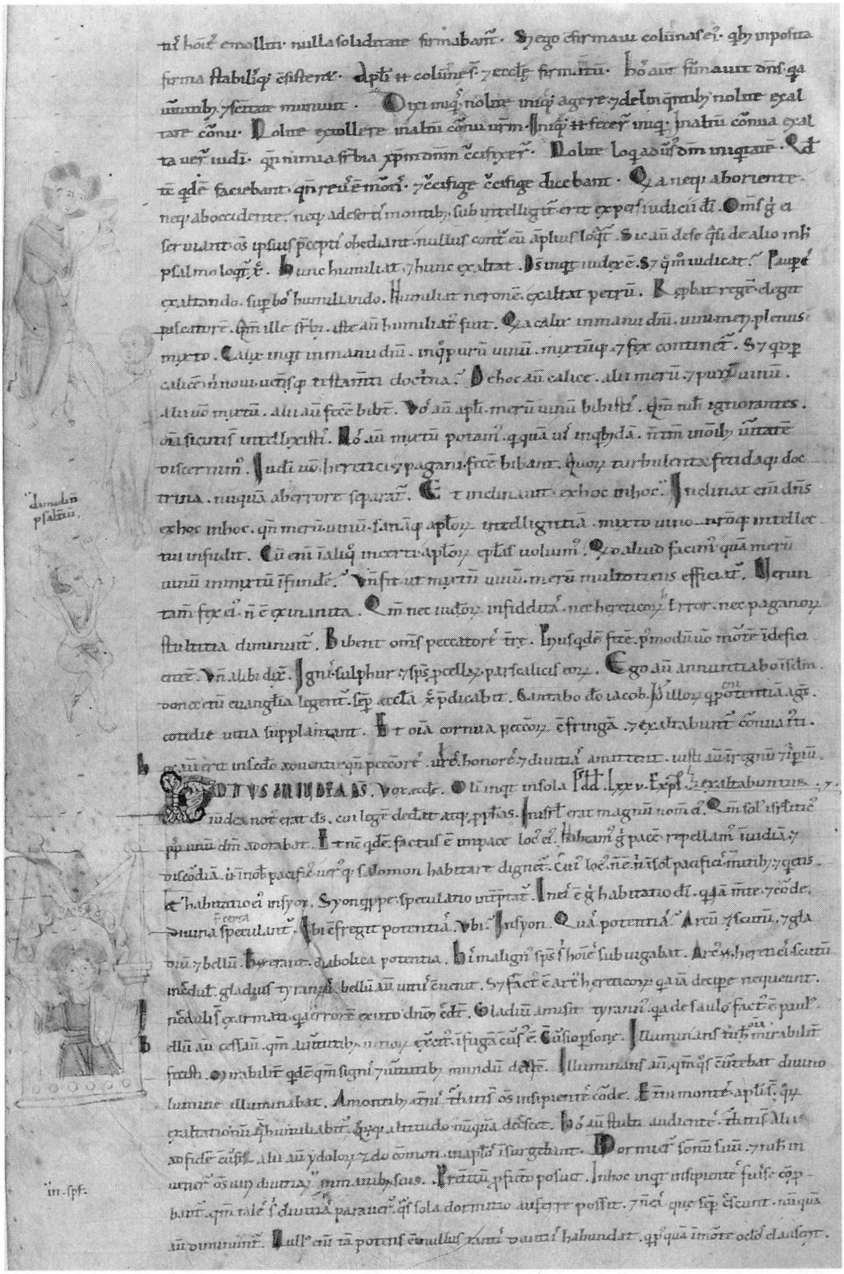

Fig. 13.6. Psalm 75 with marginal illustrations. Odo of Asti, *Commentary on Psalms,* Central Italy, twelfth century. Bib. Nat. lat. 2508, fol. 48v (Bibliothèque Nationale de France)

former, written in larger script, occupies narrow columns on each side of the central gutter, while the latter is written in a more compressed fashion in the somewhat wider columns on the outer edges of the page. The coordination of psalm text with the pertinent gloss must have presented scribes with unusual difficulties, not to say headaches. The very copious commentary must have been written first, and the psalm text adjusted to its flow as well as possible. My example is a mid-twelfth century copy of the work, likely of English origin, that a man named Hamo, who was chancellor of Lincoln Cathedral in northern England at this time, gave to the chapter library (fig. 13.7).[21] The page, with the beginning of Ps 26, shows its opening verses positively overwhelmed by the mass of neighboring gloss, a situation that the scribe has sought to counter by drawing out the psalm text as much as possible, treading water, so to speak, with the single phrase *quem timebo* ("whom shall I fear?") taking up four lines. However, the system had the advantage of great clarity, and Gilbert further innovated by identifying his sources—chiefly Augustine, Cassiodorus, and Jerome, along with a smattering of later authors—by specific marginal references. He may indeed have some claim to be remembered as the inventor of the scholarly footnote, though whether everyone would now feel grateful to him for this is doubtful. The decorative accent on Ps 26, with its two painted initials—the larger one for the psalm text, the smaller one for the gloss—alerts us to the fact that Gilbert's commentary is laid out in the manner of a liturgical psalter (Ps 26 being the second of the eight normative liturgical subdivisions). It was thus possible to use this kind of book for both prayer and study or, perhaps better, for an activity at once prayerful and meditative. However this may be, the liturgical dimension no doubt added some justification for the fastidious presentation and embellishment of the manuscript.

This combination of aims and qualities is realized to even better effect in a second manuscript of Gilbert's commentary, this one made in the early 1160s for the illustrious abbey of Corbie in Picardy.[22] The instigator of this project is depicted in a swelling of the opening letter B as he presents the volume to the saintly patrons of Corbie, and his name, *Herbertus Durus Sensus,* is given in a dedicatory poem. I take this odd nickname to mean something like "hard-headed" (or even "pig-headed"), and since he was

---

[21] *Lincoln, Cathedral Library, Ms. 174.* Rodney M. Thomson, *Catalogue of the Manuscripts of Lincoln Cathedral Chapter Library* (Cambridge: Brewer, 1989), 140.

[22] *Paris, Bib. Nat. lat. 12004.* Christian de Mérindol, *La production des livres peints á l'abbaye de Corbie au XIIe siècle: Etude historique et archéologique* (Lille: Service de reproduction des thèses de l'Université, 1976), 2:861–64.

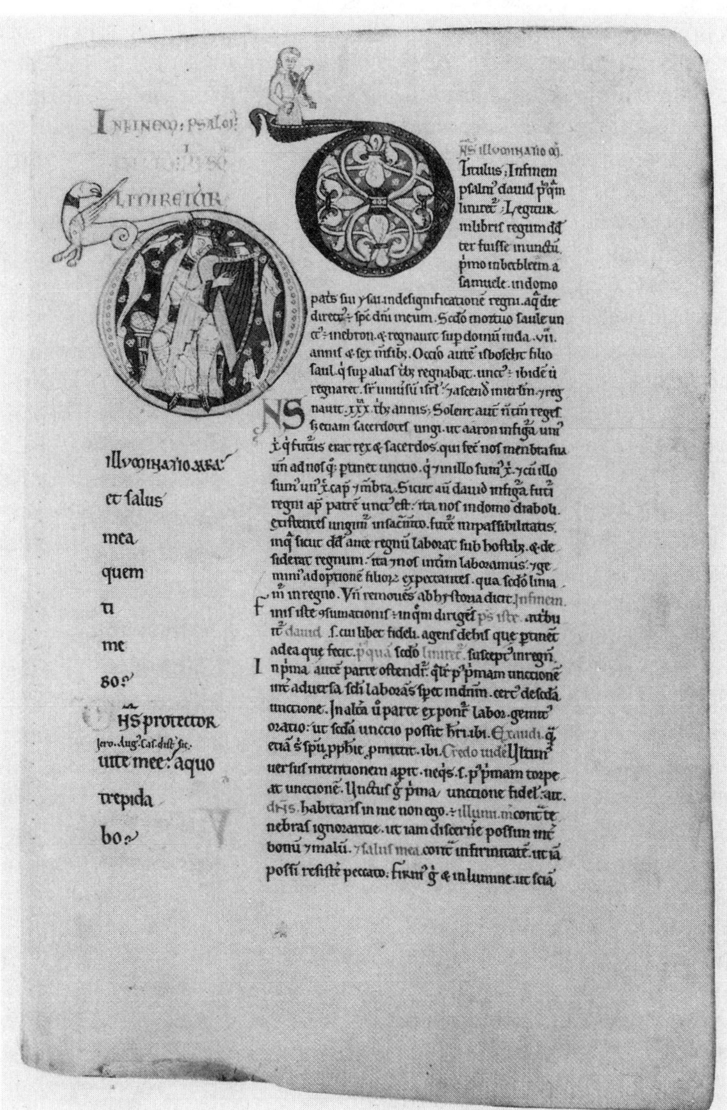

Fig. 13.7. Psalm 26. Gilbert de la Porrée, *Glossed Psalms,* Lincoln, twelfth century. Lincoln Cathedral, Chapter Library, Ms. 174, fol. 51 (after de Hamel, *Glossed Books of the Bible*).

the treasurer of the abbey, it may refer to a certain reputation for stinginess that goes with this territory. A typical page showing the beginning of Ps 26 demonstrates a now nearly perfect coordination between the psalm text and the commentary, undoubtedly the result of careful calculation and much prior practice (fig. 13.8). I would not want to pass over in silence the rather witty juxtaposition of David playing his psaltery, in the psalm initial, with an animal musician, half-lion, half-dog, playing a viol in the adjoining initial of the corresponding commentary, though the motif is something like a trademark for a style much practiced by illuminators on both sides of the English Channel during this period and the ensuing decades.

I turn next and last to the psalm commentary of Peter Lombard, of which handsomely illuminated copies were also produced in some number. How many copies of this work are still extant is difficult to determine with any accuracy, since no up-to-date census seems to exist, but it is certainly very large, and although Lombard's commentary did not altogether displace Gilbert de la Porrée's, its popularity did eventually come to overshadow it. The author was, of course, a man of greater prominence who in his *Sententiae* was to give the high and later Middle Ages its most definitive handbook of theology.[23] Thought to have been born near Novara between 1095 and 1100, he taught in Paris from the early 1140s onward, was elected bishop in 1159, and died one year later. The commentary on the psalms was his earliest work, having been completed before 1138. A nearly contemporaneous source tells us that he compiled it for his own use as a teacher, revised it, but apparently left its final editorial polish and diffusion to others. The entire process remains to be clarified, and all that can be said is that the work came into circulation endowed with prestige but not cast into a distinctive and authoritative format. As Christopher de Hamel has shown, the earliest manuscripts of the work are written in the form of a continuous sequence, the gloss following the cue given by a word or two from the biblical text, underlined, as in the older commentaries that have been mentioned. However, the scribes in due course adopted the practice of including the psalm in its entirety, alternating with or surrounded by the smaller writing of the gloss.[24]

The oldest firmly dated manuscript of it that we possess was written in 1166 by a scribe named Michael at the behest of Hartwig I, Archbishop of Bremen, for the library of his cathedral.[25] The layout of the page exemplifies this integrated manner, with the psalm text in the larger script, followed by the commentary in the smaller hand. There is a slightly

---

[23] PL 191:55–1296. Colish, "Psalterium scholasticorum"; idem, *Peter Lombard,* 1:158–88. For a provisional list of manuscripts, see Stegmüller, *Repertorium biblicum medii aevi,* 3:319–25, no. 6637.

[24] Hamel, *Glossed Books of the Bible,* 21.

[25] Bremen, Staats- und Universitätsbibliothek, Ms. a244. Hamel, *Glossed Books of the Bible,* 59, and *Heinrich der Löwe und seine Zeit* (ed. J. Luckhardt and W. F. Niehoff; 3 vols.; Munich: Hirmer, 1995), 1:488–90, no. G11.

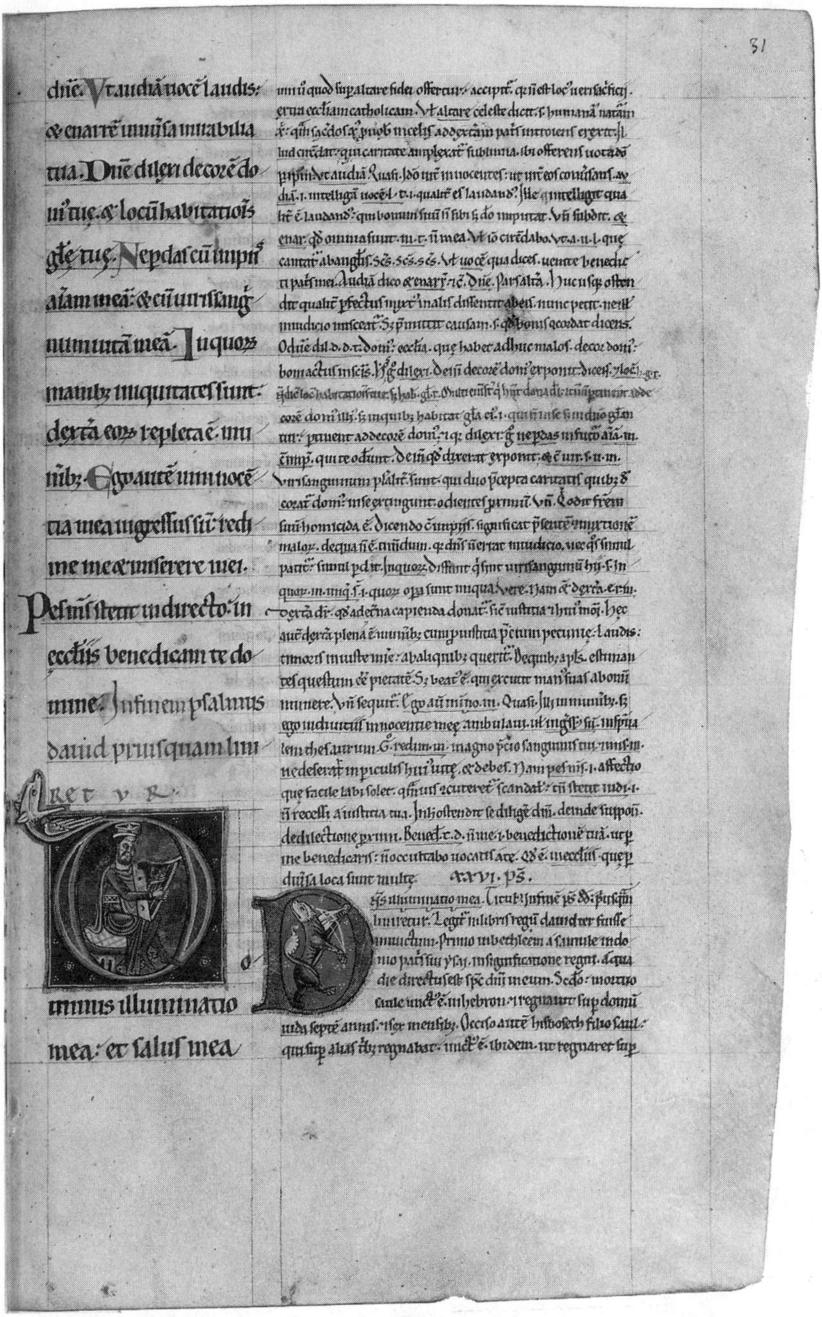

Fig. 13.8. Psalm 26. Gilbert de la Porrée, *Glossed Psalms,* Corbie, twelfth century. Bib. Nat. lat. 12004, fol. 31 (Bibliothèque Nationale de France).

irregular, ten-partite subdivision—that is, a combination of the tripartite and octopartite schemes—with imposing painted initials especially for Pss 51 and 68. The subject of the latter has a sharp, anti-Jewish edge, inspired by 68:19–29, which speak of the sufferings inflicted on the psalmist by his enemies and of his hope to be avenged for their misdeeds. Verse 22, "They gave me gall to eat and vinegar when I was thirsty," is specifically quoted by the Gospel authors in reference to the crucifixion, and this is the basis of the scene, in which two bearded men with lance and sponge, wearing Jewish hats, take the place customarily assigned to Roman soldiers as Christ's tormentors (fig. 13.9). The event is witnessed by a group of Jews at the lower left of the composition, one of them displaying a scroll on which are inscribed the dreadful words that the Gospel attributes to them (Matt 27:25): "Sanguis eius super nos" ("His blood be upon us").

What is from an artistic point of view the most elaborate and impressive presentation of the Lombard's psalm commentary to have come down to us is once again, perhaps surprisingly, a work of German origin. It is a manuscript, datable around 1170, that came into the possession of the cathedral of Bamberg in Franconia at an unknown time and was perhaps written and illuminated in that important center.[26] Its decoration consists of historiated and ornamental initials placed at the beginning of the opening words of the psalms and a prefatory cycle of the life of David spread over seven pages, for which the biblical narrative in 1 and 2 Samuel was the source. The primary agents in the diffusion of Lombard's psalm commentary, however, were the Parisian professional workshops that came to flourish in the second half of the twelfth century as a result of an increasing demand for books stimulated by the teaching activity of the Schools.[27] Unlike the German illuminators and their patrons, who were moved—exceptionally, to be sure—to issue the writings of the Lombard accompanied, as in the Bremen manuscript, with a rich and complex imagery, the Paris workshops and their imitators elsewhere gave to these books a largely aniconic embellishment, focused first and foremost on clarifying the architecture of the text and facilitating its consultation. A fine example of this textbook industry, once in the possession of the Abbot Guarinus of Saint-Victor, who died in 1193, illustrates the technical perfection achieved

---

[26] *Bamberg, Staatsbibliothek, Ms. Msc. Bibl. 59.* Gude Suckale-Redlefsen, *Der Buchschmuck zum Psalmenkommentar des Petrus Lombardus in Bamberg* (Wiesbaden: Reichert, 1986); Susanne Wittekind, *Kommentar mit Bildern: Zur Austattung mittelalterlicher Psalmenkommentare und Verwendung der Davidgeschichte in Texten und Beispiel des Psalmenkommentars des Petrus Lombardus* (Frankfurt am Main: Lang, 1994).

[27] Hamel, *Glossed Books of the Bible,* 7–13, 44–54.

Fig. 13.9. Crucifixtion. Psalm 68. Peter Lombard, *Commentary on the Psalms,* Bremen, twelfth century. Bremen, Staats- und Universitätsbib. Ms. a244, fol 113v (Staats- und Universitätsbibliothek Bremen).

by these specialized ateliers (fig. 13.10).[28] The psalm text is, here too, separated from the commentary, though a new fluidity is achieved in the coordination of these components, which are no longer merely juxtaposed but allowed to surround or interpenetrate each other. Peter's commentary on the psalms was sometimes issued and acquired by purchasers in combination with his equally admired glosses on the Pauline Epistles, a pattern that can also be observed in the diffusion of Gilbert de la Porrée's exegesis of the same biblical book.

The sumptuous yet restrained graphic embellishment perfected in the Parisian milieu is exuberantly displayed in the edition prepared by Herbert

[28] *Paris, Bib. Nat. lat. 11565.* Cahn, *Romanesque Manuscripts,* 2:111, no. 90.

Fig. 13.10. Psalm 26. Peter Lombard, *Commentary on the Psalms,* Paris, twelfth century. Bib Nat. lat. 11565, fol. 31v (Bildarchiv Foto Marburg).

of Bosham, who had been one of Peter Lombard's students and who went on to become the secretary of Thomas Becket, his companion in exile, and one of the martyred archbishop of Canterbury's biographers.[29] Undertaken

---

29 *Cambridge, Trinity College, Ms. B.5.4,* and *Oxford, Bodleian Library, Ms. Auct. E. infra 6.* Hans Hermann Glunz, *History of the Vulgate in England from Alcuin to Roger Bacon* (Cambridge: Cambridge University Press, 1933), 219–21 and 341–49; Hamel, *Glossed Books on the Bible,* 42–3, 53, 57–8.

at Thomas's request between the years 1173 and 1177, and composed of four volumes—two devoted to the psalms, and two to the Pauline Epistles—it is surely the most ambitious and complex realization of book art this side of the electronic spreadsheet, and, not surprisingly, it inspired no imitations. Herbert's edition of the psalm commentary provided prefaces of his own and parallel citations from both the Hebrew and Gallican versions, accompanied by the Lombard's glosses, along with an elaborate apparatus of cross-references. A novel element of the decoration, confined to the psalm commentary, are numerous small marginal figures or figurative compositions, many of which have unfortunately been excised. Those remaining include an allegorical triad of personified virtues, *ethica-astutia-simplicitas,* and an enigmatic male figure enveloped in flames, which I would take to be a vision of man filled by the divine spirit. Both of these compositions are repeated several times, and their relation to the text remains to be clarified. Others images show David before Christ, Solomon, the Virgin with the Christ Child, and other subjects, but most are figures of patristic authorities—Augustine, Cassiodorus, and Jerome—armed with arrows that they point toward passages in the commentary to which they lay claim. Herbert was punctilious to the point of making sure that the attributions were correct or signaling to the reader places where previous opinion diverged. Thus, some figures carry scrolls inscribed with the words "Non ego" ("I did not say that") or, like this portrait of Cassiodorus (fig. 13.11), wearing a strange, turbanlike headgear, "Non approbo" ("I do not approve," or "agree").

If Herbert of Bosham's Lombard edition displays bookmaking at its most attentive to the interests of the university-trained and philologically informed reader, my next and concluding example, produced in a monastic environment of southern Germany, meets its audience rather on the ground of typological interpretation and allegory. The work, perhaps written around 1170–80, presents the psalm text and the gloss in a continuous, integrated form, seemingly favored by more traditional readers, with ornamental initials scaled in a hierarchical fashion in accordance with the tripartite emphasis on Pss 1; 51; and 101.[30] The burden of the illumination, however, is concentrated on the highly unusual double-sided frontispiece, whose range of symbolic reference easily rivals the dense tissue of significance articulated in the commentary. Although some aspects of the imagery remain elusive, the general sense is clear enough. Its point of

---

30 *Stuttgart, Württembergische Landesbibliothek, Cod. theol.* fol. 341. Wilhelm Hoffmann, "Der Psalmenkommentar des Petrus Lombardus in einer Bilderhandschrift der Württembergischen Landesbibliothek," *Neue Heidelberger Jahrbücher,* NS (1939): 67–83.

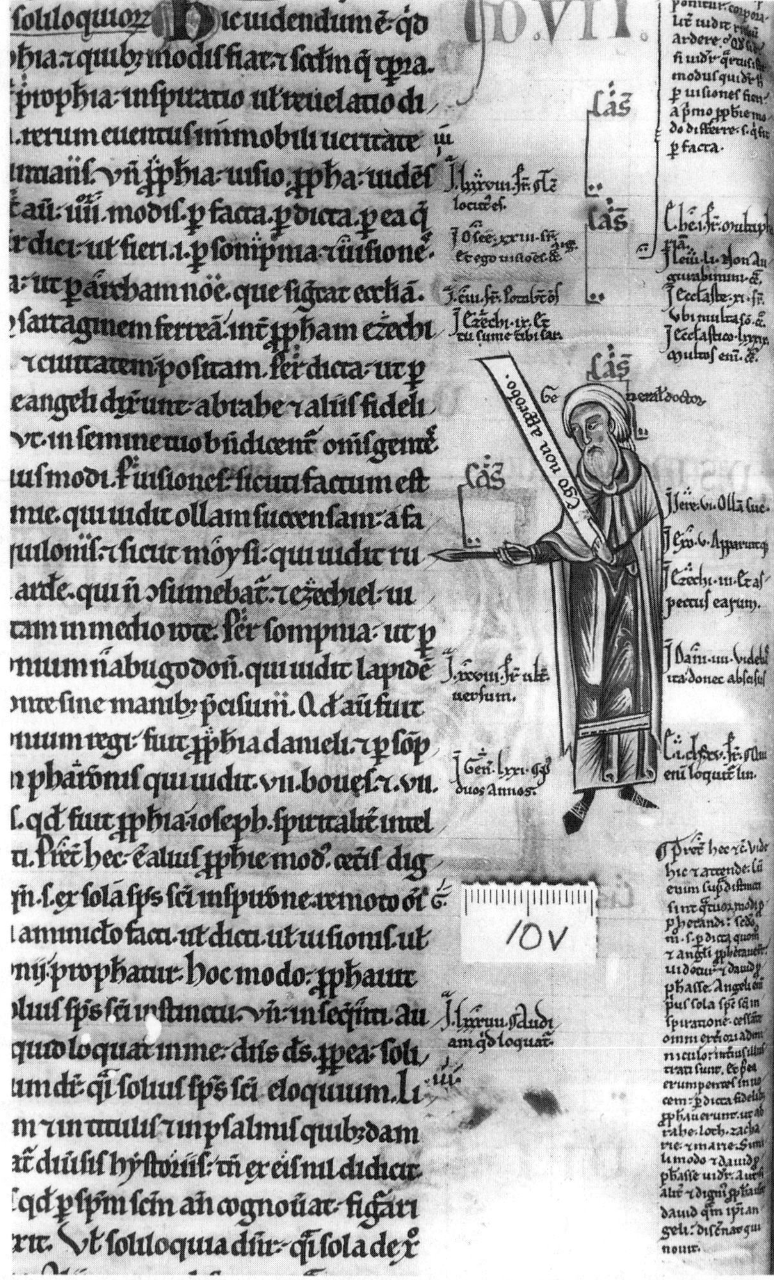

Fig. 13.11. Cassiodorus, marginal illustrations in Herbert of Bosham's edition of Peter Lombard, *Commentary on the Psalms,* Paris (?), twelfth century. Cambridge, Trinity College, Ms. B. 5.4, fol. 10v (Courtauld Institute of Art).

departure is the main thrust of Christian commentary on the psalms, which is that its prophetic utterances are to be construed as concerning Christ, that it is Christ who is speaking through the psalmist or, as Peter Lombard puts it in one of his more lapidary formulations: "Materia ... hujus libri est totus Christus" ("The subject of this book is Christ in his entirety"). The substance of this doctrine is expressed in our manuscript by the juxtaposition of images of David on the recto with the crucified Christ on the verso of the page, like two sides of a coin, as it were. Moreover, the portrait of David with his instrument is in an audacious and certainly inventive fashion configured as a crucifixion, the frontalized David displaying the wooden frame of his instrument is if it were the twin, transversal arms of the cross (fig. 13.12). The image further elaborates on the significance of the instrument, qualified in several psalms as ten-stringed (*decachordo*), the number of the strings corresponding to the Ten Commandments and being further subjected to a division into two groups of five that are attached to the side of David's body, each with its own symbolical interpretation.[31] The body of the psalmist, equated to that of Christ, is understood to signify the church, a point that is graphically expressed by the twelve windows inscribed on the figure, and said to stand for the twelve apostles.

Images such as these are rare, and we may choose to see exemplified in them the limits of an art overly reliant on the suggestive power of verbal metaphor, with which it seeks to establish a kind of parity. Perhaps the mental habits stimulated by the practice of exegesis, among which one would count associative play and speculative ingenuity, favored a parallel disposition in the illuminators to make unaccustomed leaps and inventive connections. However, the institutional framework in which exegetical activity took place contributed another dimension to the efforts of the scribes and the painters. The enormous accumulation of commentary stimulated attempts to give textual display a clearer, more rational articulation.[32] This is a process in which the short and somewhat unexpected flowering of commentary illumination that I have described was deeply implicated.

---

[31] For the symbolism of the ten-stringed psaltery (Pss 32:2; 91:4; 143:9), see Alastair J. Minnis, *Medieval Theories of Authorship* (2d ed.; Philadelphia: University of Pennsylvania Press, 1988), 46, and the references given at 237 n. 34.

[32] For these developments, see Malcolm B. Parkes, "The Influence of the Concepts of *Ordinatio* and *Compilatio* on the Development of the Book," in *Medieval Learning and Literature: Essays Presented to Richard William Hunt* (ed. J. G. Alexander and M. T. Gibson; Oxford: Clarendon Press, 1976); Michael T. Clanchy, *From Memory to Written Record: England 1066–1307* (2d ed.; Oxford: Blackwell, 1993), .

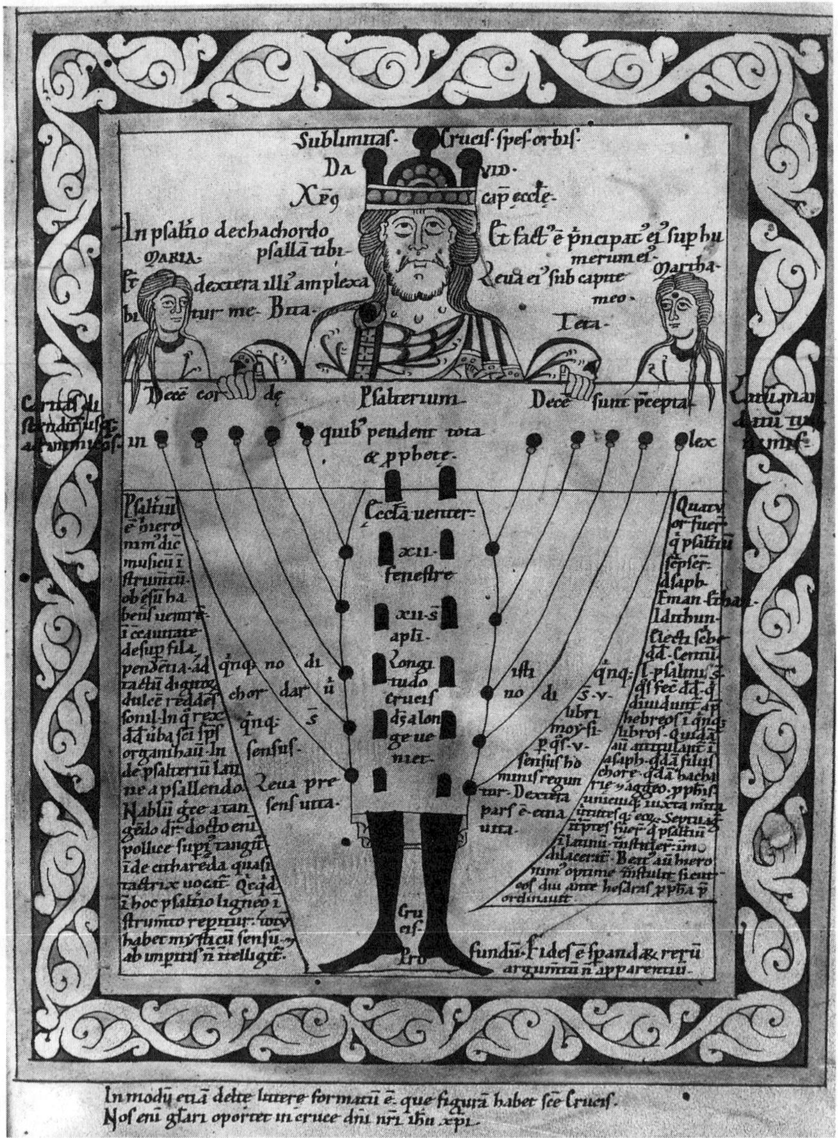

Fig. 13.12. David displaying the ten-stringed psaltery, from Peter Lombard, *Commentary on the Psalms,* Southern Germany, twelfth century. Stuttgart, Württ. Landesbib. Cod. theol. fol. 341, fol. 1v (Bildarchiv Foto Marburg).

"Soul Anatomy": Calvin's Commentary on the Psalms

Serene Jones
Yale University Divinity School

John Calvin is most famous for his work *The Institutes of the Christian Religion,* a text he wrote over and over again throughout his life, a compendium of Christian doctrine.[1] What beginning students of Reformed theology often overlook is that Calvin was quite prolific, writing volumes of tracts, lectures, letters, sermons, and, most importantly, a series of biblical commentaries. I say "most importantly" because in his preface to the *Institutes* Calvin explains that his major doctrinal work is first and foremost a tool designed to help students read the Bible. He states this clearly when he tells his readers that the content of the *Institutes* is "clearly mirrored in all my commentaries."[2] This fact has led theologians interested in Calvin's work to take seriously the volumes he devoted directly to scriptural exegesis and reflection. It is here, in volumes such as the *Commentary on the Book of Psalms,*[3] that Calvin gives us his firsthand encounter of the "Word

[1] *The Institutes of the Christian Religion* (ed. J. T. McNeill; trans. F. L. Battles; 2 vols.; LCC 20–21; Philadelphia: Westminster, 1960).

[2] "John Calvin to the Reader," *Institutes,* 1:4–5.

[3] *Commentary on the Book of Psalms* (trans. J. Anderson; 5 vols.; Edinburgh: Calvin Translation Society, 1845; Grand Rapids: Eerdmans, 1949). The commentary is a work of mammoth proportions, comprising five volumes. Calvin originally wrote it in Latin and published it, near the end of his life, in Geneva, in 1557. The text was translated into French and published in 1563; as early as 1571 we find it translated into English and being distributed widely. Much of the commentary originated as lectures he delivered in Geneva between 1553 and 1557. See James A. De Jong, "'An Anatomy of All Parts of the Soul': Insights into Calvin's Spirituality from His Psalms Commentary," in *Calvinus Sacrae Scripturae Professor: Calvin as Confessor of Holy Scripture: Die Referate des Congrès International des Recherches Calviniennes, International Congress on Calvin Research, Internationalen Kongresses für Calvinforschung vom 20. bis 23. August 1990 in Grand Rapids* (ed. W. H. Neuser; Grand Rapids: Eerdmans, 1994), 1–14. For additional discussions, see James Luther Mays, "Calvin's Commentary on the Psalms: The Preface as Introduction," in *John Calvin and the Church: A Prism of Reform* (Louisville: Westminster

of God," which stands at the foundation of Reformed theology. When we explore his commentaries we are digging into the bedrock of his thought.

In the pages of this text we see Calvin at his rhetorical and theological best. As he works through the psalms, one by one and often verse by verse, Calvin follows a pattern of interpretive procedures common among his colleagues in the French humanist academy.[4] This pattern of reading consists of four different but interrelated hermeneutical strategies. When Calvin interprets a particular psalm, he presents his readers with pertinent historical, literary, and philological evidence; this material, he believed, would help readers contextualize the psalm and clear up a variety of issues related to translation. In addition, he puts on the hat of the scholar of doctrine and examines how former doctors of the church, such as his own beloved Augustine, interpreted the text—interpretations that he is not afraid to reject or correct when he believes it necessary! He also offers his readers his own sustained reflection, as a systematic theologian (to use an anachronistic term), on the nature and reality of the God we meet in this poetry of David's and, most importantly, the testimony it offers concerning the complicated character of Christian life. Here we see Calvin at his theological best as he grapples conceptually with issues such as predestination, providence, suffering, Christology, and the character of God's sovereignty. Woven throughout these reflections is a fourth hermeneutical agenda, Calvin's work as a practical theologian (to use another contemporary term). Again and again in his readings of the psalms we meet a theologian who is not afraid to jump into the messiness of everyday life and explain how this poetry might help one negotiate tough, everyday issues and challenges. In all, it is an absolute masterpiece of Renaissance literature—a testimony to his brilliance as a humanist scholar and theologian.

What strikes me most about the *Commentary* is not its erudition but how existentially gripping it is. As I read through it in preparation for this essay, I kept thinking how relevant his analysis of the psalms seemed to my own present-day experience of living in Christian community and trying to figure out how to make sense of the world in light of faith. I thought, again and again, "This book could easily be used as a textbook for a weekly Bible study in today's inner-city New Haven."

John Knox, 1990), 195–204; Thomas H. L. Parker, *Calvin's Old Testament Commentaries* (Louisville: Westminster John Knox, 1986).

[4] For a treatment of Calvin's interpretative strategies, see David L. Puckett, *John Calvin's Exegesis of the Old Testament* (Louisville: Westminster John Knox, 1995). Puckett not only outlines the varied interpretative strategies used by Calvin in the commentaries but also develops an argument for the Jewish character of Calvin's interpretation of Hebrew texts. See Puckett's second section, pp. 52–81, where he details the "'Jewish' Appearance of Calvin's Exegesis."

Why is this book so powerful, so compelling? Why did I hear it speaking so directly to people in my own downtown New Haven church? To answer this question, the first thing one needs to understand is something about how Calvin understood and read Scripture, not just as a scholar but as a person of faith. When Calvin approached the Bible, he did not see before him just a set of simplistic propositional claims from which he could extract doctrinal truths about God. Rather, when Calvin interpreted Scripture he viewed the books of the Bible as, to use his words, "a lens which we put on" and through which we look at the world. For Calvin, sacred Scripture served as the glasses Christians wear to view reality: *the lens of faith,* he called it. Another way of saying this is that for Calvin, Scripture is a world we are invited to stand in and to inhabit as our own, a world where we encounter the God of Israel and of Jesus Christ who creates and redeems the world.

Hans Frei describes this dimension of Calvin's thought in the following way.[5] Instead of approaching Scripture as we often do in the present—we take our modern worldview as a measure of truth and then try to get Scripture to make sense in light of our experience—Calvin reverses the flow. According to Calvin, a person of faith is called to step into Scripture and to use its construal of the world as the principal measure of truth. This truth is, for Calvin, not just propositional; it is broad, all-inclusive, and deeply existential. It is the dramatic theater in which our imaginations are shaped. To use another metaphor, Calvin thinks of Scripture as a land we inhabit, a space that claims and defines us, a territory in which we live and move. Yet another way of thinking about this understanding of Scripture—a way

---

[5] See Hans Frei's description of this hermeneutical approach in *The Eclipse of the Biblical Narrative* (New Haven: Yale University Press, 1974). There are several places where Frei describes this hermeneutic in general; with specific regard to Calvin, see pages 18–26, esp. 24–25. In the latter case, Frei notes that "the text fitly rendered what it talked about in two ways for Calvin. It was in the first place a proper (literal or figurative) rather than allegorical description of the world or reality it narrated. But in the second place it rendered that reality itself to the reader, making the reality accessible to him through its narrative web.... Through the coincidence or even identity between a world being depicted and its reality being rendered to the reader..., the reader or hearer in turn becomes part of that depicted reality and thus has to take a personal or life stance toward it. For Calvin ... not the act of recital or preaching of a text, but the cumulative pattern constituting the biblical narrative ... is the setting forth of the reality which simultaneously constitutes its effective rendering to the reader by the Spirit.... It is the effective rendering of God and his real world to the reader by way of the text's appropriate depiction of the intercourse of that God and that world, engaging the reader's mind, heart, and activity."

Calvin is quite fond of—is to think of its books as a theater or stage upon which we stand and, along with the biblical characters we meet there, enact the unfolding scenes of our lives before God.

This view of Scripture dramatically affected Calvin's understanding of what theologians are called to do. He believed that the task of the theologian is to present this biblical world in as lively and vigorous a fashion as possible. This means that in the actual writing of theology theologians need to use language and images that rhetorically help readers imaginatively enter into and stand in this scriptural territory: to see, feel, touch, and taste it. This does not mean that readers must pretend that they are living in the ancient world. No, Calvin pressed his readers to live fully in the present moment, a moment given to them by God; however, to do this—to live in the moment—in and through the world of Scripture is to stand alongside the people of Israel and Christ's disciples and to enact along with them patterns of living that reflect the glory of God. As a theologian trained in the art of rhetoric, Calvin believed that his task, as an interpreter of Scripture who invited people into its world, was to form in his readers habits of thought and action that, through their textual embodiment, might actively instantiate this posture of faith. To this end, Calvin penned theological discourses designed to influence not only the thought of his readers but their character as well. To use the language of Renaissance humanism, he struggled to "make the whole reader good"; this required invoking certain "plays of mind" in his audience, as they read, certain "habits of imagination" that were conducive to faith.[6] This task of crafting character was, no doubt, a rather daunting one for Calvin. However, as we see in his rhetorically rich texts, he was more than capable of fulfilling this high calling, not only as a thinker but as a writer, an artist of language. Indeed, contemporary French literary scholars who refer to him as "the father of modern French prose" in this regard often recognize his gifts.[7]

THE PSALMS AND TRAUMA

In light of this view of Scripture and theology—Scripture as a world we enter to encounter God and theology as the enterprise of making this world come alive for readers so that it may shape them—what do we make of Calvin's *Commentary on the Psalms*? Why did he love the psalms so

---

[6] For a fuller discussion of Calvin's rhetorical training and its influence on his understanding of theology, see Serene Jones, "Calvin and the Rhetorical Tradition," in *Calvin and the Rhetoric of Piety* (Louisville: Westminster John Knox, 1995), 11–45.

[7] Francis Higman, "Calvin the Writer" (manuscript; New Haven: Yale University, 1989).

much? What kind of world does it welcome us into, and how does Calvin's interpretation of it contribute to the shaping of our, the readers', identity and our struggles faithfully to engage the challenges of everyday life? What is it about this commentary that makes it as pertinent to life in inner-city New Haven today as it was to life in downtown Geneva in 1557?

There are many ways one could answer these questions. One particular approach that has been helpful to me as I have grappled with the seemingly ageless power of the *Commentary* correlates with my interest in a field of academic research referred to as "trauma studies." This material explores the long-term personal and collective effects that events of overwhelming violence can have upon the persons and the communities who experience them. It offers insight into how people cope with such traumatic events and the processes that, at times, can heal their wounds. Below I will discuss some of the most significant findings of this work, but for now I want to suggest that Calvin's psalms commentary is a text that seeks to address, theologically, the reality of such traumatic violence, its emotional aftermath, and the character of its eventual healing. In the *Commentary* we find Calvin trying to speak pastorally to a community of persons who find themselves in the midst of a violent social crisis and who are asking questions about what it means to be faithful in this context. Using the gifts of his theological and rhetorical genius, he interprets the psalms in a manner that invites his suffering readers into plays of mind and vistas of faith's imagination that he believes offer them hope and healing. To use the dramatic metaphor I discussed earlier, he uses the psalms as a textual theater wherein traumatized persons can adopt identity scripts that strengthen their faith, even in the midst of the harm they are experiencing.[8]

I want to suggest, further, that part of the unique brilliance of this work is not just the "ideas" it offers about how one might cope in the aftermath of violence and its healing. More powerfully, it is a text that dares to take us on a strange and haunting journey deep into the heart of trauma itself and to look boldly at what it means to do theology therein. Here we see Calvin engaged in the art of theological soul-craft as he attempts to actually

---

[8] In this regard, it is a text that had the capacity not only to speak to the profound spiritual challenges that violence raised for Calvin's community; it addresses, in real and substantive ways, faith questions raised in a place such as New Haven—as well as many other communities around the world—where the ongoing effects of debilitating violence are daily evident. In doing so, the text speaks across the centuries by bearing witness to the many ways in which harm done to persons affects how they view the world around them and their understanding of God; even more important, the *Commentary* continues to speak to us by testifying to the ever-gracious and healing presence of God in the midst of such suffering.

inhabit the psychic space occupied by persons who have been traumatized and, standing in this space, to offer his readers a set of "imaginative practices" designed to comfort them, to strengthen them, and, most crucially, to make grace alive for them as they dwell in this terrifying space. By focusing on this dimension of Calvin's enterprise I do not mean to imply that we best understand the *Commentary* by haphazardly applying to it the contemporary psychological categories used by trauma theorists. Rather, I want to suggest something methodologically much looser, namely, that when we read Calvin's writings with the Bible in one hand and the work of trauma theorists in the other, we are able to identify certain resonant patterns of meaning that might otherwise not come to the foreground of our theological reflections. At the center of these resonant patterns is Calvin's remarkable capacity to enter the violence-torn world of his readers' imagination and to speak, in this space, a theologically powerful—and timeless—word of hope and healing.

To see how Calvin accomplishes this, let us now turn to the *Commentary* and explore some of these resonant patterns. Let me begin by looking at Calvin's situation and what trauma studies can tell us about the nature of the task Calvin undertakes. As students of Calvin's theology are well aware, in his introduction to the psalms Calvin offers his readers a rare autobiographical glimpse of his own violent exile from France and the ongoing agonies that accompanied his life as a controversial reformer of the church. It is notable that in this preface Calvin makes it clear that this particular story is going to set the stage decisively for what he has to say about the biblical text before him. In this context, his life story as a persecuted, struggling reformer frames the psalmic story. Correlatively, he also makes it clear that the psalmic story itself frames his own autobiographical account. In a compelling rhetorical move, he uses the tale of King David's life as a template for this dramatic and unambiguously traumatic narrative. He writes of David, "In considering the whole course of the life of David, it seemed to me that by his own footsteps he showed me the way, and from this I have experienced no small consolation."[9] Like David, Calvin describes himself as being called from humble origins to defend the cause of a persecuted people, a people he portrays as maimed, executed, tortured, burned, and assailed on all sides by the wicked. As he narrates his journey as a leader of this people, Calvin divides the world into two sets of persons: the faithful who are being unjustly assaulted by "the evil ones,"

---

9 "The Author's Preface," *Commentary,* 1:xliv. For a broader discussion of the role of David in early modern literature, see Stephen Greenblatt, *Renaissance Self-Fashioning: From More to Shakespeare* (Chicago: University of Chicago Press, 1980), 118.

and the evil perpetrators who forcefully seek to do the faithful harm.[10] As Carlos Eire has explained, this account of Calvin's "people" resonates with what we know about his actual historical context.[11] The Geneva in which Calvin wrote was being flooded by exiled and fleeing French evangelicals who, because of their faith (as they perceived it), sought refuge in this Swiss city from the violence inflicted upon them in their homeland, France.[12]

As a theologian trained in the art of rhetoric, Calvin was well aware of the distinct needs and expectations of such a community, a community under siege. In addressing this audience he is quite insistent that he is not speaking about suffering in general, in all its varied forms (many of which he takes up in other texts). Rather, he insists that he is speaking to people who are suffering specifically from harm done *to* them by others. Further, he sees his audience principally (although not exclusively) as victims and not as perpetrators of violence, although he is willing to admit that the line between the two is often slim and that harm done to us can cause us to reciprocally harm others. He describes the victims as suffering from "terrorized conscience" and as living in a world marked by "mental distress" and "protracted sorrow," a world where it seems as if "hell opened to receive them."[13] Note that, contrary to most popular readings of Calvin that interpret his "terrorized conscience" as referring to an internal, deep-seated, individual "furnace of sin" that leads us to sin constantly against God and our neighbors, here he assumes that the "terror of mind" his audience suffers from is provoked, in part, by the external persecution they are experiencing. It is a terror produced by the violence done *to* them and not necessarily *by* them. By focusing on the mental distress

---

[10] Calvin also identifies his position with the specific leadership challenges faced by David. As Calvin describes it, they both were caught in the midst of an ongoing social crisis in which they had to make life-and-death decisions without having the time they needed to reflect upon them. They both had to decide to take lives—to inflict violence on others—and did so "faithfully," even though they found it painful. They both faced constant betrayal by their closest friends and saw themselves as not just socially but also personally living in a state of constant siege and personal isolation. As they grappled with this, they both understood faith in God to be "not just a matter of cold reason" but, more importantly, a matter of a "warm heart." In this regard Calvin celebrates the fact that David was emotional and not distant from the suffering around him but immersed himself in it and spoke to and about God out of it. See "Author's Preface," *Commentary,* 1:xxxix–xl, xliv–xlviii.

[11] See his essay in this volume, pp. 285–91.

[12] Barbara Diefendorf, *Beneath the Cross: Catholics and Huguenots in Sixteenth-Century Paris* (Oxford: Oxford University Press, 1991).

[13] *Commentary,* 1:72–73.

caused by this violence, Calvin also makes it clear that he wants to help his readers cope not just with the physical effects of violence but also with its deeply emotional effects as well. This meant, for him, speaking to the complex weave of feelings and psychic agonies that haunted his readers, as well as the more obviously rational, ideational questions raised for them by their persecution.

In speaking to this audience, Calvin seems aware, as well, of the fact that these victims suffer from *ongoing* (and not just "past") and *collective* (not just individual and personal) experiences of social, cultural violence, and he crafts his language appropriately. He assumes that his readers are persons whose meaning systems exist outside the dominant systems of meaning in which they find themselves in France. They are "evangelicals" (Protestants) living in a culture whose main discursive forms are structured according to the logic of Roman Catholicism and a growing French nationalism. Knowing this, Calvin appears to take up that task of articulating an alternative discursive world that they might inhabit. Again, he had found in the figure of David an image of a leader with whom he could identify as he engaged in this process, a leader struggling to speak meaningfully to a community whose imaginations had been profoundly marked by the systemic, cultural violence of others, a community that had undergone a kind of discursive as well as physical undoing. All this is to say that when Calvin stepped into the world of Scripture via the psalms, he stepped into a world consonant with his own: a collective, social world that collective, social violence had knocked out of kilter.

Against the backdrop of these comments about Calvin's context, let me say a few words about how trauma theorists describe the effects that events of overwhelming violence have upon people's capacity to cope. By looking at this material, I hope to highlight what might have been some of the specific psychic dynamics Calvin had to deal with when he spoke to this French community. As I said earlier, the field as a whole is rich with insights, the most profound of which, for me, is the growing awareness that such violence creates in human beings a kind of cognitive breakdown that is as neurological and physical as it is emotional and intellectual. Persons or communities marked by such violence often lose their capacity to make sense of their world, to impose order on it. They suffer massive cognitive breakdown followed by a profound loss of trust in the world around them. This breakdown of meaning-structures often causes survivors of traumatic violence to lose their capacity to speak coherently; their capacity for linguistic trust as well as social trust deteriorates. To use a phrase invoked often by trauma theorists, they are "undone selves." Further, survivors of traumatic violence often get caught in a kind of time warp, where the violence that unhinges their world is forever reenacted in their present-day attempts at meaning-making: intrusive memories of the violence inform all that they do, even if, as is often the case, the event of violence itself has been forgotten or repressed. Judith Herman, one of the most influential theorists in the field, summarizes these complex dynamics in the following manner:

> Traumatized people feel utterly abandoned, utterly alone, cast out of the human and divine systems of care and protection that sustain life. Thereafter, a sense of alienation, of disconnection, pervades every relationship, from the most intimate familial bonds to the most abstract affiliations of community and religion. When trust is lost, traumatized people feel that they belong more to the dead than to the living.[14]

In a remarkable passage in which he reflects on the lament of Ps 88, Calvin uses strikingly similar language to describe what his persecuted readers and the lamenting psalmist must have been experiencing in the midst of their traumatic suffering. After using 88:5 to depict them as living a state in which one feels "free among the dead, like the slain who lie in the grave, whom thou rememberest no more, and who are cut off from thy hand," Calvin offers his own interpretation of this particular plight. He tells us that the psalmist stands "with those who have been wounded, [as] he bewails his condition as worse than if, enfeebled by calamities, he were going down to death by little and little; for we are naturally inspired with horror at the prospect of a violent death."[15] What more powerful testimony could one give to the reality described by Herman than this?

How does one speak a word of hope to this situation? to selves undone? The literature on trauma gives us some interesting clues. In her unpublished book *Alphabets of the Night,* Annie Rogers describes working with a group of teenage incest survivors. She tells us that for several months she tried unsuccessfully to get them to talk about their lives and the harm done to them. All her efforts failed until one night she tried beginning class with a reading of poetry. That night, and then in the subsequent nights when students were asked to bring in their own or others' poetry, she found that the dam of silence broke. Somehow, the space of speaking created by the poetic genre allowed their silenced voices to reach articulate expression. Why? I believe it is because for the trauma survivor whose world is "out of kilter," where regular structures of meaning are always being undone by the disruptive recall of the violence (a world of dissociation), the cadence of poetry and its associative structure invite the voice of the shattered to unfold in its space because it does not assume

---

[14] Judith Herman, *Trauma and Recovery: The Aftermath of Violence—From Domestic Abuse to Political Terror* (New York: Basic Books, 1977), 52.

[15] *Commentary* 3:409–10. Calvin uses *vulneratis* ("wounded") here for "trauma."

regular patterns of coherence; it does not assume narrative closure; it does not assume a world unfolding in perfect order.[16] Because of its nonnarrative structure, poetic language is free to ramble, weave, and be moved in unanticipated ways by passions that are often conflicting and disordered. Given the curious power of poetry to usher such speech into existence, it is not surprising to me that Calvin found David's poetry providing a powerful linguistic arena for grappling theologically with the traumatic speech of his own traumatized community. Might we imagine that uniquely here, in the poetic, nonnarrative space of the psalms, Calvin and his community found an invitation to speak their story in a manner resonant with their own experience of a world unhinged?

In his description of the overarching purpose of the psalms, Calvin offers an account of this poetry that suggests he might have seen its power in just this way, as a context in which conflicting and often incoherent feelings and thoughts can be given over to speech. He writes:

> I have been accustomed to call this book, I think not inappropriately, "An Anatomy of all Parts of the Soul;" for there is not an emotion of which any one can be conscious that is not here represented as in a mirror. Or rather, the Holy Spirit has here drawn to the life all the griefs, sorrows, fears, doubts, hopes, cares, perplexities, in short, all the distracting emotions with which the minds of men are wont to be agitated. The other parts of Scripture contain the commandments which God enjoined his servants to announce to us. But here [in the psalms] the prophets themselves, seeing they are exhibited to us as speaking to God, and laying open all their inmost thoughts and affections, call, or rather draw, each of us to the examination of himself in particular, in order that none of the many infirmities to which we are subject, and of the many vices with which we abound, may remain concealed. It is certainly a rare and singular advantage, when all lurking places are discovered, and the heart is brought into the light, purged from that most baneful infection, hypocrisy.[17]

Bringing to light sorrows and fears hidden away in "lurking places." Speaking the unspeakable. Giving language to a heart whose pain has made it speechless. Is this not what Calvin here describes as the remarkable and rare power of the psalmist—that he can express the agonies of

---

[16] David Read Johnson makes a similar point when he suggests using the creative arts to work with persons suffering from posttraumatic stress disorder. He states that contemporary research has shown that "traumatic experience and associated distorted schemas may be stored in ... non-lexical forms" in the psyche ("Creative Therapies," in *Effective Treatments for PTSD* [ed. E. B. Foa et al.; New York: Guilford, 2000], 305).

[17] *Commentary,* 1:xxxvi–xxxvii.

those whose innermost emotional world has become, for them, a source of their deepest infirmity? Calvin makes this point later in the *Commentary* using the words of another teacher of the church to describe what the psalmist accomplishes in speech. He tells us that the Davidic poet offers up the "kind of complaint [that] justly deserves to be reckoned among the unutterable groaning of which Paul makes mention."[18]

Healing The Wounds

Having briefly explored similarities between Calvin's understanding of the plight of his audience and the insights of trauma theorists into the challenges of dealing with traumatized persons, let me now say something about Calvin's theological response to the existential challenges raised by violence as it lives in the depths of people's souls. It is crucial that we turn to this topic because, for Calvin, articulating the unutterable groaning of those who suffer is only a part of the theological work undertaken in the psalms. To provide a full "anatomy of all parts of the soul," Calvin also insists that persons of faith must not only speak outwardly about the violence that haunts them but must also come to grips with the healing power of grace in their lives. For Calvin, this means coming to grips with the promise that God has made to be ever-present to them in their suffering and, in being present, to redeem and transform them as they stand "groaning" before the Divine.

As to how this redemption and transformation happen, Calvin offers his readers no trivial answer, no easy outs, no abstract platitudes. Like the psalmist, he refuses blithely to tell readers that their faith will carry them through hard times if they just believe strongly enough or that God has preordained that they be persecuted and they should therefore endure it patiently. Even more important, he does not attempt to glorify their suffering or to make it appear as if their mental anguish is a test designed by God to measure the depth of their piety. No, he enters into the depths of the traumatic anguish they are experiencing and, instead of trying to explain *why* they are suffering, offers them a concrete "practice"—a collective pattern of thinking, acting, and feeling—that he believes has the power to transform their mental distress even as they continue to stand in the midst of traumatic events and experience their ravaging force. The practice he offers is a deceptively simple one; it is the practice undertaken by the psalmist himself: prayer.

In a section that immediately follows his description of the psalms as "an anatomy of all parts of the soul" (the section quoted above),

[18] Ibib., 3:416.

Calvin explains to his readers why prayer holds out such promise for their healing.

> In short, as calling upon God is one of the principal means of securing our safety, and as a better and more unerring rule for guiding us in this exercise cannot be elsewhere than in the Psalms, it follows, that in proportion to the proficiency which a man shall have attained in understanding them, will be his knowledge of the most important part of celestial doctrine. Genuine and earnest prayer proceeds first from a sense of our need, and next, from faith in the promises of God. It is by perusing these inspired compositions [the psalms], that men will be most effectually awakened to a sense of their maladies, and, at the same time, instructed in seeking remedies for their cure. In a word, whatever may serve to encourage us when we are about to pray to God, is taught us in this book.[19]

Why is it that prayer has the power to offer such hope to the wounded? The entire body of Calvin's *Commentary* is devoted to showing his readers the transformation of imagination that happens when we lift up our groaning to the Divine. Even more important, by showing his readers the dispositions that psalmlike prayer evokes in its practitioners, Calvin tries to actually inculcate in his readers the very disposition he describes. In other words, he pragmatically demonstrates through the play of his own rhetoric the discursive mechanism by which prayer, as the paradigmatic Christian practice, reconfigures the experience of trauma itself.

Rather than tracing the conversion of imagination Calvin is trying to elicit as he carefully works through the psalmist's prayers, one by one, bringing into focus as he goes along the varied dimensions of this transformative practice, I want to turn briefly, once again, to the literature on trauma and to explore the deep resonance between what this contemporary material says about the dynamics of traumatic healing and Calvin's own account of the psalmist's practice of prayer.

Although scholars in the field of trauma studies acknowledge that there are myriad ways in which persons learn to survive and, at times, even flourish in the aftermath of traumatic violence, there is general consensus that healing unfolds—at the very least—as a three-staged process. Judith Herman describes this process as follows: "Recovery unfolds in three stages. The central task of the first stage is the establishment of safety. The central task of the second stage is remembrance and mourning. The central task of the third stage is reconnection with ordinary life."[20] She and others

---

[19] Ibib., 1:xxxvii.

[20] Herman, *Trauma and Recovery,* 155.

also argue that as this process unfolds, there needs to be an ongoing, dynamic conversation taking place between a testifier and a witness—between the survivor who offers testimony to the harm endured and the person who, having helped establish a sense of safety for the survivor, witnesses the traumatic speech.[21] In testifying, the survivor gives voice to the previously unspeakable agony of the plight, and in witnessing the receiver of the testimony is able to confirm that the survivor's voice is heard and that the plight no longer needs to be hidden in a dark corner of the soul but can now be pulled into the light of day and affirmed as a reality worthy of sustained lamentation and possible redress. As this reciprocal play of speaking and hearing unfolds, the two conversation partners together begin to undertake the task of writing a story about the trauma that allows it, in the long run, to be integrated into a broader, more expansive story of hope and hence of future possibilities for fullness of life.

How do these insights relate to Calvin's reading of the psalms? I find similarities between the two discussions at several levels. First, it is striking that throughout the *Commentary* Calvin uses the language of testifying and witnessing to describe what happens when a person turns to God in prayer. When one dares to lift up to God the most painful and often unseemly torments of one's soul, one engages in an act of testifying to the suffering one has undergone. In so doing, one is testifying to God—speaking directly to the Divine—the story that holds one's deepest affections and emotions. In prayer, one tells God the tale of one's trauma, a tale that is often impossible to tell, at least initially, in the language of everyday experience. Calvin also insists on referring to God as the one who "witnesses" this story, in all its messy indeterminacy. For example, in his reading of Ps 10:13, Calvin states forthrightly that God is "the witness of all our affections."[22] When we pray, God is the one who receives our speaking and, in so doing, affirms the reality of our suffering. Calvin insists further that when this dynamic of testifying and witnessing transpires in prayer, a person's own story undergoes a transformation as it is pulled into and redefined by the divine story of God's constant presence with us and God's promise ultimately to redeem the harm done to us and thus make "all things right." In this way, the practice of prayer allows our broken speech to be knit together in the space of divine speech. It allows as well for our experiences of isolation and hopelessness to be recast in the space of divine grace as experiences in which we are not alone but rather exist with a God who offers us, unceasingly, a future.

---

21 Shoshana Felman and Dori Laub, *Testimony: Crises of Witnessing in Literature, Psychoanalysis, and History* (New York: Routledge, 1992).

22 *Commentary,* 1:150.

The similarities between trauma studies and Calvin become apparent, secondly, when we compare Herman's account of the three stages of healing to Calvin's standard division of the psalms into three basic types of prayers: psalms of deliverance, psalms of lamentation, and psalms of thanksgiving. It seems to me that in his analysis of the three different functions of the psalms, he describes a mode of divine presence and human response that resonates well with Herman's framework.

PSALMS OF DELIVERANCE: ESTABLISHING SAFETY, PROVIDENCE, AND DIVINE WITNESSING

In his exploration of psalms of deliverance, Calvin describes a form of praying in which a person asks God for support in and rescue from the calamities of life. In such prayers, the psalmist invokes the reality of a God who has the power and the compassion necessary to respond to such beseeching. When Calvin reads these psalms, he focuses on what they tell us about God's sovereign power and merciful love. He repeatedly tells his readers that in the verses of these psalms we see clearly that God desires to deliver us from the evil of those who assail us and that ultimately God has the power to do this because God is ruler of the universe in all its vast complexity and mystery. By emphasizing God's goodness and righteous power, Calvin creates a theological framework designed to assure his readers that in the midst of their trauma they are safe and can trust God. Why is this important for his traumatized readers to hear? Following the insights of Herman into the first stage of healing, it seems to me that this type of praying forms in its practitioner three habits of imagination crucial to beginning the process of recovering from traumatic stress.

First, it is crucial that Calvin invoke, at the beginning of his training in the art of prayer, the reality of God's sovereignty, because this dimension of divine identity provides for the traumatized a profound sense of safety, that which they so profoundly lack as they wander in the world of the dead. Calvin makes this point when he stresses the fact that if this God, the ultimate determiner and orderer of all, is in control of everything, then we can rest assured that the forces of violence that assail us will not, in the final analysis, determine our ultimate reality. For persons whose world has been knocked out of kilter by traumatic events, the invocation of divine control can serve to stabilize their seemingly unstable reality by bringing order into the midst of their experiences of profound disorder. With this stabilization comes the possibility of imagining that one is, in the most ultimate of senses, safe. It becomes possible to imagine a world where the deepest truth about who they are is that God loves them—and the order of this love stabilizes and thus relativizes the disorder of the violence that lives around them and within them.

Second, by stressing that we can earnestly "trust" this God who determines the ultimate order of things, Calvin not only stabilizes our discursive environment but also makes it a place in which we can imagine that our traumatic speech is actively received by a powerful but also open, accepting, and witnessing God. Calvin thus invokes an imaginative space in which the traumatized self can experience the protection of God's enveloping arms and receptive ear. In such a space, he suggests, we should feel free to bring expression to those unutterable groans that violence has stifled in our souls. In this regard, prayers of deliverance provide a space where trust ushers repressed voices into speech, a space where those who feel isolated and silenced by the world find permission to express unguardedly their formerly inexpressible agony of spirit to a God who stands before them as witness.

Out of this sense of safety and trust comes a third important disposition performed by the psalmist in his psalms of deliverance. By assuring readers that God is in control and that they are protected and heard by God, Calvin creates an imaginative space within which it is possible for those who have felt helplessness in the face of violence to imagine themselves once again as agents, as actors, as persons whose actions in the world matter. On the surface, it might seem counterintuitive that giving control of one's life over to God can have the inverse effect of increasing one's sense of personal agency and control, but the literature on trauma suggests otherwise. It proposes that trauma survivors desperately need to believe that the world is fundamentally ordered and trustworthy if they, in turn, are to have the capacity to imagine themselves as meaningful actors within it. The literature suggests further that this enabling order can take many forms; parents, communities, nations, and myriad other institutions and persons can provide the contextual arena within which this can happen. What Calvin teaches his readers in the psalms of deliverance is that the most enduring context for establishing this sense of human agency is the context of divine agency.

PSALMS OF LAMENT AND MOURNING: REMEMBERING AND OFFERING TESTIMONY

In Calvin's discussion of the second form of psalmic prayer—prayers of lamentation—he moves into a textual world where the sentiments invoked by the psalmist resonate well with Herman's description of the second stage of healing: the stage of remembrance and mourning. After trauma survivors have become empowered to speak, to trust, and to act in the first stage, they then begin a long, arduous process of actually speaking about the original traumatic events and their aftermath. They begin the process of remembering what happened to them and grieving the losses they have sustained. When this activity of remembering starts, the victim need not get all the facts correct. It is often the case that the events themselves cannot be "accurately" retrieved because, in the originary experience of violence, one's usual mechanisms of cognition and memory may have been disabled or overwhelmed by the magnitude of the event. When this occurs, the events do not mentally register. Hence, there is often no straightforward memory to excavate; there are only gaps, silences, and a vast range of emotions and vague, dreamlike images that move in and out of one's consciousness. To remember, in this context, is to give linguistic shape and substance to these silences, emotions, and dreams, to pull them out of the "lurking corners" Calvin describes, and to do so in a manner such that one "is effectually awakened to a sense of [one's] maladies."

In describing the psalms as "awakening us" to a sense of our "maladies," Calvin rightly discerns that in this activity of remembering one is not engaged in a straightforward process of simply recollecting previously known subject matter. The act of speaking, at this stage in the healing process, involves actively creating a new discursive awareness of something previously unknown. As Calvin often reminds his readers, it is only when they hear the psalmist lament the harm done to him that they, by mimicking his words as they pray, find a language for and an awareness of the trauma they have endured. As the trauma literature further tells us, it is important that these emerging sentiments not be negatively judged or criticized as inappropriate, false, immoral, or incoherent; they simply are what they are: the groans of the violated. Further, when the groans are heard in all their incoherence and emotional volatility, the traumatized person begins to develop the capacity to mourn the harm done. In this regard, along with remembering comes the process of grieving—of deeply lamenting—the traumatic reality to which one is testifying.

When I first ventured into Calvin's analysis of the psalms of lamentation, the degree to which he encourages his readers to identify with the often violent rage of the psalmist and to hate viciously the "wicked ones" who have hurt him made me very uncomfortable. In these psalms Calvin fully shares the writer's sense that the world can be sharply divided into two groups of people, the good and the evil, and that the good people who have suffered the oppression of the evil ones have every right to want their oppressors to suffer, to be punished by God, to be annihilated by divine wrath. As he reads through these psalms, he refuses to remove the sharp edges of these feelings; in fact, he often goes further than the psalmist in expressing his anger, outrage, despair, urge for revenge, and desire for unspeakable harm to befall the wicked. In this respect, his account of these psalms is uncomfortably rough, assaultive, emotional, and irrationally rage filled.

When I began to read these psalms in light of trauma literature, however, my assessment shifted; I was less troubled and more intrigued by the rhetorical force of Calvin's interpretation. I began to understand that by allowing the full range of human emotions to surface in his reading of these psalms, Calvin creates a vivid imaginative space within which his readers can similarly experience, without negative judgment, the outrage and grief that emerge as they remember and name the traumatic harm they have suffered. Moreover, I began to appreciate how his own articulation of these sentiments may have provided his readers with a language that they might not initially have possessed but that they could now actively inhabit as they struggled to speak. I began to see as well that demonizing their perpetrators may have been an essential part of their healing process and that admitting the depth of their anger toward their persecutors might have been a necessary precursor to his community's return to the land of the living. Given this, Calvin's skills at vitriolic oration began to impress me as a theological strength rather than as a discomforting theological weakness. I began to see that perhaps the more caustic the language became, the more expansive the possibilities of healing.

PSALMS OF THANKSGIVING: REINTEGRATION OF THE MUNDANE AND THE SCOPE OF DIVINE GRACE

These prayers of lamentation are not the last word with which Calvin leaves his readers, however. He also devotes his attention to the third category, psalms of thanksgiving. Like the two previous categories of psalms, his interpretation of these prayers bears striking resemblance to Herman's schema, in this case the third stage of healing: reconnection with everyday life. According to Herman, what needs to happen in this stage of healing is that the trauma survivor and the witness need to undertake together the task of telling a story in which the now-articulated experience of trauma is woven into an account of daily life that allows the person to reenter the land of living. Herman suggests that central to this activity of storytelling is the ability of trauma survivors to reconnect with the regular and often rather mundane patterns of meaning-making that constitute the linguistic stage of everyday life. This requires telling a story in which the survivor's tale of the violence done is not forgotten or unrealistically glorified but is, rather, integrated into patterns of speech and forms of knowledge that are broader, more complex, and experientially more comprehensive than the disrupted discourse of trauma.

Given its scope, this third stage of healing often takes a lifetime to enact. It consists of such simple things as learning how a person can at one and the same time remember seeing the violent death of a friend and enjoy such tasks as baking bread, caring for children, and going to a Sunday morning psalm-sing. To be able to see all these experiences as constitutive of one's lived reality is difficult, not only at a practical level, but, perhaps even more importantly, at the level of imagination. It requires having an interior landscape of imagination capable of holding together images of both haunting violence and kneading bread, each envisioned in its fullness as well as in its relativized relation to the other. It is only when their imagination has been so capacitated, Herman suggests, that trauma survivors retrieve their ability to hope and to act subsequently in a world that had been marked by broken speech, lost memory, and failed agency.

I want to suggest that this integration unfolds powerfully for readers as they move through Calvin's interpretations of David's psalms of thanksgiving. Calvin not only shows readers of these poems how to render God praise for their deliverance from the harm that threatens them; he also uses very commonplace references to ground his descriptions of the activity of praising. At times he beckons his reader to give God thanks for God's mighty acts against vast nations and grand enemies, while at other times he uses details taken from daily life as the occasion for offering thanks. These psalms are rich in references to the majesty and splendor of nature as a hallmark of God's continued presence with us. Imagery of eating, of feasting, of resting, of walking safely, of sleeping peacefully, of life lived in a web of secure relations and hope—all these serve as reminders to his readers that the God whose providence protects us, and whose witnessing ears and eyes receive us, is also a God who offers to us a future in which violence need no longer be the determinative reality of our imaginative landscapes, a God who gives to us food, sleep, daily work, and the bonds of human community. In other words, through these psalms Calvin takes a world that has been thrown out of kilter and not only stabilizes it but also weaves it back into a worldview where violence itself no longer determines the central features of one's ongoing experience.

What is also remarkable about these psalms is that Calvin accomplished this reintegration into the mundane world of everyday life not by pollyanishly pretending as if the trauma his readers have suffered never happened or has somehow magically disappeared just because it has been remembered and mourned. Rather, Calvin allows the reality testified to in the first two types of psalms to continue to echo through the praising prayers of this third type of psalm. He admits that praise itself must often emerge in the midst of continued suffering and persecution. What is crucial, therefore, is not that the pain disappears or that the forces of violence cease to bear down upon us but that there is a shift with respect to the hold that traumatic violence has upon the imaginative capacity of the one who suffers. In these psalms of the third kind, hope returns not because evil is explained or immediate justice is invoked but because through the activity of psalmic thanksgiving the goodness of God is publicly attested to and reaffirmed. By invoking such goodness, the world in all its complex wonder returns to the traumatized as a gift of God.

Conclusion

In this essay I have only just begun to explore the riches held in Calvin's reading of the psalms. If you find this discussion compelling, you might benefit most not from more academic reflection on the theological world Calvin renders in these texts but from actually reading parts of the *Commentary* yourself and, in doing so, experiencing the power of Calvin's poetic voice. It is in the texture of his language and the play of mind it invokes that one comes to understand the prayerful disposition that Calvin believes can heal the wounds of traumatic violence.

For those who choose to embark on such a reading, let me close with several questions raised for me as I worked with this material, questions to which I have no answers but which directly relate to how we understand the relation of theology to traumatic violence in today's world. The first concerns the performative character of psalmic interpretation. In his introduction to the *Commentary* as well as throughout the body of his readings, Calvin refers repeatedly to his text as a "performance" and to himself as a "performer."[23] What insights might we gain into the nature and task of theological reflection if we took, as Calvin bids, its performative dimensions more seriously? This question relates back to my initial claim that dramatic imagery captures, for Calvin, the true scope and function of theological discourse and its relation to scriptural exegesis. In this context, let us ask what it might mean to "perform the psalms," to take them on as dramatic roles and to let them become the script of action? Would this not raise for us important questions about the relation between aesthetics, theological discourse, and the nature of social action and practice?

Related to this is a second question. Though in this essay I have mainly focused on Calvin's written commentary on the psalms, it is not the only context in which he engaged the poetic prayers of David. Calvin regularly preached on the psalms in the afternoon service of the worship community of Geneva. Liturgically, they also constituted the substance of congregational hymn singing. In his Geneva articles on church organization and worship, Calvin describes this activity as a crucial part of the communal prayers that the faithful perform together with patterned regularity. As he explains it, singing the psalms would edify them, "so that the hearts of all be roused and incited to make like prayers and render like praises and thanks to God with one accord."[24] In other words, singing the psalms is one of the central ways in which Calvin imagined people collectively lifting up to God their innermost thoughts as well as their shared and spoken yearnings.

If my analysis of the psalms and trauma were to have extended to include this dimension of psalmic practice, I would have moved more

---

[23] See, for example, ibid., 1:xlii.

[24] John Calvin, "Articles concerning the Organization of the Church and of Worship at Geneva Proposed by the Ministers at the Council January 16, 1537," in *Calvin: Theological Treatises* (trans. J. K. S. Reid; Philadelphia: Westminster, 1954), 48.

directly into a discussion of liturgy and the role it plays in the collective healing of traumatic violence. It seems to me that it may have been in the actual, embodied performance of the psalms that Calvin helped the whole body of Christ undergo a healing process that was as physical as it was emotional. Might we imagine that by singing the psalms the church performed itself into a new and ever-renewed form of embodied community? The possibilities for expanding our interpretation of the psalms in this direction are exciting not only for our understanding of ecclesiology but for eschatology as well. It bids us to consider the nature of hope performed and the physical, embodied dimensions of theological transformation.

This brings me to a final question—a question less hopeful and more sobering to consider. While it is inspiring to think of a community of people performing themselves into a new community through their collective reenactment of psalmic praise, we must face the possibility that these poems/songs might also be performed in a manner that forcefully reinscribes the violence articulated rather than healing it. Recall in my earlier discussion of the literature on trauma the claim that, when persons experience overwhelming violence, there is often a tendency compulsively to reenact the originary scene of the trauma without interrupting its dramatic unfolding. If this is true—if people who have suffered traumatic events can become caught in a time warp where the violence done to them is constantly reenacted in the present, often in a manner unknown to them or in ways that pass as "normal"—it may well be that a community could use the often vengeful rhetoric of the psalms to fuel hate rather than transform it into healing praise of God. History testifies well to the fact that Reformed theology and its liturgies have been used, at times, to encourage rather than disrupt the force of collective violence. When this occurs, the psalms themselves risk becoming a weapon that actually inflicts trauma instead of serving as its calming balm, as Calvin would have it. This raises, then, a most pressing question: When is a theological testimony to violence the source of healing, and when is it the cause of harm? As to the answer, perhaps it requires a form of theological discernment that Calvin himself teaches us in his interpretation of the prayerful, psalmic play of mind, a discernment that is as attentive to power and context as it is to the heavenly truths its professes. This is doubtless a complicated challenge, but it is surely one worthy of David—and of Calvin—and the present-day church that lives, as it always has, in a world where trauma and hope remain conflicted but constant companions.*

---

* I want to thank Susan Pfeil, whose course work on Calvin, the psalms, and trauma theory played a crucial role in helping me conceptualize the central argument of this essay.

Calvin's Geneva and the Psalms

Carlos Eire
Yale University

You are living in exile, in a city that remains foreign to you and that you don't like very much. Few people seem to genuinely like you. Many distrust you and are busy doing everything within their power to run you out of town, back to wherever you came from, which in your case happens to be Noyon, in Picardy.[1] The problem is that if you go back to Noyon, you will be killed for your beliefs. Your native land is ruled by a monarch who is God's enemy and an unrepentant idolater, bent on making all his subjects follow a false, humanly devised religion that dishonors God. The price for refusing to worship as an idolater is death.[2]

Those psalms, they keep you going. You sing along with David: "The Lord is my light and my salvation; whom do I fear? The Lord is my life's refuge; of whom am I afraid? When evildoers come at me to devour my flesh, these my enemies and foes themselves stumble and fall" (Ps 27:1–2).

Your life is dedicated entirely to your work, a work that many around you seem not to appreciate or, worse, to despise. You work around the clock. You write tirelessly: theological treatises, Bible commentaries, letters by the hundreds. You keep several scribes busy, day in day out, except on

---

[1] On Calvin's life, see Bernard Cottret, *Calvin: A Biography* (trans. M. W. McDonald (Grand Rapids: Eerdmans, 2000); William G. Naphy, *Calvin and the Consolidation of the Genevan Reformation* (Manchester; Manchester University Press, 1994); William Bouwsma, *John Calvin: A Sixteenth Century Portrait* (New York: Oxford University Press, 1988); Alister McGrath, *A Life of John Calvin* (Oxford: Blackwell, 1990); and Thomas H. L. Parker, *John Calvin* (Philadelphia: Westminster, 1977).

[2] On persecution and religious violence in Calvin's France, see Denis Crouzet, *Les guerriers de Dieu: La violence au temps des troubles de religion, 1525–1610* (2 vols.; Seyssel: Champ Vallon, 1990); Mark Greengrass, *The French Reformation* (Oxford: Blackwell, 1987); Francis Higman, *La diffusion de la Réforme en France, 1520–1565* (Geneva: Labor et Fides, 1992); and J. H. M. Salmon, *Society in Crisis: France in the Sixteenth Century* (New York: St. Martins, 1978).

the Sabbath. But you also lead worship. You write sermons and deliver them, three times a week. You oversee admission to the communion table. You share in the deliberations of a court that oversees everyone's behavior in town. In spite of pouring yourself out like this, you are also convinced that many around you would like to see you dead. Your own relatives cause you trouble and embarrass you beyond what is bearable.[3]

If it weren't for those psalms, you might give up. "God is present as my helper; the Lord sustains my life" (Ps 54:6).

As if this were not enough, you suffer from various ailments, all of them serious. You are plagued by migraine headaches, ulcers, kidney stones, indigestion, high blood pressure, hemorrhoids of the worst sort, and all the remedies offered by sixteenth-century medicine. You especially remember that time that the stones and the hemorrhoids hit you at the same time, and the doctor prescribed horseback riding as a means of shaking loose the stones. You remember obeying the doctor. You remember the torture imposed on you by nature and the physicians. You always obey. Always. You always do what is right. Pain is beside the question.[4]

But those psalms, they bear you up,[5] and you hope they do the same for everybody else. "God's faithfulness is a protecting shield. You shall not fear the terror of the night, nor the arrow that flies by day, nor the pestilence that roams in darkness, nor the plague that ravages at noon. Though a thousand fall at your side, ten thousand at your right hand, near you it shall not come. You need simply watch; the punishment of the wicked you will see" (Ps 91:4–8).

You are John Calvin, the leader of the church in Geneva. You have already been kicked out of the city once and have returned only because you are convinced God wants you there. You actually hate the place and have no clue how long you will remain there. You don't know, of course, that you will die there while still a young man at the age of fifty-five, in 1564, while you still dictate letters to scribes and your friends ask you to take it easy.

---

[3] See William Monter, *Calvin's Geneva* (New York: Wiley, 1967).

[4] Calvin gave intimate details about his ailments in his correspondence, but we also have the testimony of his first biographer, Theodore Beza, who knew him intimately. See Beza's *Vita Calvini,* available in John Calvin, *Joannis Calvini opera quae supersunt omnia* (ed. W. Baum et al.; 59 vols.; Corpus reformatorum 29–87; Braunschweig: Schwetschke, 1863–1900), vol. 21; English translation in John Calvin, *Tracts and Treatises* (3 vols.; Endinburgh, 1851; repr., Grand Rapids: Eerdmans, 1958), 1:lvii–cxxxviii.

[5] See Ford Lewis Battles, trans. and ed., *The Piety of John Calvin: An Anthology Illustrative of the Spirituality of the Reformer* (music edited by Stanley Tagg; Grand Rapids: Baker, 1978).

You rely on the psalms to get you through every single day. God speaks to you, and you speak back to God. You sing back to God, in public, too. You love and live the psalms. No wonder you reveal so much more about yourself in the preface to your commentary on the psalms than you do anywhere else in the thousands of pages that you write.

> Praise the Lord, all you nations!
> Give glory, all you peoples! (Ps 117:1)

You have no way of knowing that when your best friend and associate asks you to stop working, while you are on your deathbed, you will snap at him and say, "What? Would you have God find me idle?" You will say this to the man responsible for creating the Geneva Psalter, Theodore Beza. You will say this to the man who has helped turn your love for the psalms into what will become the heart of worship for thousands upon thousands of people for centuries to come.[6]

You are the author of the *Institutes,* an incredible compendium of Christian theology, unlike any other ever written, and you are responsible for creating a unique Christian society in an independent city-state that will always consider you a foreigner. A Scotsman passing through your beleaguered city, John Knox, will pay you the ultimate compliment. He will say that not since the time of the apostles has there ever been any community on earth that follows the gospel as well as Geneva. Knox will be especially pleased by the way in which worship is conducted in Geneva. He will especially love the fact that the psalms are the backbone of the ritual life of Geneva. All the senseless idolatrous braying of the Roman Catholic Church replaced by the simple singing of the psalms—imagine that.

Calvin's Geneva deserves attention in any book dedicated to the psalms for one very simple reason. Geneva was a city in which the psalms were the language of communication with God. God spoke through the psalms, and the people prayed to God through the psalms. In a city committed to ordering every aspect of life around the Word of God and to accepting no worship except demanded by God, what better set of words could there be but the psalms?

The psalms were the only extensive example of the right kind of worship found in the Bible that could still apply to Christians, now that temple

---

[6] On the Geneva Psalter, see *Le Psautier de Genève, 1562–1865: Images commentées et essai de bibliographie* (Geneva: Droz, 1986); Orentin Douen, *Clément Marot et le Psautier huguenot: Étude historique, littéraire, musicale et bibliographique* (2 vols.; Paris: Imprimerie Nationale, 1878–79); Waldo Selden Pratt, *The Significance of the Old French Psalter* (New York: The Hymn Society, 1933).

worship was impossibly obsolete.[7] As the heart of Scripture, they brought the elect as close to God as was possible. Scripture, it must be remembered, "keeps us under control and makes us walk in the fear and obedience of God; it makes us put all our trust in him so that we invoke Him" (*Institutes,* 2.2.25)—and invoking was done so well, and so thoroughly, by the psalms themselves.

Yet my focus will not be the way in which the psalms were integrated into worship or how worship was conducted but rather the way in which Geneva sought to embody the psalms and everything contained within them. I am convinced, after twenty-five years of working on Calvin and Calvinism, that the psalms were a constant frame of reference for Calvin, in a personal and communal sense. Geneva was not just the city of God's elect; it was also necessarily the city of the psalms.

As Calvin saw it, the psalms were key (1) to understanding how God is worshiped; (2) to understanding how God's elect must behave; and (3) to communicating with God.

On the first point, Calvin framed much of his understanding of the nature and purpose of worship on the language of the psalms. John Calvin was convinced that the most important thing in life was to have the right relationship with God. He begins the *Institutes* (1.1.1) by saying that what matters most in life can be summed up in two questions: Who is God? And who am I? The fact that Saint Francis had summed it up the same way did not matter to Calvin. Francis was part of a church that Calvin considered fallen and idolatrous. The Roman Catholic Church was wrong on all accounts: it worshiped incorrectly because it had come up with the wrong answer to those two basic questions. Saint Francis was wrong, and so was his whole church.

As Calvin said in his commentary on Ps 123:3 ("Show us favor, Lord, show us favor for we have our fill of contempt"), the true church was "deprived of all worldly protection and lying under the feet of enemies who abound in all things and are armed with fearful power."

For Calvin, God was a transcendent being who could only be approached as spirit. Material points of contact with the divine were not to be sought out. God mixed with these as much as fire mixes with water. He had commanded total reverence in his revealed Word, the Bible. There were no compromises to be had. He was Other and unapproachable by any means invented by humans. Anything other than what God had commanded was idolatry. Moroever, if one did not worship correctly, everything else was wrong. True piety begets true confession—this was

---

[7] See Richard R. Terry, ed., *Calvin's First Psalter: 1539* (with critical notes and modal harmonies to the melodies; London: Benn, 1932).

one of Calvin's guiding principles—and he found that much of what he saw in the Catholic Church in which he had been reared resembled the religion of the Canaanites and Egyptians:[8]

> Their idols are silver and gold, the work of human hands. They have mouths but do not speak, eyes but do not see. They have ears but do not hear, noses but do not smell. They have hands but do not feel, feet but do not walk, and no sound rises from their throats. Their makers shall be like them, all who trust in them. (Ps 115:4–8).

It was that black and white for Calvin. Do not let anyone argue otherwise. God's elect were a chosen few, surrounded by idolatry on all sides, numerically inferior, always on the brink of extinction by the world's standards, but always protected directly by the hand of God. One crucial item ensured that the covenant between God and his people worked the right way, as in the case of the ancient Israelites: the chosen must worship correctly. Calvin was convinced that anything other than correct worship would surely bring out God's wrath.[9]

This is why anyone who was suspected of attending Mass outside Geneva could be brought to justice, fined, even expelled from the city. And the temptation was always there, just a few miles away, in places such as at Annency, where the exiled bishops of Geneva resided.

On the second point, Geneva was the city of exclusion par excellence. It was the city of the elect, and the elect observed God's law as closely as possible. God demanded right worship and right behavior. The sinner had no place in Geneva—no comfortable place, anyway.

> Rejoice, you just, in the Lord; praise from the upright is fitting. (Ps 33:1)

One of Calvin's sturdiest safety nets, when it came to ensuring proper behavior among the elect, was the creation of the Consistory, the tribunal that oversaw behavior and made sure that the upright retained the upper hand in town.[10] The consistory made sure that the wicked would be

---

[8] See Carlos M. N. Eire, *War against the Idols: The Reformation of Worship from Erasmus to Calvin* (New York: Cambridge University Press, 1986), 195–275.

[9] Calvin describes the threats God makes against idolaters in *Institutes,* 2.18–21. In his *On the Necessity of Reforming the Church* Calvin was succinct: "We know how hateful idolatry is to God; and we know what awful punishments he has sent because of it, both to the Israelites and to the gentiles, as narrated by various histories" (Calvin, *Joannis Calvini opera,* 6:502).

[10] The records kept by this court are now available in a printed edition: *Registres du Consistoire de Genève au temps de Calvin* (ed. R. M. Kingdon et al.; Geneva:

stripped of their delusions: "Sin directs the heart of the wicked; their eyes are closed to the fear of God. For they live with the delusion: their guilt will not be known and hated" (Ps 36:2–3).

Geneva knew and hated the guilt of all of the wicked brought before the Consistory. Calvin wanted none of the elect in Geneva to be accused by the psalmist as they sang out in church: "When you see thieves, you befriend them; with adulterers you throw in your lot" (Ps 50:18). The elect in Geneva could feel at one with the Lord and his purposes when they sang out against the wicked in church: "Now God will strike you down, leave you crushed forever ... uproot you from the land of the living. The righteous will look on with awe; they will jeer and say, 'That one did not take God as a refuge'" (Ps 52:7–9).

Expulsion from Geneva was routine for the wicked. Excommunication, imprisonment, and public humiliation were more commonly used, and, rarely, the death penalty. However, identifying and shunning the ungodly was deemed absolutely necessary. This notion of separating the righteous and wicked drew from the language of the psalms and was reinforced in the psalms sung in church:

> The wicked have been corrupt since birth; liars from the womb, they have gone astray. Their poison is like the poison of a snake, like that of a serpent stopping its ears, so as not to hear the voice of the charmer who casts such cunning spells. O God, smash the teeth in their mouths; break the jaw-teeth of these lions, Lord! Make them vanish like water flowing away; trodden down, let them wither like grass. Let them dissolve like a snail that oozes away, like an untimely birth that never sees the sun.... Then the just shall rejoice to see the vengeance, and bathe their feet in the blood of the wicked. Then it will be said: "Truly there is a reward for the just; there is a God who is judge on earth!" (Ps 58:4–12).

Among the types of wickedness not tolerated in Geneva were swearing, taking the name of the Lord in vain, breaking the Sabbath, adultery, all the Ten Commandments, and then some. Names for children were carefully regulated, as were names for pets; clothing was regulated as well, and so were leisure-time activities.[11] Among the rules for innkeepers,

---

Droz, 1996–2001). These records are now being translated into English: *Registers of the Consistory of Geneva in the Time of Calvin* (ed. R. M. Kingdon et al.; trans. M. W. McDonald; Grand Rapids: Eerdmans, 2000–).

[11] See Robert M. Kingdon, *Adultery and Divorce in Calvin's Geneva* (Cambridge: Harvard University Press, 1995); idem, "The Control of Morals in Calvin's Geneva," in *The Social History of the Reformation* (ed. L. P. Buck and J. W. Zophy; Columbus: Ohio State University Press, 1972); and William Monter, "The

one said it all: "No one is allowed to stay up past nine at night, except informers."

On the third point, the psalms were the heart of worship in Geneva. The sermon was the head, thinking in terms of bodily metaphors, but the psalms were the heart. The very sense of a chosen people, hemmed in all sides by dangers, burst forth from almost every psalm. The very sense of a righteous individual, much like David, beset by sin but always properly contrite, and of an individual close to God, confident in his benevolent guidance, also oozed from every psalm sung in church.

> God alone is my rock and salvation, my secure height; I shall never fall. (Ps 62:3)
> The Lord is our God who rules the whole earth. He remembers forever his covenant, the pact imposed for a thousand generations. (Ps 105:7–8)

Genevans were the spiritual children of Abraham—better even than physical children, given the superiority of the spiritual over the material in Calvin's mind. The covenant, the pact, the law: these ruled in Geneva,[12] and Genevans sang of their obedience and their close relationship with God in the only way in which God would have wanted, through the psalms.

> Happy those whose way is blameless, who walk by the teaching of the Lord. Happy those who observe God's decrees, who seek the Lord with all their heart. They do no wrong; they walk in God's ways. (Ps 119:1–3).

Consistory of Geneva, 1559–1569," *Bibliothèque d'Humanisme et Renaissance* 38 (1976): 467–84.

[12] See Harro Höpfl, *The Christian Polity of John Calvin* (Cambridge: Cambridge University Press, 1982).

Feathered Psalms: Old World Forms in a New World Garb

Jaime Lara
Yale University Divinity School

An essay on the importance of the book of Psalms in the New World of sixteenth-century Latin America may seem like a bit of a stretch. After all, what would the songbook of ancient Israel have to do with maritime exploration, conquest, political hegemony, or religious conversion? Indeed, I know of no one who has dealt with the topic, and the reader will please forgive me if my approach here is somewhat eclectic and suggestive rather than diachronic and conclusive, more like notes to myself for further research. As with most issues dealing with the unique encounter of peoples, languages, religions and cosmologies that we call the "Discovery"—or as we prefer to call it today, the "Contact"—the last word is far from having been said. In the research on the New World, new discoveries are being made constantly. Native voices are now being recognized as subtexts within the Euro-Christian telling of the story; these voices speak of resistance to or negotiation with the European interlopers and their new God. However, they also speak of native appropriation of Euro-Christian culture and religion as well as the convergence of root metaphors and a resulting religious inculturation.[1] I would like to look at the use of the psalms within

[1] The convergence of native and Christian root metaphors in the New World is elaborated in my forthcoming book, *City, Temple, Stage: Eschatological Architecture and Liturgical Theatrics in New Spain*. On the power of metaphor, especially visual metaphors, in Nahua society, see Doris Heyden, "Metaphors, Nahualtocaitl, and Other 'Disguised' Terms among the Aztecs," in *Symbol and Meaning beyond the Closed Community: Essays in Mesoamerican Ideas* (ed. G. Gossen; Albany: Institute for Mesoamerican Studies, State University of New York, 1986), 35–43. On the metaphoric power of Aztec myths, see David Carrasco, "The Sacrifice of Tezcatlipoca" in *To Change Place: Aztec Ceremonial Landscapes* (ed. D. Carrasco; Niwot: University of Colorado Press, 1991), 31–57. On Nahua floral metaphors, see Louise Burkhart, "Flowery Heaven: The Aesthetic of Paradise in Náhuatl Devotional Literature," *Res* 21 (1992): 89–109; idem, "The Amanuenses Have Appropriated the

this unique context, and I will make two presuppositions that the reader may or may not share with me.

First, I recognize that the discovery of the New World was not so much the first deed of the modern age by a scientific rebel who refused to accept that the world was flat but rather that the event of 1492 was the last dramatic gesture of the Middle Ages by the last of the medieval explorers in the line of a Marco Polo. The conquest, conversion, and urbanization of the Americas by Iberians was the last flowering of a medieval culture that began with Augustine's *City of God*.[2] No better example of that medieval mind exists than Christopher Columbus, about whom I will speak in a moment.

My second supposition has to do with the very term that we use: "New World." Modern, scientifically minded scholarship has tended to understand that phrase in terms of politics and economics and, for want of a better word, in terms of "turf." Capitalist and Marxist societies have conceived the New World purely in terms of real-estate adventures: Spain's acquiring of new real-estate properties or a shorter route to commerce with China and the beginnings of a global economy. I hold that that is only a partial and impoverished explanation and does not capture the elements of the fantastic and the marvelous or the mystical aspects of something more akin to a new cosmic order.

For medieval men and women that new world order had to be found in some way and somewhere within the Judeo-Christian story of salvation history, which is to say that this brave new world, America, and its novel peoples had to be found in the Bible. To the medieval mind, Holy Scripture was the history book par excellence, the book that explained not only the past but the present and future as well. It is no wonder, then, that a hidden identity of Amerindian peoples and places would be discovered in the ancient biblical texts.[3] Divine Providence had to have foreseen what

---

Text: Interpreting a Náhuatl Song of Santiago," in *On the Translation of Native American Literatures* (ed. B. Swann; Washington, D.C.: Smithsonian Institution Press, 1992), 339–55. On the metaphoric quality of Nahua language and art in general, see José Alcina Franch, "Lenguaje metafórico e iconografía en el arte mexica," *Anales del Instituto de Investigaciones Estéticas* 66 (1995): 7–44.

[2] See, e.g., Luis Weckmann, *The Medieval Heritage of Mexico* (New York: Fordham University Press, 1992), esp. 3–135 and *passim.*

[3] On the eschatological dimension of the discovery of America, see, e.g., Marcel Bataillon, "Nouveau Monde et Fin du Monde," *L'Education Nationale* 32 (11 dic. 1952): 3–6; idem, "Evangelisme et millénarisme au Nouveau Monde," in *Courants religieux et humanisme a la fin du XVe siècle* (Colleque Strasbourg; Paris: Presses universitaires de France, 1959); John Leddy Phelan, *The Millennial Kingdom of the Franciscans in the New World* (2d ed.; Berkeley and Los Angeles: University of

the sixteenth-century chronicler López de Gómora claimed to be the second most momentous event of all time: "The greatest thing since the creation of the world, save the Incarnation and death of Him who created it, is the discovery of the Indies that are thus called the New World."[4] This discovery included the disclosure of the hitherto hidden lands mentioned in Scripture as the prelude to the final age of world history. It is worth noting that of all the books of the Bible quoted to explain the traumatic events of 1492 and thereafter, the most often quoted books are: (1) the prophets, especially Isaiah and Ezekiel, but equally the Minor Prophets who predicted the restoration of Jerusalem and its temple in a golden, utopian age; (2) the book of Revelation, or the Apocalypse; and (3) the book of Psalms.

Prophecy, prediction, and psaltery were the exegetical tools used to explain the why and wherefore of the discovery of America. We see hints of this already in the Old World, particularly in the Spanish monarchs and their mystical vision of Spain's bravura and destiny.

The *Isabella Breviary,* one of the gems of Flemish bookmaking, is now owned by the British Library (fig. 16.1).[5] It was written and illuminated in Flanders during the last decade of the fifteenth century. Its owner, Queen Isabella of Castille, was one of the most influential figures in Europe, though today she is most widely remembered for her patronage of Columbus's momentous voyage. The tome was presented to her in 1497 to commemorate the marriages of her two children to the son and daughter

---

California Press, 1975); Luis Weckmann, "Las esperanzas milenaristas de los franciscanos en la Nueva España," *Historia Mexicana* 32 (1982): 89–105; José Sala Catala y Jaime Vilchis Reyes, "Apocalíptica Española y Empresa Misional en los Primeros Franciscanos de Mexico," *Revista de Indias* 45/176 (1985): 421–47; Delno West, "Medieval Ideas of Apocalyptic Mission and the Early Franciscans in Mexico," *The Americas* 45 (1989): 293–313; Juana Maria Arcelus Ulibarrena, "La esperanza milenaria de Joaquín de Fiore y el Nuevo Mundo: Trayectoria de una utopia," *Florensia* 1 (1987): 47–79; idem, "Cristobal Colón y los primeros evangelizadores del Nuevo Mundo: Lección de profetismo joaquinista," in *Il profestismo gioachimita tra Quattrocento e Cinquecento: Atti de III Congresso Internazionale di Studi Gioachimiti* (ed. G. L. Potestà; Genova: Marietti, 1991), 475–504; Marjorie Reeves, *The Influence of Prophecy in the Later Middle Ages: A Study in Joachimism* (Oxford: Clarendon Press, 1969); Marjorie Reeves, ed., *Prophetic Rome in the High Renaissance Period: Essays* (Oxford: Clarendon Press, 1992); and David Carrasco, *Quetzalcóatl and the Irony of Empire: Myths and Prophecies in the Aztec Tradition* (Chicago: University of Chicago Press, 1982), 11–12.

[4] Father Francisco López de Gómora, chaplain to Hernán Cortes, wrote the *Historia General de las Indias* (Zaragosa, 1552).

[5] The following figures appear in the color insert: 16.1, 16.2, 16.3, 16.4, 16.5, 16.6, 16.8, 16.9, 16.10, 16.11, 16.12, 16.13, 16.14, 16.15, 16.16, 16.17, 16.18, 16.21, 16.22, 16.23. Figures 16.7, 16.19, and 16.20 appear within the text of this essay.

of the Holy Roman Emperor, Maximilian of Austria. The first of these marriages gave her, in the person of the future Emperor Charles V, a grandson who was to unite under his rule not only the greater part of Europe but also the immensity of the territories of the New World.[6]

The two folios for the First Sunday of the eschatological season of Advent pair the twelve Sibyls of the mystical Sibylline Oracles with King David, who is seen on his deathbed (fig. 16.2).[7] The Sibyls foretell the events of the future, while David reminisces how he built the first altar on the future site of the temple seen in the theatrical cutaway above. The psalm is number 146, "My soul, give praise to the Lord." There is a foreshadowing here, for in the New World enterprise both the Sibylline Oracles and the temple of Jerusalem would be an obsession of Christopher Columbus and of the mendicant missionary friars who followed in his wake.

In this Book of Hours an extraordinary amount of space is devoted to David (seen here at his coronation) as well as to Solomon and the temple, more so than in other late medieval illuminated prayer books. At Ps 120, marking the beginning of the fifteen gradual psalms, David and his musicians are shown ascending the fifteen steps (*gradus,* in Latin) of the temple, while on the right Solomon oversees its construction (fig. 16.3).

We are in the realm of prophecy and prediction, for David never lived to see the temple completed. It is as if he had written his psalms in mystic anticipation of the temple's processional liturgy—a kinesthetic liturgy and temple space soon to be re-created for the Mexica (Aztecs) in the New World.

At Ps 80, David and his musicians have moved into the very holy of holies to make music in front of the tablets of the covenant, which Moses had received on Sinai, while—anachronistically again—Abraham prepares to sacrifice Isaac outside on Mount Moriah (fig. 16.5). Time has been collapsed by the singing of the psalm; the past has been pulled forward into the present, while the future is anticipated in the here and now.

At Ps 68, David conducts the choristers in "flower and song" beneath a spectacular vision of the passion (like the beads of a rosary), which includes a large roundel with the events of the year 70 of the Common Era: the destruction of Jerusalem and the burning of its temple (figs. 16.1 and 16.6). The choir members vocalize while holding lilies in their hands. Mesoamerican scholars will catch my reference to "flower and song," a phrase translated from the Náhuatl language (that is, the language of the

---

[6] Janet Backhouse, *The Isabella Breviary* (London: British Library, 1993), 8–17.

[7] For the prevalence of these oracles in the Middle Ages and in the age of exploration, see Ernst Sackur, *Sibyllinsiche Texte und Forschungen: Pseudomethodius Adso und Die tiburtinische sibylle* (Halle: Niemeyer, 1898).

Mexica), which summed up the poetry, mythology, and worship of the Aztec civilization of central Mexico, soon to be encountered by an envoy of Queen Isabella's grandson.[8]

The Isabella Book of Hours is a beautiful testimony to the Psalter, but it is also a witness to the political and mystical concerns of the Catholic kings. Isabella's husband, Ferdinand of Aragón, held the title "King of Jerusalem," and the monarchs were hopeful that the reconquest of the Iberian peninsula from the Moors would be the beginning of a last crusade to regain the Holy Land.[9]

Another person who dreamed of the Holy Land was Christopher Columbus. In fact, the "Admiral of the Ocean Sea" left money gained from his voyages of exploration in a revolving bank account in Genoa to finance a last crusade that never took place, and he firmly held that King Ferdinand would fulfill his destiny and rightly take back his Palestinian possession as monarch of Jerusalem. In 1502 Columbus composed *El Libro de las Profecias* (*The Book of the Prophecies*) with the help of his son, also named Ferdinand, and his chaplain, Fray Gaspar Gorricio.[10] The text was only translated into English in 1992 and is still by and large unexamined by scholars. It is a masterful compilation of biblical texts and commentaries as well as ancient and medieval writers who speculated on geography and eschatology. Columbus combed the Scriptures for every passage he could find relating to "islands," especially those mythical islands of Seba, Ophir, and Tarshish mentioned in relation to Solomon, because Columbus believed that he himself had now rediscovered them.[11] He found the core of this insular exegesis in the prophets and, of course, the psalms, such as in Ps 72:10: "The kings of Tarshish and the islands shall pay him tribute; the kings of Sheba and Seba shall bring gifts." This verse he exegeted as referring to the Spanish monarch. Or in Ps 97:1: "The LORD is king; let the

---

8 Burkhart, "Flowery Heaven."

9 Pauline Moffitt Watts, "Prophecy and Discovery: On the Spiritual Origins of Christopher Columbus's Enterprise of the Indies," *AHR* 90 (1985): 73–102; Delno West, "The Abbot and the Admiral: Joachite Influences in the Life and Writings of Christopher Columbus," in *Il profetismo gioachimita tra Quattrocento e Cinquecento, Atti del III Congresso Internazionale di Studi Gioachimiti* (ed. G. L. Potestà; Genova: Marietti, 1991), 461–73.

10 Christopher Columbus, *Libro de las Profecias* (ed. and trans. Delno West and August King; Gainsville: University of Florida Press, 1991).

11 On Columbus as an exegete, see John Fleming, "Christopher Columbus as a Scriptural Exegete," *LQ* 5 (1991): 187–98; Hector Avalos, "Columbus as Biblical Exegete: A Study of the *Libro de las profecías*," in *Religion in the Age of Exploration: The Case of Spain and New Spain* (ed. B. Le Beau et al.; Omaha: Creighton University Press, 1996), 59–80.

earth rejoice, let the many islands be glad." These islands were the West Indies through which Columbus sailed and which he explored on four voyages. The medieval commentaries that he used, including that of Rabbi Samuel of Fez, all claimed that the island nations were real locations to the west of Europe and that they would receive the gospel message near the end of time. With this biblical confirmation, the explorer developed a geo-eschatology to describe the relationship between geographic lore and a theology of the end times.[12]

Columbus seems to have been obsessed by Ps 2, applying verses 7 and 8 both to the Spanish monarchy and to himself. "The LORD said to me: 'You are my son. It is I who have begotten you this day. Ask and I shall bequeath you the nations and put the very ends of the earth in your possession.'" Christopher Columbus's very name "Christ-bearer" and his distinctive signature bear witness to his understanding of himself as an individual with a divine mission. Quoting Isa 61, the Admiral of the Ocean Sea claims that he himself is none other than the prophet of the last days, the one foretold in Scripture to bring the good news to the nations and thus initiate the final age.[13]

So startling were the American discoveries that they sent Europe into a frenzy of speculation about a proximate return of Christ. Cardinal Francisco Ximénez de Cisneros commissioned a translation of the Bible into Aramaic (*Biblia Polyglota*) so that, upon Christ's second advent, European scholars would be able to converse with him in his own native language![14] Likewise, there arose an eschatological desire on the part of Europeans to read the world-discoverer himself, Christopher Columbus, into the biblical prophecies. In 1516, another edition of the polyglot Psalter was published in Genoa (fig. 16.7). Psalm 19:4 reads as follows: "No speech, no word, no voice is heard, yet their span extends through all the earth, their words go out to the utmost bounds of the world." It is at this precise point that the commentator added an entire vita of Columbus and his accomplishments that runs on for several more folios.[15] Christopher Columbus himself was exegeted into the book of Psalms.

---

12 Columbus, *Libro de las Profecias,* 7–40, 261 n. 18.

13 Alain Milhou, *Colón y su mentalidad mesiánica en el ambiente franciscanista español* (Valladolid: Casa-Museo Colón, 1983), 79–91 and *passim.*

14 Richard Popkin, "Jewish Christians and Christian Jews in Spain, 1492 and After," *Judaism* 41 (1992): 248–68.

15 The polyglot psalter, *Psalterium Hebreum, Grecum, Arabicum et Chaldaeum* (Genoa, 1516), contains the complete vita of Columbus immediately after Ps 19:5. See Adriano Prosperi, "New Heaven and New Earth: Prophecy and Propaganda at the Time of the Discovery and Conquest of the Americas," in *Prophetic Rome and the Renaissance* (ed. M. Reeves; Oxford: Clarendon Press, 1992), 279–303, esp. 281 n. 4.

Psalterium, Hebręum, Gręcū,
Arabicū, & Chaldęū, cū tribus
latinis iterp̄tatōibus & glossis.

תהלים עברי יואני ערבי עם
תרגום ושלשה תרגומים
מלטין עם פרושן

Ψαλτήριον ἑβραϊκὸν ἑλληνικὸν, ἀρα
βικὸν, χαλδαϊκὸν μετὰ τριῶν ἑρ
μηνειῶν λατινικῶν καὶ γλωσσημάτων.

مزامير عبراني يوناني
عرابي وقصداني بثلث
ترجمة لطين وتفسيرهم

ספרא דתהלאי יהודאי יונאי
ערבאי וכשדאי עם תלת
תרגומא מן לטין ובאוריהון

Fig. 16.7. Title page. *Psalterium Hebricum, Grecii, Arabicum et Chaldicii* (Genoa, 1516)
(The Bancroft Library, University of California Berkeley. Used with permission.)

We usually think of the explorer as seeking a new route to China, and that is true in part. However, it was Jerusalem that he was really after, the same Jerusalem that had always been the umbilical center of the world for the medieval mind. The artist of a 1582 map, or world schema, still had trouble integrating America into his Jerusalem-centered world (fig. 16.4),[16] and a 1571 map, by the librarian of the Escorial Palace in Spain, identifies North and South America with the mysterious sites mentioned in reference to Solomon, his mines, and the Lost Tribes of the Jews (figs. 16.8 and 16.9).[17]

The supposed Jewish origin of the American Indians was no afterthought in the New World but continued with greater or lesser credence from the sixteenth century into the beginning of the twentieth century. Anthropologists at a certain university in Cambridge, Massachusetts, held to the Hebraic origin of the American Indians well until the 1920s. Moreover, Mesoamericans had practiced things that seemed to the first missionaries to point to a Jewish or Judeo-Christian prehistory, such as circumcision, a ritual priesthood for sacrifice, and a liturgical calendar. The Aztecs practiced forms of public confession, penance, self-flagellation, and communion. They had divinely inspired scriptures, a liturgical calendar, a ritual priesthood, vestments, relics, and circumcision.[18] Their native priests lived as mendicant beggars and as temporary celibates in monastery-like settings.[19] There were military-monastic orders and consecrated virgins.[20] Their altar sacrifices, accomplished in the body and blood of the deified victim, were a seemingly debased parody of the Catholic sacrifice of the Mass. These practices confused the friars, raising in their minds the possibility of an earlier evangelization and a subsequent demonic perversion, but they also opened up for their neophytes points of association to the new religion.[21]

---

16 Heinrich Bünting, *Intinerarium sacrae Scripturae* (Helmstadt: Siebenburger, 1582); see Ronald Schaer et al., eds. *Utopia: The Search for the Ideal Society in the Western World* (New York: Oxford University Press, 2000), 50–51.

17 The world map was created by the erudite orientalist, Benedictus Arias Montanus, OSB, librarian to King Phillip II in his *Humanae salutis monumenta* (Antwerp, 1571).

18 See, e.g., the similarities to Catholicism mentioned by Diego Durán, *Book of the Gods and Rites and The Ancient Calendar* (trans. and ed. F. Horcasitas and D. Heyden; Norman: University of Oklahoma Press, 1977), 100–111.

19 López Austin, *Human Body and Ideology: Concepts of the Ancient Nahuas* (2 vols.; Salt Lake City: University of Utah Press, 1988), 1:306.

20 Diego Durán, *Book of the Gods and Rites.*

21 For pre-Hispanic religious practices and Judeo-Christian legends, see Jacques Lafaye, *Mesías, cruzadas, utopias* (Mexico: Fondo de la Cultura Económica, 1988),

It also appeared to some that there were native linguistic characteristics similar to spoken Hebrew or Aramaic.[22] Indeed, an analysis of ancient Náhuatl poetry shows the use of many of the same lyrical devices as the Hebrew psalms: repetition, parallelism, internal rhyme, cantillation.[23] It is no wonder, then, that the mendicant friars would treat the Indians like Iberian *conversos,* Jewish converts to Christianity, and they would even go so far as to adapt the architecture of the ancient Jerusalem temple for the outdoor liturgical worship of these New Israelites/New Christians of the New World.[24]

Meanwhile, back in Europe a new Solomon had come to the throne, one who possessed the same global aspirations as the earlier Catholic kings. Charles V, Holy Roman Emperor, lord of the islands of the Indies, was likewise the titular king of Jerusalem. This new European Solomon was depicted as such in liturgical manuscripts and in theatrical productions. His distinctive profile appears at the incipit of the seven penitential psalms of the *Sforza Hours,* completed for his coronation celebration (fig. 16.11).[25] In 1520 another Book of Hours was created for the emperor's seaward visit to his home town of Ghent, en route to his coronation at Aachen (fig. 16.12). It contains only three liturgical hours:

57–64. For modern scientific studies of Aztec rituals, see Inga Clendinnen, *Aztecs: An Interpretation* (Cambridge: Cambridge University Press, 1991), 236–66; David Carrasco, *Religions of Mesoamerica* (San Francisco: Harper & Row, 1990), esp. 58–91; James Lockhart, *The Nahuas after the Conquest: A Social and Cultural History of the Indians of Central Mexico, Sixteenth through Eighteenth Centuries* (Stanford, Calif.: Stanford University Press, 1992). On anthropophagia as communion, see López Austin, *Human Body and Ideology,* 1:382.

22 For the supposed Jewish origins of Native Americans, see L. Huddleston, *Origins of the American Indian: European Concepts, 1492–1929* (Austin: University of Texas Press, 1965), esp. 33–47, 83–128; "Tribes, Lost Ten," *JE* 12:249–53; Lynn Glaser, *Indians or Jews? An Introduction to Manasseh Ben Israel's "The Hope of Israel"* (Gilroy, Calif.: Boswell, 1973), 3–32; and Ronald Sanders, *Lost Tribes and Promised Lands: The Origins of American Racism* (Boston: Little Brown & Co., 1978, 1992), 43–46. Early Puritians in New England also shared this belief; see Djelal Kadir, *Columbus and the Ends of the Earth* (Berkeley and Los Angeles: University of California Press, 1992), 178–92.

23 Miguel León Portilla, ed., *Native Mesoamerican Spirituality: Ancient Myths, Discourses, Stories, Doctrines, Hymns, Poems from the Aztec, Yucatec, Quiche-Maya and Other Sacred Traditions* (New York: Paulist, 1980).

24 The adaptation of late medieval plans of the temple of Jerusalem is documented in my *City, Temple, Stage.*

25 The *Sforza Hours,* originally begun ca. 1466–76 for the Duke of Sforza and later enlarged, was a gift to Charles V from his aunt, Margaret of Austria. It is now in the British Library.

Matins, for the departure of the monarch from the Spanish port of Coruña; Vespers, to pray for a safe journey; and Compline, as preparation for the "new Solomon" to build the temple of God. In the illuminated initial, Charles V sits enthroned between his biblical predecessors David and Solomon.[26]

On stage, Charles was also portrayed by thespian impersonators as a new Solomon in triumph, frequently surrounded by the prophetic Sibyls or as the conqueror of the Holy Land receiving the keys and crown of the city of Jerusalem (fig. 16.13).[27]

Charles lacked, however, the wisdom of Solomon and his juridical success. In 1548 he attempted to solve the problem of religious dissent and division in Germany by convoking a commission of Catholic and Protestant theologians at Augsburg to elaborate a compromise known as the Interim. The compromise, however, satisfied no one and was the subject of ridicule and satire, as we see in a comical broadsheet (fig. 16.14). The Catholics on the left are joining the Protestants on the right in a feigned psalm fest. Note the stereotypical Catholic fool and the Protestant beer guzzler. Was this type casting? Everyone is singing—in Latin and German—Ps 1 *Beatus Vir* as a protest against the Interim.[28] "Blessed is the man who follows *not* the counsel of the wicked" (that is, the Interim of the Emperor) nor lingers in the way of sinners, nor sits in the company of scorners."

Back in the New World the process of Christian evangelization was at its most robust around mid-century, impelled by the fervor of the Franciscans, Dominicans, and Augustinians. By then, the polytheistic religion of the Aztecs and Maya had been suppressed for the most part and their temples demolished. On the same sites and platforms of those former temples there now arose replicas of the new temple foretold by the prophet Ezekiel (chs. 40–43) and by medieval prophetic voices such as that of Joachim of Fiore, the twelfth-century abbot who had predicted an

---

[26] The work is entitled *Salomonis tria offici ex sacris derupte navigation Carli V Imperatoris*. Biblioteca Escorial, Mss. III-D-9, fol. 22. This illuminated manuscript was given by Robert of Keyser to the emperor at his formal entry into the city of Ghent in 1520. See Hugo Soly, *Charles Quint, 1500–1558: L'Empereur et son temps* (Arles: Actes Sud, 2000), 45.

[27] Fernando Checa Cremades, *Carlos V y la imagén del héroe en el Renacimiento* (Madrid: Taurus, 1987); idem, *Carlos V: La imagén del poder en el Renacimeinto* (Madrid: Ediciones del Viso, 1999); and Reny de Puys, *La tryumphante Entre de Charles Prince des Espagnes en Bruges 1515* (facsimile with introduction by Sydney Anglo; Amsterdam: Theatrum Orbis Terrarum, 1973).

[28] Satirical broadsheet on the Interim. Woodcut, Madgenburg 1548, now in the Germanisches Nationalmuseum, Nuremburg. See Soly, *Charles Quint,* 361.

approaching Third Age of the Holy Spirit—a utopian era in which all humankind would sing psalms.[29]

The spiritual conquest of the New World was underway, and its most powerful weapons of conversion were music, architecture, and art, including some adapted indigenous media. For example, for Mesoamericans, feathers were much more than bodily adornment (fig. 16.15). They were sacred objects and attributes of aerial divinities or associated with the souls of the dead. They were also indicators of status and power as well as of royalty and divinity. It is no wonder, then, that feathers were worked into images of Christ and stone crosses or used to decorate the miters of bishops, the new lords of the Christianized Aztecs (figs. 16.16 and 16.18).[30]

Another conversion tool was music and the pomp and splendor of the liturgy. In fact, it would not be unreasonable to state that the Aztecs of central Mexico, or the Incas of the central Andes, may have finally appropriated Christianity because of the audio and visual appeal of medieval Catholic worship; however, in appropriating the faith, they created their own indigenous version of it.[31] Musical instruments and hymnody had a lot to do with this. It was not too much of a stretch for a Jesuit missionary to boast in 1549: "Give me an orchestra of musicians and I will convert all the Indians for Christ."[32]

The Amerindians had previously had flutes and percussion, but the missionaries delighted them by introducing the full range of European instruments and polyphony (fig. 16.17). Music soon became all the rage, so much so that, within a few years of the conquest, the Mexican council of bishops had to enact legislation limiting the exaggerated size of parish choirs and church orchestras. One of the reasons for the enthusiasm might also have been that musicians were exempt from taxation and hence eager to join a choir or play an instrument regardless of talent, although it has to be said that all the chroniclers remark on the uncanny ability of the natives to imitate, and to imitate well. Those Indian choristers, many of whom were bilingual, trilingual, or even quatralingual, sang the psalms of the daily Office and the Little Hours of the Virgin in Latin or in the vernacular, just like the monks or nuns in monasteries; by mid-century natives were

---

29 Henri de Lubac, *La posteridad espiritual de Joaquín de Fiore* (2 vols.; Madrid: Encuentro Editiones, 1989), 1:52.

30 Heyden, "Metaphors."

31 Jaime Lara, "Precious Green Jade Water: A Sixteenth-Century Adult Catechumenate in the New World," *Worship* 71 (1997): 415–29.

32 Robert Stevenson, *Music in Aztec and Inca Territory* (Berkeley and Los Angeles: University of California Press, 1968), 154–72.

composing Latin Masses, motets, and psalm settings in a mixture of chant and elaborate polyphony.[33]

Early missionaries composed entire hymnals in indigenous languages. We can gain insight into the developing inculturation of the Nahua-Christian liturgy by examining the collection of liturgical canticles written for Sundays and major feasts of the church year by Fray Bernardino de Sahagún and his elite native translators (fig. 16.19). His *Psalmodia Christiana* was published in Mexico City in 1583 but was already in use in manuscript form as early as the 1550s.[34] It was composed in the Náhuatl language in an effort to replace the precontact hymns that were still dear to the indigenous population. This book of "psalms" is not so much the biblical collection of songs attributed to David but rather something akin to doctrinal and liturgical paraphrases. Like David's Psalms, though, it was meant to be sung while dancing. The book contains a brief catechism, basic prayers, the commandments, and then fifty-four compositions that follow the liturgical year from the Circumcision (Jan. 1) to the Nativity (Dec. 25). The style of the songs attempts as closely as possible to follow the rhythms, characteristics, and metaphors of Náhuatl poetry.[35]

The Lenten set of hymns is entitled *Tlauculcuical,* or "Songs of Lamentation," and was begun on Septuagesima Sunday (seventy days before Easter). Sahagún incorporates material from the book of Genesis, in which there are lamentations for the sins that brought suffering to humanity, all done with local flavor. For example, the ark of Noah is described in Náhuatl as a canoe. The trials of this life, the suffering of the church, and the

---

[33] Robert Ricard, *The Spiritual Conquest of Mexico: An Essay on the Apostolate and the Evangelizing Methods of the Mendicant Orders in New Spain, 1523–1572* (trans. L. B. Simpson; Berkeley and Los Angeles: University of California Press, 1974), 176–93.

[34] Bernadino de Sahagún, *Psalmodia christiana, y sermoniario de los sanctos del año en lengua mexicana* (Mexico City: Pedro Ocharte, 1583). In English, Arthur Anderson, trans., *Bernardino de Sahagún's Psalmodia Christiana* (*Christian Psalmody*) (Salt Lake City: University of Utah Press, 1993). For studies on the *Psalmodia* and Sahagún's other works, see the collection of essays in Ascensión Hernández de León-Portilla, ed., *Bernardino de Sahagún: Diez estudios acerca de su obra* (Mexico City: Fondo de La Cultura Económica, 1990).

[35] Louise Burkhart, "A Doctrine for Dancing: The Prologue to the Psalmodia Christiana," *Latin American Indian Literatures Journal* 11 (1995): 21–33; idem, "El Tlauculcuicatl de Sahagún: Un lamento Náhuatl," in León-Portilla, *Bernardino de Sahagún,* 219–64. In praising God for creation, special thanks are offered for "the gold, the jade, the feathers of the Quetzal bird." Or when lauding the Virgin, Sahagún has his faithful sing: "You are, O Virgin Mary, like precious jade, like the finest turquoise." Also see Arthur Anderson, "La Enciclopedia Doctrinal de Sahagún," in León-Portilla, *Bernardino de Sahagún,* 164–79.

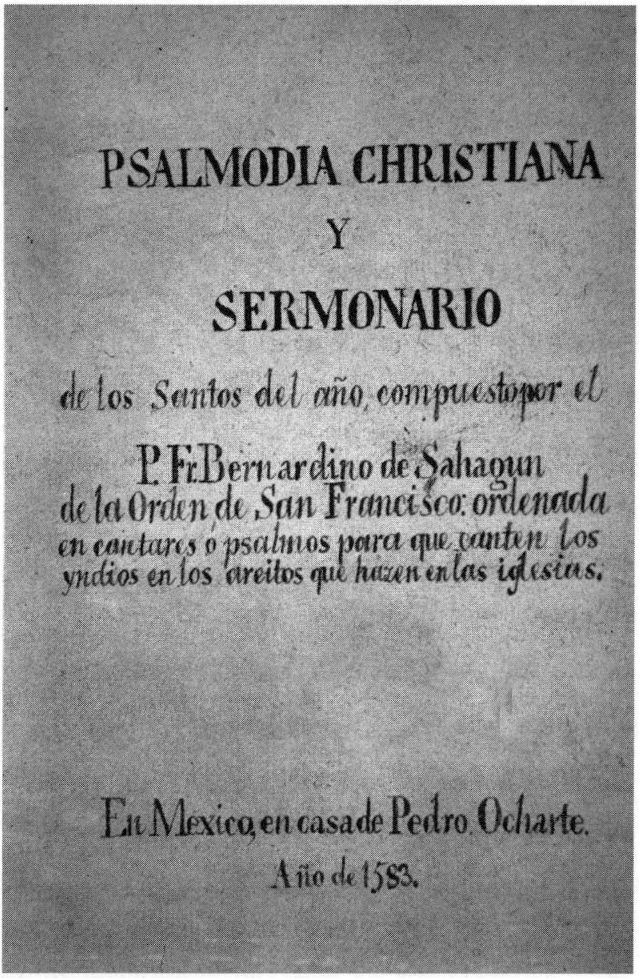

PSALMODIA CHRISTIANA
Y
SERMONARIO
de los Santos del año, compuesto por el
P. Fr. Bernardino de Sahagun
de la Orden de San Francisco: ordenada
en cantares ó psalmos para que canten los
yndios en los areitos que hazen en las iglesias.

En Mexico, en casa de Pedro Ocharte.
Año de 1583.

Fig. 16.19. Title page. Bernardino de Sahagún, *Psalmodia christiana,* 1583 (Courtesy of the John Carter Brown Library, Brown University.)

death of Christ culminate in the hymns that meditate on the mysteries of Passion Week.[36] However, of more interest are the *Xochicuicatl,* or "Florid Songs," of Eastertide. They are all based on the book of the Apocalypse, and they describe the city of God, the celestial Jerusalem. The Florid Songs hymn the glories of heaven and the final triumph of good over evil.[37] Here

---

[36] Sahagún, *Psalmodia christiana,* 62–77; Burkhart, "El Tlauculcuicatl," 221.
[37] Sahagún, *Psalmodia christiana,* 108–39; Burkhart, "El Tlauculcuicatl," 222.

we observe the development of Nahua-Christian metaphors that culminates in a paraphrase of Rev 21 with literal and metaphorical interpretations simulating the activity of the Aztecs themselves in the evangelization centers.

> And these city walls are constructed all of precious stones; all the various kinds of stones are placed in the wall. The first kind of precious stones of which it is constructed is called precious flint. It is very precious, much like copal incense. It is called jasper. It benefits the eyes, and it signifies the Faith. The second kind of precious stones of which the walls are made is fine turquoise. It is very smoky; it is brightly gleaming.... It denotes desire for heavenly things.... And the city of our Lord has courtyards in many places, and has courtyards that are totally of gold, translucent, very yellow, most beautifully resplendent.... they are brilliant there. And in your midst is always joyous song, and there will always be dancing also.[38]

The mention of jewels and sparkle would appeal to the Nahuas' propensity for baubles, bangles and beads. Objects, deities, and persons who were perceived as precious or mirrorlike had an in-built sacredness for the Mexica. The iridescent blue-green plumes of the quetzal bird, for instance, were believed to have divine qualities. Thus the Nahua emphasis on glitter, sheen, and luminosity coincided, by chance, with the biblical concept of divine glory (*kābôd* in Hebrew; *doxa* in Greek), which likewise was imagined as brilliant and reflective of light.

After quoting from the literal text of Revelation, Sahagún's elite translators continued to meditate on the heavenly city theme with a paraphrase of the medieval hymn *Urbs Beata Hierusalem,* which they certainly knew in Latin. This song for the dedication of a church, which originated in Carolingian Europe, is the Christian appropriation of Jerusalem imagery as a trope on the liturgical building and the utopian metropolis of the present dispensation. We know it in English as "Blessed City, Heavenly Zion" or as "Christ Is Made the Sure Foundation." The hymn was especially fitting for the eschatological last age that the early missionaries believed they were initiating in the New World. It speaks of the heavenly Jerusalem with all its glitter and sparkle being built here and now in the church on earth.

> Ah, you are in Heaven, O Jerusalem, made of precious stones, and the angels form your crown. Your gates shine brightly; they are like precious pearls. They always remain open. There many enter who live here in earth. The stones are living. By suffering, by misery they are polished. And when they are prepared for temple building, they give them their

[38] Anderson, *Bernardino de Sahagún's Psalmodia Christiana,* 132–35.

Fig. 16.1. Psalm 68: David and the Temple singers, f. 146v. *The Isabella Breviary,* detail of fig. 16.6 (The British Library. Used with permission.)

Fig. 16.2. Advent I: The twelve Sibyls foretell the birth of Christ, and David on his deathbed; ff. 8v-9. *The Isabella Breviary* (The British Library. Used with permission.)

Fig. 16.3. Psalms 119-121 David and musicians ascend temple steps; Solomon oversees the building of the temple; ff. 184v–185 *The Isabella Breviary* (The British Library. Used with permission.)

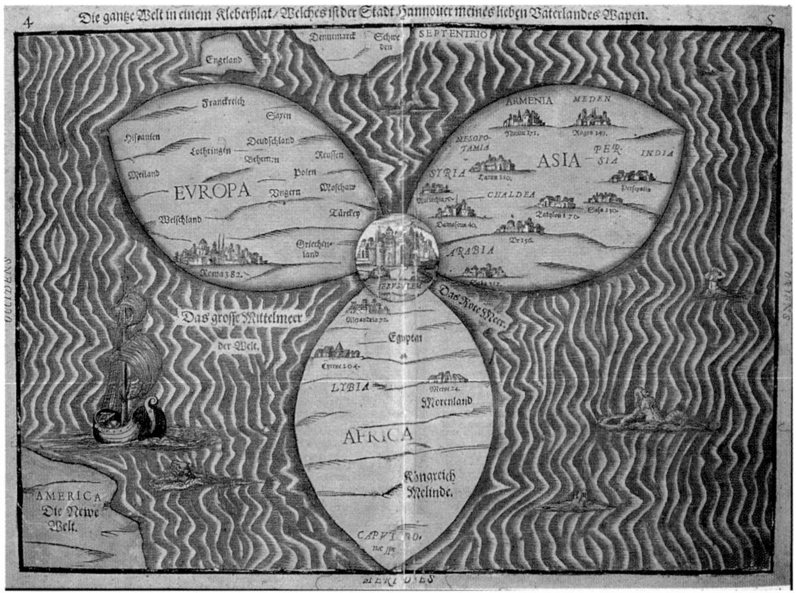

Fig. 16.4. Heining Bünting, *Itinerarium Sacrae Scripturae* (Helmstadt, 1582) hand-colored engraving. (The Jerusalem Map Project, Hebrew University, Jerusalem. Used with permission.)

Fig. 16.5. Psalm 80: David and musicians in temple; Sacrifice of Isaac in background; f. 155v. *The Isabella Breviary* (The British Library. Used with permission.)

Fig. 16.6. Psalm 68: David and temple singers carrying metaphorical flowers beneath a vision of the Passion and the destruction of Jerusalem; f. 146v. *The Isabella Breviary* (The British Library. Used with permission.)

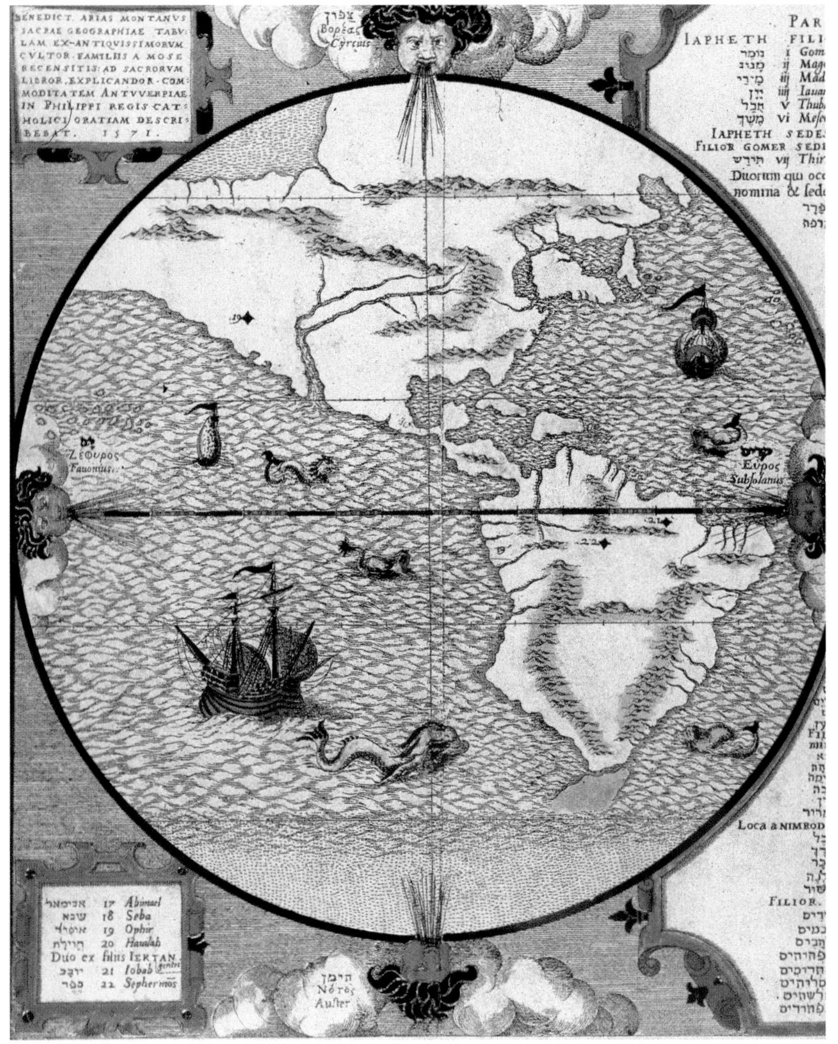

Fig. 16.8. Benedictus Arias Montano, *Humanae salutis monumenta* (Antwerp, 1571). Hand-colored engraving. (The Jerusalem Map Project, Hebrew University, Jerusalem. Used with permission.)

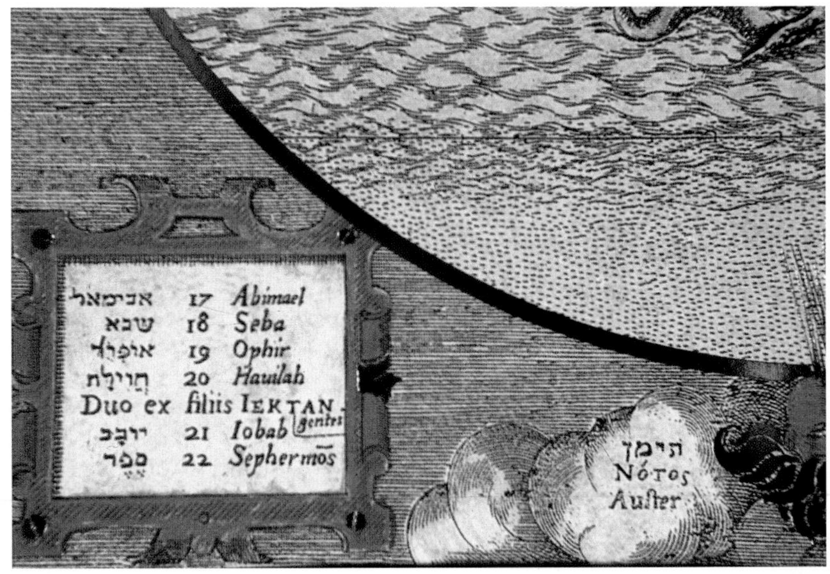

Fig. 16.9. Detail of fig. 16.8.

Fig. 16.10. Cloister of the Augustinian evangelization center at Malinalco, Morelos. (Photo: J. Barry Kiracofe. Used with permission.)

Fig. 16.11. Incipit of the seven penitential psalms, *Sforza Hours* (The British Library. Used with permission.)

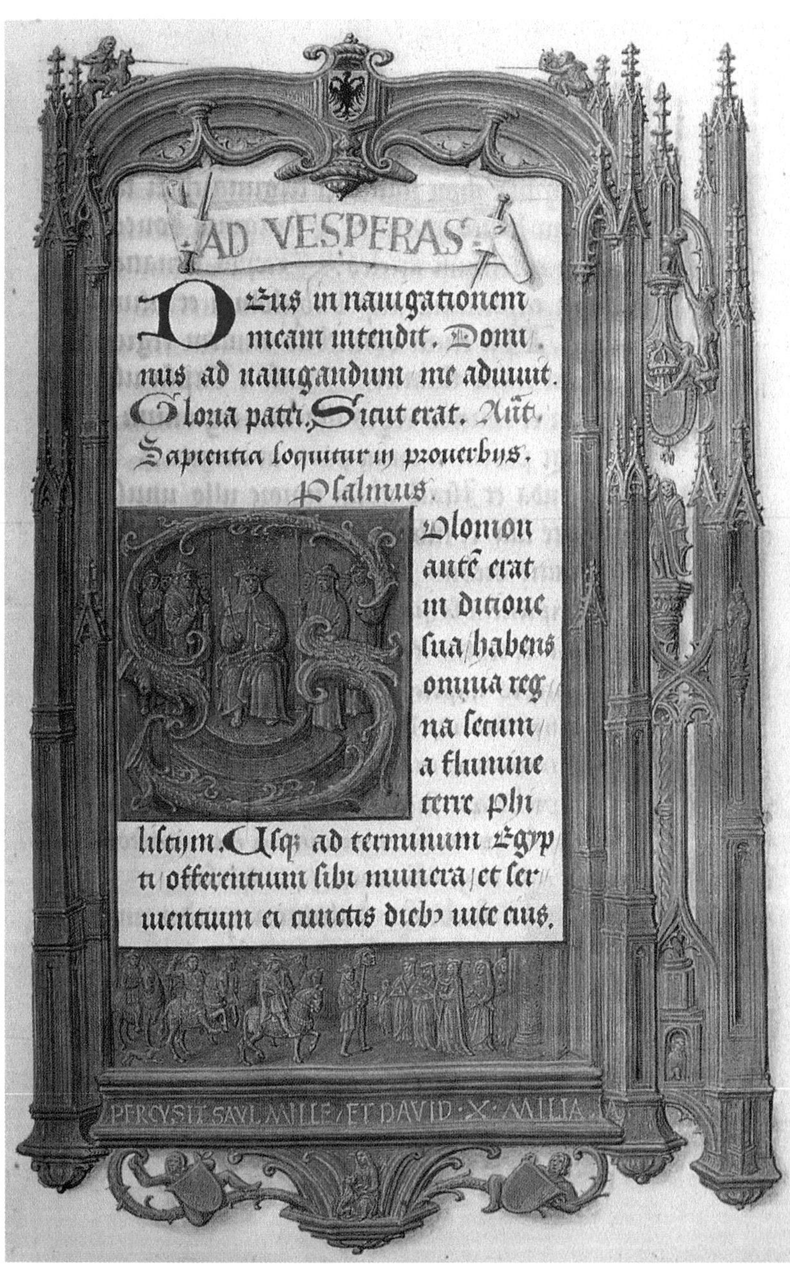

Fig. 16.12. *Salomonis tria official ex sacris derupte navigationis Caroli Imperatoris,* 1520. Escorial Library, Mss. III-D-9, fol. 22)
(© Patrimonio Nacional. Used with permission.)

Fig. 16.13. Emperor-elect Charles V at the gates of the city of Jerusalem. Stage set from Reny de Puys, *La tryumphante Entre de Charles Prince des Espagnes en Bruges,* 1515. (Österreichische Nationalbibliothek, Vienna. Used with permission.)

Fig. 16.14. Satire on the *Interim*. Woodcut. Madgenburg 1548.
(Germanisches Nationalmuseum, Nuremburg. Used with permission.)

Fig. 16.15. Bernardino de Sahagún, *Florentine Codex* (ca. 1579). (Paso y Troncoso, *Sahagun's Historia General de las Cosas,* 1905. Public domain.)

Fig. 16.16. Atrial cross at Huandacareo, Michoacán with sculpted plumes terminating the shafts; mid-sixteenth century. (Photo: author)

Fig. 16.17. Native dancers and instruments, *Codex Tovar,* ca. 1585. (The John Carter Brown Library at Brown University. Used with permission.)

Fig. 16.18. Feather miter, sixteenth-century, central Mexico. (Photo: author)

Fig. 16.21. Atrium of the evangelization center at Copacabana, Bolivia, with *Miserére* chapel, seventeenth century. (Photo: author)

Fig. 16.22. Malinalco, cloister murals.
(Photo: J. Barry Kiracofe. Used with permission.)

Fig. 16.23. Native musicians. Bernardino de Sahagún, *Florentine Codex* (ca. 1579). (Paso y Troncoso, *Sahagun's Historia General de las Cosas,* 1905. Public domain.)

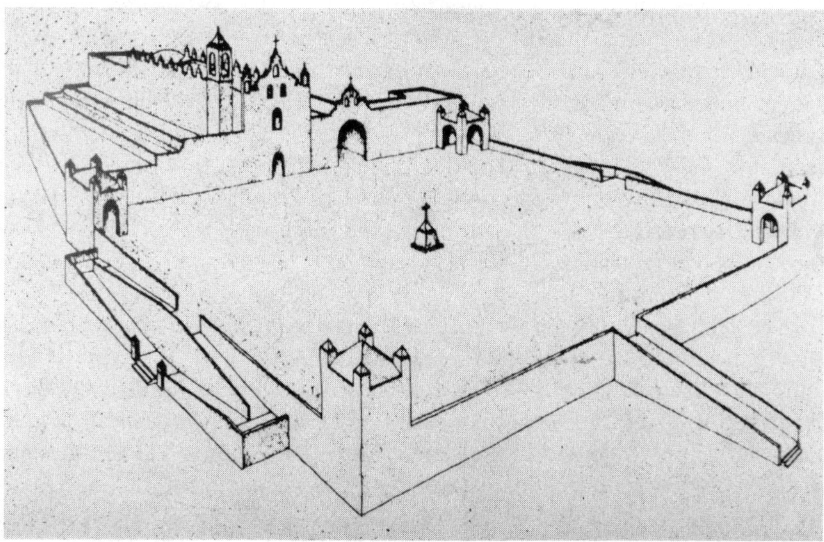

Fig. 16.20. Drawing of the Franciscan evangelization center at Izamal, Yucatan (after John McAndrew, *The Open Air Churches of Sixteenth-Century Mexico*)

> own place apart in the heavenly city. God's blessed city full of song, full of (the sound of) flutes.[39]

The imagery of precious jewels, sacred trees, and Nahua luxury objects testifies to the desire to indigenize the Christian message in an appealing way that would guarantee that the message take root in the visual imagination.

The *Psalmodia Christiana* was composed to be sung while dancing in the church yards or atria, which were modeled on the courts of the Jerusalem temple (fig. 16.20). The atrium housed an outdoor altar in an apse, four corner chapels (posas) with double entryways, and, at the center, a monumental cross referred to as if it were the ancient altar of holocausts. The use of the *Psalmodia* in this context testifies to a stational and liturgical event that utilized the four posa chapels and the atrial cross at the patio's heart for kinetic worship. The assembly danced past or through the four posas in a counterclockwise fashion, in one door and out the other, in a sort of liturgical conga line.[40]

---

[39] Ibid., 138–39.

[40] Dancing in a counterclockwise direction around a central object, such as an altar or a cosmic tree, was an important aspect of Aztec mythology and cult. Power was thought to be transmitted or increased by such circumambulation.

In the Andean countries, the atrium cross was often covered by a baldachin and used as a mortuary chapel to wake the dead (fig. 16.21).[41] There it is called the Miserére Chapel in reference to Ps 51 *Miserére mei Deus,* "Have mercy on me O God," the psalm that the medieval liturgical texts indicate for the stations on the procession to the cemetery. So commonly used was the psalmodic title of this chapel, *Miserére,* that until relatively recently young Andean lovers—who were never allowed to rendezvous without the presence of a chaperon—would often whisper fleetingly to one another: "Meet me tonight at the Miserére!" I know of no other such romantic use of a psalm title.

For the Mesoamerican, nature with its birds and flowers was both sacred and tragic. To live in this world was to be planted, grow, bud, blossom, wither, and finally die. Therefore, gardens were intrinsically holy places to the Aztecs. In this, Amerindians shared a common metaphor with the Judeo-Christian paradise garden of Eden. The Augustinian monastery of Malinalco reproduced this in a unique way. The site of Malinalco had been chosen for a friary because of a famous psychotropic plant garden that the Aztec royalty had there in preconquest times.[42] The cloister paintings, created by the christianized natives after 1560, acted as a stage set re-creating in monotones of black, white, and teal a dense junglelike garden within a garden (fig. 16.10). Throughout the entire building even in the friars' cells, Latin inscriptions in the bandings at ceiling level recount verses from the Psalms. Here, in the cloister, Ps 84 is painted in handsome script, a reference to the ancient temple of Jerusalem: "How lovely is your dwelling place, LORD God of hosts.... The sparrow herself finds a home and the swallow a nest for her brood; she lays her young by your altars, my king and my God . . ." (fig. 16.22). The cloister was meant to be experienced by the friars and by their trusted Indian catechists, who sang that same psalm during their liturgical processions through a fictive Paradise.

The psalms of David found their way into the consciousness and subconscious of the New World in unique ways. They were first used to explain the designs of divine providence in what seemed like an eschatological moment when time appeared to be moving toward its climax and conclusion. Exegesis of the Psalter yielded a rich, albeit *sui generis* application to a novel event.

Later the Indians were taught the psalms as part of their daily prayers. Still later, when the missionary church had been fully institutionalized,

---

[41] Teresa Gisbert and José de Mesa, *Arquitectura Andina* (La Paz: Colección Arsanz, 1985), 133.

[42] Jeanette Favrot Peterson, *The Paradise Garden Murals of Malinalco: Utopia and Empire in Sixteenth-Century Mexico* (Austin: University of Texas Press, 1993).

cathedral canons and cloistered nuns sung the psalms daily in the Liturgy of the Hours at morning, noon, and night. Their praying of the Psalter was public, and although in Latin, it allowed the laity to enter the prayer even if only vicariously: standing, sitting, and bowing at the appropriate moments. During this rich colonial period of the Baroque (1625–1750), professional musicians, both European and native, composed psalm settings in the style of the period. The works of native musicians, who spontaneously seem to have learned the techniques of European composition, are still be discovered today and brought to light.

However, the moment that I find most interesting is earlier in the evangelization process, in the more experimental and freer years before the decrees of the Council of Trent (1545–63) took effect. In those pioneer days in New Spain, Israel's songs were translated and paraphrased in the many indigenous languages, and Native American Christians appropriated those songs with dancing and the use of native instruments and costume—even feathers (fig. 16.23)! I think that King David, who was not averse to kicking up his heels now and then, would have been very happy.

PART 5
CASE STUDIES OF CONTEMPORARY PRACTICE

Psalms in a Contemporary African American Church

Gilbert I. Bond
Yale University Divinity School

Let the words of my mouth and the meditation of my heart be acceptable in thy sight, O Lord, my rock and my redeemer.

These words from Ps 19:14 can be heard in the sanctuaries of African American churches of different denominations throughout this country. They are uttered before and after testimony, the reading of Scriptures, and seemingly mundane announcements and belong to one of the many enduring traditions of psalmody that persist among Christians of African descent in North America.

In this essay I want to address the history of the psalms in the liturgical life of African American Christians and the context in which the psalms are enacted; I also want to attempt a theological explanation as to why the psalms have been and remain of crucial significance to African American Christians across the denominational spectrum.

History

Slaves from Africa, imported between 1620 and 1807 to the British colonies of what eventually became the United States, were imported into a colonial culture. The large plantation estates of the Caribbean and of Central and South America continued to import millions of Africans across the four centuries of the North Atlantic slave trade into the mid-nineteenth century, while approximately 400,000 slaves were brought into this country. Seventy-five percent of the slaves lived on farms whose owners held from five to ten slaves.[1]

---

[1] Philip D. Curtin, *The Atlantic Slave Trade: A Census* (Madison: University of Wisconsin Press, 1969). Curtin sets the figure slightly below 400,000 imported Africans. Higher figures often include those Africans who were brought to Jamaica, West Indies. See John B. Boles, *Black Southerns: 1619-1869* (Lexington: University of Kentucky Press, 1984), 30–31.

This colonial culture was predominately Protestant.[2] In northern colonies Congregational and Dutch Reform worship depended upon the singing of metrical psalm texts to then-familiar melodies such as Windsor, Cambridge Short, and York.[3] The seventeenth-century manner of singing in this style required one person chanting a line and the congregation imitating the chanter's lead, a style called "lining out." Slaves were forced to attend predominately White churches, and they participated in this form of psalm singing. The Bay Psalm Book, published in 1640, rendered the psalms in metrical verse, so that, for example, Ps 19 in the King James Version:

> The heavens declare the glory of God
> And the firmament sheweth his handywork

becomes

> Declare abroad the heavens do, The majesty of God;
> And forth the firmament doth show, His handywork abroad.[4]

At the same time, the evidence of the first baptism of a slave in America, in 1641, indicates that the female candidate's preparation included instruction in the psalms. We can thus see that the psalms were part of both the catechetical and liturgical life of slaves in early colonial America.

The majority of slaves, however, resided in the Southern colonies, which created a different environment for the transmission of Christian culture. During the seventeenth and early eighteenth centuries the majority of slave owners, if they were practicing Christians, were Anglicans. The Anglican church leadership, on the whole, did not demonstrate an interest in the religious instruction of the slaves, turning their missionary attention to the plantations only after they were rejected by the White colonists and Native Americans. When they did, the results were negligible. The style of Anglican worship at the time was remote, affectively attenuated, and theologically encumbered by the uncertainty of the effects of baptism upon the status and behavior of the slaves.

---

[2] The exception among the thirteen colonies was Maryland, and later Louisiana, where Catholicism established an early presence. See Nelson Rightmyer, *Maryland's Established Church* (Baltimore: Church Historical Society for the Diocese of Maryland, 1956), and Gwendolyn Midlo Hall, *Africans in Colonial Louisiana: The Development of Afro-Creole Culture in the Eighteenth Century* (Baton Rouge: Louisiana State University Press, 1992).

[3] Eileen Southern, *The Music of Black Americans: A History* (New York: Norton, 1971), 31–32.

[4] Ibid., 32.

During the first part of the eighteenth century a number of important developments took place, among them the Great Awakening and the publication of Dr. Isaac Watts's hymnal.[5] The Great Awakening emphasized the importance of affective religious experience in the conversion of the believer. The leadership, including George Whitefield, demonstrated a more inclusive missionary zeal than the Anglican Church and therefore reached out to the slaves and created a cognate liturgical style that allowed the African Americans to participate in a more holistic form of worship. This was ecstatic, kinetic, bodily animated, interactive, and bore the hallmark of African communion with the divine: Spirit-possession, Protestant style.[6]

The first edition of *The Psalms of David Imitated in the Language of the New Testament and Apply'd to the Christian State and Worship* (otherwise known as Dr. Watts's hymnal) to appear in the colonies was printed by Benjamin Franklin in 1729. Franklin did not print another edition until 1741, the period of the Great Awakening. The Rev. Samuel Davies, a Presbyterian minister and missionary among the slaves in Virginia during the Great Awakening, wrote letters requesting copies of Dr. Watts's hymnal in 1755:

> The books were all very acceptable, but none more so than the Psalms and Hymns, which enable [the slaves] to gratify their peculiar taste for psalmody. Sundry of them have lodged all night in my kitchen, and sometimes when I have awaked about two or there-o'clock in the morning, a torrent of sacred harmony has poured into my chamber and carried my mind away to heaven. In this seraphic exercise some of them spend almost the whole night. I wish, Sir, you and other benefactors could hear some of these sacred concerts. I am persuaded it would surprise and please you more than an Oratorio or a St. Cecilia's day....
>
> The Books I principally want for the slaves are the Watts's Psalms and Hymns.... I am rather importunate for a good Number of these, as I cannot but observe that the Negroes, above all the Human Species that I ever knew, have an Ear for musick, and a kind of extatic Delight in Psalmody; and there are no Books they learn so soon and take so much pleasure in, as those used in that heavenly Part of divine Worship.[7]

---

[5] Isaac Watts, *The Psalms of David Imitated in the Language of the New Testament and Apply'd to the Christian State and Worship* (Philadelphia, 1729).

[6] Wesley M. Gewhehr, *The Great Awakening in Virginia, 1740–1790* (Durham, N.C.: Duke University Press, 1930).

[7] Eileen Southern, ed., *Readings in Black American Music* (New York: Norton, 1983), 27–28. This letter originally appeared in Charles Colcok Jones, *Religious Instruction of the Negroes in the United States* (Savanna, Ga.: Purse, 1842). Jones, a Presbyterian, was a zealous leader in the plantation missions to the slaves in the South.

A year after the second printing of Dr. Watts's hymnal, Rev. Charles Wesley's *Collection of Psalms and Hymns* was published by his brother John.[8] These two collections of psalms and hymns became the most popular mainstays among the converted slaves. The Wesley collection also became the forerunner of the first Methodist Church hymnal.

In 1804 the following description of the style of singing appears in a report by Clement Caines:

> The slaves then work in a long string, and follow each other in regular order. Some one takes the lead and breaks out with a song, to which there is always a chorus. In this they all join, and the union of such a number of voices produces a very animated and pleasing effect.[9]

Both hymnals utilized this antiphonal style of "lining out," which resembled the style of singing found among West Africans, and would have been a recognizable pattern among eighteenth-century imported Africans and their descendants.

Eileen Southern offers three additional reasons for the popularity of this style and these hymnals: the vitality of the words; wider use of intervals than in the psalm tunes of the Bay Colony Psalter; and rhythmic freedom (see fig. 17.1).[10]

One of the examples of the Wesley hymns that has endured is "Father, I Stretch My Hands to Thee."

> Father, I stretch my hands to Thee, No other help I know:
> If Thou with-draw Thyself from me, Ah! Whither shall I go?
>
> What did Thine only Son endure, Before I drew my breath!
> What pain, what labor, to secure My soul from endless death!
>
> Surely Thou canst not let me die; O speak, and I shall live;
> And here I will unwearied lie, Till Thou Thy Spirit give.
>
> Author of faith! To thee I lift My weary, longing eyes:
> O let me now receive that Gift! My soul without it dies.

---

8 John Wesley, *A Collection of Psalms and Hymns* (Charlestown, S.C., 1737).

9 Clement Caines, *The History of the General Council and General Assembly of the Leeward Islands, Which Were Convened for the Purpose of Investigating and Meliorating the Condition of the Slaves throughout Those Settlements, and of Effecting a Gradual Abolition of the Slave Trade* (St. Christopher: Cable, 1804), 1:110–11, quoted in Dena J. Epstein, *Sinful Tunes and Spirituals: Black Folk Music to the Civil War* (Urbana: University of Illinois Press, 1977), 71.

10 Southern, *Music of Black Americans,* 35.

"A Morning Hymn," Isaac Watts, based on
Psalm 19; "One Hundredth Tune"

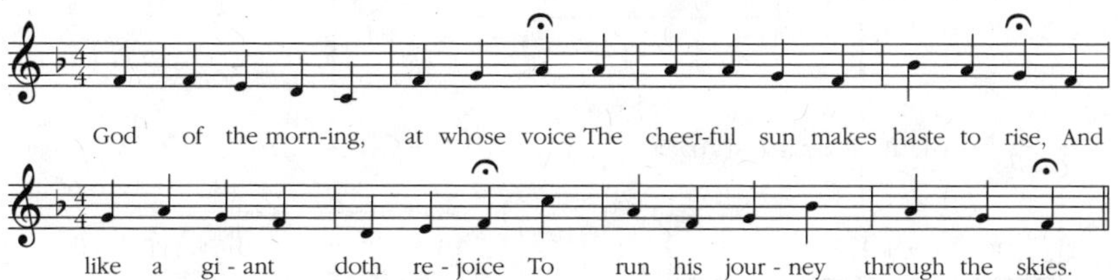

2. From the fair chambers of the east
The circuit of his race begins,
And without weariness or rest
Round the whole earth he flys and shines.

Fig. 17.1. Eileen Southern, *The Music of Black Americans: A History* (New York: Norton, 1971), 40.

At first this hymn may seem to be a departure from the psalms, but upon closer examination its composition reveals its dependence. Look at the first verse and compare Ps 74:11: "Why withdrawest thou thy hand, even thy right hand?" and from Ps 88: "Mine eye mourneth by reason of affliction: Lord, I have called daily upon thee, I have stretched out my hands unto thee," and from Ps 123, "Behold, as the eyes of servants look unto the hand of their masters, and as the eyes of a maiden unto the hand of her mistress; so our eyes wait upon the Lord our God, until that he have mercy upon us."

With the development of independent Black churches, the traditions of psalm singing, and older and newer forms, coexisted and emerged within liturgical practices (see fig. 17.2). Figure 17.3 provides an approximate sense of these developments. Whereas the psalms were part of the congregational singing, they eventually became part of the repertoire of the spiritual leaders of the church: the deacons.

Deacon's Devotion

The following rite is representative of a style of worship that can still be found throughout the South, especially in rural areas, and is a trans-denominational phenomenon within the African American Christianity of this region. This form of worship can be found especially during revival season, which usually occurs in July and August. The site of my analysis is Salem Baptist Church, in Atlanta, Georgia. Salem is part of the National Baptist Convention, a denominational body of over six million members.

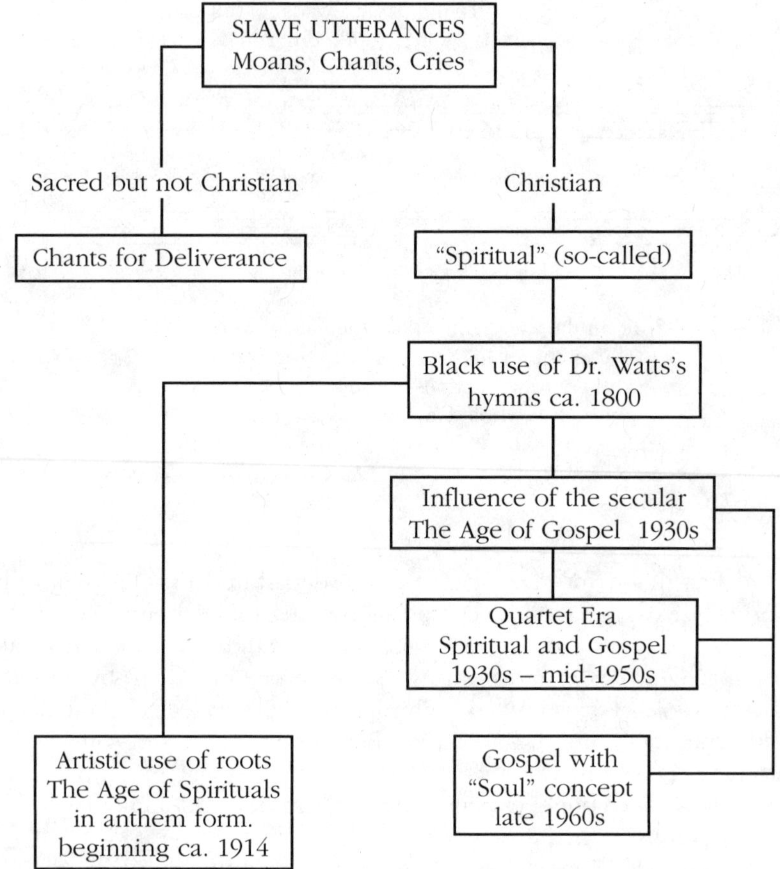

Fig. 17.2. See Wendel Phillips Whalum, "Black Hymondy," *Review and Expositor* (Summer 1973): 343.[11]

Founded in 1891 in Atlanta by former slaves, Salem has had only five pastors in over one hundred years. At the time of my original study, in the first few years after 1990, Salem held approximately two thousand members attending two services each Sunday.

---

[11] This chart, which appears on page 343 of the article, is erroneously cited in both *Lead Me, Guide Me: The African American Catholic Hymnal* (Chicago: G.I.A. Publications, 1987), 5; and in Wyatt Tee Walker, *Somebody's Calling My Name* (Valley Forge, Pa.: Judson, 1979), 146, as *Review and Expositor* (Spring 1972): 581 (*errata*).

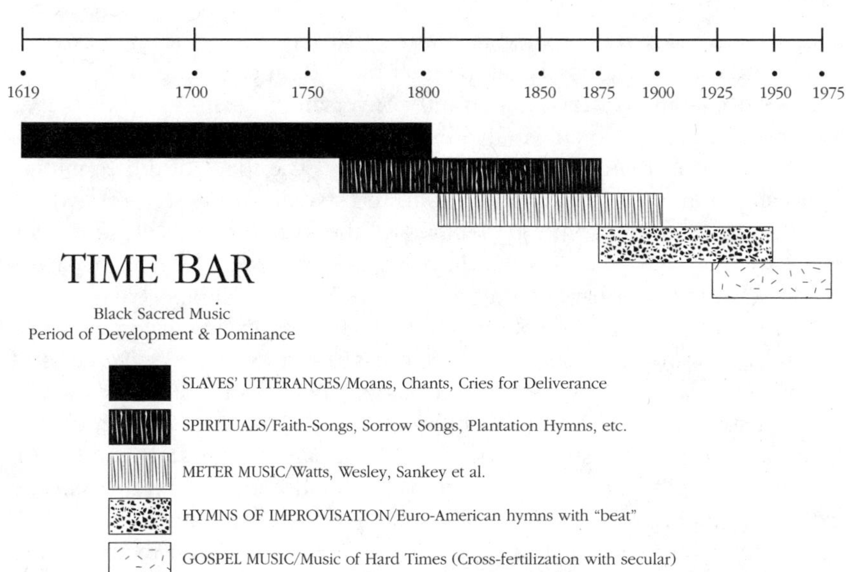

Fig. 17.3. Wyatt Tee Walker, *Somebody's Calling My Name* (Valley Forge, Pa.: Judson, 1979), 129.

The Deacon's Devotion usually began one-half hour to forty-five minutes before the commencement of the larger congregational worship. Salem's original sanctuary is one of the best-designed churches I have attended; style of architecture and style of worship are thoroughly integrated. Rather than being a typical Protestant-style rectangle, Salem is constructed like an amphitheater, with pews that radiate concentrically in ever-widening arcs toward the balcony. The rear of the nave is therefore a wide concave wall. The longest and widest pews are closest to this wall, with each succeeding pew slightly shorter than the one behind it, each with the same degree of curvature. The floor of the sanctuary is built upon a descending grade. Each of the six aisles moves toward the apex of the chancel, a point located right behind the pulpit. Thus all lines converge upon this place of prominence, commanded by the pastor or whoever is presiding. Instead of having to turn to view the pastor, a worshiper is automatically positioned and focused upon him as long as he stays within the pulpit area. Further, upon entering the sanctuary, one is literally pulled toward this focal point by the floor's incline. Physically and visually one is drawn toward the center of activity and attention.

Members who enter move toward the center without the encouragement of ushers or the exhortation of ministers. These members want to be as close as possible to the Deacon's Devotion. With its enormous size—it is equipped with a balcony under a vaulted ceiling—Salem is a commodious church. The aisles are carpeted in a warm maroon-beige, and the pews are cushioned on the back and seat in a soft blue. Both carpeting and padding dampen the sound of movement and conversation, giving the sanctuary's acoustics an intimate quality. Given the radiating design, the chancel has a smaller diameter than the rest of the sanctuary. The focus of the congregation's attention, therefore, contributes to the spatial closeness.

In contrast to the comfortable finery of the furniture, a single drab grey metal folding chair stands alone in the space immediately in front of the pulpit. The chair appears ugly in its stark and inharmonious coarseness of color and shape. As the members settle into silence, Deacon Napper stands and turns toward the members. He is dressed in the conservative cloth of his office: a dark-grey wool suit, conservatively cut without concession to modern style. Deacon Napper is president of the Deacon Board, a church elder, and a highly respected person within Salem's hierarchy and community. His gifts as a leader, both spiritual and organizational, are extremely important to the life of the church and the vitality of its worship.

Deacon Napper holds an open copy of John Wesley's hymnal, containing compositions by Isaac Watts and Charles Wesley,[12] and begins "lining" a hymn. He sings the first verse, followed by the congregation the song; he then talks the second verse, followed by singing. He is the only one with a hymnal, which leaves everyone else free to focus upon him and the singing. The hymns are never posted in advance, since the leader is given the latitude to select them according to the mood and needs of those members gathered at the moment. "A Charge to Keep I Have" is an example. It is not a psalm, but it is the same style in which the psalm selections are performed: the common style, or heterophany, which is described by David Reck as "the weaving of melodic strands around a central core of a melody; it is melody-based—rather than harmony-based—and its strands happening simultaneously, all relate to the central melody in some way: they may be variations of it, they may ornament it, they may scan or punctuate its important notes."[13]

Not only is the performance style the same, but the inverted sentence order is common to this style:

A charge to keep I have, A God to glorify,
Who gave His Son my soul to save,
And fit it for the sky.

---

[12] John Wesley, *Collection of Psalms and Hymns.*

[13] David Reck, *Music of the Whole Earth* (New York: Scribner's, 1977), 312. See also Edith Borroff and Marjory Irvin, *Music in Perspective* (New York: Harcourt Brace Jovanovich, 1976), 33–35, for a heterophanic application of the definition of heterophany to music from different cultures.

As the congregation responds musically to Deacon Napper, the other deacons, who have been seated in the first pew, stand. One has removed his suit coat before rising, and he is approached by his fellow deacons, who begin to shake and grasp his hands. Each of the six other deacons performs this gesture with the divested deacon. As this ceremony proceeds, Deacon Napper makes a gesture and the church members rise, still singing. Once everyone is standing and the deacons have completed the rite of preparation, the designated deacon kneels before the metal chair; he faces the congregation, resting his elbows on the seat of the chair. When he is settled at his station, Deacon Napper signals the congregation to be seated. They sing a few more words before growing silent. The church is hushed. Into the silent sanctuary emerges the sonority of a voice full of pleading and praise. The prayer that unfolds is another presentation, but let me just say that the prayer is in continuity with the musical style and the content of the selections, including the psalms.

Another example is "Before Jehovah's Awful Throne" by Isaac Watts. This is based on Ps 100 and sung to the melody of the "Old Hundredth."[14] I bring to your attention the first verse:

> Before Jehovah's awful throne, Ye nations, bow with sacred joy;
> Know that the Lord is God alone, He can create and He destroy.

In the four years since my study was completed, Salem Baptist Church has undergone a number of significant changes. The congregation has grown to eight thousand. The church consists of two sanctuaries, the new one located in an adjacent city.[15] They now have two sets of deacons, the elder ones and a younger generation. The deacons now include men and women who lead the Deacon's Devotion together. The younger deacons

---

[14] This example is found in *The African Methodist Episcopal Zion Bicentennial Hymnal: The Official Hymnal of the African Methodist Episcopal Zion Church* (October, 1996) and was used at Salem Baptist Church as well.

[15] Salem Baptist Church has entered into the twenty-first century. It has kept its original sanctuary on the west side of Atlanta, historically the section of the city reserved for its Black residents during segregation, and constructed a new sanctuary in Lithonia, Dekalb County, which is undergoing a second Northern invasion with accompanying rapid population growth. Each sanctuary schedules worship at 8:00 A.M., 10:15 A.M., and 12:30 P.M. to accommodate the expanding church attendance. In addition to growth in attendance, Salem now broadcasts its services on cable television (AIB Cable TV on Sunday evenings at 7:30 P.M.); on radio on Sunday morning at 10:00 A.M. (WAOK-AM); has an Internet website (www.salembaptistchurch.org); and has an extensive collection of Pastor Williams's sermons on video and audiocassette in its library.

do not kneel but remain standing throughout the devotional service, a style adopted by a number of churches with younger members. Most significantly, Deacon Napper died in 1996, and while the older deacons still utilize the psalmody tradition of Wesley and Watts, the younger deacons do not.

Psalms can still be found in the hymnal, such as "This Is the Day," which belongs to the new genre of "praise songs."[16] While based on Ps 118:24, it is lacking in the textual richness and theological ambiguity of the psalms that used to characterize the worship:

This is the day, this is the day that the Lord hath made,
    That the Lord hath made.
Let us rejoice, let us rejoice and be glad in it,
    And be glad in it.
This is the day that the Lord hath made;
    Let us rejoice and be glad in it.
This is the day, this is the day that the Lord hath made
        [repeated indefinitely]

One can also find the psalms in the responsive readings of the congregation, which are still a part of worship in the major denominations in African American Christianity. Further, the tradition of the Deacon's Devotion lives on in rural churches in the South, where the pattern of singing, standing, kneeling, and praying continues.

At Salem Baptist the most important vessel of continuity in the traditional sensibility of the psalms, and the textual richness that characterized the traditions that emerged in eighteenth-century worship, is the pastor, Rev. Jasper Williams Jr. Pastor Williams has presided at Salem Baptist for thirty-seven years and has been preaching for fifty years; he began his precocious and gifted vocation at the age of nine. He is a liturgical genius and the subject of a much wider study.[17]

As an example of his use of the psalms, Pastor Williams inserted a sermonic exegesis of Ps 23 in the middle of a sermon on suffering and spiritual growth. An embodiment and recapitulation of the ethos of the psalms as they were redacted and adapted within the context of mainline African American Protestant Christianity was here enacted and articulated within Pastor Williams's interpretation of Ps 23, with the culminating and concluding movements of completed transformation and divine deliverance. The sermonic exegesis of Ps 23 is an answer to the prayers of supplication

---

[16] Les Garrett, "This is the Day" (Laguna Hills, Calif.: Maranatha Music, 1977).

[17] Gilbert I. Bond, *Community, Communitas, and Cosmos: Toward a Liturgical Theology of Afro-Christian Worship* (Lanham, Md.: Catholic Scholar's Press, 2002).

initiated in the Deacon's Devotion. The movement of radical contingency to divine intervention was the basic structure of worship at Salem until recently. Now that pattern has come to reside in the person and the liturgical enactments of Pastor Williams. He has become the primary vessel for the continuity of the tension-wrought range of devotional dispositions so richly represented in the Psalter.

The adoption of the psalms as redacted by Watts and Wesley in the devotional life of the emerging slave Christians revealed a critical selection process at work. Watts's and Wesley's juxtaposition of the psalm material, containing the movement of suffering supplication, with the movement of the cross looking toward redemption, provided a theological texture rich enough for the slaves to identify their lives of tribulation and their experience of transformation within the static structures of slavery. Holding these heterogeneous sensibilities together is the strength of the psalms and the strength of traditional African American liturgy, piety, and practice. One may ask if this premodern style and sensibility will survive its entry into modernity or undergo the fate that befell certain varieties of mainline American Christianity when they forgot the relationship between tragedy and transformation and underwent the unraveling of the tension-wrought tapestries of dissimilar divine sensibilities into separated and weakened stands of enthusiastic praise shorn of its solid moorings in divine and human suffering. Only time will tell.

Chanting Psalms Today: The *Zemirot* in Syrian Sabbath Prayers

Mark Kligman

Psalm recitation is an active component of Syrian Jewish prayer.[1] Like other Jewish communities, Syrians use psalms prominently in their morning service, *Shaḥarit*.[2] Over ten psalms are part of the morning liturgy and twenty in the Shabbat morning liturgy (see table 18.1 for a listing of psalms chanted in *Shaḥarit*). Unique to the Syrian community is how they recite the psalms. After residing in Syria for over two thousand years, Syrian Jews were deeply immersed in Middle Eastern culture; we see this in their dress, language, food, and music, and although adapted, their Arab-influenced way of life persists in Brooklyn.[3] In the musical expression of the liturgy Syrian Jews draw from Arab musical styles and aesthetics to create a Judeo-Arab synthesis.[4] This essay will focus on the recitation of psalms in the

---

[1] Research for this study was conducted between 1990 and 1992 and culminated in my doctoral dissertation ("Modes of Prayer: Arabic Maqamat in the Sabbath Morning Liturgical Music of the Syrian Jews in Brooklyn" [Ph.D. diss., New York University, 1997)]). Funding for the writing of the dissertation, which made the present study possible, was provided by the Memorial Foundation for Jewish Culture and the National Foundation for Jewish Culture.

[2] *Shaḥarit* is one of the three required daily times of prayer: *Shaḥarit* takes place in the morning, *Minḥa* is the afternoon prayer, and *Ma'ariv* the evening prayer. *Musaf* is an added time of prayer for the Sabbath, holidays, and Rosh Ḥodesh newmoon celebration. These times of prayer stem from the sacrifices of the temple. Psalm chanting is most prominent in *Shaḥarit*. On holidays Hallel is recited; it consists of Pss 113–118. For more on psalms in Jewish liturgy, see Louis Isaac Rabinowitz, "Psalms, Book of, in the Liturgy," *EncJud* 13:1323–25.

[3] Walter P. Zenner and Mark Kligman, "Brooklyn's Syrian Sephardim in the 1990s: Diversification and Ethnic Persistence," in Zenner, *A Global Community: The Jews from Aleppo, Syria* (Detroit: Wayne State University Press, 2000), 155–76.

[4] Mark Kligman, "Modes of Prayer"; and Kay Kaufman Shelemay, *"Let Jasmine Rain Down": Song and Remembrance among Syrian Jews* (Chicago Studies in Ethnomusicology; Chicago: University of Chicago Press, 1998).

Table 18.1. *Zemirot* Liturgical Section on Shabbat

LITURGICAL SECTION	SOURCE OF TEXT	WEEKDAY LITURGY	MAQAM
1. *Hodu la-Shem Kir'u bi-Shemo Va-Ya'amideha le-Ya'akov le-Ḥok*	1 Chr 16:8–15	yes	*seyga*
2. *Kel Nekamot Ha-Shem*	various psalm passages	yes	"
3. *Aromimkha Ha-Shem*	Ps 30	yes	"
4. ***Ha-Shem Melekh***	various biblical passages	yes	Maq of Day**
5. *Lamnazze'aḥ Mizmor le-David*	Ps 19	no	*seyga*
6. *Rannenu Zaddikim*	Ps 33	no	"
7. *Le-David, be-Shannoto et Tamo*	Ps 34	no	"
8. *Tefillah le-Moshe*	Ps 90	no	"
9. *Yoshev be-Seter Elyon*	Ps 91	no	"
10. *Mizmor, Shiru la-Shem*	Ps 98	no	"
11. *Shir la-Ma'alot, Essa Einai*	Ps 121	no	"
12. *Shir ha-Ma'alot le-David, Samaḥti*	Ps 122	no	"
13. *Shir ha-Ma'alot, Elekha*	Ps 123	no	"
14. *Shir ha-Ma'alot le-David, Lulei*	Ps 124	no	"
15. *Halleluyah, Hallelu et Shem*	Ps 135	no	"
16. *Hodu la-Shem Ki Tov*	Ps 136	no	"
17. ***Barukh she-Amar***	verses of praise	yes	fixed tune
Blessing [continuation]		Contrasting Maqam	
18. *Mizmor Shir le-Yom ha-Shabbat*	Ps 92	no	"
19. *Ha-Shem Malakh Ge'et Lavesh*	Ps 93	no	"
20. *Yehi Khavod*	various biblical passages	yes	"
21. *Ashrei Yoshvei*	Ps 145	yes	"
22. *Halleluyah, Halleli Nafshi*	Ps 146	yes	"
23. *Halleluyah, Ki Tov Zamrah*	Ps 147	yes	"
24. *Halleluyah, hallelu et Ha-Shem*	Ps 148	yes	"
25. *Halleluyah, Shiru la-Shem*	Ps 149	yes	"
26. ***Halleluyah, Hallelu Kel be-Kadsho***	Ps 150	yes	varies
27. *Barukh Ha-Shem le-Olam*	four psalm phrases; 1 Chr 29:10–13; Neh 9:5–11	yes	*seyga*
28. *Az Yahir Moshe (Shirat ha-Yam)*	Exod 14:30–15:19	yes	"

Bold items are highlighted musically. Psalm number is in accordance with the Hebrew Bible.

Shaḥarit service of Shabbat by Syrian Jews in Brooklyn, emphasizing the organizational structure of their musical rendering.

The Syrian Community in Brooklyn

Syrian immigration to America started over one hundred years ago and has been ongoing. At present the Syrian Jews in Brooklyn are estimated at forty thousand, thus constituting the largest group anywhere in the world. The community resides predominantly in the Flatbush section of Brooklyn, where they support fifteen synagogues, of which thirteen follow the Aleppo customs and two the traditions of Damascus. My research has focused on the Aleppo tradition.

My informants were lay cantors who are now in their seventies and eighties. These men were all born in Brooklyn and come from families immersed in the liturgical and paraliturgical singing of *bakkashot* and *pizmonim,* two genres of liturgical poetry.[5] The primary progenitor of the Aleppo tradition was Raphael Antebi Taboush, who immigrated to Israel prior to his death; he was the teacher of Moses Ashear (1877–1940),[6] a cantor who left Aleppo for Brooklyn in 1912. Several members of the Tawil family were students of Ashear, prominent among them Naftali Tawil (1902–63), whose two younger brothers, Moses and David, credit their knowledge and love of the tradition to their older brother. Moses and David Tawil were main informants for my work with the Syrian liturgical tradition.

One hears in the prayers by Syrian cantors a fluid recitation in a *maqâm* (pl. *maqâmât*) Arabic mode, which may contain pitches that do not appear on Western instruments. Syrian liturgy makes use of eleven *maqâmât* (table 18.2),[7] of which *maqâm seyga* is the most prominent. A variety of Arab musical styles serve as a basis for Syrian liturgy: the *murattal* and *mujawwad* style of qur'anic recitation;[8] the improvisatory singing

---

[5] While my work focuses on the practices of this tradition in the synagogue, Kay Shelemay's delves into the paraliturgical practice of the *pizmonim* (see *"Let Jasmine Rain Down"*).

[6] His Hebrew name was Moshe Ashkar.

[7] This use of eleven *maqâmât* is consistent with pan-Arab usage. See Scott L. Marcus, "Arab Music Theory in the Modern Period" (Ph.D. diss., University of California, Los Angeles, 1989); Mark Kligman, "Modes of Prayer"; idem, "The Bible, Prayer and Maqam: Extra-Musical Associations of Syrian Jews," *Ethnomusicology* 45 (2001): 443–79.

[8] Lois Ibsen al-Faruqi, "The Cantillation of the Qur'an," *Asian Music* 19 (1987): 2–25; Kristina Nelson, "Reciter and Listener: Some Factors Shaping the Mujawwad Style of Qur'anic Reciting," *Ethnomusicology* 26 (1982): 41–47; idem, *The Art of Reciting the Qur'an* (Austin: University of Texas Press, 1985).

Table 18.2. Eleven *Maqamat* Used by Syrian Jews in Brooklyn

ajam	B♭	C	D	E♭	F	G	A	B♭			
rast		C	D	E𝄳	F	G	A	B𝄳	C		
mahur		C	D	E𝄳	F	G	A	B♭	C		(starts on upper C)
nahawand		C	D	E♭	F	G	A♭	B♭	C		
rahaw nawa		G	A	B♭	C	D	E♭	F	G		
bayat			D	E𝄳	F	G	A	B𝄳	C	D	
muḥayyar			starts on upper D and focuses on upper tetrachord								
ḥuseini						starts on A					
saba			D	E𝄳	F	G♭	A	B𝄳	C	D	
hijaz			D	E♭	F♯	G	A	B♭	C	D	
seyga				E𝄳	F	G	A	B𝄳	C	D	E𝄳

found in Arabic vocal music; and, interaction between the leader and listeners or, in the context of Syrian liturgy, the cantor and the congregation.

Syrian Sabbath Morning Service

Shaḥarit, the Sabbath morning service of the Syrian Jews in Brooklyn, consists of six distinct sections, like other traditional Jewish liturgies.[9] Each section makes use of a variety of musical performance styles, including recitation, song (both fixed and improvised), and spoken discourse. Variety is achieved through the use of a different leader, or leaders, for each section, and through the *maqâm* employed in singing or improvising (table 18.3). Psalm recitation takes place in the *Zemirot* section, the portion of the *Shaḥarit* service that will be discussed in detail below.

First some comments on the musical organization of the entire morning service. The use of a *maqâm,* and its variously rendered styles, is determined by text and liturgical section. The first liturgical section, *Birkhot ha-Shaḥar,* makes use of a recitation formula in *maqâm seyga;* the

[9] The canonization of the text in Jewish liturgy took place between the eighth and eleventh centuries C.E.; see Lawrence A. Hoffman, *The Canonization of the Synagogue Service* (University of Notre Dame Center for the Study of Judaism and Christianity in Antiquity 4; Notre Dame, Ind.: University of Notre Dame Press, 1979), 8–9. Two rites developed: the Ashkenazic in continental Europe; and the Sephardic, in Spain and the Middle East (ibid., 46–59). Syrian liturgy closely resembles the Sephardic rite, with minor modifications.

Table 18.3. Liturgical Sections of the Syrian Sabbath Morning Service

LITURGICAL SECTION	LEADER	*MAQĀM*	LENGTH
1. *Birkhot ha-Shaḥar* [Introductory morning blessings]	none	mainly *seyga*	15 min.
2. *Zemirot* [Psalms]	2 congregants	*seyga* contrasting *maqām*	30 min.
3. *Shaḥarit*	*ḥazzan*	*maqām* of the day	45 min.
4. Torah reading	Torah reader	*seyga*	60–75 min.
5. Sermon	rabbi	———	15 min.
6. *Musaf* [Additional service]	*ḥazzan* or skilled congregant	varies *seyga*	15 min.

second and fourth sections, *Zemirot* and the Torah reading respectively, make use of different melodic formulas also in *maqâm seyga*. *Birkhot ha-Shaḥar* has no designated leader, and men lead portions from their seats. During *Zemirot* two men walk to the *teiva,* a raised platform in the middle of the sanctuary (see fig. 18.1 below), and lead from there.

Shaḥarit is unusual because it is led by the *ḥazzan* and makes use of a special *maqâm* of the day, determined by the biblical reading; a biblical reading is associated with a particular *maqâm* because of a perceived affect of that *maqâm* or another principle (table 18.4). For example, the biblical reading *ḥayyei Sarah* (Gen 23:1–15:18, the fifth biblical reading in Genesis) uses *maqâm hijaz* because both are associated with sadness. This subject has been much discussed.[10] *Bayat, saba,* and *seyga* are used most

[10] A. Z. Idelsohn, "Die Makeman in der hebraischen Poesie der orientalischen Juden," *MGWJ* 57 (1913): 314–25; idem, *Gesange der orientalischen Sefardim* (Hebraish-orientalischer Melodienschatz; Jerusalem: Harz, 1923); Macy Nulman, "Musical Service of Syrian Synagogue: Its Structure and Design," *Journal of Jewish Music and Liturgy* 2 (1977–78): 34–56; Kligman, "Modes of Prayer," 248–305. Elsewhere I have shown that three principles are at work in the *maqâm* and biblical reading associations: affect—including *saba* for the seriousness of circumcision, *hijaz* for sadness, *ajam* for happiness; theory—*rast* as the first *maqâm* used for each of the five books of Moses similar to *rast* as the first *maqâm* discussed in Arabic theoretical writings; variety—the desire never to have the same *maqâm* two weeks in a row. See Kligman, "Modes of Prayer," 258–75; idem, "Bible, Prayer and Maqam"; and Ezra Barnea, "The Tradition of the Jerusalemite-Sephardic Hazzanut:

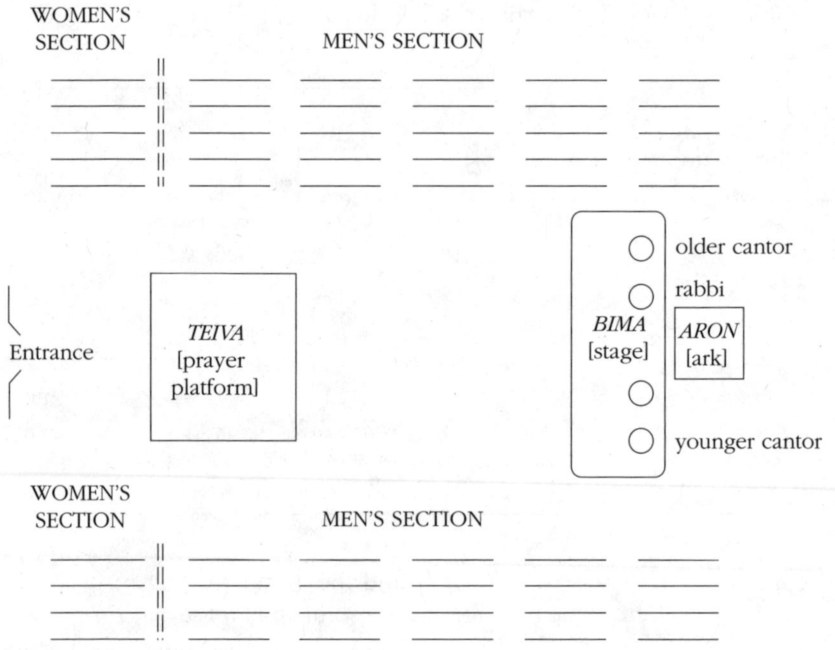

Fig. 18.1. Diagram of Congregation Beit Torah

often during *Shaḥarit,* with over 50 percent of the *pizmonim* in Brooklyn in these three *maqâmât.* Seven sung textual portions of *Shaḥarit* are initiated by the *ḥazzan.* The melodic content of *Shaḥarit* includes sung melodic portions, which are often adaptations of known Arab melodies, and improvisations. *Shaḥarit* is the most musically elaborate service. The remaining portions are similar to earlier sections. The Torah reading is based on a formula in *maqâm seyga,* yet different from *Zemirot.* The rabbi's sermon is spoken, and the *Musaf* section makes use of both the recited and sung sections heard earlier in *Zemirot* and *Shaḥarit.*[11]

Zemirot

Psalm chanting during the *Zemirot* section of *Shaḥarit* provides an introduction to the main liturgy of the day. *Zemirot* ("songs," in this context

A Clarification of Nusah Hatefillah as Dominant in Our Era" (trans. from Hebrew by W. Wolfson), *Journal of Jewish Music and Liturgy* 19 (1996–97): 19–29.

[11] For a further description of the melodic organization of the Syrian morning service, see Kligman, "Modes of Prayer," 181–247, 306–65.

Table 18.4. *Maqam* and Biblical Reading Associations

	BIBLICAL READING	*MAQAM*
	GENESIS	
1.1	*Bereshit*	*rast*
1.2	*No'aḥ*	*seyga*
1.3	*Lekh Lekha*	*saba*
1.4	*Va-Yera*	*rahaw* (*nawa*)
1.5	*Ḥayye Sarah*	*hijaz*
1.6	*Toledot*	*mahur*
1.7	*Va-Yeze*	*ajam*
1.8	*Va-Yishlaḥ*	*saba* or *seyga*
1.9	*Va-Yeshev*	*rahaw* or *nahawand*
1.10	*Mi-Kez*	*seyga*
1.11	*Va-Yiggash*	*bayat*
1.12	*Va-Yeḥi*	*hijaz*
	EXODUS	
2.1	*Shemot*	*rast* or *bayat*
2.2	*Va-Era*	*ḥuseini* or *rast*
2.3	*Bo*	*seyga*
2.4	*Be-Shallaḥ*	*ajam*
2.5	*Yitro*	*ḥuseini*
2.6	*Mishpatim*	*saba*
2.7	*Terumah*	*ḥuseini*
2.8	*Tezavveh*	*seyga*
2.9	*Ki Tissa*	*hijaz*
2.10	*Va-Yakhel*	*ḥuseini*
2.11	*Pekudei*	*rahaw* (*nawa*)
2.12	*Va-Yakhel-Pekudei*	*bayat*
	LEVITICUS	
3.1	*Va-Yikra*	*rast*
3.2	*Zav*	*rahaw* (*nawa*)
3.3	*Shemini*	*ḥuseini*
3.4	*Tazri'a*	*saba* or *bayat*
3.5	*Taḥor*	*nahawand* or *seyga*
3.6	*Tazri'a-Taḥor*	*saba*
3.7	*Aḥarei Mot*	*hijaz*
3.8	*Kedoshim*	*saba*
3.9	*Aḥarei Mot-Kedoshim*	*bayat-hijaz*
3.10	*Emor*	*seyga ḥuseini*
3.11	*Be-Har*	*saba* or *nahawand*
3.12	*Be-Ḥukkotai*	*nahawand*
3.13	*Be-Har-Be-Ḥukkotai*	*saba*
	NUMBERS	
4.1	*Be-Midbar*	*ḥuseini* or *rast*
4.2	*Naso*	*rast-saba*
4.3	*Be-Ha'alotkha*	*seyga*
4.4	*Shelaḥ Lekha*	*hijaz*
4.5	*Koraḥ*	*nahawand*
4.6	*Ḥukkat*	*ḥuseini*
4.7	*Balak*	*mahur*
4.8	*Ḥukkat-Balak*	*ḥuseini*
4.9	*Pinḥas*	*saba*
4.10	*Mattot*	*nahawand* or *rahaw*
4.11	*Masei*	*saba*
4.12	*Mattot-Masei*	*nahawand*
	DEUTERONOMY	
5.1	*Devarim*	*hijaz*
5.2	*Va-Etḥannan*	*ḥuseini*
5.3	*Ekev*	*seyga*
5.4	*Re'eh*	*rast*
5.5	*Shofetim*	*ajam*
5.6	*Ki Teze*	*saba*
5.7	*Ki Tavo*	*seyga*
5.8	*Nizzavim*	*nahawand*
5.9	*Va-Yelekh*	*hijaz*
5.10	*Nizzavim-Va-Yelekh*	*nahawand*
5.11	*Ha'axinu*	*muḥayyar*
5.12	*Ve-zot Ha-Brakhah*	*ajam*

"songs of praise") contrasts with *Birkhot ha-Shaḥar.* The twenty-eight texts of *Zemirot* consist of chapters from the psalms, combined with other biblical passages (table 18.1).[12] Like *Birkhot ha-Shaḥar, Zemirot* is recited during the week, but unlike *Birkhot ha-Shaḥar, Zemirot* contains additional psalm texts for the Sabbath while omitting certain texts that appear on weekdays.[13] The additional psalms for the Sabbath (see table 18.1, Liturgical Sections [hereafter referred to as LS] 5–16, 18, and 19) are placed in the middle of the *Zemirot* section. These added psalms focus on three things: the remembrance that God finished creation in six days and rested on the Sabbath; the remembrance of the exodus from Egypt; and the idea that the Sabbath is a semblance of the world to come.[14]

Zemirot begins at the conclusion of the recitation of *Kaddish* with the congregation singing a fixed melody to *Hodu la-Shem Kir'u bi-Shemo,* "Praise the Lord, call on his name" (LS 1). The same melody is used from week to week; no single individual initiates the singing. Next follows a recitation of the remaining portion of the text, by a seated congregant, to the same *seyga* pattern used in *Birkhot ha-Shaḥar* (see fig. 18.2). The next two texts (LS 2 and 3) are recited similarly.

The *Ha-Shem Melekh,* "The Lord is King" text (LS 4), is sung by the *ḥazzan* of the day. The text reads: "Ha-Shem melekh, ha-Shem malakh, ha-Shem yimlokh le-olam va-ed," "The Lord reigns, The Lord has reigned, The Lord will reign for ever and ever."[15] The *ḥazzan,* from his seat on the *bima* (see fig. 18.1), sings this single line of text, which is repeated by the congregation; the *ḥazzan* repeats it, as does the congregation. The melody is in the *maqâm* of the day for use during *Shaḥarit;* like the *maqâm* it changes from week to week (see fig. 18.3). A proficient *ḥazzan* tries to offer variety by changing the melody when the same *maqâm* is used in a subsequent week. More importantly, Moses Tawil has pointed out to me that the goal is to use the *maqâm* of the day to foreshadow

---

[12] See Ismar Elbogen, "The Morning Psalms," in *Jewish Liturgy: A Comprehensive History* (trans. R. P. Scheindlin; Philadelphia: Jewish Publication Society, 1993; based on *Der judische Gottesdienst in seiner geschichtlichen Entwicklung* [Leipzig: Fock, 1913; repr., Hildesheim: Olms, 1962]), §11:72–76, 95; Hoffman, *Canonization,* 127–34; Herman Kieval, "Pesukei De-Zimra," *EncJud* 13:335. The *Zemirot* section of a Sephardic liturgy has a different order, and includes more psalms, than the corresponding Ashkenazic *Pesukei de-Zimra.*

[13] Pss 67 and 100 are omitted on the Sabbath. See Elbogen, *Jewish Liturgy,* 95.

[14] Nosson Scherman, trans., *Sidur Kol Ya'akov: hol/Shabat/Shalosh regalim* [*The Complete ArtScroll Siddur: Weekday/Sabbath/Festival*] (Brooklyn: Nesorah, 1984), 374.

[15] This text combines three separate biblical phrases: Pss 10:16 and 93:1 and Exod 15:18.

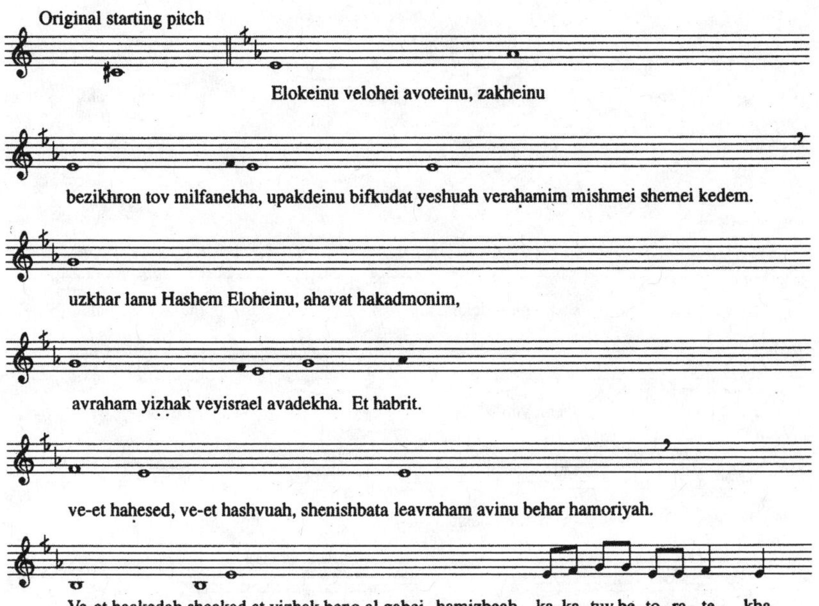

Fig. 18.2. *Birkot ha-Shaḥar* Formula. Applied to *Eloheinu ve-elokei avoteinu*. Sung by D. Tawil, 28 July 1995.

what will be heard later in *Shaḥarit*. See figure 18.3 for *Ha-Shem Melekh* melody in *bayat*.

After *Ha-Shem Melekh*, two congregants walk to the *teiva* (raised platform) and recite alternately most of the remaining *Zemirot*. The twelve psalms (LS 5–16) between *Ha-Shem Melekh* and *Barukh she-Amar* (LS 17) are recited in the *maqâm seyga* formula. See figure 18.4 for an illustration of the *Zemirot* seyga formula applied to *Lamnaẓẓe'aḥ Mizmor le-David,* Ps 19 (LS 5). This formula can be characterized as an even recitation, giving equal prominence to each word, with clear enunciation. The melodic components of the *Zemirot* formula consists of an emphasis on the first and third notes of *maqâm seyga* (E-quarter flat and G respectively) for each verse of the psalm text. Occasionally one verse may emphasize the first note of the *maqâm* and the next verse the third. The formula is adapted to fit the text. It differs from the *maqâm seyga* recitation used for *Birkhot ha-Shaḥar* (see fig. 18.2) in that there is a greater emphasis in melodic shape. Ends of psalm texts are slightly melodically embellished. Occasionally the leader gestures for someone else to continue, calling upon a member of the congregation to recite a psalm from his seat.

The design of *Zemirot,* thus far, consists of the three texts that precede *Ha-Shem Melekh* and twelve that follow. On the Sabbath, three

Fig. 18.3. *Ha-Shem Melekh* sung in *maqām bayat*.
Sung by D. Shiro, 6 October 1999

preceding texts are led from within the congregation and are rendered in the same manner as on weekdays. *Ha-Shem Melekh* serves as an introduction to the following twelve texts, which are specific to the Sabbath (see table 18.1). These twelve are rendered more formally by two leaders standing at the *teiva* rather than from within the congregation. While *Ha-Shem Melekh* is also recited on the weekday, it is singled out on the Sabbath as an important text, most likely for its present-, past-, and future-tense references to the "reigning of the Lord." This important text is highlighted musically by the *ḥazzan,* the important musical reciter, who signals a change in the manner of recitation to follow and announces the *maqâm* to be used later.

Similarly, *Barukh she-Amar* (LS 17) acts as a transition. It is sung by the entire congregation to a fixed melody in *nahawand* (see fig. 18.5),

Fig. 18.4. *Zemirot* formula. Applied to *Lamnaẓẓe'ah Mizmor le-David.* Sung by D. Tawil, 28 July 1995.

and, as with the singing of *Hodu la-Shem Kir'u bi-Shemo* (LS 1), is performed to a melody for the congregation to sing together. The *Barukh she-Amar* melody is not initiated by a leader since it is widely known. The first part of this text[16] is sung by the congregation; the second is led by the *ḥazzan* or another knowledgeable member of the congregation. It is set to a contrasting *maqâm*.

When *ḥazzan* Moses Tawil attends Congregation Shaarei Zion, the largest Syrian synagogue in Brooklyn, as a congregant—he no longer serves as a *ḥazzan* of the congregation—he begins with the second part of *Barukh she-Amar* after the congregational singing. The new *maqâm* that he establishes will be used thereafter, up to and including *Halleluyah,*

[16] *Barukh she-Amar* is unlike the other texts in *Zemirot* since it is not taken from the Bible. It is a composed text of two parts: the first praises God, and the second lauds and exalts God as ruler of the universe. It is variously dated to the period between the sixth and ninth centuries C.E. See Elbogen, *Jewish Liturgy,* 74, 405 n. 4.

Fig. 18.5. *Barukh she-Amar.* Sung by M. Tawil, 6 October 1991 (*Siddur kol ya'akov* 1995:465 [LS 2.17]).

Hallelu Kel be-Kadsho (LS 26). In a conversation on 6 October 1991, *Ḥazzan* Moses Tawil elaborated further on the prescribed change of *maqâm* and on the participation of others who recite from this point on during *Zemirot:*

> MT: If I am present, I will take over from after the whole *kahal* [congregation] says *Barukh she-Amar* together until the *Berakha* [blessing].[17] So at about the middle of the *Barukh she-Amar,* in this portion . . . we establish the *maqâm* that we are going to say the *Zemirot*. . . . It is not the same *maqâm* that we are going to pray from *Nishmat*[18] and onwards, in order not to overdo the *maqâm* and, on the other hand, give a chance to the *ḥazzan* that is going to start *Nishmat* to elaborate himself on that particular *maqâm*. . . . Very often when it comes to *Mizmor Shir le-Yom ha-Shabbat* (LS 18), if there is someone who is proficient he is invited to say it out loud—to sing it. There it depends on the proficiency of the *ḥazzan,* how much he can elaborate on it.
>
> MK: What *maqâm* would that be in?

[17] This is his reference to the second part of *Barukh she-Amar.*

[18] *Nishmat* refers to the first liturgical text, *Nishmat Kol Ḥai,* "the soul of every living thing," of the *Shah'arit* portion of the morning service (see table 18.3, LS 3).

MT: The *maqâm* that they establish for the rest of the *Zemirot*. For example, this past Shabbat they sang it in *nahawand*. The *tefilah* [the prayers from *Shaḥarit*], the body of it was in *rast*. The *Zemirot* before [*Barukh she-Amar*] were said in *seyga,* and soon as we got to *Barukh she-Amar* I started and I switched to *nahawand,* and I made *Mizmor Shir le-Yom ha-Shabbat* in *nahawand,* and we finished the rest of these *Halleluyot* [LS 20–26] in *nahawand* until we get to this [*Halleluyah, Hallelu Kel be-Kadsho* (LS 26)], which is sung by the general public. Also in *nahawand*.

MK: Now this [*Halleluyah, Hallelu Kel be-Kadsho* (LS 26)] uses the same melody [from week to week] too?

MT: No, it varies. There are many tunes one can use in *nahawand*.... This is sung by the general public, and you set the pattern and you set the pace for it.

When the *ḥazzan* takes over from the blessing in *Barukh she-Amar,* the rendering is distinct from the even-paced, formulaic style already heard during the *Zemirot*. The *ḥazzan* has a strong voice, and the improvisational style contrasts with the preceding application of the *seyga* formula: the cantor emphasizes certain words over others, elaborates some words melodically, and recites others very quickly. One of the other significant differences in the *ḥazzan*'s performance is the manner in which he sings the cadences at the ends of texts. In a cadence, the *ḥazzan* pauses before the last two or three words, which are recited by the congregation. The *ḥazzan* then repeats these words in an elaborate fashion, producing a distinctive melodic cadence. This, like *Ha-Shem Melekh,*[19] foreshadows what is to come during the *ḥazzan*'s rendering of *Shaḥarit*.

The remaining texts (LS 20–28), also part of the weekday liturgy, are rendered in a manner that is not unique to the Sabbath. At this point in the service a less musically proficient reciter may continue in the *seyga* formula rather than continue in the contrasting *maqâm*. The manner of recitation changes despite the return to the *seyga* formula. The reciters at the *teiva* try to emulate the *ḥazzan,* usually by adding some slight cadential elaborations—although none as elaborate as the cantor's. This is typically applied to the psalms that both begin and end with the word "Halleluyah,"

[19] Both *Ha-Shem Melekh* and *Barukh she-Amar* are highlighted through a different manner of presentation from the preceding texts. *Ha-Shem Melekh* is initiated by the *ḥazzan* and sung to a melody in the *maqâm* of the day, whereas *Barukh she-Amar* starts in a fixed melody sung by the congregation and is then improvised by the *ḥazzan,* or proficient leader, in a contrasting *maqâm*.

"Praise the Lord" (LS 22-25).[20] The word "Halleluyah" is emphasized melodically by a slight melisma and is often repeated or stated at the same time by the congregation.

It is during these sections of the service that members of the congregation who are proficient at reciting psalms are designated by the leader, who signals in a nonverbal manner such as a hand gesture or a nod. Sometimes the leader may gesture to one of the two cantors to render a psalm. On the rare occasion when a guest cantor was present, he was designated to lead the text *Yehi khavod,* "May the Glory" (LS 20), which is comprised of sentences or phrases from various psalms. The textual incipit reads, "May the glory of the Lord endure forever." The word *khavod,* translated here as "glory," can also be understood as "honor." Perhaps the honor of giving the guest *ḥazzan* this passage to read is reflected in the word *khavod* at the beginning of its text. Another reason the *Yehi khavod* may be chosen for the guest cantor is that this is the first text that continues in the contrasting *maqâm.* This assumes that the guest cantor is capable of continuing in the new *maqâm* earlier established by the *ḥazzan.*

The next liturgical text emphasized is the final Halleluyah psalm (Ps 150), *Halleluyah, Hallelu Kel be-Kadsho,* "Hallelujah, praise God in his sanctuary" (LS 2.26). This last psalm in the Psalter praises God by listing various musical instruments and, appropriately, is sung by the congregation. See figure 18.6 for an illustration of this liturgical section sung in *maqâm nahawand.* The text reads:

> Praise God.
> Praise the Almighty in His sanctuary—
> praise Him in the firmament of His might.
> Praise Him for His mighty deeds—
> praise Him according to the abundance of His greatness.
> Praise Him with the blowing of the shofar—
> praise Him with lyre and harp.
> Praise Him with drum and dance—
> praise Him with stringed instruments and flute.
> Praise Him with resounding cymbals—
> praise Him with clanging cymbals.
> Let every soul praise God—praise God.
> Let every soul praise God—praise God.[21]

---

[20] These are Pss 146–149; see table 18.1, LS 22–25.

[21] Translation taken from *Siddur kol ya'akov* (1995): 480. This prayerbook is commonly used in the Syrian community in Brooklyn.

Fig. 18.6. *Halleluyah, Hallelu Kel be-Kadsho* in *Maqām Nahāwand*. Sung by M. Tawil, 6 October 1991.

The two concluding texts of *Zemirot* (LS 27 and 28), taken from biblical passages, are typically recited in *maqâm seyga*. *Ḥazzan* Moses Tawil points out that the reciter can vary the *maqâm* in the first of these two passages. When Tawil leads this passage, he starts in *seyga,* then goes to another *maqâm,* and returns to *seyga*. The last text (LS 28) is recited in *seyga* because it is a passage from the Torah, always recited in this *maqâm*.[22] Taken from Exod 14:30–15:19, this final text is known as *Shirat*

[22] The Torah is always read in the *seyga* formula, while the Torah portion determines the *maqâm* for *Shaḥarit*. Idelsohn refers to *maqâm seyga* as mode II (*Jewish Music in Its Historical Development* [New York: Holt, 1929; repr., New York: Tudor, 1944, 1948], 25–26), stating that for the recitation of the Torah it is "common in all Oriental and Italian synagogues with the exception of the Yemenite and Spanish-Oriental" (43). For further discussion of Syrian cantillation practice, see Avishai Ya'ar, "The Cantillation of the Bible: The Aleppo Tradition (Pentateuch)" (Ph.D. diss., City University of New York, 1996).

ha-Yam, "Song of the Sea"; it is said to have been sung by the Israelites after crossing the Red Sea following the exodus from Egypt. The leader may embellish the song by decorating certain passages melodically.

Conclusions

In general, the *Zemirot* section of the service contains an increased level of musical activity or texture from the previous section (*Birkhot ha-Shaḥar*). A full range of recitation and vocal styles are employed throughout *Zemirot.* It is noteworthy that the manner of delivery articulates specific textual additions. Changes in recitation style, placement of the leader, and melodic choices all serve to accommodate psalms added to the liturgy for the Sabbath and make this organization of *Zemirot* unique for the day. The *Zemirot* section thus provides contrast. At certain times it allows for variety and personal expression.

The *ḥazzan* has a limited but important role in *Zemirot.* He recites the important textual portions, thereby signaling a change in the nature of the liturgical text and manner of recitation to follow. It is significant that the three portions of the *ḥazzan*'s *Zemirot* activity express different musical elements: the responsorial singing of *Ha-Shem Melekh* (LS 4) introduces the *maqâm* of the day; the second half of *Barukh she-Amar* (LS 17) and the two following psalms (18–19) introduce a contrasting *maqâm* and an improvisatorial style; and *Halleluyah, Hallelu Kel be-Kadsho* (LS 26) introduces a song that is sung by the entire congregation with a different melody each week. All three of these elements, integrated strategically within *Zemirot,* offer to the congregation a taste of what is to come in the *Shaḥarit* section. Variety of textual type does not determine the type of melodic style; function of the text is the determinant. Psalms added for the Sabbath receive more musical prominence.

Tradition and Renewal in Contemporary Greek Orthodox Psalmody

Alexander Lingas
Arizona State University

What is Greek Orthodox psalmody? A logical and seemingly self-evident answer is provided by Robert Taft in the *Oxford Dictionary of Byzantium.* There he defines ψαλμῳδία as "the use of the 150 Psalms of the Bible in worship."[1] However, if one were to ask the same question of the average churchgoer in Greece, there is a good chance that his or her definition of *psalmōdia* would be some variant on "Byzantine music" (Βυζαντινὴ μουσική), the strictly (at least in theory) unaccompanied chant of the Greek Orthodox Church. This is always sung, not by a "singer" or "cantor," as in the West, but by a *psaltēs* (ψάλτης) or psalmist.[2] The gap between liturgiology and common usage is significant but cannot be dismissed as simply an instance of disjunction between elite theology and popular piety in the Orthodox East.[3] On the contrary, these two definitions of psalmody mark out the ends of a whole spectrum of ways in which psalmody has been understood and practiced by Greek-speaking Christians over the last two millennia.[4]

---

[1] Robert F. Taft, "Psalmody," in *Oxford Dictionary of Byzantium* (ed. A. Kazhdan et al.; New York: Oxford University Press, 1991), 1752.

[2] See David Melling, "Music," in *The Blackwell Dictionary of Eastern Christianity.* (ed. K. Parry et al.; Oxford: Blackwell, 1999), 328–31.

[3] The literature on popular piety is vast, but probably the most famous instance of such a disjunction is belief in the "evil eye" (Richard P. H. Greenfield, "Evil Eye," in *Encyclopedia of Greece and the Hellenic Tradition,* [ed. G. Speake; London: Fitzroy Dearborn, 2000], 1:596-97). For other examples from the Byzantine period, see Jane R. Baun, "Middle Byzantine Tours of Hell: Outsider Theodicy?" in *Strangers to Themselves: The Byzantine Outsider* (ed. D. Smythe; Aldershot: U.K.; Burlington, Vt.: Variorum, 2000), 47–60; and Tia M. Kolbaba, *The Byzantine Lists: Errors of the Latins* (Urbana: University of Illinois Press, 2000).

[4] For a general introduction to the historical use of the term ψαλμῳδία, see Athanasios Th. Vourles, *Δογματικοηθικαὶ ὄψεις τῆς Ὀρθοδόξου ψαλμῳδίας* (Athens:

In the first instance, one may discern in modern Greek usage an echo of the fluid musical terminology employed by the earliest Christians, for whom the noun ψαλμός had not yet acquired its later and more particular definition as one of the 150 (or 151!) poetic texts found in the biblical book attributed to David.[5] Eventually the doctrinal concerns that motivated the church to form its canon of Scripture also led it in some locations to ban nonscriptural texts from worship, a stance enshrined in the late fourth-century Council of Laodicea's Canon 59, which prohibited "privately composed psalms" (ἰδιωτικοὺς ψαλμούς).[6] Byzantine Christians, however, continued to use "psalm" occasionally in its earlier broad sense of "sacred song." Thus, *psalmos* is only one of a number of labels applied by Saint Romanos the Melodist and his colleagues to the elaborate strophic hymns that eventually became known as kontakia.[7]

Second, Greek-speaking Christians' use through the centuries of the term *psalmōdia* to describe all forms of liturgical singing is a witness to the fact that specifically biblical psalmody has been central to their cycles of private devotion and common worship ever since the emergence of what James McKinnon called a "psalmodic movement" in late antiquity.[8] The origins and immediate consequences of this movement—namely, the decision by Egyptian monks to recite the Psalter in its entirety, followed by the rapid diffusion of biblical psalmody throughout the Mediterranean basin—have been discussed elsewhere and need not detain us here.[9] Rather, the

---

Theological School of the University of Athens, 1994), 17–26. On pages 11–69 of *Θέματα ἱερᾶς ψαλμῳδίας*, vol. 1 (Athens: n.p., 2000), the same scholar meticulously examines references to psalmody in the writings of Gregory of Nyssa, showing how he uses the term in ways that cover nearly the full range of its present meanings.

[5] E.g. Eph 5:18–20 and Col 3:16–17, passages that tempted earlier generations of scholars to make anachronistic musical distinctions between "psalms, hymns, and spiritual songs." See Egon Wellesz, *A History of Byzantine Music and Hymnography* (2d ed.; Oxford: Clarendon Press, 1961), 33–43.

[6] *MECL* §119.

[7] Others include hymn (ὕμνος), poem (ποίημα or ἔπος), ode (ᾠδή), song (ᾆσμα), praise (αἶνος), prayer (προσευχή), and supplication (δέησις). See Wellesz, *History of Byzantine Music,* 179.

[8] James McKinnon, "Desert Monasticism and the Late Fourth-Century Psalmodic Movement," *Music and Letters* 75 (1994): 505–19.

[9] E.g., Joseph Dyer, "Monastic Psalmody of the Middle Ages," *RBén* 99 (1989): 41–74; idem, "The Singing of Psalms in the Early-Medieval Office," *Spec* 64 (1989): 535–78; James McKinnon, "Christian Antiquity," in *Antiquity and the Middle Ages: From Ancient Greece to the Fifteenth Century* (ed. J. McKinnon; Englewood Cliffs, N.J.: Prentice Hall, 1991), 68–87; idem, "Desert Monasticism"; Edward Nowacki, "Antiphonal Psalmody in Christian Antiquity and the Early Middle Ages," in *Essays*

significance of these ancient precedents to our present discussion lies in their persistent influence on the life and spirituality of Orthodox Christianity. The meditative and often private psalmody pioneered by early ascetics, for example, has been cultivated in one form or another by Orthodox anchorites, cenobites, and other "spiritual athletes" until the present day.[10] Likewise, the practice of gathering in urban churches to sing psalms appropriate to the hour, found in such early sources as the *Apostolic Constitutions,* is maintained by the modern Orthodox Liturgy of the Hours, the major offices of which are regularly celebrated in both parishes and monasteries.[11]

The Development of the Received Tradition

By emphasizing continuity in this manner, I do not to wish to reinforce the common misconception that liturgy in the Byzantine rite is characterized chiefly by rigid immobility. Indeed, Greek Orthodox psalmody has, along with the other elements of the Byzantine rite, undergone periods of vigorous development.[12] Antiphonal psalmody flowered in Late Antique

---

on Medieval Music in Honor of David G. Hughes (ed. G. M. Boone; Isham Library Papers 4; Cambridge: Harvard University Department of Music, 1995), 287–315; and Robert F. Taft, *The Liturgy of the Hours in East and West: The Origins of the Divine Office and Its Meaning for Today* (Collegeville, Minn.: Liturgical Press, 1986), 31–213.

[10] See the entries for "psalmody" in the indices to the four-volume English edition of the *Philokalia* (G. E. H. Palmer et al, eds. and trans., *The Philokalia: The Complete Text Compiled by St. Nikodimos of the Holy Mountain and St. Makarios of Corinth* [4 vols.; London: Faber & Faber, 1979–95]), an eighteenth-century anthology of texts on prayer from the fourth to fifteenth centuries that is today perhaps Orthodoxy's most authoritative guide to the contemplative life known as "hesychasm." On the relationship between this tradition and that of liturgical psalmody, particularly in late Byzantium, see Alexander Lingas, "Hesychasm and Psalmody," in *Mount Athos and Byzantine Monasticism* (ed. A. Bryer and M. Cunningham; Brookfield, Vt.: Variorum, 1996), 155–68.

[11] The chapters "Sunday in the Byzantine Tradition" and "The Spirit of Eastern Christian Worship" in Robert F. Taft, *Beyond East and West: Problems in Liturgical Understanding* (NPM Studies in Church Music and Liturgy; Washington, D.C.: Pastoral Press, 1984), are good introductions to liturgical practice and piety in the churches employing the Byzantine rite. Kallistos Ware ("The Theology of Worship," in *Collected Works* [Crestwood, N.Y.: St. Vladimir's Seminary Press, 2000], 1:59–68) provides a complementary theological perspective.

[12] The long and complicated development of the Byzantine rite as a whole is the subject of Robert F. Taft, *The Byzantine Rite: A Short History* (American Essays in Liturgy Series; Collegeville, Minn.: Liturgical Press, 1992). More narrowly focused treatments of the subject including material relevant to the study of psalmody

Jerusalem and Constantinople within the context of rapidly developing stational liturgies.[13] In the latter city, frequent psalmodic processions (still sixty-eight per year in the tenth century)[14] played a vital role in the formation of a distinct Rite of the Great Church of Hagia Sophia, shaping both the form and the original architectural contexts of its eucharistic liturgies.[15] The characteristically Constantinopolitan predilection for antiphonal psalmody and processions was equally important to the formation of Hagia Sophia's cycle of daily prayer. Known collectively as the Sung Office (ᾀσματικὴ ἀκολουθία), it featured services that were direct descendents of the popular psalmodic assemblies of late antiquity, consisting almost entirely of blocks of antiphonal psalms, diaconal litanies, and presidential prayers separated at symbolically significant points by processions.[16]

Not long after the Rite of the Great Church reached its apogee of ceremonial magnificence under the emperor Heraclius, psalmody in the Holy Land began to grow in other directions. Beginning in the seventh century, the churches of Jerusalem and the nearby monastery of Saint Sabas fostered the composition of hymns for intercalation between the biblical psalms and canticles of the Horologion (the "Book of the Hours" containing the Palestinian Divine Office).[17] Initially limited to Sundays and feasts,

---

include Miguel Arranz, "Les grandes étapes de la Liturgie Byzantine: Palestine-Byzance-Russie. Essai d' aperçu historique," in *Liturgie de l'église particulière et liturgie de l'église universelle* (Bibliotheca Ephemerides Liturgicae, Subsidia 7; Rome: Edizioni Liturgiche, 1976), 43–72; Robert F. Taft, "Mount Athos: A Late Chapter in the Byzantine Rite," *DOP* 42 (1988): 179–94; idem, "How Liturgies Grow: The Evolution of the Byzantine Divine Liturgy" in *Beyond East and West,* 167–92.

13 John F. Baldovin, *The Urban Character of Christian Worship: The Origins, Development, and Meaning of Stational Liturgy* (OCA 228; Rome: Pontificium Institutum Studiorum Orientalium, 1987).

14 Ibid., 211–14.

15 Summarized in Taft, *Byzantine Rite,* 30–36. See also Thomas F. Mathews, *The Early Churches of Constantinople: Architecture and Liturgy* (University Park: Pennsylvania State University Press, 1971).

16 On the use of psalmody in these services, see Oliver Strunk "The Byzantine Office at Hagia Sophia," *DOP* 9–10 (1956): 175–202; repr. in Strunk, *Essays on Music in the Byzantine World* (New York: Norton, 1977), 112–50; Kosmas I. Georgiou, "'Η ἑβδομαδιαία ἀτφωνικὴ κατανομὴ τῶν ψαλμῶν καὶ τῶν ᾠδῶν εἰς τὰς 'ΑΙσματικὰς 'Ακολουθίας ἑσπερινοῦ. 'Ελλήικοὶ Μουσικοὶ Κώδικες 2061–2062 'Εθνικῆς Βιβλιοθήκης 'Αθήῶν" (Ph.D. diss., Pontifical Oriental Institute, 1976); Alexander Lingas, "Sunday Matins in the Byzantine Cathedral Rite: Music and Liturgy" (Ph.D. diss., University of British Columbia, 1996), and idem, "Festal Cathedral Vespers in Late Byzantium," *OCP* 63 (1997): 421–59.

17 The Constantinopolitan kontakia of the previous century were originally paraliturgical compositions intended for performance between the offices of a vigil. See

the replacement of the old antiphonal refrains with melodious exegeses of Christian theology by such luminaries as Sophronios of Jerusalem, Andrew of Crete, and John of Damascus proved to be enormously popular. The adoption in 799 of the Sabaïtic Divine Office by the Studios monastery in Constantinople—an event precipitating the formation of a mixed Studite rite, a preliminary synthesis between Palestinian and Constantinopolitan liturgical traditions that coexisted for centuries alongside the cathedral Rite of the Great Church—further accelerated the growth of the new hymnodic repertories of stichera and canons. By the twelfth century the process of farcing Studite psalmody with hymnody was virtually complete, bequeathing to subsequent generations over sixty thousand proper hymns[18] for the eight-week resurrectional and yearly fixed and movable cycles of the Byzantine liturgical year.[19] Hymnody thereafter was assimilated so completely to the concept of Greek Orthodox *psalmōdia* that it became customary in many places to abridge or even omit the scriptural texts that the hymns were originally meant to adorn.[20]

The Latin occupation of Constantinople (1204–61) marked the beginning of a period of precipitous and ultimately terminal decline for the venerable Sung Office, which disappeared completely following the Ottoman conquest in 1453. Its retreat left a void that was filled by the monastic rite of Saint Sabas in its fourteenth-century Athonite recension, a Neo-Sabaïtic synthesis that also replaced most Studite usages.[21] Rising monastic

---

Alexander Lingas, "The Liturgical Use of the Kontakion in Constantinople," in *Liturgy, Architecture and Art of the Byzantine World: Papers of the XVIII International Byzantine Congress (Moscow, 8–15 August 1991) and Other Essays Dedicated to the Memory of Fr. John Meyendorff* (ed. C. C. Akentiev; Byzantinorossica 1; St. Petersburg: Vizantinorossika, 1995), 50–57.

[18] Kenneth Levy and Christian Troelsgård, "Byzantine Chant," in *The New Grove Dictionary of Music and Musicians* (ed. S. Sadie and J. Tyrell; rev. ed.; London: Macmillan, 2001), 4:743. This figure is based on a count of incipits in published sources alone.

[19] These hymns dominate the fifteen volumes containing the most important proper texts used in modern Byzantine worship: the Octoechos (Book of the Eight Modes) or Paraklitike (Book of Supplication), containing an eight-week cycle of hymns beginning with the Saturday-evening Vigil of the Resurrection arranged according to musical mode; the Menaia (Book of the Months), twelve volumes of propers for fixed commemorations; and the (Lenten) Triodion and Pentecostarion, books containing propers for the movable season centered on Easter.

[20] E.g., the so-called Antiphons of the Octoechos for Sunday and festal matins, which were originally sung with Pss 119–30. See Oliver Strunk, "The Antiphons of the Octoechos," *Journal of the American Musicological Society* 13 (1960): 50–67; repr. in Strunk, *Essays on Music*, 165–90.

[21] Taft, *Byzantine Rite*, 78–84.

influence in the church hierarchy undoubtedly played a role in these developments, but it is worth noting that Archbishop Symeon of Thessalonica (d. 1429), the Constantinopolitan cathedral rite's last and most prolific apologist, reports that some members of his flock were actively seeking to abolish the cathedral rite on the pretext that they were being deprived of the canons sung elsewhere.[22] Symeon's solution was to supplement the Sung Office's old-fashioned antiphonal psalms with dogmatically rich and tuneful monastic hymnody, thereby producing what he saw as a more pleasing union of Old Testament typology and New Testament revelation.[23] Sadly, his reformed cathedral rite did not survive the fall of Thessalonica to the Ottoman Turks in 1430, at which time Symeon's provincial cathedral of Hagia Sophia was turned into a mosque.

Of more lasting significance was the replacement of Studite forms of the Divine Office with their Neo-Sabaïtic counterparts in the contemporary monastic tradition. The total number of psalms heard in offices remained about the same, but changes in performance practice and compositional style drastically shifted musical emphasis away from the majority of psalms. Whereas documents of the Studite tradition indicate that many psalms, including some from the weekly cycle of continuous psalmody, were formerly sung in imitation of cathedral practice,[24] they came to be recited simply (χῦμα) and without refrains (as in modern Greek usage). The newfound austerity of most ferial psalmody was, however, balanced by the emergence of new varieties of florid psalmody concentrated in the Neo-Sabaïtic All-Night Vigil, an ancient concatenation of evening and morning offices revived for celebration on Saturday evenings and the eves of major solemnities.[25]

Formerly, the cathedral and Studite rites of Byzantium had shared repertories of anonymous melismatic chants for choirs and soloists transmitted in notated collections known, respectively, as the Asmatikon and the Psaltikon. These volumes—together with the majority of their stately and highly formulaic melodies for such psalmodic genres as the Byzantine Divine Liturgy's Prokeimenon, Alleluiarion, and Communion (corresponding to the Gradual, Alleluia, and Communion of the Roman Mass)—were replaced during the fourteenth century by a new collection usually entitled Akolouthiai or "Orders of Service," the compilation of which was attributed

[22] PG 155:556.

[23] Symeon's reforms are discussed in Lingas, "Sunday Matins," 191–278.

[24] Arranz, "Les grandes étapes," 64.

[25] Discussed most extensively in Nicholas Uspensky, "Chin vsenoshchnogo bdeniia (ἡ ἀγρυπνία) na pravoslavnom vostoke i v russkoï tserkvi," *Bogoslovskie Trudy* 18 (1977): 5–117; 19 (1978): 3–69. On the music, see Lingas, "Hesychasm and Psalmody," 160–68 and idem, "Sunday Matins," 157–69.

to the saint, monk, composer, and theorist John Koukouzeles (ca. 1280–ca. 1341).[26] Akolouthiai manuscripts contained within a single cover all the ordinary chants and psalmodic propers of the Byzantine monastic offices and eucharistic liturgies, including not only new redactions of certain chants formerly contained in the Asmatikon and Psaltikon but also many previously unnotated psalms, some of which were presented in multiple versions reflecting regional or functional variations in practice (Thessalonian, Athonite, monastic, etc.). These anonymous repertories, however, were overshadowed musically by numerous musical settings of ordinary and (especially) festal psalms by Koukouzeles and his Late Byzantine colleagues. These were written in a new, distinctly personal, and often highly virtuosic "kalophonic" or "beautified" idiom distinguished variously by virtuosic vocal ranges, textual troping, extended melismas, and vocalizations on nonsense syllables (teretisms).

The Neo-Sabaïtic and Koukouzelian reforms succeeded in establishing jointly the range of psalmodic forms found today in Greek Orthodox worship. After the fall of the Byzantine Empire their music was modified only in detail as cantors enriched older works with orally transmitted formulae and composed new settings reflecting contemporary tastes.[27] Liturgical changes during the post-Byzantine period were similarly minor in scope and may, in some instances, even reflect the survival of older urban usages. Thus most Greek churches today, unlike their Russian counterparts, celebrate the All-Night Vigil infrequently, choosing instead to separate the evening and morning offices in the Studite manner. Similarly, Greek parishes tend to prefer beginning the Divine Liturgy with the singing

---

[26] For summary discussions of the Koukouzelian reforms and their liturgical context, see Edward V. Williams, "A Byzantine *Ars Nova:* The Fourteenth-Century Reforms of John Koukouzeles in the Chanting of Great Vespers," in *Aspects of the Balkans: Continuity and Change: Contributions to the International Balkan Conference Held at UCLA, October 23–28, 1969* (ed. H. Birnbaum and S. Vryonis Jr.; The Hague: Mouton, 1972), 211–29; and Lingas, "Hesychasm and Psalmody." Dimitri E. Conomos, *The Late Byzantine and Slavonic Communion Cycle: Liturgy and Music* (Dumbarton Oaks Studies 21; Washington, D.C.: Dumbarton Oaks Research Library and Collection, 1985), contains a detailed discussion of Communion settings in the Asmatikon and Akolouthiai, as well as representative lists of these manuscripts and the composers represented in them.

[27] The musical history of this period is recounted in Manolis Chatziagiakoumes, *Χειρόγραφα ἐκκλησιαστικῆς μουσικῆς (1453–1820)* (Athens: National Bank of Greece, 1980); and Dimitri E. Conomos, "Sacred Music in the Post-Byzantine Era," in *The Byzantine Legacy in Eastern Europe.* (ed. L. Clucas; Eastern European Monographs 230; Boulder, Colo.: East European Monographs; New York: Columbia University Press, 1988), 83–105.

of Constantinopolitan antiphons rather than the Palestinian *Typika* (Pss 102 [103] and 145, followed by a farced rendition of the Beatitudes).

Equally common but of greater concern is the abbreviation or total omission from Greek Orthodox services today of particular psalmodic elements for reasons of (real or perceived) pastoral need, local custom, or convenience. Certain cuts to the funeral service and the morning office of Orthros, a service that can run well over three hours when celebrated in its entirety, are officially mandated by the Ecumenical Patriarchate's modern parochial *Typikon of the Great Church*.[28] However, the rubrics of the *Typikon* account for only a fraction of the bewildering array of abbreviations that one may encounter in virtually every service, many of which reinforce the longstanding Byzantine tendency to omit biblical psalmody rather than the hymnody attached to it (although significant quantities of the latter are often left out of parochial celebrations of Orthros).

This may be observed in contemporary Greek Orthodox celebrations of the Divine Liturgies of Saint John Chrysostom and Saint Basil, which often deemphasize or suppress virtually all of the Byzantine Eucharist's remaining biblical psalmody.[29] In the Greek Archdiocese of America, for example, the Constantinopolitan Antiphons are often reduced in practice to a two- or threefold repetition of their refrains, leading even church musicians to reclassify the latter as "hymns."[30] Nearly everywhere the refrain and verse of the Prokeimenon are performed sequentially (i.e., without repetition of the refrain) in a monotone, while the following Alleluiarion—originally comparable in form to the medieval Roman Alleluia[31]—is customarily represented

---

[28] Giorgios Violakis, ed., *Τυπικὸν τῆς τοῦ Χριστοῦ Μεγάλης Ἐκκλησίας* (Constantinople: n.p., 1888; repr., Athens: Saliveros, n.d.).

[29] I.e., after the Trisagion and Cherubic Hymn were shorn of their original psalm verses; see Juan Mateos, *La célébration de la parole dans la liturgie byzantine: Étude historique* (OCA 191; Rome: Pontificium Institutum Studiorum Orientalium, 1971), 106–14; Taft, *Beyond East and West,* 176–82. At all events, the quantity of psalmody sung in Constantinopolitan eucharistic liturgies was, in comparison with the Roman Mass, never very extensive (for comparative statistics, see Strunk, *Essays on Music,* 317).

[30] E.g., Tom Pallad, ed., *A Guide to Congregational Singing* (National Forum of Greek Orthodox Musicians; [n.p.]: National Forum of Greek Orthodox Church Musicians, 1991), 9; Sophronia Tomaras, ed., *Hymns from the Liturgy, Book 1: A Beginner's Hymnal Arranged for Church School and Home Use* (2d field-test ed.; San Francisco: Greek Orthodox Diocese of San Francisco Religious Education Commission, 1986), 5:1–6.

[31] On the form of the medieval Alleluiarion, see Christian Thodberg, *Der byzantinische Alleluiarionzyklus: Studien im kurzen Psaltikonstil* (MMB, Subsidia 8; Copenhagen: Munksgaard, 1966). The relationship of Western Alleluias to their

by a threefold repetition of the word "Alleluia" lasting approximately five seconds. Consequently, the symbolically rich censing that formerly accompanied the singing of the Alleluiarion has, at best, been replaced by a few token but nevertheless distracting swings of the censer during the preceding reading.[32] An unintentionally comical result of drastically abbreviating the Alleluiarion and its prefatory dialogue between reader and celebrant is that the response to "Peace be to you [the reader]" is no longer generally perceived to be "and to your spirit," but "Alleluia! Alleluia! Alleluia!"[33] Finally, in place of the received repertory of melismatic settings of twenty-two scriptural and two nonscriptural proper communion texts, one may hear seemingly random combinations of hymns from the offices, excerpts of festal psalms from the All-Night Vigil, and paraliturgical songs.[34] The moment of communion has in some Greek churches become effectively an excuse for the performance of a sacred concert related only tangentially to the liturgical action, a stage of disintegration reached approximately two centuries before in Russia with the rise of the sacred Choral Concerto.[35]

Greek Orthodox Psalmody Today: Revival and Restoration

Despite differences of detail in liturgical and musical usage, modern Greek Orthodox psalmody has clearly been afflicted by the same problems that Alexander Schmemann diagnosed in contemporary Russian worship: tokenism, indifference, and ignorance contributing to structural and ultimately spiritual incoherence.[36] Schmemann's solution to what he called

---

Byzantine counterparts is reexamined by James McKinnon, *The Advent Project: The Later-Seventh-Century Creation of the Roman Mass Proper* (Berkeley and Los Angeles: University of California Press, 2000), 249–79, who suggests that the latter exercised a decisive influence on the former.

32 See the discussion of this action in the liturgical commentary of the eighth-century patriarch Germanus of Constantinople in Paul Meyendorff, ed. and trans., *On the Divine Liturgy* (Crestwood, N.Y.: St. Vladimir's Seminary Press, 1984), 78–81.

33 This may be seen from the insertion in some modern Greek books of threefold Alleluias after the Apostolic readings of the Royal Hours on Good Friday, for which no Alleluiaria are in fact prescribed.

34 Probably the most common paraliturgical song heard today is the Marian carol "Ἁγνὴ Παρθένε" on a text by Saint Nektarios of Aegina (1846–1920) set to music by Fr. Gregorios Simonopetrites (*Ψαλτήριον τερπνόν* [Mount Athos: Holy Monastery of Simonos Petras, 1991], 637–40).

35 Vladimir Morosan, ed., *One Thousand Years of Russian Church Music* (Monuments of Russian Sacred Music 1/1; Washington, D.C.: Musica Russica, 1991), xlix.

36 Alexander Schmemann, *Introduction to Liturgical Theology* (trans. A. E. Moorhouse; 3d ed.; Crestwood, N.Y.: St. Vladimir's Seminary Press, 1986), 35–39.

"the problem of the Ordo" was the cultivation of a liturgical theology defined as "the systematic study of the *lex orandi* of the Church,"[37] beginning with inquiry into the "concrete data of the living tradition of worship," followed by investigation of its history and, finally, discernment of its inner meaning.[38] With the benefit of hindsight, we can see that just such a program of study, of which Schmemann's own work forms an important part, was undertaken during the twentieth century. Operating in parallel with such other movements as the revival of patristics, it advanced not only on a pan-Orthodox basis but on also an ecumenical one, as liturgiology, historical musicology, patristics, and theology all contributed to progressively fuller understanding of the forms, functions, and meaning of biblical psalmody used in the Christian East over the last two millennia. Recognition of the degree to which later developments have obscured or otherwise altered earlier psalmodic forms has allowed scholars to consider the impact of such changes on particular services and liturgical cycles[39] as well as their relationship to concurrent changes in other elements (e.g., iconography and mystagogy) of Byzantine worship.[40] Viewed within the context of the "eucharistic theologies" advanced by certain modern Orthodox theologians, it becomes apparent that such concerns are ultimately inseparable from the Church's ecclesiological, social, and cosmological consciousness.[41]

Elegant and inspiring as such holistic theological visions may be, the renewal of psalmody in actual Greek Orthodox worship has proven to be

---

[37] Ibid., 39.

[38] Ibid., 40.

[39] In the United States, St. Vladimir's Seminary (Orthodox Church in America) has been particularly active in this regard. See, e.g., David Drillock, *Orthodox Church Music* (2 vols.; Crestwood, N.Y.: St. Vladimir's Seminary Press, 1984–85); idem, "Liturgical Song in the Worship of the Church," *St. Vladimir's Theological Quarterly* 41 (1997): 183–218; Mark Bailey, "Psalmic Music in Orthodox Liturgy as Foundation, Movement, and Ministry," *Jacob's Well* (Spring-Summer, 2000); online at http://jacwell.org/spring_summer2000/psalmic_music_in_orthodox_liturg.htm.

[40] E.g., Hans-Joachim Schulz, *The Byzantine Liturgy: Symbolic Structure and Faith Expression* (trans. M. J. O'Connell; New York: Pueblo, 1986); Hugh Wybrew, *The Orthodox Liturgy: The Development of the Eucharistic Liturgy in the Byzantine Rite* (Crestwood, N.Y.: St. Vladimir's Seminary Press, 1990).

[41] A classic statement of this is Alexander Schmemann, *For the Life of the World: Sacraments and Orthodoxy* (4th printing of the rev. 2d ed.; Crestwood, N.Y.: St. Vladimir's Seminary Press, 1988). See also Metropolitan John of Pergamon Zizioulas, "Συμβολισμὸς καὶ Ρεαλισμὸς στὴν Ὀρθόδοξη λατρεία," *Σύναξη* 71 (1999): 6–21; David Drillock, "Liturgical Song in the Worship of the Church," *St. Vladimir's Theological Quarterly* 41 (1997): 183–218.

a painfully slow process.[42] The decentralized nature of Orthodox church administration, the low level of training (if any) given to most church musicians, and the sheer force of inertia in a church that continues to suffer dissension from a partial shift away from the Julian calendar in the 1920s have until recently precluded the emergence of anything but isolated initiatives. Among the first were efforts to preserve traditional forms of Byzantine psalmody by Konstantinos Psachos (ca. 1866–1949), who vehemently defended the integrity of the received tradition of chanting in the face of Westernization,[43] and the priest George Rigas of Skiathos (1884–1961), a spiritual descendant of the Athonite Kollyvadist movement, which promoted its conservative psalmodic practices as part of a broader effort to encourage fidelity to the traditions enshrined in the *Typikon*.[44]

A similarly preservationist agenda may be observed in the work of Simon Karas (1905–99), a scholar of Greek folk and ecclesiastical music. He taught students at his Society for the Dissemination of National Music strict adherence to the received traditions of chanting, including the singing at communion of only the appointed melismatic verse and the performance of the poetic Praises of Holy Saturday Orthros without, as had unfortunately become customary, omitting the verses of Ps 118. Karas, however, went beyond Psachos and Rigas to embrace mild forms of musical and liturgical restorationism, ranging from the historically informed performance of forgotten psalmodic settings contained in premodern manuscripts to the composition of neomedieval Prokeimena and Alleluiaria for the Divine Liturgy. Initially appreciated primarily by a narrow circle of connoisseurs, Karas's work began to circulate more widely in the mid-1970s through gramophone recordings, books, and other publications.[45] During the 1980s and 1990s Karas's ideas achieved even greater

---

[42] Cf. Taft's observation ("Sunday in the Byzantine Tradition," in idem, *Beyond East and West,* 47) that the Orthodox are often better at articulating beautiful liturgical ideals than realizing them in practice.

[43] Psachos's work is summarized in Markos Ph. Dragoumis, "Constantinos A. Psachos (1869–1949): A Contribution to the Study of His Life and Work," in *Studies in Eastern Chant* (ed. D. Conomos; Crestwood, N.Y.: St. Vladimir's Seminary Press, 1990), 5:77–88.

[44] A selection of Kollyvadist melodies from Giorgios Rigas, *Μελῳδήματα Σκιάθου* (Athens: n.p., 1958), has recently (2001) been recorded (Ioannis Arvanitis, dir., *Under the Shadow of Mount Athos: Orthodox Hymns from Skiathos Monasteries* [The Hellenic Music Archives CD AEM 019]). *Τύπικον* (Liturgica Vlatadon 1; Thessalonica: Patriarchal Institute for Patristic Studies, 1994) is the imposing result of Rigas's efforts to promote the careful celebration of services.

[45] Especially Simon Karas, *Μέθοδος ἑλληνικῆς μουσικῆς* (8 vols.; Athens: Society for the Dissemination of National Music, 1982–85), and the series of recordings he

currency through the efforts of his students, some of whom assumed prominent cantorial posts, taught in conservatories accredited by the Greek state, published scholarly or pedagogical writings, and founded choirs with international reputations.[46]

The advent of a distinct "Karas school" of chanting was but one of several factors accelerating the renewal of Greek Orthodox psalmody during the last quarter of the twentieth century. Equally important were the concurrent revival of monasticism and the institutionalisation of chant scholarship in Greek universities. Among the first communities to promote the renewal of liturgical psalmody were the Athonite monastery of Simonopetra and its dependent convent of the Annunciation located near Ormylia, Chalkidiki. In addition to running fully staffed choral offices throughout the week, these monasteries have produced—often in cooperation with the Athenian musicologist Gregorios Stathis or the Thessalonian liturgiologist Ioannis Phountoulis—a steady stream of service books, musical settings, and recordings. As with Karas and his school, the members of these monastic communities have generally sought to deepen appreciation of received psalmodic traditions while also seeking to restore certain other ancient customs, most notably through the setting to music of full psalms with Alleluia refrains for use at communion.[47] Other monasteries have since issued recordings and publications in emulation of Simonopetra, but only Vatopaidi on Athos has been comparable in its scholarly ambitions, adopting the Simon Karas model in its entirety and producing a remarkable series of historically informed recordings.[48]

When working within an academic or public (as opposed to a monastic) setting, members of Greece's first generation of chant scholars with university posts have been far more daring in their attempts to revitalize and restore various psalmodic forms. Antonios Aligyzakes, for example, produced for use in the chapel of the University of Thessalonica a pastorally

---

made with the support of the Ford Foundation. The latter are currently being reissued on compact disc by the Society for the Dissemination of National Music.

[46] Lycourgos Angelopoulos (b. 1941), founder of the Greek Byzantine Choir, is but the most prominent example.

[47] Simonopetrites, *Ψαλτήριον τερπνόν*.

[48] The monastery has issued two series of recordings with extensive notes and scores in Byzantine notation: the self-published *Musical Bible* with works by composers from the monastery and a newer series for the University of Crete Press presenting "textbook" versions of Holy Week services. From the latter series, Holy and Great Monastery of Vatopaidi, *Holy Saturday: Service of the Epitaphios*. The Holy Week 6. University of Crete Press CD CUP 26 (1999), is notable for its restoration of psalm verses to the Praises (Engomia) and Alleluiarion of Holy Saturday Orthros.

oriented collection of chants designed to accompany Phountoulis's important series of liturgical texts.[49] Its music for the Divine Liturgy of Saint John Chrysostom includes newly composed Alleluias in all eight modes, simpler and less self-consciously neomedieval than those written by Karas, as well as a series of responsorial communion psalms. Even more unusual is its provision of psalmody for such rare services as the Divine Liturgies of the Apostolic Constitutions, Saint Mark, Saint James (both regular and presanctified), as well as the minor cathedral-rite offices of Pannychis and Trithekte. Elaborate settings of the latter two services have been composed by Gregorios Stathis of the University of Athens, whose choir "The Maestors of the Psaltic Art" has participated annually in public celebrations of Pannychis since 1994, and Trithekte—altered from its original Lenten form for performance during Advent, and with the addition of Romanos's Christmas Kontakion—since 1999.[50]

The Frontiers of Psalmodic Renewal

The celebrant at the première of Stathis's setting of Trithekte was His Beatitude Christodoulos, enthroned as Archbishop of Athens and All Greece in 1998. Having publicly advocated the renewal of the Church's psalmodic traditions since at least 1971 (the year he published the first edition of his *Cantor's Handbook: Basic Obligations of the Cantor as a Contribution to the Liturgical Renaissance*[51]), Archbishop Christodoulos now promotes this cause at the highest levels; he commissioned from Stathis a set of Sunday Alleluias,[52] approved the celebration in all churches

[49] Antonios E. Alygizakes, *Μελωδήματα ἀσκήσεων λειτουργικῆς* (Thessalonica: Dedouses, 1992).

[50] Grigorios Stathis, *Παννυχίς, ἤτοι Νυκτερινὴ Ἀσματικὴ Ἀκολουθία κατὰ τὸ Βυζαντινὸν Κοσμικὸν Τυπικὸν τῆς Μεγάλης Ἐκκλησίας Ἁγίας Σοφίας* (Athens: Apostolike Diakonia, 1999); idem, *Τριθέκτη, ἤτοι Ἀκολουθία τοῦ Βυζαντινοῦ Κοσμικοῦ Τυπικοῦ τῆς Μεγάλης Ἐκκλησιά Ἁγίας Σοφίας καὶ τὸ Κοντάκιον τῶν Χριστουγέννων τοῦ Ρωμανοῦ τοῦ Μελῴδοῦ* (Λατρειολογήματα 2; Athens: Institute of Byzantine Musicology, 2000); Pannychis: A Byzantine "Chanted" Office of the Great Church of Saint Sophia (CD Recording with booklet; National and Kapodistrian University of Athens, Department of Musical Studies, 2000).

[51] Archbishop Christodoulos (Pareskeviades), *Ἐγχειρίδιον ἱεροψάλτου· Βασικαὶ τοῦ ἱεροψάλτου ὑποχρεώσεις ὡς συμβολὴ εἰς τὴν Λειτουργικὴν ἀναγέννησιν* (3d ed.; Athens: Apostolike Diakonia, 2001).

[52] Grigorios Stathis, *Κυριακὰ Ἀλληλουϊάρια τοῦ Εὐαγγελίου διὰ τὸν καιρὸν τῆς προσφορᾶς τοῦ θυμιάματος μελισθέντα κατ' ἦχον μετὰ τῶν ἁρμοδίων στίχων αὐτῶν παρὰ Γρηγορίου Θ. Στάθη καθηγητοῦ τῆς Βυζαντινῆς Μουσικολογίας καὶ Ψαλτικῆς Τέχνης ἐν τῷ Πανεπιστημίῳ Ἀθηνῶν, τάχα καὶ μαΐστορος, κατ' εἰσήγησιν καὶ*

of Trithekte on the Friday before Christmas,[53] and sponsored a major conference on church music.[54] Although the audience's contributions to the open discussion that followed this conference's concluding round-table demonstrated that a sizable number of Greek cantors are, to say the least, uncomfortable with some recent developments,[55] the continuing appearance of a steady stream of publications pondering even more radical initiatives to renew Greek Orthodox liturgy and its psalmody makes further alterations to received practice seem inevitable.

One particular area of concern that has yet to be addressed significantly in practice is the virtual absence of congregational singing, the promotion of which may require changes to received musical and psalmodic forms.[56] Recognizing this, some authors have turned to the offices of the Constantinopolitan cathedral rite for alternative models.[57] However, a full-scale revival of the old Sung Office, or, indeed, any other such attempt to displace completely the received tradition, is highly unlikely to succeed. Not only would the usual Orthodox patterns of resistance to change make radical reform virtually impossible, but the current mixed rite and its exuberant hymnography remain both popular and spiritually powerful, making the cathedral offices' more restricted offerings of biblical psalmody seem dry in comparison.[58] It therefore seems probable

---

εὐλογίαν τοῦ μακαριωτάτου Ἀρχιεπισκόπου Ἀθηνῶν καὶ πάσης Ἑλλάδος κυρίου Χριστοδούλου, εἰς ὃν καὶ ἀφιεροῦνται προφρόνως τὰ νεωστὶ ποιηθέντα, εἰς ἦχον πλ. β', βαρὺν καὶ πλ. δ΄, κατὰ τὴν ε΄ καὶ ϛ τοῦ μηνὸς Φεβρουαρίου τοῦ σωτηρίου ἔτους βα΄ (Athens: Apostolike Diakonia, 2001).

53 The encyclical, issued in the name of the Holy Synod of Greece, is reprinted on pages 7–8 of Stathis, *Τριθέκτη*.

54 Proceedings in Achilles G. Chaldaiakis, ed., *Θεωρία καὶ Πράξη τῆς Ψαλτικῆς Τέχνης· Πρακτικὰ Α΄ Πανελληνίου Συνεδρίου Ψαλτικῆς Τέχνης (Ἀθῆνα, 3–5 Νοεμβρίου)* (Athens: Institute of Byzantine Musicology of the Holy Synod of the Church of Greece, 2001).

55 Chaldaiakis, *Θεωρία καὶ Πράξη,* 201–15. The round-table is also discussed on pages 119–37 of Philippos Ath. Oikonomou, *Το Νέο «Μουσικό Ζήτημα» στην Ορθόδοξη Εκκλησία* (Eliki, Aegio: n.p., 2002), which is a polemic against the Karas school.

56 Metropolitan Aimilianos (Timiades) of Selybria has been a particularly harsh critic of the status quo. See *"ΑΙσατε τῷ Κυρίῳ—Σκέψεις γιὰ τὴν ἀναζωπύρηση τῆς θείας λατρείάς* (Preveza: Holy Metropolis of Nikopolis, 1990); "*Ἡ ὑμνολογία ὅμηρος τῆς μουσικῆς,*" *Σύναξη* 81 (2002): 5–17.

57 See the articles by Pinakoulas (48–54) and Balageorgos (55–62) as well as the following discussion (63–69) in *Σύναξη* 71 (1999), an issue devoted to the question "Liturgical Renaissance: Need or Luxury?"

58 One participant in a "Sung" Vespers reconstructed by the author for celebration in the chapel of St. Peter's College, Oxford, on 26 May 2001, remarked afterwards that he felt it to have been a very "low-church" experience.

that the renewal of psalmody in Greece will continue to follow its current trajectory, emphasizing revitalization of the received tradition and greater respect for its forms of biblical psalmody.

The situation is somewhat different in the Greek Orthodox Archdiocese of America, where some members of the clergy and the laity have also expressed a desire for increased congregational participation. Historical circumstances such as the coincidence of Greek immigration's height in the early twentieth century with the period of Greek music's maximal Westernization,[59] as well as the pressures of assimilation, contributed to the development of a distinctly Greek-American tradition of Orthodox liturgical music.[60] In many American parishes, plainchant—often sung by cantors who have received only limited training in Byzantine music—is used only for offices and weekday services. This is because the Sunday Divine Liturgy has generally become the preserve of mixed choirs with electronic organs, who sing musical settings influenced strongly by Russian and Western prototypes.[61] Most attempts to foster congregational singing in America have therefore not been inspired by the traditions and history of Orthodox psalmody but by Protestant hymnals.[62]

---

[59] The Westernization of Greek music, both sacred and secular, during this period is briefly surveyed by Alexander Lingas, "Music," in Speake, *Encyclopedia of Greece and the Hellenic Tradition,* 2:1102.

[60] The development of liturgical music in the United States is surveyed in Frank Desby, "The Growth of Liturgical Music in the Iakovian Era," in *History of the Greek Orthodox Church in America* (ed. M. B. Ephthimiou and G.A. Christopoulos; New York: Greek Orthodox Archdiocese of North and South America, 1984), 303–23; George Raptis, ed., *National Forum of Greek Orthodox Church Musicians Silver Anniversary 1976–2001* (Bloomington, Ind.: National Forum of Greek Orthodox Church Musicians, 2002); and in the booklet to Alexander Lingas, dir., *Tikey Zes: Choral Works*. Cappella Romana. Gagliano GR501-CD (1999), 1–2.

[61] See, e.g., Christos Vrionides, *Byzantine Hymnology: The Divine Services of the Greek Orthodox Church* (2d ed.; repr., Brookline, Mass: Holy Cross Orthodox Press, 1980); Perecles P. Phillips, *ΜΕΓΑ ΣΑΒΒΑΤΟΝ ΠΡΩΙ: The Holy Saturday Morning Service* (Junior Choir Series; Denver: Federation of Greek Orthodox Choirs of the Western States–East, 1980); and Frank Desby, ed., *Communion Hymns of the Pentecost Season* (Federation Choral Series; Los Angeles: Greek Sacred and Secular Music Society, 1986).

[62] Tom Pallad, ed., *A Guide to Congregational Singing* (n.p.: National Forum of Greek Orthodox Musicians, 1991). Examples of such hymnals are Ernest A. Villas, *The Divine Liturgy of St. John Chrysostom Hymnal: A Hymnal with Texts in Greek, English and English Phonetics* (2d ed.; Brookline, Mass.: Greek Orthodox Archdiocese of North and South America Department of Religious Education, 1982); Nicolas E. Maragos, *Holy Cross Liturgical Hymnal: Containing the Divine Liturgy of Saint John Chrysostom in Greek and English, the Resurrectional Apolytikia, Hymns*

There are, however, now tentative signs—most visibly the increased space devoted in recent editions of the National Forum of Greek Orthodox Church Musicians' annual *Liturgical Guidebook* to rubrics for psalm verses that were customarily omitted—that a revival of psalmody may also be occurring in the Greek Archdiocese of America. Presently observable trends that would appear to be contributing to the renewal of Greek Orthodox psalmody in North America include greater familiarity with liturgical structures brought about by the use of English in worship, more frequent contact with church musicians from other Orthodox jurisdictions,[63] the recent establishment of a significant number of Greek Orthodox monasteries, and the growing popularity of recordings of chant, especially those featuring adaptations of traditional melodies to English.[64] One should also not discount the missionary zeal of those who have experienced the newly revitalised psalmodic traditions of Greece at first hand. Like the emissaries of Prince Vladimir who wished to recapture the experience of worship at the Constantinopolitan Hagia Sophia in their native Kievan Rus, a small but significant group of American clergy and church musicians are now working hard to restore a sense of heavenly glory to psalmody in their own Greek Orthodox parishes.*

---

of the Menaion, Hymns of Lent and Easter, Hymns of the Pentecostal Season, the Memorial Service, and the Service of Thanksgiving Following Holy Communion (Brookline, Mass.: Holy Cross Orthodox Press, 1988); and Tikey Zes, arr., *The Divine Liturgy Arranged for Congregational Participation* (San Francisco: Diocese of San Francisco, 1984).

63 Collaborations between musicians of different jurisdictions have occurred at the local level for such events as joint celebrations of Vespers on the Sunday of Orthodoxy. Thanks in part to the recent establishment of the Pan-Orthodox Society for the Advancement of Liturgical Music (PSALM), cross-jurisdictional contacts now also occur frequently at the highest levels. Further particulars are available at PSALM's web site: www.orthodoxpsalm.org, which includes a link to its lively listserver.

64 Recordings made by the Boston Byzantine Choir and the three sisters who form the ensemble EIKONA have circulated widely. Publications of chant in English include *The Divine Liturgy of Our Father among the Saints John Chrysostom, Archbishop of Constantinople* (Seattle: St. Nektarios Press, 1982), and *Selected Byzantine Hymns according to the Tradition of the Great Church of Christ, Including Troparia Taken from Vespers, Great Lent, Holy Week, and Pascha, Transcribed from the Chrysanthine Byzantine Notation* (Brookline, Mass.: Holy Transfiguration Monastery, 1986).

*The author gratefully acknowledges the support of the British Academy in the form of a Postdoctoral Fellowship.

PART 6
TEXTUAL TRADITION IN CHURCHES AND SYNAGOGUES

Texts and Translations in Tension

Richard J. Clifford, S.J.
Weston Jesuit School of Theology

The project of translating the Hebrew Bible into the vernacular (Greek) changed the very concept of translation in antiquity. As Sebastian Brock has pointed out, the Septuagint translators in the third and second centuries B.C.E. replaced the prevailing classical ideal of *sensus e sensu,* "sense for sense," with a new ideal of *verbum e verbo,* "word for word." Then, as now, not everyone was happy with the translation, for copyists kept correcting the Greek to make it conform more closely to the Hebrew text. Translating the Septuagint was a part of a large cultural shift in which Judaism adapted itself to a new culture and language.[1]

Another great translation project is taking place in our day in anglophone Roman Catholic as well as in other churches, involving both biblical and liturgical texts. It is the result of two decisions by the pope and the Second Vatican Council: translate the Bible from the original Hebrew and Greek; use the vernacular in the liturgy. The massive task of translating and composing liturgical texts, which is being done by the International Committee for English in the Liturgy (ICEL), is beyond the scope of this essay. For the Bible, the encyclical of Pope Pius XII in 1943, *Divino afflante Spiritu,* directed scholars to translate the Hebrew and Greek texts instead of the Latin Vulgate, and the Council reaffirmed that decision.[2] The Vulgate had been the official version for Catholics, meaning that it was used in the liturgy, cited in church documents, and served as the basis for official translations. Previous official English versions by Roman Catholics—the Douay-Rheims version (New Testament 1582; Old Testament 1609), its revision by Bishop Challoner (1750), and the Ronald Knox version (late 1940s)—were all made from the Vulgate. In the late

---

[1] Sebastian Brock, "Translating the Old Testament," in *It Is Written: Scripture Citing Scripture: Essays in Honour of Barnabas Lindars, SSF* (ed. D. A. Carson and H. G. M. Williamson; Cambridge: Cambridge University Press, 1988), 87–98.

[2] *Divino afflante Spiritu: Encyclical Letter of Pope Pius XII on Promotion of Biblical Studies* (Washington, D.C.: National Catholic Welfare Conference, 1943).

1940s, the Catholic Biblical Association of America embarked on a translation of the entire Bible from Hebrew and Greek, which appeared in 1970 as the New American Bible (NAB).

The Revision of the New American Bible and Its Psalter

As planning went forward for a revision of the NAB in the early 1980s, much had happened in the theory and practice of translation that would affect the project. Protestant Bible societies preparing translations for non-Western cultures had shifted attention from the text as such to how people hear the text in their cultural context, and the Chicago Bible had broken definitively with "bibelese," inspiring translators with new ideals. The Catholic bishops decided to begin the revision with the New Testament; it was completed in 1986. To lead off the revision of the Old Testament, they chose the Psalter. The NAB Psalter of 1950 was outdated and not made for singing, and the Grail Psalter used in the breviary since 1963 was, despite its many virtues, often inaccurate and mechanical in its strophic divisions. A new Psalter was badly needed.

Special problems faced the bishops as they planned the Psalter, however, among them inclusive language (already raised in the New Testament translation) and singability, so that the psalms could be sung in the liturgy and used in religious communities singing the Divine Office. Discussion among translators and bishops led to the publication of the *Criteria for the Evaluation of Inclusive Language Translation of Scriptural Texts Proposed for Liturgical Use*.[3] It was approved by the bishops in 1990 by an 84 percent margin. The document takes note of peculiarly American problems: (1) sensitivity to "exclusive language"; (2) loss of a sense of grammatical gender in American English; (3) words that once referred to all human beings (*man* and *he*) had become gender-specific and thus exclusive; (4) the multiplication of do-it-yourself renderings that offended taste and sometimes doctrine, which the bishops charitably describe as "impromptu efforts." The bishops propose two principles for biblical texts for liturgy: fidelity to the word of God (= accuracy) and the nature of the liturgical assembly (= all, women and men, should hear themselves called to participate in worship). The document encourages inclusive translation and gives examples of what might be done, such as occasionally substituting second for third-person singular when the original text alternates grammatical persons (as Hebrew poetry frequently does), occasionally substituting plural for singular, though without resorting to blanket substitutions. No

[3] Dated 15 November 1990 (Washington, D.C.: National Conference of Catholic Bishops, 1991).

changes in divine names or titles are permitted, including "Lord"; christological references in Old Testament texts are to be retained for the sake of intertextuality, such as Pss 2 and 110 and the Son of Man passages in Dan 7.

Using these guidelines, the six-member committee to revise the Psalter (four men, two women, one a Protestant scholar) set to work in 1989. It met one weekend a month for two years revising (twice) the drafts provided by thirty scholars. Though it spent most of its time on revising the drafts for accuracy and English idiom, it devoted considerable energy to singability (e.g., ending lines with a strong, accented syllable; avoiding successions of weak syllables and accumulation of sibilants) and inclusive language. For inclusive language, the bishops' *Criteria* was the guide. The translation was finished in 1991. The American Bishops approved the revised Psalter for the lectionary in the same year, approving as well the NRSV. (The RSV had long been used in an official Roman Catholic lectionary, and the NRSV had been used without controversy in the Canadian lectionary for several years.) The bishops forwarded the package to the Congregation for Divine Worship in Rome for confirmation, which was promptly given. This confirmation, however, was withdrawn in 1994 by the Congregation for the Doctrine of the Faith (headed by Cardinal Ratzinger) for doctrinal reasons: inclusive language obscured intertextual christological references, was not faithful to the text, and was "ideological" in that it seemed to cater to extreme feminism. Matters were taken out of the hands of the revision committee, the Catholic Biblical Association, and the bishops' Committee on the Liturgy. Several years of negotiation produced a compromise lectionary that the American bishops approved provisionally in 1997. Not all the bishops were happy with the lectionary. Bishop Donald Trautman, former chair of the Bishops Committee on the Liturgy, judged that it "has been substantially and radically altered, rendering it no longer an inclusive-language text."[4] Unfortunately, the approved lectionary adopted the old NAB Psalter of 1950. It is now in use for Sunday readings.

A Reflection and a Few Suggestions

A Reflection

After many years of translating and responding to criticisms, I have come to the conclusion that the chief difference between proponents and opponents of inclusive language in biblical translation is this: proponents see the issue as primarily linguistic, whereas opponents see it as primarily

---

[4] See Richard J. Clifford, "The Rocky Road to a New Lectionary," *America* 174/4 (16–23 August 1997): 18.

cultural. For proponents, accuracy in modern English is the watchword and goal. For opponents, inclusive language is an alien language imposed on them; familiar texts are "altered" by people with a modernist or feminist ideology with the goal of eliminating all male references. The differences are deep. To borrow a line from G. K. Chesterton, justice and peace have not only not kissed (Ps 84:10), but they are not even on speaking terms. It is clear that producing an acceptable translation in a time of cultural change is an ongoing process; it will take time. In the course of time, some translations will be recognized as "right" and others will be regarded as failures in being cumbersome and calling attention to themselves. Scholars will have to try, try again. During the process, it is important that there be at hand carefully made translations to serve as models. Without wishing to endorse every translation decision, one can point to two useful exemplars for scholars, the *Psalter for the Christian People* and the ICEL Psalter.[5] If one takes this long view, one recognizes that at the present stage not every word can be translated inclusively. Some words resist. One such word, in my view, is "son" in Proverbs, which refers to a young man old enough to marry and build a household. "Child" does not work as a translation. One has to interpret the "son" as referring to any adult or young adult engaged in building a house, choosing life companions, seeking God.

A FEW SUGGESTIONS

Though inclusive language is important, it should not be allowed to push other important matters to the margin, such as accuracy, contemporary idiom, felicity, and rhythm. The decision to reject the NAB Psalter for liturgical use, for example, was based narrowly on its inclusive language. The unintended consequence was that a Psalter was chosen for the lectionary that is below par in accuracy and singability.

Some opposition to inclusive language comes from people who are unaware of the linguistic problems. For them, translators need to do "language catechesis," explaining what the issues are and how they intend to address them. Let me mention the topics a catechesis might address today: register, the ambiguities inherent in the English language (*man,* pronoun concord), Hebrew kinship terms (*brother, son, fathers*), male

---

[5] Gail Ramshaw and Gordon Lathrop, eds., *Psalter for the Christian People: An Inclusive Revision of the Psalter of the Book of Common Prayer 1979* (Collegeville, Minn.: Liturgical Press, 1993); Gabe Huck, ed., *The Psalter: A Faithful and Inclusive Rendering from the Hebrew into Contemporary English Poetry, Intended Primarily for Communal Song and Recitation* (Chicago: Liturgy Training Publications, 1995).

language for God, and the focus on male agents. Linguistic issues have plagued translators from time immemorial, among them the proper rendering of the imperfect and perfect tenses in Hebrew, of long Hebrew and Greek sentences (in, e.g., Deuteronomy, Paul's letters), and of parallel verses in Hebrew poetry, but they do not raise hackles in the way that inclusive language does.

Let me comment on the linguistic issues noted above. The first is register, which in linguistic usage means a variety of language used in a specific social setting, such as speaking in an informal register, writing in a proverbial register or a scientific register. Register is important in the current debate about inclusive language and has not received the attention it deserves. Though they do not use the term, the Catholic bishops raise the issue in their *Criteria* when they introduce the principle of "the nature of the liturgical assembly." By this phrase they mean that each person, male and female alike, should feel addressed in the readings and the prayers of the liturgy. Perhaps one ought to propose the register "oral liturgical usage."

The second problem translators must deal with is two ambiguities in the English language: *man* and pronoun concord. In English, *man* can mean a human being as well as an adult male. All the Germanic languages except English transferred the original generic sense of *man* to a new word (e.g., *Mensch* in German), thereby freeing *man* in these languages to mean "adult male." Not so in English. If one renders Gen 1:26, "Let us make man in our image, after our likeness," many people will "hear" *man* as adult male, for that is the contemporary English meaning. As long ago as 1908 the authoritative *Oxford English Dictionary* noted that *man* in the meaning "human being" was obsolete in many contexts. In the interests of accuracy, therefore, NRSV and the revised NAB properly render, respectively, "humankind" and "human beings."

The second English ambiguity is grammatical concord in the pronoun system. Though some languages, including the Germanic, have grammatical concord in nouns and articles, English has it only in the pronoun system, where *he* can refer to a male or be used in a generic sense or when the sex of the person is unspecified. North Americans not used to grammatical concord "hear" a male in a phrase such as "he who has ears to hear, let him hear." To avoid this misunderstanding translators often use the plural pronoun *they,* which includes male and female. Excessive use of the plural can be problematic, however, for it can diminish the specific and singular emphasis of biblical books such as the wisdom literature. The problem is the English language, not the Bible, and, alas, no universal formula will solve the problem. Parenthetically, I would like to make a plea for rendering Hebrew participles in the psalms having God as subject by "who does such and such" rather than, as is customary, "he does such and such." Though seemingly a small point, the Psalter has many such participles, and translating them in this way makes a considerable difference. An example is Ps 136:4–5, "Who alone has done great wonders ... who skillfully made the heavens" (NAB). Contrast the Revised English Bible: "He alone works wonders.... In wisdom he made the heavens."

Another linguistic problem is Hebrew kinship terms that can have a different reference than in English. The chief examples are *ʾāḥ,* "brother," "blood relation," "fellow member of the tribe" (male and female)"; *ʾāb,* "father," "ancestor" (male and female)"; *ben,* "male offspring," "member of a class" (male and female, as in "sons of Israel" = "Israelites"). When kinship terms include female referents, the primary dictionary translations, "brother," "son," "father," "forefather," are inaccurate, the proper translation in such cases being "kin," "ancestor," and "member of" or the like.

The last problem mentioned above, male language for God and the predominance of male actors in the Bible, is not strictly a translation issue. The huge number of male images and metaphors, however, makes it imperative to find solutions to the linguistic problems. One reason for the predominance of male metaphors and images was Israel's monotheism, which forbade a female consort for Yahweh. Neighboring religions had such female consorts, thereby assuring feminine images and metaphors for the deity. The predominance of males is the result of the Bible's preference for the public sphere (worship, warfare, kingship) over the private sphere, the household, the domain of women. In that culture, men ordinarily had the public roles. English speakers unaware of the difference in grammatical and personal gender (because of its small role in English) may too easily conclude that God is male and that God's ideal worshipers are also male.

Singing God's Praises: The Translation and Liturgical Uses of Hallel Psalms 113 and 114

Elliot L. Stevens
Central Conference of American Rabbis

No text has had a greater impact on humanity than the Bible, and, within the Bible, no text resonates with us more deeply than the Psalms. Through the almost ubiquitous use of psalm texts in Jewish and Christian prayerbooks and hymnals, their lofty themes and poetic expressions have become embedded in our culture as have no other texts, biblical or otherwise. Those who prepare translations of psalms face the challenge of providing accurate, faithful renditions that are yet poetic and literary, accessible and idiomatic, and conform to the religious teachings of a particular ideology. Since some of these goals seem mutually contradictory, translators choose their point of emphasis; a comparison of various translations can be instructive in pointing to ideological bias or to comfort with a particular style of worship.

Before turning to this comparison, let us consider the translator's challenge. That no translation can utterly convey the fine nuances of an original text is a truism. A single word holds within it, like a note on the keyboard of a piano, layers of meaning and overtone. The rhythm and poetry, the multiple meanings and plays on words of biblical Hebrew can never be fully captured outside the original. A few examples will suffice.

In Hebrew, names usually carry meanings. Adam is rooted in the words for "earth," "land," "red," and others. Eve is cognate to "life" or "being," while Isaac signifies "laughter"; his name literally is "he will laugh." Knowing the root meanings of names in Hebrew already deepens one's experience in reading a text. Words can also carry theological overtones. Thus translating the very first verse of Genesis as "In the beginning God created the heaven and the earth. Now the earth was unformed and void..." is quite different from "When God began to create heaven and earth—the earth being unformed and void...." The first raises questions about what came *before* "the beginning" and whether God is or is not outside of time, while the second more accurately points to God's operating within time, and forever. In the next verse, translating *rûaḥ ʾĕlōhîm* as "a wind from God" is very different from translating "the spirit of God" or even "the Spirit of God." Just that capital S, not represented in the Hebrew, brings in theological notions of *logos* or of some entity operating as God's agent apart from God. For that matter, the designation of God in Hebrew, *ʾĕlōhîm,* is actually a plural noun better translated as "gods," not "God," perhaps hinting at an early polytheistic Israelite worldview. On the other hand, translating it as "the Lord" is ambiguous in English, since "the Lord" is often taken by Christians as a reference to Jesus.

One final example of how translations can be used in support of ideology is Isa 7:14, which states: *hinnēh hāʿalmâ hārâ wəyōledet bēn* ("The young woman shall conceive and bear a son"). The Greek Septuagint (third century B.C.E.) translated *ʿalmâ* as *parthenos,* an ambiguous term that supported the translation in English as "virgin." Now Isaiah seems to declare that "the virgin shall conceive and bear a son," as if predictive of the divine birth of Jesus. This example suggests the endless possibilities for polemical use of biblical translations.

Multiple meanings can also inhere in liturgical expressions. Thus, *bərākâ* is commonly understood as "blessing." Less well known is its root meaning, "knee" (*berek*). Knowing that, one can imagine the worshipers bowing and prostrating, or going down on their knee(s), as they approach the ark or bring a sacrifice to the temple. The experience of reciting a blessing is changed when one thinks of the "knee" at its root.

The psalms present a special challenge, in that psalms are used liturgically more than any other biblical texts. The aural experience of chanting psalms in Hebrew during modern worship has as its context, and brings to mind, the pomp and circumstance of the Levitical processional ascending the steps of Jerusalem's temple, singing God's praises during the sacred and celebratory occasions of Israelite worship, surrounded by worshipers standing in awe of their surroundings as the ceremonies of the sacrificial cult commence. Can any English translation chanted or sung convey these exalted overtones?

The challenge of translating from Hebrew into English for Jewish congregations is especially daunting. Many Jews know Hebrew. Congregations familiar with the cadences of the original Hebrew revere the texts in a special way.

The psalms recited in Jewish worship as a part of festival services are collectively called Hallel (Pss 113–118). The Hallel provides us with some wonderful examples of how different translations convey different experiences or theological overtones. These psalms present the translator with a range of problems and possibilities. We will consider two of these psalms in particular: Ps 113 and Ps 114.

The Hallel (also called the Egyptian Hallel, based on the reference to the exodus in Ps 114) is recited after the morning service on the three pilgrim festivals and on Hanukkah.[1] Originally Hallel was chanted during the offering of the pilgrims' sacrifices; on other occasions it was chanted in order that the people of Israel should be redeemed from potential misfortune.[2] By talmudic times the recitation of Hallel was also included in the Passover Seder, Pss 113 and 114 being recited at the second cup of wine. Hallel is recited in different communities standing or sitting, in unison or antiphonically (reader and congregation chant alternate verses[3]), or recited by a reader while the congregation responds "halleluyah" after each verse, as in Yemenite communities. In some Ashkenazic communities the congregation recites each silently, and the reader repeats the response aloud, while some passages are sung jointly. Hallel may be recited in any language.[4]

In Ps 113, an elaborate call to prayer that summons the people to perform acts of praise, God is both transcendent and immanent—exalted but also concerned with human beings and the needs of each individual. Rashi, the great medieval Jewish commentator, writes that this psalm expresses Israel's gratitude for the restoration from Babylonian captivity. Psalm 113 is apparently a cultic hymn, intoned by choirs of priests,[5] perhaps antiphonally. The song is addressed to the Shem Adonai (name of God). The "name" stands as a substitute term in place of the person and becomes the embodiment of the presence and power of God.[6]

In Ps 114, the exodus, revelation, and Israel's sustenance in the wilderness are all sketched (e.g., "mountains skipping like rams" is taken to refer to earthquakes at the time of the revelation at Sinai).

Consider how different is our experience as we read three different translations. The first is a traditional Christian translation, the New King James Version of 1979 as published in the Nelson Study Bible of 1997.[7]

---

[1] See *t. Sukkah* 3:2 and *b. Taʿan.* 28b.

[2] *b. Pesaḥ.* 117a.

[3] See *Tosef. Sotah* 6:2.

[4] *b. Soṭah* 32a, *Tosafot.*

[5] Hans-Joachim Kraus, *Psalms 60–150: A Commentary* (trans. H. C. Oswald; Minneapolis: Augsburg, 1989), 367.

[6] Ibid., 368.

[7] *The Nelson Study Bible: New King James Version* (ed. E. D. Radmacher et al.; Nashville: Nelson, 1979). In the introduction we read: "The translators…, while sensitive to the late-twentieth-century English idiom, and while adhering faithfully to the Hebrew, Aramaic, and Greek texts, have sought to maintain those lyrical and devotional qualities that are so highly regarded in the Authorized Version. This devotional quality is especially apparent in the poetic and prophetic books."

Praise the LORD! Praise, O servants of the LORD, Praise the name of the LORD!
Blessed be the name of the LORD from this time forth and forevermore!
From the rising of the sun to its going down, the LORD's name *is* to be praised.
The LORD is high above all nations, His glory above the heavens.
Who is like the LORD our God, Who dwells on high,
Who humbles Himself to behold *the things that are* in the heavens and in the earth?
He raises the poor out of the dust, *and* lifts the needy out of the ash heap,
That He may seat *him* with princes—with the princes of His people.
He grants the barren woman a home, like a joyful mother of children. Praise the LORD!

When Israel went out of Egypt, the house of Jacob from a people of strange language,
Judah became His sanctuary, *and* Israel His dominion.
The sea saw *it* and fled; Jordan turned back.
The mountains skipped like rams, the little hills like lambs.
What ails you, O sea, that you fled? O Jordan, *that* you turned back?
O mountains, *that* you skipped like rams? O little hills, like lambs?
Tremble, O earth, at the presence of the LORD, at the presence of the God of Jacob,
Who turned the rock *into* a pool of water, the flint into a fountain of waters.

The commentary on this version clearly perceives Christian significance, when it emphasizes, for example, "God's mercy in Jesus" in 113:7 when God "raises the poor," or when it holds that 114:2 anticipates the New Testament sense of God living among his people rather than in a shrine. The commentary uses terms such as "grace," "salvation," and "Redeemer," all of which have Christian theological significance and all of which are missing from the Hebrew. The commentary describes Ps 114 in particular as "arresting" and "somber."

Now a contemporary, Jewish, gender-inclusive translation intended for liturgical use. This excerpt is published in a new Haggadah with a decidedly feminist perspective.[8]

Halleluyah!
Sing praises to God, O servants of the Holy One.
May God's name be praised, now and forever.

---

8 *The Open Door* (ed. S. L. Elwell; New York: Central Conference of American Rabbis, 2001).

From the rising of the sun to its setting,
From east and to west, God's name is praised.
Greater than all the nations is the Wondrous One,
God's glory surpasses heaven.
Who is like our God, enthroned on high,
You are present in the most humble dwellings,
Surveying both heaven and earth.
You raise the lowly from the dust, the needy from the ash-heap;
You seat them with the generous ones, those with open hearts.
You give a place of honor to those who create a home.
Let the ones who nurture children rejoice.
Halleluyah!

When Israel went forth from Egypt,
When the house of Jacob emerged from a babel of tongues,
Judah became God's dwelling place,
Israel, God's dominion.
The sea looked and fled,
The Jordan looked back.
The mountains danced like lambs,
The hills like young sheep.
Why do you flee, O sea?
O Jordan, why do you change your course?
Why do you frolic, O mountains,
Why do the hills tremble?
In God's presence, the earth moves
Before the God of Jacob.
You transform rocks into pools of water,
You turn flint to flowing springs.

This translation is anything but "arresting" and "somber." Here we have images of "open hearts," "children rejoicing," dancing and frolicking mountains. "Princes" becomes "the generous ones," and the poetic use of language enhances the aural experience for reader and listener.

Finally, listen to Stephen Mitchell's recent translation.[9]

Praise the Lord, you who love him;
    Praise him who is beyond praise.
Bless him, sing out his praises
    Now and to the end of time.

---

[9] *A Book of Psalms: Selected and Adapted from the Hebrew* (New York: HarperCollins, 1993). Mitchell "has paraphrased, expanded, contracted, deleted, and freely improvised on the themes of the originals" (from the introduction). Mitchell is also author of *The Gospel according to Jesus.*

Let all beings on earth and in heaven
  Fill the world with his praise.
Praise him, praise him, the Unnamable,
  The All-Perfect, the Inconceivable,
Who, higher than the highest heavens,
  Stoops to the lowest of the low,
Who raises the poor from the dunghill
  And lifts the wretched from the dust,
Who grants them his infinite abundance
  And showers them with all good things,
Who gives the barren wife children
  And overwhelms her with joy.

When Israel went forth from Egypt,
  When a people of slaves was set free,
God was their only guardian,
  The Unnamable was their guide.
The Red Sea saw it and ran back;
  The mighty waters took flight.
Like rams the mountains leaped up;
  The small hills frolicked like lambs.
What made you run back, sea?
  Why did you take flight, waters?
What made you leap, mountains,
  And made the hills frolic like lambs?
The whole earth trembles and dances
  When the God of freedom appears,
Who made the rock a clear pool
  And the boulder a bubbling spring.

Who cannot be moved by the transporting poetry of these psalms, no matter that considerable liberties have been taken in the translation?

Psalms 113 and 114 were chosen as an example for this discussion precisely because neither presents insurmountable difficulties in translating, yet points of difference abound. The first term, *Halleluyah,* commands us to praise God. Our translators commonly use the term "Lord" but also use "the Eternal," "Adonai," "Eternal One," "Holy One," or leave it untranslated as "Halleluyah." Those for whom all translations, but especially those used liturgically, must be gender-inclusive point out that terms such as "Lord" and "Adonai" convey a maleness in God that is both anthropomorphic and sexist. They point out that seeing both genders in the Godhead, and understanding the patriarchal nature of biblical society, are needed to speak to contemporary sensitivities.

The selective use of capitalization shows translators' religious emphases. Consider the rendering "praise the Name of Hashem!" in the

ArtScroll Tehillim.[10] "Hashem"—literally, "the name"—is a locution or euphemism used by Orthodox Jews to avoid writing or saying the word "God," which itself is already a step removed from the Hebrew. This phrase therefore means, "praise the Name of the Name." The theological distance between ourselves and God implied by the double use of "Name," both capitalized, is profound.

We expect "Lord" to be capitalized, and sometimes divine pronouns (e.g., "His" sanctuary), but we also find these capitalized terms: the Unnamable, the All-Perfect, the Inconceivable, Presence, Master, Glory, People, Dominion, Sacred Mission, Sea, House (of Jacob).

Psalms were composed for oral recitation or for chanting. Speak some of these verses aloud, in several translations, and immediately recognize differences in cadence, which either help or hinder the experience. Compare—aloud—"Which turned the rock into a standing water, the flint into a fountain of waters" (*Interpreter's Bible*) with "Who made the rock a clear pool, And the boulder a bubbling spring" (Mitchell). Compare the stodginess of "When Israel left Egypt, the house of Jacob left a people of a strange tongue" (Rosenberg[11]) with the poetry of "When Israel went forth from Egypt, Jacob's house from the alien nation" (Bronstein).[12] One unnecessary syllable in Rosenberg interrupts the poetic flow.

The setting of the psalm on the page and the headings are also of some importance. The use of instructional markers (Company, Leader, Minister, Congregation) or of indented verses set in italics sets up a mode of responsive reading not indicated in the original, even though these psalms were probably recited antiphonally. Responsive readings used liturgically are often less meaningful than the book's designers intended. In some liturgical situations the need to focus on the process of responsive reading distracts rather than enhances the worship experience. Those who wish to be full participants sometimes voice resentment that only the leader has the privilege of holding the primary position; in some Jewish congregations everyone reads in unison, in Hebrew or English, either silently or aloud, but never responsively.

A few particular terms are of interest. In Ps 114, the house of Jacob went forth *mēʿam lōʿēz,* literally "from a foreign people." The term is a *hapax legomenon,* the only biblical usage of the term. Midrashically *lōʿēz*

---

10 The *ArtScroll Tehillim* [= *Sefer Tehillim*] (trans. H. Danziger with N. Scherman; Brooklyn: Mesorah, 1988).

11 A. J. Rosenberg, ed., *Psalms: A New English Translation* (New York: Judaica, 1991).

12 Herbert Bronstein, ed., *A Passover Haggadah: The New Union Haggadah* (for the Central Conference of American Rabbis; New York: Grossman, 1974).

is sometimes taken as an acronym for *lāšôn ʿăbōdâ zārâ,* "the language of idol worship." Our translations include such expressions as "people of strange language," "a people of slaves," "a people of strange speech," "a people of alien speech," "the alien nation," "a babble of tongues," "a people of babbling tongue," "an alien people," and several variations of the same. What is the import of such differences? Some are clearly pejorative: "strange" and "alien" connote the second-class status of the Egyptians in the eyes of the Israelites. "Alien speech" seems not as pejorative as "alien people." "A babble of tongues" seems the most neutral, in the contemporary sense of the term, until we recall the tower of Babel story in Gen 11. The least pejorative term—"foreign people"—is also the most literally correct and the one missing from our set of translations. The most pejorative translation is in the Greek Septuagint, which translates "barbaric people."[13]

Midrash is a wonderful way to add layers of meaning to a text. Consider the command at the beginning Ps 113: "Hallelu-yah," "Praise God." However, as the rabbis who wrote the midrash point out, "Yah" is only half the name of God. Why not "Hallelu-yahweh"? Rabbi Jeremiah explained in the name of Rabbi Eleazar: "The world is not worthy enough to praise God with His whole name, but with only half of His name, as is said in Psalm 150, 'Let every thing that has breath praise Yah.' Hence it is said here, 'Praise ye Yah.' "[14]

The midrash also points out that the psalms of praise, when used in Jewish worship (as the Hallel is on the pilgrimage festivals and at home on Passover eve), must be recited by at least three together. Why? Because "Hallelu" is in the plural, indicating no fewer than two listeners, plus the speaker or leader. Indeed, one's spirit is elevated by being part of a community, even of three, reciting the psalms together.

We have seen that even the smallest turn of phrase carries great import. Given the difficulties of translating texts deemed holy by our religious traditions, those who carry on the sacred task of translating scriptures for each new generation merit our highest esteem. However, as we learn from a dispute and its resolution described in the Talmud: "Eilu v'eilu divrei Elohim chayim," "These and those are both the words of the living God."

---

[13] The Midrash on Psalms, incidentally, understands this text completely differently: "When Israel went forth out of Egypt, the house of Jacob from a people that was glad." The midrashic understanding here is that *lōʿēz,* "foreign," should be *ʿālēz,* "glad." Why? Because the Egyptians were glad to see the Israelites go! See *The Midrash on Psalms* (trans. W. G. Braude; New Haven: Yale University Press, 1959), 2:215.

[14] Ibid., 2:213.

Texts in Tension: Translations for Contemporary Worship

Gordon Lathrop
Lutheran Theological Seminary

In the response to the 1995 Berakah Award of the North American Academy of Liturgy, Harold Daniels, the recipient of the award and one of the principal architects of the remarkable Presbyterian *Book of Common Worship,* tells this story about the origin of that book's psalter:

> The Psalms which were not included in the [1970] *Worshipbook* are now restored. Behind this lies a wonderful example of ecumenism.
>
> One of the guidelines for preparing the book was that its language be gender-inclusive. There seemed to be no satisfactory inclusive-language psalter text available that met the criteria until we discovered the psalter of the Church of the Province of New Zealand (Anglican) released in 1989. So, this psalter was included in the final draft of the service book. At the Fall 1992 meeting of the Consultation on Common Texts, I shared our decision. David Holeton quietly responded, "Are you prepared to handle the charges that the New Zealand psalter is anti-Semitic?" What a bombshell! He later informed me of the controversy surrounding the New Zealand psalter and agreed to obtain information for me. This was particularly discouraging, for by this date the publishers had the service book manuscript in hand.
>
> It was at the January 1993 meeting of the North American Academy of Liturgy in Albuquerque that the solution unfolded. One day I was met in the hall by Alan Detscher, who informed me that he might have the solution. Gail Ramshaw and Gordon Lathrop had just completed a gender-inclusive revision of the psalter from the [1979] *Book of Common Prayer*. Even then they were to see Michael Naughton of Liturgical Press to make final arrangements for its publication. I immediately talked with Gordon and Gail and with Michael. After the Academy meeting, Gail and Gordon sent me a copy of the psalter on a computer diskette. By then I had the articles David Holeton had gotten for me giving both sides of the New Zealand debate. This led to a decision that, if it was not too late in the publishing schedule, we would not use the New Zealand psalter and use the text Gail and Gordon had prepared.

> Fortunately, the publisher had not yet begun copy editing the psalter section of the *Book of Common Worship* manuscript, and was willing to permit us to substitute the new text. Permission was obtained from Liturgical Press. In two weeks, the text was pointed, the psalm prayers moved into place, and 350 substitute manuscript pages were given to the publisher. Four months later the book was in print.
>
> This is ecumenism. A Canadian Anglican alerted us to a problem. A Roman Catholic pointed us to the solution—an Episcopalian text, revised by Lutherans, destined for publication by Roman Catholic Benedictines, and first incorporated into a service book by Presbyterians. It is an example of the way service book revision should work in an ecumenical time.[1]

This little story is amply full of some of the tensions and concerns that must mark the use of the psalms in worship today. The questions are there, before the book publishers and even more before the worship planners: Is the psalm translation faithful to the original text, yet does it make the psalms available to the current community of singers? Does it overclaim the psalms for this community, in such a way that its avoidance of such words as "Zion" or of the ancient images for the people and their leaders with which the text is full could be regarded as anti-Jewish? Or does it underclaim the psalms, making them appear simply as ancient and odd remnants from a very different time and culture, noninclusive of the present community? Does it understand that this reuse of the psalms in a new community and new situation is as old as the psalms themselves? And is the translation able, indeed, to be communal speech, communal song? Does it avoid an idiosyncratic style more appropriate to individual expression? Does it find a beautiful—even elegant—communal English?

I am very proud of my own small role in the story that Harold Daniels tells. The psalter of which he speaks was indeed published in the *Book of Common Worship* (1993) and, only a few months later, as the *Psalter for the Christian People,* by the Liturgical Press.[2] In both cases it appeared as the fruit of ecumenical cooperation and of an ecumenical interest in responding to the challenges and tensions alive in contemporary Christian psalm-singing. However, this psalter is only one example of such a response. There are many others, most notably the remarkable ICEL psalter, the subject of much recent debate. Still, as one of the two editors of this psalter, and in the name of us both, I am glad to set before the readers of

---

[1] Harold M. Daniels, "Service Books and Ecumenism: Response to the Berakah Award," in *Proceedings of the North American Academy of Liturgy 1995* (Valparaiso, Ind.: The Academy, 1995), 39–40.

[2] Gordon Lathrop and Gail Ramshaw, eds., *Psalter for the Christian People* (Collegeville, Minn.: Liturgical Press, 1993).

this volume the solutions of this one translation as a small part of the continuing interest in those tensions.

The three-year lectionary now used by a wide variety of churches in North America for their Sunday celebrations of the Eucharist calls always for a psalm to be sung in response to the first reading of the day. Furthermore, many of those same churches are engaged in a widespread recovery of the Liturgy of the Hours in congregational use. The psalms are newly alive in the weekly and even daily worship of Episcopalians, Lutherans, Roman Catholics, Methodists, Disciples, Presbyterians, and many, many more. Then these are the issues: gracious, communal, singable English; faithful translation; responsible liturgical theology; and inclusivity.

And inclusivity—this issue does not arise as some nod toward "political correctness." Rather, it is an urgent question precisely because of the theology of the Christian assembly and because of issues in American linguistics. Christians use the psalms in an assembly in which all the participants, women and men, adults and children, people of all races and physical abilities, gather in the dignity given them in their baptism. There is no rank here, no gender preference, no inside track. As Paul says of this same baptismal dignity, "As many of you as were baptized into Christ have clothed yourselves with Christ. There is no longer Jew nor Greek, there is no longer slave or free, there is no longer male or female; for all of you are one in Christ Jesus" (Gal 3:27–28). The language of the community in prayer before God, to the extent that faithful translation allows, must reflect that identity of the communal "we."

Furthermore, this assembly gathers in and proclaims what Christians call the "triune God." God, for these Christians, is not an eternal and absolute monad but a rich "perichoretic" dance of relationships that draw us into God's very life. The assembly gathers in memorial of the man Jesus, with a sense of his presence and, at the same time, a sense of his identification in suffering and death with all of needy humanity, especially the marginalized, outsiders, the dying and the poor. To encounter Jesus Christ, for these Christians, is to encounter God. However, such an encounter is possible because there is a Spirit enlivening this meeting, a Spirit flowing from the resurrection of Jesus Christ to become the Spirit of the assembly itself. To encounter this Spirit is to encounter God. Gathered in the power of this Spirit, in the presence of Jesus Christ, the assembly stands before the Ancient One, the Eternal Majesty, the One who sends Jesus—and so encounters God. Yet there are not three gods but one God. Of course, the community will refer to Jesus, who was indeed a human male, as "he," though with economy and care, since the community's faith is that all of humanity is gathered up in his identity. However, "he" or "him" is hardly adequate for this triune God as God, nor for reference to the Spirit, nor to the Ancient One.

This need for gender inclusivity is heightened by the development of American English. Without entering into historical arguments, one can simply affirm that grammatical gender simply does not exist in current American English, except as a very rare archaism. That absence of grammatical gender means that gender reference almost always implies sex. For speech intended to bring the baptized liturgical assembly to expression, as for speech intended to articulate theology in the context of trinitarian faith, that sexual reference is a problem. Neither the representative member of that assembly nor the God in whom that assembly gathers is a male.

So what does one do with the psalms?

Psalter for the Christian People represents one response to these issues. It is a conservative emendation, disciplined to liturgical intention and to theologically grounded inclusive language, created for ecumenical Christian use. This solution, therefore, will not be for everyone. It is one attempt, with Christian Sunday assemblies specifically in mind. However, its proposals may assist us in discussing some of the tensions involved in using the psalms in worship.

This proposal begins with the psalter of the *Book of Common Prayer* rather than that of any of the current Bible translations, since that psalter already represents years of tradition in trusted liturgical language, intended for common song or common recitation. The prayerbook tradition is a tradition of elegant, communal speech. The further principles of the *Psalter for the Christian People* are then forthright. Still, they could not be applied in a mechanical way, requiring instead in each case—in each psalm—consideration of original context, original language, and current liturgical use. The principles are these:[3]

1. The use of "LORD" as the translation of the Tetragrammaton and "Lord" as the translation of *Adonai* was retained. The conservative character of this psalter may be apparent here: these are words deeply embedded in Christian prayer and custom. Of course, God is not a "lord" in any conventional sense. This word, then, is the "wrong word" as the translation of the unpronounceable name of God. However, these words will require years of reflection and of teaching in order for them to yield to a profound change.

2. The metaphor "king" when referring to God was rendered "Sovereign," and God's "kingdom" was translated as God's "reign."

3. Masculine pronouns referring to God were eliminated.

4. In any psalm in which the Hebrew uses both "God" and "LORD" as divine designations, the translation alternated these titles as one way to eliminate the third-person masculine pronoun.

---

[3] Ibid., v–vii.

5. "Hebrew poetry allows a switching of grammatical person ... in a manner considered grammatically unacceptable in modern English. Some biblical scholars suggest that [in the case of reference to God] this alternation of person provides a meaningful distinction between proclamation (God as third person) and prayer (God as second person). The editors of this volume find this distinction strained and unsupported by the Hebrew itself. Rather, person in ancient Hebrew was grammatically fluid. This fact allows modern liturgical usage to substitute second person (God as *you*) in some cases as a technique to eliminate masculine pronouns. The rule of this revision is to make such substitutions only in those psalms that already include second person in the original Hebrew."[4]

6. The masculine possessive pronoun and the masculine objective pronoun, when referring to God, were rendered in various ways: the former as "God's," "of the Lord," "the holy," "divine," or "the chosen"; and the latter in the way demonstrated by rendering "praise him" as simply "give praise!"

7. Although the psalter of the *Book of Common Prayer* had already made great strides in making the language for the human community inclusive, some further attention was needed. Thus "brethren" became "kin" or "community," the city was always an "it," a "forefather" was an "ancestor," a "watchman" became a "sentry," and so forth. On the other hand, in some cases the gender of the metaphor is part of the essential aspect of the poem. "For example, Ps 45 is an epithalamion for a king and a princess. No attempt has been made to make it inclusive. The churches must decide in what contexts these psalms are appropriate prayer."[5]

There are the proposals, grounded in one Christian conception of the liturgical assembly. Still, the proposals themselves would be clearer—and the tensions may begin to resolve into active praise!—if examples of the psalms are set before us. So here, from Ps 19:[6]

> The heavens declare the glory of God,
> and the firmament shows forth the work of God's hands....
> In the deep has God set a pavilion for the sun;
> it comes forth like a bridegroom out of his chamber;
> it rejoices like a champion to run its course....
> The fear of the Lord is clean and endures forever;
> the judgments of the Lord are true and righteous altogether.
> More to be desired are they than gold, more than much fine gold,
> sweeter far than honey, than honey in the comb.

---

[4] Ibid., vi.

[5] Ibid.

[6] Ibid., 30.

By them also is your servant enlightened,
    and in keeping them there is great reward.
Can people tell how often they offend?
    Cleanse me from my secret faults.

And, as a last word, Ps 150:[7]

Hallelujah!
Praise God in the holy temple;
    give praise in the firmament of heaven.
Praise God who is mighty in deed;
    give praise for God's excellent greatness.
Praise God with the blast of the ram's-horn;
    give praise with lyre and harp.
Praise God with timbrel and dance;
    give praise with strings and pipe.
Praise God with resounding cymbals;
    give praise with loud-clanging cymbals.
Let everything that has breath
    praise the LORD.
    Hallelujah!

---

[7] Ibid., 150.

PART 7
THE PSALMS IN PREACHING AND POETRY TODAY

Singing a New Song: The Poetic Afterlife of the Psalms

Peter S. Hawkins
Boston University

There is a long history in our language of turning to the Psalter not only as a resource for prayer but as a sourcebook for poetry. It is not difficult to see why. Many of the psalms foreground the act of speech or song, the activity of utterance itself, as the chief end of everything that has breath. In this universal work of praise the poet leads the cosmic chorus, giving voice not only to "kings of the earth and all people" but to "mountains, and all hills; fruitful trees ands cedars" (Ps 148:9, 11). In addition to the vocation of thanksgiving—the joyful noise of words and music—the poet is confronted in the Psalter with the sheer power of the psalmist's "I," his alternation between worlds public and private, his broad spectrum of emotion. There is also a stockpile of images and metaphors that continues with astonishing vigor to fly with the wings of the morning despite three millennia of such flight, so that the Psalter's ancient singing somehow remains perpetually a "new song."

Where else in Scripture, then, to look for suitable words to speak to God than in the psalms of David, God's preeminent artist and the model for anyone whose ten-stringed instrument would soar heights and plumb depths, to adore the Almighty "enthroned upon the praises of Israel" or boldly call God into the dock for things done or left undone? "How long wilt thou forget me, O Lord? Forever? How long wilt thou hide thy face from me?" (Ps 13:1).[1]

---

[1] For the literary art of the Psalms, see Robert Alter, *The Art of Biblical Poetry* (New York: Basic Books, 1985); idem, "The Psalms," in *Literary Guide to the Bible* (ed. R. Alter and F. Kermode; Cambridge: Harvard University Press, 1987); idem, *The World of Biblical Literature* (New York: Basic Books, 1992). See also James L. Kugel, *The Idea of Biblical Poetry: Parallelism and Its History* (New Haven: Yale University Press, 1981); and John Hollander, "The Psalms," in *Congregation: Contemporary Writers Read the Jewish Bible* (ed. D. Rosenberg: San Diego: Harcourt Brace Jovanovich, 1987), 244–62.

Such a model for divine address has by no means been the special prerogative of word crafters. For centuries, the faithful as a whole have looked to the Psalter as hymnal and prayerbook, as prophecy and moral guide. Clergy and religious, moreover, were bound to say the psalms through every week, until David's words were hid in the heart, to become linguistic second nature, an undersong audible within virtually all devotional language. Nonetheless, for those whose "tongue is the pen of a ready writer" (to recall Ps 45:1), perhaps the most compelling way to pray the psalms has been to rewrite them, that is, to translate them out of David's biblical speech and into one's own language.

In the first instance, this meant bringing the Bible into the language of the people. While the biblical translator did this work in prose, the poet imitated the sacred text not only by taking it out of Hebrew, Greek, or Latin and bringing it into English but also by refashioning it within the modes and conventions of vernacular versification. Here I am thinking in part of Middle English works by Lydgate, Langland, and Richard Rolle, but even more of the spate of poetry that issued from the English Reformation, stretching from the sixteenth century and into the early eighteenth. Poets who translated the whole Psalter into English verse include (in chronological order) Philip Sidney and his sister Mary Sidney Herbert, George Wither, George Sandys, and Christopher Smart. Many others, however, tried their hand at parts of the whole.[2] George Herbert's "Twenty-Third Psalm," for instance, provides an excellent example of what this versification could offer—in Herbert's case, a portrait of the psalmist as a seventeenth-century country parson who, surviving the earlier efforts of Sternhold and Hopkins, discovered how to make an English psalm truly capable of song:[3]

---

[2] For Middle English paraphrases of the psalms, see Michael P. Kuczynski, *Prophetic Song: The Psalms as Moral Discourse in Late Medieval England* (Philadelphia: University of Pennsylvania Press, 1995), 120–48. For a collection of later renderings of all 150 psalms, see Laurance S. Wieder, *The Poets' Book of Psalms: The Complete Psalter as Rendered by Twenty-Five Poets from the Sixteenth to the Twentieth Centuries* (Oxford: Oxford University Press, 1995). In addition to paraphrases, Robert Atwan and Laurance Wieder (*Chapters into Verse: Poetry in English Inspired by the Bible* [Oxford: Oxford University Press, 1993], 1:290–338) gather poems more loosely based on psalms. See also Bernhard Kytzler, "Moderne Psalmen," in *Bibel und Literatur* (ed. J. Ebach and R. Faber; Munich: Fink, 1995), 157–81.

[3] Chana Bloch studies Herbert's relation to the Bible as a whole and to the psalms in particular in *Spelling the Word: George Herbert and the Bible* (Berkeley and Los Angeles: University of California Press, 1985), esp. 231–43. For what a "Protestant poetics" might offer the biblically minded poet, see Barbara Lewalksi, *Protestant Poetics and the Seventeenth-Century Religioius Lyric* (Princeton: Princeton University Press, 1979).

The God of love my shepherd is,
    And he that doth me feed:
While he is mine, and I am his,
    What can I want or need?

He leads me to the tender grass,
    Where I both feed and rest;
Then to the streams that gently pass:
    In both I have the best.

Or if I stray, he doth convert
    And bring my mind in frame:
And all this not for my desert
    But for his holy name.

Yea, in death's shady black abode
    Well may I walk, not fear:
For thou art with me; and thy rod
    To guide, thy staff to bear.

Nay, thou dost make me sit and dine,
    Ev'n in my enemy's sight:
My head with oil, my cup with wine
    Runs over day and night.

Surely thy sweet and wondrous love
    Shall measure all my days;
And as it never shall remove,
    So neither shall my praise.

"Green pastures" in Herbert's rendering becomes "the tender grass," and God's "goodness and mercy," "thy sweet and wondrous love." The effect of the paraphrase is to naturalize the Scripture, planting it unmistakably in England's green and pleasant land—an excellent place to "sit and dine." This also means a "conversion" of the psalm into the paths of quatrains and alternating rhymes, in order to bring the poem (along with the mind of the speaker) "in frame." David sings the "new song" of Herbert's time, place, and language, while Herbert in some sense becomes a biblical poet, co-author with the psalmist, his version of the sacred text at once a prayer and an achievement—a (re)new(ed) singing of the Lord's song.

Other kinds of psalm imitation are more limited or oblique; they range further afield from Scripture's model than does paraphrase. A single verse might give rise to an entirely new poem or a text find its interpretative grounding in familiar figures of speech, or in a cluster of metaphors, that invoke a particular psalm and thereby establish an intertextual relationship with it. Finally, a poem might include only a distant echo of the Psalter, one that may not point to any specific text as much as suggest the spirit of the psalms as a whole or evoke the entire enterprise of psalm making. Often the connection seems especially powerful for being only implicit and unspoken, the imitation of the sacred text more profound because it is atmospheric. Who, when reading Donne's Holy Sonnets or so many poems in George Herbert's *The Temple,* can fail to recognize something very like the psalmist's full-throttle displays of emotion, his sudden turns from sorrow to joy, his lover's quarrel with the Lord, his full range of intimacy? Such poems strike the reader as what David might well have said under similar circumstances, had he been burdened by Donne's particular sense of guilt or able to praise God with Herbert's "utmost art." Thus, the writer of devotional verse could do no better than to study the Psalter, whose author was, in the words of Christopher Smart's "A Song to David," "The minister of praise at large" (iii): "His muse, bright angel of his verse, / Gives balm for all the thorns that pierce, / For all the pangs that rage" (xvii).[4]

The Davidic muse of "thorns that pierce" and "pangs that rage" presides over the tortured poems written by Gerard Manley Hopkins toward the end of his life, when the poetry of praise that takes such radiant form in sonnets such as "Pied Beauty"—"Glory be to God for dappled things"—darkens into the world of what Hopkins himself called his Terrible Sonnets. Whereas the psalmist typically ends even his most despairing laments with an affirmation, and often one that has no other rationale than a leap of faith, Hopkins remains in the pit, his strength dried up like a potsherd. Yet speaking *de profundis,* and at a depth that apparently affords no exit, he nonetheless manages to keep talking to a God who seems to hide in the shadows, beyond his grasp.

In a sonnet written in mid-March of 1889, prefixed with a text from Jeremiah (12:1–3), we find a Hopkins version of the psalmist's plangent talking back to the Almighty:

[4] Marcus Walsh and Karina Williamson give a helpful introduction to "A Song of David" in *Religious Poetry 1763–1772* (vol. 2 of *The Poetical Works of Christopher Smart;* Oxford: Clarendon Press, 1983), 99–126; they highlight the poet's appreciation of what Smart called "the prodigious grandeur and genuine majesty" of David's poetry; see also Walsh's introduction to vol. 3, *A Translation of the Psalms of David* (Oxford: Clarendon Press, 1987); and Harriet Guest on "A Song to David," in *A Form of Sound Words: The Religious Poetry of Christopher Smart* (Oxford: Clarendon Press, 1989), 241–87.

Justus quidem tu es, Domine, si disputem tecum: verumtamen justa loquar ad te: Quare via impiorum prosperatur? &c.

Thou art indeed just, Lord, if I contend
With thee; but, sir, so what I plead is just.
Why do sinners' ways prosper? And why must
Disappointment all I endeavour end?
  Wert thou my enemy, O thou my friend,
How wouldst thou worse, I wonder, than thou dost
Defeat, thwart me? Oh, the sots and thralls of lust
Do in spare hours more thrive than I that spend,
Sir, life upon thy cause. See, banks and brakes
Now, leavèd how thick! lacèd they are again
With fretty chervil, look, and fresh wind shakes
Them; birds build—but not I build; no, but strain,
Time's eunuch, and not breed one work that wakes.
Mine, O thou lord of life, send my roots rain.

Hopkins's words echo with the complaints of Jeremiah and Job, as well as of the psalmist—all friends of God who found themselves seduced and abandoned. Life has been "spent" in the Lord's service, but in the end, what has it amounted to? "Why must / Disappointment all I endeavour end?" The contrast with the wicked could not be starker: "sinners' ways prosper," "the sots and thralls of lust / Do in spare hours . . . thrive." In the words of Ps 92, the workers of iniquity spring up like grass in the rainy season, they flourish. But not I.

The speaker pleads his case by contending respectfully: he uses the word "sir" twice when addressing his Lord. Still, what all but overwhelms the poem is the speaker's sense not only of having been disappointed in his hopes but having been actively defeated, thwarted, "worsted" by the One he has been trying to serve. Rendered sterile, dried up, he looks around and sees the abundance of the natural world: the banks and brakes of even the meanest roadway are leaved and laced with green life; wind moves like breath through everything; birds build their nests and await their young. "[B]ut not I build; no, but strain, / Time's eunuch, and not breed one work that wakes."

The "work" Hopkins speaks of here is no doubt his ill-fated teaching career in Dublin: "Five wasted years almost have passed in Ireland," he notes during what was to be his last spiritual retreat, on New Year's Day 1889, three months before composing this sonnet. "I am ashamed of the little I have done, of my waste of time. . . . All my undertakings miscarry: I am like a straining eunuch."[5] Along with this feeling of having been

---

[5] *The Sermons and Devotional Writings of Gerard Manley Hopkins* (ed. C. Devlin; London: Oxford University Press, 1959), 262. See Paul Mariani, *A Commentary on*

thwarted and defeated in his profession there is almost certainly a sense of the loss of his poetic vocation as well, the drying up of the inspiration that once enabled him to hymn "God's grandeur" (with its final line, "Praise him") or to harvest "Christ my saviour" in the Welsh landscape of his Jesuit novitiate. Nothing grows in this desert.

And yet, Hopkins does not end his sonnet with an abrupt switch to affirmation, as we find in Ps 22, but rather with a supplication to the Lord of life: "send my roots rain." The showers of blessing never fall in this psalm of complaint. However, with the prayerful turn to God in the final line we perhaps find a root of faith struck so deep into bedrock that the poet's withered tree can outlast the drought. At least this is the witness of Hopkins's parent text, the Psalter, where David affirms that what is sown in tears can in time be reaped with shouts of joy, that those now mute in the pit of miry clay can yet have a new song put in their mouth, "even praise unto our God" (Ps 40:3).

To identify the psalms as a "parent text" requires no stretch of the imagination for any of the poets named thus far. They all participated in a biblical culture so pervasive as to be a second nature. For them to speak of God, therefore, involves what amounts to an unconscious ventriloquism of the Scripture's voices. Texts known by heart, recited week by week and year by year, would not require deliberate citation in order to be recalled; rather, they would always and *already* be there, implicitly present between the lines as well as on the surface of the text—a shared language of common prayer that also affords expression for the subjective, individual "I."[6]

What happens subsequently, however, when the Bible's hold on the poetic imagination loosens in the Enlightenment and the romantic, lyrical "I" replaces the communal subjectivity represented in earlier poet psalmists? I think we can see this turn in mid-twentieth-century writers such as John Berryman and Anne Sexton, categorized along with Robert Lowell and several others as "Confessional Poets," who in effect reinvented the psalmic poem in the late 1960s. Both were readers of Scripture, both intimate with God in their later verse. Gone, however, is the communal force of the original psalms or the liturgical context of praise-making so powerful in Herbert, Smart, or Hopkins. Instead, the self is primary: the "I" expresses itself, in full subjectivity and without restraint, on its own. The *Sitz im Leben* of the poem, in other words, is none other than the poet: his or her welter of personal history, sexual conflict, terror, and exaltation.

---

the Complete Poems of Gerard Manley Hopkins (Ithaca, N.Y.: Cornell University Press, 1970), 301–4.

[6] See Peter S. Hawkins, "The Scriptural Self," in idem, *Dante's Testaments: Essays in Scriptural Imagination* (Stanford, Calif.: Stanford University Press, 1999), 19–35.

God, for Berryman, is the "Adonai of Rescue" who brought him out of the pit and with whom he carries on intermittent conversation in his posthumously published *Love and Fame* (1971). For Anne Sexton, God is an island she struggles to row toward, a card shark that bests her at poker, a household deity as familiar as the "godhead of the table that I set my silver, plate, cup upon / each morning."

All this is God,
right here in my pea-green house
each morning
and I mean,
though I often forget,
to give thanks,
to faint down by the kitchen table
in a prayer of rejoicing
as the holy birds at the kitchen window
peck into their marriage of seeds.

So while I think of it,
let me paint a thank-you on my palm
for this God, this laughter of the morning,
lest it go unspoken.

The Joy that isn't shared, I've heard,
dies young.[7]

Although the spirit of lament pervades these Confessional Poets—who divulge their broken past, the terrors of their present—the works that most directly recall the psalms are poems of praise, what Anne Sexton calls "thank-you notes." Here preoccupation with the self turns outward, to address a personal relationship with God that wants and needs to be shared. Take, for instance, the first of John Berryman's *Eleven Addresses to the Lord,* a sequence that appears in the 1971 collection, *Love and Fame:*

Master of beauty, craftsman of the snowflake,
inimitable contriver,
endower of Earth so gorgeous & different from the boring Moon,
thank you for such as it is my gift.

I have made up a morning prayer to you
containing with precision everything that most matters.

---

[7] "Welcome Morning," 455.

"According to thy will" the thing begins.
It took me off & on two days. It does not aim at eloquence.

You have come to my rescue again & again
in my impassable, sometimes despairing years.
You have allowed my brilliant friends to destroy themselves
and I am still here, severely damaged, but functioning.

Unknowable, as I am unknown to my guinea pigs:
how can I "love" you?
I only as far as gratitude & awe
confidently & absolutely go.

I have no idea whether we live again.
It doesn't seem likely
from either the scientific or philosophical point of view
but certainly all things are possible to you,

and I believe as fixedly in the Resurrection-appearances to Peter and to Paul
as I believe I sit in this blue chair.
Only that may have been a special case
to establish their initiatory faith.

Whatever your end may be, accept my amazement.
May I stand until death ever at attention
for any your least instruction or enlightenment.
I even feel sure you will assist me again, Master of insight & beauty.[8]

In his "morning prayer" Berryman begins the day with an attempt to live it "according to Thy will." This entails, in the first place—and then again in the final line—a naming of the Lord and his attributes. Using the inclusio structure so beloved of the psalmist, Berryman ends exactly where he begins, in praise of God as "Master of beauty." Yet this master of the beautiful is also a "craftsman," a "contriver," an "endower," a rescuer "again and again." Just as the psalmist often links God's praiseworthiness to his own making of praise, that is, connects the Creator to the creature's linguistic creation, so Berryman thanks the "inimitable contriver" by offering up this particular verbal contrivance: "thank you for such as it is my gift. / I have made up a morning prayer to you / containing with precision everything that matters most."

The point of this seven-quatrain instance of the gift, however, is not to court the Lord with "flattering speeches" (to recall Donne in the Holy

---

8 *Eleven Addresses to the Lord,* 1, 215–16.

Sonnets); it is, rather, to say only what he means, to be precise. This requires that praise be qualified: Berryman carefully measures out the *hallel* he renders. The one thing that he can give God wholeheartedly is sheer astonishment: "I only as far as gratitude & awe / confidently & absolutely go." But what about his heart? How can he ever say that he loves the Unknowable One, who is as inscrutable to him as he is to his pet guinea pigs? Love, in fact, may simply be too much to offer: hence the scare marks that surround the word ("how can I 'love' you?"), and the avoidance of empty, sentimental avowals that characterize so much pious talk.

Berryman affirms, doubts, waffles, and defines his terms, presuming to share with God the ebb and flow of faith's tide within him. The breezy nonchalance of his rhetorical stance is unimaginable in the psalmist—"it doesn't seem likely"—let alone in Herbert or Hopkins, however doubt-driven they may present themselves in any given poem. We have little sense of the fear of the Lord that is the beginning of wisdom. In the end, however, Berryman accepts God's otherness and alludes to his own vulnerability. The poem concludes with his version of David's patient watching, his "waiting upon the Lord" at the dawn of a new day:

> Whatever your end may be, accept my amazement.
> May I stand until death forever at attention
> for any your least instruction or enlightenment.
> I even feel sure you will assist me again, Master of insight & beauty.

The intensely autobiographical "I" of the Confessional Poets shows the extent to which the psalms could be adapted to a modern American culture largely cut off from ancient traditions or the experience of common prayer. The personal power inherent in the poet's "addresses" to the Lord remains a link with the Psalter, but so much else in the psalms is lost, as it were, in translation. This is not the case with Jacqueline Osherow, a Philadelphia-bred, Harvard- and Princeton-educated professor in the English department of the University of Utah. Like so many of the American poets of her generation, she inherited from forebears such as Lowell, Berryman, and Sexton an ease with self-disclosure, with the colloquial and apparently off-the-cuff. What distinguishes her, however, is her deep knowledge of the Jewish Bible. She has learned Hebrew, knows the psalms by heart, and not merely as texts to be read but as lyrics to be sung. With that singing comes the liturgical context of home and synagogue, of feast days and seasons, of a lost temple and centuries of Diaspora spent chanting the Lord's song in lands as strange as Salt Lake City.

This is not to say that tradition obscures Osherow's individual talent. Her idiosyncratic "I" leaves an indelible impression of her own singularity.

She constantly refers to her family and friends, her reading, her love for Italy, for all that constitutes her self:

> My jokey, too self-conscious sabotage,
> My father-in-law, my husband, my unsalvageable Europe,
> My terza rima poem, my camouflage.[9]

However, this "personification" is always grounded in a "we" that speaks a language far older than English and participates in a history of Hallelujah-making that ultimately makes a Jew a Jew. For Osherow, then, the "annoying epithet chosen" signifies the Jew's election to divine praise. Like the generations upon generations of "dead men" before her, she knows herself to have been singled out for *hallel:*

> chosen for this
> tenacious language,
> to be the *we*
> who get to say this word
> and live forever,
>
> and it makes me pity Handel,
> Gospel singers, televangelists—
> belting out their hearts for a borrowed word—
>
> when I have the whole thing,
> one hundred and fifty psalms,
> every single syllable a *hallelujah*
>
> and not—you have to understand—
> an English hallelujah
> with its vague exultation and onomotopoeia
>
> but a word composed of holy signs
> that could actually spell God's name
> if they weren't ordering the universe
> to praise Him.[10]

The "we / who get to say this word" constitute the audience for Osherow's fourth collection, *Dead Men's Praise* (1999). Her book's title, like its epigraph, points us to Ps 115:17: "The dead praise not the Lord, neither any that go down into silence." Dedicating the book to two sets of

---

[9] "One Last Terza Rima/Italian Train," 102.
[10] "XI (Dead Men's Praise)," 80–81.

grandparents, she aims to rescue the dead from silence, to give them her voice and, with it, the power to praise. Osherow's bloodlines, however, extend beyond her own family to a larger "we"—notable Jews such as Rabbi Schneerson ("the old bearded rebbe to whom my grandma used to point / From her Parkway bench on Shabbos afternoon")[11] or others for whom she has no proper name. In one of thirteen poems she calls "Scattered Psalms," she conjures up the world of Auschwitz, wonders about the pale Torah scholar starving to death as, over and over again, he sings a verse from Ps 37, "Nourish yourself with faith." She also imagines others in the camp:

> I know it sounds crazy, but couldn't one of them—
> Not that it matters, they all died anyway—
> But still, so many people, and enough time
> For reciting what the dying are supposed to say
>
> (*Hear, O Israel,* et cetera) *and* a psalm.
> Or not even a whole psalm. Just one line.
> All those people waiting. Couldn't one of them
> Have mumbled to a brother, a father, a son,
>
> (The women, of course, were on another line
> And this was not a psalm they would have known),
> *Just a little longer and there will be no wicked one;*
> *Just a little longer . . . he'll be gone.*[12]

Osherow gives voice to these dead men, lost in the ashes of silence, still waiting for deliverance. In so doing, she refutes Adorno's claim that there can be no poetry after Auschwitz. Against odds, she continues to write as a Jew, and that, for her, means rendering praise, making psalms, and bringing worlds to pass through her words. Take, for instance, the following.

> I (HANDIWORK/GLORY)
>
> *To the Conductor: A song of David.*
> *The heavens declare the glory of God,*
> *the firmament tells His handiwork.*
> *Day on day utters speech,*
> *night on night announces knowledge.*
> *There is no speech and there are no words*
> *Without hearing their voice.*
> (Psalm 19:1–4)

---

[11] "XII (Science Psalm)," 87.
[12] "V (Psalm 37 at Auschwitz)," 64.

Dare I begin: a song of Jacqueline?
But what, from my heart of hearts, do I say?
Not that it matters, since every line
Will murmur with the heavens, sotto voce,
The knowledgeable night, the chatty day,
Their information constant, simultaneous:
The glory of the Lord and then *His handiwork.*
Indulge them: theirs is undiluted lyric
And we can't utter speech without its voice . . .

So how hard could it be to write a psalm?
Think of David's fairly modest territory,
There are other trees than cedar, willow, palm
(*The handiwork of God* and then *His glory*),
So many kinds of praise he couldn't know:
the ferns on their unfinished violins,
The jonquils on their giddy, frail trombones,
The aspens shaking their silver tambourines,
Then yellow-gold ones, then letting go.

What did David know about such changes?
The top arc of the spectrum gone beserk?
That when some skyward barricade unhinges
Without even a breath, a noise, a spark
(*The glory of the Lord* and then *His handiwork*),
No single earthly thing stays as it was,
Except insofar as it still sings.
Hand me an instrument of ten strings;
Everything was put on earth to praise.

The crocodile. The cheetah. Hallelujah.
The nightingale. The lynx. The albatross.
The pine tree. Fir tree. Glacier. Hallelujah.
The hornet's diligence. The gibbon's voice.
The pale reprieve of snow. Hallelujah.
The volcano's unrestricted exultation.
The forest's lazy ease. The desert's fury.
Our own extraneous efforts at creation.
(*The handiwork of God* and then *His glory*).

This first of Osherow's thirteen "Scattered Psalms" opens with the initial verses of Ps 19, where David proclaims that the creation itself declares, tells, speaks "the *handiwork of God* and then *His glory.*" These italicized phrases then become a refrain, slightly modulated, that occupies a different place in each of the four stanzas—a thread of scriptural language that runs through the text, joining David's ancient, oft-declared—told—spoken psalm with something brand new, "a song of Jacqueline."

"Dare I begin?" starts us off with a question, which the rest of the poem answers in the affirmative. She may dare to speak, even as David dared before her, knowing that human speech is at best but a descant to the "undiluted lyric" of the heavens. The witness of day and night, of the circuit-riding sun (like a bridegroom, "coming out of his chamber," 19:5), compose their spectacular lines, give voice in their own way to God's glory. Nonetheless, because we too have the ability to declare and tell, we also have a part to play in this orchestration. As Osherow says in another poem, "the endless business of creation requires our participation."

And so Jacqueline dares to sing along with David, wondering how difficult it is, after all, to write a psalm. Come to think of it, she has resources to draw upon that are richer than his "fairly modest territory." "There are so many kinds of praise he couldn't know," restricted as he was to the Holy Land. Take trees, for instance. He had the "utterance" of cedar, willow, and palm, but no idea whatsoever about the botanical *hallel* implicit in violin-ferns and trombone-jonquils, or the sustained hallelujah of Utah trees making their transition from summer to fall, "The aspens shaking silver tambourines, / Then yellow-gold ones, then letting go."

The "modesty" of David's territory becomes even more apparent when one looks up from the earth, higher even than the "firmament" of yore, to notice that the heavens have gotten infinitely bigger, "The top arc of the spectrum gone beserk." The ancient sky is no longer the limit. Yet none of these expansions of the imagination cause this psalmist to lose her voice. Yes, the "skyward barricade unhinges," now opening wide David's little world—but not upon a void, a black hole of silence. Rather, precisely because of this explosion of immensity, there is more of "the *handiwork of God* and then *His glory*" than there used to be, and therefore still more of a reason to take up the ten stringed instruments of old. "Everything was put on earth to praise."

Osherow ends her psalm by fulfilling this injunction. As a new, daredevil David (American, female, at once reverent and sassy), she gives us a roll call of creatures, each of which makes its own joyful noise. Some are merely named, their utterance implied only by genus or species: the crocodile, the cheetah, the pine tree, the fir. Others sing a more particular tune, and so we hear of the hornet's "diligence," the gibbon's "voice." Whole landscapes join in: there is the "pale reprieve" of snow, the forest's "lazy ease," the volcano's "unrestricted exaltation," "the desert's fury." In the end, though, Osherow comes to humankind, uniquely endowed with the language of nouns and verbs, stanzas and hallelujahs, a learned Hebrew and an American English acquired at the breast.

God's glory is expressed in his handiwork, firmament and all, but what we have to offer is what Osherow presents here, in this collection of her scattered psalms, a human effort to speak the praises of the heavens, "Our own extraneous efforts at creation." If no one were to make this utterance, day and night would nonetheless keep on singing: as Jesus said, even the stones would cry out. Yet for the human psalmist such silence would be a horribly lost opportunity—a tongue shriveled up, a right hand withered. No matter how bleak the prospect, it turns out that there is always a new song to be sung, "a song of praise to our God" (Ps 40:3).[13]

---

[13] The psalms have not only provided inspiration for "high art" poets but for popular songwriters such as Bono, leader singer with the group U2. In his "Pocket Canon" introduction to *The Book of Psalms* (New York: Grove, 1999), xi–xii, he writes: "Years ago, lost for words and with 40 minutes of recording time left before the end of our studio time, we were still looking for a song to close our third album, War. We wanted to put something explicitly spiritual on the record to balance the politics and romance of it; like Bob Marley or Marvin Gaye would. We thought about the psalms—Ps 40. There was some squirming. We were a very 'white' group, and such plundering of the scriptures was taboo for a white group unless it was in the service of 'Satan.' Psalm 40 is interesting in that it suggests a time when grace will replace karma, and love will replace the very strict laws of Moses (in other words, fulfill them). I love that thought. David who committed some of the most selfish as well as selfless acts, was depending on it. That the scriptures are brim full of hustlers, murderers, cowards, adulterers and mercenaries used to shock me. Now it is a source of great comfort.

"'40' became the closing song at U2 shows, and on hundreds of occasions, literally hundreds of thousands of people of every size and shape of T-shirt have shouted back the refrain, pinched from Psalm 6: 'How long (to sing this song)'. I had thought of it as a nagging question, pulling at the hem of an invisible deity whose presence we only glimpse when we act in love. How long hunger? How long hatred? How long until creation grows up and the chaos of its precocious hell-bent adolescence has been discarded? I thought it odd that the vocalizing of such questions could bring such comfort—to me, too."

Osherow encounters the Psalter against the backdrop of Auschwitz and Bono in the midst of the Northern Irish "Troubles."

MIZMOR L'DAVID

Rabbi Margaret Moers Wenig
Beth Am, The People's Temple, New York City

The LORD is my shepherd, I shall not want. (Ps 23:1)

Today George W. Bush was inaugurated as president. That is not what I want. And he has nominated, as Secretary of the Interior, one who would drill oil in green pastures and allow pollution in undisturbed waters. As Attorney General, he has nominated a man who would reverse traffic on the paths of righteousness, turning back progress in civil rights and gun control. Sometimes I feel like a lamb in the jaws of a lion.

How can we sing "He makes me lie down in green pastures" when Salvadoran earthquake victims lie trapped under rubble? The composer Leonard Bernstein could barely get through the psalm. In his setting, the boy's solo and the angelic choir are interrupted by warlike sounds, angry men singing (from Ps 2): "Why do the nations rage?"[1]

In a world in which enemies cannot occupy the same holy ground or sit down together at the negotiating table, the absence of fear in Ps 23 seems naive. Like Bernstein, Martin Luther sensed the contrast between the quiet confidence of this psalm and the anxiety many feel:

> If the Lord is my shepherd, . . . [w]hy does He permit the devil to harm me so greatly with terror and doubts? Besides, I find myself quite unfit, weak, impatient, still laden with many sins. I feel no security, but only doubt, no comfort but only fear and trembling because of God's wrath. When will He ever begin to manifest in me that He is my shepherd?[2]

Even our mundane problems—trying to earn a living in academics or in the not-for-profit world, caring for a chronically ill child or parent, burying friends before you turn fifty, fighting with the church council, with the

---

[1] Leonard Bernstein, "Chichester Psalms," composed in 1965.

[2] Martin Luther, *Selections from the Psalms* (vol. 12 of *Luther's Works;* ed. J. Pelikan; St. Louis: Concordia, 1955), 158–599.

pastor, with your teenager, or with your partner—all these can wear us down and make us afraid.

For Luther, however, a proper reading resolves the apparent contradiction between our experience and the world portrayed in this bucolic poem. For Luther, God's flock is the people of the church. The fertile field is the gospel or any place in which the Word is preached and confessed. The table is the communion table. The overflowing cup is the church filled with the Holy Spirit. The enemies are the flesh, the devil, sin, Romans, Jews, Turks, and the pope. The shepherd is the Good Shepherd, Jesus.

> This shepherd ... is Christ ... who is a shepherd much different from Moses. Moses is harsh and unfriendly toward his sheep. He drives them away into the desert, where they will find neither pasture nor water but only want (Exod 3:1). Christ, however, is the good, friendly shepherd, who goes after a famished and lost sheep in the wilderness, seeks it there, and when he has found it, lays it on His shoulder rejoicing (Luke 15:4). He even "gives his life for His sheep" (John 10:12).[3]

Luther continues:

> "thy rod and thy staff they comfort me" ... Moses is also a shepherd and also has a rod and a staff. But he does nothing with them but drive and plague and burden his sheep ... (Acts 15:10, Isa 9:3). Therefore he is a terrible, horrible shepherd whom the sheep only fear and from whom they flee. But thou, O Lord, does not drive and frighten Thy sheep with Thy rod and Thy staff, nor dost Thou burden them, but dost only comfort them.[4]

Jewish commentators read "rod and staff" as references to the Torah, but Luther disagrees:

> The law cannot restore the soul for it is a word that makes demands on us that we shall love God with all our hearts, etc., and our neighbors as ourselves (Matt 22:37, 39). It damns him that does otherwise and pronounces this sentence upon him (Gal 3:10, Deut 27:26). "Cursed be everyone who does not do all the things written in the Book of the Law."[5]

I think Martin Luther was wrong about Moses, whom Jewish tradition describes as a loving shepherd, wrong about the desert, where God provided manna and Torah, and wrong about the law, which Jews do not consider to be a burden but a gift.

---

[3] Ibid., 154–55.
[4] Ibid., 170–71.
[5] Ibid., 164–65.

But I think Luther was right—to contrast the curses in Deuteronomy with the reassurance of this psalm. Yet, I wonder what Luther would have thought of Judaism had he known what this psalm means to Jews, particularly what it means to Sephardic and Hasidic Jews?

In their liturgy, Ps 23 is the quintessential Sabbath psalm, appearing more often than Ps 92, "The Song for the Sabbath Day." Some recite Ps 23 five times: on Friday night before the conclusion of the service,[6] at dinner before Kiddush,[7] again at lunch before Kiddush,[8] during Seudat Shelishit,[9] and as part of the Melave Malka.[10] Every Sabbath meal includes this psalm, and many of the *zemirot* (table songs) use its images: the cup overflowing (with God's mercy);[11] the table, laden with meat, fowl, fish, and sweets;[12]

---

[6] Philip Birnbaum, trans., *Daily Prayer Book/HaSiddur HaShaleim* (annotated with an introduction; Sephardic edition; New York: Hebrew Publishing Company, 1969), 309–10; *Siddur Tehilat Hashem: Al Pi Nusach HaAri Z'L,* according to the text of Rabbi Shneur Zalman of Liadi (new, emended Hebrew edition with an English translation by Rabbi Nissen Mangel; Brooklyn: Merkos L'Inyonei Chinuch, 1995), 143.

[7] Zalman, *Siddur,* 146; *From the Rebbe's Table: Sabbath and Festival Songs and Blessings* (Brookline, Mass.: New England Chassidic Center, 1983), 18–19.

[8] Birnbaum, *Daily Prayer Book,* 475–76; Zalman, *Siddur,* 201; *From the Rebbe's Table,* 34–35; Rabbi Nosson Scherman, trans., *Zemiroth: Sabbath Songs with Additional Sephardic Zemiroth* (a new translation with a commentary anthologized from talmudic, midrashic and rabbinic sources; Brooklyn: Mesorah, 1979), 158–61.

[9] Birnbaum, *Daily Prayer Book,* 593; Zalman, *Siddur,* 210; *From the Rebbe's Table,* 50–51; Scherman, *Zemiroth,* 222–23.

[10] Scherman, *Zemiroth,* 256–57.

[11] In its commentary on Ps 23, the Art Scroll *Zemiroth* notes "that the numerical value of *kos,* cup and *Elohim,* the Divine name signifying strict justice are identical, eighty-six. Just as a cup holds a precise measure, so God's justice is precisely meted out according to the deeds of a person. In justice, there is no place for mercy. But, when God acts mercifully, His generosity exceeds the precise limits of the law. Thus metaphorically, His cup of justice overflows [with mercy]" (Scherman, *Zemiroth,* 160). The overflowing cup appears in Sabbath *zemirot,* e.g., *cosi revaya* in the *zemer* "Ma Yafit" (ibid., 108).

[12] "Yirv'yun mideshen beytecha, v'nachal adanecha tashkeim, May they overflow from the fat of your house, and you make them drink from the river of your Eden" (from "Kol M'kadeish" [*From the Rebbe's Table,* 22; Scherman, *Zemiroth,* 86]); "Yirv'yun mideshen beytecha / They are filled to overflowing from the fat of your house" (from "Yah Echsof" [*From the Rebbe's Table,* 28]); "Lo techsar kol bo / you shall lack nothing on [the Sabbath]" (from "Yom Zeh Mechubad" [*From the Rebbe's Table,* 42]); "Laaroch l'fanai maseyt vaarucha shabbat menucha / To spread before me courses and banquets of sabbath rest" (in the *zemer* "Yom Zeh L'Yisrael" by Isaac Luria [Scherman, *Zemiroth,* 112]); "B'mishneh lechem, v'kiddush

rest (the sleep that is praiseworthy on the Sabbath);[13] and the soul revived (through study).[14] These *zemirot* address God as "Shepherd" more than any other liturgy at any other time of the year, except on Yom Kippur (which is after all the "Sabbath of Sabbaths"). One *zemer* (song), "Chai Hashem," from the 1600s, written by Chaim Yitzhok, quotes almost all of Ps 23.[15] An earlier composition by Israel Najara, who was born only a decade after Martin Luther died,[16] addresses God as "The Lord, my shepherd" in every refrain of his song: "My innermost thoughts shall praise you, Lord who is my shepherd on the holy Sabbath day, the seventh day."[17] In a liturgical tradition in which God is most often addressed as "King," the Sabbath use of *Adonai roi* stands out.[18]

---

rabbah / b'rovmatamim v'ruach n'divah / with double loaves and the Great Kiddush / with abundant delicacies and a generous spirit" (from the *zemer* "Menucha v'Simcha" (Scherman, *Zemiroth,* 94]).

13 The phrase *mey menuchot* ("still waters") in Ps 23 contains the same root as the word used to describe Sabbath rest (*menucha*). In many *zemirot*—such as "Menucha V'simcha," "Ma Yedidut," "Yom Zeh L'Yisrael," "Yom Shabbaton"—the word *menucha* ("rest") figures prominently. Moreover, "he makes me lie down in green pastures" is also taken to refer to Sabbath rest/sleep. Some Jews consider sleep during the week to be a waste of precious time that otherwise could be spent in study. On the Sabbath, however, even these Jews consider sleep to be praiseworthy; see "V'hasheina m'shubachat / Sleep is praiseworthy" from "Ma Yididut" (*From the Rebbe's Table,* 24; Scherman, *Zemiroth,* 98]).

14 "K'dat [kama d'teymar] nefesh m'shivat / As it says in scripture: the soul is restored" from the *zemer* "Ma Yedidut," referring to Ps 19:8, "Torat Adonai temimah, meshivat nafesh / The Torah of the Lord is pure, reviving the soul."

15 The phrases *Adonai roi, lo echsar / al mey menuchot yinahaleini / taaroch l'fanai shulchan / t'dashen beshemen roshi* from Ps 23 are all quoted in the *zemer* "Chai Hashem" (Scherman, *Zemiroth,* 152 [152–61]; *From the Rebbe's Table,* 34–35).

16 Luther lived from 1483 to 1546; Najara, a student of Isaac Luria's in Tzfat and later a rabbi in Gaza, ca. 1555–1625.

17 From the *zemer* "Yoduca rayonai" (Scherman, *Zemiroth,* 292–95). Najara is also the composer of "Yah Ribon Olam." During Shabbat, God is described as "shepherd." As soon as the Sabbath is over, however, the *zemirot* contain images of sheep who are "scattered and cast out" (see "B' motzaei yom menucha" in Scherman, *Zemiroth,* 159). Most of these *zemirot* consist of petitions for the coming of the Messiah and the redemption of Israel. Metaphors of sheep in need of a shepherd replace the Sabbath images of sheep protected by the Shepherd, e.g., "Establish your settled home to settle your sheep there" and "Redeem your sheep from the hand of the shearers" (in "Adir ayom v'nora," Scherman, *Zemiroth,* 270–71). *Lo ira* ("I will not fear") is replaced by *al tira* ("Do not fear)" ("Amar hashem l'yaakov, al tira avdi yaakov," Scherman, *Zemiroth,* 276–81).

18 The *zemer* "Tzur Mishelo" refers to God as *Roeinu, Avinu* ("Our Shepherd, Our Father"). The liberal movements of Judaism, deriving their liturgical tradition

Martin Luther was also right that no one can fulfill all that is written in the law. Six days a week we wrestle with our demons, fight to subdue our evil inclination, engage in the endless task of healing the sick and feeding the hungry, try to build God's kingdom on earth and in the halls of our government, or merely try to finish the administrative work of a little parish church, but we will never complete the task. Are we doomed to eternal guilt, frustration, and failure with no relief for our bodies or souls? Such was the case in this family in which

> we could only have fun after the work was done and the work was never done. We could only relax and take care of our personal needs when the chores were completed ... and when that was done we were much too tired to do anything else.[19]

Martin Luther understood that such an attitude renders human beings slaves, working hopelessly to earn our freedom, and God—a relentless taskmaster, not a loving shepherd.[20]

Perhaps for this reason the second-century Mishnah taught, "It is not upon you to complete the work" (*m. ʾAbot* 2:21). Rabbi Abraham Joshua Heschel understood this too. In his commentary on Exod 30:8 ("Six days shalt thou do all thy work") he asks, "Is it possible for a human being to

---

from the Ashkenai rite, not the Shephardi rite, do not include Ps 23 in their Sabbath liturgy. The Reform prayer book *Gates of Prayer* includes Ps 23 only in its memorial service or service in the home of mourners. Even though all Orthodox *bentschers* (books containing the grace sung after meals as well as sabbath table songs), even Ashkenazi *bentschers,* do contain Ps 23 among their table songs, the *bentschers* of the liberal movements do not. Even the beautiful new *bentscher* published by the Reconstructionist movement (*Kol Haneshamah: Nashim Unevareh/ Songs and Grace after Meals* [Wyncote, Pa.: Reconstructionist Press, 1991]) omits *Mizmor L'David* (Ps 23). I would be very happy if this sermon encourages liberal Jews to reintroduce Ps 23 into their Sabbath synagogue or table rites.

19 Anne Wilson Schaef, *Meditations for Women Who Do Too Much* (San Francisco: HarperCollins, 1990), from the entry for 3 January.

20 Jewish tradition and Jewish liturgy do describe us as God's slaves/servants and God as our master (*anu avadecha v'ata adoneinu*) but not as our taskmaster who works us to an unbearable extent. When Jewish liturgy does speak of us as God's servants it is in the context of a series of metaphors for our relationship with God making clear that servant/master by no means says it all. ("We are your people, you are our God. We are your children, and you are our Father. We are your servants, and you are our Lord.... We are your flock, and you are our shepherd. We are your vineyard, and you are our keeper. We are your work, and you are our creator. We are your faithful, and you are our beloved. We are your chosen, and you are our friend. We are your subjects, and you are our king.").

do all his work in six days? Does not work always remain incomplete? What the verse means to convey is: 'Rest on the Sabbath as if all your work were done.' "[21]

Neither the work of repairing the world, nor the work of earning a living, is the purpose for which we were created. We were planted in the garden of Eden to rest in the fields God created for us, to sit at the table God prepared for us, to study the word God gave to us, and to sing love songs to God.

Outside of Eden, our mission is necessarily different. Still, God gave us the Sabbath as a reminder of Eden and as a foretaste of the world to come[22] and to assure us that while the yoke may be heavy, we were not created to be beasts of burden.[23]

Sam Levenson, describes what Shabbat meant to his father:

> Making a living, being a sweatshop slave 16 hours a day, this was profane time. But come *Erev Shabbos* with the candles lit on the table, I could see my father change from a sweatshop slave into an angelic figure who had something to do with eternity. Suddenly the wrinkles came out of his face, and he became again a holy man who was related to the whole universe and to God's destiny for man—which was greater than sitting over a sewing machine.[24]

The members of my family do not sweat over sewing machines, but every dinner is followed by homework—except on Shabbes. Nearly every night we eat pasta, but on Shabbat salmon. Every morning the alarm goes off at 6:30 A.M.; on Shabbat we sleep until 9:00. And every three days my kids schlep stuff from their mothers' home to their father's home and back again. But on many a Shabbat morning our kids sit in synagogue, surrounded by their mothers and their father, all in the same pew.

Those of you who lead multiple services of worship each Sabbath day, those for whom the Sabbath is anything but a day of rest, know that

---

[21] Abraham Joshua Heschel, *The Sabbath,* in *The Earth Is the Lord's; and The Sabbath* (New York: Harper Torchbooks, 1966), 32.

[22] "Meyeyn olam habah yom shabbat menucha / a taste of the world to come is the day of sabbath rest" from the *zemer* "Ma Yedidut" (Scherman, *Zemiroth,* 96ff.). This reminded the Rev. Barbara Lundblad of the Lutheran hymn sung before communion, "Grace our table, give us a foretaste of the feast to come."

[23] "Man is not a beast of burden, and the Sabbath is not for the purpose of enhancing the efficiency of his work" (Heschel, *Sabbath,* 14).

[24] A passage sent me by the late Sidney Greenberg, intended for his *Treasury of the Sabbath* (now out of print). Shabbat does not make one's problems disappear, but it can remind us that these problems do not define us in God's eyes.

change is needed. So deprived have modern clergy been of leisurely Sabbath meals, long walks, unrushed sex, and sleep that there is now talk in the Reform movement of giving rabbis and cantors at least one Shabbat off a month.[25] The purpose of this Sabbath rest is not to enable clergy to be more productive. The purpose, in Heschel's words, is "not to recover one's lost strength and become fit for forthcoming labor.... [For] the Sabbath is not for the purpose of enhancing the efficiency of [our] work.... [Shabbat] is not an interlude but the climax of living."[26]

So, our quintessential Sabbath psalm—is it history or is it prophecy? How shall we read all of its imperfect verbs? As affirmations of faith in a certain future? As petitions for a longed-for time? As descriptions of a continuous present?

Two settings, sung at Seudat Shelishit, offer different answers. In the Bostoner Rebbe's,[27] joy spills over as the psalm is sung three times. If Friday night is the time of welcoming the bride, Shabbat morning the time of rejoicing with the bride, and Shabbat musaf (the additional service) the wedding feast, then the conclusion of the Sabbath is the consummation of the marriage, the climax of the day.[28] In this setting the verbs are understood in the present tense. So palpable is God's presence that you cannot imagine such a time will ever end.

In contrast, the awareness that the Sabbath will soon end is the feeling of the most commonly sung melody, composed by Ben Zion Shenker, a hasid of the Modzitzer sect,[29] and sung widely even in non-Hasidic families.

---

[25] See "The Rabbi's Shabbat," by President Charles Kroloff, in the *Newsletter of the Central Conference of American Rabbis* 48/5 (January 2001).

[26] Heschel, *Sabbath,* 14.

[27] I know this melody from the singing of former Beth Am member Rabbi Michael Michlin, who first sang it to me over a decade ago. The melody comes from the Hasidic sect of Lelov, whose rebbe, David Zevi Solomon Biderman (1844–1918), was the leader of the Hasidim in Jerusalem at the beginning of the twentieth century (Chemjo Vinaver, *Anthology of Hassidic Music* [ed. E. Schleifer; Jerusalem: Jewish Music Research Center of the Hebrew University, 1985], 96). Moses of Lelov (1778–1850) had settled in Eretz Yisrael toward the end of his life (*EncJud* 11:9). A transcription of the melody can be found in *From the Rebbe's Table,* 20–22. The book can be purchased from The New England Chassidic Center, 1710 Beacon Street, Brookline, Mass., 02146, with tapes. The Rebbe's melody for Mizmor L'David (Ps 23) is included on the tape, but you must imagine it sung, not by a single voice as on the tape, but by a room full of voices.

[28] Heschel, *Sabbath,* 55.

[29] Shenker was born in 1925. This melody has been transcribed in many collections of *zemirot,* including Velvel Pasternak, ed., *Melodies of Modzitz: Classics from the Hassidic Music Masters* (Cedarhurst, N.Y.: Tara Publications, 1998), 42–43. The tape that accompanies the book does not include Shenker's setting, however.

Unlike the Bostoner's melody, Shenker's is slow. Some call it "comforting," others say "sad." This melody is full of longing—like a woman standing in a train station bidding her lover goodbye. In Shenker's setting the verbs are petitions: we are living in the Sabbath's embrace, and before its departure we already yearn for its return.

Some Jewish commentators claim that Ps 23 recounts actual events in David's life or in the life of Israel. However, does the slow movement of Beethoven's *Fifth Piano Concerto* recount an actual experience of tranquility? Or did the composer create sublime tranquility that, in his God-given soul, he was able to imagine? Did the psalmist report an experience or create one? The composer of Ps 23 could surely see the enemies in the new government. He could surely hear the fighting in the Holy Land. He was well aware of all the unfinished work of the world. Nonetheless, he was also able to imagine. He could *imagine* God singing to him and to us:

> There's a place for us…
> A time and place for us…
> Peace and quiet and open air…
> hold my hand and I'll take you there.[30]

I like to think that Ps 23 was David's reply. Singing his song on Shabbat is all it takes to make it real for me.

---

[30] Excerpted from "Somewhere," lyrics by Stephen Sondheim, music by Leonard Bernstein, from their musical *West Side Story.* In the preaching of the sermon, I actually sang these lines.

Evening Prayer, Sunday, 21 January 2001: Psalm 103

Ellen Davis
Duke Divinity School

> Bless the LORD, O my soul,
> and all that is within me bless his holy Name.
> Bless the LORD, O my soul,
> and forget not all his benefits. (Ps 103:1–2)

This evening we hear the psalmist at her most exuberant, turned almost inside out with exhilaration: "All that is within me, bless his holy Name." The cause for exhilaration is the extravagance of God's kindness to us—most of all, in freeing us from sin. It seems that God makes a complete break between ourselves and our sin:

> As far as East is from West,
> so far has he removed from us our transgressions. (Ps 103:12)

But in a cooler mood than the psalmist's own, you have to ask: Really? *Has* God set us a world away from our transgressions? For that claim seems to contradict one of the elemental facts of human existence: our sins, once committed, are with us for the rest of our lives. The consequences of sin remain permanent facts on the ground, even though the sins themselves may be long ago regretted and forgiven. I dare say that for every one of us, among the outstanding facts of our personal history are the consequences of sins we committed and sins by which we were victimized: a marriage was damaged or broken, a friendship lost; a child was neglected, a body abused; a good mind achieved only a fraction of its potential; years were wasted in empty pleasures or work that did not bring us closer to God.

What does it mean, then, to say that God removes our sins far from us, if we live always with their memory and their effects? This is, I think, the question that our psalm answers—not in so many words, but as the psalms always answer big questions, in the language of poetry: metaphorical, more suggestive than explanatory, in language that is surprised and surprising. Here, for instance, is something surprising:

> *Not* according to our sins has [God] done to us,
> and not according to our iniquities has he recompensed us. (Ps 103:10)

It seems that God is not keeping such close score of our iniquities as we often suppose. This is a common but often overlooked error in the spiritual life: treating sin as though it were the most interesting thing about myself or any other human being, harboring guilt for my own sins and grudges about theirs, imagining that God is eternally occupied with plans to get us back for them. But in fact, "[God] does not deal with us according to our sins." The psalm reveals that sin is essentially boring, to God as it should be to us; quite literally, it is deadly dull.

God is not interested in sin because God is so interested in us, with the fascination characteristic of parents. The psalmist puts it thus:

> As a father has compassion on children,
> God has compassion on those who fear him. (Ps 103:13)

God's parental compassion for us means this at least: our sins cause God pain. (The English word "compassion" literally means "suffering with" someone.) God suffers over our sins, probably more than we do; therefore, God has a personal interest in getting rid of them. We may understand this from family experience. The loving parent's response to the worst sins of the child is less anger than pained bewilderment: How could you have done this? I have seen that look on my mother's face, the bewilderment borne out of bone-deep knowledge that her children were formed in the womb for goodness, not evil. Maybe that is why God has to be imaged as mother or father, because, as the psalm says, "he knows our formation" (103:14). Only a parent has the long memory and the patience to make a firm distinction, day by day—to distinguish and separate our created selves, formed in God's own image, from our evil actions.

It takes a parent's love to do for us what we generally fail to do: to see ourselves as separate from our sins. Our confusion in this is common, but tragic nonetheless. We come to think of our sins as our real selves, and therefore we are stuck with them. We even stick up for them. Probably all of us have defended one or another damaging behavior with the remark, "That's just the way I am.... Sure, I have a bad temper; yes, I drink (or gossip, or flirt, or spend, or nag, or sulk) a little too much, but after all, I'm only human." Accepting our own evil with a shrug or even tears of frustration is a lie, a lie about our humanity. From the perspective of Christian faith, the incarnation of God in Jesus Christ is the definitive exposure of that lie.

The good news revealed in Jesus Christ is that we are far more like God than like our sins. No one has shown that more graphically than Michelangelo, in his Sistine Chapel painting of Adam and Eve being expelled from Eden. These are not the bewildered childlike figures who often appear in medieval art. Michelangelo gave Adam and Eve the same magnificent musculature as he painted for God, even the same gestures. He put the power and beauty of divinity into these first humans; they are truly God's image and likeness, and therefore it is especially horrible when they misuse that wonderful power to their own misery.

Christians speak of Jesus Christ as the second Adam, meaning that in him we see for once God's image without any distortion. God's purpose in showing us that perfect image was not to sink us in despair; years, or tens of thousands of years, of sin had already dragged us down into that pit. Rather, God means to draw us up into the genuinely human life that the biblical writers call "God's kingdom" (Ps 103:19) or sometimes, "eternal life"—that abundant life[1] that does not begin when we die but rather when we start focusing on what God is doing, living no longer out of our own whims and fears, but out of the possibilities that God's action opens up for us. That life of abundance is what the psalmist celebrates, calling forth everything she's got to bless the LORD

> who forgives all your sins
> and heals all your infirmities,
> who redeems your life from the pit,
> and crowns you with steadfast love and mercy,
> and satisfies you with good as long as you live. (Ps 103:3–5)

The work of ministry—what one person of faith can do for another person—is to make more real the possibility of that abundant life, life in which we are separated from our sins. One of the kindest works of ministry is to help another see that sin is not just bad (that's obvious enough). It is also incongruous. Change becomes possible when we see that our sins have no genuine place in our lives; there is no real "fit" between them and us. My first confessor helped me see that. I only spoke with him once. He was a monk who heard confessions at the convent where I often made retreats, and I asked if he would listen to mine. I am told that hearing the confessions of cloistered nuns is like being stoned with cotton balls. I was lobbing real stones—metaphorical stones, but real nonetheless. Yet when I had finished, he looked at me with a mildness I did not deserve and asked: "Tell me, did these things surprise you?" Up to that moment I had thought of my sins only as cause for guilt, not surprise. But now I saw for the first time how surprising sin always is, because we were made for glory. "Did these things surprise you?" Once we have seen each of our sins

---

[1] See Jesus' saying in John 10:10: "I came that they might have life, and have it abundantly."

for what it is, an absurd accretion to our souls that defeats our deepest purposes—when we have seen that, then one by one the sins lose their compelling interest and thus the power to do real harm, through either tortuous memories or fresh repetitions.

God is bored by sin but fascinated beyond all reason by our potential for goodness, so God bends every effort to create the conditions in which that potential can develop. There is just one thing that makes human goodness possible, and that is what the psalmist calls God's *ḥesed,* the covenant love that is, to this poet's eyes, the biggest fact on the ground. God's *ḥesed,* steadfast love, dominates the horizon:

> Yes, as high as the heavens are above the earth,
> So does his steadfast love tower over those who fear him. (Ps 103:11)

"So does his steadfast love tower over those who fear him." God's steadfast love spreads over us high and wide, like a shade tree in the summer heat. The invitation of the gospel, the good news as it comes to us in both Testaments, is to come off the long hot road and spend the rest of our lives in that refreshing shade. We are tired, for we have carried too much with us: old guilt and shame whose usefulness has passed, unhealed anger that is doing us harm, defenses and denials that offer no genuine relief. Come, the place is ready, stay here; you will find rest for your soul. Amen.

Bibliography

The bibliography is divided into two sections. The first section contains primary sources, catalogues, and multivolume reference works. Citations from classical sources are taken from the Loeb Classical Library unless otherwise stated. English translations of early Christian writings can be found in one or more of the following series: *Ante-Nicene Fathers, Nicene Fathers and Post-Nicene Fathers,* Ancient Christian Writers, Fathers of the Church, and Library of Christian Classics. Texts published in James Mckinnon's *Music in Early Christian Literature* are not listed in the bibliography. In the second section of the bibliography, secondary works are listed according to Society of Biblical Literature style guidelines. It is not difficult, therefore, for the reader to know which of the two sections to consult.

Primary Sources, Catalogues, and Multivolume Reference Works

Alcinous. *The Handbook of Platonism.* Translated by John Dillon. Oxford: Clarendon Press, 1993.

Alygizakes, Antonios E. *Μελωδήματα άσκήσεων λειτουργικῆς*. Thessalonica: Dedouses, 1992.

Amalarius. *Opera liturgica omnia.* Edited by Jean Michel Hanssens. Città del Vaticano: Biblioteca apostolica vaticana, 1948–50.

Ambrose, Saint. *Opera.* 27 vols. Milan: Città Nuova; Rome: Bibliotheca Ambrosiana, 1977.

Anastasius of Sinai. *Quaestio 2.* PG 89:344–52.

Apophthegmata Patrum, Alphabetical Collection. Translated by Benedicta Ward in *The Desert Christian: Sayings of the Desert Fathers: The Alphabetical Collection.* New York: Macmillan, 1980.

Aristeas. *Aristeas to Philocrates (Letter of Aristeas).* Edited and translated by Moses Hadas. Jewish Apocryphal Literature. New York: Harper & Brothers for The Dropsie College for Hebrew and Cognate Learning, 1951.

———. *Lettre d'Aristée à Philocrate.* Edited and translated by André Pelletier. SC 89. Paris: Cerf, 1962.

Aristides Quintilianus. *La Musique.* Translation and commentary by François Duysinx. Bibliothèque de la Faculté de Philosophie et Lettres de l'Université de Liège 276. Geneva: Droz, 1999.

———. *On Music in Three Books.* Translated, with introduction, commentary, and annotations by Thomas J. Mathiesen. Music Theory Translation Series. New Haven: Yale University Press, 1983.

Aristoxenus. *Elementa Rhythmica: The Fragment of Book II and the Additional Evidence for Aristoxenean Rhythmic Theory.* Edited by Lionel Pearson. Oxford: Clarendon Press, 1990.

Arvantis, Ioannis, dir. [2001]. *Under the Shadow of Mount Athos: Orthodox Hymns from Skiathos Monasteries.* The Hellenic Music Archives CD AEM 019.

Asterius. *Commentariorum in Psalmos quae supersunt accedunt aliquot homiliae anonymae.* Edited by Marcel Richard. Symbolae Osloenses fasc. supplet. 16. Oslo: Brøgger, 1956.

———. *Psalmenhomilien.* Translated by Wolfram Kinzig. 2 vols. Bibliothek der griechischen Literatur 56. Stuttgart: Hiersemann, 2002.

Athanasius, Saint. *The Letter to Marcellinus.* Pages 101–29 in *The Life of Antony and the Letter to Mercellinus.* Translated by R. C. Gregg. Classics of Western Spirituality. New York: Paulist, 1980.

Atwan, Robert, and Laurance Wieder. *Chapters into Verse: Poetry in English Inspired by the Bible.* 2 vols. Oxford: Oxford University Press, 1993.

Backhouse, Janet. *The Isabella Breviary.* London: British Library, 1993.

Barker, Andrew, ed. *Greek Musical Writings.* 2 vols. Cambridge Readings in the Literature of Music. Cambridge: Cambridge University Press, 1984.

Barsanuphius and John of Gaza. *Correspondence.* Translated by Lucien Régnault. 2 vols. in 4 tomes. SC 426–427, 450–451. Paris: Cerf, 1997, 2001.

Basil, Saint. *Exegetical Homilies.* Translated by Agnes Clare Way. FC 46. Washington, D.C.: Catholic University of America Press, 1963.

———. *Sur le Saint-Esprit.* 2d ed. Edited by Benoît Pruche. SC 17bis. Paris: Cerf, 1968.

Benedict, Saint. *Rule.* In *RB 1989: The Rule of St. Benedict in Latin and English with Notes.* Edited by Timothy Fry. Collegeville, Minn.: Liturgical Press, 1981.

Bernstein, Leonard. *Chichester Psalms.* 1965.

Berryman, John. *Collected Poems of John Berryman, 1937–71.* Edited by Charles Thornbury. New York: Farrar, Straus & Giroux, 1989.

Beza, Theodore. *Vita Calvini.* Vol. 21 in *Joannis Calvini opera quae supersunt omnia.* Edited by William Baum, Edward Cunitz, and Edward Reuss. Corpus Reformatorum 29–87. Braunschweig: Schwetschke. 1863–1900. English translation, pages lvii–cxxxviii in vol. 1 of John Calvin, *Tracts Relating to the Reformation.* Translated by Henry Beveridge. 3 vols. Edinburgh: Calvin Translation Society, 1844–51. Repr., *Tracts and Treatises.* Grand Rapids: Eerdmans, 1958.

Birnbaum, Philip, ed. *Birnbaum Haggadah*. New York Hebrew Publishing Co., 1953.

———. *Daily Prayer Book: Ha-siddur Ha-shalem*. New York: Hebrew Publishing Co., 1948, 1977.

Braude, William G., trans. *The Midrash On Psalms*. 2 vols. Yale Judaica Series 13. New Haven: Yale University Press, 1959.

Buber, Solomon, ed. *Midrash Tehillim*. Vilna: Wittwe & Gebrüder Romm, 1891. Repr., 1966.

Bünting, Heinrich. *Intinerarium sacrae Scripturae*. Helmstadt: Siebenburger, 1582.

Caines, Clement. *The History of the General Council and General Assembly of the Leeward Islands, Which Were Convened for the Purpose of Investigating and Meliorating the Condition of the Slaves throughout Those Settlements and of Effecting a Gradual Abolition of the Slave Trade*. St. Christopher: Cable, 1804.

Calvin, John. "Articles concerning the Organization of the Church and of Worship at Geneva Proposed by the Ministers at the Council January 16, 1537." Pages 47–55 in *Calvin: Theological Treatises*. Translated by J. K. S. Reid. LCC 22. Philadelphia: Westminster, 1954.

———. *Calvin's First Psalter: 1539*. Edited with critical notes and modal harmonies to the melodies by Richard R. Terry. London: Benn, 1932.

———. *Commentary on the Book of Psalms*. Translated by James Anderson. 5 vols. Edinburgh: Calvin Translation Society, 1845. Repr., Grand Rapids: Eerdmans, 1979.

———. *The Institutes of the Christian Religion*. Edited by John T. McNeill. Translated by Ford Lewis Battles. 2 vols. LCC 20–21. Philadelphia: Westminster, 1960.

———. *Opera quae supersunt omnia*. Edited by William Baum, Edward Cunitz, and Edward Reuss. 59 vols. in 26. Corpus Reformatorum 29–87. Brunswick: Schwetschke, 1863–1900.

———. *The Piety of John Calvin: An Anthology Illustrative of the Spirituality of the Reformer*. Translated and edited by Ford Lewis Battles. Music edited by Stanley Tagg. Grands Rapids: Baker, 1978.

Cassiodorus. *Explanation of the Psalms*. Translated by P. G. Walsh. 3 vols. ACW 51–53. New York: Paulist, 1990–91.

Central Conference of American Rabbis. *Union Haggadah*. Rev. ed. Cincinnati: Conference of American Rabbis, 1923.

Columbus, Christopher. *Libro de las Profecias*. Edited and translated by Delno West and August King. Gainesville: University of Florida Press, 1991.

Cyril of Scythopolis. *Life of St. Sabas; Life of St. Theodosius*. In *Kyrillos von Skythopolis*. Edited by Eduard Schwartz. TU 49/3. Leipzig: Hinrichs, 1939.

———. *The Lives of the Monks of Palestine.* Translated by Richard M. Price. Cistercian Studies 114. Kalamazoo, Mich.: Cistercian Publications, 1991.

Cyril/John II of Jerusalem. *Catéchèses mystagogiques.* Edited by Auguste Piédagnel. SC 126bis. Paris: Cerf, 1966.

Dagron, Gilbert, ed. *Vie et miracles de Sainte Thecle: texte grec, traduction et commentaire.* Subsidia hagiographica 62. Brussels: Société des Bollandistes, 1978.

Desby, Frank. "The Growth of Liturgical Music in the Iakovian Era." Pages 303–23 in *History of the Greek Orthodox Church in America.* Edited by M. B. Ephthimiou and G. A. Christopoulos. New York: Greek Orthodox Archdiocese of North and South America, 1984.

Diodorus. *Commentarii in Psalmos* 1. In *Commentarii in Psalmos I–L.* Edited by Jean-Marie Olivier. CCSG 6. Turnhout: Brepols, 1980.

Dionysius of Halicarnassus. *Dionysii Halicarnassi opera.* Edited by Herman Usener and Ludwig Radmacher. 2 vols. Leipzig: Teubner, 1904.

———. *La composition stylistique.* Vol. 3 of *Opuscules rhétoriques.* Edited by Germaine Aujac and Maurice Lebel. Collection des Universités de France. Paris: Les Belles Lettres, 1981.

Egeria. *Egeria's Travels to the Holy Land.* Translated by John Wilkinson. Rev. ed. Jerusalem: Ariel, 1981; 3d ed., Warminster, U.K.: Aris & Phillips, 1999.

———. *Journal de voyage: Itinéraire.* Edited by Pierre Maraval. SC 296. Paris: Cerf, 1982.

Einhorn, David. *Olat Tamid: Book of Prayers for Jewish Congregations.* Chicago: Ettinger, 1896.

Eustratius. *Vita et conversatio S. Eutchii 78* (= *BHG* 657). PG 86.2:234B.

From the Rebbe's Table: Sabbath and Festival Songs and Blessings. Brookline, Mass.: New England Chassidic Center, 1983.

Funk, Franz X. von, ed. *Didascalia et Constitutiones apostolorum.* 2 vols. Paderborn: Schoeningh, 1905, Repr., Turin: n.p., 1964.

Germanus of Constantinople, Saint. *On the Divine Liturgy.* Edited and translated by Paul Meyendorff. Crestwood, N.Y.: St. Vladimir's Seminary Press, 1984.

Goldschmidt, Ernst Daniel, ed. *Mechkarei Tefillah Ufiyut.* Jerusalem: Magnes, 1979.

Gregory of Nazianzus, Saint. *Autobiographical Poems.* Translated and edited by Carolinne White. Cambridge: Cambridge University Press, 1996.

Gregory of Nyssa, Saint. *Commentary on the Inscriptions of the Psalms.* Translated by Casimir McCambley. Brookline, Mass.: Hellenic College Press, 1990.

Hamman, Adalbert-G. *Les trois premiers siècles.* Vol. 2 of *La prière.* Paris: Desclée, 1963.

Hänggi, Anton, and Irmgard Pahl, eds. *Prex eucharistica.* 3d ed. Spicilegium Friburgense 12. Fribourg: Universitätsverlag, 1998.

Herbert, George. *The Poems of George Herbert.* From the text of Francis E. Hutchinson, with an introduction by Helen Gardner. London: Oxford University Press, 1961.

Hesbert, René-Jean, ed. *Corpus antiphonalium officii.* 6 vols. Rerum ecclesiastiarum documenta, Series maior, Fontes 7–12. Rome: Herder, 1963–79.

Hildegard of Bingen, Saint. *Lieder.* Edited and transcribed by Prudentiana Barth, M. Immaculata Ritscher, and Josef Schmidt-Görg. Salzburg: Mueller, 1969.

———. *On Natural Philosophy and Medicine.* Translated by Margret Berger. Rochester, N.Y.: Brewer, 1999.

———. *Scivias.* Translated by Columba Hart and Jane Bishop. Classics of Western Spirituality. New York: Paulist, 1990.

———. *Symphonia* [*Symphony of the Harmony of Celestial Revelations*]. Translated by Barbara Newman. Ithaca, N.Y.: Cornell University Press, 1988; rev. ed., 1998.

———. *Symphonia hamoniae caelestium revelationum.* Edited by Peter van Poucke. Peer, Belgium: Alamire, 1991.

Hippolytus. *Hippolytus: A Text for Students.* Introduction, translation, commentary and notes by Geoffrey J. Cuming. Grove Liturgical Studies 8. Bramcote, Nottingham: Grove Books, 1976.

———. *On the Apostolic Tradition.* Translated by Alistair Stewart-Sykes. Crestwood, N.Y.: St. Vladimir's Seminary Press, 2001.

———. *The Statutes of the Apostles, or, Canones ecclesiastici.* Edited with translation and collation from Ethiopic and Arrabic manuscipts by George W. Horner. London: Williams & Norgate, 1904.

———. *La Tradition apostolique de S. Hippolyte: Essai de reconstitution par Bernard Botte.* LQF 39. Münster Westfalen: Aschendorff, 1963.

———. *The Treatise on the Apostolic Tradition of St. Hippolytus of Rome, Bishop and Martyr.* Edited by Gregory Dix. Revised by Henry Chadwick. London: Alban, 1992.

Hoeg, Casten, Gunther Zuntz, and Gudrun Engberg, eds. *Prophetologium.* Monumenta musicae byzantinae Lectionaria 1. 2 vols. Copenhagen: Munksgaard, 1939–81.

Holy Transfiguration Monastery. *The Divine Liturgy of Our Father among the Saints John Chrysostom, Archbishop of Constantinople.* Seattle: St. Nektarios Press, 1982.

——— *Selected Byzantine Hymns according to the Tradition of the Great Church of Christ, Including Troparia Taken from Vespers, Great Lent, Holy Week, and Pascha, Transcribed from the Chrysanthine Byzantine Notation.* Brookline, Mass.: Holy Transfiguration Monastery, 1986.

Hopkins, Gerard Manley. *The Poetry of Gerard Manley Hopkins.* Edited by W. H. Garner and N. H. Mackenzie. 4th ed. Oxford: Oxford University Press, 1967.

——— *The Sermons and Devotional Writings of Gerard Manley Hopkins.* Edited by Christopher Devlin. London: Oxford University Press, 1959.

Huck, Gabe, ed. *The Psalter: A Faithful and Inclusive Rendering from the Hebrew into Contemporary English Poetry, Intended Primarily for Communal Song and Recitation.* Chicago: Liturgy Training Publications, 1995.

Joannou, Pericles-Pierre, ed. *Discipline générale antique.* 3 vols. in 4. Fonti codificazione canonica orientale 9. Grottaferrata (Rome): Tipografia Italo-Orientale "S. Nilo," 1962–64.

Jonkers, Engbert J., ed. *Acta et Symbola Conciliorum quae saeculo quarto habita sunt.* Testus minores in usum academicum 19. Brill: Leiden, 1954.

Josephus, *Judean Antiquities 1–4.* Translation and Commentary by Louis H. Feldman. Flavius Josephus Translation and Commentary 3. Edited by Steve Mason. Leiden: Brill, 2000.

Karas, Simon. *Μέθοδος ἑλληνικῆς μουσικῆς.* 8 vols. Athens: Society for the Dissemination of National Music, 1982–85.

Kingdon, Robert M., ed. *Registres du Consistoire de Genève au temps de Calvin.* Geneva: Droz, 1996–2001. English translation in *Registers of the Consistory of Geneva in the Time of Calvin.* Edited by Robert M. Kingdon et al. Translated by M. Wallace McDonald. Grand Rapids: Eerdmans, 2000–.

Kraft, Robert A., Harold Attridge, Russell Spittler, and Janet Timbie, eds. *The Testament of Job according to the SV Text.* SBLTT 5; Pseudepigrapha Series 4. Missoula, Mont.: Scholars Press, 1974.

Lampe, Geoffrey, ed. *A Patristic Greek Lexicon.* Oxford: Oxford University Press, 1961.

Lathrop, Gordon, and Gail Ramshaw, eds. *Psalter for the Christian People: An Inclusive Revision of the Psalter of the Book of Common Prayer 1979.* Collegeville, Minn.: Liturgical Press, 1993.

Lingas, Alexander, dir. 1999. *Tikey Zes: Choral Works.* Cappella Romana. Gagliano GR501–CD.

Longinus. *On Sublimity.* Pages 143–87 in *Classical Literary Criticism.* Edited by Donald Russell and Michael Winterbottom. The World's Classics. Oxford: Oxford University Press, 1989.

Longo, Augusta, ed. "Il testo della «Narrazione degli abati Giovanni e Sofronio» attraverso le <<Jemhnei ai>> di Nicone." *Revista di studi bizantini e neoellenici,* NS 2–3 = 12–13 (1965–66): 223–67.

López de Gómora, Francisco. *Historia General de las Indias.* Zaragosa, 1552.

Luckhardt, Jochen, and Franz Niehoff, eds., *Heinrich der Löwe and seine Zeit: Herrschaft und Repräsentation der Welfen 1125–1235.* 3 vols. Munich: Hirmer, 1995.

Luther, Martin. *Selections from the Psalms.* Vol. 12 of *Luther's Works.* Edited by Jaroslav Pelikan. St. Louis: Concordia, 1955.

Maclean, Arthur. *East Syrian Daily Offices.* London: Rivingtons, 1894.

Manuscrits normands, XI–XIIe siècles. Exhibition catalogue. Rouen, Musée des BeauxArts, 1975.

Maragos, Nicolas E. *Holy Cross Liturgical Hymnal: Containing the Divine Liturgy of Saint John Chrysostom in Greek and English, the Resurrectional Apolytikia, Hymns of the Menaion, Hymns of Lent and Easter, Hymns of the Pentecostal Season, the Memorial Service, and the Service of Thanksgiving Following Holy Communion.* Brookline, Mass.: Holy Cross Orthodox Press, 1988.

Mateos, Juan, ed. *Le Typicon de la Grande Église. Ms. Sainte-Croix no. 40, Xe siècle. Introduction, texte critique, traduction et notes.* 2 vols. OCA 165–166. Rome: Pontificium Institutum Orientalium Studiorum, 1962–63.

McKinnon, James, ed. *Music in Early Christian Literature.* Cambridge Readings in the Literature of Music. Cambridge: Cambridge University Press, 1987.

Metzinger, Joseph, et al., eds. *The Zwiefalten Antiphoner: Karlsruehe, Badische Landesbibliothek, Aug. perg.LX: Printouts from an Index in Machine-Readable Form: A CANTUS Index.* Introduction by Hartmut Möller. Musicological Studies 55/5. Ottawa: Institute of Mediaeval Music, 1996.

Michael the Studite. *Vita 1* (= *BHG* 1754). PG 99:312C–313B; *Vita 3* (= *BHG* 1755d).

Mitchell, Stephen. *A Book of Psalms, Selected and Adapted from the Hebrew.* New York: HarperCollins, 1993.

Montanus, Benedictus Arias. *Humanae salutis monumenta.* Antwerp, 1571.

Morosan, Vladimir, ed. *One Thousand Years of Russian Church Music.* Monuments of Russian Sacred Music 1/1. Washington, D.C.: Musica Russica, 1991.

Niceta of Remesiana. *De psalmodiae bono.* Edited by A. E. Burn. Cambridge: Cambridge University Press, 1905.

Origen. *Sur les Écritures: Philocalie, 1–20.* Translated by Marguerite Harl. SC 302. Paris: Cerf, 1983.

Osherow, Jacqueline. *Dead Men's Praise.* New York: Grove, 1999.

Palladius. *La Storia lausiaca.* Edited by Gerhardus J. M. Bartelink. Translated by Mariano Barchiesi. Vite dei santi 2. Milan: Modadori, 1974, 1990.

Palmer, Gerald E. H., Philip Sherrard, and Kallistos Ware, eds. and trans. *The Philokalia: The Complete Text Compiled by St. Nikodimos of the*

Holy Mountain and St. Makarios of Corinth. 4 vols. London: Faber & Faber, 1979–95.

Phillips, Perecles P. *ΜΕΓΑ ΣΑΒΒΑΤΟΝ ΠΡΩΙ: The Holy Saturday Morning Service*. The Junior Choir Series. Denver: Federation of Greek Orthodox Choirs of the Western States–East, 1980.

Philo of Alexandria. *About the Contemplative Life, or The Fourth Book of the Treatise Concerning Virtues*. Edited by Frederick C. Conybeare. Oxford: Clarendon Press, 1895.

———. *Concerning the Contemplative Life*. Translated by Frederick C. Conybeare. N.p. 1895.

———. "The Contemplative Life." Pages 41–57 in *The Contemplative Life; The Giants; and Selections*. Translated by David Winston. Classics of Western Spirituality. New York: Paulist Press, 1981.

———. *Les oeuvres de Philon d'Alexandrie*. Edited by Roger Arnaldez, Jean Pouilloux, and Claude Montdésert. 36 vols. in 35. Paris: Cerf, 1961–92.

Philodemus. *On Poems*. Edited by Richard Janko. Oxford: Oxford University Press, 2000.

Pietersma, Albert, ed. *The Psalms: A New English Translation of the Septuagint and Other Greek Translations Traditionally Included under That Title*. New York: Oxford University Press, 2000.

Pius XII, Pope. *Divino afflante Spiritu: Encyclical Letter of Pope Pius XII on Promotion of Biblical Studies*. Washington, D.C.: National Catholic Welfare Conference, 1943.

Plato. *The Dialogues of Plato*. Translated Reginald E. Allen. 4 vols. New Haven: Yale University Press, 1984–97.

———. *The Laws*. Translated by Thomas L. Pangle. New York: Basic Books, 1980.

———. *The Republic*. Translated by Richard W. Sterling and William C. Scott. New York: Norton, 1985.

Porphyry. *Kommentar zur Harmonielehre des Ptolemaios*. Edited by Ingemar Düring. Göteborg: Elanders, 1932. Repr., New York: Garland, 1980.

Portilla, Miguel León, ed. *Native Mesoamerican Spirituality: Ancient Myths, Discourses, Stories, Doctrines, Hymns, Poems from the Aztec, Yucatec, Quiche-Maya and Other Sacred Traditions*. New York: Paulist, 1980.

Presbyterian Church (U.S.A.). *Book of Common Worship*. Louisville: Westminster John Knox, 1993.

Le Psautier de Genève, 1562–1865: Images commentées et essai de bibliographie. Geneva: Droz, 1986.

Ptolemy. *Harmonics: Translation and Commentary*. Translated by Jon Solomon. Mnemosyne: Bibliotheca Classica Batava, supplementum 203. Leiden: E. J. Brill, 2000.

Pudichery, Sylvester. *Ramsa*. Palchalam: Dharmaram College, 1972.

Puys, Reny de. *La tryumphante Entre de Charles Prince des Espagnes en Bruges 1515.* Facsimile with introduction by Sydney Anglo. Amsterdam: Theatrum Orbis Terrarum, 1973.

Radmacher, Earl D., ed. *The Nelson Study Bible.* Nashville: Nelson, 1997.

Rhamani, Ignatius Ephrem II, ed. "Ritus receptionis episcopi et celebrationis liturgiae catechumenorum." Pages 1–22 in *Vetusta documenta liturgica*. Fasc. 3 of *Studia Syriaca*. Monte Libano: Typis Patriarchalibus in Seminario Scharfensi, 1908.

Rigas, Giorgios. *Μελῳδήματα Σκιάθου*. Athens: n.p., 1958.

———. *Τύπικον*. Liturgica Vlatadon 1. Thessalonica: Patriarchal Institute for Patristic Studies, 1994.

Rozenberg, Martin S., and Bernard M. Zlotowitz. *The Book of Psalms: A New Translation and Commentary.* Northvale, N.J.: Aronson, 1999.

Sackur, Ernst. *Sibyllinsiche Texte und forschungen: Pseudomethodius Adso und Die tiburtinische sibylle*. Halle: Niemeyer, 1898.

Sahagún, Bernadino de. *Bernardino de Sahagún's Psalmodia Christiana* (*Christian Psalmody*). Translated by Arthur Anderson. Salt Lake City: University of Utah Press, 1993.

———. *Psalmodia christiana, y sermoniario de los sanctos del año en lengua mexicana.* Mexico City: Pedro Ocharte, 1583.

Saurma-Jeltsch, Lieselotte E. *Die Miniatauren im "Liber Scivias" der Hildegard von Bingen: Die Wucht der Vision und die Ordnung der Bilder.* Wiesbaden: Reichert, 1998.

Scherman, Nosson, trans. *Sidur Kol Ya'akov: Hol, Shabat, Shalosh Regalim = The Complete ArtScroll Siddur: Weekday, Sabbath, Festival.* Brooklyn: Mesorah, 1984.

———. *Zemiroth: Sabbath Songs with additional Sephardic Zemiroth.* Brooklyn: Mesorah, 1979.

Severus. *The Hymns of Severus and Others in the Syriac Version of Paul of Edessa as Revised by James of Edessa*. Edited by Ernest W. Brooks. PO 6.1 and 7.5. Paris: Firmin-Didot, 1911.

Sexton, Anne. *The Complete Poems.* Boston: Houghton Mifflin, 1981.

Simonopetrites, Grigorios. *Ψαλτήριον τερπνόν*. Mount Athos: Holy Monastery of Simonos Petras, 1991.

Skard, Eiliv, ed.. *Index Asterianus.* Symbolae Osloenses 17. Oslo: Universitetsforlaget, 1962.

Smart, Christopher. *The Poetical Works.* Edited by Karina Williamson. 6 vols. Oxford: Clarendon Press, 1980–96.

Southern, Eileen, ed. *Readings in Black American Music.* New York: Norton, 1983.

Stathis, Grigorios. *Κυριακὰ Ἀλληλουϊάρια τοῦ Εὐαγγελίου διὰ τὸν καιρὸν τῆς προσφορᾶς τοῦ θυμιάματος μελισθέντα κατ' ἦχον μετὰ τῶν ἁρμοδι-΄ων στίχων αὐτῶν παρὰ Γρηγορίου Θ. Στάθη καθηγητοῦ τῆς Βυζαντινῆς*

Μουσικολογίας καὶ Ψαλτικῆς Τέχνης ἐν τῷ Πανεπιστημίῳ Ἀθηνῶν, τάχα καὶ μαΐστορος, κατ' εἰσήγησιν καὶ εὐλογίαν τοῦ μακαριωτάτου Ἀρχιεπισκόπου Ἀθηνῶν καὶ πάσης Ἑλλάδος κυρίου Χριστοδούλου, εἰς ὃν καὶ ἀφιεροῦνται προφρόνως τὰ νεωστὶ ποιηθέντα, εἰς ἦχον πλ. β', βαρὺν καὶ πλ. δ', κατὰ τὴν ε' καὶ ς τοῦ μηνὸς Φεβρουαρίου τοῦ σωτηρίου ἔτους βα'. Athens: Apostolike Diakonia, 2001.

———. *Παννυχίς, ἤτοι Νυκτερινὴ Ἀσματικὴ Ἀκολουθὶα κατὰ τὸ Βυζαντινὸν Κοσμικὸν Τυπικὸν τῆς Μεγάλης Ἐκκλησίας Ἁγίας Σοφίας*. Athens: Apostolike Diakonia, 1999.

———. *Pannychis: A Byzantine "Chanted" Office of the Great Church of Saint Sophia.* CD recording with booklet. National and Kapodistrian University of Athens, Department of Musical Studies, 2000.

———. *Τριθέκτη, ἤτοι Ἀκολουθία τοῦ Βυζαντινοῦ Κοσμικοῦ Τυπικοῦ τῆς Μεγάλης Ἐκκλησιά Ἁγίας Σοφίας καὶ τὸ Κοντάκιον τῶν Χριστουγέννων τοῦ Ρωμανοῦ τοῦ Μελώδου.* Λατρειολογήματα 2. Athens: Institute of Byzantine Musicology, 2000.

Stegmüller, Friedrich, ed. *Repertorium biblicum medii aevi.* 11 vols. Madrid: Consejo Superior de Investigaciones Cientificas, Instituto Francisco Súarez, 1940–80.

Symeon of Thessalonika. *De sacra precatione.* PG 155:535–670.

Tarchnishvili, Michel, ed. *Le Grande lectionnaire de l'église de Jérusalem.* CSCO 188–189, 204–205 = Scriptores Iberici 9–10, 13–14. Leuven: Secrétariat du CSCO, 1959–60.

———. *Liturgiae Ibericae antiuiores.* CSCO 122–23 = Scriptores Iberici 1–2, ser. 1, vol. 1. Leuven: Durbecq, 1950.

Theodore Daphnopates. *Life of St. Theodore Studites* (= *Vita* 2). PG 99: 216B–17A.

Theodore of Mopsuestia. *Commentarium in Habacucum prophetam.* PG 66:423–50.

Tomaras, Sophronia, ed. *Hymns from the Liturgy, Book One: A Beginner's Hymnal Arranged for Church School and Home Use.* 2d field-test ed. San Francisco: Greek Orthodox Diocese of San Francisco Religious Education Commission, 1986.

Trésors des abbayes normandes. Exhibition catalogue. Caen, Musée des Beaux-Arts. Rouen: Musée des Antiquités, 1979.

Vatopaidi, Holy and Great Monastery of. *Holy Saturday: Service of the Epitaphios.* The Holy Week 6. University of Crete Press, 1999, CD CUP 26.

Vermes, Geza. *The Complete Dead Sea Scrolls in English.* New York: Penguin, 1997.

Villas, Ernest A. *The Divine Liturgy of St. John Chrysostom Hymnal: A Hymnal with Texts in Greek, English and English Phonetics.* 2d ed. Brookline, Mass.: Greek Orthodox Archdiocese of North and South America Department of Religious Education, 1982.

Violakis, Georgios, ed. *Τυπικὸν τῆς τοῦ Χριστοῦ Μεγάλης Ἐκκλησίας*. Constantinople: n.p., 1888. Repr., Athens: Saliveros, n.d.

Vitruvius. *Ten Books on Architecture.* Translated by Ingrid D. Rowland. Commentary and illustrations by Thomas Noble Howe et al. Cambridge: Cambridge University Press, 1999.

Vrionides, Christos. *Byzantine Hymnology: The Divine Services of the Greek Orthodox Church.* Reprint of the 2d ed. Brookline, Mass: Holy Cross Orthodox Press, 1980.

Watts, Issac. *The Psalms of David Imitated in the Language of the New Testament and Apply'd to the Christian State and Worship.* Philadelphia: Thomas Godfrey, 1729.

Wesley, John. *A Collection of Psalms and Hymns.* Charleston, S.C.: Louis Timothy, 1737.

Wieder, Laurance. *The Poets' Book of Psalms: The Complete Psalter as Rendered by Twenty-Five Poets from the Sixteenth to the Twentieth Centuries.* Oxford: Oxford University Press, 1995.

Württembergisches Landesmuseum. *Die Zeit der Staufer. Geschichte, Kunst, Kultur.* Exhibition catalogue. 5 vols. Stuttgart: Württembergisches Landesmuseum, 1977–79.

Zalman, Shneur, *Siddur Tehilat Hashem: Al Pi Nusach HaAri Z'L.* New, emended Hebrew edition with an English translation by Rabbi Niseen Mangel. Brooklyn: Merkos L'Inyonei Chinuch, Inc. 1995.

Zes, Tikey, arr. *The Divine Liturgy Arranged for Congregational Participation.* San Francisco: Diocese of San Francisco, 1984.

Secondary Sources

Abegg, Martin G. "Who Ascended to Heaven? 4Q491, 4Q427 and the Teacher of Righteousness." Pages 61–73 in *Eschatology, Messianism, and the Dead Sea Scrolls.* Edited by Criag A. Evans and Peter W. Flint. Grand Rapids: Eerdmans, 1997.

Aberbach, David. *Imperialism and Biblical Prophecy, 750–500 BCE.* New York: Routledge, 1993.

Adams, J. N. *The Latin Sexual Vocabulary.* London: Duckworth, 1982.

Albright, William Foxwell. *Yahweh and the Gods of Canaan.* Garden City, N.Y.: Doubleday, 1968.

Alcina Franch, José. "Lenguaje metafórico e iconografía en el arte mexica." *Anales del Instituto de Investigaciones Estéticas* 66 (1995): 7–44.

Alexander, Jonathan J. G. *Insular Manuscripts, Sixth to the Ninth Century (A Survey of Manuscripts Illuminated in the British Isles).* London: Miller, 1978.

———. "A Twelfth-Century Augustine on the Psalms, Perhaps from the Area of Soissons, Containing an Unpublished Library Catalogue." Pages

13–22 in *Florilegium in honorem Carl Nordenfalk Octogenarii Contextum.* Edited by Per Bjurström, Nils-Göran Hökby, and Florentine Mütherich. Stockholm: Nationalmuseum, 1987.

Alter, Robert. *The Art of Biblical Poetry.* New York: Basic Books, 1985.

———. *Literary Guide to the Bible.* Cambridge: Harvard University Press, 1987.

———. *The World of Biblical Literature.* New York: Basic Books, 1992.

Alter, Robert, and Frank Kermode, eds. *Literary Guide to the Bible.* Cambridge: Harvard University Press, 1987.

Anderson, Arthur. "Egypt, Arab Republic of: Ancient Music." Pages 1–7 in vol. 8 of *The New Grove Dictionary of Music and Musicians.* Edited by Stanley Sadie. 2d ed. 29 vols. London: Macmillan, 2001.

———."La Enciclopedia Doctrinal de Sahagún." Pages 164–79 in *Bernardino de Sahagún: Diez estudios acerca de su obra.* Edited by Ascensión Hernández de León-Portilla, Mexico City, Fondo de Cultura Económica, 1990.

Anderson, Warren D. *Music and Musicians in Ancient Greece.* Ithaca, N.Y.: Cornell University Press, 1994.

Arangassery, Lonappan. "The Odes of Solomon and the Psalms of David [Thematic Comparison]." *Christian Orient* 19 (1998): 63–72.

Arcelus Ulibarrena, Juana Maria. "Cristobal Colón y los primeros evangelizadores del Nuevo Mundo: Lección de profetismo joaquinista." Pages 475–504 in *Il profestismo gioachimita tra Quattrocento e Cinquecento: Atti de III Congresso Internazionale di Studi Gioachimiti.* Edited by Gian Luca Potestà. Genova: Marietti, 1991.

———. "La esperanza milenaria de Joaquín de Fiore y el Nuevo Mundo: Trayectoria de una utopia." *Florensia* 1 (1987): 47–79.

Arranz, Miguel. "Les grandes étapes de la Liturgie Byzantine: Palestine-Byzance-Russie. Essai d' aperçu historique." Pages 43–72 in *Liturgie de l'église particulière et liturgie de l'église universelle.* Bibliotheca Ephemerides Liturgicae, Subsidia 7. Rome: Edizioni Liturgiche, 1976.

Ashby, Clifford. *Classical Greek Theatre: New Views of an Old Subject.* Studies in Theatre History and Culture. Iowa City: University of Iowa Press, 1998.

Assaf, Simchah. "Miseder Hatefillah Me'erets Yisra'el." In *Sefer Dinabourg.* Edited by Yitzhak Baer, Joshua Gutman, and Moses Schwabe. Jerusalem: Kiryat Sefer, 1949.

Atkins, John W. H.. *Literary Criticism in Antiquity: A Sketch of Its Development.* Cambridge: Cambridge University Press, 1934.

Attridge, Harold W. *The Epistle to the Hebrews: A Commentary on the Epistle to the Hebrews.* Hermeneia. Philadelphia: Fortress, 1989.

Austin, López. *The Human Body and Ideology: Concepts of the Ancient Nahuas.* 2 vols. Salt Lake City: University of Utah Press, 1988.

Avalos, Hector. "Columbus as Biblical Exegete: A Study of the *Libro de las profecías.*" Pages 59–80 in *Religion in the Age of Exploration: The Case of Spain and New Spain.* Edited by Bryan F. Le Beau and Menachem Mor. Omaha: Creighton University Press, 1996.

Avril, François. *Manuscrits normands, XI–XIIe siècles.* Exhibit catalogue. Rouen: Musée des Beaux-Arts, 1975.

———. "Notes sur quelques manuscrits bénédictins normands du XIe au XIIe siècle." *Mélanges d'archéologie et d'histoire publiés par l'École Française de Rome* 77 (1965): 209–48.

Avril, François, and Zaluska, Yolanta. *VIe–XIIe siècles.* Vol. 1 of *Manuscrits enluminés d'origine italienne.* Paris: Bibliothèque Nationale, Département des manuscrits, 1980.

Aylen, Leo. *The Greek Theater.* Madison, N.J.: Fairleigh Dickinson University Press, 1985.

Bader, Günter. *Psalterium affectuum palaestra.* Tübingen: Mohr Siebeck, 1996.

Baer, Seligman. *Seder Avodat Yisrael.* Rödelheim: Lehrbeger, 1868.

Bailey, Mark. "Psalmic Music in Orthodox Liturgy as Foundation, Movement, and Ministry." *Jacob's Well* (Spring-Summer, 2000). Online at http://jacwell.org/spring_summer2000/psalmic_music_in_orthodox_liturg.htm

Baillet, Maurice *Qumrân Grotte 4.III (4Q482–4Q520).* DJD 7. Oxford: Clarendon Press, 1982.

Baldovin, John F. *The Urban Character of Christian Worship: The Origins, Development, and Meaning of Stational Liturgy.* OCA 228. Rome: Pontificium Institutum Studiorum Orientalium, 1987.

Barker, Andrew. "*Heterophonia* and *Poikilia:* Accompaniments to Greek Melody." Pages 41–60 in *Mousike: Metrica, ritmica e musica greca in memoria di Giovanni Comotti.* Edited by Bruno Gentili and Franca Perusino. Pisa: Instituti editoriali e poligrafici internazionali, 1995.

Barnea, Ezra. "The Tradition of the Jerusalemite-Sephardic Hazzanut: A Clarification of Nusah Hatefillah as Dominant in Our Era." Translated from Hebrew by Wilfred Wolfson. *Journal of Jewish Music and Liturgy* 19 (1996–97): 19–29

Bastiaensen, A. "Psalmi, Hymni, and Cantica in Early Jewish Tradition." Pages 15–26 in *Second Century: Tertullian to Nicaea in the West, Clement of Alexandria and Origen, Athanasius.* Vol. 3 of *Papers Presented to the Tenth International Conference on Patristic Studies Held in Oxford, 1987.* Edited by Elizabeth A. Livingstone. StPatr 21. Leuven: Peeters, 1989.

Bataillon, Marcel. "Evangelisme et millénarisme au Nouveau Monde." In *Courants religieux et humanisme a la fin du XVe siècle.* Colloque Strasbourg. Paris: Presses universitaires de France, 1959.

———. “Nouveau Monde et Fin du Monde.” *L’Education Nationale* 32 (11 dic. 1952): 3–6.

Baumstark, Anton. *Comparative Liturgy*. Translated by F. L. Cross. Revised by Bernard Botte. Westminster, Md.: Newman, 1958. 3d edition of *Liturgie comparée*. Chevetogne: Éditions de Chevetogne, 1939.

———. *Festbrevier und Kirchenjahr der syrischen Jakobiten*. Studien zur Geschichte und Kultur des Altertums 3/3–5. Paderborn: Schönigh, 1910.

———. “Das Gesetz der Erhaltung des Alten in liturgisch hochwertiger Zeit.” *Jahrbuch für Liturgiewissenschaft* 7 (1927): 1–23.

Baun, Jane R. “Middle Byzantine Tours of Hell: Outsider Theodicy?” Pages 47–60 in *Strangers to Themselves: The Byzantine Outsider*. Edited by Dion Smythe. Aldershot, U.K.: Ashgate; Burlington, Vt.: Variorum: 2000.

Becker, J. *Das Heil Gottes*. Göttingen: Vandenhoeck & Ruprecht, 1964.

Bell, Richard H. *Provoked to Jealousy: The Origin and Purpose of the Jealousy Motif in Romans 9–11*. WUNT 2/63; Tübingen: Mohr Siebeck, 1994.

Berg, Knut. *Studies in Twelfth-Century Tuscan Illumination*. Oslo: Universitetsforlaget, 1968

Berger, Klaus. “Hellenistische Gattungen im Neuen Testament.” *ANRW* 25.2:1031–1885.

Beutler, Johannes. “Greeks Come to See Jesus (John 12.20f).” *Bib* 71 (1990): 333–47.

———. “Psalm 42/43 im Johannesevangelium.” *NTS* 23 (1978–79): 33–57.

Bieber, Margarete. *The History of the Greek and Roman Theater*. Princeton: Princeton University Press, 1961.

Bieri, Anton. *Der Chor in der alten Komödie: Ritual und Performativität (unter besonderer Berücksichtigung von Aristophanes’ Thesmophoriazusen und der Phalloslieder fr. 851 PMG)*. Munich: Saur, 2001.

Bieringer, Reimund, Didier Pollefeyt, and Frederique Vandecasteele-Vanneuville. “Wrestling with Johannine Anti-Judaism: A Hermeneutical Framework for the Analysis of the Current Debate” Pages 3–37 in *Anti-Judaism and the Fourth Gospel: Papers of the Leuven Colloquium, 2000*. Edited by Reimund Bieringer, Didier Pollefeyt, and Frederique Vandecasteele-Vanneuville. Jewish and Christian Heritage Series 1. Assen: Van Gorcum, 2001.

Blank, Debra Reed. “It’s Time to Take Another Look at ‘Our Little Sister’ Soferim: A Bibliographical Essay.” *JQR* 90 (1999): 1–26.

Bloch, Chana. *Spelling the Word: George Herbert and the Bible*. Berkeley and Los Angeles: University of California Press, 1985.

Bloemendaal, Willem. *The Headings of the Psalms in the East Syrian Church*. Leiden: Brill, 1960.

Boles, John. *Black Southerns: 1619–1869*. Lexington: University of Kentucky Press, 1984.

Bond, Gilbert I. *Community, Communitas, and Cosmos: Toward a Phenomenological Interpretation and Theology of Traditional Afro-Christian Worship.* Lanham, Md.: Catholic Scholar's Press, 2003.

Bono. "Pocket Canon" introduction to *The Book of Psalms.* New York: Grove, 1999.

Borrof, Edith, and Marjory Irvin. *Music in Perspective.* New York: Harcourt Brace Jovanovich, 1976.

Boutemy, Andre. "Les enlumineurs de l'abbaye de Saint-Amand." *Revue belge d'archéologie et d'histoire de l'art* 12 (1942): 131–67.

Bouwsma, William. *John Calvin: A Sixteenth Century Portrait.* New York: Oxford University Press, 1988.

Bowie, Ewen L. "Greek Sophists and Greek Poetry in the Second Sophistic." *ANRW* 33.1:209–58.

Bradshaw, Paul F. *Daily Prayer in the Early Church: A Study of the Origin and Early Development of the Divine Office.* London: SPCK, 1981.

———. "From Word to Action: The Changing Role of Psalmody in Early Christianity." Pages 21–37 in *Like a Two-Edged Sword: The Word of God in Liturgy and History: Essays in Honor of Canon Donald Gray.* Edited by Martin R. Dudley. Norwich, Norfolk: Canterbury, 1995.

———. *The Search for the Origins of Christian Worship: Sources and Methods for the Study of Early Liturgy.* New York: Oxford University Press, 1992.

Bradshaw, Paul F., and Lawrence A. Hoffman, eds. *The Changing Face of Jewish and Christian Worship in North America.* Notre Dame, Ind.: University of Notre Dame Press, 1991.

Bradshaw, Paul F., Maxwell E. Johnson, and L. Edward Phillips. *The Apostolic Tradition: A Commentary.* Edited by Harold W. Attridge. Minneapolis: Fortress, 2002.

Brakke, David. "Jewish Flesh and Christian Spirit in Athanasius of Alexandria." *JECS* 9 (2001): 453–81.

Braun, Joachim. "Some Remarks on the Music History of Ancient Israel/Palestine: Written or Archaeological Evidence?" Pages 135–39 in *Musikarchäologie früher Metallzeiten.* Vol. 2 of *Studien zur Musikarchäologie.* Edited by Ellen Hickmann, Ingo Laufs, and Ricardo Eichmann. Orient-Archäologie 7. Rahden: Leidorf, 2000.

Brent, Allen. "John as Theologos: The Imperial Mysteries and the Apocalypse." *JSNT* 75 (1999): 87–102.

Brightman, Frank E., ed. *Liturgies Eastern and Western: Being the Texts, Original or Translated, of the Principal Liturgies of the Church.* Based on the former work by C. E. Hammon. Oxford: Clarendon Press, 1896.

Brock, Sebastian. "Translating the Old Testament." Pages 87–98 in *It Is Written: Scripture Citing Scripture: Essays in Honor of Barnabas Lindars,*

SSF. Edited by D. A. Carson and H. G. M. Williamson. Cambridge: Cambridge University Press, 1988.

Bronstein, Herbert. *A Passover Haggadah.* New York: Grossman, 1974.

Brown, Raymond E. *The Birth of the Messiah: A Commentary on the Infancy Narratives in Matthew and Luke.* Garden City, N.Y.: Doubleday, 1977.

———. *The Community of the Beloved Disciple: The Life, Loves, and Hates of an Individual Church in New Testament Times.* New York: Paulist, 1979.

———. *The Death of the Messiah: From Gethsemane to the Grave, A Commentary on the Passion Narratives in the Four Gospels.* 2 vols. ABRL. New York: Doubleday, 1994.

Brucker, Ralph. *"Christushymnen" oder "epideiktische Passagen"? Studien zum Stilwechsel im Neuen Testament und seiner Umwelt.* FRLANT 176. Göttingen: Vandenhoeck & Ruprecht, 1997.

Burkhart, Louise. "The Amanuenses Have Appropriated the Text: Interpreting a Náhuatl Song of Santiago." Pages 339–55 in *On the Translation of Native American Literatures.* Edited by Brian Swann. Washington, D.C.: Smithsonian Institution Press, 1992.

———. "A Doctrine for Dancing: The Prologue to the Psalmodia Christiana." *Latin American Indian Literatures Journal* 11 (1995): 21–33.

———. "Flowery Heaven: The Aesthetic of Paradise in Náhuatl Devotional Literature." *Res* 21 (1992): 89–109.

———. "El Tlauculcuicatl de Sahagún: Un lamento Náhuatl." Pages 219–64 in *Bernardino de Sahagún: Diez estudios acerca de su obra.* Edited by Ascensión Hernández de León-Portilla, Mexico City, Fondo de Cultura Económica, 1990.

Burkhart, Louise, and James T. Burtchaell. *From Synagogue to Church: Public Services and Offices in the Earliest Christian Communities.* Cambridge: Cambridge University Press, 1992.

Buttenwieser, Moses. 1969. *The Psalms, Chronologically Treated with a New Translation.* New York: Ktav, 1969.

Cahn, Walter. "Heresy in the Interpretation of Romanesque Art." Pages 27–33 in *Romanesque and Gothic: Essays for George Zarnecki.* Edited by N. Stratford. Woodbridge, Suffolk: Boydell, 1987.

———. *Romanesque Manuscripts: The Twelfth Century.* 2 vols. London: Miller, 1996.

———. *Studies in Medieval Art and Interpretation.* London: Pindar, 2000.

Calame, Claude. *Choruses of Young Women in Ancient Greece: Their Morphology, Religious Role, and Social Functions.* Rev. ed. Translated by Derek Collins and Janice Orion. Lanham: Rowman & Littlefield, 2001.

———. "Performative Aspects of the Choral Voice in Greek Tragedy: Civic Identity in Performance." Pages 125–53 in *Performance Culture and*

Athenian Democracy. Edited by Simon Goldhill and Robin Osborne. Cambridge: Cambridge University Press, 1999.

Carrasco, David. *Quetzalcóatl and the Irony of Empire: Myths and Prophecies in the Aztec Tradition*. Chicago: University of Chicago Press, 1982.

———. *Religions of Mesoamerica*. San Francisco: Harper & Row, 1990.

———. "The Sacrifice of Tezcatlipoca." Pages 31–57 in *To Change Place: Aztec Ceremonial Landscapes*. Edited by David Carrasco. Niwot: University of Colorado Press, 1991.

Chadwick, Henry. *The Early Church*. Harmondsworth: Penguin, 1967.

Chaldaiakis, Achilles G., ed. *Θεωρία καὶ Πράξη τῆς Ψαλτικῆς Τέχνης· Πρακτικὰ Α΄ Πανελληνίου Συνεδρίου Ψαλτικῆς Τέχνης ('Αθῆνα, 3–5 Νοεμβρίου)*. Athens: Institute of Byzantine Musicology of the Holy Synod of the Church of Greece, 2001.

Charlesworth, James H. "A Prolegomenon to a New Study of the Jewish Background of the Hymns and Prayers in the New Testament." *JJS* 33 [*Essays in Honour of Yigael Yadin*] (1982): 265–85.

Chatziagiakoumes, Manolis. *Χειρόγραφα ἐκκλησιαστικῆς μουσικῆς (1453–1820)*. Athens: National Bank of Greece, 1980.

Chazon, Esther G. "Hymns and Prayers in the Dead Sea Scrolls." Pages 244–70 in vol. 1 of *The Dead Sea Scrolls after Fifty Years: A Comprehensive Assessment*. Edited by Peter W. Flint and James C. VanderKam. Leiden: Brill, 1998.

Checa Cremades, Fernando. *Carlos V: La imagén del poder en el Renacimeinto*. Madrid: Ediciones del Viso, 1999.

———. *Carlos V y la imagén del héroe en el Renacimiento*. Madrid: Taurus, 1987.

Childs, Brevard. "Psalms Titles and Midrashic Exegesis." *JSS* 16 (1971): 137–50.

Chira, Robert. *From Aleppo to America: The Story of Two Families*. New York: Rovercross, 1994.

Christodoulos (Pareskeviades), Archbishop. *'Εγχειρίδιον ἱεροψάλτου· Βασικαὶ τοῦ ἱεροψάλτου ὑποχρεώσεις ὡς συμβολὴ εἰς τὴν Λειτουργικὴν ἀναγέννησιν*. 3d ed. Athens: Apostolike Diakonia, 2001.

Clanchy, Michael T. *From Memory to Written Record: England 1066–1307*. 2d ed. Oxford: Blackwell, 1993.

Clendinnen, Inga. *Aztecs: An Interpretation*. Cambridge: Cambridge University Press, 1991.

Clifford, Richard J. "The Case for Inclusive Language in the Lectionary." *Church* 16/2 (2000): 21–24.

———. "The Rocky Road to a New Lectionary." *America* 174/4 (16–23 August 1997): 18–22.

Cody, Aelred. "The Early History of the Octoechos in Syria." Pages 89–113 in *East of Byzantium: Syria and Armenia in the Formative Period*.

Edited by Nina G. Garsoïan, Thomas F. Mathews, and Robert W. Thomson. Washington, D.C.: Dumbarton Oaks, Center for Byzantine Studies, 1982.

Colish, Marcia. *Peter Lombard.* 2 vols. Leiden: Brill, 1994.

———. "'Psalterium scholasticorum.' Peter Lombard and the Development of Scholastic Psalms Exegesis." *Spec* 67 (1992): 531–48.

Collamore, Lila. "Prelude: Charting the Divine Office." Pages 3–11 in *The Divine Office in the Latin Middle Ages.* Edited by Margot E. Fassler and Rebecca A Baltzer. New York: Oxford University Press, 2000.

Collins, John J. *Apocalypticism in the Dead Sea Scrolls.* London: Routledge, 1997.

———. *The Scepter and the Star.* New York: Doubleday, 1995.

Colombás, García M. *El monacato primitivo.* 2 vols. Madrid: Biblioteca de autores cristianos, 1975.

Conomos, Dimitri E. *The Late Byzantine and Slavonic Communion Cycle: Liturgy and Music.* Dumbarton Oaks Studies 21. Washington, D.C.: Dumbarton Oaks Research Library and Collection, 1985.

———. "Sacred Music in the Post-Byzantine Era." Pages 83–105 in *The Byzantine Legacy in Eastern Europe.* Edited by Lowell Clucas. Eastern European Monographs 230. Boulder, Colo.: East European Monographs; New York: Columbia University Press, 1988.

Cooper, Allan. "The Life and Times of King David according to the Book of Psalms." Pages 117–31 in *The Poet and the Historian: Essays in Literary and Historical Biblical Criticism.* Edited by Richard Elliot Friedman. Chico, Calif.: Scholars Press, 1983.

Corrigan, Kathleen A. *Visual Polemics in the Ninth-Century Byzantine Psalters.* New York: Cambridge University Press, 1992.

Cottret, Bernard. *Calvin: A Biography.* Translated by M. Wallace McDonald. Grand Rapids: Eerdmans, 2000.

Creach, Jerome F. D. *Yahweh as Refuge and the Editing of the Hebrew Psalter.* JSOTSup 217. Sheffield: Sheffield Academic Press, 1996.

Cross, Frank Moore. *Canaanite Myth and Hebrew Epic.* Cambridge: Harvard University Press, 1973.

Cross, Frank Moore, and David Noel Freedman. *Studies in Ancient Yahwistic Poetry.* Grand Rapids: Eerdmans, 1997.

Crouzet, Denis. *Les guerriers de Dieu: La violence au temps des troubles de religion, 1525–1610.* 2 vols. Seyssel: Champ Vallon, 1990.

Csapo, Eric, and William J. Slater. *The Context of Ancient Drama.* Ann Arbor: University of Michigan Press, 1995.

Curtin, Philip D. *The Atlantic Slave Trade: A Census.* Madison: University of Wisconsin Press, 1969.

Daly-Denton, Margaret. *David in the Fourth Gospel: The Johannine Reception of the Psalms.* AGJU 47. Leiden: Brill, 2000.

Daniels, Harold M. "Service Books and Ecumenism: Response to the Berakah Award." In *Proceedings of the North American Academy of Liturgy 1995*. Valpraiso, Ind.: The Academy, 1995.

Danzinger, Hillel. *The Art Scroll Tehillim*. Brooklyn, N.Y.: Mesorah, 1988.

Davidson, Israel, Assaf Assaf, and Issachar Joel, eds. *Siddur Rav Saadiah Gaon*. Jerusalem: Mekitse Nirdamim, Re'uben Mas, 1963.

Davila, James R. *Liturgical Works*. Eerdmans Commentaries on the Dead Sea Scrolls 6. Grand Rapids: Eerdmans, 2000.

De Jongh, James A. "'An Anatomy of All Parts of the Soul': Insights into Calvin's Spirituality from His Psalms Commentary." Pages 1–14 in *Calvinus Sacrae Scripturae Professor: Calvin as Confesor of Holy Scripture*. Edited by Wilhelm H. Neuser. Grand Rapids: Eerdmans, 1994.

Dekkers, Eligius. "Were the Early Monks Liturgical." *Collectanea Cisterciensia* 22 (1960): 120–37.

Delling, Gerhard. "ὕμνος, κ.τ.λ." *TDNT* 8:489–503.

Desby, Frank. "The Growth of Liturgical Music in the Iakovian Era." Pages 303–23 in *History of the Greek Orthodox Church in America*. Edited by M. B. Ephthimiou and G. A. Christopoulos. New York: Greek Orthodox Archdiocese of North and South America, 1984.

deSilva, David. *Perseverance in Gratitude: A Socio-rhetorical Commentary on the Epistle "to the Hebrews."* Grand Rapids: Eerdmans, 2000.

Deutsch, Diana, ed. *The Psychology of Music*. 2d ed. San Diego: Academic Press, 1999.

Diefendorf, Barbara. *Beneath the Cross: Catholics and Huguenots in Sixteenth-Century Paris*. Oxford: Oxford University Press, 1991.

Dodd, C. H. *According to the Scriptures: The Sub-structure of New Testament Theology*. London: Nisbet, 1952.

Dolbeau, Frangois. "La bibliothèque de l'abbaye de Hasnon, O.S.B., d'après un catalogue du XIIe siècle." *Revue des études augustiniennes* 34 (1988): 209–29.

Dorival, Giles, and Alain Le Boulluec. *Origeniana Sexta: Origène et la Bible*. Leuven: Leuven University Press, 1995.

Douen, Orentin. *Clément Marot et le Psautier huguenot: Étude historique, littéraire, musicale et bibliographique*. 2 vols. Paris: Imprimerie Nationale, 1878–79.

Douglas, Michael C. "The Teacher Hymn Hypothesis Revisited: New Data for an Old Crux." *DSD* 6 (1999): 239–66.

Dover, Kenneth J. *Greek Homosexuality*. Cambridge: Harvard University Press, 1978.

Dragoumis, Markos Ph. "Constantinos A. Psachos (1869–1949): A Contribution to the Study of His Life and Work." Pages 77–88 in vol. 5 of *Studies in Eastern Chant*. Edited by Dimitri Conomos. Crestwood: St. Vladimir's Seminary Press, 1990.

Drillock, David. "Liturgical Song in the Worship of the Church." *St. Vladimir's Theological Quarterly* 41 (1997): 183–218.

———. *Orthodox Church Music.* 2 vols. Crestwood, N.Y.: St. Vladimir's Seminary Press, 1984–85.

Durán, Diego. *Book of the God and Rites and The Ancient Calendar.* Edited and translated by Fernando Horcasitas and Doris Heyden. Norman: University of Oklahoma Press, 1977.

Dyer, Joseph. "Monastic Psalmody of the Middle Ages." *RBén* 99 (1989): 41–74.

———. "The Singing of Psalms in the Early-Medieval Office." *Spec* 64 (1989): 535–78.

Ebach, Jürgen, and Richard Faber, eds. *Bibel und Literatur.* Munich: Fink, 1995.

Eckman, Barbara. "A Quantitative Metrical Analysis of the Philippians Hymn." *NTS* 26 (1980): 258–66.

Eire, Carlos M. N. *War against the Idols: The Reformation of Worship from Erasmus to Calvin.* New York: Cambridge University Press, 1986.

Eisenbaum Pamela Michelle. *The Jewish Heroes of Christian History: Hebrews 11 in Literary Context.* SBLDS 156. Atlanta: Scholars Press, 1997.

Eisenstein, Judah David. *Otsar Dinim Uminhagim.* New York: Aizenshtain, 1917.

Elazar, Daniel J. *The Other Jews: The Sephardim Today.* New York: Basic Books, 1989.

Elbogen, Ismar. *Jewish Liturgy: A Comprehensive History.* Translated by Raymon P. Scheindlin. Philadelphia: Jewish Publication Society, 1993. Based on *Der judische Gottesdienst in Seiner Geschichtlichen, Entwicklung.* Leipzig: Fock, 1913. Repr., Hildesheim: Olms, 1962.

Ellis, Earl E. *Paul's Use of the Old Testament.* Grand Rapids: Eerdmans, 1985.

Engberg-Pedersen, Troels. "Philo's *De vita contemplativa* as a Philosopher's Dream." *JSJ* 30 (1999): 40–64.

Engdahl, Richard. *Beiträge der byzantinischen Liturgie.* Berlin: Trowitzsch, 1908.

Epstein, Dena J. *Sinful Tunes and Spirituals: Black Folk Music to the Civil War.* Urbana: University of Illinois Press, 1977.

Erwin, H. M. "Theological Aspects of the Septuagint of the Book of Psalms." Ph.D. diss. Princeton University, 1962.

Eshel, E. "The Identification of the 'Speaker' of the Self-Glorification Hymn." Pages 619–35 in *The Provo International Conference on the Dead Sea Scrolls.* Edited by Donald W. Parry and Eugene Ulrich. STDJ 30. Leiden: Brill, 1999.

Falk, Daniel F. *Daily, Festival, and Sabbath Prayers from Qumran.* STDJ 27. Leiden: Brill, 1997.

Faruqi, Lois Ibsen al-. "The Cantillation of the Qur'an." *Asian Music* 19 (1987): 2–25.

Fassler, Margot. "Composer and Dramatist: 'Melodious Singing and the Freshness of Remorse.'" Pages 149–75 in *Voice of the Living Light: Hildegard of Bingen and Her World.* Edited by Barbara Newman. Berkeley and Los Angeles: University of California Press, 1998.

———. "Music for the Love Feast: Hildegard of Bingen and the Song of Songs." In *Women's Voices across Musical Worlds.* Edited by Jane Bernstein. Boston: Northeastern University Press, 2003.

Fee, Gordon D. "Philippians 2:5–11: Hymn or Exalted Pauline Prose?" *BBR* 2 (1992): 29–46.

Feldman, Louis H. "Philo's Views on Music." Pages 504–28 in idem, *Studies in Hellenistic Judaism.* AGJU 30. Leiden: Brill, 1996. Repr. from *Journal of Jewish Music and Liturgy* 9 (1986–87): 36–54.

Felman, Shoshana, and Dori Laub. *Testimony: Crises of Witnessing in Literature, Psychoanalysis, and History.* New York: Routledge, 1992.

Ferguson, Everett. "Psalm-Singing at the Eucharist: A Liturgical Controversy in the Fourth Century." *Austin Seminary Bulletin* 98 (1983): 52–77.

Ferrari, Giovanni R. F. *Listening to the Cicadas: A Study of Plato's Phaedrus.* Cambridge Classical Studies. Cambridge: Cambridge University Press, 1987.

Fiedrowicz, Michael. *Psalmos vox totius Christi: Studien zu Augustine "Enarrationes in Psalmos."* Freiburg im Breisgau: Herder, 1997.

Fiensy, David A. *Prayers Alleged to be Jewish: An Examination of the Constitutiones Apostolorum.* BJS 65. Chico, Calif.: Scholars Press, 1985.

Fischer, Balthasar. "Die Psalmenfrömmigkeit der Märtyrerkirche." Pages 17–18 in *Die Psalmen als Stimme der Kirche.* Edited by Andreas Heinz. Trier: Paulinus-Verlag, 1982.

Fitzmyer, Joseph A. "The Aramaic Background of Philippians 2:6–11." *CBQ* 50 (1988): 470–83.

Fleischer, Ezra. "Chadashot L'inyan 'Rosh Roshei Chodashim.'" In *Mechkarim B'aggadah, Targumim, Ut'fillot Yisrael L'zekher Yosef Heinemann.* Edited by Ezra Fleischer and Jakob Petuchowski. Jerusalem: Magnes, 1981.

———. "Chekrei Fiyut V'shirah." *Tarbiz* 39 (1970): 19–38, 248–67.

———. "Rosh Roshei Chodashim." *Tarbiz* 37 (1968): 265–78.

———. *T'fillah Uminhagei T'fillah Erets Yisra'eliyim Bit'kufat Hagenizah.* Jerusalem: Magnes, 1988.

Fleming, John. "Christopher Columbus as a Scriptural Exegete." *LQ* 5 (1991): 187–98.

Flesher, Paul Virgil McCracken. "Palestinian Synagogues before 70 C.E.: A Review of the Evidence." Pages 67–81 in *Studies in the Ethnography and Literature of Judaism.* Vol. 6 of *Approaches to Ancient Judaism.*

Edited by Jacob Neusner and Ernest S. Frerichs. BJS 192. Atlanta: Scholars Press, 1989.

Flint, Peter W. *The Dead Sea Psalms Scroll and the Book of Psalms.* STDJ 17. Leiden: Brill, 1997.

Flint, Valerie J. "Some Notes on the Early Twelfth-Century Commentaries on the Psalms." *Recherches de théologie ancienne et médiévale* 38 (1971): 80–88.

Flusser, David. "Psalms, Hymns, and Prayers." Pages 551–77 in *Jewish Writings of the Second Temple Period: Apocrypha, Pseudepigrapha, Qumran, Sectarian Writings, Philo, Josephus.* Edited by Michael E. Stone. CRINT 2/2. Assen: Van Gorcum; Minneapolis: Fortress, 1984.

Foley, Edward. *Foundations of Christian Music: The Music of Pre-Constantinian Christianity,* American Essays in Liturgy. Collegeville, Minn.: Liturgical Press, 1996.

Follieri, Enrica. "L'innografia bizantina dal contacio al canone." Pages 1–32 in *Da bizanzio a San Marco: Musica e liturgia.* Edited by Giulio Cattin. Quaderni di "Musica e storia" 2. Venice: Societá editrice "Il mulino," 1997.

Follis, Elaine R., ed. *Directions in Biblical Hebrew Poetry.* JSOTSup 40. Sheffield: JSOT Press, 1987.

Fonrobert, Charlotte Elisheva. "The *Didascalia Apostolorum:* A Mishnah for the Disciples of Jesus." *JECS* 9 (2001): 483–509.

Fontaine, J. *Naissance de la Poésie dans l'Occident Chrétien.* Paris: Études augustiniennes, 1981.

Freedman, David Noel. "Divine Names and Titles in Early Hebrew Poetry." Pages 55–107 in *Magnalia Dei, the Mighty Acts of God: Essays on the Bible and Archaeology in Memory of G. Ernest Wright.* Edited by Frank Moore Cross, Werner E. Lemke, and Patrick D. Miller Jr. Garden City, N.Y.: Doubleday, 1976.

Freedman, Jacob. *Polychrome Historical Haggadah for Passover.* Springfield, Mass.: Jacob Freedman Liturgy Research Foundation, 1974.

Freehof, Solomon B. *The Book of Psalms: A Commentary.* Cincinnati: Union of American Hebrew Congregations, 1938.

Freeman, Barbara. "Practicing Christian Rock." Pages 221–31 in *One Nation Under God? Religion and American Culture.* Edited by Marjorie Garber and Rebecca L. Walkowitz. New York: Routledge, 1999.

Frei, Hans. *The Eclipse of Biblical Narrative.* New Haven: Yale University Press, 1974.

Frenske, W. "'Das Lied des Mose, des Knechtes Gottes, und das Lied de Lammes' (Apokalypse de Johannes 15,3f). Der Text und seine Bedeutung für die Johannes-Apokalypse." *ZNW* 90 (1999): 250–64.

Fritsch, Charles T. "Studies in the Theology of the Greek Psalter." Pages 729–41 in *Zer li-qevurot.* Edited by Ben-Zion Luria. Jerusalem: World Union of Jewish Studies, 1973.

Froyshov, Stig S. “La réticence à l’hymnographie chez les anchorètes de l’Égypte et du Sinaï du 6e au 8e siècles.” Pages 229–45 in *L’hymnographie: Conférences Saint-Serge.* Edited by Achille M. Triacca and Alessandro Pistoia. BEL.S 105. Rome: CLV-Edizioni liturgiche, 2000.

Fujita, Neil S. *A Crack in the Jar: What Ancient Jewish Documents Tell Us about the New Testament.* New York: Paulist, 1986.

Gager, John G. “Jews, Gentiles, and Synagoges in the Book of Acts.” Pages 91–99 in *Christians among Jews and Gentiles: Essays in Honor of Krister Stendahl on His Sixty-Fifth Birthday.* Edited by George W. E. Nickelsburg and George W. MacRae. Philadelphia: Fortress, 1986.

Gain, Benoît. *L’église de Cappadoce au IVe siècle d’après la correspondance de Basile de Césarée (330–379).* OCA 225. Rome: Pontificium Institutum Orientale, 1985.

Galavaris, George. *Bread and the Liturgy: The Symbolism of Early Christian and Byzantine Bread Stamps.* Madison: University of Wisconsin Press, 1970.

Gamble, Harry Y. *Books and Readers in the Early Church: A History of Early Christian Texts.* New Haven: Yale University Press, 1995.

García Martínez, Florentino, and Eibert J. Tigchelaar. *The Dead Sea Scrolls Study Edition.* 2 vols. Leiden: Brill, 1997.

Garitte, Gerard. “Un fragment grec attribué à S. Antoine l’Ermite.” *Bulletin de l’Institut historique belge de Rome* 20 (1939): 165–70

Garrigues, Jean-Miguel, and Jean Legrez. *Moines dans l’assemblée des fidèles à l’époque des pères: IVe–VIIIe siècle.* Théologie historique 87. Paris: Beauschesne, 1990.

Garrison, Edward B. *Studies in the History of Medieval Italian Painting.* 4 vols. Florence: L’Imprenta, 1953–63.

Gélineau, Joseph. “Les psaumes à l’époque patristique,” *La Maison-Dieu* 135 (1978): 99–116.

Gentili, Bruno, and Roberto Pretagostini, eds. *La Musica in Grecia.* Bari: Laterza, 1988.

Georgiou, Kosmas I. “ Ἡ ἑβδομαδιαία ἀτφωνικὴ κατανομὴ τῶν ψαλμῶν καὶ τῶν ᾠδῶν εἰς τὰς Ἀσματικὰς Ἀκολουθίας ἑσπερινοῦ. Ἑλλήικοὶ Μουσικοὶ Κώδικες 2061–2062 Ἐθνικῆς Βιβλιοθήκης Ἀθήῶν.” Ph.D. diss. Pontifical Oriental Institute, 1976.

Gerald, Wilson. *The Editing of the Hebrew Psalter.* SBLDS 76. Chico, Calif.: Scholars Press, 1985.

Gerstenberger, Erhard S. *Psalms: Part I with an Introduction to Cultic Poetry.* FOTL 14. Grand Rapids: Eerdmans, 1988.

Gewhehr, Wesley M. *The Great Awakening in Virginia, 1740–1790.* Durham, N.C.: Duke University Press, 1930.

Gibson, Margaret T., Timothy A. Heslop, and Richard A. Pfaff. *The Eadwine Psalter: Text Image and Monastic Culture in Twelfth-Century*

Canterbury. Publications of the Modern Humanities Research Association 14. University Park: Pennsylvania State University Press, 1992.

Gillingham, Susan E. *The Poems and Psalms of the Hebrew Bible*. Oxford: Oxford University Press, 1994.

Gisbert, Teresa, and José de Mesa. *Arquitectura Andina*. La Paz: Colección Arsanz, 1985.

Glaser, Lynn. *Indians or Jews? An Introduction to Manasseh Ben Israel's "The Hope of Israel."* Gilroy, Calif.: Boswell, 1973.

Glaze, Florence Eliza. "Medical Writer: 'Behold the Human Creature.'" Pages 125–48 in *Voice of the Living Light: Hildegard of Bingen and Her World*. Edited by Barbara Newman. Berkeley and Los Angeles: University of California Press, 1998.

Glunz, Hans Hermann. *History of the Vulgate in England from Alcuin to Roger Bacon*. Cambridge: Cambridge University Press, 1933.

Goldhill, Simon, and Robin Osborne. *Performance Culture and Athenian Democracy*. Cambridge: Cambridge University Press, 1999.

Goldschmidt, Ernst Daniel. "Seder Hatefillah shel Harambam." In *Mechkarei Tefillah Ufiyut*. Edited by Ernst Daniel Goldschmidt. Jerusalem: Magnes, 1979.

———. *Seder Rav Amram Gaon*. Jerusalem: Magnes, 1971.

Grabar, André. *Christian Iconography: A Study of Its Origins*. Bollingen Series 35/10. Princeton: Princeton University Press, 1968.

Greenblatt, Stephen. *Renaissance Self-Fashioning: From More to Shakespeare*. Chicago: University of Chicago Press, 1980.

Greenfield, Richard P. H. "Evil Eye." Pages 596–97 in vol. 1 of *Encyclopedia of Greece and the Hellenic Tradition*. Edited by Graham Speake. London: Fitzroy Dearborn, 2000.

Greengrass, Mark. *The French Reformation*. Oxford: Blackwell, 1987.

Grisbrooke, W. Jardine, and Alexander Schmemann. "Liturgical Reform: A Debate." *St. Vladimir's Theological Quarterly* 13 (1969): 212–24. Repr., *Liturgy and Tradition: Theological Reflections of Alexander Schmemann*. Edited by Thomas Fisch. Crestwood, N.Y.: St. Vladimir's Seminary Press, 1990.

Gross-Diaz, Theresa. *The Psalms Commentary of Gilbert of Poitiers: From Lectio Divina to the Lecture Room*. Leiden: Brill, 1996.

Gruenwald, Ithamar. "God the 'Stone/Rock': Myth, Idolatry, and Cultic Fetishism in Ancient Israel." *JR* 76 (1996): 428–49.

Guest, Harriet. *A Form of Sound Words: The Religious Poetry of Christopher Smart*. Oxford: Clarendon Press, 1989.

Guinot, Jean Nöel. "L'*In Psalmos* de Théodoret: Une relecture critique du Commentaire de Diodore de Tarse." Pages 97–134 in *Le Psautier chez les Pères*. Introduction by Pierre Maraval. Cahiers de Biblia Patristica 4. Strasbourg: Centre d'analyse et de documentation patristiques, 1994.

Gunkel, Hermann. *An Introduction to the Psalms.* Completed by Joachim Begrich. Translated by James D. Nogalski. Macon, Ga.: Mercer University Press, 1998.

Gurrieri, John. "The Perception of Jews in Christian Liturgy: Then and Now." Pages 46–65 in *The Changing Face of Jewish and Christian Worship in North America.* Edited by Paul F. Bradshaw and Lawrence A. Hoffman. Notre Dame, Ind.: University of Notre Dame Press, 1991.

Guthrie, William Keith Chambers. "Hymns." *OCD,* 534.

Gutmann, Joseph, ed. *The Synagogue: Studies in Origins, Archaelogy and Architecture.* New York: Ktav, 1975.

Hall, Gwendolyn Midlo. *Africans in Colonial Louisiana: The Development of Afro-Creole Culture in the Eighteenth Century.* Baton Rouge: Louisiana State University Press, 1992.

Hamel, Christopher de. *Glossed Books of the Bible and the Origins of the Paris Booktrade.* Woodbridge, Suffolk: Brewer, 1984.

Hanke, Gregor. "Der Odenkanon des Tagzeitenritus Konstaniopels im Licht der Beiträge H. Schneiders und O. Strunks—eine Relectur." Pages 345–67 in *Crossroad of Cultures: Studies in Liturgy and Patristics in Honor of Gabriele Winkler.* Edited by Hans-Jürgen Feulner, Elena Velkovska, and Robert F. Taft. OCA 260. Rome: Pontificium Institutum Orientalium Studiorum, 2000.

Häring, Nikolaus M. "Commentary and Hermeneutics." Pages 173–200 in *Renaissance and Renewal in the Twelfth Century.* Edited by Robert L. Benson and Giles Constable. Cambridge: Harvard University Press, 1982.

Harper, John. *Forms and Orders of Western Liturgy from the Tenth to the Eighteenth Century: A Historical Introduction and Guide for Students and Musicians.* New York: Oxford University Press, 1991.

Harrison, Martin. *A Temple for Byzantium: The Discovery and Excavation of Anicia Juliana's Palace Church in Istanbul.* Austin: University of Texas Press, 1989.

Harvey, A. E. "The Classification of Greek Lyric Poetry." *CQ* 49 (1955): 157–75.

Hawkins, Peter S. *Dante's Testaments: Essays in Scriptural Imagination.* Stanford, Calif.: Stanford University Press, 1999.

Hay, David M. *Glory at the Right Hand: Psalm 110 in Early Christianity.* SBLMS 18. Nashville: Abingdon, 1973.

Hays, Richard B. *Echoes of Scripture in the Letters of Paul.* New Haven: Yale University Press, 1989.

Heinemann, Joseph. *Prayer in the Talmud Forms and Patterns.* Translated by Richard S. Sarason. SJ 9. Berlin: de Gruyter, 1977.

Herman, Judith. *Trauma and Recovery: The Aftermath of Violence—From Domestic Abuse to Political Terror.* New York: Basic Books, 1977.

Hertz, Joseph H. *The Authorised Daily Prayer Book*. Rev. ed. New York: Bloch, 1948.

Heschel, Abraham Joshua. *The Earth Is the Lord's and the Sabbath*. New York: Harper Torchbooks, 1966.

Heyden, Doris. "Metaphors, Nahualtocaitl, and Other 'Disguised' Terms among the Aztecs." Pages 35–43 in *Symbol and Meaning beyond the Closed Community: Essays in Mesoamerican Ideas*. Edited by Gary Gossen. Albany: Institute for Mesoamerican Studies, State University of New York, 1986.

Higman, Francis. "Calvin the Writer." Unpublished manuscript. New Haven: Yale University, 1989.

———. *La diffusion de la Réforme en France, 1520–1565*. Geneva: Labor et Fides, 1992.

Hiley, David. *Western Plainchant: A Handbook*. Oxford: Clarendon Press, 1993.

Hill, C. E. "Chrysostom's Commentary on the Psalms: Homilies or Tracts?" Pages 301–17 in *Prayer and Spirituality in the Early Church*. Edited Pauline Allen et al. Queensland: Australian Catholic University, 1998.

Hoffman, Lawrence A. *Beyond the Text: A Holistic Approach to Liturgy*. Bloomington, Ind.: Indiana University Press, 1987.

———. *The Canonization of the Synagogue Service*. University of Notre Dame Center for the Study of Judaism and Christianity in Antiquity 4. Notre Dame, Ind.: University of Notre Dame Press, 1979.

———. "What Is a Liturgical Tradition?" Pages 3–25 in *The Changing Face of Jewish and Christian Worship in North America*. Edited by Paul F. Bradshaw and Lawrence A. Hoffman. Notre Dame, Ind.: University of Notre Dame Press, 1991.

Hoffmann, Wilhelm. "Der Psalmenkommentar des Petrus Lombardus in einer Bilderhandschrift der Württembergischen Landesbibliothek." *Neue Heidelberger Jahrbücher* NS (1939): 67–83.

Hollander, John. "The Psalms." Pages 244–62 in *Congregation: Contemporary Writers Read the Jewish Bible*. Edited by David Rosenberg. San Diego: Harcourt Brace Jovanovich, 1987.

Holm-Nielsen, Svend. *Hodayot. Psalms from Qumran*. Acta theologica Danica 2. Aarhus: Universitetsforlaget, 1960.

Höpfl, Harro M. *The Christian Polity of John Calvin*. Cambridge: Cambridge University Press, 1982.

Horbury, William. "Old Testament Interpretation in the Writings of the Church Fathers." Pages 727–87 in *Mikra: Text, Translation, Reading and Interpretation of the Hebrew Bible in Ancient Judaism and Early Christianity*. CRINT 2/1. Edited by Martin Jan Mulder. Assen: Van Gorcum; Minneapolis: Fortress, 1990.

Horsley, Richard A. *Jesus and the Spiral of Violence.* San Francisco: Harper & Row, 1987.

Horst, Pieter W. van der. "The Greek Synagogue Prayers in the Apostolic Constitutions." Pages 19–46 in *From Qumran to Cairo: Studies in the History of Prayer: Proceedings of the Research Group Convened under the Auspices of the Institute for Advanced Studies of the Hebrew University of Jerusalem, 1997.* Edited by Joseph Tabory. Jerusalem: Orhot Press, 1999.

Hossfeld, Frank-Lothat, and Erich Zenger. "Die Psalmen 1–50." In *Die Neue Echter Bibel: Kommentar zum Alten Testament mit der Einheits Übersetzung.* Würzburg: Echter, 1993.

Huddleston, Lee Eldridge. *Origins of the American Indian: European Concepts, 1492–1929.* Austin: University of Texas Press, 1965.

Husmann, Heinrich. "Hymnus und Troparion: Studien zur Geschichte der musikalischen Gattungen von Horologion und Tropologion." Pages 7–86 in *Jahrbuch des Staatlichen Instituts für Musikforschung Preußischer Kulturbestitz 1971.* Berlin: de Gruyter, 1972.

Idelsohn, Abraham Z. *Gesange Der orientalischen Sefardim.* Hebraish-orientalisher Melodienschatz. Jerusalem: Hartz, 1923.

———. *Jewish Music in Its Historical Development.* New York: Holt, 1929. Repr., New York: Dover, 1992.

———. "Die Makeman in der hebraischen Poesie der orientalischen Juden." *MGWJ* 57 (1913): 314–25.

Ingalls, Wayne B. "Ritual Performance as Training for Daughters in Archaic Greece." *Phoenix: Journal of the Classical Association of Canada* 54 (2000): 1–20.

Irigoin, Jean. "Il salterio nella versione dei Settanta: Alla ricerca di una poetica." Pages 23–34 in *La traduzione dei testi religiosi: Atti del convegno tenuto a Trento il 10–11 febbraio 1993.* Edited by Claudio Moreschini and Giovanni Menestrina. Collana "Religione e Cultura" 6. Brescia: Morcelliana, 1994.

———. "Le Psaume 26 dans la Septante: Étude de compositions rythmique." Pages 287–97 in *Κατά τούς ό = Selon les Septante: Trente études sur la Bible grecque des Septante en hommage à Marguerite Harl.* Edited by Gilles Dorival and Olivier Munnich. Paris: Cerf, 1995.

Jacob, André. "Une version géorgienne inédite de la Liturgie de S. Jean Chrysostome." *Mus* 77 (1964): 65–117.

Jacobs, Joseph. "Tribes, Lost Ten." *JE* 12:249–53.

Jakab, Attila. "Le judaïsme hellénisé d'Alexandrie depuis la fondation de la ville jusqu'à la révolte sous Trajan." *Hen* 21 (1999): 147–64.

Janowski, Bernd. "Die 'Kleine Biblia': Zur Bedeutung der Psalmen für eine Theologie des Alten Testaments." Page 403 in *Der Psalter in Judentum und Christentum.* Edited by Erich Zenger. Herder's Biblical Studies 18. Freiburg: Herder, 1998.

Jeannin, Jules, and Julien Puyade. "L'Octoëchos syrien." *OrChr* NS 3 (1913): 82–104, 277–98.

Jeannin, Jules. "Octoëchos surien." *DACL* 12/2:1888–1900

Jeffery, Peter. "Monastic Reading and the Emerging Roman Chant Repertory." Pages 45–103 in *Western Plainchant in the First Millenium: Studies of the Medieval Liturgy and Its Music in Memory of James W. McKinnon.* Aldershot, U.K.: Ashgate; Burlington, Vt.: Variorum, 2003.

———. *A New Commandment: Toward a Renewed Rite for the Washing of Feet.* Collegeville, Minn.: Liturgical Press, 1992.

———. "The Sunday Office of Seventh-Century Jerusalem in the Georgian Chantbooks (Iadgari): A Preliminary Report." *Studia liturgica* 21 (1991): 52–75.

———. "Werner's *The Sacred Bridge* Volume 2: A Review Essay." *JQR* 77 (1987): 283–98.

Jenny, M. "Cantica." *TRE* 7:624–28.

Jeremias, G. *Der Lehrer der Gerechtigkeit.* Göttingen: Vandenhoeck & Ruprecht, 1963.

Johnson, David Read. "Creative Therapies." In *Effective Treatments for PTSD.* Edited by Edna B. Foa, Terence M. Keane, and Matthew J. Friedman. New York: Guilford, 2000.

Jones, Charles Colock. *Religious Instruction of the Negroes in the United States.* Savanna, Ga.: Purse, 1842.

Jones, Serene. *Calvin and the Rhetoric of Piety.* Louisville: Westminster John Knox, 1995.

Joubert, S. J. "A Bone of Contention in Recent Scholarship: The 'Birkat ha-Minim' and the Separation of Church and Synagogue in the First Century AD." *Neot* 27 (1993): 351–63.

Jungmann, Joseph A. *The Mass of the Roman Rite: Missarum sollemnia.* 2 vols. New York: Benziger, 1951–55. Repr., Westminster, Md.: Christian Classics, 1986.

Kadir, Djelal. *Columbus and the Ends of the Earth.* Berkeley and Los Angeles: University of California Press, 1992.

Kamesar, Adam. "Philo and the Literary Quality of the Bible: A Theoretical Aspect of the Problem." *JJS* 46 (1995): 55–68.

Karff, Samuel E. "The Perception of Christians in Jewish Liturgy: Then and Now." Pages 31–45 in *The Changing Face of Jewish and Christian Worship in North America.* Edited by Paul F. Bradshaw and Lawrence A. Hoffman. Notre Dame, Ind.: University of Notre Dame Press, 1991.

Karris, Robert J. *Luke: Artist and Theologian: Luke's Passion Account as Literature.* New York: Paulist, 1985.

Kerby-Fulton, Kathryn. "Prophet and Reformer: 'Smoke in the Vineyard.'" Pages 70–90 in *Voice of the Living Light: Hildegard of Bingen and Her World.* Edited by Barbara Newman. Berkeley and Los Angeles: University of California Press, 1998.

Kessler, Herbert L. *The Illustrated Bibles from Tours.* Studies in Manuscript Illumination 7. Princeton: Princeton University Press, 1977.

Kieval, Herman. "Pesukei De-Zimra." *EncJud* 13:335.

Kingdon, Robert M. *Adultery and Divorce in Calvin's Geneva.* Cambridge: Harvard University Press, 1995.

———. "The Control of Morals in Calvin's Geneva." Pages 3–16 in *The Social History of the Reformation.* Edited by Lawrence P. Buck and Jonathan W. Zophy. Columbus: Ohio State University Press, 1972.

Kinzig, Wolfram. *In Search of Asterius: Studies on the Authorship of the Homilies on the Psalms.* Forschungen zur Kirchen- und Dogmengeschichte 47. Göttingen: Vandenhoeck & Ruprecht, 1990.

Kistemaker, Simon J. *The Psalm Citations in the Epistle to the Hebrews.* Amsterdam: van Soest, 1961.

Kittel, Bonnie. *The Hymns of Qumran.* SBLDS 50. Missoula, Mont.: Scholars Press, 1981.

Klauser. Theodor. *A Short History of the Western Liturgy.* Oxford: Oxford University Press, 1979.

Klemm, Elisabeth. *Die romanischen Handschriften der Bayerischen Staatsbibliothek.* Wiesbaden: Reichert, 1980.

Klentos, John E. *Byzantine Liturgy in Twelfth-Century Constantinople: An Analysis of the Synaxarion of the Monastery of the Theotokos Evergetis* (codex *Athens Ethnike Bibliotheke 788).* Ph.D. diss. University of Notre Dame, 1995; Ann Arbor: University Microfilms International Dissertation Service, 1997.

Kligman, Mark. "The Bible, Prayer, and Maqam: Extra-Musical Associations of Syrian Jews." *Ethnomusicology* 45 (2001): 443–79.

———. "Modes of Prayer: Arabic Maqamat in the Sabbath Morning Liturgical Music of the Syrian Jews in Brooklyn." Ph.D. diss. New York University, 1997.

Knohl, Israel. *The Messiah before Jesus: The Suffering Servant of the Dead Sea Scrolls.* Berkeley and Los Angeles: University of California Press, 2000.

Knowles, Michael P. "'The Rock, His Work is Perfect': Unusual Imagery for God in Deuteronomy XXXII." *VT* 39 (1989): 307–22.

Kock, Dietrich-Alex. *Die Schrift als Zeuge des Evangeliums: Untersuchungen zur Verwendung und zum Verstandnis der Schrift bei Paulus.* Tübingen: Mohr Siebeck, 1986.

Koester, Craig R. *Hebrews: A New Translation with Introduction and Commentary.* AB 36. New York: Doubleday, 2001.

———. *Symbolism in the Fourth Gospel: Meaning, Mystery, Community.* Minneapolis: Fortress, 1995.

Kolbaba, Tia M. *The Byzantine Lists: Errors of the Latins.* Urbana: University of Illinois Press, 2000.

Kratz, Reinhard Gregor. "Die Tora Davids. Psalm 1 und die doxologisch Fünfteilung des Psalters." *ZTK* 93 (1994): 1–34.

Kraus, Hans-Joachim. *Psalms 60–150: A Commentary.* Translated by Hilton C. Oswald. Minneapolis: Augsburg, 1989.

Kuczynski, Michael P. *Prophetic Song: The Psalms as Moral Discourse in Late Medieval England.* Philadelphia: University of Pennsylvania Press, 1995.

Kugel, James L. "David the Prophet." Pages 45–55 in *Poetry and Prophecy: The Beginning of a Literary Tradition.* Edited by James L. Kugel. Ithaca, N.Y.: Cornell University Press, 1990.

———. *The Idea of Biblical Poetry: Parallelism and Its History.* New Haven: Yale University Press, 1981.

Kuhn, Heinz-Wolfgang. *Enderwartung und Gegenwärtiges Heil.* SUNT 4. Göttingen: Vandenhoeck & Ruprecht, 1966.

Kytzler, Bernhard. "Moderne Psalmen." Pages 157–81 in *Bibel und Literatur.* Edited by Jürgen Ebach and Richard Faber. Munich: Fink, 1995.

Lafaye, Jacques. *Mesías, cruzadas, utopias.* Mexico: Fondo de la Cultura Económica, 1988.

Lafont, Ghislain. "The Eucharist in Monastic Life." *Cistercian Studies* 19 (1984.): 296–318.

Lamb, John A. *The Psalms in Christian Worship.* London: Faith Press, 1962.

Lamberton, *Robert. Homer the Theologian.* Berkeley and Los Angeles: University of California Press, 1986.

Lanne, Emmanuel. "Les dix leçons de *Liturgie Comparée* d'Anton Baumstark au Monastère d'Amay-sur-Meuse en 1932: Leur contexte et leur publication." Pages 145–61 in *Acts of the International Congress Comparative Liturgy Fifty Years after Anton Baumstark (1872–1948).* Edited by Robert F. Taft and Gabriele Winkler. OCA 265. Rome: Pontificium Institutum Orientalium Studiorum, 2001.

LaPorte, Jean. *Eucharistia in Philo.* Studies in the Bible and Early Christianity 3. New York: Mellen, 1983.

Lara, Jaime. *City, Temple, Stage: Eschatological Architecture and Liturgical Theatrics in New Spain.* Notre Dame, Ind.: University of Notre Dame Press, forthcoming.

———. "Precious Green Jade Water: A Sixteenth-Century Adult Catechumenate in the New World," *Worship* 71 (1997): 415–29.

Latyshev, Vasilij. "Zhitie prep. Feodora Studita v mjunzenskoj rukopisi No 467." *Vizantijshij Vremennik* 21 (1914): 222–54.

Lauterbach, Jakob Z., ed. *Mekilta d'Rabbi Ishmael.* 3 vols. Philadelphia: Jewish Publication Society of America, 1949.

Leclercq, Henri. "Communion (Rite et antienne de)." *DACL* 3/2:2427–33.

Leclercq, Jean. *The Love of Learning and the Desire for God.* 3d ed. Translated by Catherine Misrahi. New York: Fordham University Press, 1982.

Leeb, Helmut. *Die Gesänge im Gemeindegottesdienst von Jerusalem (vom 5. bis 8. Jahrhundert).* Wiener Beiträge zur Theologie 28. Vienna: Herder, 1970.

———. *Die Psalmodie bei Ambrosius.* Wiener Beiträge zur Theologie 18. Vienna: Herder, 1967.

Leonhardt, Jutta. *Jewish Worship in Philo of Alexandria.* Texts and Studies in Ancient Judaism 84. Tübingen: Mohr Siebeck, 2001.

León-Portilla, Ascensión Hernández de, ed. *Bernardino de Sahagún: Diez estudios acerca de su obra.* Mexico City: Fondo de Cultura Económica, 1990.

Levarie, Siegmund. "Philo on Music." *Journal of Musicology* 9 (1991): 124–30.

Levine, Lee I. *The Ancient Synagogue: The First Thousand Years.* New Haven: Yale University Press, 2000.

Levy, Kenneth, and Christian Troelsgård. "Byzantine Chant." Pages 734–56 in vol. 4 of *The New Grove Dictionary of Music and Musicians.* Edited by Stanley Sadie. 2d ed. 29 vols. London: Macmillan, 2001.

Levy, Kenneth. "A Hymn for Thursday in Holy Week." *Journal of the American Musicological Society* 16 (1963): 127–75.

Lewalksi, Barbara. *Protestant Poetics and the Seventeenth-Century Religious Lyric.* Princeton: Princeton University Press, 1979.

Lewy, Hans. *Sobria ebrietas: Untersuchungen zur Geschichte der antiken Mystik.* BZNW 9. Giessen: Töpelmann, 1929.

Leyerle, Blake. "Meal Customs in the Greco-Roman World." Pages 29–61 in *Passover and Easter: Origin and History to Modern Times.* Edited by Paul F. Bradshaw and Lawrence A. Hoffman. Two Liturgical Traditions 5. Notre Dame, Ind.: Notre Dame University Press, 1999.

Lingas, Alexander. "Festal Cathedral Vespers in Late Byzantium." *OCP* 63 (1997): 421–59.

———. "Hesychasm and Psalmody." Pages 155–68 in *Mount Athos and Byzantine Monasticism.* Edited by Anthony Bryer and Mary Cunningham. Brookfield, Vt.: Variorum, 1996.

———. "The Liturgical Use of the Kontakion in Constantinople." Pages 50–57 in *Liturgy, Architecture and Art of the Byzantine World: Papers of the XVIII International Byzantine Congress (Moscow, 8–15 August 1991) and Other Essays Dedicated to the Memory of Fr. John Meyendorff.* Byzantinorossica 1. Edited by Constantin C. Akentiev. St. Petersburg: Vizantinorossika, 1995.

———. "Music." Pages 1097–1104 in vol. 2 of *Encyclopedia of Greece and the Hellenic Tradition.* 2 vols. Edited by Graham Speake. London: Fitzroy Dearborn, 2000.

———. "Sunday Matins in the Byzantine Cathedral Rite: Music and Liturgy." Ph.D. diss. University of British Columbia, 1996.

Lissarrague, François. *The Aesthetics of the Greek Banquet: Images of Wine and Ritual.* Translated by Andrew Szegedy-Maszak. Princeton: Princeton University Press, 1990.

Lockhart, James. *The Nahuas after the Conquest: A Social and Cultural History of the Indians of Central Mexico, Sixteenth through Eighteenth Centuries.* Stanford, Calif.: Stanford University Press, 1992.

Lohfink, Norbert. "Psalmen in Neuen Testament: Die Lieder in der Kindheitsgeschichte bei Lukas." Pages 105–25 in *Neue Wege der Psalmenforschung.* Edited by Klaus Seybold and Erich Zenger. Herders Biblical Studies 1. Freiburg: Herder, 1994.

Lohmeyer, Ernst. *Kyrios Jesus: Eine Untersuchung zu Phil. 2,5–11.* Heidelberg: Winter, 1928. Repr., Darmstadt: Wissenschaftliche Buchgesellschaft, 1961.

Lohse, Eduard. *Colossians and Philemon: A Commentary on the Epistles to the Colossians and to Philemon.* Hermeneia. Philadelphia: Fortress, 1971.

Louf, André, et al. *The Message of Monastic Spirituality.* New York: Desclée, 1964.

Lubac, Henri de. *La posteridad espiritual de Joaquín de Fiore.* 2 vols. Madrid: Encuentro Editiones, 1989.

Mann, Jacob. "Genizah Fragments of the Palestinian Order of Service." Pages 379–448 in *Contributions to the Scientific Study of Jewish Liturgy.* Edited by Jakob J. Petuchowski. New York: Ktav, 1970.

Manniche, Lise. *Music and Musicians in Ancient Egypt.* London: British Museum Press, 1991.

Marcus, Scott L. "Arab Music Theory in the Modern Period." Ph.D. diss. University of California-Los Angeles, 1989.

Mariani, Paul. *A Commentary on the Complete Poems of Gerard Manley Hopkins.* Ithaca, N.Y.: Cornell University Press, 1970.

Mariès, Louis. *Études préliminaires à l'édition de Diodore de Tarse sur les Psaumes: La tradition manuscrite, deux manuscrits nouveaux, le caractère diodorien du commentaire.* Collection d'Études anciennes, publiée sous le patronage de l'Association Guillaume Budé. Paris: Les Belles Lettres, 1933.

Marrou, Henri-Irénée. *Histoire de l'éducation dans l'antiquité.* 6th ed. Paris: Seuil, 1964.

Martin, Ralph P. *A Hymn of Christ: Philippians 2:5–11 in Recent Interpretation and in the Setting of Early Christian Worship.* Downers Grove, Ill.: InterVarsity Press, 1997.

Mateos, Juan. *La célébration de la parole dans la liturgie byzantine: Étude historique.* OCA 191. Rome: Pontificium Institutum Orientalium

Studiorum, 1971. Pages 7–26, "La psalmodie: ses genres," were first published as "La psalmodie dans le rite byzantin." *Proche-orient chrétien* 15 (1965): 107–26.

———. "Une collection syrienne de «prières entre les marmyata»." *OCP* 31 (1965): 53–75, 304–35.

———. *Lelya-Sapra: Les offices chaldéens de la nuit et du matin.* 2d ed. OCA 156. Rome: Pontificium Institutum Orientalium Studiorum, 1972.

———. "The Origins of the Divine Office." *Worship* 41 (1967): 477–85.

———. "La psalmodie variable dans l'office byzantin." *Societas Academica Dacoromana Acta philosophica et theologica* 2 (1964): 325–39.

———. "La synaxe monastique des vêpres byzantines." *OCP* 36 (1970): 248–72.

Mathews, Thomas F. *The Early Churches of Constantinople: Architecture and Liturgy.* University Park: Pennsylvania State University Press, 1971.

Mathiesen, Thomas J. *Apollo's Lyre: Greek Music and Music Theory in Antiquity and the Middle Ages.* Publications of the Center for the History of Music Theory and Literature, Indiana University 2. Lincoln: University of Nebraska Press, 1999.

———. "Harmonia and Ethos in Ancient Greek Music." *Journal of Musicology* 3 (1984): 264–79.

———. "Hermes or Clio? The Transmission of Ancient Greek Music Theory." Pages 3–35 in *Musical Humanism and Its Legacy: Essays in Honor of Claude V. Palisca.* Edited by Barbara R. Hanning and Nancy K. Baker. New York: Pendragon, 1992.

———. "Rhythm and Meter in Ancient Greek Music." *Music Theory Spectrum* 7 (1985): 159–80.

Mays, James L. "Calvin's Commentary on the Psalms: The Preface as Introduction." Pages 195–204 in *John Calvin and the Church: A Prism of Reform.* Louisville: Westminster John Knox, 1990.

———. "The Center of the Psalms: 'The Lord Reigns' as Root Metaphor." Pages 12–22 in *The Lord Reigns: A Theological Handbook to the Psalms.* Edited by James L. Mays. Louisville: Westminster John Knox, 1994.

———. "The David of the Psalms." *Int* 40 (1986): 143–55.

———, ed. *The Lord Reigns: A Theological Handbook to the Psalms.* Louisville: Westminster/John Knox, 1994.

McCann, J. Clinton. "Books I–III and the Editorial Purpose of the Psalter." Pages 93–107 in *The Shape and Shaping of the Psalter.* Edited by J. Clinton McCann. JSOTSup 159. Sheffield: JSOT Press, 1993.

McCarter, P. Kyle. *1 Samuel: A New Translation with Introduction and Commentary.* AB 8. Garden City, N.Y.: Doubleday, 1980.

McGrath, Alister. *A Life of John Calvin.* Oxford: Blackwell, 1990.

McKinnon, James. *The Advent Project: The Later-Seventh-Century Creation of the Roman Mass Proper.* Berkeley and Los Angeles: University of California Press, 2000.

———. "Christian Antiquity." Pages 68–87 in *Antiquity and the Middle Ages: From Ancient Greece to the Fifteenth Century.* Edited by James McKinnon. Englewood Cliffs, N.J.: Prentice Hall, 1991.

———. "Desert Monasticism and the Later Fourth-Century Psalmodic Movement." *Music and Letters* 75 (1994): 505–19. Repr. as ch. 11 in McKinnon, *The Temple.*

———. *The Temple, the Church Fathers and Early Western Chant.* Brookfield, Vt.: Ashgate, 1998.

McNeil, Brian. "The Odes of Solomon and the Scriptures." *OrChr* 67 (1983): 104–22.

Meeks, Wayne. "Breaking Away: Three New Testament Pictures of Christianity's Separation from the Jewish Communities." Pages 89–113 in *Essential Papers on Judaism and Christianity in Conflict: From Late Antiquity to the Reformation.* Edited by Jeremy Cohen. Essential Papers on Jewish Studies. New York: New York University Press, 1991.

Melling, David. "Music." Pages 328–31 in *The Blackwell Dictionary of Eastern Christianity.* Edited by Ken Parry et al. Oxford: Blackwell, 1999.

Menken, Maarten J. J. "The Translation of Psalm 41:10 in John 13:18." *JSNT* 40 (1990): 61–79.

———. "The Use of the Septuagint in Three Quotations in John: Jn 10, 34; 12, 38; 19, 24." Pages 367–93 in *The Scriptures in the Gospels.* Edited by Christopher M. Tuckett. BETL 131. Leuven: Leuven University Press, 1997.

Menn, Esther M. "No Ordinary Lament: Relecture and the Identity of the Distressed in Psalm 22." *HTR* 93 (2000): 301–41.

———. "Praying King and Sanctuary of Prayer, Part I: David and Temple Origins in Rabbinic Psalms Commentary (*Midrash Tehillim*)." *JJS* 52 (2001): 1–26.

———. "Praying King and Sanctuary of Prayer, Part II: David's Deferment and the Temple's Dedication in Rabbinic Psalms Commentary (*Midrash Tehillim*)." *JJS* 53 (2002): 298–323.

Merindol, Christian de. *La production des livres peints à l'Abbaye de Corbie au XIIe siècle: Étude historique et archéologique.* 3 vols. Lille: Service de reproduction des thèses de l'Université, 1976.

Metzger, Marcel. "Expressions hymniques dans les *Constitutions apostoliques.*" Pages 59–71 in *L'hymnographie: Conférences Saint-Serge.* Edited by Achille M. Triacca and Alessandro Pistoia. BEL.S 105. Rome: CLV-Edizioni liturgiche, 2000.

Mews, Constant J. "Religious Thinker: 'A Frail Human Being' on Fiery Life." Pages 52–69 in *Voice of the Living Light: Hildegard of Bingen and Her*

World. Edited by Barbara Newman. Berkeley and Los Angeles: University of California Press, 1998.

———, ed. *Listen, Daughter: The Speculum Virginum and the Formation of Religious Women in the Middle Ages*. Basingstoke: Palgrave, 2001.

Michaelides, Solon. *The Music of Ancient Greece: An Encyclopedia*. London: Faber, 1978.

Milhou, Alain. *Colón y su mentalidad mesiánica en el ambiente franciscanista español*. Valladolid: Casa-Museo Colón, 1983).

Millar, Fergus. *The Roman Near East 31 B.C.–A.D. 337*. Cambridge: Harvard University Press, 1993.

Miller, Patrick D. "The Beginning of the Psalter." Pages 83–92 in *The Shape and Shaping of the Psalter*. Edited by J. Clinton McCann. JSOTSup 159. Sheffield: JSOT Press, 1993.

———. "Kingship, Torah Obedience, and Prayer: The Theology of Psalms 15–24." Pages 127–42 in *Neue Wege der Psalmenforschung*. Edited by Klaus Seybold and Erich Zenger. Herders Biblical Studies 1. Freiburg: Herder, 1994.

———. "The Poetry of Creation: Psalm 104." Pages 87–103 in *God Who Creates: Essays in Honor of W. Sibley Towner*. Edited by William P. Brown and Sean D. McBride Jr. Grand Rapids: Eerdmans, 2000.

———. *They Cried to the Lord: The Form and Theology of Israelite Prayer*. Minneapolis: Fortress, 1994.

Milovanović-Barham, Čelica. "Gregory of Nazianzus: Ars Poetica (In suos versus: Carmen 2.1.39)." *JECS* 5 (1997): 497–510.

Minnis, Alastair J. *Medieval Theories of Authorship*. 2d ed. Philadelphia: University of Pennsylvania Press, 1988.

Mitchell, Linda, ed. *Women in Medieval Western European Culture*. New York: Garland, 1999.

Mitchell, Nathan. "The Liturgical Code in the Rule of Benedict." Pages 379–414 in *RB 1980: The Rule of St. Benedict in Latin and English with Notes*. Edited by Timothy Fry. Collegeville, Minn.: Liturgical Press, 1981.

Monter, William. *Calvin's Geneva*. New York: Wiley, 1967.

———. "The Consistory of Geneva, 1559–1569." *Bibliothèque d'humanisme et renaissance* 38 (1976): 467–84.

Moran, Neil K. "Byzantine Castrati." In *XXe Congrès international des études byzantines: Collège de France-Sorbonne, 19–25 août 2001: Pré-Actes 3: Communications libres*. Paris: Collège de France, 2001.

———. *Singers in Late Byzantine and Slavonic Painting*. Byzantina Neerlandica, Fasc. 9. Leiden: Brill, 1986.

Motyer, Stephen. "The Fourth Gospel and the Salvation of Israel: An Appeal for a New Start." Pages 92–110 in *Anti-Judaism and the Fourth Gospel: Papers of the Leuven Colloquium, 2000*. Edited by Reimund

Bieringer, Didier Pollefeyt, and Frederique Vandecasteele-Vanneuville. Jewish and Christian Heritage Series 1. Assen: Van Gorcum, 2001.

Mueller, Joel, ed. *Chiluf Minhagim Bein Bavel V'erets Yisra'el.* 1870. Repr., Jerusalem: Makor, 1970.

Mullen, William. *Choreia: Pindar and Dance.* Princeton: Princeton University Press, 1982.

Murray, Oswyn, ed. *Sympotica: A Symposium on the Symposion.* Oxford: Clarendon Press, 1990.

Naphy, William G. *Calvin and the Consolidation of the Genevan Reformation.* New York: Manchester University Press, 1994.

Nasuti, Harry. *Defining the Sacred Songs: Genre, Tradition, and the Post-Critical Interpretation of the Psalms.* Sheffield: Sheffield Academic Press, 1999.

Nelson, Kristina. *The Art of Reciting the Qur'an.* Austin: University of Texas Press, 1985.

———. "Reciter and Listener: Some Factors Shaping the *Mujawwad* Style of Qur'anic Reciting." *Ethnomusicology* 26 (1982): 41–47.

Neusner, Jacob. *The Formation of the Jewish Intellect.* BJS 151. Atlanta: Scholars Press, 1988.

———. *The Glory of God Is Intelligence: Four Lectures on the Role of Intellect in Judaism.* Salt Lake City: Religious Studies Center, Brigham Young University, 1978.

———. "System or Tradition? The Babli and Its Sources." Pages 127–83 in *Judaic and Christian Interpretations of Texts: Contents and Contexts.* Edited by Jacob Neusner and Ernest S. Frerichs. New Perspectives on Ancient Judaism 3. Lanham, Md.: University Press of America, 1987.

Newman, Barbara. *Sister of Wisdom: St. Hildegard's Theology of the Feminine.* 2d ed. Berkeley and Los Angeles: University of California Press, 1997.

———, ed. *Voice of the Living Light: Hildegard of Bingen and Her World.* Berkeley and Los Angeles: University of California Press, 1998.

Newsom, Carol. *Songs of the Sabbath Sacrifice: A Critical Edition.* HSS 27. Atlanta: Scholars Press, 1985.

Nilsson, Martin P. *Geschichte der griechischen Religion.* 3d ed. 2 vols. Munich: Beck, 1974.

Nordenfalk, Carl. *Die spätantiken Zierbuchstaben.* Stockholm: Egnellska boktr., 1970.

Nowacki, Edward. "Antiphonal Psalmody in Christian Antiquity and the Early Middle Ages." Pages 287–315 in *Essays on Medieval Music in Honor of David G. Hughes.* Edited by Graeme M. Boone. Isham Library Papers 4. Cambridge: Harvard University Department of Music, 1995.

Nulman, Macy. "Musical Service of Syrian Synagogue: Its Structure and Design." *Journal of Jewish Music and Liturgy* 2 (1977–78): 34–56.

Oikonomou, Philippos Ath. *Το Νέο «Μουσικό Ζήτημα» στην Ορθόδοξη Εκκλησία*. Eliki, Aegio: n.p., 2002.

Olofsson, Staffan. *God Is My Rock: A Study of Translation Technique and Theological Exegesis in the Septuagint*. Stockholm: Almqvist & Wiksell, 1990.

Pallad, Tom, ed. *A Guide to Congregational Singing*. N.p.: National Forum of Greek Orthodox Musicians, 1991.

Parenti, Stefano. "La celebrazione delle Ore del Venerdì Santo nell'eucologio G.b.X. di Grottaferrata (X–XI sec.)." *Bolletino della Badia Greca di Grottaferrata* 44 (1990): 81–124.

Parker, L. P. E. *The Songs of Aristophanes*. Oxford: Clarendon Press, 1997.

Parker, Thomas H. L. *Calvin's Old Testament Commentaries*. Louisville: Westminster John Knox, 1986.

———. *John Calvin*. Philadelphia: Westminster, 1977.

Parkes, Malcolm B. "The Influence of the Concepts of *Ordinatio* and *Compilatio* on the Development of the Book." Pages 115–41 in *Medieval Learning and Literature: Essays Presented to Richard William Hunt*. Edited by Jonathan G. Alexander and Margaret T. Gibson. Oxford: Clarendon Press, 1976.

Patai, Raphael. *The Messiah Texts: Jewish Legends of Three Thousand Years*. Detroit: Wayne State University Press, 1979.

Pearson, Birger A. "Christians and Jews in First-Century Alexandria." Pages 206–16 in *Christians among Jews and Gentiles: Essays in Honor of Krister Stendahl on His Sixty-Fifth Birthday*. Edited by George W. E. Nickelsburg and George W. MacRae. Philadelphia: Fortress, 1986.

Peterson, Jeanette Favrot. *The Paradise Garden Murals of Malinalco: Utopia and Empire in Sixteenth-Century Mexico*. Austin: University of Texas Press, 1993.

Peterson, Norman. *The Gospel of John and the Sociology of Light: Language and Characterization in the Fourth Gospel*. Valley Forge, Pa.: Trinity Press International, 1993.

Petuchowski, Jakob J. "The Liturgy of the Synagogue: History, Structure, and Contents." Pages 1–64 in *Studies in Liturgy, Exegesis, and Talmudic Narrative*. Vol. 4 of *Approaches to Ancient Judaism*. Edited by William Scott Green. BJS 27. Chico, Calif.: Scholars Press, 1983.

Phelan, John Leddy. *The Millennial Kingdom of the Franciscans in the New World*. 2d ed. Berkeley and Los Angeles: University of California Press, 1975.

Pickard-Cambridge, Arthur. *The Dramatic Festivals of Athens*. 2d ed. with supplement, revised by John Gould and D. M. Lewis. Oxford: Clarendon Press, 1988.

Pierik, Marie. *The Psalter in the Temple and the Church*. Washington, D.C.: Catholic University of America Press, 1957.

Platzner, Robert L. "In the Cleft of a Rock: Metaphors of Divine Concealment and Disclosure in the Hebrew Bible." Pages 29–37 in *Metaphor, Canon, and Community: Jewish, Christian, and Islamic Approaches.* Edited by Ralph Bisschops and James Francis. New York: Lang, 1999.

Pleket, H. W. "An Aspect of the Emperor Cult: Imperial Mysteries." *HTR* 58 (1965): 331–47.

Pöhlmann, Egert, and Martin L. West, eds. *Documents of Ancient Greek Music: The Extant Melodies and Fragments Edited and Transcribed with Commentary*. New York: Oxford University Press, 2001.

Popkin, Richard. "Jewish Christians and Christian Jews in Spain, 1492 and After." *Judiasm* 41 (1992): 248–68.

Porter, James. "Content and Form in Philodemus: The History of an Evasion." Pages 97–147 in *Philodemus and Poetry*. Edited by Dirk Obbink. New York: Oxford University Press, 1995.

Pott, Thomas. *La réforme liturgique byzantine: Étude du phénomène de l'évolution non-spontanée de la liturgie byzantine*. BEL.S 104. Rome: CLV-Edizioni liturgiche, 2000.

Powers, Harold S. "Melody." Pages 481–84 in *The New Harvard Dictionary of Music*. Edited by Don Michael Randel. Cambridge: Harvard University Press, 1986.

Pratt, Waldo Selden. *The Significance of the Old French Psalter*. New York: The Hymn Society, 1933.

Price, S. R. F. *Rituals and Power: The Roman Imperial Cult in Asia Minor*. Cambridge: Cambridge University Press, 1984.

Prosperi, Adriano. "New Heaven and New Earth: Prophecy and Propaganda at the Time of the Discovery and Conquest of the Americas." Pages 279–303 in *Prophetic Rome and the Renaissance*. Edited by Majorie Reeves. Oxford: Clarendon Press, 1992.

Pucket, David L. *John Calvin's Exegesis of the Old Testament*. Louisville: Westminster John Knox, 1995.

Puech, E. *La croyance des Esséniens en la vie future*. Paris: Gabalda, 1993.

Quasten, Johannes. *Music and Worship in Pagan and Christian Antiquity*. Translated by Boniface Ramsey. NPM Studies in Church Music and Liturgy. Washington, D.C.: National Association of Pastoral Musicians, 1983.

Rabinowitz, Louis Isaac. "Psalms, Book of, in the Liturgy." *EncJud* 13:1323–25.

Raft, Robert. *The Precommunion Rites*. OCA 261. Rome: Pontificium Institutum Orientalium Studiorum, 2000.

Rappaport, Roy. *Ecology, Meaning and Religion*. Berkeley, Calif.: North Atlantic Books, 1979.

Raptis, George, ed. *National Forum of Greek Orthodox Church Musicians Silver Anniversary 1976–2001*. Bloomington, Ind.: National Forum of Greek Orthodox Church Musicians, 2002.

Raven, D. S. *Greek Metre.* 2d ed. London: Faber & Faber, 1968. Repr., London: Bristol Classical Press, 1998.

Reeves, Marjorie. *The Influence of Prophecy in the Later Middle Ages: A Study in Joachimism.* Oxford: Clarendon Press, 1969.

Reeves, Marjorie, ed. *Prophetic Rome in the High Renaissance Period: Essays.* Oxford: Clarendon Press, 1992.

Régnault, Lucien. *La vie quotidienne des Pères du déserte en Égypte au IVe siècle.* Paris: Hachette, 1990.

Reichert, Andreas. "The Song of Moses (Duet 3) and the Quest for Early Deuteronomic Psalmody." Pages 53–60 in *August 1985 Proceedings: Ninth World Congress of Jewish Studies, Jerusalem.* Jerusalem: World Union of Jewish Studies, 1986.

Reif, Stefan C. *Judaism and Hebrew Prayer.* Cambridge: Cambridge University Press, 1993.

Reim, Günter. "Vom Hebräerbrief zum Johannesevangelium, anhand der Psalmzitate." *BZ* NS 44 (2000): 92–99.

Rendtorff, R. *Kanonische Grundlegung.* Vol. 1 of *Theologie des Alten Testaments: Ein kanonischen Entwurf.* Neukirchen-Vluyn: Neukirchener Verlag, 1999.

Renoux, Athanase Charles. ed. *Le codex arménien Jérusalem 121.* PO 36/1. Turnhout: Brepols, 1971.

Reynolds, Roger. "Divine Office." Pages 221–31 in vol. 4 of *Dictionary of the Middle Ages.* Edited by Joseph Strayer et al. 13 vols. New York: Scribner, 1982–89.

Ricard, Robert. *The Spiritual Conquest of Mexico: An Essay on the Apostolate and the Evangelizing Methods of the Mendicant Orders in New Spain, 1523–1572.* Translated by Lesley Byrd Simpson. Berkeley and Los Angeles: University of California Press, 1974.

Rightmyer, Nelson. *Maryland's Established Church.* Baltimore: Church Historical Society for the Diocese of Maryland, 1956.

Rock, David. *Music of the Whole Earth.* New York: Scribners, 1977.

Rooy, H. F. van. *Studies on the Syriac Apocryphal Psalms.* JSSSup 7. Leiden: Brill, 1999.

Rosenberg, A. J., ed. *Psalms: A New English Translation.* New York: Judaica, 1991.

Rosenberg. David, ed. *Congregation: Contemporary Writers Read the Jewish Bible.* San Diego: Harcourt Brace Jovanovich, 1987.

Rowley, H. H. *Worship in Ancient Israel: Its Forms and Meaning.* London: SPCK, 1967, 1981.

Ruiten, J. T. A. G. M. van. "The Use of Deuteronomy 32:39 in Monotheistic Controversies in Rabbinic Literature." Pages 223–41 in *Studies in Deuteronomy.* Edited by Florentino Garcia Martinez. VTSup 53. Leiden: Brill, 1994.

Runia, David T. *Philo in Early Christian Literature: A Survey.* CRINT 3/3. Assen: Van Gorcum; Minneapolis: Fortress, 1993.

Russell, Donald A. "Aristides and the Prose Hymn." Pages 199–219 in *Antonine Literature.* Edited by D. A. Russell. Oxford: Clarendon Press, 1990.

———. *Criticism in Antiquity.* Berkeley and Los Angeles: University of California Press, 1981.

Rutherford, Ian. *Pindar's Paeans.* Oxford: Oxford University Press, 2001.

Sala Catala, José, and Jaime Vilchis Reyes. "Apocalíptica Española y Empresa Misional en los Primeros Franciscanos de Mexico." *Revista de Indias* 45/176 (1985): 421–47

Salmon, J. H. M. *Society in Crisis: France in the Sixteenth Century.* New York: St. Martins, 1978.

Sanders, E. P. *Jesus and Judaism.* Philadelphia: Fortress, 1985.

Sanders, Jack T. "Nag Hammadi, the Odes of Solomon and NT Christological Hymns." Pages 51–66 in *Gnosticism and the Early Christian World: In Honor of James M. Robinson.* Edited by James E. Goehring et al. Sonoma, Calif: Polebridge, 1990.

Sanders, James A. *Canon and Community.* Philadelphia: Fortress, 1983.

———. *From Sacred Story to Sacred Text.* Philadelphia: Fortress, 1987.

Sanders, James, ed. *The Psalms Scroll of Qumran Cave 11 (11QPs^a).* Oxford: Clarendon Press, 1965.

Sanders, Paul. *The Provenance of Deuteronomy* 32. OTS 37. Leiden: Brill, 1996.

Sanders, Ronald. *Lost Tribes and Promised Lands: The Origins of American Racism.* Boston: Little Brown & Co., 1978, 1992.

Sarason, Richard S. "On the Use of Method in the Modern Study of Jewish Liturgy." Pages 97–172 in *Theory and Practice.* Vol. 1 of *Approaches to Ancient Judaism.* Edited by William Scott Green. BJS 1. Missoula, Mont.: Scholars Press, 1978.

Sarason, Richard S. "Religion and Worship: The Case of Judaism." Pages 59–65 in *Take Judaism, For Example.* Edited by Jacob Neusner. Chicago: University of Chicago Press, 1983.

Sarna, Nahum M., et al. "Psalms Book of." *EncJud* 13:1303–22.

Schade, Herbert. "Zur 'beseelten Säule' (=lithos empsychos) als Ursprung des Gottesbildes: Ein Beitrag zur kosmologisch-psychologischen Hermentituk der älteren Kunnstgeschichte." Pages 1–32 in *Aufsätze zur Kuntsgeschichte: Festrschift für Herman Bauer zum 60. Geburtstag.* Edited by Karl Möseneder and Andreas Praber. Hildesheim: Olms, 1991.

Schaef, Anne Wilson. *Meditations for Women Who Do Too Much.* San Francisco: HarperCollins, 1990.

Schaer, Ronald, et al., eds. *Utopia: The Search for the Ideal Society in the Western World.* New York: Oxford University Press, 2000.

Scheiber, A. *Geniza Studies.* Hildesheim: Olms, 1981.

Schiffman, Lawrence H. "The Dead Sea Scrolls and the Early History of Jewish Liturgy." Pages 33–48 in *The Synagogue in Late Antiquity.* Edited by Lee I. Levine. Philadelphia: ASOR, 1987.

Schmemann, Alexander. *For the Life of the World: Sacraments and Orthodoxy.* 4th printing of the rev. 2d ed. Crestwood, N.Y.: St. Vladimir's Seminary Press, 1988.

———. *Introduction to Liturgical Theology.* Translated by Asheleigh E. Moorhouse. 3d ed. Crestwood, N.Y.: St. Vladimir's Seminary Press, 1986.

Schmid, Wilhelm. *Die nachklassische Periode der griechischen Literatur.* Vol. 2 of *Wilhelm von Christs Geschichte der griechischen Literatur.* Edited by Walter Otto. Rev. ed. Handbuch der Altertumswissenschaft 7. Munich: Beck, 1924

Schmidt, Margot. "Maria: 'materia aurea' in der Kirche nach Hildegard von Bingen." Pages 262–83 in *Hildegard von Bingen: Prophetin durch die Zeiten.* Edited by Edeltraud Forster. Freiburg im Breisgau: Herder, 1997.

Schneider, Heinrich. "Die biblischen Oden im christlichen Altertum." *Bib* 30 (1949): 28–65.

Schnusenberg, Christine Catharina. *The Relationship between the Church and the Theatre, Exemplified by Selected Writings of the Church Fathers and by Liturgical Texts until Amalarius of Metz—775–852 AD.* Lanham, Md.: University Press of America, 1988.

Schuller, Eileen M. "Hodayot." Pages 69–254 in *Qumran Cave 4.XX: Poetical and Liturgical Texts, Part 2.* Edited by Esther Chazon. DJD 29. Oxford: Clarendon Press, 1999.

———. *Non-canonical Psalms from Qumran: A Pseudepigraphic Collection.* HSS 28. Atlanta: Scholars Press, 1986.

———. "Prayer, Hymnic, and Liturgical Texts from Qumran." Pages 153–71 in *The Community of the Renewed Covenant.* Edited by Eugene Ulrich and James VanderKam. Notre Dame, Ind.: University of Notre Dame Press, 1994.

Schulz, Frieder. "Die jüdischen Wurzeln des christlichen Gottesdienstes." Pages 15–36 in *Synaxis: Beiträge zur Liturgik: Zum 80. Geburtstag des Autors im Auftrag der Evangelischen Landeskirche in Baden.* Edited by Gerhard Schwinge. Göttingen: Vandenhoeck & Ruprecht, 1997.

Schulz, Hans-Joachim. *The Byzantine Liturgy: Symbolic Structure and Faith Expression.* Translated by Matthew J. O'Connell. New York: Pueblo, 1986.

Scott, William C. *Musical Design in Aeschylean Theater.* Hanover, N.H.: University Press of New England for Dartmouth College, 1984.

———. *Musical Design in Sophoclean Theater.* Hanover, N.H.: University Press of New England for Dartmouth College, 1996.

Sève, Michel, and Patrick Weber. "Un monument honorifique au forum de Philippes." *Bulletin de correspondence hellénique* 112 (1988): 467–79.

Shelemay, Kay Kaufman. *"Let Jasmine Rain Down": Song and Remembrance among Syrian Jews.* Edited by Philip V. Bohlman and Bruno Nettl. Chicago Studies in Ethnomusicology. Chicago: University of Chicago Press, 1998.

Sheridan, Susan Guise. "Biocultural Reconstruction of Kneeling Pathology in a Byzantine Judean Monastery." *American Journal of Physical Anthropology* Supplement 24 (1996): 209.

———. "'New Life the Dead Receive': The Relationship between Human Remains and the Cultural Record for Byzantine St. Stephen's." *RB* 106 (1999): 1–34.

Sheridan, Susan Guise, and Michael S. Driscoll. "Every Knee Shall Bend: A Biocultural Reconstruction of Liturgical and Ascetical Prayer in 5–7 Century Palestine." *Worship* 74 (2000): 453–68.

Sheridan, Susan Guise, and Sarah E. Niebuhr. "Vertebral Pathology from a Byzantine Judaean Monastery." Abstract, *American Journal of Physical Anthropology,* Supplement 26 (1996): 170.

Shewring, Walter Hayward, and Kenneth James Dover. "Prose-Rhythm." *OCD,* 888–90.

Sigal, Phillip. "Early Christian and Rabbinic Liturgical Affinities: Exploring Liturgical Acculturation." *NTS* 30 (1984): 63–90.

Simon, Uriel. *Four Approaches to the Book of Psalms: From Saadiah Gaon to Ibn Ezra.* Albany: State University of New York Press, 1991.

Slater, William J., ed. *Dining in a Classical Context.* Ann Arbor: University of Michigan Press, 1991.

Sly, Dorothy. *Philo's Perception of Women.* BJS 209. Atlanta: Scholars Press, 1990.

Smalley, Beryl. *The Study of the Bible in the Middle Ages.* Oxford: Blackwell, 1941; 2d ed., 1952.

Smith, J. A. "The Ancient Synagogue, The Early Church and Singing." *Music and Letters* 65 (1984): 1–16.

———. "First-Century Christian Singing and Its Relationship to Contemporary Jewish Religious Song." *Music and Letters* 75 (1994): 1–15.

Smith, Michael R. "In the 'Christian Rock' Sound You Can Hear God Whisper." *Fundamentalist Journal* 5/2 (1986): 22–23.

Smith, Morton. "Ascent to the Heavens and Deification in 4QM[a]." Pages 181–88 in *Archaeology and History in the Dead Sea Scrolls: The New York University Conference in Memory of Yigael Yadin.* Edited by Lawrence H. Schiffman. JSPSup 8; JSOT/ASOR Monographs Series 2. Sheffield: JSOT Press, 1990.

Smyth, Herbert Weir. *Greek Grammar.* Cambridge: Harvard University Press, 1966.

Snyder, Bob. *Music and Memory: An Introduction.* Cambridge, Mass.: MIT Press, 2000.

Soly, Hugo. *Charles Quint, 1500–1558: L'Empereur et son temps.* Arles: Actes Sud, 2000.

Southern, Eileen. *The Music of Black Americans: A History.* New York: Norton, 1971.

Spinks, Bryan D. *The Sanctus in the Eucharistic Prayer.* Cambridge: Cambridge University Press, 1991.

Stansbury, Mark. "Early Medieval Biblical Commentaries, Their Writers and Readers." *Frühmittelalterliche Studien* 33 (1999): 49–82.

Steiner, Ruth. "Antiphons for the Benedicite at Lauds." *Journal of the Plainsong and Mediaeval Music Society* 7 (1984): 1–17.

Stendahl, Krister. *The School of St. Matthew and Its Use of the Old Testament.* 2d ed. Philadelphia: Fortress,1968.

Stern, Chaim, ed. *Gates of Prayer: The New Union Prayer Book.* New York: Central Conference of American Rabbism, 1975.

Stevenson, Robert. *Music in Aztec and Inca Territory.* Berkeley and Los Angeles: University of California Press, 1968.

Stewart, Columba. *Cassian the Monk.* Oxford: Clarendon Press, 1998.

Stichel, Rainer. "Homiletik, Hymnographie und Hagiographie im früybzantinischen Palästina." Pages 389–406 in *ANDRIAS: Herbert Hunger zum 80. Geburtstag = Jahrbuch der österreichischen Byzantinistik* 44. Edited by Wolfram Hörander, Johannes Koder, and Otto Kresten. Vienna: Verlag de Österreichischen Akademie der Wissenschaften, 1994.

Stirnemann, Patricia. "Où ont été fabriqués les livres de la Glose Ordinaire dans la première moitié du XIIe siècle?" Pages 257–301 in *Le XIIe siècle: Mutations et renouveau en France dans la première moitié du XIIe sicèle.* Edited by Françoise Gasparri. Cahiers du Lêopard d'or 3. Paris: Le Léopard d'or, 1994.

Stock, Brian. *Listening for the Text.* Baltimore: Johns Hopkins University Press, 1990.

Storey, William F. "The Liturgy of the Hours: Cathedral Versus Monastic." *Worship* 50 (1976): 50–70.

Strunk, Oliver. "The Antiphons of the Octoechos." *Journal of the American Musicological Society* 13 (1960): 50–67. Repr. as pages 165–90 in Strunk, *Essays on Music.*

———. "The Byzantine Office at Hagia Sophia." *DOP* 9–10 (1956): 175–202. Repr. as pages 112–50 in Strunk, *Essays on Music.*

———. *Essays on Music in the Byzantine World.* New York: Norton, 1977.

Suckale-Redlefsen, Gude. *Der Buchschmuck zum Psalmenkommentar des Petrus Lombardus in Bamberg.* Wiesbaden: Reichert, 1986.

Sukenik, E. L. *The Dead Sea Scrolls of the Hebrew University.* Jerusalem: Magnes, 1955.

Swancutt, Diana M. "*Pax Christi*: Romans as Protrepsis to Live as Kings." Ph. D. diss. Duke University, 2001.

Taft, Robert F. "Anton Baumstark's Comparative Liturgy Revisited." Pages 135–61 in *Acts of the International Congress Comparative Liturgy Fifty Years after Anton Baumstark (1872–1948).* Edited by Robert F. Taft and Gabriele Winkler. OCA 265. Rome: Pontificium Institutum Orientalium Studiorum, 2000.

———. *Beyond East and West: Problems in Liturgical Understanding.* NPM Studies in Church Music and Liturgy. Washington, D.C.: Pastoral Press, 1984; 2d ed., Rome: Edizione Orientalia Christiana, Pontifical Oriental Institute, 1997.

———. *The Byzantine Rite: A Short History.* American Essays in Liturgy. Collegeville, Minn.: Liturgical Press, 1992.

———. "Comparative Liturgy Fifty Years after Anton Baumstark (d. 1948): A Reply to Recent Critics." *Worship* 73 (1999): 521–40.

———. "'Eastern Presuppositions' and Western Liturgical Renewal." *Antiphon* 5 (2000): 10–22.

———. *The Great Entrance: A History of the Transfer of Gifts and Other Preanaphoral Rites of the Liturgy of St. John Chrysostom.* OCA 200. Rome: Pontificium Institutum Orientalium Studiorum, 1978.

———. *The Liturgy of the Hours in East and West: The Origins of the Divine Office and Its Meaning for Today.* Collegeville, Minn.: Liturgical Press, 1986; 2d ed., 1993.

———. "Mount Athos: A Late Chapter in the History of the 'Byzantine Rite.'" *DOP* 42 (1988): 179–94.

———. *The Precommunion Rite.* Vol. 5 of *A History of the Liturgy of St. John Chrysostom.* OCA 261. Rome: Pontificium Institutum Orientalium Studiorum, 2000.

———. "Psalmody." Page 1752 in *Oxford Dictionary of Byzantium.* Edited by Alexander Kazhdan et al. New York: Oxford University Press, 1991.

———. "Über die Liturgiewissenschaft heute." *TQ* 177 (1997): 243–55.

———. "Women at Church in Byzantium: Where, When—and Why." *COP* 52 (1998): 27–87.

———. "The βηματίκιον in the 6/7th c. Narration of the Abbots John and Sophronius (BHGNA 1438w): An Exercise in Comparative Liturgy." Pages 674–92 in *Crossroad of Cultures: Studies in Liturgy and Patristics in Honor of Gabriele Winkler.* Edited by Hans-Jürgen Feulner, Elena Velkovska, and Robert F. Taft. OCA 260. Rome: Pontificium Institutum Orientalium Studiorum, 2000.

Terrien, Samuel. "The Metaphor of the Rock in Biblical Theology." Pages 157–71 in *God in the Fray: A Tribute to Walter Brueggemann.* Edited by Tod Linafelt and Timothy K. Beal. Minneapolis: Fortress, 1998.

Thodberg, Christian. *Der byzantinische Alleluiarionzyklus: Studien im kurzen Psaltikonstil.* MMB, Subsidia 8. Copenhagen: Munksgaard, 1966.

Thomson, Rodney M. *Catalogue of the Manuscripts of Lincoln Cathedral Chapter Library.* Cambridge: Brewer, 1989.

Timiades, Metropolitan Aimilianos of Selybria. *Ἄσατε τῷ Κυρίῳ—Σκέψεις γιὰ τὴν ἀναζωπύρηση τῆς θείας λατρείας.* Preveza: Holy Metropolis of Nikopolis, 1990.

———. "Ἡ ὑμνολογία ὅμηρος τῆς μουσικῆς." *Σύναξη* 81 (2002): 5–17.

Toubert, Hélène. "Contribution à l'iconographie des psautiers: Le commentaire des psaumes d'Odon d'Asti, illustré à l'abbaye de Farfa." *MEFR* 88 (1976): 581–619.

Uspensky, Nicholas. "Chin vsenoshchnogo bdeniia (ἡ ἀγρυπνία) na pravoslavnom vostoke i v russkoï tserkvi." *Bogoslovskie Trudy* 18 (1977): 5–117; 19 (1978): 3–69.

Van den Eynde, Damien. "Literary Notes on the Earliest Scholastic Commentarii In Psalmos." *Franciscan Studies* 14 (1954): 121–54.

Van Deusen, Nancy, ed. *The Place of the Psalms in the Intellectual Culture of the Middle Ages.* Albany: State University of New York Press, 1999.

Velkovska, Elena. *Il Praxapolstolos A.b.V (XI sec.) della Biblioteca di Grottaferrata.* Excerpta ex dissertatione ad doctoratum. Rome: Pontificio Istituto Orientale, 1994.

Vogüé, Adalbert de. "Le sens d''antifana' et la longueur de l'office dans la 'Regula Magistri.'" *RBén* 71 (1961): 119–24.

Vollenweider, Samuel. "Der 'Raub' der Gottgleichheit: Ein religionsgeschichtlicher Vorschlag zu Phil 2.6(–11)." *NTS* 45 (1999): 413–33.

Vööbus, Arthur. *History of Asceticism in the Syrian Orient: A Contribution to the History of Culture in the Near East.* 3 vols. CSCO 184, 197, 500, subsidia 14, 17, 81. Leuven: Secrétariat du CSCO, 1960.

Vourles, Athanasios Th. *Δογματικοηθικαὶ ὄψεις τῆς Ὀρθοδόξου ψαλμῳδίας.* Athens: Theological School of the University of Athens, 1994.

———. *Θέματα ἱερᾶς ψαλμῳδίας.* Athens: n.p., 2000.

Wagner, J. Ross. "'Not Beyond Things Which Are Written': A Call to Boast Only in the Lord (1 Cor. 4.6)." *NTS* 44 (1998): 279–87.

Walker, Wyatt Tee. *"Somebody's Calling My Name": Black Sacred Music and Social Changes.* Valley Forge, Pa.: Judson, 1979.

Ware, Kallistos. "The Theology of Worship." Pages 59–86 in vol. 1 of idem, *Collected Works.* Crestwood, N.Y.: St. Vladimir's Seminary Press, 2000.

Watts, James W. *Psalm and Story: Insert Hymns in Hebrew Narrative.* JSOTSup 139. Sheffield: JSOT Press, 1992.

Watts, Pauline Moffitt. "Prophecy and Discovery: On the Spiritual Origins of Christopher Columbus's Enterprise of the Indies." *AHR* 90 (1985): 73–102.

Weckmann, Luis. "Las esperanzas milenaristas de los franciscanos en la Nueva España." *Historia Mexicana* 32 (1982): 89–105

———. *The Medieval Heritage of Mexico.* New York: Fordham University Press, 1992.

Weitzman, Michael P. "The Origin of the Peshitta Psalter." Pages 277–98 in *Interpreting the Hebrew Bible.* Edited by J. Emerton and S. Reif. Cambridge: Cambridge University Press, 1982.

———. "The Peshitta Psalter and Its Hebrew *Vorlage.*" *VT* 35 (1985): 341–54.

Weitzman, Steven. *Song and Story in Biblical Narrative: The History of Literary Convention in Ancient Israel.* Indiana Studies in Biblical Literature. Bloomington: Indiana University Press, 1997.

Welker, Michael. *Creation and Reality.* Translated by John F. Hoffmeyer. Minneapolis: Fortress, 1999.

Wellesz, Egon. *A History of Byzantine Music and Hymnography.* 2d ed. Oxford: Clarendon Press, 1961.

Werner, Eric. "Hebrew and Oriental Christian Metrical Hymns: A Comparison." *HUCA* 23 (1950–51): 414–15.

———. *The Sacred Bridge: The Interdependence of Liturgy and Music in Synagogue and Church during the First Millennium.* Vol. 1. New York: Columbia University Press, 1959, 1984. Partially reprinted (omitting much of the musical material) as *The Sacred Bridge: Liturgical Parallels in Synagogue and Early Church.* New York: Columbia University Press, 1970.

West, Delno. "Medieval Ideas of Apocalyptic Mission and the Early Franciscans in Mexico." *The Americas* 45 (1989): 293–313.

West, Delno. "The Abbot and the Admiral: Joachite Influences in the Life and Writings of Christopher Columbus." Pages 461–73 in *Il profetismo gioachimita tra Quattrocento e Cinquecento: Atti del III Congresso Internazionale di Studi Gioachimiti.* Edited by Gian Luca Potestà. Genova: Marietti, 1991.

———. "Medieval Ideas of Apocalyptic Mission and the Early Franciscans in Mexico." *The Americas* 45 (1989): 293–313.

West, Frederick S. *Anton Baumstark's Comparative Liturgy in Its Intellectual Context.* Ann Arbor, Mich.: University Microfilms International Dissertation Services, 1988.

West, Martin Litchfield. *Ancient Greek Music.* Oxford: Clarendon Press, 1992.

Westermann, Claus. "The Formation of the Psalter." Pages 250–58 in idem, *Praise and Lament in the Psalms.* Translated by Keith R. Crim and Richard N. Soulen. Atlanta: John Knox, 1981.

Whalum, Wendel Phillips. "Black Hymnody." *RevExp* (1973): 341–55.

Wieder, Laurance. *The Poets' Book of Psalms: The Complete Psalter as Rendered by Twenty-Five Poets from the Sixteenth to the Twentieth Centuries.* Oxford: Oxford University Press, 1999.

Wigodsky, Michael. "The Alleged Impossibility of Philosophical Poetry." Pages 58–68 in *Philodemus and Poetry*. Edited by Dirk Obbink. New York: Oxford University Press, 1995.

Wilken, Robert. *John Chrysostom and the Jews: Rhetoric and Reality in the Late Fourth Century*. Berkeley and Los Angeles: University of California Press, 1983.

Williams, Craig A. *Roman Homosexuality: Ideologies of Masculinity in Classical Antiquity*. Oxford: Oxford University Press, 1999.

Williams, Edward V. "A Byzantine *Ars Nova:* The 14th-Century Reforms of John Koukouzeles in the Chanting of Great Vespers." Pages 211–29 in *Aspects of the Balkans: Continuity and Change: Contributions to the International Balkan Conference Held at UCLA, October 23–28, 1969*. Edited by Henrik Birnbaum and Speros Vryonis Jr. The Hague: Mouton, 1972.

Willis, John T. "The Song of Hannah and Psalm 113." *CBQ* 35 (1973): 139–54.

Wilmart, André. "La tradition des grands ouvrages de Saint Augustin." *Miscellanea augustiniana* 11 (1931): 295–315.

Wilson, Gerald. *The Edition of the Hebrew Psalter*. SBLDS 76. Chico, Calif.: Scholars Press, 1985.

Wilson, Peter. "The *aulos* in Athens." Pages 58–95 in *Performance Culture and Athenian Democracy*. Edited by Simon Goldhill and Robin Osborne. Cambridge: Cambridge University Press, 1999.

Winterbottom, Michael. *Classical Literary Criticism*. Oxford: Oxford University Press, 1989.

Wise, Jennifer. *Dionysus Writes: The Invention of Theatre in Ancient Greece*. Ithaca, N.Y.: Cornell University Press, 1998.

Wise, Michael O. "מי כוני באלים: A Study of 4Q491c, 4Q471b, 4Q427 7 and 1QHa 25:35–26:10." *DSD* 7 (2000): 173–219.

Wittekind, Susanne. *Kommentar mit Bildern: Zur Austattung mittelalterlicher Psalmenkommentare und Verwendung der Davidgeschichte in Texten und Bildern am Beispiel des Psalmenkommentars des Petrus Lombardus*. Europäische Hochschulschriften 28/212. Frankfurt am Main: Lang, 1994.

Wright, George E. "The Lawsuit of God: A Form-Critical Study of Deuteronomy 32." Pages 26–67 in *Israel's Prophetic Heritage: Essays in Honor of James Muilenberg*. Edited by Bernhard W. Anderson and Walter Harrelson. New York: Harper, 1962.

Wulf, Friedrich. "Priestertum und Rätestand." *Geist und Leben* 33 (1960): 250.

Wybrew, Hugh. *The Orthodox Liturgy: The Development of the Eucharistic Liturgy in the Byzantine Rite*. Crestwood, N.Y.: St. Vladimir's Seminary Press, 1990.

Ya'ar, Avishai. "The Cantillation of the Bible: The Aleppo Tradition (Pentateuch)." Ph.D. diss. City University of New York, 1996.

Yee, Gale. *Jewish Feasts in the Gospel of John.* Wilmington, Del.: Glazier, 1989.

Zenger, Erich. "The God of Israel's Reign over the World (Psalms 90–106)." Pages 161–190 in *The God of Israel and the Nations: Studies in Isaiah and the Psalms.* Edited by Norbert Lohfink and Erich Zenger. Collegeville, Minn.: Liturgical Press, 2000.

———. "Der Psalter als Buch: Beobachtungen zu seiner Enstehung, Komposition und Funktio." Pages 1–57 in *Der Psalter in Judentum und Christentum.* Edited by Erich Zenger. Herder's Biblical Studies 18. Freiburg: Herder, 1998.

Zenner, Walter, and Mark Kligman. "Brooklyn's Syrian Sephardim in the 1990s: Diversification and Ethnic Persistence." Pages 155–76 in *A Global Community: The Jews from Aleppo, Syria.* Edited by Walter Zenner. Detroit: Wayne State University Press, 2000.

Zenner, Walter, ed. *A Global Community: The Jews from Aleppo, Syria.* Detroit: Wayne State University Press, 2000.

Zimmermann, Heidy. *Tora und Shira: Untersuchungen zur Musikauffassung des rabbinischen Judentums.* Publikationen der Schweizerischen Musikforschenden Gesellschaft. 2/40. Bern: Lang, 2000.

Zizioulas, Metropolitan John of Pergamon. "Συμβολισμὸς καὶ Ρεαλισμὸς στὴν Ὀρθόδοξη λατρεία." *Σύναξη* 71 (1999): 6–21.

Index of Canonical and Deuterocanonical References

Hebrew Bible

APOCRYPHA

NEW TESTAMENT

General Index

Contributors

Harold W. Attridge, Dean of Yale Divinity School and Lillian Claus Professor of New Testament. His publications include *First-century Cynicism in the Epistles of Heraclitus* (HTS 29; Scholars Press, 1976); *The Interpretation of Biblical History in the Antiquitates Judaicae of Flavius Josephus* (Scholars Press, 1976); *Nag Hammadi Codex I: The Jung Codex* (Brill, 1985); *Hebrews: A Commentary* (Hermeneia; Fortress, 1989). He has served on the editorial boards of the *Journal of Biblical Literature,* the *Catholic Biblical Quarterly, The Second Century* (now the *Journal of Early Christian Studies*), The Society of Biblical Literature's Texts and Translations Series, Nag Hammadi and Manichaean Studies, and the Hermeneia commentary series.

Gilbert Bond, Professor of Theology, Yale University Divinity School. His publications include *Community, Communitas, and Cosmos: Toward a Phenomenological Interpretation and Theology of Traditional Afro-Christian Worship* (University Press of America, 2002) and *In Christos as Creolization: A Phenomenology of Reconciliation* (Westminster John Knox, 2004). In 1993, he received the Assistant Instructor Award for Excellence in Teaching from Emory.

Walter Cahn, Carnegie Professor of the History of Art (emeritus) at Yale University. Publications include *Studies in Medieval Art and Interpretation* (Pindar, 2000); *A Survey of Manuscripts Illuminated in France: Romanesque Manuscripts, 1100–1200* (Harvey Miller, 1996); *Romanesque Bible Illumination* (Cornell University Press, 1982); *Masterpieces: Chapters on the History of an Idea* (Princeton University Press, 1979); and *The Romanesque Wooden Doors of Auvergne* (New York University Press, 1974). He has been a Fulbright and Guggenheim Fellow.

Richard Clifford, Professor of Old Testament, Weston Jesuit School of Theology. Publications include *Psalms 1–72* (Abingdon, 2002); *Wisdom Literature* (Abingdon, 1998), *Book of Proverbs and Our Search for Wisdom* (Marquette University Press, 1995); and *Psalms 73–150* (Liturgical Press, 1986). Professor Clifford entered the Jesuits and was ordained in 1966. He has a doctorate in biblical studies from Harvard Divinity School.

Adela Yarbro Collins, Buckingham Professor of New Testament, Yale University Divinity School. Publications include *Cosmology and Eschatology in Jewish and Christian Apocalypticism* (Brill, 1996); *The Beginning of the Gospel: Probings of Mark in Context* (Fortress, 1992); *Crisis and Catharsis: The Power of the Apocalypse* (Westminster, 1984); *The Apocalypse* (Michael Glazier, 1979); and *The Combat Myth* *in the Book of Revelation* (Scholars Press, 1976). She holds the Ph.D. from Harvard University and an honorary doctorate from the University of Oslo, Norway. She was awarded a Fellowship by the National Endowment for the Humanities for 1995–96.

John J. Collins, Holmes Professor of Old Testament Criticism and Interpretation, Yale University Divinity School. Books include *Between Athens and Jerusalem: Jewish Identity in the Hellenistic Diaspora* (revised ed.; Eerdmans, 2000); *The Apocalyptic Imagination* (revised ed.; Eerdmans, 1998); *Seers, Sibyls and Sages* (Brill, 1997); *Jewish Wisdom in the Hellenistic Age* (Westminster, 1997); *Apocalypticism in the Dead Sea Scrolls* (Routledge, 1997); *The Scepter and the Star: The Messiahs of the Dead Sea Scrolls* (Doubleday, 1995); and a commentary on *The Book of Daniel* (Hermeneia; Fortress, 1993). He has served as editor of the *Journal of Biblical Literature,* as president of the Catholic Biblical Association (1997), and as president of the Society of Biblical Literature (2002).

Brian E. Daley, S.J., Catherine F. Huisking Professor of Theology, University of Notre Dame. Recent books include *The Hope of the Early Church* (1991; Hendrickson, 2003) and *On The Dormition of Mary: Early Patristic Homilies* (St. Vladimir's Seminary Press, 1997). Presently he is working on a commentary on the book of Psalms drawn from patristic exegetical sources, as well as a book on Gregory of Nazianzus. A past president of the North American Patristic Society, he is an editor of the journal *Traditio* and also serves on the editorial board of the *Journal of Early Christian Studies.*

Ellen F. Davis, Associate Professor of Bible and Practical Theology, Duke Divinity School. Among her recent publications are *Who Are You, My Daughter: Reading Ruth through Image and Text* (Westminster John Knox, 2003); *Getting Involved with God* (Cowley, 2001); *Proverbs, Ecclesiastes, and the Song of Songs* (John Knox, 2000); and *Imagination Shaped: Old Testament Preaching in the Anglican Tradition* (Trinity Press International, 1995). She received a Ph.D. (Old Testament) from Yale University in 1987 and subsequently taught at Union Theological Seminary (New York City), Yale Divinity School, and Virginia Theological Seminary.

Carlos M. N. Eire, Riggs Professor of History and Religious Studies at Yale University. Publications include his memoir of the Cuban Revolution, *Waiting for Snow in Havana* (Free Press, 2003); *Jews, Christians, Muslims: An Introduction to Monotheistic Religions* (with Martin S. Jaffee; Prentice Hall, 1998); *From Madrid to Purgatory: The Art and Craft of Dying in Sixteenth Century Spain* (Cambridge University Press, 1995); *War against the Idols: The Reformation of Worship from Erasmus to Calvin* (University Press, 1986); and *Reformations: Early Modern Europe 1450-1700* (Yale University Press, forthcoming).

Margot E. Fassler, Director of the Yale Institute of Sacred Music and Robert S. Tangeman Professor of Music History, Yale Divinity School, School of Music, and Music Department. She has co-edited *Divine Office in the Latin Middle Ages: Methodology and Source Studies, Regional Developments, Hagiography: Written in Honor of Professor Ruth Steiner* (Oxford University Press, 2000, with Rebecca A.

Baltzer) and has just completed a book on the cult of the Virgin Mary at Chartres (Yale University Press, forthcoming). Her book *Gothic Song: Victorine Sequences and Augustinian Reform in Twelfth-Century Paris* (Cambridge University Press, 1993) has received awards from both the American Musicological Society and the Medieval Academy of America.

Peter S. Hawkins, Professor of Religion and Director of Luce Program in Scripture and Literary Arts, Boston University. In addition to his work on Dante—*The Poets' Dante: Twentieth-Century Reflections* (with Rachel Jacoff; Farrar, Straus & Giroux, 2001) and *Dante's Testaments: Essays in Scriptural Imagination* (Stanford University Press, 1999), winner of the American Academy of Religion's 2001 Excellence in the Study of Religion Constructive-Reflective Studies award—he is co-editor with Paula Carlson of the four-volume series, *Listening for God: Contemporary Literature and the Life of Faith* (Augsburg Fortress; 1994–2003). Professor Hawkins supervises the graduate concentration in religion and literature at Boston University.

Lawrence A. Hoffman, Barbara and Stephen Friedman Professor of Liturgy, Worship and Ritual, Hebrew Union College, New York School. Recent publications include *The Journey Home: Discovering the Deep Spiritual Wisdom of the Jewish Tradition* (Beacon, 2002); *My People's Prayerbook* (Jewish Lights, 1997, 2002); and *Sacred Sound and Social Change: Liturgical Music in Jewish and Christian Experience* (ed. with Janet R. Walton; University of Notre Dame Press, 1992). An ordained rabbi, he is past president of the North American Academy of Liturgy and a co-founder of Synagogue 2000, a transdenominational project to envision and implement the North American synagogue as a moral and spiritual center for the twenty-first century.

Peter Jeffery, Scheide Professor of Music History, Princeton University. His publications include *The Study of Medieval Chant: Paths and Bridges, East and West* (Boydell, 2000); *Ethiopian Christian Liturgical Chant: An Anthology* (3 vols. + CD-ROM; A-R Editions, 1993–97; Kay Kaufman Shelemay); and *Re-envisioning Past Musical Cultures: Ethnomusicology in the Study of Gregorian Change* (University of Chicago Press, 1992). Professor Jeffery has won fellowships from the MacArthur and Guggenheim Foundations. He is a Benedictine Oblate of St. John's Abbey, Collegeville, Minnesota.

Serene Jones, Professor of Theology, Yale University Divinity School, Yale Law School, Yale Department of African American Studies. Recent publications include *Feminist Theory and Christian Theology: Cartographies of Grace* (Fortress, 2000) and *Calvin and the Rhetoric of Piety* (Westminster John Knox, 1995). In addition, she is a contributor to *Dictionary of Feminist Theologies* (ed. L. M. Russell and J. S. Clarkson; Westminster John Knox, 1996). Professor Jones is ordained in both the Christian Church (Disciples of Christ) and the United Church of Christ and serves on the Advisory Committee for the Wabash Center for Teaching and Learning in Theology and Religion and on the Yale University Women's and Gender Studies Council.

Mark Kligman, Associate Professor of Jewish Musicology, Hebrew Union College-Jewish Institute of Religion, School of Sacred Music, New York. Publications include *Maqam and Liturgy: Ritual, Music andAesthetics of Syrian Jews in Brooklyn* (under consideration) and several articles on the liturgy of Syrian Jews and on the historical trends in the liturgical music of Ashkenazic and Sephardic traditions. His entry "Music in Judaism" was recently published in *The Encyclopedia of Judaism* (ed. J. Neusner et al.; Continuum, 1999). He was the editor of the Jewish terms in *Worship Music: A Concise Dictionary* (ed. E. Foley; Liturgical Press, 2000).

Jaime Lara, Associate Professor of Christian Art and Architecture, Yale University Divinity School, Institute of Sacred Music. His book *City, Temple, Stage: Eschatology and Architecture in New Spain* is forthcoming from the University of Notre Dame Press. Another book, *A Volcano and Two Saints: Francis of Assisi and Joachim of Fiore in Latin American Art,* is reaching completion. He focuses on medieval continuities in colonial Latin America. His interests and academic studies have attempted to create bridges between history, theology, liturgy and anthropology.

Gordon W. Lathrop, Charles A. Schieren Professor of Liturgy, Lutheran Theological Seminary at Philadelphia. He is the author of several books, including most recently *Holy Ground: A Liturgical Cosmology* (Fortress: 2003); *Holy People: A Liturgical Ecclesiology* (Fortress, 1999); and *Holy Things: A Liturgical Theology* (Fortress, 1993). He was the tenth president of the North American Academy of Liturgy and is on the editorial board of the journal *Worship.*

Alexander Lingas, Assistant Professor of Music History, Arizona State University's School of Music; Fellow, European Humanities Research Centre, Oxford University. Publications include *An Introduction to Byzantine Chant* (Yale University Press, forthcoming); "Preliminary Thoughts on the Liturgical Use of Melismatic Chant in the Byzantine Tradition," in *Paleobyzantine Notations III: Acts of the Congress Held at Hernen Castle in March 2001* [tentative title] (ed. G. Wolfram; Bredius Foundation, forthcoming); "Festal Cathedral Vespers in Late Byzantium,"*OCP* 63 (1997); and "Hesychasm and Psalmody," in *Mount Athos and Byzantine Monasticism* (ed. A. Bryer and M. Cunningham; Variorum, 1996). He is the founder and director of the professional vocal ensemble Cappella Romana and has served the Orthodox Church as a cantor, choir director, and clinician for twenty years. He has received British Academy, Dumbarton Oaks, Onassis, and Fulbright fellowships for his study of the past and present traditions of Byzantine chanting.

Esther M. Menn, Associate Professor of Old Testament, Lutheran School of Theology at Chicago. She is the author of *Judah and Tamar (Genesis 38) in Ancient Jewish Exegesis: Studies in Literary Form and Hermeneutics* (Brill, 1997). She serves on the Consultative Panel on Lutheran-Jewish Relations for the Evangelical Lutheran Church in America. She received her Ph.D. from the University of Chicago Divinity School. Previously, she taught in the Christianity and Judaism in Antiquity program at the University of Virginia.

Patrick C. Miller, Professor of Old Testament Theology, Princeton Theological Seminary, where he has taught for eighteen years. Among his publications are *The Religion of Ancient Israel* (Westminster John Knox, 2000); *They Cried to the Lord: The Form and Theology of Biblical Prayer* (Fortress, 1994); *Deuteronomy* (John Knox, 1990); *Interpreting the Psalms* (Fortress, 1986); and *Sin and Judgment in the Prophets* (Scholars Press, 1982). In 1998, Miller served as President of the Society of Biblical Literature, having previously been the Society's Secretary-Treasurer.

Bryan D. Spinks, Professor of Liturgical Studies; chair, Program in Liturgical Studies, Yale Institute of Sacred Music, Yale Divinity School. His most recent book is entitled *Sacraments, Ceremonies and the Stuart Divines: Sacramental Theology and Liturgy in England and Scotland 1603–1662* (Ashgate, 2002). Recent essays have been published in *Christian Worship in Reformed Churches Past and Present* (ed. L. Vischer; Eerdmans, 2003) and in *Lord Jesus Christ, Will You Not Stay: Essays in Honor of Ronald Feuerhahn* (Concordia, 2002). He is currently writing a book on the history and development of baptismal rites. He is a Fellow of the Royal Historical Society and an ordained priest of the Church of England.

Rabbi Elliot L. Stevens, Executive Secretary, Director of Publications, Central Conference of American Rabbis. The CCAR is the international professional association of Reform rabbis. Rabbi Stevens edits the CCAR *Yearbook,* is managing editor of the *CCAR Journal,* and is on the editorial board of *Reform Judaism* and the management board of Transcontinental Music Publications. He also edited *Rabbinic Authority: Papers Presented before the Ninety-First Annual Convention of the Central Conference of American Rabbis* [1980] (Central Conference of American Rabbis, 1982), an anthology of scholarly papers. Rabbi Stevens was ordained in 1975 by the Hebrew Union College-Jewish Institute of Religion. He has been president of the Association of Jewish Book Publishers and served on the Jewish Book Council.

Diana Swancutt, Assistant Professor of New Testament, Yale University Divinity School. She is a Society of Biblical Literature Regional Scholar who combines interests in gender, Judaica, rhetoric, ideological criticism, and ancient social practices in her interdisciplinary research. She focuses on early Christian identity formation in Pauline communities, particularly the resocialization of Gentiles into complex patterns of identity, molded—within the Greco-Roman milieu—by the movement's Jewish roots and worldview. Her current writing projects include a book on the rhetoric of Romans and articles on the early Christian use of the Psalms, Paul's ethnic stereotyping, the charge of effeminacy in Pauline rhetoric, and queer theory and the New Testament.

Robert F. Taft, S.J., Professor Emeritus of Oriental Liturgy at the Pontifical Oriental Institute, Rome. He is a Jesuit priest ordained in the Byzantine Slavonic (Russian) Rite in 1963. He has also served as Visiting Professor in the Graduate School of the University of Notre Dame since 1974. A prolific writer, his bibliography comprises over 630 titles, including fourteen books of his own plus seven others edited in collaboration with other authors. Several of his writings have been translated into Arabic, Bulgarian, Czech, Dutch, French, German, Greek, Italian,

Malayalam, Portuguese, Russian, Slovak, Spanish, and Ukrainian. In recognition of his work, Fr. Taft has received numerous academic awards, including two honorary doctorates. In 2001, he was elected Corresponding Fellow of the British Academy, the highest honor conferred in the U.K. on non-British scholars. He is the only U.S. Jesuit in history to have received this distinction.

Margaret Moers Wenig, Rabbi Emerita, Beth Am, The People's Temple, New York City; Instructor in Liturgy and Homiletics, Hebrew Union College-Jewish Institute of Religion, New York City. Ordained in 1984, Rabbi Wenig revitalized the congregation at Beth Am while continuing to teach and to conduct workshops for Christian clergy. Her sermon, "God Is a Woman and She Is Growing Older," won a HarperCollins' Best Sermons Award in 1991. Other writings have appeared in journals such as *Reform Judaism, The Reconstructionist, Journal of Feminist Studies in Religion, The Living Pulpit,* and *National Bulletin on Liturgy,* and in anthologies published by HarperCollins, Jewish Lights, Riverhead Books (Penguin Putnam), UAHC, Chalice, Abingdon, Routledge, and Westminster John Knox. Her undergraduate honors thesis on Mishnah *Bikkurim* has been published, in sections, by, among others, Scholars Press, Ktav, and Yale University Press.